THE

EPISTLE OF PAUL

TO THE

PHILIPPIANS.

BY

KARL BRAUNE, D.D.

GENERAL SUPERINTENDENT AT ALTENBURG, SAXONY.

TRANSLATED FROM THE GERMAN, WITH ADDITIONS,

BY

HORATIO B. HACKETT, D.D.

PROFESSOR IN THE THEOLOGICAL SEMINARY, ROCHESTER, N. Y.

Wipf & Stock

PUBLISHERS

Eugene, Oregon

Wipf and Stock Publishers
199 W 8th Ave, Suite 3
Eugene, OR 97401

The Epistle of Paul to the Philippians and Colossians
An Exegetical and Doctrinal Commentary
By Braune, Karl
ISBN 13: 978-1-55635-411-3
ISBN 10: 1-55635-411-8
Publication date 4/6/2007
Previously published by Charles Scribner, 1871

THE

EPISTLE OF PAUL TO THE PHILIPPIANS.

INTRODUCTION.

CONTENTS OF THE EPISTLE.

The following schedule exhibits to us the heads under which these may be arranged:—

SEC. I. ADDRESS AND SALUTATION (i. 1, 2).

SEC. II. SITUATION AND LABORS OF THE APOSTLE AT ROME (i. 3-26).

(1) The Apostle's gratitude and joy before God on account of the church at Philippi (i. 3–11).

After joyful thanksgiving for the fellowship of the church in the gospel (3–5), and the expression of his confident hope that God will make this perfect (6–8), he offers a fervent prayer for them (9–11).

(2) The gospel, in spite of insincere or false brethren and threatening danger of death, makes progress during the Apostle's captivity at Rome (i. 12–26).

After referring to the happy effects of his ministry in bonds (12–14), among sincere and insincere witnesses for Christ (15–17), he expresses his views respecting this varied experience (18–20), and calmly revolves the question whether life or death may be better for him (21–26).

SEC. III. THE LORD'S EXAMPLE AND PATTERN FOR THE OBSERVANCE OF THE CHURCH (i. 27—ii. 18).

(1) A true Christian deportment the condition of the Apostle's joy in the church (i. 27–30). Characteristics of a Christian walk (27, 28 *a*); encouraging motives (28 *b*–30).

(2) Christ's example on the way through humiliation to exaltation (ii. 1–11).

After entreating them earnestly and eloquently to stand together in harmony (1–4), he holds up to view the person of the Redeemer (5, 6), His state of humiliation (7, 8), and His state of exaltation (9–11).

(3) God strengthens believers to walk in Christ's footsteps along the painful way of obedience (12–14), to its glorious end (15–18).

SEC. IV. PAUL'S ASSISTANTS AND CO-LABORERS (ii. 19–30).

(1) Timothy and his speedy mission to Philippi (19–24).

(2) Sending back of Epaphroditus (25–30).

SEC. V. WARNING AGAINST JUDAISTIC FALSE TEACHERS AND WICKED DECEIVERS IN CONTRAST WITH THE APOSTLE (iii. 1—iv. 1).

(1) The spirit of these teachers as distinguished from that of Paul (iii. 1–16).

He warns them against the disposition of such errorists, especially their pride (2–7), points out the opposition between the righteousness of the law and that of faith (8–11), and speaks of his humble striving after perfection (12–14), with an exhortation to harmony among the Philippians (15–16).

(2) Opposite destiny of false and true Christians (iii. 17—iv. 1).

He confirms his exhortation to imitate himself and others like-minded (17) by two contrasts: the destruction of the worldly, and the glorification of the righteous believers (18–21); and concludes (iv. 1) with an exhortation to steadfastness.

SEC. VI. FINAL EXHORTATION TO CO-OPERATION BETWEEN HIMSELF AND THE PHILIPPIAN CHURCH (iv. 2–20).

(1) Individuals exhorted to harmony (2, 3).

(2) General exhortation to joyfulness (4–7).

(3) General and final summons to Christian progress (8, 9).

(4) Thanksgiving for the gifts of love from them (10–20).

His joy on this account (10), caution against misapprehension (11–13), grateful recognition of their kindness (14–17), and assurance of the Divine blessing (18–20).

SEC. VII. SALUTATION AND BENEDICTION (iv. 21–23).

The ground tone of this Epistle is found in the antithesis of joy and sorrow which runs through every part of it, not only in Paul's references to his own joy in his diversified relations (i. 4, 18; ii. 2, 17; iv. 1, 10), but also in his exhortations to the church to cherish this spirit. The feeling of joy animates the Apostle in his darkest hours, and that joy is the mark which he has always in view. With ZÖCKLER (VILMAR'S *Pastoraltheologische Blätter*, 1864, *Heft* 5 and 6, p. 239 sq.) we shall find the ground-thought in that divine mystery which Peter (1 Pet. i. 11) designates as "the sufferings of Christ and the glory that should follow" (τὰ εἰς Χριστὸν παθήματα καὶ τὰς μετὰ ταῦτα δόξας), and describes as an object of hope and longing to the angels in heaven. Expressed in one sentence it is this: Only humble, loving self-denial, after the example of Christ, who has passed through the condition of self-abasement to His exaltation in heaven, can lift us up to true honor, to a full, abiding enjoyment of the Christian life.

§ 2. CHARACTER AND IMPORTANCE OF THE EPISTLE.

(1) The character of the letter distinguishes it in a marked way from the letters to the Ephesians and Colossians. The theme is not here as in those letters divided in its treatment into a theoretical and a hortatory part. It is a genuine outgush of the heart, and bears more than any other a familiar character (WIESINGER). It is a natural and unstudied expression of feeling, without doctrinal purpose or strict plan (ZÖCKLER), although the beautiful organism of the letter is not to be overlooked, and HOLTZMANN (HERZOG'S *Real-encyk.* Vol. XX. p. 401) should not say that it is wanting in close connection and progress of the thought. Even the single but extremely important doctrinal passage (ii. 5–11) is ethically conceived, and bears directly with all its force upon practical life. As MEYER well remarks: "The entire contents breathe an inmost and touching love for this favorite Church. No other letter is so rich in heartfelt expressions and tender allusions—none so characteristically epistolary, without exact arrangement, without doctrinal discussions, without Old Testament citations and dialectic argumentations. None is so completely a letter of the heart, an outburst of passionate longing for the fellowship of love amid outward desertion and affliction; so that although at times almost elegiac in its tone, it is a model of the union of tender love with apostolic dignity and boldness." Although the letter of a prisoner near death, it is *melior alacriorque et blandior ceteris* (GROTIUS). Written in view of death, yet full of unshaken hope of life, under heavy oppression, yet full of unbending courage, amid grievous conflicts, yet full of fresh zeal, it passes from expressions of tender love for the church to the severest denunciations of dangerous adversaries. With passages full of elegant negligence (i. 29), like Plato's dialogues, and Cicero's letters, it has passages of wonderful eloquence, and proceeds from entirely outward, special, relations and circumstances to wide-reaching thoughts and grand conceptions.

(2) Hence the importance of the letter, apart from the one doctrinal passage (ii. 5–11), lies in the province of practical life. It treats of the mutual relations of the minister and his church, and also of the general Christian life, especially in regard to self-discipline and proper demeanor in circumstances of difficulty and towards various persons.

The Church has therefore selected from it four portions to be read on the fourth Sunday after

Advent (iv. 4–7), on Palm-Sunday (ii. 5–11), on the twenty-second (i. 3–11) and the twenty-third Sunday after Trinity (iii. 17–21).

§ 3. UNITY OF THE EPISTLE.

This unity appears from §§ 1, 2, and it would be unnecessary to refer to it, had not HEINRICHS (*Novum Testamentum ed. Koppe* VII. *Proleg.* p. 31 sqq.) and Paulus (*Heidelb. Jahrb.* 1817, 7, p. 702 sq.) brought forward the idea that there were two letters here, the one (i. 1—iii. 1, as far as χαίρετε ἐν κυρίῳ, and iv. 21–23) addressed to all the Philippians, and the other (iii. 1 *b*—iv. 20) addressed to his more intimate friends, the ἐπίσκοποι and διάκονοι; and that the exoteric and esoteric parts were first united by another hand. This view finds no exegetical support in λοιπόν (iii. 1), τέλειοι (iii. 15), as the explanation of the passages shows. It deserves to be forgotten, or to be mentioned only as a curiosity.

§ 4. AUTHOR OF THE EPISTLE.

(1) The letter itself designates the Apostle Paul as the author (i. 1), represents Timothy as one of his associates (i. 1; ii. 19), and refers to his imprisonment (i. 7), and to his former preaching in Macedonia (iv. 15), in a manner entirely natural and in harmony with his actual relations. On this point, therefore, there is no room for doubt.

(2) The external testimonies maintain Paul's authorship. Polycarp cites it (ad Phil. iii. 11) as a letter of Paul's, according to its position in MURATORI's Canon, after the Epistle to the Ephesians, and before that to the Colossians (Eph. § 4, 2), and in this he is followed by IGNATIUS, IRENÆUS, CLEMENS of Alexandria, ORIGEN, TERTULLIAN, and EUSEBIUS who reckons it among the ὁμολογούμενα. MARCION also regards it as an epistle of Paul.

(3) It bears undeniably the Pauline impress in its contents and spirit, its delicate turns and allusions, its language and mode of representation (MEYER, comp. § 2, 1). It should be remarked too that from the subordination of the doctrinal element, as also from the prominence of its characteristics as fresh, original, and called forth by a special occasion, all suspicion of forgery in the interest of doctrine is excluded (MEYER). Hence OLSHAUSEN could still say that this letter belongs to the few writings of the New Testament of which the genuineness has never been disputed.

(4) SCHRADER leads the way to the more recent assaults on this Epistle (*Der Apostel Paulus*, V. p. 233 sq.). According to his view, the passage iii. 1—iv. 9 is interpolated between ii. 30 and iv. 10, destroying the symmetry of the letter and its character as a letter of friendship. This arbitrary assumption falls away at once before an unprejudiced interpretation of the passage in question.

The leader of the Tübingen School, BAUR (especially in his *Paulus*, 1845, pp. 458–475) whom his pupil, SCHWEGLER (*Nachapost. Zeitalter* II. 133–135), ably supports, makes the attack in a different way. BAUR's arguments group themselves under three heads:—

(*a*) The letter moves in the circle of Gnostic ideas, not combating them, but attaching itself to them. Consequently the passage, ii. 5 sq., must have this import: ἁρπαγμός points to the Valentinian Sophia, which strives to force itself into the being of the Father (ἴσα τῷ θεῷ εἶναι) and thus sinks down from the πλήρωμα into the κένωμα; "Being found in the likeness of men," *etc.* (ἐν ὁμοιώματι ἀνθρώπων and σχήματι εὑρεθεὶς ὡς ἄνθρωπος) are *Docetic;* and the division into the three regions of ἐπουρανίων, ἐπιγείων, καταχθονίων is purely Gnostic. This view also is utterly untenable in the light of impartial exegesis.

(*b*) The character of the letter justifies a doubt of its Pauline origin. The expression κύνες (iii. 2) is indelicate; and the antithesis of κατατομή and περιτομή forced and out of place. The statement in iii. 2 sq. is copied from 2 Cor. xi. 18 sq., and that in iv. 15 contradicts 1 Cor. ix. 15 (ἐγὼ δὲ οὐ κέχρημαι οὐδενὶ τούτων), or at least 2 Cor. xi. 9, according to which the contribution did not reach him at the beginning of his Macedonian labors, but at a later period. The passage in Philippians arose probably from that in Corinthians by an exaggeration. The passage iv. 16 is not historically correct, since Paul did not make a long stay there; further iii. 1 (τὰ αὐτὰ γραφεῖν) indicates poverty of thought; and iii. 6 (δικαιοσύνη ἐν νόμῳ) is un-Pauline. These charges also prove unfounded when we examine the passages.

(*c*) The historical relations all point to a post-Pauline period. Κλήμεντος (iv. 3), in connection with ἐκ τῆς Καίσαρος οἰκίας (iv. 22), compels us to think of the relation of the Emperor TIBERIUS, FLAVIUS CLEMENS, who on account of impiety (ἀθεότης) was condemned to death, and thus for the first time the προκοπὴ τοῦ εὐαγγελίου (i. 12) becomes clear, together with Paul's joyful hope of a speedy release (ii. 24). Further, in the fact that this CLEMENS, a genuine disciple of Peter, had become a συνεργός of Paul, we see the writer's tendency to harmonize the representatives of the Jewish and Gentile Christians, Εὐοδία and Συντύχη (iv. 2). 'Επισκόποις καὶ διακόνοις (i. 1) is an anachronism in a Pauline Epistle. As to these objections also an unbiassed exegesis removes every difficulty.

Such objections to the genuineness of the letter become in reality vouchers for it. If there are no others against Paul's authorship, we need not be concerned. They serve only to make us feel how uncertain are the decisions of critics who recognize such delicacy of feeling on the part of the writer, and yet complain of monotonous repetitions, poverty of thought, and a want of any definite theme or purpose. LÜNEMANN (*Pauli ad Phil. Ep. contra Baurium defendit*, 1847) and BRÜCKNER (*Ep. ad Phil. Paulo auctori vindicata contra Baurium defendit*, 1848) have triumphantly vindicated the genuineness of this letter.

§ 5. RELATIONS OF THE READERS.

(1) Their external relations. Not merely in the superscription (i. 1, ἐν Φιλίπποις) does the Apostle designate the place of the church, but also (which he seldom does except under deep emotion) in the body of the letter, where he mentions their gifts of love to him (iv. 15: Φιλιππήσιοι). Philippi is first mentioned in Acts xvi. 12. It was originally called Κρηνίδες from the great number of fountains in that region, afterwards Δάτος, and finally, when Philip, the son of Amyntas, king of Macedonia, enlarged and fortified it as a bulwark against the Thracians, about B. C. 358, it was named Φίλιπποι. It became still more celebrated on account of the battle fought there B. C. 42 between the Triumviri and Brutus and Cassius (which decided the fate of the republic), after which it was made a Roman *colonia* (κολωνία, Acts xvi. 12) with the *jus italicum;* but it obtained its greatest glory as the first city of Europe in which the gospel was preached with great success by Paul (A. D. 53) on his second missionary journey (Acts xvi. 9–40). When it is said (Acts xvi. 12): ἐκεῖθεν εἰς Φιλίππους, ἥτις ἐστὶν πρώτη τῆς μέριδος τῆς Μακεδονίας πόλις, this πρώτη evidently designates only its local position (ἐκεῖθεν, *i. e.*, from Neapolis), not its political importance. It lies not far from the sea,* and after Neapolis, the port of Philippi, reckoned at that time as in Thrace (VAN HENGEL *Comment. Ep. ad. Phil.* p. 4), is the first city reached on coming from Neapolis to Macedonia. The capital of Macedonia was Amphipolis (Liv. 45, 29). Comp. Acts of the Apostles, LANGE'S Series, p. 304. Paul, along with the happy results of his preaching in the conversion of Lydia and the jailor, had suffered many trials there (1 Thess. ii. 2: προπαθόντες καὶ ὑβρισθέντες). After probably a short stay at Philippi on his third missionary journey (Acts xx. 1, 2), he remained there somewhat longer on his return, though still not a long time (Acts xx. 6).

[Some of the later commentators (even MEYER, *Comment. über die Briefe an die Philipper*, etc., p. 1, 1859) speak of a village, *Felibah*, as still occupying the ancient site. This is incorrect. COUSINÉRY wrote nearly forty years ago: *"La ville célèbre de Philippi ne renforme aujourd'hui que des animaux sauvages; l' oiseau de Minerva se y régénère au milieu des debris"* (*Voyage dans la Macedonie*, p. 17, tome 2, Paris, 1831). The nearest human habitation at present is a Greek κατάλυμα, or caravansary, a mile or more from the ruins, though the ancient name undoubtedly still lingers among the peasants of the country. The nearest village is *Bereketli*, several miles distant. The ruins consist principally of the remains of a theatre or amphitheatre on the side of the hill which formed the acropolis of Philippi, mounds of rubbish containing broken columns and fragments of marble, two lofty gateways supposed to have belonged to a colossal temple of the emperor CLAUDIUS, and a portion of the ancient city wall on the east side towards *Kavalla* (Neapolis). Latin inscriptions are still found there, which show that the place

[* It is somewhat less, certainly, than 10 miles. The recent French explorers (*Mission Archéologique*) make the distance from 12 to 13 kilomètres, *i. e.*, about 9 Roman miles. From the crags which overlook the road across Symbolum from *Kavalla*, the ancient Neapolis, to the site of Philippi, the traveller has both places in sight at the same time.—H.]

was once occupied by Romans. (See the addition to COLONY in the American edition of SMITH'S *Bible Dictionary*, Vol. I. p. 447).

The river of which Luke speaks in Acts xvi. 13 is undoubtedly the Gangas or Gangites mentioned by ancient writers (Herod. vii. 113), and said to be known still as Anghista. It is not a permanent stream, but, like many of the so-called rivers (*ποταμοί*) in the East, may be entirely dry in summer, but flow with water in the rainy season. When the writer was there on the 13th of December, 1859, it was a rapid torrent, rushing and foaming over its rocky bed, varying in depth at different points from one and two feet to four and five feet, and covering a bed of about thirty feet in width. The stones at the bottom showed the action at times of a still more powerful current. The channel of this stream is only a few rods beyond the circuit of the city, as indicated by the parts of the wall which still remain. For other information respecting the site of Philippi and its harbor, Neapolis, the present *Kavalla*, see *Bibl. Sacra*, Vol. XVII. 873 ff. It was on the bank of this stream that the Jews or Jewish proselytes assembled for worship (Acts xvi. 13), and hence, as Luke's expression indicates (for we are to read there, *ἐκ πύλης*, *out of the gate* and not *ἐκ πόλεως*, *out of the city*), they had only to pass out of the gate, and would then come at once to the river-side.—H.]

Nearly all the inhabitants of Philippi were heathen, among whom were a few Jews, who did not have even a synagogue, but only a place of prayer (Acts xvi. 13, LANGE'S Series, p. 304), without the city, near the river, where also a few proselytes worshipped with them. Among these undoubtedly the Apostle gained his first converts. The church must have been composed principally of Gentiles. We cannot infer, on sufficient grounds, that the church was wealthy, either from the case of Lydia or the jailor, or from their gifts to the Apostle. Polycarp indeed, in his letter to the Philippians, censures their love of money; but he died A. D. 168 at the age of 86, and wrote his letter at least fifty or sixty years after Paul wrote to the Philippians. During this period great changes may have taken place even in the outward circumstances of the church.*

2. The internal condition of the church was, on the whole, very favorable. The church could not have remained weak, as the Jewish congregation there had been; for it had *ἐπίσκοποι καὶ διάκονοι* (i. 1). It must therefore have been also well regulated. We must not overlook the fact that Paul writes *πᾶσιν τοῖς ἁγίοις ἐν Χριστῷ Ἰησοῦ* (i. 1). This *πᾶσιν* is omitted in his letter to the Colossians, who were known to him, and in his letter to the Ephesians, while in his letter to the Romans, who were as yet unknown to him, and in his second letter to the Corinthians, it occupies a different position. He also not merely salutes *πάντα ἅγιον* (iv. 21), but rejoices in them *all* (ii. 17). In like manner Epaphroditus longs earnestly, not after Philippi merely, but even after them all (ii. 26), and is anxious because they have heard of his sickness. More than once, before the Apostle arrived at Corinth, did they contribute to his support (iv. 15, 16), nor did they probably fail to share in the gifts of love which were sent from Macedonia to Corinth (2 Cor. xi. 9), and now again they have forwarded by a messenger their gifts to him at Rome (iv. 10–20). It was this last act, together with the return of Epaphroditus (ii. 25–30), which gave occasion for the letter. They have their trials (i. 29), but remain faithful. Adversaries (*ἀντικείμενοι*) come among them (i. 28), also false teachers (iii. 2 sq.), and enemies to Christ (iii. 18, 19), but it is always evident that they do not come forth from them nor succeed among them. He has no fear of intellectual or doctrinal errors among them, but only calls their attention to the approaching danger. The false teachers are Judaistic, as among the Galatians, but with this difference, that among the latter they had arisen in the church itself, and had met with success, whereas here they had entered the church from without, and had hitherto met with no success. He is obliged indeed to exhort them to harmony (ii. 1–4; iv. 2, 3), to pray for their furtherance in knowledge and experience (i. 9), to warn them against strife and vanity (ii. 3, 4); but not in a tone of accusation or of reproach on account of grievous errors, as in the case of the Corinthians and others. If therefore officiousness or a striving for pre-eminence existed among them, or the conceit of moral perfection (WIESINGER), the rivalship of spiritual pride, which leads one by turns to arrogate to himself or to disclaim Christian perfection (MEYER), the

* POLYCARP charges two members of the Philippian church with the vice of avarice, but exonerates the church as a whole from any participation in their sin. See Prof. LIGHTFOOT'S *Commentary*, p. 63, note 1.—H.]

tinder of this pride, ever ready for the spark, namely, a tendency to excessive self-estimation (SCHENKEL), or ascetic jealousy (DE WETTE), we are to understand this as applicable to single persons, or occurrences, or as pertaining to the natural man, from whom even the true Christian is not freed. Without this view of the case, Paul's high commendation of the Philippians (iv. 1, χαρὰ καὶ στεφανος μου), the praise awarded to them at the beginning of the letter (i. 3–11), the account of his external condition (i. 12–20), and also of his state of mind (i. 21–26; iii. 7–15), become unintelligible.

§ 6. TIME AND PLACE OF COMPOSITION.

(1) Facts of the letter. According to i. 7, 13–20; iv. 22, it is evident that Paul is a prisoner: that he has freedom and opportunity to preach: that he has been in that situation for some time, and is in such relations with the well-known Prætorium (τῷ πραιτορίῳ) that his person and work have become known throughout that camp (ἐν ὅλῳ) and among all the others (τοῖς λοιποῖς πᾶσιν) who would here come into question. There is a church there, which is also not without witnesses for Christ, of whom some indeed are "contentious" (οἱ ἐξ ἐριθείας), so that we are to think of an important place in which such dissension would be comparatively of little account; and as, finally, the imperial palace (ἡ Καίσαρος οἰκία) is there, the place thus variously indicated must be Rome.

Since Paul has been there for some time, he cannot have written this letter in the beginning of his imprisonment, but must have written it towards its close;—an inference which is confirmed by his uncertainty as to whether he will be finally released, or meet with a martyr's death. Hence we conclude that this letter was written at Rome, A. D. 63 or 64; a year after that to the Colossians, and in the spring, which we infer not from ἀνεθάλετε (see on iv. 10), but from the return of Epaphroditus, which the opening of the spring navigation rendered practicable. The subscriptions of the Codices from the fourth century and onwards (B. and others at the end) favor this conclusion.

The Church, which divided the letters of Paul into those addressed to churches and those addressed to individuals, arranged them according to their *stichometric* length, and thus our letter stands before Colossians. Only the epistle to the Ephesians, which with its 155 verses contains only six more verses than Galatians (in the *cod. Sin.* however, 48 στοῖχοι), is placed after Galatians, because in comparison with the latter composition the difference in length was of minor importance. (LAURENT, *Neutestamentliche Studien*, p. 43 sq.).

(2) The following are different views: OEDER (*De tempore et loco epistolæ ad Phil. scriptæ.* ONOLDI, 1731), transfers the letter to the time of Paul's sojourn of a year and a half at Corinth (Acts xviii. 11). But the Apostle was not then in prison, and not in danger of death, as at Rome.

D. PAULUS (1799), BÖTTGER, (*Beiträge*, GÖTTINGEN, 1837), and others, refer the letter to the time of Paul's imprisonment at Cæsarea. BÖTTGER, not without acuteness and learning, founds his argument upon the misunderstood judicial procedure, according to which an appeal must be answered within five or ten days. Maintaining that Paul's imprisonment at Rome, resulting from his appeal to the emperor, could last only five days, he assumes (since Paul was in prison there during two years, Acts xxviii. 30), a second imprisonment, and by a forced explanation understands τῷ πραιτωρίῳ (i. 13), and ἡ Καίσαρος οἰκία (iv. 22), of imperial edifices out of Rome, and on account of ἐν τῷ πραιτωρίῳ Ἡρώδου (Acts xxiii. 35) he places these at Cæsarea. But on this view he does not explain the other indications (above noticed) which point out the time and place of composition, and creates a new perplexity, namely, how Luke (Acts xxviii. 16–23) forgot to mention that Paul was released, and was not imprisoned at Rome until a later period.

§ 7. LITERATURE.

For GENERAL WORKS see the Introduction to Ephesians, § 7.

SPECIAL WORKS.—MELANCHTHON:—*Argumentum Ep. Pauli ad. Phil.* (*Corp. Ref.* XV. pp. 1283–1294).—MUSCULUS: *Comment.*—AM ENDE: *Ep. ad. Phil. Græce, nova versione lat. et annot. perpet. illustr.*, 1789.—HEINRICHS, *in N. T. ed.* KOPPE, vol. VII. p. II. 1826.—RHEINWALD: *Comment. über den Brief an die Philipper*, 1827.—MATTHIES: *Erklärung des Briefes Pauli an die Philipper* 1835.—VAN HENGEL: *Comm. perpet. in Ep. ad. Phil.* 1838, (distinguished for philological accuracy).—HÖLEMANN: *Comm. in Ep. D. Pauli ad. Phil.* 1839 (too artificial).—RILLIET: *Commentaire sur l'épître de l'apôtre Paul aux Philippiens* 1841.—WIESINGER in OLSHAUSEN'S *Commentary on the N. T.*, vol. 5, 1850, (with fine remarks).—CONR. MÜLLER: *Commentatio de locis quibusdam Ep. ad. Phil.* 1843.—SCHINZ: (of Zürich) *die christliche Gemeinde zu Philippi*, 1833.

On the important passage ii. 5–11, compare especially the following: UMBREIT, in the review of RHEINWALD'S *Commentar in "Studien und Kritiken," pp.* 593–596.—STEIN, *ibid.* 1837, pp. 165–180. ERNESTI, *ibid.*, 1848, pp. 858–924; 1851, pp. 595–630; and THOLUCK'S *Pfingstprogramm*, 1847: *Disputatio christologica de loc. Paul. Phil. II.* 6–9.

For a practical exposition see, besides those mentioned in the Introduction to Ephesians, [§ 7], which include our epistle, SCHLEIERMACHER: *Predigten über den Brief an die Philipper Werken.* 2 *Abtheilung*, 10 *Band, S.* 337–804.—PASSAVANT: *Versuch einer practischen Auslegung des Briefes Pauli an die Philipper*, 1834.—MENKEN: *In Homiletischen Blättern*, 1835, *S.* 300–419.—KÄHLER: *Auslegung der Epistel Pauli an die Philipper in* 25 *Predigten*, 1855.

[The following additional works may be mentioned:

IN GERMAN:

1) DR. AUGUST NEANDER: *Der Brief Pauli an die Philipper praktisch erläutert*, with Luther's version corrected by F. Th. Schneider (pp. 1–162; Berlin, 1849). This work is translated by Mrs. H. Conant (pp. 1–140; New York, 1851). The quotations from NEANDER in the pages which follow are to be accredited to this translation.

2) GR. FR. JATHO: *Pauli Brief an die Philipper* (1857).

3) DR. BERNHARD WEISS: *Der Philipper Brief ausgelegt und die Geschichte seiner Auslegung kritisch dargestellt* (Berlin, 1859). An important work for illustrating the relations of the epistle to dogmatic theology.

4) DR. D. SCHENKEL: *Die Briefe an die Epheser, Philipper, und Colosser* (1862).

IN ENGLISH:

1) REV. JOHN TRAPP, A. M.: *Commentary upon the Epistle of St. Paul to the Philippians*, contained in his *Commentary on the New Testament* (edited by Rev. W. Webster, Lond., 1865). Some extracts from this work are given among the Homiletic and Practical remarks.

2) REV. ROBERT HALL, A.M.: *A Practical Exposition of the Epistle to the Philippians*, in Twelve Discourses, delivered at Cambridge in 1801 and 1802. (Stenographic notes, but very full, with reference both to the ideas and the language of the preacher. They are good specimens of pulpit exposition by one of the great masters of sacred eloquence).

3) REV. FR. D. MAURICE: *Epistle to the Philippians*, pp. 549-558, in his *Unity of the New Testament* (1854).

4) WEBSTER AND WILKINSON: *New Testament, with Notes Grammatical and Exegetical*, II. 506–528 (London, 1861).

5) T. B. LIGHTFOOT, D. D.: *St. Paul's Epistle to the Philippians.* A Revised Text, with Introduction, Notes, and Dissertations (London, 1868).

6) PROF. JOHN EADIE: *A Commentary on the Greek Text of the Epistle of Paul on Philippians* (Edinburg and New York, 1859).

The remarks of Professor Stuart on Philip. ii. 5–8 are in the best style of that eminent interpreter (*Miscellanies*, Andover, 1846).

The older Commentaries of CALVIN, BENGEL, HENRY, MACKNIGHT, DODDRIDGE, and the later Commentaries of BARNES, BLOOMFIELD, ALFORD, ELLICOTT, and WORDSWORTH, are too well known to be formally cited.

LECTURES ON THE CHARACTER OF ST. PAUL. By the Rev. J. Howson, D. D. (2d ed., London, 1864). The author has drawn some of his finest illustrations from the Epistle to the Philippians. He shows that the heart of the great Apostle, that the distinctively personal traits of his character, are revealed more fully in this letter than in any of his other writings.

The articles on Philippi and Neapolis in HERZOG'S *Real-Encyklopädie* and in SMITH'S *Dictionary of the Bible* may be consulted with advantage on the persons and places mentioned in the Epistle.—H.]

THE

EPISTLE OF PAUL TO THE PHILIPPIANS.*

SECTION I.

I. ADDRESS AND SALUTATION.

CHAPTER I. 1, 2.

1 Paul and Timotheus [Timothy],[1] the [omit the] servants of Jesus Christ[2] [Christ
Jesus], to all the saints in Christ Jesus, which [who] are at Philippi, with the
2 [omit the] bishops[3] [overseers] and deacons[4] [helpers]: Grace (*be*)[5] unto you and
peace, from God our Father and *from* [omit *from*] the Lord Jesus Christ.

* Πρὸς Φιλιππησίους, ℵ, A B F S K, *et al.;* D E have πρὸς Φιλιππηνσίους preceded by ἄρχεται (found also in F G). There are fuller titles, as in the case of the Epistle to the Ephesians.

1 Ver. 1. [Timotheus occurs in the A. V. seventeen times and Timothy seven times, for Τιμόθεος, in Acts and the Epistles. The anglicized form is the easier one.—H.]

2 *Ibid.* Χριστοῦ Ἰησοῦ, ℵ B D E, *et al.;* A is uncertain. F S K L have Ἰησοῦ Χριστοῦ. [LACHMANN, TISCHENDORF, MEYER, WORDSWORTH, LIGHTFOOT and others adopt the former collocation.—H.]

3 *Ibid.* Σὺν ἐπισκόποις, B, *et al.;* συνεπισκόποις is a correction [and arose probably, says ELLICOTT, from the epistolary style of later times. The A. V. translates this Greek title by "overseers" in Acts xx. 28.—H.]

4 *Ibid.* [Instead of "deacons" (διακόνοις), as in A. V., BRAUNE renders "helpers" (*Helfern*), but LUTHER "servants" (*Dienern.*)—H.]

5 Ver. 2. [The Greek has no verb after χάρις. LUTHER, whom BRAUNE follows, omits the copula here. The A. V. in this elliptical form of salutation omits or supplies "be" without any rule. In respect to the nature of the ellipsis, see remarks on Philem., ver. 4 (Vol. VIII., p. 12 *b*).—H.]

EXEGETICAL AND CRITICAL.

Ver. 1. **Paul and Timothy, servants of Christ Jesus.**—(Παῦλος καὶ Τιμόθεος δοῦλοι Χριστοῦ Ἰησοῦ.) See on Eph. i. 1 and Col. i. 1. Timothy is not mentioned here as joint writer of the Epistle (MEYER), for the first person singular immediately follows in ver. 3, and in ii. 19 Paul appears as his director, nor for the sake of honoring him and of securing him greater influence in the church (SCHENKEL). [It has excited surprise that Luke is not named here as well as Timothy, since he was with Paul at Philippi, when the church was gathered (Acts xvi. 11), and was with Paul at Rome shortly before the time when he wrote to the Colossians (iv. 14). It is conjectured that some unknown exigency may have called him away from Paul just at the time when he wrote this epistle.—H.] The designation *servants* (δοῦλοι) marks their common relation to the Lord of the church, and corresponds to the familiar character of the epistle, as well as its object, which was to express his thanks for the supplies sent to him from Philippi. The church has by this act served not merely Paul and Timothy, but the Lord whose servants they are. BENGEL: *Familiarius scribit ad Philippenses, quam ad eos, ubi se apostolum nominat. Sub hoc prædicato communi discipulum Timotheum mediate vocatum sibi humanissime adjungit, qui recens Paulo adjunctus Philippos venerat* (Acts xvi. 3–12).—[We certainly miss here Paul's customary official title of Apostle, omitted elsewhere only in his two earliest Epistles, namely, those to the Thessalonians, and that to Philemon, which relates to a private matter. We are to attribute this, says SCHENKEL (*Briefe an die Epheser, etc.*, p. 112), not to his courteous regard for Timothy, for he assumes the title in Col. i. 1, where, as here, he associates Timothy with himself; but to the almost purely personal occasion of the letter, and its tone of familiarity, which naturally left out of view his official position. Besides, no one here at Philippi had assailed his apostolic authority, and hence he had no reason for giving prominence to his official dignity.—H.]—**To all the saints in Christ Jesus, who are at Philippi.**—Comp. Eph. i. 1. Πᾶσι τοῖς ἁγίοις, comprises all the members of the church. It is worthy of notice that this "all" recurs again and again, as in i. 4, 7, 8, 25; ii. 17, 26; iv. 22. We are to attribute this to the orderly condition of the church, which rendered exceptions unnecessary; not to the ardor of his love (MEYER), or his impartiality with respect to the disagreement (iv. 2, 3) which existed in the church (DE WETTE), or by way of emphasis with respect to his more confidential friends, for whom chaps. iii. and iv. are intended (HEINRICHS), or because he would include also those who had not contributed to his support (HENGEL). On τοῖς οὖσιν ἐν Φιλίπποις see Introduction, § 5, and on Eph. i. 1, and Coloss. i. 1.—**With bishops and assistants**—σὺν ἐπισκόποις καὶ διακόνοις. The ἐπίσκοποι are the πρεσβύτεροι (Acts xx. 28), ποιμένες (Eph. iv. 11), the presbytery. At the head of the church stood, therefore, not one bishop, but several elders. Concerning the διάκονοι see Acts vi. 1, 2; 1 Tim. iii. 8, 9. *Illi tum interna, hi externa curabunt proprie* (1 Tim. iii. 2, 8), *nec tamen hi non interna, neque illi non externa. Hæc una ad Philippenses epistola ita inscribitur, ut cum emphatica paraphrasi conjungatur mentio episcoporum et diaconorum* (BENGEL). Paul indicates that as the individual members are united to each other (πᾶσι), so the church with its officers forms a living, beautiful unity, as evinced also by the contribution sent to the Apostle and collected in the church by its officers. More remote, if at all involved, are the supposed references to the fact that it was a regularly constituted church (RHEINWALD), which is not to be presumed as true only of the one at Philippi; to the recognition of officers in the church (WIESINGER); to the special zeal of the bishops and deacons (MATTHIES); to Epaphroditus, as one who belonged to the ἐπισκόποις (GROTIUS, *et al.*), or to the fact that the collection came from the members of the church, without its having an official character (SCHENKEL).

Ver. 2. **Grace (be) unto you and peace, from God our Father and from the Lord Jesus Christ,** Χάρις ὑμῖν καὶ εἰρήνη ἀπὸ θεοῦ πατρὸς ἡμῶν καὶ Κυρίου Ἰησοῦ Χριστοῦ.—This accords with Eph. i. 2, which compare.

DOCTRINAL AND ETHICAL.

Comp. on Eph. i. 1, 2, and Col. i. 1, 2.

1. Paul comprises under δοῦλος Χριστοῦ Ἰησοῦ the relation of both Timothy and himself as servants. So great and glorious is their Master that before Him all distinctions in rank and importance vanish. These distinctions are authorized, and yet care is to be taken that they be not overstrained, or hierarchically established, or abused. It is one thing for the Apostle in his humility to associate himself with his assistant, and quite another for the latter to arrogate to himself an equality with the former.

2. The Apostle in the first place distinguishes between the church and its servants; but, secondly, he does not separate the two, so that the servants stand exalted *above* the church, but places them *in* the church, *from* which they are taken, and *for* which they are employed. Thirdly, he distinguishes also the different servants of the church, and names some ἐπίσκοποι and others διάκονοι, without stating any thing more definite in regard to them, except that the former are employed especially in the training and instruction of the Church, the latter in the care of the poor and sick. But, fourthly, he unites these together as belonging to one body and subordinate to one head. Fifthly, he speaks of a single church as having not merely διάκονοι, but also ἐπίσκοποι, so that we do not discover here the beginning of the Episcopal system, but find rather a college of presbyters at the head of a single congregation.

HOMILETICAL AND PRACTICAL.

Comp. on Eph. i. 1, 2; Col. i. 1, 2.

Be not confused by the distinctions among men, nor in the presence of them, that thou mayest clearly recognize the common position of all before the Lord. But do not, on account of this equality in His sight, despise the distinctions which He has appointed. Thou who art more highly honored, follow Paul; and thou who art less elevated follow Timothy. The pastor is not lord over the church which has a claim upon him and his office. The church may have stronger grounds of complaint against him than he against the church.

STARKE:—One must not seek for saints in heaven only, but find them already upon earth. He who does not become a saint here will not be one there.

RIEGER:—Paul places himself here by the side of his young co-laborer, Timothy, that others also may feel a well grounded confidence in him. The kingdom of Christ is throughout a kingdom of love. No one there desires to be alone, or misuses his gifts and advantages for the injury or depreciation of another, but, on the contrary, every one desires to lift up the younger and weaker ones, and to draw them after him. The welfare of the church is the main work. Bishops and servants are appointed to care for its interests and to maintain good order in it.

SCHLEIERMACHER:—When we say "peace," we know that it is the deepest, grandest, expression of our hearts for the soul's true welfare.

[ROBERT HALL:—"*Peace*," ver. 2. This was the term in which the primitive Christians were accustomed to salute each other in the common meetings, and in the streets, and market places. This was sanctified by Jesus Christ. He said: "My peace I leave with you, my peace I give unto you, not as the world giveth give I unto you (by compliment, *etc.*): let not your heart be troubled, neither let it be afraid." They were accustomed to express all this by the term peace; and the best thing we can wish for our fellow-Christians and for ourselves is, that "peace may be multiplied."—H.]

SCHENKEL:—The true importance of the office in its relation to the church: (1) as an office in the church; (2) as an office from the church; (3) as an office for the church.

SECTION II.

Situation and Labors of the Apostle at Rome.

CHAPTER I. 3–26.

(1) *The Apostle's gratitude and joy before God on account of the church* (i. 3-11).

After joyful thanksgiving for the fellowship of the church in the gospel (3–5), and the expression of his confident hope that God will make it perfect (6–8), he offers a fervent prayer for them (9–11).

3, 4 I thank my God upon every [all] remembrance of you, Always in every prayer
5 of mine for you all making [the] request [prayer] with joy, For your fellowship in
6 [unto] the gospel from the first[1] day until now; Being confident of this very thing that
he which [who] hath begun [began] a good work in you will perform [complete] it un-
7 til [up to] the day of Jesus Christ;[2] Even as it is meet [just] for me to think this of you
all, because I have you in my heart; inasmuch as both in my bonds and in the defence
and confirmation of the gospel ye all are partakers of my grace [of the grace with
8 me]. For God is my record [witness][3] how greatly I long after you all in the bow-
9 els [heart] of Jesus Christ. And this I pray, that your love may abound yet more
10 and more in knowledge and *in* [omit] all judgment [discernment or experience]; That
ye may approve things that are excellent [or, prove things that differ]; that ye
11 may be sincere [pure] and without offence till [unto] the day of Christ; Being
filled with the fruits [fruit] of righteousness which are [is][4] by [through] Jesus
Christ,[5] unto the glory and praise of God.

[1] Ver. 6. [A few of the oldest MSS. insert τῆς before πρώτης. Some copyist may have thought it necessary, but the grammar does not require it. See the exegetical remarks.—H.]

[2] *Ibid.* [Instead of Ἰησοῦ Χριστοῦ (T. R.) some copies invert the order as in ver. 1 (LACHMANN, ELLICOTT, TISCHENDORF, ALFORD). The evidence seems not to be conclusive.—H.]

[3] Ver. 8. [MEYER, TISCHENDORF and others, reject ἐστίν in μου ἐστίν of the T. R. The omission, on the whole, is very doubtful. See ELLICOTT's statement of the testimony.—H.]

[4] Ver. 11. Καρπὸν δικαιοσύνης τόν in ℵ A B (which last, however, omits the article τόν) and many others. The plural καρπῶν—τῶν is not duly attested. [The A. V. therefore requires correction here.—H.]

[5] *Ibid.* [Whether the order here is Jesus Christ or Christ Jesus, with the present evidence, is uncertain.—H.]

EXEGETICAL AND CRITICAL.

Ver. 3. **I thank my God** (*εὐχαριστῶ τῷ θεῷ μου*). Exactly like Rom. i. 8; 1 Cor. i. 4; Phil. 4. Comp. Col. i. 3.—**Upon all** [or **the whole**] **remembrance of you.**—Ἐπί states the ground or basis (*πάσῃ τῇ μνείᾳ*) on which the thanksgiving rests. This remembrance of Paul extends through his life; he contemplates it as one, as a whole. LUTHER well says: "As often as I think of you." See WINER's *Gram.* pp. 110, 392.* MEYER, urging the force of *πᾶς* with the article, explains: My remembrance of you is entirely and throughout connected with thanksgiving to God; and SCHENKEL: So far as he remembers them. These explanations are wrong; for the thanksgiving and the supplication go together. Still less can *ὑμῶν* be *gen. subj.*, as if Paul were giving thanks for their remembrance of him (BRETSCHNEIDER). Further, *μνεία* is not=mention (WINER, VAN HENGEL), as in *μνείαν ποιεῖσθαι* (Rom. i. 9; Eph. i. 16; 1 Thess. i. 2; Phil. 4). Comp. *μνείαν ἔχειν* (1 Thess. iii. 6; 2 Tim. i. 3).

* [The reference here and elsewhere is to the translation of the seventh edition of WINER'S *Grammar of the Idiom of the New Testament*, revised and edited by Prof. J. HENRY THAYER (Andover, 1869).—H.]

Ver. 4. **Always in every prayer of mine for you all** (*πάντοτε ἐν πάσῃ δεήσει μου ὑπὲρ πάντων ὑμῶν*). In Rom. i. 8 we have *πάντων ὑμῶν*; in 1 Cor. i. 4, *πάντοτε περὶ ὑμῶν*; and in Eph. i. 16, only *ἐπὶ τῶν προσευχῶν μου* after *οὐ παύομαι*. Here, after *πάσῃ τῇ μνείᾳ* (ver. 3) we have the idea of totality repeated three times: *πάντοτε, πάσῃ, πάντων*. *Latum erat cor Pauli* (BENGEL), by his joy in the church.—This clause is to be joined with the following: **Making the prayer with joy** (*μετὰ χαρᾶς τὴν δέησιν ποιούμενος*). [The article before *δέησιν* recalls *δεήσει* as *the prayer* in each instance which he offers in their behalf.—H.] *Πάντοτε* in the preceding clause shows that his thankfulness goes hand in hand with his constant prayer, and *ἐν πάσῃ δεήσει* that his prayer for the church, and indeed for all its members, never ceases; while here in *μετὰ χαρᾶς* we have his frame of mind disclosed to us, and the prayer noted as a fact. It is peculiar to this place. THEOPHYLACT: *τὸ μετὰ χαρᾶς μεμνῆσθαι σημεῖον τῆς ἐκείνων ἀρετῆς*. BENGEL: *summa epistolæ: gaudeo, gaudete! Nam perpetua gaudii mentio* (ver. 18 ff.; ii. 2, 19, 28; iii. 1; iv. 1, 4). *Preces imprimis gaudium animat.* For *δέησις* and *προσευχή* see on Eph. vi. 18. It is incorrect to join *πάντοτε* (WIESINGER), or *ὑπὲρ πάντων ὑμῶν* (HÖLEMANN), with *εὐχαριστῶ* (ver. 3). It is wrong also to make the participial clause parenthetical (HEINRICHS). [Taking this verse and the preceding one together, we have then three steps in the development of the thought: First, the apostle never remembers the Philippians but with thanksgiving; secondly, he remembers them in fact as often as he prays; and, thirdly, this remembrance of them was always a source of joy to himself, as well as a cause of thanksgiving to God.—H.]

Ver. 5 brings forward the cause of his thanks. —**For your fellowship unto the gospel.** —Ἐπί with the dative (preceded by εὐχαριστεῖν) quite often indicates the object of the thanksgiving (1 Cor. i. 4). See WINER's *Gram.* p. 393. —Τῇ κοινωνίᾳ ὑμῶν represents the fellowship of the Philippians as already existing, and not now as first to be prayed for, and the object of this fellowship is the gospel (εἰς τὸ εὐαγγέλιον). Κοινωνία is found without the *gen. obj.* in Gal. ii. 9 and in 2 Cor. ix. 13, where we have also εἰς αὐτούς, analogous to κοινωνεῖς εἰς λόγον (iv. 15). The article is not repeated before εἰς εὐαγγέλιον, because it appears as one conception, gospel-fellowship. The connection of this clause with the participle is incorrect (CALVIN, *et al.*), for we expect here a statement of the ground of his thanksgiving, and τὴν δέησιν has already been defined as ὑπὲρ ὑμῶν. It is wrong also to take κοινωνία actively, as *support, contribution* (ESTIUS, *et al.*), as in Num. xv. 26 (κοινωνίαν τινὰ ποιεῖσθαι), Heb. xiii. 16 (εὐποιΐας καὶ κοινωνίας), where the context demands that meaning; to refer it to their fellowship with Paul (CHRYSOSTOM, VAN HENGEL), for μετ' ἐμοῦ (1 John i. 3) is wanting; to regard it as = ἡ ἀγάπη ὑμῶν in ver. 9 (MEYER); to refer it to the fellowship of the Philippians with other Christians (WIESINGER); or to render it: *quod evangelii participes facti estis* (GROTIUS, *et al.*).—**From the first day until now,** ἀπὸ πρώτης ἡμέρας ἄχρι τοῦ νῦν, marks with emphasis this well-tried fellowship of faith and love as existing from the first preaching of the gospel among them (Acts xvi. 13) until the moment of Paul's writing the letter. [The church at Philippi had existed now about ten years. Among the proofs of this spirit of fellowship and zeal for the gospel (though not limiting himself to them) Paul no doubt had more or less distinctly in view the supplies which the Philippians had sent to him; first, once and again at Thessalonica, soon after his first departure from them (iv. 16), and still more recently at Rome, by the hand of Epaphroditus (iv. 18). Nothing but the want of an opportunity on the part of the Philippians to transmit their gifts, had prevented his receiving still others during the intermediate period (iv. 10). The recorded instances of their liberality, therefore, might well be mentioned as characteristic of their later history as a church. The article before πρώτης is unnecessary, the ordinal being sufficiently definite by itself. See WINER's *Gram.* p. 124.—H.]. It is incorrect to connect *from the first day, etc.*, with εὐχαριστῶ (BENGEL), or with πεποιθώς (MEYER). The aim is to characterize the fellowship, but not the thanksgiving or confidence of the apostle.

Ver. 6. The apostle is *confident* (πεποιθώς) that God will still work for them and in them. This participle marks his confidence as antecedent to the εὐχαριστῶ. *Hæc fiducia nervus est gratiarum actionis* (BENGEL). Αὐτὸ τοῦτο shows that his confidence rests upon God and nothing else (Eph. vi. 18, 22; Col. iv. 8).—**That he who began a good work in you will complete [or finish] it,** ὅτι ὁ ἐναρξάμενος ἐν ὑμῖν ἔργον ἀγαθὸν ἐπιτελέσει. Without doubt God is meant (ii. 13), and ἐν ὑμῖν is *in animis vestris* (ii. 13), while the context requires us to think of all the members of the church as addressed (vers. 4, 7). Comp. Gal. iii. 3; 2 Cor. viii. 6 (var. προενήρξατο. To explain it as meaning "among the Philippians" (HÖLEMANN) is against the context. Not only the context, but Paul's doctrine forbids us to understand "every good one" with ὁ ἐναρξάμενος (WAKEFIELD). By ἔργον ἀγαθόν is meant not "the good work" (LUTHER), but the κοινωνία ὑμῶν εἰς εὐαγγέλιον (ver. 5), a work which is not finished at a single blow, but is carried forward through a gradual development from step to step, through many a fluctuation and danger from within and without, to be made complete in eternity. BENGEL: *Initium est pignus consummationis: Ne homo quidem temere aliquid incipit.*—**Up to the day of Jesus Christ,** ἄχρις ἡμέρας Ἰησοῦ Χριστοῦ. The day of the Lord's coming for judgment is meant (ver. 10; ii. 16; 2 Cor. i. 14). The nearness of the day is not indicated (MEYER), or the day of each one's death intended* (ESTIUS, *et al.*).—**Even as it is just for me to think this of you all.**—Καθώς gives the reason for the subjective confidence in the objective fact (Eph. i. 4). Ἐστὶν δίκαιον ἐμοὶ τοῦτο φρονεῖν describes this confidence, which extends to each individual (ὑπὲρ παντῶν ὑμῶν), as a duty and obligation which he owes to his readers (vers. 4, 8; Eph. vi. 1; Col. iv. 1). To withhold it seems to him a wrong against them (BENGEL: *justas invenio causas*). — **Because I have you in my heart**—διὰ τὸ ἔχειν με ἐν τῇ καρδίᾳ ὑμᾶς. The context demands με as the subject; with this agrees the sing. καρδίᾳ. See WINER's *Gram.*, p. 329. It is contrary to the order of the words, as well as to the context, to take ὑμᾶς as subject (AM ENDE, FLATT, *et al.*). He has them in his heart, because he is separated from them. This certainly shows his deep, abiding affection for them. But this again would be only a subjective matter, like his confidence. Hence what follows is to be closely joined with it: He has them in his heart, and loves them as sharers of the grace of God.—**Inasmuch as both in my bonds and in the defence and confirmation of the gospel, ye all are partakers of my grace**—lit., *grace with me;* ἔν τε τοῖς δεσμοῖς μου καὶ ἐν

* [ALFORD (*in loc.*) supposes Paul to assume here "the nearness of the coming of the Lord." But that view is apparently inconsistent with 2 Thess. ii. 2; for the Apostle there declares this opinion (which some had falsely imputed to him) to be unfounded and without sanction in any thing that he had said or written. If at that early period (2 Thess. being the second of all his extant Epistles) Paul did not entertain that definite expectation, much less should we ascribe it to him after the lapse of so many years, during which this visible coming of Christ had been delayed. The reason why Paul refers here to a more distant event, instead of saying that God would strengthen the Philippians and enable them to persevere to life's end, may be that the day of one's death coincides so essentially in its moral consequences with the Lord's final advent, and hence was habitually near (as it should be to us all) to the feelings and consciousness of the first Christians. On this topic see remarks of the writer in his *Commentary on the Acts*, pp. 80–82 (revised ed.). See also ELLICOTT's notes on Phil. i. 6, in opposition to ALFORD's view. —H.]

τῇ ἀπολογίᾳ καὶ βεβαιώσει τοῦ εὐαγγελίου συγκοινωνούς μου τῆς χάριτος πάντας ὑμᾶς ὄντας. The nerve of the argument lies in συγκοινωνούς μου τῆς χάριτος πάντας ὑμᾶς ὄντας; πάντας ὑμᾶς corresponds to ὑπὲρ πάντων ὑμῶν, and they are all characterized as fellow-partakers (συγκοινωνοί) with the Apostle in the grace of God. The pronoun μου depends in sense upon σύν, τῆς χάριτος upon κοινωνούς: they share with Paul in the same grace, which he has received. [For the dependence of the two genitives on συγκοινωνούς (comp. also ii. 25, 30), see WINER's *Gram.*, p. 191—H.] The context (vers. 6, 7), defines it as the grace of God mediated through the gospel, *i. e.*, salvation and blessedness in eternity. It is thus not suffering for the gospel (v. 29, 30), as MEYER thinks, or merely *gratiosa evangelii donatio*, (HÖLEMANN), or the apostolic office upheld and made more efficient by the liberality of the Philippians (STORR, AM ENDE), gratitude—*i. e.*, to them (RILLIET), or *gaudii* (Vulg.), [which seems to rest on the assumed reading, χαρᾶς.—H.]. The importance of this co-partnership is the greater on account of Paul's situation at the time. Hence he characterizes the situation under two aspects before he speaks of their personal relation to each other: ἔν τε τοῖς δεσμοῖς μου and ἐν τῇ ἀπολογίᾳ καὶ βεβαιώσει τοῦ εὐαγγελίου. The first expression refers to his imprisonment, and the second to his work as a prisoner, embracing his labors both in opposition to adversaries, and for the confirmation of Christians (Acts xxviii. 23). It is not therefore merely his judicial defence that is meant (VAN HENGEL), or his general Christian activity alone (WIESINGER), but both together. It is incorrect also to regard the last two substantives as ἓν διὰ δυοῖν (HEINRICHS), or to separate τοῦ εὐαγγελίου from ἀπολογίᾳ, and to refer this last only to his person (ESTIUS), since neither ἐν, nor the article before βεβαιώσει, is repeated. The explanation which makes the two entirely synonymous (RHEINWALD) has as little in its favor as that which makes the one a defence by word, the other a confirmation by act (ERASMUS). The most natural connection is with ὑμᾶς συγκοινωνοὺς-ὄντας and not with ἔχειν ἐν τῇ καρδίᾳ (CHRYSOSTOM, also MEYER). [We prefer with CHRYSOSTOM, NEANDER, DE WETTE, MEYER, ALFORD, and others, to connect the words in question with what precedes, and not so closely with what follows. Nothing surely could be more pertinent here as a proof of Paul's affection for the Philippians (ἔχειν—ὑμᾶς), than to say, that not all his trials and anxieties as a prisoner at Rome, and not all his arduous labors in the church and for the conversion of sinners, could divert his thoughts from them or interrupt or weaken at all his attachment to them. This view of the connection, too, better explains the solemn appeal in μάρτυς—ὁ θεός, which (note the γάρ, ver. 8) seems too impressive to be referred merely to διά τὸ ἔχειν—ὑμᾶς.—H.] To infer from vers. 29, 30, that the bonds and the defence and confirmation of the gospel were common to Paul and the Philippians, (SCHENKEL) is not permitted either by δεσμοῖς μου, or by πάντες.

Ver. 8. **For God is my witness,** μάρτυς γάρ μου ὁ θεός. Comp. Rom. i. 9. He would confirm here his declaration that he has them in his heart. [His earnest desire to see the Philippians was both a proof and a consequence of his earnest affection for them.—H.]—**How I long after you all.**—Ὡς shows the degree, the prep. in ἐπιποθῶ, the direction of the ποθεῖν, ii. 26; 1 Thes. iii. 6; 2 Tim. i. 4. The object of ἐπιποθῶ is πάντας ὑμᾶς, none being excepted. Observe the energetic repetition of the πάντας.—**In the heart of Jesus Christ,** ἐν σπλάγχνοις Χριστοῦ Ἰησοῦ, characterizes the ἐπιποθεῖν of Paul. Σπλάγχνα, רַחֲמִים, *viscera*, is the physical designation of the inmost seat of the affections, of the emotional life in the soul (Col. iii. 12: οἰκτιρμῶν; Luke i. 78: ἐλέους); hence ἐν local. BENGEL explains it well: *In Paulo non Paulus vivit, sed Jesus Christus; quare Paulus non in Pauli, sed Jesu Christi movetur visceribus. Nexus hic est: ego vos tamquam consortes gratiæ in corde meo habeo* (2 Cor. vii. 3) *atque desidero, neque id affectu naturali, sed pietate Jesu Christi, inde persentisco eodem erga vos affectu esse ipsum potius dominum, qui rem a principiis ad suos exitus est deducturus.** See ἐμοὶ γὰρ τὸ ζῆν Χριστός, in ver. 21, and comp. ζῇ ἐν ἐμοὶ Χριστός (Gal. ii. 20). WINER's *Gram.* p. 189. It is incorrect to regard ἐν as the rule or norm, (RILLIET), for it is not=κατά; or to explain the genitive as, *in animo penitus affecto, ut animus fuit Christi.* (VAN HENGEL). It is incorrect to join the word with ὑμᾶς, and to supply ὄντας (STORR). We are to reject every such weakened explanation as *amore vere Christiano* (GROTIUS), or *digna Jesu Christi affectione* (CASTALIO).

Ver. 9. **And this I pray.**—To the prayer of thanksgiving in vers. 3, 8, καί adds further, the fact that he prays, and what he prays for, in behalf of the church (τοῦτο προσεύχομαι). The subject or contents of this prayer are first stated with emphasis, and therefore placed in connection with the subject and ground of his thanks; hence not προσεύχομαι τοῦτο. It is not true that καί connects what follows with ver. 8, and joins still another act, *i. e.*, προσεύχομαι, with μάρτυς μου ὁ θεός, ὡς ἐπιποθῶ. (RILLIET).—**That your love may abound yet more and more.**—Ἵνα points out the direction, purpose, of the prayer, and so the contents, purport of it. Comp. Eph. i. 17; Col. i. 9. Ἡ ἀγάπη ὑμῶν ἔτι μᾶλλον καὶ μᾶλλον περισσεύῃ, pre-supposes this love to be already existing, and that in no small degree, like ἵνα πληρωθῆτε. Col. i. 9. BENGEL: *Ignis in apostolo nunquam dicit, sufficit.* Love of the church is meant, which, as shown by the cause of his joyful thanksgiving (ἐπὶ τῇ κοινωνίᾳ ὑμῶν εἰς τὸ εὐαγγέλιον, ver. 5), and by the ground of his confidence and longing (συγκοινωνούς μου τῆς χάριτος, ver. 7), is more exactly defined to be Christian love. It is therefore neither merely love towards one another (MEYER), nor works of love for the cause of the gospel (SCHENKEL), nor love to the Apostle (CHRYSOSTOM, *et al.*), nor to God and Christ (CALOV), although all these are involved. The accumulative, ἔτι μᾶλλον καὶ μᾶλλον, marks the earnestness of the supplication. Comp. πολλῷ μᾶλλον κρεῖσσον, ver. 23. Περισσεύῃ indicates an increase of this love of the church

* ['Did I speak of having you in my heart? I should rather have said that in the heart of Christ Jesus I long for you.' A powerful metaphor describing perfect union. The believer has no yearnings apart from his Lord; his pulse beats with the pulse of Christ; his heart throbs with the heart of Christ (LIGHTFOOT).—H.]

above the ordinary measure of its possession. (Comp. 1 Thes. iv. 1, 10, περισσεύειν μᾶλλον).—How that shall take place is shown by what follows: **In knowledge and in every perception, or discernment**, ἐν ἐπιγνώσει καὶ πάσῃ αἰσθήσει. The first (see Eph. i. 17) is a more perfect knowledge of the truth in contrast with a knowledge which is defective, uncertain, confused; and therefore an intellectual act and intensive. The other (αἴσθησις, here only in the N. T.) is the perception by the mind or senses of what takes place or exists around us; here in its ethical sense as opposed to a weak judgment, to inexperience, inconsiderate conduct, and, having to do with the entire range of man's acts and relations, is therefore *extensive*, on which account also πάσῃ (=*every form of*) is added. [This faculty (αἴσθησις), as WORDSWORTH remarks, is that delicate tact and instinct which almost intuitively perceives what is right, and almost unconsciously shrinks from what is wrong.—H.] Both of these, the theoretical knowledge and the ethical tact, belong and go together. The prep. ἐν marks each as the sphere, or element, in which the increase of love is to take place. The progress is also a natural one, from knowledge to knowledge, from experience to experience, each promoting the other. Comp. Col. ii. 7. It is incorrect to deny here an increase of love, as if that were already complete (MEYER), or to find that the Philippians were not wanting in love, but in knowledge, their zeal being still *οὐ κατ' ἐπίγνωσιν* (Rom. x. 2), *i. e.*, blind, undiscriminating, liable to error (SCHENKEL).

Ver. 10. **That ye may prove things that differ.**—Εἰς τὸ δοκιμάζειν denotes the immediate end of the περισσεύῃ. It is in practice, the conduct of life that we are to prove τὰ διαφέροντα. As the senses are to be exercised, πρὸς διάκρισιν καλοῦ τε καὶ κακοῦ (Heb. v. 14), so here love should increase in knowledge and experience, that we may prove the things in regard to which we are to decide or act. Δοκιμάζειν means to test, distinguish the genuine from the spurious (χρυσίον, 1 Pet. i. 7), to distinguish between things which are different (τὰς καρδίας ἡμῶν, 1 Thess. ii. 4; πάντα δὲ δοκιμάζετε, τὸ καλὸν κατέχετε, v. 21), or between men who differ (1 Tim. iii. 10). The things which experience presents to us are different in degree as well as kind. *Non modo præ multis bona, sed in bonis optima.* (BENGEL). The rendering *ut probetis potiora* (Vulg., *et al.*) is incorrect.—The purpose of this increase of love is: **That ye may be pure and without offence unto, or against the day of Christ.** Ἵνα points out the direction of the prayer for the increase of their love. A firm decision for the good follows a correct judgment respecting what is good and evil. The knowledge and experience brought into activity lead to a certain condition and conduct (ἦτε): (εἰλικρινεῖς καὶ ἀπρόσκοποι). The first (Grimm, *Clavis* s. v: *ab.* εἵχη s. ἕλη, *splendor solis, et* κρίνω, *qui ad solis lucem explicatus et examinatus purus deprehenditur*,* *ex aliorum conjectura ab* εἶλος, εἵλειν, *volubile agitatione secretus et purgatus*) elsewhere only in 2 Pet. iii. 1, is positive, internal; the second, negative, outward, as referring to persons and relations; hence active, as in 1 Cor. x. 32, while in Acts xxiv. 16, it is passive. We are to look here not to the church or the world, not to the present or the past, but to God who ἐπιτελέσει ἄχρις ἡμέρας Χριστοῦ Ἰησοῦ (v. 6); hence εἰς ἡμέραν Χριστοῦ, **against, for the day of Christ** [not *until*, A.V.] in which this character will be made manifest. They should prepare for this as their great aim (see ii. 16: Eph. iv. 30).—**Being filled**, πεπληρωμένοι. The passive refers to what has been experienced or attained, and the perfect to the continued effects of this experience, and thus the participle characterizes the ἦτε εἰλικρινεῖς καὶ ἀπρόσκοποι.—**The fruit of righteousness which is by or through Jesus Christ** (καρπὸν δικαιοσύνης τὸν διὰ Ἰησοῦ Χριστοῦ). The *acc.*, as in Col. i. 9, points out that with which they are filled. The *sing.* καρπόν marks the harmonious unity, as Gal. v. 22. Comp. v. 19; Rom. vi. 22; James iii. 18. The gen. δικαιοσύνης indicates the cause, source. The omission of the article makes it a single conception: righteousness-fruit, more strongly descriptive of the character of the fruit: this fruit is itself righteousness in its very nature. Hence we must not think here of justification (HÖLEMANN). But this fruit of righteousness is not produced by the unaided strength of the Christian without the mediation of Jesus. See Eph. iv. 7, 8; Gal. ii. 20, iii. 22. This truth humbles us because it rebukes self-exaltation, but makes us rejoice also because it shows how glorious this fruit is.—**Unto the glory and praise of God** (εἰς δόξαν καὶ ἔπαινον θεοῦ) is an addition to πεπληρωμένοι. Comp. Eph. i. vi., 12, 14. Such fulness is of itself the glory of God, because it shows His excellence, and leads to His praise, because men declare it in every way. ["Herein is my Father glorified," says Christ, "that ye bear much fruit; so shall ye be my disciples" (John xv.).—H.]

* [The above is the generally received etymology. But some derive εἰλικρινεῖς from εἵλη=ἴλη, '*band*,' '*troop*,' and κρίνω, '*to separate*,' and hence *gregatim*, 'distinct,' 'unmixed.' HESYCHIUS defines: εἰλικρινές· τὸ καθαρὸν καὶ ἀμιγὲς ἑτέρου. LIGHTFOOT adopts this derivation. ELLICOTT prefers the second of the views mentioned in the text (see *in loc.*).—H.]

DOCTRINAL AND ETHICAL.

1. The salvation of individuals is the chief topic of this section, viewed however not theoretically, but practically, in its relation to a living body of Christians. It is a work, a *good work*, (ἔργον ἀγαθόν), wrought in the individual (v. 6: ἐν ὑμῖν), in whose inmost personality it is accomplished. Hence in its first province it is a human work.

2. In its nature salvation is righteousness, the fruit of which appears in the life (ver. 11: καρπὸν δικαιοσύνης), and love (ver. 9: ἡ ἀγάπη ὑμῶν), which is self-sacrificing. Hence it is opposed to self-seeking and self-will, and is fellowship with God, Christ, and the brethren. It is, then, in its next effect, a social work.

3. The source of salvation is to be sought in God alone (ver. 6: ὁ ἐναρξάμενος) without any merit or worthiness on the part of the subject who needs salvation, and is capable of receiving it, so that he is only the object, the recipient, of the blessing (συγκοινωνοὺς τῆς χάριτος, ver. 7). Hence in its beginning it is a divine work, which excludes as well the αὐτεξούσιον of the Greek Fathers, especially Clemens and Origen, as it does

Pelagianism, denying the transmission of sin (which Socinianism warmed again into life), and Semi-pelagianism (which Arminianism revived), weakening the conviction of this sinfulness in conformity with its idea of universal grace.

4. Nor in its entire progress is this less a work of God who does not draw back where He has put His hand, who, in the realm of creation and of redemption, in all His works in nature, and in the lives and hearts of men, is ever present, not only as a witness (*μάρτυς μου ὁ θεός*, v. 8) but to complete also (*ἐπιτελέσει*, ver. 6), what He has begun.

5. The work of salvation is mediated, objectively, through the person of Jesus Christ (ver. 11), the preaching of the gospel (ver. 5), and supplication. With regard to the *how* nothing more definite is here said, because it does not come into question.

6. The subjective mediation is indicated under different aspects, (*a*) Christ, He who is preached coming near to us in the preaching, and received in us by His word, becomes our life, His heart our heart, His pity our pity, so that we love with Him, with His heart, with His love (ver. 8: *ἐν σπλάγχνοις Χριστοῦ Ἰησοῦ*); (*b*) He who does not resist Him, receives His strength and gifts, so that by means of these he works in turn; won for Him, drawn to Him, united with those who are like-minded, he lives, and acts, and walks in love (ver. 9: *ἡ ἀγάπη ὑμῶν* ver. 5: *ἐπὶ τῇ κοινωνίᾳ ὑμῶν εἰς τὸ εὐαγγέλιον*); (*c*) Personal activity is not excluded, but called forth (vers. 9–11), self-exaltation is destroyed, and Synergism has no place here.

7. Love, combined with an active faith, is the central force which penetrates the inmost personality, directs the life, and goes forward step by step towards its perfection. This progress shows itself in a two-fold way: *a*) *Internally*, the Christian becomes intellectually more intimate with God and with His thoughts (*ἐπίγνωσις*). Love thus becomes clearer, deeper, stronger. It increases in knowledge, grows in that and with that. As an ethical effect, also, the love perceives, experiences, feels (*πᾶσα αἴσθησις*), the power of the kingdom of God with its manifold ordinances, and richly endowed membership. It thus becomes stronger, fuller, riper. It increases in experience, grows in that and with that. Thus Christians come to a surer judgment respecting the things which are about them, and concern them (*εἰς τὸ δοκιμάζειν τὰ διαφέροντα*) within and without, good and bad. The result is *purity* (*εἰλικρινεῖς*). *b*) *Externally*, love acts spontaneously, without calculation, with nice moral tact, with tender conscientiousness, giving no offence, (*ἀπρόσκοποι*). The eye ever directed to the end (*εἰς ἡμέραν Χριστοῦ*) animates this love thus progressive to the final day (*ἄχρις ἡμέρας Χριστοῦ*). Pantheistic necessity, all physical compulsion in the Christian's progress, are excluded. Our moral responsibility remains entire.

8. Love in two respects is an object of the Apostle's joy. It actuates all, one as well as another (ver. 7 *a*, and 7 *b*, 8), and redounds to the honor of God (ver. 11). First, though there is a difference in the strength, purity, breadth, and capacity of this love, from Lydia (Acts xvi. 14, 15) and the jailer (*ib.* 30–34) down to the weakest member, the fellowship between them is not disturbed. Every one looks upon the other with humility, and without envy, and cleaves to him. Secondly, the majesty of love becomes manifest, while gratitude for God's gifts is shown in word and work.

9. It is instructive to observe how the Apostle demeans himself here. He is thankful for what is given or done to him; God's act is final; his own doing is as nothing. He rejoices in spite of his imprisonment, since the internal welfare and the salvation of the church are of more importance to him than his own outward suffering. He is full of confidence, for, amid all the dangers to which the members of the church are exposed, from flesh and blood, as well as from the world about them, he has cast his cares upon Him who is greater than he that is in the world, and greater than his own heart. (Comp. 1 John iii. 20; iv. 4). He prays for them heartily, as well as confidently. Without pride of office, without selfishness, without carnal calculation, without meagre consolation, or satisfaction in comparing them with other churches, as in Galatia and Corinth, he looks with grand humility, with noble joy, with childlike confidence, and paternal care, upon the condition of this particular church.

10. [NEANDER:—Paul here (vers. 9–11) gives to love the first place, and ascribes to its quickening presence the knowledge and capacity required for distinguishing the good and the bad, the true and the false; as he himself expresses it, "that your love may more and more abound in all knowledge;" meaning, that *therein* its effect is seen—that increase of knowledge is the fruit of more abundant love. But as here the theoretical proceeds from the practical, the new direction of the judgment from the new direction of the will, of the moral disposition; so is the theoretical in like manner to react upon the practical, the enlightened judgment upon the conduct. Hence Paul adds, as the object to be thus attained, that they should continue "pure and irreproachable" in their Christian walk, until all shall appear before the Lord; "being filled with the fruit of righteousness, which is by Jesus Christ, to the glory and praise of God."—H.]

HOMILETICAL AND PRACTICAL.

The minister, in view of the past, should have reason to give thanks for the success of the divine word, and in view of the present should rejoice in the growth of love, and in view of the future be consoled as to more immediate danger, and hope for a glorious end. The church should find in him a helper of their joy; ever active, yet without official conceit, a friend, full of sympathy, without selfishness, a hero who lifts praying hands over them, a father who cares earnestly for their future inheritance, vers. 3–11.

STARKE:—God has indeed deserved our thanks: He never ceases to do us good. So also our thanks should have no end. Ps. c. 5.—He will be able to pray to God with joy who regards his prayer not merely as a duty, but also as a gospel right, in virtue of which he may come to the throne of grace, and be looked upon graciously.—To begin is well and necessary, but to complete still better, and more necessary.—The more thou art pressed the more cry out. Remain firm, and be not deterred. Through scorn we come to the crown.—The longer in the Christian life the happier, the better, is the true testimony. He who does not increase, decreases; at least, standing still is not the right way.—Since the chief powers of the soul are understanding and will, the growth must show itself in them both: the one can no more be separated from the other than understanding from the will.

HEUBNER:—If men do not recognise God as their God, they have no religion at all. It is not a living piety unless they have found God in their inner and outer life.—True love and friendship is ever a religious, mutual remembrance. Remembrance of God is a holy admonition that we live for, with, and in one another. Thus we see how Christianity enlarges the heart. Christian love embraces many; yea, all. (Vers. 4–7.)—Every shepherd must pray daily for his church. Paul had much to do, but he always had time for prayer.—True, inward fellowship of hearts, is a cause for thanksgiving. It is a source of true happiness which nothing can surpass. In our days a repugnance to the closer religious associations often shows itself; for in them religion comes nearer to men, and touches the heart. In like manner too great an equality of many with each other is offensive to some. Among ministers a dread of work is often the cause of this aversion.—There are special days of salvation and grace in our life. These memorable days are not merely birth-days, but rather those in which we have been awakened to a spiritual life.—We have still *churchly* assemblies, but those really Christian are rare.—For progress in what is good one needs grace as much as at the beginning: it is this which accomplishes all. God's Spirit leaves nothing half done. He completes His work if man only lets Him rule. It is disgraceful to us, after God has begun the building, to allow it to stop, or to tear it down. God does not destroy His work, we destroy it.—If thou art anxious about thy progress, cling only to God.—Christian love should not make blind, but clear-sighted. Love lifts up the spirit. The truth is always better discerned through love, and the medium of a practical Christianity. When borne up by others, one sees further, more clearly, (ver. 9.)—Love has a keen, critical character. The Christian has a delicate sensibility, by means of which he finds the right. A Christian's growth is growth in the spirit of examination, and the more the Christian discriminates, the freer does he become from all blemishes. It is only the pure, clean heart, which makes us blameless before Christ, (ver. 10.)—Paul gives here a definition of good works: they correspond to the law, spring from the Spirit of Christ, and redound to the honor of God: this last is their highest object, (ver. 11.) But measured by this rule, many good works so-called lose their value. The Christian should have also not merely single, isolated, good works, but a fullness of them (ver. 12.)—As the Epistle for the 22d Sunday after Trinity: The intimate connection of the Apostle with his church.

1) Ground: faith and love. 2) Effects: growth, new zeal.—Christian friendship: 1) Its nature; 2) Blessing; 3) Conditions.

PASSAVANT:—Without His grace over us, and His Spirit within us, all in us is vain and impure.

SCHLEIERMACHER:—The beginning, though very often the most difficult, is also in many cases the easiest, and not until afterwards do the difficulties which must be overcome, appear. The former exertions then seem, as it were, mere play in comparison with the persistent zeal, which must be shown, if the work is to be brought to an end.—If a man is impelled by the power of genuine love, he is not content with mere experience of life, or with a knowledge of the divine word, by itself, but he seeks to bind both together, so that the one shall ever accompany, support, and promote the other.

KRUMMACHER:—Love for all the saints urges, 1) to thorough self-examination; 2) to joyful emulation; 3) to hearty and humble praise of the free grace of God.—The fellowship of the saints: 1) The duty of thankfulness towards God; 2) Communications from the history of His kingdom; 3) Well-meant counsel: pray and watch.

ASHFELD:—At the end of the church year we observe a thanksgiving festival for the spiritual blessings of the year. 1) We give thanks for the gifts bestowed; 2) We trust God, that He will continue them to us; 3) We pray that we may constantly adorn our faith with richer fruits of righteousness.

LÖHE:—1) The Apostle's joyful thanksgiving for the fellowship of the Philippians in the Gospel; 2) His joyful confidence that the good work which has been begun, will be completed until the day of Christ; 3) His great longing for the Philippians, and for their perfection.

RAUTENBERG:—The signs of genuine thankfulness for the precious gift of the gospel: 1) Hearts which beat for it; 2) Lips which testify for it; 3) Hands which work for it.

OETTINGER:—The greatest joy of the faithful is fellowship in the gospel: 1) Of the perfect joy in pure fellowship; 2) of the incomplete joy in mixed fellowship.

MUENKEL:—The good work: 1) Begun through the gospel; 2) Proved in sorrow; 3) Completed in the love that gives no offence.

The priestly heart of the Apostle Paul: 1) A mirror for repentance; 2) A copy for faith; 3) A pattern for sanctification.

PRÖHLE:—True Christian friendship: 1) The source whence it flows; 2) The signs by which it verifies itself; 3) The blessing which rests upon it.—Most holy thought: God is my witness! 1) A thought of delight; 2) or of fear.—The way to a right understanding of Christian truth is through the heart: 1) It inclines the understanding aright; 2) takes away the bandage which keeps it from discerning divine things in their true form; 3) adds an inward experience to the testimony of the convictions of the understanding.

[NEANDER:—It is customary with Paul to commence his letters with a recognition of whatever is praiseworthy in the church to which he is writing. In this appears his wisdom as a spiritual guide. The confidence of men is far more easily won, and a hearing secured for whatever one has to say in the way of admonition and rebuke, if it appears that he nowise overlooks or undervalues what is good in them, that he does not willingly find fault, but is ready to acknowledge every real excellence with cordial approbation. Good and bad, moreover, stand frequently in close connection with each other. The good lies at the foundation; but the evil mingles its disturbing influence with the good, and hence it is through the latter that we can best reach and remedy the former. It is in the clear perception of this relation, and in the skilful use of it for the correction of error, that Paul manifests his wisdom (see vers. 5-7).—H.]

---

(2) *The gospel, in spite of insincere or false brethren and threatening danger of death, makes progress during the Apostle's captivity at Rome* (i. 12–26).

After referring to the happy effects of his ministry in bonds (12–14) among sincere and insincere witnesses for Christ (15–17) he expresses his views respecting this varied experience (18–20) and calmly revolves the question whether life or death may be better for him (21–26).

12 But I would that ye should understand [know], brethren, that the things which
happened unto me [my affairs] have fallen out rather to the furtherance of the
13 gospel; so that my bonds in Christ are [have become] manifest in all the palace[1]
14 [Prætorium, *or* Prætorian camp] and in all other places [to all the rest]; and many
[the greater part] of the brethren [in the Lord], waxing confident [in the Lord]
15 by my bonds, are much more bold to speak the word without fear. Some indeed
16 preach Christ even of envy and strife; and [but] some also of good will. The one[2]
17 of love, knowing that I am set for the defence of the gospel; but the other [others][3]
preach Christ of contention [contentiousness *or* party spirit] not sincerely, sup-
18 posing [thinking] to add[4] [raise up] affliction to my bonds. What then? notwith-
standing[5] every way, whether in pretence or in truth, Christ is preached; and
19 I therein do rejoice, yea, and will [shall] rejoice. For I know, that this shall
[will] turn to my salvation through your prayer, and the supply of the Spirit
20 of Jesus Christ, according to my earnest expectation, and (*my*) hope, that in nothing
I shall be ashamed, but (*that*) with all boldness, as always, (*so*) now also, Christ shall
21 be magnified in my body, whether (*it be*) by life, or by death. For to me to live is
22 Christ, and to die (*is*) gain. But if I live in the flesh, this is the fruit of my labor;
23 yet what I shall choose I wot [know] not. For[6] I am in a strait betwixt two, having
24 a [the] desire to depart, and to be with Christ; which is far better. Nevertheless, to
25 abide in the flesh is more needful for you. And having this confidence, I know that I
26 shall abide and continue with you all for your furtherance and joy of faith; that
your rejoicing may be more abundant in Jesus Christ, for [in] me by my coming
to you again.

[1] Ver. 13.—[Our English version assumes that ἐν ὅλῳ τῷ πραιτωρίῳ refers to the palace of the emperor at Rome. But there is no adequate proof that this Greek term ever designated the imperial palace in that city. The majority of the best interpreters discard that view. See notes below.—H.]

[2] Vers. 16, 17 are so arranged in ℵ A B, *et al.* A few copies have them inverted, as in LUTHER'S version, evidently to conform with ver. 15. [The A. V. transposes the verses in accordance with the received Greek text. The object of the transposition was to introduce the subjects of the verbs in verses 16 and 17 in the order in which they occur in verse 15; whereas in the text the subject last mentioned is taken up first.—H.]

[3] Ver. 17.—["Other" occurs here in the A. V. (as in Josh. viii. 22; 2 Chron. xxxii. 22; Job xxiv. 24) in the plural by an old usage for "others." The form has been silently changed in some later editions.—H.]

[4] *Ibid.*—'Εγείρειν is found in ℵ A B, *et al.*; ἐπιφέρειν is a gloss, with very slight support.

[5] Ver. 18.—Πλήν, D E K L, πλὴν ὅτι ℵ, ὅτι B. These last have arisen from the first. [LIGHTFOOT regards πλὴν ὅτι as more probably correct. Some texts have πλήν alone, others ὅτι alone; both which readings appear like attempts to smooth the construction.—H.]

[6] Ver. 23.—Δέ is found in ℵ and the majority of MSS.; γάρ has but slight support. [It is found in some of the best MSS., and "yet a reading, which comes to the relief of a disjointed syntax, must be regarded with suspicion" (LIGHTFOOT). MEYER regards δέ as the true reading.—H.]

EXEGETICAL AND CRITICAL.

Ver. 12. **But I would that ye should know, brethren.**—The position of γινώσκειν renders it emphatic: *contrariis rumoribus præoccupari potuissent ecclesiæ* (BENGEL). Δέ marks the transition from the condition of the church at Philippi to that of the Apostle at Rome. Ὑμᾶς βούλομαι, together with the friendly address ἀδελφοί, shows that this desire springs from Paul's heart. Comp. 1 Cor. xi. 3; 2 Tim. iii. 1.—**That my affairs** (ὅτι τὰ καὶ ἐμέ, as in Eph. vi. 21; Col. iv. 7,) **have fallen out rather to the furtherance of the gospel.** The comparative μᾶλλον refers to the anxiety of the Apostle and the Philippians. (WINER'S *Gram.*, p. 243). [The result was favorable rather (μᾶλλον) than adverse, as Paul and the Philippians had feared. —H]. The perf. (ἐλήλυθεν) indicates an effect which still continues. Comp. ver. 25. HÖLEMANN'S explanation *quam antea contigerat*, is wrong, for there is no comparison here of past and present.

Ver. 13. **So that my bonds in Christ have become manifest.**—Ὥστε explains how it was that his imprisonment at Rome had contributed to the progress of the gospel (εἰς προκοπὴν τοῦ εὐαγγελίου ἐλήλυθεν). Τοὺς δεσμούς μου φανεροὺς ἐν Χριστῷ γενέσθαι mentions the first result of his imprisonment in regard to hearers who were not Christians. As in 1 Cor. iii. 13; xi. 19; xiv. 25, φανεροὺς γενέσθαι means *to become manifest.* It is incorrect to explain φανερός as *illustris, conspicuus* (CALVIN). It is the opposite of κρυπτός, ἀπόκρυφος. The order of the words demands the connection of ἐν Χριστῷ with φανερούς. *Paulus cum aliis captivis traditus par eis visus est; deinde innotuit, aliam esse Pauli causam et sic invaluit evangelium.* (BENGEL). The nature of the information thus diffused, is shown by ἐν Χριστῷ. Paul's bonds are those of a Christian. He is δέσμιος τοῦ Χριστοῦ, ἐν Κυρίῳ (Eph. iii. 1; iv. 1; Philem. 9; 2 Tim. i. 8). His bonds had indeed been manifest before this time, but had not been manifest ἐν Χριστῷ. The emphasis lies on the fact that in this relation they had become manifest or known, and on that account φανερούς precedes.—**In all the Prætorium** *or* **Prætorian camp,** (ἐν ὅλῳ τῷ πραιτωρίῳ) designates the place where this knowledge had spread. On the subject, see Acts xxviii. 16–31.* The *castrum prætorianorum* (SUETON. *Tib.* 37, *Tac. Ann.* 42) is meant, (which was built by Sejanus in the reign of Tiberius, near the *porta Viminalis*), not the *aula Cæsaris* (BENGEL); for πραιτώριον is not the same as Καίσαρος οἰκία (iv. 22), as many hold. "*Repressaque in præsens exitiabilis superstitio rursus erumpebat, non modo per Judæam, originem ejus mali, sed per urbem etiam.*" (TACITUS *Ann.* 15, 40). [Prof. LIGHTFOOT at present understands πραιτωρίῳ in the sense of "*prætorians,*" and not "*prætorian camp,*" as formerly. (See his Commentary *in loc.*). But with that direct personal sense we might have expected the dative without ἐν, as in the other clause (comp. Acts iv. 16; vii. 13; 1 Tim. v. 15); whereas with the local sense as the direct one, and the personal as indirect, the change of construction becomes perfectly natural. EWALD'S periphrastic rendering "in all the *Prætorium* among the soldiers" (*Sendeschreiben des Apostel Paulus*, p. 441), gives the correct sense. —H.]—**And to all the rest,** καὶ τοῖς λοιποῖς πᾶσιν, points to others besides the Prætorians, for many besides these could hear, and did hear Paul preach. But we are not to think of heathen merely (VAN HENGEL), regarding the expression as analogous to 1 Thess. iv. 13. The prep. ἐν should not be repeated, and τόποις supplied (CHRYSOSTOM, *et al.*); for that would be making the circuit too extensive. It is plain from ὅλῳ and πᾶσιν (which shows how widely the gospel had become known) that the letter could not have been written very soon after Paul's arrival, but at a later period.

[Paul (if we make a distinction between ξενίαν, Acts xxviii. 23, and μισθώματι, ver. 30) may have spent a few days after his arrival at Rome at some place of public or of private hospitality; but after that he "dwelt in his own hired house," yet under the surveillance of soldiers, who, according to the Roman custom, were detailed from the Prætorian camp to attend him as a guard. But the Prætorian camp occupied an extensive circuit, and "might have contained within its precincts lodgings rented by prisoners under military custody" (LIGHTFOOT). Hence as different Prætorians relieved each other in the performance of this office, Paul would in the course of time become favorably known to many of them, and through these to other comrades. Thus it was soon understood far and wide that Paul had been imprisoned not for any immorality or crime alleged against him, but for preaching the gospel of Christ.—H.]

Ver. 14. Here we learn another fact which was a consequence of the Apostle's captivity, and favorable to the gospel: **And the greater part of the brethren** (καὶ τοὺς πλείονας τῶν ἀδελφῶν). [LUTHER renders πλείονας *many,* as does also the A. V. They constituted the majority, but Paul intimates at the same time that all the Roman Christians did not derive the same benefit from his example.—H.] The reference is to Christians, members of the church, who stood at the Apostle's side as assistants, co-laborers; not to teachers (SCHENKEL).—**Waxing confident in the Lord by my bonds** (ἐν κυρίῳ πεποιθότας τοῖς δεσμοῖς μου) explains why they acted thus. The perf. part. marks this confidence as already attained, and still in operation; ἐν κυρίῳ is the nearest object of the verb (Philem. ver. 21). OECUMENIUS well remarks: εἰ γὰρ μὴ θεῖον ἦν, φησί, τὸ κήρυγμα, οὐκ ἂν ὁ Παῦλος ἠνείχετο ὑπὲρ αὐτοῦ δεδέσθαι. Paul's bonds are to those *qui antea timuerant* (BENGEL) an actual pledge of the entire truthfulness, power, and glory of the gospel (MEYER), and, indeed, as the emphatic position of ἐν κυρίῳ shows, their confidence rests entirely on Christ, and not on any human calculation or reflection. See WINER'S *Gram.* 137 sq.; Gal. v. 10; 2 Thess. iii. 4. LUTHER incorrectly connects ἐν κυρίῳ with ἀδελφῶν, while BENGEL joins it with τολμᾶν.—**Are much more bold,** (περισσοτέρως τολμᾶν), states in what degree they were animated by the Apostle's zeal. The comparative supposes the case of Paul's being free from bonds, (*i. e.*, more boldly than if he were not imprisoned) and does not refer to the time of his arrival at Rome (SCHNECKENBURGER), or to that of his former freedom (SCHENKEL).—**To speak the word without fear,** (ἀφόβως τὸν λόγον λαλεῖν) shows what they are now *much more bold* to do, though even before

* [In regard to the passage referred to, it should be said that the words "the centurion delivered the prisoners to the captain of the guard: but—" in the A. V. (Acts xxviii. 16) are probably the translation of a later addition to the Greek text. See Mr. ABBOT'S note in SMITH'S *Bible Dictionary*, Vol. I., p. 384 (Amer. ed.). At the same time the words state correctly what was unquestionably true in regard to the Roman usage of committing prisoners like Paul to the care of the Prætorian prefect or commander of the Prætorian camp. (See PLINY'S Epist. X. 65). The reference therefore to Acts xxvii. 26 is still pertinent, though not so decisive as if the words were genuine. The false rendering of ἐν ὅλῳ τῷ πραιτωρίῳ by "in all the palace" (A. V.) destroys the interesting connection between the Epistle here and that passage. See above on the text.—H.]

this time they had attempted it. Hence περισσοτέρως is not to be joined with ἀφόβως, (BAUMGARTEN-CRUSIUS). Τὸν λόγον is absolute, as Gal. vi. 6, *i. e.*, God's word, which every Christian in his sphere is to speak and to bear witness to. The article denotes, according to the context, that it is the word which the Apostle preaches. The verb is used not merely of teachers (Eph. vi. 20; Col. iv. 3, 4), but also of members of the church (Eph. v. 19).

Ver. 15. **Some indeed preach Christ, also of envy and strife** (τινὲς μὲν καὶ διὰ φθόνον καὶ ἔριν); in contrast with τοὺς πλείονας τῶν αδελφῶν we have τινὲς μὲν—τινὲς δέ, in contrast with τὸν λόγον λαλεῖν we have Χριστὸν κηρύσσουσιν—καταγγέλλουσιν (ver. 17), and in contrast with ἐν κυρίῳ πεποιθότας, we have διὰ φθόνον καὶ ἔριν. The καί, *also*, introduces something additional (MEYER) *i. e.*, others besides those mentioned in ver. 14, who are also teachers. Their motive (διά) is a base one, namely, envy, excited by the Apostle's activity, and prompting them to strife for the purpose of disturbing or checking this activity, or of injuring his person.—**And some also of good will** (τινὲς δὲ καὶ διὰ εὐδοκίαν) forms the antithesis to what precedes. We are to take εὐδοκία therefore in the sense of having pleasure or satisfaction, *i. e.*, in Paul's work and person, which includes indeed, complaisance, or a desire to please, but not exactly benevolence. Those here meant are not identical with those designated in v. 14. It is not therefore that they act from conviction: *ideo quod ipsi id probarent* (GROTIUS) nor *alios salvare volentes* (PELAGIUS). Τὸν Χριστὸν κηρύσσουσιν belongs to the two contrasted groups. In their teaching concerning Christ they do not essentially differ, but they differ entirely in their motives, their moral classification, their character. This is more clearly explained in vers. 16, 17.—**The one of love** (οἱ μὲν ἐξ ἀγάπης) points to the latter group, οἱ δέ (v. 16) to the former. See WINER'S *Gram.* p. 561. The latter are characterized as οἱ ἐξ ἀγάπης as in Gal. iii. 7: οἱ ἐκ πίστεως sc. ὄντες. They are viewed as children of love; ἀγάπη is their nature. Comp. on εἶναι ἐκ τινός in 1 John ii. 16, (LANGE'S Series, XV.) By ἀγάπη (BENGEL: *erga Christum et me*), the generic or essential characteristic is meant; by εὐδοκία the specific as a manifestation or result of the other.—**Knowing that I am set for the defence of the gospel,** εἰδότες presents the motive (as Eph. vi. 8, 9) ὅτι εἰς ἀπολογίαν τοῦ εὐαγγελίου κεῖμαι. The verb κεῖμαι (as in Luke ii. 34; 1 Thes. iii. 3; 1 Tim. i. 19) represents his bondage as a divine appointment or destiny. Incorrect and opposed to the context (ver. 12) is the idea of his being prostrate *in conditione misera* (VAN HENGEL), or in *bonds* (LUTHER), because by their preaching they make up for his impeded activity, *supplent hoc meum impedimentum sua prædicatione* (ESTIUS). The task which devolves upon him in his situation has for its object the defence of the gospel, ἀπολογίαν τοῦ εὐαγγελίου (ver. 7), in which these Christians support the Apostle by their co-operation. It is incorrect to refer this to his account before God (CHRYSOSTOM), or his defence before the court, *coram judice* (VAN HENGEL).

Ver. 16. **But the others of contentiousness or party spirit.**—οἱ δὲ ἐξ ἐριθείας, as in ver. 17. Comp. Rom. ii. 18. Out of this spirit of rivalry or ambition (ii. 3; Jas. iii. 14, 16), which is their characteristic, spring envy and strife, φθόνος καὶ ἔρις (v. 15). 'Εριθεία from ἔριθος, day-laborer, ἐριθεύω to be an ἔριθος, and then in the middle, to use unscrupulous means for one's advantage, is the *ambitus* of the Romans. See PASSOW. *Lex. s. v.* The context requires us to retain the idea of intrigue or party-spirit. SCHENKEL incorrectly assumes the meaning to be "work for pay."—These do the same as the other class: they **preach Christ** (τὸν Χριστὸν καταγγέλλουσιν, v. 15, κηρυσσουσιν). Both verbs designate preaching, but have this shade of difference, that the latter signifies to proclaim Christ to those who have a very slight, or absolutely no knowledge of Him, while the former means to announce Him as present, near. Col. i. 28; Acts xvii. 3, 23. We are to join the finite verb with ἐξ ἀγάπης (ver. 16) and ἐξ ἐριθείας (NEANDER), since otherwise we have a needless accumulation of epithets, and we miss a characteristic designation of the two different classes. The preaching of the opponents is the same in substance as that of the others, but in a different spirit: **not purely,** οὐχ ἁγνῶς, *i. e.*, properly, not untainted, not *free* from coarser, or more refined accessory motives (iv. 8; 2 Cor. vi. 6; vii. 11; xi. 2). It is saying negatively that these do not preach from pure, unalloyed love for Christ.—This is further explained, positively:—**Thinking to add affliction to my bonds** (οἰόμενοι θλῖψιν ἐγείρειν τοῖς δεσμοῖς μου). The participle as present states an attendant motive or belief which the import of the word itself characterizes as unfounded, and the result also shows to be false (vers. 18–20), in contrast with the actual knowledge of the true witnesses respecting the Apostle's work and destiny (ver. 16, εἰδότες). 'Εγείρειν refers to the stirring up of further, additional, θλῖψις, *affliction*, connected with the imprisonment (τοῖς δεσμοῖς μου), not merely the prisoner, its effect being to aggravate his sufferings. [Prof. LIGHTFOOT finds a metaphor in θλῖψιν ἐγεῖρειν=*to make my chains gall me.* "This word (θλῖψις), though extremely common in the LXX, occurs very rarely in classical writers even of a late date, and in those few passages has its literal meaning. The same want in the religious vocabulary which gave currency to θλῖψις also created '*tribulatio*' as its Latin equivalent. The reading ἐγείρειν, besides being supported, carries out the metaphor better than ἐπιφέρειν of the received text."—H.].—How this aggravation of his trials was to take place, φθόνος, ἔρις (ver. 15) and ἐριθεία (ver. 17) indicate. Though the Apostle's enemies preach Christ as do the others, they do not, like them, seek to edify the church, and to assist the Apostle, but stir up strife and hatred against him. They preach Jesus as the promised one, that those who hear may say: 'This is indeed also Christian preaching; we need not run after Paul.' They thus draw the church to themselves, and withdraw it from Paul. They preach concerning Christ essentially as he does, only either more strictly to please those who are zealous for the law, or more loosely for the sake of those who are still weak, or in a more rhetorical way, not to offend the cultivated, as does the Apostle. Thus they not merely weaken the attachment of others to him, and draw away his followers, but excite enmity against him, and thereby make his imprisonment still more oppressive. In their preaching of Christ they go beyond their convictions from dislike to Paul; they make them more Christian in form to do him injury. To understand θλῖψις of an increased severity in his imprisonment by command of the emperor Nero (the Greek commentators, and PELAGIUS, ERASMUS, GROTIUS), accords as little with the contex, as it does to limit the term to his personal mortifications.

Ver. 18. **What then?** τί γάρ;—The question implies a denial of the belief (οἰόμενοι) *Quid refert? utrinque juvor* (ver. 12). BENGEL.—**Notwithstanding every way whether in pretence or in truth, Christ is preached.** Πλήν presupposes a difference (that is, of motives), while, at the same time, it brings forward what is common to the parties. Under παντὶ τρόπῳ are included what is outward, the manner of representation, the compass, articulation, the systematic arrangement and tendency of this teaching, not its contents as being Ebionitic, or other Jewish views, or Gnostic conceptions (Gal. i. 8). The more exact definition of πᾶς τρόπος follows in εἴτε προφάσει εἴτε ἀληθείᾳ. Both mark the relation of the word preached to the character of the preacher; εἴτε προφάσει points to the difference, εἴτε ἀληθείᾳ to the harmony between the two, as regards the word, doctrine and motives of the respective preachers: on the one side, insincerity, self-seeking, party spirit; on the other, conscientiousness, faithfulness. The first description embraces those mentioned in ver. 15 *a* and ver. 17, and the second those mentioned in ver. 15 *b* and ver. 16, and also ver. 14. It is incorrect to regard προφάσει=*per occasionem* (Vulg., GROTIUS). It is also incorrect to include under προφάσει those mentioned in ver. 15 *b*, as if these also merely showed themselves pleased with the apostolic type of doctrine (SCHENKEL). Χριστὸς καταγγέλλεται in ver. 17, sets forth what is common to the different witnesses.—**And I therein do rejoice**, καὶ ἐν τούτῳ χαίρω. For the construction see iii. 1; iv. 4, 10; Col. i. 24. The cause of his joy is that in every way Christ is proclaimed. The difference in the mode of proclamation cannot disturb his joy, though he must condemn the unworthy motives of his opponents. This joy is not merely a present, but an abiding one.—**Yea, and I shall rejoice** (ἀλλὰ καὶ χαιρήσομαι)—let the result of it as to himself be what it may. In like manner ἀλλά (iii. 8) opposes the pres. ἡγοῦμαι to the perfect ἥγημαι. We supply mentally a negative clause—'I do not merely at present rejoice.' Hence we are not to insert a period after χαίρω, as in LACHMANN'S N. T., see WINER'S *Gram.*, p. 442. We are not to think here of its being less difficult for Paul to show a spirit of resignation or acquiescence because the danger at Rome did not concern his apostolic authority as in some other instances (MEYER); for joy and an elevated tone of mind pervade the entire letter, and the Roman church was an object of the Apostle's special regard and solicitude, as the Epistle to the Romans testifies. Manifestly the teachers are not like those spoken of in iii. 2 sq., nor are they Judaizers, or Jewish Christians, disinclined to the Pauline view of Christianity (SCHENKEL). They must have been inclined to Paul's system of doctrine, and have approximated to it, but they were unfavorable to his mode of treatment, and unfriendly to his person. Their motives were corrupt (ii. 21), and they were not sincere friends of the Apostle. [For NEANDER'S views on this question see note below.*]

Ver. 19.—**For I know** (οἶδα γάρ) emphasizes the declaration as to his joy.—**That this shall result to me** (ὅτι τοῦτο μοι ἀποβήσεται). The demonstrative (τοῦτο) refers to ver. 18 (παντὶ τρόπῳ Χριστὸς καταγγέλεται), and explains why he rejoices, and not to θλῖψιν ἐγείρειν (ver. 17), as CALVIN, VAN HENGEL and others think. The use of the verb is similar to that of ἐλήλυθεν in ver. 12. [It explains why nothing hereafter can occur to rob him of this assurance and joy

* [NEANDER'S views respecting the character and object of those at Rome to whom Paul refers as seeking by their preaching to add affliction to his bonds, deserve to be considered here.—"Are we to suppose that these men, without personal love to the gospel, without personal conviction of its truth, preached Christ for no other reason than to add to the hardship of Paul's situation, and to bring him into greater danger by the wider extension of the gospel at Rome—thus rendering him, as the origin of it all, more obnoxious to the Roman civil power? It appears at once how unnatural and intrinsically improbable is such a supposition. If they would thus bring Paul into greater peril, they would by so doing plunge themselves into equal danger. Can it be imagined that one would play so hazardous a game, simply from hatred to another? He who at that time did not himself believe in the gospel, must be enlisted against it; and would certainly not have given himself up to the business of preaching it merely as the means to another end. We must seek, then, another explanation of this difficulty. When it is said of an individual that he preaches the gospel only in appearance, this need not be understood as necessarily meaning that he has no concern whatever in regard to the subject of his preaching; that he has no personal interest in it, no conviction of its truth, that he makes use of it only as a means to another end. It may mean that he preaches it, not in its purity and completeness, but as an adulterated, mutilated gospel. And when, moreover, he says of such that they were actuated by party zeal and hatred against him, desiring to add new affliction to his sufferings, it is not necessary to understand by this that their witness for the gospel was mere pretence, a form of hypocrisy to which the circumstances of the time afforded no occasion and no ground; but that their ruling motive in preaching was not from love of the Lord; that it was their aim, consciously or unconsciously to themselves, by their manner of preaching, to give offence to Paul, and to raise up for themselves a party against him. . . . We know that Paul had to contend with opposers, to whom all that has been here said is applicable. There were those who did acknowledge and preach Jesus as the Messiah, but a Messiah in the Jewish sense; who acknowledged Him, not as that which He has revealed Himself to be, the only ground of salvation for man; who, in connection with the one article of faith, that Jesus was the Messiah promised in the Old Testament, still adhered to the Jewish legal position; who understood nothing of the new creation of which Christ was the author, and to whom faith in Jesus as the Messiah was only a new patch upon the old garment of Judaism. These were the opposers, with whom we so often find Paul contending in his Epistles. Of such he might justly say, that they preached the gospel not purely and sincerely, but only in appearance; for indeed they were far more concerned for Judaism than for Christianity, and their converts became Jews rather than Christians. Of such he might also say that they sought to form a party against him, and to add affliction to his bonds; for those persons every where seem chiefly animated by jealousy of Paul, through whom the gospel was preached to the heathen world as freed from all dependence upon Judaism, and standing upon its own foundation. They oppose themselves to him on all occasions, contest his apostolic dignity, seek to encroach on his sphere of labor, to draw over the people from him to themselves, from that pure and complete gospel to their own mutilated one. And it need not surprise us to meet such even in Rome; for Paul's Epistle to the church at Rome, written some years previous to his imprisonment there, shows us in this church, consisting chiefly of Gentile converts, a small party of such Judaizing Christians who were in conflict with the rest. It was a matter of course then, that when the pure gospel in the sense of Paul was preached by the one party, the other, provoked to rivalry, should rise up in opposition and seek to give currency to their own corrupted form of the gospel." (*Epistle of Paul to the Philippians*, translated by MRS. H. C. CONANT, N. Y., 1851.)—H.]

of which he speaks. He feels assured that the opposition of his enemies will be the means not only of advancing the cause of Christ (ver. 18), but, as stated here, of exciting him to greater zeal and activity, and thus also indirectly of promoting his own spiritual welfare and ultimate salvation. The reference of *τοῦτο* to the opposition of Paul's enemies (so also LIGHTFOOT) is the most natural, both on account of the sequel, and because the statement that the preaching of Christ must advance the cause of Christ is too obvious to need a formal confirmation (*γάρ*).—H.]—**Unto salvation** (*εἰς σωτηρίαν*), like *εἰς προκοπὴν τοῦ εὐαγγελίου* in ver. 12, with the meaning (comp. also ver. 20), that in himself Christ and His gospel will be glorified and advanced. Hence it does not refer to his release from imprisonment (CHRYSOSTOM, *et al.*), to the preservation of his life (OECUMENIUS), to his victory over his enemies (MICHAELIS), *ad salutem multorum hominum* (GROTIUS), to *salus vera et perennis* (VAN HENGEL), or to his own salvation in a spiritual sense (RHEINWALD). [Among others, ELLICOTT and LIGHTFOOT adopt this last explanation. The pronoun (*μοι*) indicates a personal result, and the future of the verb shows it to be one not yet secured. This meaning, too, of *σωτηρία* is the prevailing one in Paul's Epistles; comp. ver. 28; ii. 12; Rom. i. 16; 2 Thess. ii. 13. See further on ver. 20.—H.]—**Through your prayer and assistance of the Spirit of Jesus Christ.**—The way to this result (*ἀποβήσεται*) is, first, through (*διά*) the supplication of the Philippians (*τῆς ὑμῶν δεήσεως*), to which the Apostle attaches great value (Philem. 22; Rom. xv. 30, 31; 2 Cor. i. 11); secondly, through the assistance of the Spirit of Jesus Christ (*καὶ ἐπιχορηγίας τοῦ πνεύματος Ἰησοῦ Χριστοῦ*), which therefore the Holy Spirit affords, who is indeed the Spirit of Jesus Christ, directs His cause, and hence is designated as His Spirit. The genitive makes it unnecessary to repeat the article (*τῆς*), as also the close connection of the two substantives makes it unnecessary to repeat *διά*. On *ἐπιχορηγία* see Eph. iv. 16; comp. Rom. viii. 9, 10; Gal. iv. 6, 7. *Precationem in cœlum ascendentem, exhibitionem de cœlo venientem* (BENGEL). Hence it is wrong to regard *καί* as epexegetical, and *ἐπιχορηγία* as the contents of *δέησις* (MEYER); nor can *τοῦ πνεύματος* be shown to be *gen. obj.* from Gal. iii. 5. [Yet the close connection of the nouns indicates that the gifts and guidance of the Spirit were among the favors for which they prayed in his behalf.—H.]

Ver. 20.—**According to my earnest expectation and hope** (*κατὰ τὴν ἀποκαραδοκίαν καὶ ἐλπίδα μου*). Having stated the end or result (*εἰς σωτηρίαν*), and the means (*διὰ τῆς ὑμῶν δεήσεως*), he now presents the measure (*κατά*) of the *ἀποβήσεται*. The first substantive (*ἀποκαραδοκία*, see Rom. viii. 19) denotes the soul's subjective, intenser longing (*ἀποκαραδοκέω*, *erecto capite specto*); the second (*ἐλπίς*) the more objective, outward, ground or object of expectation.—The object of this longing and expectation is: **That in nothing I shall be ashamed** (*ὅτι ἐν οὐδενὶ αἰσχυνθήσομαι*). Ὅτι is declarative, not argumentative (ESTIUS); for *οἶδα γάρ* brings forward the reason of his rejoicing. Αἰσχύνεσθαι=בּוֹשׁ (Ps. xxxiv. 4, 29; Rom. ix. 33; 2 Cor. x. 8) is *to become ashamed*, to fail of one's purpose, be disappointed. The meaning is not *pudore confusus ab officio deflectam* (VAN HENGEL), since, as MEYER well observes, it relates not so much to the conduct as to the fate of Paul. Still less does it refer to an ignominious issue of his trial. Ἐν οὐδενί excludes the being put to shame in any particular, as *ἐν μηδενί* in ver. 28. It is incorrect to regard it as masculine, and to apply it to his opponents (HÖLEMANN, LIGHTFOOT), especially as the case is one not of individuals, but of parties.—**But** (*ἀλλ'*) joins the positive side to the negative.—**That with all boldness as constantly, so now also Christ shall be magnified in my body** (*ἐν πάσῃ παῤῥησίᾳ ὡς πάντοτε καὶ νῦν μεγαλυνθήσεται ὁ Χριστὸς ἐν τῷ σώματί μου*). *Ignominiam a sese removet; sibi parrhesiam, Christo ipsi gloriam tribuit* (BENGEL). In the person of the Apostle who is in bonds Christ is to be thus glorified. This positive statement shows fully what is meant by the preceding negative statement. Παῤῥησία is not=joyfulness, for see 1 John ii. 28, where *σχῶμεν παῤῥησίαν* is opposed to *καὶ μὴ αἰσχυνθῶμεν*, as here. Ἐν πάσῃ corresponds to *ἐν οὐδενί*, and the *μεγαλύνεσθαι* of Christ in Paul's person, to Paul's *αἰσχύνεσθαι* designed and sought by his enemies. As formerly this had been done in many a difficult position, amid great obstacles, so also now in this severest crisis (*καὶ νῦν*) will Christ be glorified in him. He desires for himself what he entreats for the church (see ver. 11). On *μεγαλυνθήσεται* comp. Luke i. 46; Acts x. 46. This exaltation of Christ is effected as much indeed through Paul's activity and boldness (*ἐν πάσῃ παῤῥησίᾳ*), in word and deed, before individuals and crowds, friends and foes, as through his sufferings (hence *ἐν τῷ σώματί μου* instead of *ἐν ἐμοί*). It is not, therefore, the *παῤῥησία* of the teachers (vers. 15–18) (HÖLEMANN), nor does the verb (contrary to usage) refer to the growth of Christ in Paul (RILLIET), which surely does not take place in Paul's body. [He says *ἐν τῷ σώματί μου*, not *ἐν ἐμοί*, because he is thinking of the possibility of a violent death.—H.]—Both clauses: **Whether by life or by death** (*εἴτε διὰ ζωῆς εἴτε διὰ θανάτου*) are conditioned by *ἐν τῷ σώματί μου*. The meaning is, that whether he is to live or suffer death, the result will be for the glory of Christ. In the first case, by the Apostle's activity; in the second, by his joyful death. In either case, his *παῤῥησία* or 'boldness' would be made manifest. [The manner, therefore, in which the Apostle's trials, his perplexities and annoyances (*τοῦτο*, ver. 19) might be made to conduce to his salvation (*εἰς σωτηρίαν*) is evident. If, on the one hand, they should discourage him and lead him to relax his efforts, and render him unfaithful, they would endanger his hopes and safety, or at all events dim the lustre of his crown of glory in the heavenly world. So, on the other hand, if, through the prayers of his friends and the assistance of the Holy Spirit, these same trials should be overruled (as he was confident they would be) so as to strengthen in him the graces of the Christian and excite him to greater fortitude and zeal as a preacher of the gospel, they would then render the fact of his salvation more certain, and in the measure of its fullness more complete and glorious.

And it was not a vain confidence which the Apostle has expressed here. At a later period, on the eve of his actual martyrdom, he was enabled to exclaim: "I have fought a good fight, I have kept the faith. Henceforth there is laid up for me a crown of righteousness, which the Lord, the righteous Judge, shall give me at that day; and not to me only, but unto all them also that love his appearing" (2 Tim. iv. 6, 7).—H.]

Ver. 21. [The Apostle is uncertain whether in a personal point of view he should choose to live or to die (vers. 21-24).—H.]—**For to me to live (is) Christ, and to die (is) gain.**—'Εμοὶ γάρ introduces a confirmation of the thought that it is entirely the same to him whether Christ be glorified through his life and activity, or by his death; with others (hence ἐμοί at the beginning) it may indeed be different. Τὸ ζῆν, which is made more specific by ἐν σαρκί, ver. 22, defines the nature of the preceding ζωή: this is Χριστός (predicate). *Quidquid vivo (vita naturali), Christum vivo, Christi causam, dum vitam in mundo ago, meam esse censeo* (BENGEL). [Living consists only in union with and devotion to Christ: my whole being and activities are His. The context shows that Χριστός, besides the idea of union with Him, must also involve that of devotion to His service (ELLICOTT).—H.] Καὶ τὸ ἀποθανεῖν κέρδος imports: If the imprisonment end with my being condemned to death, even this as regards my person is also gain, as more fully explained in ver. 23. Hence the inf. aorist is used to mark the simple fact, while ζῆν is a continuative present. It is incorrect to understand ζῆν of the spiritual life (RILLIETT), or to make Χριστός the subject in the sense of preaching Christ, κέρδος the predicate, and τὸ ζῆν καὶ τὸ ἀποθανεῖν as accusative relations, *tamen vita, quam in morte* (CALVIN, *et al.*). It is also wrong to make it parenthetic: His assurance that death will be gain will give him strength to die joyfully, and so he will glorify Christ (MEYER, *et al.*). [Since κέρδος is defined as σὺν Χριστῷ εἶναι in ver. 23, 'the gain' cannot be a result viewed simply as advantageous to the cause of Christ or the salvation of others.—H.]

Ver. 22. **But if the living in the flesh, this (is) the fruit of my labor.**—Εἰ δέ begins the comparison of two cases. Εἰ pre-supposes an undoubted fact, in opposition (δέ) to the last thought (τὸ ἀποθανεῖν κέρδος). Τὸ ζῆν is more fully defined by ἐν σαρκί, because there is a life out of the flesh which ἀποθανεῖν calls to mind. Τοῦτο rhetorically brings the two antecedent words together, and μοί, *for me*, is placed emphatically before the predicate without the copula (ἐστί): καρπὸς ἔργου. In καρπός we have a parallel to κέρδος (ver. 21), and τὸ ζῆν ἐν σαρκί is thus also a gain, a living, ever ripening fruit, the nature of which the *genit.* of apposition more closely defines, like *flumen Rheni, virtus liberalitatis* (BENGEL), and comp. Eph. i. 14; vi. 14, 16 f.; Col. ii. 24. See WINER'S *Gram.* p. 531. So that Paul *ipsum opus pro fructu habet, alius ex opere fructum quærit* (BENGEL). Ἔργον is the Apostolic activity. It is wrong to regard εἰ=*an* (BEZA) [*whether* (LIGHTFOOT)]; τοῦτο ἔργου as the apodosis=*this is fruit, etc.* (PELAGIUS, BENGEL, A. V.); καρπὸς ἔργου=*operæ pretium* (GROTIUS); or to suppose an *aposiopesis: non repugno, non ægre fero* (CONR. MUELLER, RILLIET). HÖLEMANN translates against the context and the language: If to live is a fruit, in the flesh, death is a fruit indeed. [Instead of ἔργου as *genit.* of apposition, we prefer that of origin or source: *If the living in the flesh* (εἰ, not hypothetical, but syllogistic=since it is, *etc.*) *this* (which simply repeats and emphasizes τὸ ζῆν) is (brings forth, secures) *fruit, i. e.*, the salvation of men, *from work* (his continued Apostolic activity; comp. ii. 30; 1 Thess. v. 13; 2 Tim. iv. 5), *also then, etc.* (as in the next clause). With this modification the explanation of Dr. BRAUNE as above agrees essentially with that of DE WETTE, MEYER, ELLICOTT, ALFORD, and many other interpreters.—H.]—**Then also what** (*i. e.*, **which of the two**) **I should choose I know not** (καὶ τὸ αἱρήσομαι, οὐ γνωρίζω). To the supposition τὸ ζῆν—καρπός Paul now adds *also* or *then* (καί) the uncertainty of the choice to be made (οὐ γνωρίζω). For this use of καί comp. 2 Cor. ii. 2. It is not a Hebraistic form of the apodosis. [TISCHENDORF has correctly only a comma after ἔργου. In this concomitant use of καί, as we may term it, its proper force is not wholly lost. It implies that if one theory be true, then another will be true also: if the life be thus useful, the choice must *also* (καί) be difficult. See ELLICOTT *in loc.*—H.] On τί αἱρήσομαι, see WINER'S *Gram.* p. 229. It is a future with the force of the conjunctive, the two being closely related; and τί is for πότερον, as in Matth. xxi. 31. See WINER'S *Gram.* p. 169. The middle denotes the choosing for himself, with γνωρίζω=*non definio mihi* (BENGEL). [In the first edition of his Commentary, MEYER renders 'I am uncertain,' but in the second and third editions he renders 'I do not make known,' 'give no decision.' The latter is the prevalent sense in the N. T.—H.]

Ver. 23. **For I am in a strait betwixt the two** (συνέχομαι δὲ ἐκ τῶν δύο).—The negative statement in οὐ γνωρίζω passes here to a positive statement in συνέχομαι, and the latter is made emphatic by its position and strengthened by δέ=rather. The verb means *to be held together*, to be pressed hard (2 Cor. v. 14; Luke viii. 45 (συνέχουσί σε καὶ ἀποθλίβουσι), xii. 50), and is followed by the instrumental dative (Matth. iv. 24; Luke iv. 38; viii. 37; Acts xviii. 5; xxviii. 8). Here the preposition with the genitive (ἐκ τῶν δύο) marks the origin or source of his perplexity about the two conditions, *i. e.*, ζῆν and ἀποθανεῖν already mentioned. The sense of the verb (see above) is manifest from ver. 24. It cannot refer to outward affliction or anxiety.—**Having the desire to depart** (τὴν ἐπιθυμίαν ἔχων εἰς τὸ ἀναλῦσαι).—Paul is in a strait or perplexity, since for himself he prefers death to life. The article marks the desire as the one which Paul feels, not one already mentioned (HÖLEMANN), which is not the case. The prep. εἰς points out the direction; whereas the genit. τοῦ would represent death as the object of his desire. Paul is not wearied of life, but his thoughts pass beyond death as a transition, and fix upon that which is to follow. Death is conceived of under a similar figure, *viz.*, that of a journey (Matth. xxvi. 24, ὑπάγειν), that of a voyage (2 Tim. iv. 6, *solvere ancoram*), and also without a figure, as *decedere*

(Luke xii. 36, BENGEL).—**And to be with Christ**—καὶ σὺν Χριστῷ εἶναι.—Comp. 2 Cor. v. 8 (ἐνδημῆσαι πρὸς κύριον); Heb. xii. 22, 23; Acts vii. 59. The departure (ἀναλῦσαι) brings him into this higher life of fellowship with Christ. There is no thought here of an intermediate state.—**Which is far better**—πολλῷ γὰρ μᾶλλον κρεῖσσον.—The accumulation of comparatives (2 Cor. vii. 13; Mark vii. 36) indicates the strength of his desire. WINER's *Gram.* p. 240.

Ver. 24. **Nevertheless to abide in the flesh is more needful for you**—Τὸ ἐπιμένειν δέ stands opposed to ἀναλῦσαι. Ἐν τῇ σαρκί has the article here in the correct text (not ἐν σαρκί, as in ver. 22); hence in *his flesh* as it now is. This remaining is more necessary (ἀναγκαιότερον) as distinguished from his departing (ἀναλῦσαι), which is better (κρεῖσσον), as far as relates to his own preference. But here a calm survey and consideration of the circumstances, a regard for the welfare of others, beloved ones, among whom are to be named especially those to whom he writes (δι' ὑμᾶς), decide the question. His Apostolic calling and his service to the church, which are of far greater importance to him than his own heart's desire, control his decision. It is incorrect to explain ἀναγκαιότερον=*præstat* (HEINRICHS), as "too necessary" (VAN HENGEL), or to consider the glory of Christ as the ground of his wish to live longer (CALVIN).

Ver. 25. **And having this confidence I know** (καὶ τοῦτο πεποιθὼς οἶδα). Τοῦτο points back to ἀναγκαιότερον, and indicates the ground of his confidence, and the perf. part. marks this confidence as one which he has had, and still entertains. We are not to join τοῦτο with οἶδα (ERASMUS, *et al.*) or to explain this last as *probabiliter sperare* (BEZA, VAN HENGEL, RILLIET). Comp. Philem. ver. 22. Though uncertain as to what he ought to choose for himself, yet he is quite sure that he will remain.—**That I shall abide and continue with you all.**—Ὅτι μενῶ is the opposite of ἀναλῦσαι. On μένειν comp. 1 Cor. xv. 6; John xxi. 22, 26. It is more fully explained by καὶ συμπαραμενῶ πᾶσιν ὑμῖν. Παραμένειν is to remain here, while σύν adds the idea of association with others (πᾶσιν ὑμῖν). This fellowship helps him to give up the more desired ἀναλῦσαι, especially as his remaining has its consequence and fruit, as well as the being with Christ (σὺν Χριστῷ εἶναι).—**For your furtherance and joy of faith.**—This is explanatory of δι' ὑμᾶς (ver. 24). Εἰς states the purpose of Paul's remaining; it is twofold: their furtherance in the faith, and their joy in the faith, τὴν ὑμῶν προκοπὴν καὶ χαρὰν τῆς πίστεως. This is Paul's life—to preach Christ and to strengthen the faith of others. On προκοπή see ver. 12; 1 Tim. iv. 15. Nothing is here said of a favorable termination of his imprisonment (BEZA). It is also incorrect to assume a hendiadys: *in incrementum gaudii vestri, quod ob agnitum evangelium accepistis* (HEINRICHS); or to understand it of Paul's joy on account of the faith of the Philippians (ERASMUS), or to connect τῆς πίστεως only with χαράν (VAN HENGEL); for in this case the pronoun would need to be repeated with πίστεως.

Ver. 26. **That your rejoicing may be more abundant.**—Ἵνα states the final purpose of the subordinate one, expressed by εἰς; comp. vers. 9, 10, 11. Τὸ καύχημα ὑμῶν is *significatio gaudii, affectus gaudii pleni* (BENGEL), glorying, as 1 Cor. v. 6. It is the natural result of the increase and joy of their faith (τὴν ὑμῶν προκοπὴν καὶ χαρὰν τῆς πίστεως), but it is not the object of them. Hence καύχημα is not *materies gloriandi* (MEYER), nor is it boasting against Judaizing teachers (FLATT), or Paul's glorying (CHRYSOSTOM). But this glorying, as well as faith, is to increase (περισσεύῃ) **in Christ Jesus** (ἐν Χριστῷ Ἰησοῦ) as its sphere.—**In me** (ἐν ἐμοί) points to the Apostle's person and activity as the outward sphere of this glorying which admits of increase in Christ. Neither ἐν Χριστῷ (CALVIN), nor ἐν ἐμοί (FLATT), belongs to καύχημα. The idea expressed by ἐν ἐμοί is rendered still more definite by the statement of the means.—**Through my return to you** (διὰ τῆς ἐμῆς παρουσίας πάλιν πρὸς ὑμᾶς)—by which the faith of the Philippians shall be confirmed and their joy be increased. On πάλιν, which has here the force of an adjective, see 2 Cor. xi. 23. Paul is thinking of his release from imprisonment; but no safe conclusion can be drawn from this as to the fulfilment of this expectation.

DOCTRINAL AND ETHICAL.

1. The evil and sorrow of the world, as imprisonment, and death, become a trial, a cross, on which hang victory and a glorious issue, only then, when he who experiences them can say: "For me to live is Christ" (ἐμοὶ τὸ ζῆν Χριστός). Not the sorrow which men experience makes a bearer of the cross, with its power of attraction, the sign in which we conquer; but the Christian's disposition and behaviour in sorrow make the sorrow a cross. In this consists the true value of martyrdom, and not in the fact alone of suffering and dying. Like the cross of Christ, it must also be a necessity, imposed by the Father, from which we can withdraw only by a violation of conscience, and a refusal to deny self, and to seek our own and our neighbor's edification. See HARLESS, *Ethik*, § 39.

2. The Christian shows himself, in calamity, to be one who is not overpowered, vexed, swept away by sorrow, or engulfed by it, like one who toilsomely wades through deep water, but he compels it to yield him strength and joy, like the stars of heaven in the night, after he has conquered it and made it his attendant. He is not the object of weak compassion and pity, but of admiration and love, like a conquering hero. He is like a praying one who speaks to God; and as one to whom God speaks, is an object almost of religious veneration.

3. The blessing of the cross is seen in three respects—*a*) The suffering soul becomes free, more joyful, riper, stronger (ver. 19, εἰς σωτηρίαν, comp. 12, 18, 20, 21 sq.), since it becomes more closely united to the Lord, purified from what is earthly and mortal, more intimate with the Eternal Will, and more joyful in it. *b*) Men on every side, Christians (ver. 14), as well as heathen, even Prætorians (ver. 13; Matth. xxvii. 54; Mark xv. 39; Luke xxiii. 47), are improved and benefited; for the glory of the peaceful fruit of righteousness becomes better and better known, and the deep need of its possession is felt in the hearts of men. *c*) The gospel secures for itself a recog-

nition of its true character by preaching, which brings to view the person and his history (vers. 12, 20), for thus the adaptation of the gospel to the hearts and lives of men is seen and confessed.

4. Death, which, like imprisonment and the world's enmity, is an evil, becomes in the Apostle's view an insignificant event, which closes indeed the life upon earth, but changes not the essence, the life of the soul, only the place and form of its existence (ver. 21, ἀποθανεῖν; ver. 23, ἀναλῦσαι). To experience it is no merit, but to conquer it by faith and patience is a grace. Death leads the faithful from the misery of imprisonment to be more completely with Christ. In what way we pass through death into fellowship with Christ, is not said; and still less is there any indication here of an intermediate state. This agrees with the word of the Lord to the thief on the cross (Luke xxiii. 43), and with the teaching of the parable of the rich man (Luke xvi. 23); and still more significantly with the efficacy of Christ's death and resurrection in regard to the relations of life and death, in heaven and on earth (1 Cor. v. 1; Eph. iv. 8; comp. 2 Cor. v. 8; Acts vii. 58).

5. [Unless Paul believed that the death which released him from the trials of this life was to introduce him at once to the presence of Christ and a state of blessedness, we see no adequate reason for the struggle between his desire to depart and be with Christ, and his anxiety to labor still for the advancement of the Redeemer's kingdom on earth. If he believed that he was to remain for an indefinite time without consciousness in the grave, his zeal for men's salvation and his contempt of personal dangers and trials in the pursuit of that object, would lead him to desire to live as long as possible, on account of the importance of his ministry to mankind. On the other hand, if we suppose him to have regarded his attainment of the joys and rewards of heaven as simultaneous with his departure from this world, we have then an adequate explanation of his perplexity (vers. 21–24). For other passages which seem to involve the same doctrine, see Luke xxiii. 43; 2 Cor. v. 6, 7; and Rev. vi. 9.—H.]

6. The substance of Christian preaching is the person of Christ (vers. 15, 17, 18), as the exaltation of His person is the end of Christian life (ver. 20). This should be the preacher's testimony, his proclamation.

7. The difference in the teaching here consists not so much in the difference of the doctrine of Christ, as in the difference of disposition of the teachers towards Paul (vers. 15–18). The agreement in their teaching, which could scarcely fail to admit of certain variations, is of more account to him than their hostility to him. So much the more magnanimous is his joy in the doctrine which they hold in common.

8. That church fellowship (*τὸ καύχημα ὑμῶν περισσεύῃ ἐν Χριστῷ Ἰησοῦ*) should promote Christian fellowship is exemplified in the intercourse of Paul and the Philippians (*ἐν ἐμοὶ διὰ τῆς ἐμῆς παρουσίας πάλιν πρὸς ὑμᾶς*, ver. 26). It is important to observe and maintain this connection.

9. The minister of Christ is helped and served in two ways—(*a*) by the assistance of the Holy Spirit, which is the Spirit of Christ; and (*b*) by the supplications of the church: thus from above and from below. He needs the supplications of the church of Christ not less than the church needs his testimony. The protection of praying hands is no insignificant one.

10. Observe the moral greatness of the Apostle! In the constraint of a prison, in the face of death, amid the enmities of some of his associates, he exults for joy in his fellowship with Christ, and allows it to suffer no abatement on account of an error. He hopes to be able to return again to the Philippians, free from his bonds (ver. 26), as shortly before he had expressed a similar hope to Philemon (Philem. ver. 22). This hope indeed he afterwards gave up (2 Tim. iv. 6), and four years before this had declared that he should not see again the Ephesians (Acts xx. 22–25). In this uncertainty his official gift remains intact, which, as a prophetical endowment, has to do with God's word, not with times and seasons (Acts i. 7). He does not, however, declare definitely (ver. 27) that he will come, but leaves it to God's disposal.*

HOMILETICAL AND PRACTICAL.

For ministers, three teachings: 1) See that thou overcomest sorrow, and that thou art not overcome by it; 2) that Christ is praised thereby; 3) that the church by this very thing is advanced and built up in the faith.—Rejoice without envy in the preaching of thy worthy official brother. The word of God and the preaching of Christ should be to thee of too much value and importance to allow an unfriendly disposition to mortify or vex thee.—For the church, three teachings: 1) Take not offence at the greatness of the evil in the world, especially of the violent enmity which befalls thy pastor, but follow his deportment in the case; 2) persist in hearty supplication for him; 3) aid him full of confidence with thy testimony.—Only one thing must be regarded: that Christ alone, the Saviour of the world, be preached. Thou art not to judge the disposition of the preacher, but only the correctness of his preaching.—In general: Persecution or, at the utmost, death, is the greatest evil which the world can inflict upon the Christian, but this effects for him what launching does for a ship:—it brings him into his proper element. As the ship is thus sent forth upon the ocean for which it is designed, so is the Christian by this means brought to heaven, which is his home. To die, is but to come to our inheritance, if Christ is our life. From Him comes the unselfish love of life for others' sake, which is at once a joy in life and a joy in death, so that from our joy in death there comes no death to our joy. It is unchristian for one to wish for death because he is weary of life, or cowardly to fear death; and worse still are they who desire death while they fear it. Evil does not make us holy, death does not make us happy. Man does not become happy by dying, but the Christian dies, being happy.

IGNATIUS:—Let me become the prey of wild beasts, that God may become my possession. I

* [If Paul was imprisoned twice at Rome (as is almost certain), he could easily have fulfilled this hope of seeing again both the Philippians and Philemon, in the interval between his first and his second captivity. See *Commentary on Philemon* (LANGE's Series), pp. 6, 23.—H.]

am God's wheat; the teeth of the wild beasts will grind me so that I may become the purified bread of God. I shall become a true disciple of Jesus Christ when the world no longer sees my body. The iron and the cross, the breaking of the legs, the raging of the wild beasts, the mangling of the limbs, and the bruising of the body—all these diabolical torments may be exercised upon me if I but win Jesus Christ.

STARKE:—If God will make His children known, even His greatest enemies must lend their aid. Let God rule, and follow His leading.—Short but beautiful confession: Christ is our life in creation, in redemption, in regeneration, in the resurrection.

RIEGER:—For those in communion with God, in enjoyment of the life of Christ, dying is not the end; the soul's life from that point is before it, not behind (see ver. 21).

SCHLEIERMACHER:—The distressed and suffering man, be the cause of his suffering and distress what it may, attracts the earnest and anxious attention of men to himself more than all the royalty in the world. The way in which he bears his cross, the way in which he accepts his need and distress in his heavenly calling, excite the sympathy of men. If now we are all cross-bearers of our Lord, and if no one here below escapes from sorrows, then there is opened to us here at once a way in which we all, each according to his ability, may contribute to the advancement of the gospel, by bearing the troubles and adversities which the Lord sends, with patience and resignation to His will, with hope and trust in His imperishable work, with confidence and joyfulness of heart in His all-sufficient wisdom, in order that men may be thereby impelled to acknowledge and praise our heavenly Father.—Boldness on the one hand and faint-heartedness on the other, have, as it were, a diffusive and contagious power among men.—The troubles of this life will result in our highest good if we love God.—Above all things this is meet: 1) that we recognize the rough ways in which the Lord leads us as His ways, and acquiesce with our whole heart in His guidance; 2) that at the same time we look more to the internal than to the external; 3) the apostle adds, that it will turn to his salvation through the prayer of the church and through the supply of the spirit of Jesus Christ, which comes to him from the church.—This is the true happiness of the Christian, to which we should all aspire, that the longing for the greater glory which is reserved for us, shall never become so strong as to check or weaken our usefulness in the calling to which God has appointed us here on the earth.—If now we see the vineyard of the Lord so divided that to each one a task therein has been assigned, what else can we say in view of its present condition but that the vineyard is far from being wholly cultivated?—We must say then that all Christians, in whom the fear of death has been destroyed by a living and blessed fellowship with the Redeemer who has taken away the power of death, are able to withstand more firmly the assaults of earthly evil, and that their love for the perishable things of the world and enjoyment in them constantly diminish. The more this actually takes place, the more does there arise in them, even here upon earth, a higher love, a love for the Redeemer and His heavenly kingdom, in the strength of which they can regard themselves as servants of the Lord, as laborers in His vineyard, whose constantly renewed wish is, to bring forth fruit for Him unto whom all fruit belongs, as a reward for His sorrows and as a glorification of His victory.

HEUBNER:—Man often comes for the first time to know his strength when he is in misfortune.—When a friend of the truth is bound, ten others arise in his place.—The very best deeds may be done from impure motives; even Christ may be preached from ambition.—Spiritual envy and pride creep in even among preachers of the gospel, and incite them to a false and envious emulation.—When the friends of the truth are imprisoned, we ought to undertake their task, and to make good their places, that the good work may suffer no hindrance. The kindest service which can be rendered to noble martyrs in bonds, is to interest one's self in their cause, not in their person. The work is of more importance than the instrument.—The Christian commits himself wholly to God, and ought with reference to life and death to be absolutely resigned to His will. If he hopes in any respect to be useful to others, then he remains here even gladly.—WHITEFIELD once asked TENNANT, a preacher who was his friend, whether the thought that he might soon be called home, gave him joy. TENNANT replied: "I have no desire about it; my death does not concern me, my duty is to live as long as I can, as well as I can, and to serve my Master as faithfully as I can, until He calls me away. If I had sent my servant to plough, and should afterwards find him asleep, and he should say to me: 'Alas, the sun is so hot, let me go to the house!' might I not say to him, 'thou sluggard!'?"

PASSAVANT:—In steadfastness of faith the man of God holds fast joy in the faith. How little inclined we are by nature to leave this world for another better world in order to be with God, every candid mind willingly confesses to itself, and this fact holds up before us the clear mirror of our natural life, and shows us how far estranged we are from God, from His love, and the blessed life which is in Him.

NITZSCH:—How gloriously do desire for death and love of life unite in the Christian's mind! 1) The Christian shows by his faith that in death he loses nothing of that in and for which he here lives, but gains it. 2) Though it is better for him to be with Christ, yet it seems more necessary to remain in the flesh and bring forth fruit. 3) Whatever contradiction remains in his desires, he leaves God to settle, and will not choose or decide for himself.

[REV. J. TRAPP:—Two things make a good Christian, good actions and good aims. Though a good aim doth not make a bad action good, as we see in Uzzah, yet a bad aim makes a good action bad, as in these preachers (see ver. 15).—St. Paul stood, as it were, on tiptoes (*ἀποκαραδοκία*), to see which way he might best glorify God, by life or death (ver. 20)—Far, far the better (*πολλῷ μᾶλλον κρεῖσσον*, ver. 23), a transcendent expression, like Paul's *καθ' ὑπερβολὴν εἰς ὑπερβολήν*, 2 Cor. iv. 17.—H.]

[ROBERT HALL:—Paul was so intent upon the

advancement of truth, that he overlooked the malignity of the intention in the success of the cause. It is thus, my brethren, that religion lifts us above self-love and party-strife, and leads us to rejoice in every opening prospect of prosperity, and of good to others, in all public events and in every denomination (see ver. 15).—We see that with all his attainments the apostle was not lifted above them when he says, "by your prayers" (ver. 19). How much have we need to say, "Brethren, pray for us." The prayer of the obscurest Christian may procure and infuse among us the Spirit of God beyond what we could wish ourselves; for with Him all distinctions are lost but piety and necessity.—"To be with Christ," was the apostle's view of the heavenly world (ver. 23). He knew that Jesus Christ had promised that where He was there also His servants should be (John xvii. 24). He values the friendship of Christ above all the world,—to be found in His image and to be with Him, he can conceive of nothing higher.—If your attachment to this world be great, it must be cured by giving yourselves up more entirely to your Lord and Master.—H.]

SECTION III.

The Lord's Example and Pattern for the Observance of the Church.

CHAPTER I. 27—II. 18.

(1) *A true Christian deportment the condition of the Apostle's joy in the Church* (i. 27–30).

Characteristics of a Christian walk (vers. 27, 28 *a*); and the incentives to such a walk (vers. 28 *b*, 30).

27 Only let your conversation [deportment] be as it becometh the gospel of Christ:
that whether I come and see you or (*else*) be absent, I may hear of your affairs, that
ye stand fast in one spirit, with one mind striving together for the faith of the
28 gospel; and in nothing terrified by your adversaries, which is[1] to them an evident
29 token of perdition, but to you of salvation, and that of God. For unto you it is
[was] given in the behalf of Christ, not only to believe on him, but also to suffer
30 for his sake [in his behalf]; having the same conflict which ye saw[2] in me and now
hear to be in me.

[1] Ver. 28.—[The received text has μέν before ἐστιν, interpolated to respond to δέ in the next clause; and probably for a similar reason ὑμῶν was changed to ἡμῖν (MEYER, ALFORD, LIGHTFOOT). ELLICOTT would retain ἡμῖν.—H.]

[2] Ver. 30.—[The T. R. has ἴδετε after a few copies, but the correct word is undoubtedly εἴδετε. The itacism, or similar pronunciation, of the first syllable (an error of the ear in dictation) led to the interchange.—H.]

EXEGETICAL AND CRITICAL.

Ver. 27. **Only let your deportment be as it becometh the gospel of Christ.** Μόνον in this emphatic position marks the true Christian walk as the sole, indispensable condition of Paul's joy, when he should come to them, as the connection with vers. 24-26 shows. (Gal. ii. 10; v. 13). BENGEL: *hoc unum curate, nil aliud.* But this one requisition contains within itself manifold other requisitions. The verb here (*πολιτεύεσθε*) is taken from political life. The church at Philippi forms a part of the kingdom of God, of which they should prove themselves citizens. Paul uses the word elsewhere only in Acts xxiii. 1 (*πεπολίτευμαι*), in his speech before the Jewish Council, where in the presence of the civil rulers he feels himself to be but a member of the common body politic. Περιπατεῖν refers more to individual life; this verb to church-life, corresponding to *πάντες* (vers. 4, 7, 8). The fundamental law of this kingdom is denoted by *τοῦ εὐαγγελίου τοῦ Χριστοῦ*, and the corresponding deportment by *ἀξίως*. (Col. i. 10: *ἀξίως τοῦ κυρίου*; Eph. iv. 1: *ἀξίως περιπατῆσαι τῆς κλήσεως*).—**That** (*ἵνα*) states the aim or object of his exhortation, agreeably to the context (ver. 26).—**Whether I come and see you or be absent** (*εἴτε ἐλθὼν καὶ ἰδὼν ὑμᾶς, εἴτε ἀπών*). He thus leaves it uncertain how it may be, but in accordance with his hopeful desire, puts the supposition of his coming first. In both cases he presupposes his release, which might indeed lead him not to Philippi, but elsewhere.—**I may hear** (*ἀκούσω*), includes both cases, *i. e.* either from their own mouth, or from others (MEYER). BENGEL: *audiam et cognoscam.* The object is: **your affairs** (*τὰ περὶ ὑμῶν*), and this as more fully explained: **that ye stand fast in one spirit** (*ὅτι στήκετε ἐν ἑνὶ πνεύματι*), which is the subject of Paul's great anxiety. Comp. *οἶδά σε τίς εἶ*,

Luke iv. 34; xix. 3; Mark i 24. See WINER'S *Gramm.* p. 626. HÖLEMANN incorrectly joins ἵνα with στήκετε, as if it were ἀκούσας, and ὅτι simply repeated ἵνα. The construction would be confused, harsh (*hiulca*, CALVIN terms it), and the participles would be nominative absolute. The verb (iv. 1; 1 Cor. xvi. 13; Gal. v. 1; 1 Thess. iii. 8; 2 Thess. ii. 15) means to *keep one's ground in battle.* What is meant evidently is that the Philippians should cherish a spirit of unity among themselves, as in 1 Cor. iv. 21; xii. 13; 1 Pet. iii. 4. It is presupposed that this harmony, which is to be an object of such earnest endeavor, is a gift of the Holy Spirit (Eph. iv. 3, 4), but the Holy Spirit is not directly intended (VAN HENGEL).—**With one mind striving together for the faith of the gospel** (μιᾷ ψυχῇ συναθλοῦντες τῇ πίστει τοῦ εὐαγγελίου. This explains more fully στήκετε ἐν ἑνὶ πνεύματι. Here we evidently have to do with a struggle in which the main object is unity, and hence μιᾷ ψυχῇ stands with emphasis at the beginning. The πνεῦμα which is in the ψυχή, is that part of our nature which is the sphere (ἐν) of the unity. The dative ψυχῇ is the instrumental dative. The substantive ψυχή denotes that part of our being which is connected above with πνεῦμα and below with σάρξ, and constitutes the centre of man's peculiar personality,—individuality. Hence, μιᾷ ψυχῇ presents their outward manifestation.—Comp. ii. 2; Acts iv. 32, (DELITZSCH, *Psychologie*, p. 199 ff.). Repellent peculiarities may exist even where there is an agreement in principle. BENGEL: *est interdum inter sanctos naturalis aliqua antipathia.* The dative τῇ πίστει, *for the faith*, presents the object of the struggle, which the genitive τοῦ εὐαγγελίου renders more precise, and so guards it from any arbitrary misconception of friends or foes. The preposition in συναθλοῦντες refers to this co-operation of the Philippians with Paul (Col. ii. 1; 1 Tim. vi. 12; 2 Tim. iv. 7). Comp. vers. 7, 30; iv. 3, where μοί indicates what is here sufficiently plain from the connection. It is incorrect to limit σύν only to the unity of the Philippians among themselves (WIESINGER), which μιᾷ ψυχῇ after ἐν ἑνὶ πνεύματι has already pointed out, or to exclude this reference (MEYER), or to make σύν govern πίστει (GROTIUS). Τῇ πίστει is not an instrumental dative (CALVIN, *et al.*), nor should μιᾷ ψυχῇ be connected with στήκετε (CHRYSOSTOM, LUTHER).

Ver. 28. **And in nothing terrified** (μὴ πτυρόμενοι ἐν μηδενί). Καί adds another concomitant of στήκετε. The verb (properly used of horses in the race) means to *turn about*, to *start*, *spring aside.* Comp. ver. 20; 2 Cor. vi. 3.—**By your adversaries** (ὑπὸ τῶν ἀντικειμένων) gives the cause of this agitation or panic. We are to understand this of their personal enemies (comp. ver. 30), unchristian opposers of the gospel, especially among the Jews, but also among the heathen (ver. 30, *etc.;* Acts xvi. 11 sq.; xvii. 5 sq).—The Apostle proceeds to enforce his exhortation by appropriate motives, vers. 28 *b*–30.—**Which to them is an evident token of perdition** (ἥτις ἐστὶν αὐτοῖς ἔνδειξις ἀπωλείας). The argumentative ἥτις = *since it is* (Eph. iii. 13), in sense points back to the thought that the church does not allow itself to be terrified, but grammatically connects itself by a familiar attraction with ἔνδειξις (1 Tim. iii. 15). See WINER'S *Gramm.*, p. 627. The emphatic position of ἐστίν shows that even if they (οἱ ἀντικείμενοι) do not perceive it, or in their excitement do not acknowledge it, yet the fact that the church is unterrified is an evidence (comp. Rom. iii. 25; 2 Cor. viii. 24) of their destruction, of their exclusion from the blessed kingdom of God (1 Cor. i. 18). Comp. 2 Thess. i. 5-10.—**But to you of salvation** (ὑμῖν δὲ σωτηρίας). Comp. Rom. viii. 17; 2 Tim. ii. 12. For the reading see on the text. That which *should* awaken the fears of others with regard to their final destiny, even if it does not, is to believers a pledge of salvation.—**And that of God.** Καὶ τοῦτο refers equally to both clauses; for the disquietude of the adversaries before the bar of conscience, and the calmness of believers, alike come from God (ἀπὸ θεοῦ). Punishment and consolation are both from Him! To limit τοῦτο in the second member (CALVIN, *et al.*), to understand it of humility (HÖLEMANN), or to connect it with what follows (RILLIET), is incorrect.

Ver. 29. **For unto you it was given** (ὅτι ὑμῖν ἐχαρίσθη) confirms the statement in ver. 28, the last words of which (ἀπὸ θεοῦ) led the Apostle to adopt the passive form here. It is just you who are struggling and suffering together, to whom this grace [or undeserved favor] has been granted by God. Hence ὑμῖν has the emphatic position. BENGEL emphasizes the verb (*gratiæ munus signum salutis*), but without reason, while MEYER limits the confirmation to τοῦτο ἀπὸ θεοῦ.—**In the behalf of Christ, not only to believe on him, but also to suffer in his behalf** (τὸ ὑπὲρ Χριστοῦ, οὐ μόνον τὸ εἰς αὐτὸν πιστεύειν, ἀλλὰ καὶ τὸ ὑπὲρ αὐτοῦ πάσχειν). This clause forms the subject of ἐχαρίσθη. At first τὸ ὑπὲρ Χριστοῦ πάσχειν was the thought in Paul's mind (which expresses positively what is stated negatively in μὴ πτυρόμενοι); but the condition under which the suffering leads to salvation (σωτηρία) occurs to the writer's mind, and he interpolates the clause οὐ μόνον . . . . πιστεύειν in the middle of the sentence, but afterwards resumes his first thought in τὸ ὑπὲρ αὐτοῦ. The faith which works such steadfast endurance of suffering clearly proves that both are from God. Τὸ ὑπὲρ Χριστοῦ is not = what concerns Christ (BEZA, *et al.*).

Ver. 30. **Having the same conflict** (τὸν αὐτὸν ἀγῶνα ἔχοντες) presents the characteristic of this suffering, the participle agreeing with the subject understood with πάσχειν, as in Eph. iv. 2; iii. 17, 18; and Col. iii. 10. See WINER'S *Gramm.*, p. 572. It should not be connected with στήκετε (BENGEL), or be referred back to ὑμῖν for its subject (MEYER).—Τὸν αὐτόν is explained by what follows: **Which ye saw in me and now hear to be in me** (οἷον εἴδετε ἐν ἐμοὶ καὶ νῦν ἀκούετε ἐν ἐμοί). He refers in the first verb to his sojourn at Philippi (Acts xvi. 12-16 sq.), and in νῦν ἀκούετε to the information contained in the present letter (which would be read before them) and to that furnished by the report of Epaphroditus (ii. 28). Ἐν ἐμοί, **in me,** in both instances refers to a conflict which Paul suffers, to persecutions directed against himself. The Philippians also endured the same; and it is the kind of conflict which is the same in each case. The likeness does not consist merely in the similar ground of the conflict, that is in the faith for which they suffer (Meyer). The second ἐν ἐμοί is not = *de me* (Vulg., Erasmus, *et al.*), nor is allusion made here to false teachers (Heinrichs).

DOCTRINAL AND ETHICAL.

1. A right deportment of the Christian is the one thing which the Apostle demands of each member of the church. It is only this one thing, because this embraces all that belongs to the special circumstances, positions, and relations of life; just this alone, because it is the deportment of a citizen of the kingdom of God, including the relations of each one with every other, and finds its rule in the fundamental law of the people of God, the Gospel of Christ, to which it must correspond (ver. 27).

2. Four points here deserve especial attention. (*a*) The calling of the Christian is that of a warrior who retreats not; (*b*) It requires him to hold together and to agree together with the church; (*c*) It requires him to keep ever in view the object of the contest, his faith; and (*d*) It secures to him, in all outward afflictions, true soul-peace. In the first respect, it is not something to be won, but is a prize which having been won, the Christian is to defend; not salvation to be gained, but a possession to be kept. In the second respect, it is unity with the Apostle and with each member of the church, in the direction and impulse of the Spirit, in opposition to unchristian opponents. But the individual peculiarities of temperament, education, *etc.*, are not to be made an occasion for separation. In the third respect, it is the holding fast of the faith which is according to the gospel; and in the fourth respect, it is the keeping watch over the soul in order that by looking to the example of the Apostle and of the Lord Himself, we may be kept from fear and despair by reason of the adversaries.

3. The intrepidity of the Christian amid the enmities of unchristian opponents, is as certainly an evidence to him of fellowship with God, as it is for them a proof that they should and may learn therein their exposure to final destruction (ver. 28).

4. He who believes in Christ must regard it as a grace of God that he is permitted to suffer for Him (ver. 29).

HOMILETIC AND PRACTICAL.

Compare the Doctrinal and Ethical remarks.

Starke:—Brief epitome of the whole of Christianity: faith, love, patience.

Rieger:—Although we must suffer and struggle together for the gospel, yet we often become thereby more completely linked together. Since the disposition to yield to fear is planted so deeply in our nature, it becomes a part of the renewal of our souls into the image of God, to obtain again a steadfast courage to adhere to the right.

Schleiermacher:—Fearlessness with respect to all adversaries of the kingdom of God and all their efforts against it, must be peculiar to the Christian; for it has no other basis or other measure in him than his faith in the Redeemer and his love for Him and for His holy cause.

Heubner:—To believe in Christ is to make common cause with Him, hence also to suffer with Him.

Passavant:—Whenever Christians fall out with one another, it happens for the most part because they are unwilling to surrender their own self-will to the control of the one Spirit of the Lord, or to merge their individuality in His sovereignty.

[Robert Hall:—"Nothing terrified by your adversaries" (ver. 28). Having Jesus Christ present with the Father, as an advocate, what was there to terrify them? They knew that He was at the head of all—principalities and powers, thrones and dominions, being made subject to Him. That Christian, my brethren, who views Jesus Christ as the Lord of men, of angels, and of glory, how firm and undaunted may he look around him, and consider kings and princes but as common dust; for they must submit themselves to His authority or perish. See Ps. ii. 10-12.—H.]

---

(2) *Christ's Example on the Way through Humiliation to Exaltation* (ii. 1-11).

After earnestly and eloquently entreating them to stand together in harmony (1-4), he holds up to view the person of the Redeemer (5, 6), His state of Humiliation (7, 8), and His state of exaltation (9-11).

1 If there be therefore any consolation [exhortation] in Christ, if any comfort
of love, if any fellowship of the Spirit, if any[1] bowels and mercies [compassion],
2 fulfil ye [make full] my joy, that ye be like-minded [mind the same thing], having
the same love, being of one accord, of one mind [with one soul minding the one
3 thing]. Let nothing be done through strife or vain glory; but in lowliness of
4 mind let each esteem other [others] better than [superior to] themselves. Look
not every man[2] on his own things, but every man also on the things of others.
5, 6 Let this mind[3] be in you which was also in Christ Jesus; who, being in the form

7 of God, thought it not robbery to be equal with God: but made himself of no re-
putation [emptied or divested himself], and took upon him the form of a servant,
8 and was made in the likeness of men. And being found in fashion as a man, he
humbled himself, and became obedient unto death, even the death of the cross.
9 Wherefore God also hath highly exalted him, and given him a [the[4]] name which is
10 above every name; that at [in] the name of Jesus every knee should bow, of
things [beings] in heaven, and things [beings] in earth, and things [beings] under
11 the earth, and that every tongue should confess that Jesus Christ is Lord, to the
glory of God the Father.

[1] Ver. 1.—ἔι τις σπλάγχνα is found in ℵ A B C D E F K L. It is either a solecism (TISCHENDORF N. T. *ed.* VII. *maj.*) or a mistake (WINER, *et al.*) of Paul or of the transcribers for τινα. [WORDSWORTH makes here the just remark (in opposition to a possible extreme): "But this text, among others, affords evidence that it is not a sound principle of criticism, to limit the data for determining the readings of the N. T. to the most ancient extant MSS., and that it is necessary to extend the range of inquiry to the cursive MSS. and other collateral aids."—H.]

[2] Ver. 4—ἕκαστοι has stronger support in A B F G, *et al.*, than ἕκαστος in ℵ C D E, *et al.*

[3] Ver. 5.—τοῦτο γὰρ φρονεῖτε is found in D E F G; γάρ is wanting in ℵ A B C, probably because ἕκαστοι was added from ver. 4. ["As ver. 5 begins an ecclesiastical lecture, and as the explanative force of γάρ (= 'verily,' 'as the case stands') might not have been fully understood and have led to the omission of the particle, the reading γάρ seems slightly more probable" (ELLICOTT).—H.] ℵ A B C* read φρονεῖτε, others read φρονείσθω. [The former is also grammatically the more difficult, and therefore more likely to be original.—H.]

[4] Ver. 9.—τὸ ὄνομα in ℵ A B C; the article is omitted in D E F G, *et al.*

EXEGETICAL AND CRITICAL.

Ver. 1. **If there be therefore any exhortation in Christ** (εἴ τις οὖν παράκλησις ἐν Χριστῷ). Οὖν goes back to the preceding thought (i. 27-30). He now exhorts them to be united in the present conflict, in which they as well as himself are engaged, that the joy which he has felt on account of their harmony may receive no check. Εἰ presents what is actual as hypothetical for the sake of the conclusion, as in Eph. iii. 2, 4, 21; Col. i. 23; ii. 20; iii. 1. We are to supply ἐστί, but not also ἐν ὑμῖν (MEYER). It is to be taken for granted that such exhortation (παράκλησις), which by ἐν Χριστῷ (i. 26) is defined as based upon Christ, as having its sphere or element in Him, is found richly in the Apostle; but he adopts this mode of expression in his humility. Comp. Rom. xv. 30. [The A. V. renders παράκλησις *consolation*, but that sense destroys the difference between this clause and the next. The meaning here is: If those who are in Christ may address to each other exhortations and entreaties with a right to expect that they will not be unavailing, then *fulfil, etc.* We may carry forward the idea of ἐν Χριστῷ to the other clause.—H.]—**If any comfort of love** (εἴτι παραμύθιον ἀγάπης). According to 1 Thess. ii. 11: ὡς πατὴρ τέκνα ἑαυτοῦ παρακαλοῦντες ὑμᾶς καὶ παραμυθούμενοι; and 1 Cor. xiv. 3: παράκλησιν καὶ παραμυθίαν, this ἅπαξ λεγόμενον must denote *consolation of love*, friendly address, or encouragement which springs from love, as described by the genitive. We are to refer the above without doubt to the Apostle. [The Apostle would say: If it be a characteristic of true love that it is ever ready to comfort or encourage those for whom it is cherished, then comply with my request and thus manifest your love to me.—H.]—**If any fellowship of spirit** [*or* **the Spirit**] (εἴ τις κοινωνία πνεύματος). The article being omitted, we cannot compare this expression with 2 Cor. xiii. 13: κοινωνία τοῦ ἁγίου πνεύματος, and explain it as fellowship with the Holy Spirit (BENGEL, MEYER); but the κοινωνία, which was described in i 5 with reference to its object or outward action, is described here in its inward sphere: *fellowship of spirit* among themselves, and with the Apostle, by virtue of which exhortation and entreaty readily find response and acceptance as addressed to each other. That this fellowship of spirit is a gift of the Holy Spirit, is only pre-supposed, not stated. [The absence of the article does not decide against the other view; for πνεῦμα as being of the nature of a proper name may have the article or omit it. See WINER'S *Gramm.*, p. 122. Most interpreters understand the Holy Spirit to be meant.—H.]—**If any bowels and compassion** (εἴ τινα σπλάγχνα καὶ οἰκτιρμοί). The first substantive (i. 8) denotes the seat, the source, of the second; the second being in the plural represents the individual proofs, the acts as repeated, manifold. See WINER'S *Gramm.*, p. 176; Col. iii. 12; σπλάγχνα οἰκτιρμοῦ, *lect. var.* (οἰκτιρμῶν). Thus the fellowship or participation (κοινωνία) in the third clause appears in its action and effects. [The two nouns give intensity to the idea. The Apostle intimates in terms of the greatest delicacy that any reluctance to grant him the favor for which he so earnestly pleads, would have all the effect upon his feelings of unkindness and cruelty.—H.] The first two clauses we are to refer to Paul, the other two to the Philippians; the implied affirmation of the several conditions (εἴ τις . . . . οἰκτιρμοί), as respects both Paul and those addressed, enforces the exhortation (πληρώσατε) which they severally introduce. It is incorrect to regard the first and third as objective, and the second and fourth as subjective motives (MEYER), or to refer all four to the Philippians only (MEYER, SCHENKEL). That we are to supply χαρά, from ver. 2, in each of the conditional clauses ('*si quod* (gaudium) *consolatio amoris*,' *etc.*), according to BENGEL, is inadmissible.

Ver. 2. **Make full my joy** (πληρώσατέ μου τὴν χαράν). The Apostle has joy already, and it only remains that this should be full and complete (comp. i. 9; 1 John i. 4; 2 John 12). The Philippians are to make it so by allowing his appeal to prevail with them (first two clauses), and by maintaining and exhibiting the virtues to which he exhorts them (last two).—He sums up the whole as it were in one word: **That ye mind the same thing.** Ἵνα represents the harmony of the Philippians (τὸ αὐτὸ φρονῆτε), as sought by them in order [as one of its attendant aims] to fill up the measure of Paul's joy. According to iii. 15; iv. 2; Rom. xii. 16; xv. 5, *minding and striving after* the same object are meant.—This is more closely defined, first on its ethical side: **Having the same love** (τὴν αὐτὴν ἀγάπην ἔχοντες). As possessors and dispensers of that love which in its object, purity and strength, is essentially the same, they should be of one mind.—Secondly, the trait or conduct appearing on its intellectual side is: **Being of one accord** (A. V.), *or* **like-minded, pondering the one thing** (σύμψυχοι τὸ ἓν φρονοῦντες). With reference to the object had in view, the τὸ αὐτό represents it as a single thing, and the question they consider is, what *one thing* is necessary; and further, the personal unity which corresponds to this unity of aim, becomes prominent, as in i. 27: μιᾷ ψυχῇ. TITTMANN (*Syn.* I. p. 67) correctly observes: ἰσόψυχος, *est qui eodem modo est animatus* (like-minded); σύμψυχος *autem, qui idem sentit, unanimis* (harmonious); σύμψυχοι *esse possunt, qui non sunt* ἰσόψυχοι; *sunt igitur* σύμψυχοι οἱ τὸ αὐτὸ φρονοῦντες. *Sed* τὸ ἓν φρονεῖν *est unum velle, in uno expetendo consentire.* In this earnest exhortation the accumulation of terms and phrases cannot surprise us. It is incorrect to regard σύμψυχοι as independent, the subject of a separate predication (OECUMENIUS, *et al.*). To these two positive qualifications correspond the negative ones in ver. 3.

Ver. 3. **Let nothing be done through strife or vain glory.**—Μηδὲν κατ' ἐριθείαν forbids whatever is without or against τὴν αὐτὴν ἀγάπην, while μηδὲ κατὰ κενοδοξίαν forbids whatever violates τὸ ἓν φρονεῖν, μιᾷ ψυχῇ. On the first substantive see in i. 17; on the second, SUIDAS: ματαία τις περὶ ἑαυτοῦ οἴησις (Gal. v. 26, κενόδοξοι); κατά denotes rule, motive (WINER'S *Gram.*, p. 401). Without question it is more simple to continue φρονοῦντες from the preceding verse (WINER, *Gram.*, p. 587) than to supply ποιοῦντες (ERASMUS, LUTHER, *et al.*), or even to construe it with the following ἡγούμενοι (HÖLEMANN).—The positive (ver. 2 *b*) is opposed here to the negative (ver. 3 *a*).—**But in lowliness of mind** (*or* **in humility**) **let each esteem others superior to themselves.**—'Αλλά marks strongly the opposition. The instrumental dative (τῇ ταπεινοφροσύνῃ) corresponds to κατά with the accusative. See WINER'S *Gram.* p. 402, note 2. On the substantive see Eph. iv. 4; Col. ii. 18, 23; iii. 12. 'Αλλήλους ἡγούμενοι ὑπερέχοντας ἑαυτῶν teaches that humility fixes its eye on another's excellences, and judges him from this point of view. BENGEL: *Jure et dotibus fieri id potest, non extreme tantum, sed per veram* ταπεινοφροσύνην, *cum quis per abnegationem oculos avertit a suis prærogativis et alterius dotes, quibus prior est, studiose contemplatur.*

Ver. 4. **Look not every one on his own things, but every one also on the things of others** (μὴ τὰ ἑαυτῶν ἕκαστοι σκοποῦντες, ἀλλὰ καὶ τὰ ἑτέρων ἕκαστοι).—The sentence presents a general principle. The unusual plural ἕκαστοι, which is emphatic in each number, but especially in the second, where it stands at the end, indicates that this should be true of *every member* of the church. Τὰ ἑαυτῶν, τὰ ἑτέρων, signify in general *res, causa,* as in ii. 21; 1 Cor. xiii. 5 (τὰ ἑαυτῶν); x. 24 (τὸ ἑαυτοῦ, τὸ τοῦ ἑτέρου), 33 (τὸ ἐμαυτοῦ, τὸ τῶν πολλῶν), τά being used, and not τό, in order to mark the multiplicity. It is also to be noticed that ἄλλος *denotat alium, nulla diversitatis nisi numeri ratione,* ἕτερος *non tantum alium, sed etiam diversum indicat* (TITTMANN, *Syn.* I. p. 155 sq.). While in the above passages ζητεῖν is employed, we have here σκοποῦντες (iii. 17). Hence, according to the context, we are to think of the gifts and excellencies of others before our own, and of their advantage, interest, as well as our own. This distinction, however, comes out more clearly in view of what follows. 'Αλλὰ καί after μή limits or softens the antithesis. We are to think *also* of the things of others, hence not merely and exclusively of them. It is selfishness only that is forbidden. [" We are to look," says LIGHTFOOT, "*beyond* our own interest to that of others."—H.] See WINER'S *Gram.* p. 498. It is incorrect to deny this distinction between ζητεῖν and σκοπεῖν so as either to find no reference to gifts and excellencies (MEYER), or to think exclusively of these (CALVIN).

Ver. 5. **Let this mind be in you**, or, according to the better text, **have this mind in you** (τοῦτο γὰρ φρονεῖτε ἐν ὑμῖν).—Paul confirms his exhortation to unity by showing what self-denying love and humility are, as illustrated in the example of Christ. Τοῦτο has as its correlative ὃ in the following clause, while ἐν Χριστῷ 'Ιησοῦ answers to ἐν ὑμῖν. Hence the meaning must be *in animis vestris*, but not *intra vestrum cœtum* (HÖLEMANN). [For the force of γάρ see notes on the text.—H.]—**Which was also in Christ Jesus** (ὃ καὶ ἐν Χριστῷ Ιησοῦ sc. ἐφρονήθη). Καί, *also, i. e.*, as well as ἐν ὑμῖν.

Ver. 6. **Who being in the form of God, thought it not robbery to be equal with God.**—Ὅς has for its antecedent Χριστῷ 'Ιησοῦ, and points to His antemundane state, as vers. 7, 8, refer to His earthly existence, and vers. 9–11 refer to His subsequent glorified condition. The subject is the *ego* of the Lord, which is active in all the three modes of existence. It is the entire summary of the history of Jesus, including His ante-human state (MEYER). Hence neither the λόγος ἄσαρκος alone, nor the λόγος ἔνσαρκος, is to be taken as the subject. The emphatic participial clause (ἐν μορφῇ θεοῦ ὑπάρχων) connects itself with the principal clause (οὐχ ἁρπαγμὸν ἡγήσατο τὸ εἶναι ἴσα θεῷ), and the participle must be taken as imperfect, not as present (UMBREIT, *Studien und Kritiken*, 1828, p. 594). The finite verb ἡγήσατο, from its import, requires us to think of a resolution or decision to which what is stated in the participle stands related as concessive in accordance with the sense of the whole passage. (Comp. 2 Cor. viii. 9, ἐπτώχευσε πλούσιος ὤν); hence neither causal (RHEINWALD *et al.*) nor merely temporal (MEYER). If now we regard strictly the connection and drift of the context, which is to bring before us Christ's example, as a testimony in behalf of that humble self-denial which promotes harmony, and against the ἐριθείαν and κενοδοξίαν which destroy it, the meaning of this difficult passage cannot be mistaken. The words in themselves are plain. 'Υπάρχων, stronger than ὤν, denotes Christ's pre-existence, ἐν μορφῇ θεοῦ. According to Mark xvi. 12 (ἐφανερώθη ἐν ἑτέρᾳ μορφῇ), and in accordance with its use elsewhere, μορφή must be understood of the outward form, "*species externa*," and this as defined by θεοῦ, which must be understood as not of the person of God, the Father, but only of the Godhead,—is a divine *morphe* or form, that of a God. Comp. iii. 21; Rom. viii. 29: σύμμορφον. The μορφῇ θεοῦ here corresponds to μορφὴν δούλου, ver. 7, as ὑπάρχων has its parallel in λαβών there. BENGEL well observes: *ipsa natura divina decorem habebat infinitum in se, etiam sine ulla creatura illum decorem intuente.* Comp. John v. 37: εἶδος αὐτοῦ (of God); xvii. 5: τῇ δόξῃ ᾗ εἶχον παρά σοι; Col. i. 15: εἰκὼν τοῦ θεοῦ; Hebr. i. 3: ἀπαύγασμα τῆς δόξης καὶ χαρακτὴρ τῆς ὑποστάσεως αὐτοῦ. It is incorrect to regard it as equivalent to φύσις, οὐσία (the Greeks, AUGUSTINE *et al.*), *status* (CALOV, *et al.*), and to hold that Jesus, when He was on earth, caused His δόξα to be recognized through the medium of His words and works (LUTHER, *et al.*), of His miracles (GROTIUS, *et al.*), and in the transfiguration (WETSTEIN). ["Though μορφή," says LIGHTFOOT, "is not the same as φύσις or οὐσία, yet the possession of the μορφή involves participation in the οὐσία also; for μορφή implies not the external accidents, but the essential attributes. Similar to this, though not so decisive, are the expressions used elsewhere of the Divinity of the Son: εἰκὼν τοῦ θεοῦ, 2 Cor. iv. 4; Col. i. 15; and χαρακτὴρ τῆς ὑποστάσεως—τοῦ θεοῦ, Heb. i. 3. Similar also is the term which St. John has adopted to express this truth—ὁ λόγος τοῦ θεοῦ." It may be added that the word is fitly chosen for the expression of the Apostle's idea. For though μορφή denotes properly the *outline* or *shape* of an object, and not directly the *substance* or *nature* of the object, it yet presupposes the existence of that *nature* or *reality*, of which it is the manifestation, just as the figure or shadow implies a body or substance which determines the figure or outline. Besides, to deny that Christ's μορφή or *form* as God, agreed with the reality, would oblige us to deny also in the next verse that His form or condition as a *servant* agreed with the reality, and this would destroy the force of the Apostle's reasoning. The condition in both cases presupposes the corresponding nature or reality, and is called μορφή precisely on account of that condition. The Apostle seems to have chosen this peculiar word because he would provide in his mode of speaking for the fact, that though the state or manifestation was changed, the nature or essence of the personality remained unchanged.—H.]—The expression οὐχ ἁρπαγμὸν ἡγήσατο is more difficult. It denies a precedence of self, as is the case with those τὰ ἑαυτῶν σκοποῦντες (ver. 4). In its connection with ἐν μορφῇ θεοῦ ὑπάρχων, and its position before ἐκένωσεν ἑαυτόν, it points to a decision in a negative form before the incarnation. Hence it is not the same as οὐχ ἥρπασε, which did not for a moment enter into the thoughts of Christ. Ἁρπαγμός may, like πειρασμός, βαπτισμός, signify the *act* of robbery; and it would properly denote this according to the rules of derivation (WINER's *Gram.* p. 93); but usage allows it to be taken as *res rapta* or *rapienda* (BRUECKNER against MEYER); just as χρησμός may be *non vaticinatio sed vaticinium*, χρησματισμός *et negotiatio et id quod hac perpetratur*, so here also ἁρπαγμός= ἅρπαγμα (THOLUCK: *Pfingstprogramm*, 1847, pp. 17–19). Whether the meaning is *res rapta* or *rapienda*, the context must decide. Here now ἁρπαγμόν is predicate in its relation to τὸ εἶναι ἴσα θεῷ as the object (WINER's *Gram.* p. 323). On this construction καὶ ἡ βασιλεία τῶν οὐρανῶν βιάζεται βιασταὶ ἁρπάζουσιν αὐτήν in Matt. xi. 12 is very instructive. Ἁρπάζειν is not a heroic *exspoliare*, but a violent appropriating to one's self, of which the object is τὸ εἶναι ἴσα θεῷ. This is therefore not "*spolium*," "*præda*," but "*res rapienda.*" The emphasis falls here on εἶναι; ἴσα (not ἴσα—see WINER's *Gram.* p. 177) is an adverbializing accusative (BENGEL), but different from ἴσως, since it denotes several relations of likeness, and from ἴσος, since it does not point to a likeness of person, as John v. 18 (ἴσον ἑαυτὸν ποιῶν τῷ θεῷ), but to the equality of Christ's condition with that of God's. What is meant by this expression appears from vers. 10, 11: it is the κυριότης of the Lord, His worship in the church, in heaven, and upon earth. Hence the difference between ἐν μορφῇ θεοῦ ὑπάρχων and τὸ εἶναι ἴσα θεῷ is that the former denotes the Lord's mode of existence, as a divine existence for Himself apart from the world and before it, the dignity of the Son, founded upon His eternal origin or generation from the Father, but the latter His existence as the King of His people in the realm of the Father, at His right hand. It is entirely like Eph. i. 20-23; John v. 22, 23; John xx. 28; Matt. xxviii. 18-20. Accordingly it must signify "*rapiendum non duxit.*" For the former (μορφῇ θεοῦ) was His from eternity, while the latter (τὸ εἶναι ἴσα θεῷ) He had not as yet obtained. He was already enjoying the former before He had received the latter. It is not correct to regard the object of ἁρπαγμὸν ἡγήσατο as identical with what is stated concessively in the participial clause (LUTHER, MEYER, *et al.*), or ἁρπαγμόν as equivalent to "*præda, res rapta*" (AMBROSIUS, *et al.*), "*spolia*" (ERASMUS, RHEINWALD, *et al.*), "*holding tenaciously*" (HÖLEMANN), "*concealing*" (MATTHIES), "*a triumphant display*" (LUTHER, *et al.*), nor are we to understand by εἶναι ἴσα θεῷ "*plenitudinem et altitudinem dei*" (BENGEL), "*vitam vitæ dei æqualem*" (VAN HENGEL), or "*identity with the Father*" (RILLIET). It is entirely fanciful to scent Gnostic allusions in ἐν μορφῇ θεοῦ, ἴσα θεῷ εἶναι, ἁρπαγμός, as also in ἑαυτὸν ἐκένωσε and ἐν ὁμοιώματι, σχήματι εὑρεθείς (ver. 7), and in ἐπουρανίων, ἐπιγείων, κατὰ χθονίων (ver. 10), (BAUR) as BRUECKNER shows (*Ep. ad Phil. Paulo auctori vindicata*, p. 15 ff.) in his *exposé* of the difference between the doctrine of the Gnostics and the present passage, and of the contradiction between BAUR's earlier and his later representation of this doctrine, and also ERNESTI (*Studien und Kritiken*, 1848, pp. 858-924; 1851, pp. 595-630), with admirable acuteness and learning. Yet the view advanced as a conjecture by UMBREIT (*Studien und Kritiken*, 1828, p. 595) and earnestly maintained by ERNESTI, that this passage is to be explained out of Gen. ii. 3, is unnecessary and untenable.

[The view of τὸ εἶναι ἴσα θεῷ (adopted above by Dr. BRAUNE) as = "the κυριότης, or worship of Christ in the church, in heaven, and on earth" (vers. 10. 11) which He did *not* claim for Himself in His pre-existent state, makes the self-denial of Christ negative merely, not positive; as the Apostle's use of the example would seem to require Moreover, if this equality with God which Christ forbore to arrogate to Himself before the incarnation be the same as the sovereignty which God conferred on Him after His humiliation and sufferings and death, as a reward for such self-devotement (see ver. 9 and Heb. xii. 2), we cannot regard such an equality as, properly speaking, subject to acceptance or rejection till the antecedent historical condition has been fulfilled.—We subjoin a summary of the views of some of the later writers in our own language on this important passage. The meaning which Bishop ELLICOTT prefers is: "He did not deem His equality to God a prize to be seized, but emptied Himself, *etc.;* in other words, He did not insist on His own eternal prerogatives, but, on the contrary, humbled Himself to the condition and sufferings of mortal man." See his *Commentary on Philippians* (*in loc.*) for the grounds of this interpretation.—Prof. LIGHTFOOT presents the philological details at some length. Instead of *ἁρπαγμός*, "the more usual form of the word is *ἅρπαγμα*, which properly signifies simply 'a piece of plunder,' but especially with such verbs as *ἡγεῖσθαι, ποιεῖσθαι, νομίζειν, etc.*, is employed like *ἕρμαιον, εὕρημα*, to denote a highly-prized possession, an unexpected gain." He adduces examples of this usage from some of the later Greek writers. "It appears then from these writers that *ἅρπαγμα ἡγεῖσθαι* frequently signifies nothing more than 'to clutch greedily,' 'prize highly,' 'to set store by,' the idea of plunder or robbery having passed out of sight. The form *ἁρπαγμός*, however, presents a greater difficulty; for neither analogy nor usage is decisive as to its meaning: (1) The termination *-μος* indeed denotes primarily the *process*, so that *ἁρπαγμός* would be 'an act of plundering.' But as a matter of fact substantives in *-μός* are frequently used to describe a concrete thing, *e. g. θεσμός, χρησμός, φραγμός, etc.* (2) And again the particular word *ἁρπαγμός* occurs so rarely that usage cannot be considered decisive. Under these circumstances we may, in choosing between the two senses of *ἁρπαγμός*, fairly assign to it here the one which best suits the context. The meaning adopted above satisfies this condition: '*Though* He pre-existed in the form of God, yet He did not look upon equality with God as a prize which must not slip from His grasp; *but* He emptied Himself, divested Himself, taking upon Him the form of a slave.' The idea is the same as in 2 Cor. viii. 9, *δι' ὑμᾶς ἐπτώχευσεν πλούσιος ὤν*. The other rendering (adopted by the A. V.), 'thought it not robbery to be equal with God,' disconnects this clause from its context.*—ALFORD translates: 'who being' (originally) 'in the form of God regarded not as self-enrichment His equality with God.' He observes (1) that *ἁρπαγμός* holds the emphatic place in the sentence; (2) that this fact casts *τὸ εἶναι ἴσα θεῷ* into the shade as secondary and as referring to the state indicated by *ἐν μορφῇ θεοῦ ὑπάρχων* above; and (3) that *ἁρπαγμός* strictly means, as here given, the act of seizing or snatching—not from *another*, but for *one's self.* Dr. WORDSWORTH paraphrases the thought thus: "*Let this mind be in you which was also in Christ Jesus,* who subsisting from eternity in the form of God, did not think His own equality with God (*τὸ εἶναι ἴσα θεῷ*) was a spoil which He had usurped wrongfully, and of which He might justly *be divested* by another, or which on principles of justice He was Himself *obliged to give up* to another," *etc.* The following is Professor EADIE's paraphrase of the meaning: "The Apostle affirms that Jesus, in His pre-incarnate state, was 'in the form of God;' and adds, that He thought it not a seizure, or a thing to be snatched at, to be on a parity with God, but emptied Himself. Now, it seems to us very plain that the parity referred to is not parity in the abstract, or in anything not found in the paragraph, but parity in possession of this form of God. He was in the form of God, and did not think it a thing to be eagerly laid hold of to be equal with God, having or exhibiting this form. The apostle adds, *ἀλλ' ἑαυτὸν ἐκένωσεν*, but emptied Himself, and the clause is in broad and decided contrast with *ἁρπαγμὸν οὐχ ἡγήσατο τὸ εἶναι ἴσα τῷ θεῷ*. That is to say, the one clause describes the result of the other. It was because He did not think it a seizure to be equal with God, that He emptied Himself. He did not look simply to His own things—the glories of the Godhead; but He looked to the things of others, and therefore descended to humanity and death. His heart was not so set upon this glory, that he would not appear at any time without it. There was something which he coveted more—something which He felt to be truly a *ἁρπαγμός*, and that was the redemption of a fallen world by His self-abasement and death. From His possession of this "mind," and in indescribable generosity He looked at the things of others, and descended with His splendor eclipsed—appeared not as a God in glory, but clothed in flesh; not in royal robes, but in the dress of a village youth; not as Deity in fire, but a man in tears; not in a palace, but in a manger. . . And in this way He gave the church an example of that self-abnegation and kindness which the apostle has been inculcating, and which the Lord's career is adduced to illustrate and confirm" (*Commentary on the Greek Text of the Epistle to the Philippians*, pp. 108, 9).—For a list of monographs on this difficult text the reader may see MEYER's "*Briefe an die Philipper*," *etc.*, p. 63 (1859), and WIESINGER's *Commentary on Philippians* (Eng. trans.), p. 61.—H.]

Ver. 7. **But emptied** *or* **stripped himself, and took upon him the form of a servant** (*ἀλλ' ἑαυτὸν ἐκένωσε μορφὴν δούλου λαβών*). The *ἀλλά* introduces the antithesis (not *tamen, nihilominus, quin potius*). The first member corresponds to the second in ver. 6, and the second here to the first there; and at the same time unfolds further the antithesis to *οὐχ ἁρπαγμὸν ἡγήσατο*. In opposition to the *not thinking* of an act stands something done: in opposition to the unwillingness to rob another stands a giving up on His part; and in opposition to the thing which He does not even wish to arrogate to Himself stands His own person which He surrenders. This last contrast appears in *ἑαυτόν*, which precedes with emphasis, in opposition to *ἑαυτῷ τι*, and hence not Himself in opposition to another (MEYER, *et al.*), as the relations in the case and the context show; since the equality with God (*τὸ εἶναι ἴσα θεῷ*) was not to be seized from men

* [Professor LIGHTFOOT states his objections to the rendering of the A. V. in an extended note in his *Commentary* at the end of chap. ii.—H.]

or angels, nor could God be deprived of it, but He, the Son, by His own might and will could seize upon it, although it would not be withheld from Him by the Father.—'Εκένωσε=κενὸν ἐποίησεν, *exinanivit*, divested Himself, *i. e.*, of that which He had, ἐν μορφῇ θεοῦ ὑπάρχων, hence of the form of God, of the divine mode of existence. Since He has *emptied* Himself of this, as the word properly means, the μορφή is not something merely external, and since He has given up only the ἐν μορφῇ θεοῦ ὑπάρχων, it cannot be an *evacuare* of the person, as if that now had in it no longer anything divine—no δόξα which remained to Him (John i. 14; Col. ii. 9); hence the nearer limitation by μορφὴν δούλου λαβών, which is itself more closely defined. The antithesis is still μορφὴ θεοῦ, and δούλου is chosen, because according to the context (ἴσα θεῷ ver. 6, comp. vers. 10, 11) the κυριότης belongs to the θεότης. It is the *becoming man*, or the incarnation that is meant, as the sequel declares, and since λαβών (which is contemporaneous with ἐκένωσε as in Eph. i. 9, 13) must be taken as a modal limitation of the verb (ἐκένωσε), this emptying of Himself (κένωσις) is the Lord's incarnation. It is incorrect to deny here the *becoming* man, the act of incarnation, and to find only His position as a servant indicated (SCHENKEL), for in this case μορφὴν δούλου λαβών must follow ἐν σχήματι εὑρεθεὶς ὡς ἄνθρωπος, and could not stand at the beginning; Observe too, that the δούλου is without the article, and hence it does not mean the servant of God, in the sense of the Messiah. The following also are incorrect interpretations: *libenter duxit vitam inopem* (GROTIUS), *miseram sortem, qualis esse servorum solet* (HÖLEMANN), *semet ipse depressit* (VAN HENGEL), *veluti deposuit* (CALOV), *non magis ea usus est* (CLERICUS), since the subject of discourse here is not anything within the human life of Christ, the laying aside of the δόξα, or abstaining from the full use of it.—**And was made in the likeness of men, and being found in fashion as a man** (ἐν ὁμοιώματι ἀνθρώπων γενόμενος καὶ σχήματι εὑρεθεὶς ὡς ἄνθρωπος). These two clauses plainly belong together. They serve more closely to define μορφὴν δούλου λαβών. BENGEL: *forma dicit aliquid absolutum, similitudo relationem ad alia ejusdem conditionis, habitus refertur ad aspectum et sensum.* Δοῦλος is more exactly defined by ἀνθρώπων, ἄνθρωπος; ἐν ὁμοιώματι, ὡς, correspond to μορφήν and indicate the difference between the Lord in the form of a servant, as the son of man, and men. He is not indeed *purus putus homo*, but the incarnate Son of God. Γενόμενος denotes a *becoming*, the human individual development, and preserves the λαβών from being mistaken as a merely outward assumption. Hence ὁμοίωμα is to be understood of the inner and outer, the spiritual and bodily life, and ἐν points this out as the sphere of His development, and the dative σχήματι as the respect in which, or rule according to which, He is found as man. WINER'S *Gram.*, p. 215. By σχῆμα (*vultus, vestitus, victus, gestus, sermones et actiones.* BENGEL), is denoted the outward manifestation which is indicated by εὑρεθείς (not equivalent to ὤν), was recognized by all who came into contact with Him. Comp. 1 John i. 1-3. On ὡς ἄνθρωπος THEODORET observes: ἡ γὰρ ἀναληφθεῖσα φύσις ἀληθῶς τοῦτο ἦν, αὐτὸς δὲ τοῦτο οὐκ ἦν, τοῦτο δὲ περιέκειτο. BENGEL: *Vulgaris, ac si nil esset præterea, nec inter homines quidem excelleret; nil sibi sumsit eximium.* It is incorrect to regard ὁμοίωμα and σχῆμα as indistinguishable synonyms (HEINRICHS, *et al.*), or the latter as *dignitas* (GROTIUS), *dress* (ELSNER), γενόμενος as *natus* (RILLIET), ἀνθρώπων as a designation of the *debile et abjectum* (HÖLEMANN), of the *infimæ et contemtæ sortis* (WOLF), or of the first human pair, because He like them was *peccati expers* (GROTIUS).

Ver. 8. **He humbled himself** (ἐταπείνωσεν ἑαυτόν). The humiliation described by ἐκένωσε, which took place in His incarnation, because He thereby passed over from the divine into the human mode of existence, is now particularly noted. Here observe the asyndeton, the verb being also connected with ἀλλά, while the position of the verb before the pronoun renders it emphatic. The general description (ἐκένωσε) gives place to the particular one (ἐταπείνωσεν). Hence there is no climax here (MEYER), nor does the latter exceed the former (SCHENKEL), nor does it refer to any humiliation below the dignity of man (HÖLEMANN).—It is more closely defined by the following: **And became obedient unto death, even the death of the cross.** Hence it is inadmissible to find in the preceding participial clause (ver. 7) the nearer limitation of ἐταπείνωσεν (WIESINGER), since this cannot be separated from the participial clauses belonging to ἐκένωσε, while ἐταπείνωσεν receives now its limitation. It is not without reference to a μαθεῖν ὑπακοήν, His learning obedience or subjection (Heb. v. 8), that γενόμενος precedes. It is not stated to whom He became ὑπήκοος, since the design was to mark the μορφὴ δούλου, *form of a servant*, according to its nature. If it were more exactly defined the object would be God (ver. 9; Rom. v. 19), not men (GROTIUS). The extent to which this obedience was carried appears in μέχρι θανάτου, *unto death* (Acts xxii. 4; Heb. xii. 4; Matt. xxvi. 38). Hence it is not a *temporal limitation* (VAN HENGEL), nor is it to be joined with ἐταπείνωσεν (BENGEL, *et al.*). Θανάτου δὲ σταύρου, a construction like σοφίαν—σοφίαν δὲ οὐ τοῦ αἰῶνος τούτου in 1 Cor. ii. 6 (WINER'S *Gram.*, p. 443). Δέ often brings forward something new, a more precise statement as opposed to something to be denied or rejected. It is opposed here to the idea of a natural or common death. Death by crucifixion was a punishment for slaves, criminals, outcasts, and hence increased the degradation. Τουτέστι τοῦ ἐπικαταράτου, τοῦ τοῖς ἀνόμοις ἀφωρισμένου (THEOPHYLACT). See Gal. iii. 13.

Ver. 9. **Wherefore God also hath highly exalted him** (διὸ καὶ ὁ θεὸς αὐτὸν ὑπερύψωσε). This was a consequence and result (διό) of the self-renunciation and the self-abasement of the Son. To this act is joined (καί) that of the Father. On the expression see Heb. xiii. 12; Rom. i. 24; Acts x. 29; on the thought Heb. ii. 9, 10; xii. 2. The language here involves an idea of merit on the part of Christ and of recompense on the part of God. The verb marks the antithesis to ἐταπείνωσε μέχρι θανάτου σταύρου, and the preposition in the verb (ὑπερύψωσε) indicates that it is an exaltation corresponding to the ὑπεράνω πάντων in Eph. iv. 10. The reference is to the resurrection and ascension, the end of which was His sitting down at the right hand of God (Matt. xxviii. 18; Mark xvi. 19; Acts vii. 55, 56; Eph. i. 20, 21; Col. iii. 1; Heb. viii. 1). The view of GROTIUS is incorrect: *eum multo sublimiorem fecit, quam antea fuit*, for the Saviour was not *sublimis* on earth (vers. 7, 8), and did not become *sublimior* than He was before the creation of the world (ver. 6), and besides ὑπέρ will not bear that signification. BENGEL: *Exinanitionis præmium justissimum est exaltatio* (Luke xxiv. 26; John x. 17); *neque ea non potuit illam consequi* (John x. 15); *quæcunque Patris sunt, filii sunt; ea non potuere ita Patris esse, ut non essent filii* (John xvii. 5); *Christum Christus exinanivit Christum deus exaltavit* (1 Peter v. 6) *eumque facit pariter deo.*—**And given him the name which is above every name.** Καί introduces the explanation of the ὑπερύψωσε, by which was obtained the εἶναι ἴσα τῷ θεῷ (ver. 6) which Christ would not seize for Himself. Ἐχαρίσατο αὐτῷ, *denotat, quam accepta deo fuerit exinanitio* (BENGEL). Τὸ ὄνομα τὸ ὑπὲρ πᾶν ὄνομα (WINER'S *Gram.*, p. 140) designates the well-known name which transcends every name, which according to the context is received and borne in heaven and on earth, since it is the *nomen cum re* (BENGEL), which is everywhere manifest and recognized, and includes the adoration of the person of Christ in its divine dignity. It is thus not mere *dignitas* (GROTIUS), or the particular name of Jesus (MICHAELIS), or κύριος (VAN HENGEL).

Ver. 10. **That in the name of Jesus every knee should bow.**—Ἵνα points out the purpose of this exaltation, which reaches its fulfilment, not by a single step, but gradually. See 1 Cor. xv. 25, 26; Rom. xiv. 11; Is. xlv. 23. Ἐν τῷ ὀνόματι stands emphatically at the beginning, and marks the ground and occasion of the πᾶν γόνυ κάμψῃ. The bending of the knee presents "plastically" (MEYER) the act of adoration. Eph. iii. 14; Rom. xi. 4; and comp. ἐπικαλεῖσθαι τὸ ὄνομα κυρίου (Acts vii. 59; ix. 14, 21; xxii. 16; 1 Cor. i. 2; Rom. x. 12, 13; 2 Tim. ii. 22). It is therefore not merely *adhibito nomine Jesu* (VAN HENGEL), since indeed Ps. lxiii. 5: ἐν τῷ ὀνόματί σου ἀρῶ τὰς χεῖράς μου, is said of prayer to God, nor is it merely a circumlocution for ἐν Ἰησοῦ (ESTIUS), or equivalent to εἰς τὸ ὄνομα, the glorification of His dignity (HEINRICHS), or *quoties auditur nomen* (ERASMUS).—**Of beings in heaven, and beings in earth, and beings under the earth**—comprises the entire realm of worshipping creatures. Τῶν ἐπουρανίων are the angels (Eph. i. 20, 21; Heb. i. 4, 6), τῶν ἐπιγείων, men upon the earth, τῶν καταχθονίων, the dead in Hades. The following are incorrect classifications: οἱ δίκαιοι, οἱ ζῶντες, οἱ ἁμαρτωλοί (CHRYSOSTOM); the dead, the living, the embryos (STOLZ); *homines sortis nobilioris, mediocris et infimæ* (TELLER). The words must not be taken as neuter (BEZA), nor is there in καταχθονίων a reference either to the demons (the Greeks, ERASMUS), which Eph. vi. 12 forbids, or to the souls in purgatory (Catholics).

Ver. 11. **And that every tongue should confess** (καὶ πᾶσα γλῶσσα ἐξομολογήσεται).—To the outward, inarticulate expression καί adds still another, the eloquent homage breaking forth from the heart and confessing itself to Him. What the bending of the knee indicates, the tongue expresses (WIESINGER). In πᾶσα the three categories (ver. 10) are included as in πᾶν γόνυ. To refer it therefore to πάντα τὰ ἔθνη (THEODORET) is erroneous, as also to take it *pro omni idiomate* (BEZA).—**That Jesus Christ is Lord.**—Ὅτι introduces the contents of the confession. Ἰησοῦς Χριστός is the subject, and κύριος the predicate, and precedes in accordance with the scope of the context: the kingship is to be pointed out of which the realm is unlimited (Eph. i. 23; iv. 10; 1 Cor. xv. 25, 28). It is not to be limited to rational creatures (HÖLEMANN), or to the Church (RHEINWALD, SCHENKEL).—**To the glory of God the Father** (εἰς δόξαν θεοῦ πατρός) belongs properly to the verb, not to the predicate κύριος (BENGEL), from which it is separated by the subject. It presents the end, purpose, of this adoring confession. It is therefore not the same as *in gloria* (Vulg.) or even, θεῷ (VAN HENGEL, who takes ὅτι as causal), as if ἐξομολογεῖν meant *laudibus celebrare.* [In θεοῦ πατρός the first term denotes a relation which God sustains to all His creatures; the second denotes one, which is peculiar to those who believe on His Son (comp. Gal. i. 1). On the universality of this confession see the last paragraph under DOCTRINAL AND ETHICAL.—H.]

DOCTRINAL AND ETHICAL.

1. *The motives* urged in teaching and exhortation are first objective, based upon Christ and the fellowship of the Holy Spirit; and secondly, subjective, as dependent on the character of individuals. Both of these concur in the case of him who teaches and exhorts, and of those dependent on the instructions and exhortations. The objective motives occupy the first place, and to these we should always appeal first of all. Among them stands in the foremost rank the example of Christ, which vers. 5–11 bring into view especially. Among the subjective motives are love and compassion, important beyond comparison with others, for they answer to the objective which come from God, who is love, and to the character of sin, which is an evil, an injury, against which we must be preserved. All other motives are, as it were, crutches, which, as adapted to a sickly self-love, must be finally thrown away, *e. g.*, regard for the judgment of others, fear of punishment, hope of reward. For with human nature as it is, one would not willingly do right, if, without doing so, he could be happy; and he would rather do wrong, if no harm should come to him from it.

2. The Apostle appeals to various motives for the maintenance of *unanimity* in the Church. But the unanimity which he seeks is moral rather than intellectual. It is not *uniformity*, but only the possession of a common centre, around which each one moves in a common love, which, however, may exhibit different degrees of strength and purity in different individuals, just as the centripetal force is capable of manifold gradations.

3. Among the bonds of this concord is *humility*, which in its two-fold intellectual and moral sphere, recognizes clearly both its own gifts and those which others possess, and does not allow one to esteem others less than himself, but prompts him with a sense of his own unworthiness

to regard them more highly, because their unworthiness does not concern him. It is characteristic of humility that it has its centre outside of itself, and includes the great whole of which it is a member within itself; while pride makes the individual himself the centre, and not only breaks loose from the whole, but stands opposed to it, and so becomes the source of all discord and enmity.

4. *Party spirit* and *vain glory* are excluded. The former misuses its neighbor, the latter its own possessions and those of the world; the former presses others down in order to raise itself; the latter draws others to itself in order to please them. The one exalts itself at the expense of others; and the other at the expense of its own real worth; party spirit often brings into action great talents and energy; self contents itself with the mere appearance. However sharply the former may spy out the weaknesses of others and the advantages of particular relations, it is yet sure to destroy itself; or it may be happy in the present moment, while blinded to the evils which follow in its train.

5. *The example of Christ* is here presented to the Church with a fullness and completeness such as is found nowhere else. The whole life, not merely the sufferings of Christ (1 Pet. ii. 21–25), enforces the doctrine, that we ought to deny self in humble love towards our neighbor, and only in such a way desire to share in his glory. If Christ existing in the form of God (*ἐν μορφῇ θεοῦ ὑπάρχων*, ver. 6), not seeking the things of Himself (*τὰ ἑαυτοῦ σκοπῶν*), but also those of others (*τὰ ἑτέρων*, ver. 4), resolved not to seize for Himself the sovereignty of a God over His creatures (ver. 6), but *in love* (*ἐν ἀγάπῃ*, ver. 2) and *lowliness of mind* (*ταπεινοφροσύνῃ*), ennobled and exalted those of mankind, made through Him in His image, and emptied Himself (*ἐκένωσεν ἑαυτόν*) by becoming a man (ver. 7), obedient in all things, even unto the death of the cross; and God has now exalted Him as the object of worship (vers. 9–11); then we also have no other way open to us to the glory with Him, except through humble self-denying love in fellowship and unity with the brethren.

6. [NEANDER:—That we rightly understand the use made of the example of Christ, as the model after which the Christian life is formed, we must first endeavor to bring the model itself clearly and distinctly before our minds. Before the eye of the Apostle stands the image of THE WHOLE CHRIST, the Son of God, appearing in the flesh, manifesting Himself in human nature. From the human manifestation he rises to the Eternal Word (as John expresses it), that Word which was, before the appearance of the Son of God in time—yea, before the *worlds* were made; in whom before all time God beheld and imaged Himself; as Paul in the Epistle to the Colossians calls Him, in this view, the image of the invisible, *i. e.*, the incomprehensible God. Then, after this upward glance of his spiritual eye, he descends again into the depths of the human life, in which the Eternal Word appears as man. He expresses this in the language of immediate perception, beholding the divine and the human as one; not in the form of abstract truth, attained by a mental analysis of the direct object of thought. Thus he contemplates the entrance of the Son of God into the form of humanity as a self-abasement, a self-renunciation, for the salvation of those whose low estate He stooped to share. He whose state of being was divine, who was exalted above all the wants and limitations of the finite and earthly existence, did not eagerly claim this equality with God which He possessed; but, on the contrary, He concealed and disowned it in human abasement, and in the form of human dependence. And as the whole human life of Christ proceeded from such an act of self-renunciation and self-abasement, so did His whole earthly life correspond to this one act even to His death; the consciousness on the one hand of divine dignity which it was in His power to claim, and on the other the concealment, the renunciation of this, in every form of humiliation and dependence belonging to the earthly life of man. The crowning point appears in His death—the ignominious and agonizing death of the cross. Paul then proceeds to show what Christ attained by such self-renunciation, thus carried to the utmost limit, by such submissive obedience in the form of a servant; the reward which He received in return, the dignity which was conferred upon Him. Here, too, is presented the universal law, laid down by Christ Himself, that whoso humbles himself, and in proportion as he humbles himself, shall be exalted.—H.]

7. Concerning the *person of Christ*, the passage before us states the following truths: (*a*) His *ego*, His essential entity, is an antemundane person, who had a divine mode of existence (*ἐν μορφῇ θεοῦ ὑπάρχων*). He is thus to be conceived of as existing within the being of God, as *πρὸς τὸν θεόν* (John i. 1), yet not merely as a thought, a principle, but as a person, *λόγος ἄσαρκος*. (*b*). Before the world was, before any creature existed, there was still wanting to Him who is *ἴσος θεῷ*, the *τὸ εἶναι ἴσα θεῷ*, a kingdom, and a people over which He might rule as the Anointed One at the right hand of the majesty of the Father. (*c*) He gave up His *μορφὴν θεοῦ*, *the form of God*, not His *ego*, not the possession of the glory, the *κτῆσις* of the *δόξα*. He assumed *a servant's form* (*μορφὴν δούλου*), not sin, in becoming man. With the incarnation His humiliation began, in which He exhibited obedience even to the death of the cross, the shameful death of a slave. Within the human life also, which began with the incarnation, there were degrees of exinanition or self-divestment from Bethlehem to Golgotha. (*d*) He humbled not His nature, but only His personal existence, Himself, by the assumption of human nature and by His entrance into the life of men, so as to subject Himself to ignominy and death. He thus humbled Himself not *through* the obedience, but *in* the obedience which He rendered to the Father's will, without sin, even in the most extreme trials that befell Him. (*e*) Such merit was followed by exaltation, which consisted in this, that He now became as *κύριος*, the object of worship for the whole realm of created spirits unto the praise of God the Father. (*f*) Into this position of exaltation the Father has placed the loved and loving Son. (*g*) In the worship of Jesus Christ the glory of the Father is constantly to be kept in view, as is the case in the public prayers and collects of the Evangelical Churches of the Reformation.

8. Our passage teaches nothing concerning the relation of the divine and the human nature, and of their attributes, to each other, of the relation of the two natures to the personal unity, or of the κτῆσις, or possession of the divine δόξα, or glory, to the χρῆσις, or use, of the same. Here we have opened to the efforts of Christological inquiry a wide and important domain which was measured and is measured or limited only by the fundamental conditions or outposts of Christianity, such as the hypostatic union, and based upon this the real communion of natures, which includes both the divine δόξα, as opposed to Ebionitism, Pelagianism, Socinianism, Rationalism, and the human development against Docetism and Romanism, and so the immutability as well as the self-limitation of the absolute God.

9. *History* of the interpretation of the text and of its doctrinal application. (*a*) The ancient Church almost throughout, before and after the Council of Nicæa, taught that the λόγος ἄσαρκος did not retain the divine δόξα for Himself, for His own advantage, while yet He did not cease, as λόγος ἔνσαρκος, to be what He was. His incarnation was not a yielding up of His divinity, but an assumption of humanity, which was taken up into His divinity. Only AMBROSIASTER, PELAGIUS, NOVATIAN, maintained opposite views. (*b*) The middle ages honored the divine nature at the expense of the human. THOMAS AQUINAS admitted only an outward development, in age and wisdom, with reference to men to whom He daily gave new proofs of it. (*c*) The Reformation harmonizes in general in the true confession of faith, yet the Lutherans, upon the fundamental principle, *finitum capax esse infiniti*, which the Reformed (Calvinists) denied, extended further the doctrine of the two natures and conditions of Christ. Thus LUTHER, led by his doctrine on the Lord's Supper, concludes from the form which Christ possesses, exalted at the right hand of God (which is conceived of, not as a place of abode, but as a mode of existence), that the humanity was taken up into the divine glory, and that from the incarnation onwards the condition of humiliation appears more as a veiling, self-limitation, that of exaltation as a complete, visible revelation of the divine life. So in the *Formula Concordiæ*, VIII., which, by "its very indefiniteness allows room for further examination," concerning which see FRANK, *Theologie der F. C.*, III., pp. 165 ff. The controversy of the theologians of Giessen and Tübingen, since 1607, did not concern itself about the κτῆσις, the possession of the divine glory, which was undisputed, but only about the χρῆσις, the use of it. The former, MENZER and FEUERBORN, with the F. C., maintained a κένωσιν χρήσεως, the latter, HAFFENREFFER, THUMMIUS, NICOLAI, only a κρύψιν χρήσεως, in respect to which the *Decisio Saxonica*, 1624, places itself on the side of the Giessen theologians, without reaching any very important result. (*d*) The modern development of Christology began with regarding the Son of God, the pre-existent God-man, as *being* in the perfect man (GOSCHEL), then attempted to conceive of the same as *becoming* the God-man (ROTHE, DORNER). THOMASIUS (*Christi Person and Werk*, II., §§ 40, 43), following HOFMANN (*Schriftbeweis* II.), went farther, since he supposed a self-abdication of the real attributes of the divine nature, amounting to a συγκοπή of the divine life of the Logos, or a sleep-like unconsciousness, and thus both impaired the *unio personalis* and assumed an exclusion of the Son from the Trinity during the earthly life of Christ. GESS (*Die Lehre von der Person Christi*), and GEORG LUDW. HAHN (*Theologie des N. T.* 1.) suppose a self-abnegation also of the immanent attributes, while SCHENKEL (*Die Christ. Dogmatik*, II.) does not proceed beyond the mere human nature, and falls into Socinianism. Others again revive Apollinarism. Comp. DORNER, *Entwicklungsgeschichte der Lehre von der Person Christi*, II., pp. 1203 ff.

9. The correct standpoint even for our time which, in the effort to conceive of the human development of the Redeemer, is in danger of lowering His divine personality, is shown by CHEMNITZ: *Reliqua vero, quæ vel quæri vel disputari possunt, et in verbo non habent expressam patefactionem, cum magni hujus profunditatem in hac vita exhaurire et pervidere non possimus, ita me differre et rejicere ad magnam illam cœlestem, æternam et illustrem scholam, ubi gloriam Christi salvatoris et fratris nostri ad faciem sicut est videbimus. Nec propter ea, quæ explicare non possum, ab illis, quæ expresso verbo patefacta sunt, discedere me debere. Hæc responsio, si videbitur rudior, simplicior et puerilior, non pugnabo, sed scio veram, certam, firmam et omnium tutissimam esse.* It is important to hold fast the ethical and practical sense of the passage, and to deny neither the constant unchangeableness of the divinity of the Son in itself (John i. 1, 18; iii. 13), nor His real, loving, self-denying, and self-abasing entrance into fellowship with sinful humanity in life and in death (John i. 14; xvii. 5).

10. [The final and universal acknowledgment of Christ's sovereignty (ver. 10) is affirmed also in Rom. xiv. 11. All the hosts of heaven and the myriads of the human race who still live, or have lived, or shall live, are to "bend the knee" before Him who bears the "name which is above every name," who, as the Apostle John has said, wears "the title written on His vesture and His thigh, 'King of kings and Lord of lords'" (Rev. xix. 16). But this language is to be understood in harmony with the teachings of other passages. "Even the enemies of Christ," says Dr. THOLUCK, "who reject the gospel, acknowledge the reality of His power, if they are unable to resist the decisions of His justice, *i. e.*, if at the end of the world they are excluded from all part in the blessings of His Kingdom; while those who have repented and submitted to His claims are received to the joys and the rewards of heaven. Both classes in this case yield to Him the homage of their submission. But according to a just distinction which some of the older writers have made, that of the one is *obedientia ex animo*, *i. e.*, a voluntary, hearty obedience; that of the other, *obedientia cum tremore*, a subjection reluctant, extorted by fear." Viewed in this light, the passage in our Epistle is parallel entirely to that in 2 Thess. i. 7–10. (*Disputatio Christologica de loc. Paul Phil.* II. 2 ff.—H.]

HOMILETICAL AND PRACTICAL.

Motives (ver. 1), aim (vers. 2–4), and method

(vers. 5–11) of a Christian teacher, a spiritual father.—We must ever start from what we have in order to get forward and upward. First, fulfil thine own duty, which should be to thee a pleasure, not a burden, and then lay hold of the good that is in others, be it ever so little, or merely supposed to be there; yet assume it, use it without complaint or mistrust.—Truth is one, simple, and yet so infinitely rich that there can be *unanimity* and yet no *monotony*, like the harmony in a choir of many voices. Most controversies in the church have moved and still move *around* the germ of the truth, *around* the fundamental doctrine, but do not touch exactly the thing itself. They have reference only to the *human* confirmation of the truth, its mediation through conceptions, or mode of apprehension, and affect not the Christian character of the individual, provided only he abides in love.—Not, how art thou esteemed by thy neighbor, but, how dost thou serve him, is the main point.—He is great who humbles himself in obedience, but disobedience dishonors and degrades; the former recognises the higher will, and looks forward to the glorious end; the latter is concerned only with itself, and does not get beyond self.—Self-seeking is a deadly plague to the soul.—The example of Jesus Christ instructs, directs, leads, makes the way of the cross a path of light; He went no other way, and the Christian also, His disciple, may not go a different one.

Starke:—If we would make people religious we must not use the wheel and the sword in the church, or fight them with the iron Bible, or preach fables; but build our exhortation upon Christ, the fellowship of the Spirit, the fellowship of God, for such arguments pierce through bone and marrow.—Love of honor in a preacher is a baneful poison, a prolific source of dissension in the church of God.—Self-seeking destroys country and people, churches and schools, cities and houses.—Who has knees to bend, let him bend them! Christ is the One most worthy of glory, the One whom we can never fully honor.

[Robert Hall:—Christianity was never intended to destroy the different stations and gradations of life; but it is intended to destroy that arrogance and superciliousness with which rank and splendor are too often borne. As it teaches the poor humility and submission, so it teaches the rich humanity, gentleness, and compassion. In this respect it merges all distinctions (ver. 3).—H.].

Rieger:—He who exalts himself above others, thinks that others also must accommodate themselves to him, acts as if they must regard his rights and their maintenance as of the first importance. With respect to the self-abasement of Christ, the language always was: He humbled Himself in order to show His obedient, willing spirit; but with reference to His exaltation, the language is: God has raised Him up, placed Him at His right hand, *etc.*, in order to distinguish Him as the Author and Finisher of our faith, the pioneer in the way of faith by which we must now come to God.

Schleiermacher:—Unity of mind among all Christians can be nothing else than unity in the knowledge that Christ is the Redeemer of the world, and in the disposition to recognize Him as such, and to accept Him as Leader in the way of salvation. 1) In what respects especially the Redeemer is our example. 2) How can we imitate this example?

Heubner:—It is characteristic of the Christian that he does not think highly of himself, but is disposed to regard others as more important, more deserving. He acknowledges gladly their excellencies and gives way to them. Such humility towards men, unaffected, and yielding the pre-eminence which pride arrogates to itself, flows from humility towards God.

[Neander:—One's judgment of another (see ver. 3) is not within the control of his own will. How can he esteem his brother higher than himself, if this is not in accordance with the truth, if he cannot but perceive in himself excellencies which are wanting in the other, and defects in the other from which he himself is free. Is humility to be grounded upon falsehood? Most certainly not. But there is here presupposed, as resulting from the development of the Christian life, a pervading temper of heart, of which such a judgment of one's self in comparison with others is but the necessary and natural expression. The Christian's love will lead him first of all to discern what is good in another; to discover even in his blemishes his peculiar gifts, that in which he is really superior to himself; while on the other hand, through a self-scrutiny, sharpened by the Spirit which quickens him, he detects with rigorous exactness his own faults. And this self-rigor, united with love, will give leniency to his judgment of whatever may obscure the divine life in others.—H.].

Passavant:—Strife and vain glory are pests in hearts, houses, families, congregations, cities, the state, the church.

As the Epistle for Palm Sunday (vers. 5–11).

Rautenberg:—The Mediator crowned with praise and honor on account of His sufferings and death. 1) By the world before God; 2) by God before the world.

Zeiss:—Royal image of the Christian who consecrates his life to the Lord; 1) Humility of heart is his costly adornment; 2) the blessing of love his joyful delight; 3) pleasing God his exalted aim; and 4) harvesting of the seed his heavenly reward.

Law and Testimony:—What a Christian shares with his Lord Jesus: 1) the cross; 2) the glory. Conditions of the church of Christ; 1) its servitude; 2) its glory. The palms which we strew in the path of the Lord Jesus: 1) That we believe in the Crucified One; 2) that we trust in the Exalted One. The five-fold hosanna with which we prepare the way of the Lord Jesus: hosanna (1) of humility, (2) of patience, (3) of faith, (4) of prayer, and (5) of hope.

Prohle:—The Epistle on Palm Sunday an earnest reminder of the entrance into the passion week. It reminds us, 1) of the cross and death of Christ; 2) of His innocence and holiness; 3) of His divine dignity; 4) of His complete subjection to God's will; 5) of the triumphant end of His sufferings.—The traits of a true imitation of Christ: 1) Humility; 2) Self-denial; 3) Obedience unto death.

God helps believers in their endeavors to imitate Christ.

(II. 12–18.)

12 Wherefore, my beloved, as ye have always obeyed, not as in my presence only,
but now much more in my absence, work out your own salvation with fear and
13 trembling. For it is God who worketh in you both to will and to do of (*or* for)
14 his good pleasure. Do all things without murmurings and disputings [doubtings].
15 That ye may be [become][1] blameless and harmless [pure] (the) sons [children] of
God, without rebuke,[2] in the midst of a crooked and perverse nation [generation],
16 among whom ye shine [appear] as lights [luminaries][3] in the world, holding forth
the word of life; that I may rejoice in the day of Christ, that I have not run in
17 vain, neither labored in vain. Yea, and if [But, if also] I be offered upon [in] the
18 sacrifice and service of your faith, I joy [rejoice], and I rejoice with you all. For
the same cause (also) do ye [also] joy [rejoice], and rejoice with me.

[1] Ver. 15. Γενέσθαι in ℵ B, *et al.* has better support than ἦτε in A, *et al.*

[2] *Ibid.* Ἄμωμα, found in ℵ A B C *et al.*, is better supported than ἀμώμητα, but as the more common form in the N. T. might more readily displace the latter, than the reverse.

[3] [*Ibid.* The Greek for *luminaries* (φωστῆρες), says Lightfoot, is used almost exclusively of the heavenly bodies. It occurs again in the N. T. only in Rev. xxi. 11, where also it should be so rendered.—H.].

EXEGETICAL AND CRITICAL.

Ver. 12. **Wherefore,** ὥστε, refers to what precedes, as in iv. 1. See WINER'S *Gram.* p. 301. Ὑπηκούσατε is correlative with γενόμενος ὑπήκοος, and τὴν ἑαυτῶν σωτηρίαν corresponds to vers. 9–11. The exhortation borrows its coloring indeed from vers. 8-11, but, like the example of Christ adduced as an illustration, it reaches back to the entire course of thought (vers. 1-11), and hence does not attach itself merely to ver. 11 (SCHENKEL), to the last thing discussed (vers. 6-11, MEYER) or to i. 27 ff. (DE WETTE).—**My beloved** (ἀγαπητοί μου) shows the Apostle's joy and deep interest in them (ver. 2).—**As ye have always obeyed** (καθὼς πάντοτε ὑπηκούσατε) singles out the act on the part of the Philippians, upon which he now builds his hope that his exhortation will not be in vain. *Mihi ad salutem vos hortanti, ipsique deo* (BENGEL). The context requires this explanation.—**Not as in my presence only.** Μὴ belongs to the following imperative (κατεργάζεσθε); for if the negative belonged to ὑπηκούσατε, with which Luther wrongly connects it, οὐ would have been used. Ὡς, according to its use in a participial clause, points out a possible idea of the Philippians, that such compliance with Paul's admonition must be necessary only in his presence. See WINER'S *Gram.* p. 617. Hence it is not a term of comparison (HÖLEMANN).—**But now much more in my absence** (ἀλλὰ νῦν πολλῷ μᾶλλον ἐν τῇ ἀπουσίᾳ μου) urges the stronger necessity for self-exertion, because they are left to themselves, without the assistance of the Apostle who is now far distant. *Quia ego vobis non adesse possum, ipsi vos curateeo magis* (BENGEL).—**Work out your own salvation with fear and trembling.** Μετὰ φόβου καὶ τρόμου refers (as in Eph. vi. 5) to that tender conscientiousness, that fear in the presence of the omnipresent God, which feels that no effort or solicitude can be too great. It does not refer to a servant's relation (BENGEL: *servi esse debetis, examplo Christi,* ver. 8), nor to spiritual pride (RILLIET), nor to resignation to God's will (MATTHIES). Τὴν ἑαυτῶν σωτηρίαν marks the salvation as that of the Philippians themselves (ἑαυτῶν not being here used for ἀλλήλων, FLATT, *et al.*), who in this case ought to regard the things of themselves (τὰ ἑαυτῶν σκοπεῖν) as the glorious end of the κατεργάζεσθε. On ἑαυτῶν see WINER'S *Gram.*, p. 150 sq. Κατεργάζεσθαι means *to bring to pass* (*perficere usque ad metam,* BENGEL), for which energetic perseverance is requisite. The mode of this is indicated by ὑπηκούσατε, as also by the example of Christ (ver. 8).

Ver. 13. **For it is God who worketh in you** (θεὸς γάρ ἐστιν ὁ ἐνεργῶν ἐν ὑμῖν). The Apostle strengthens his exhortation here by reminding them that if they disregard it they will not merely suffer personal loss, (τὴν ἑαυτῶν σωτηρίαν), but strive against another, the Highest, whose work and working they would disturb and bring to naught. It confirms the entire exhortation, though it designates only the τὴν ἑαυτῶν σωτηρίαν specially as their aim and labor. Thus it is neither a ground of encouragement (CHRYSOSTOM, MEYER, *et al.*), nor an incentive to humility (CALVIN, SCHENKEL, *et al.*); for it is not designed to confirm exclusively either κατεργάζεσθε or μετὰ φόβου καὶ τρόμου. Notwithstanding God's activity, which is shown by ἐστὶν ὁ ἐνεργῶν to be constant, and by ἐν ὑμῖν to be exerted in the hearts of individuals, every one should be careful both as to what he does or omits to do. Of God it is not said that He *effectually* works (κατεργάζεται) to will and to do, since He does not indeed accomplish this result in all; but He is only said ἐνεργεῖν, because where it is effected, it is not without His assistance; which of course to be effective (κατεργάζεσθαι) requires obedience on their part (ὑπακούειν). HÖLEMANN wrongly explains ἐν ὑμῖν as *intra cœtum vestrum* [and others 'among you.'—H.]. What God works is especially—**Both to will and to do,** καὶ τὸ θέλειν καὶ τὸ ἐνεργεῖν. The first is the self-determination, the second the personal exertion: both take place in the heart of the believer. The first originates, the second carries out in the life; both are conditions of the κατεργάζεσθαι.—**Of** *or* **for his good pleasure** ὑπὲρ τῆς εὐδοκίας is a nearer limitation of ἐνεργῶν. God's working has its ground within Himself (His εὐδοκία), and is not occasioned or controlled by anything out of Himself, and in man. The article defines the disposition as well known. Comp. Rom. xv. 8: ὑπὲρ ἀληθείας θεοῦ. See WINER'S *Gram.* p. 383. [The preposition ὑπέρ does not represent the εὐδοκία as the mere *ratio* of the action, or the mere *norma* according to which it is done, but as the *interested cause* of it; the *commodum* of the εὐδοκία was that which the action was designed to subserve (ELLICOTT).—H.]. On εὐδοκία see i. 15; Eph. i. 5. The meaning of ὑπέρ cannot be κατά, *secundum*, nor can the εὐδοκία of the Philippians be meant (ERASMUS, *et al.*)

Ver. 14. **Do all things without murmurings and doubtings.** Πάντα is limited only by the context: all which is to be done in reference to salvation, for which God gives the willing and the working. [The verb (ποιεῖτε) here comprehends in its full compass suffering as well as doing. The patience with which the Christian endures the trials to which God may call him illustrates his character not less decisively than the habit of active obedience.—H.] Ποιεῖτε marks only the act, the nature and mode of which are determined by the disposition of the doer (χωρὶς γογγυσμῶν καὶ διαλογισμῶν). The preposition denotes, like ἄνευ (1 Pet. iv. 9) a separation, but the difference between them is, that the former represents the subject, the latter the object as distant. The Philippians ought to be distant, separated, from murmurings and doubtings; ἄνευ would indicate that these ought to be far from the Philippians (Eph. ii. 12); and see TITTMANN *Syn.*, 1, pp. 93-97. The distinction between the two substantives is, that the first (γογγυσμοί) belongs to the unwilling, weak, and still stubborn spirit, the second (διαλογισμοί) to the doubtful spirit, which does not see its way clearly. The former proceeds from the will, the latter from the intellect. SCHENKEL refers the first to the defiant, the second to the timid heart. BENGEL supposes the ἄμεμπτοι in ver. 15 to refer back to γογγυσμοί, and ἀκέραιοι to διαλογισμῶν. We are not to understand by the latter term *disputation, controversy* (WIESELER, ERASMUS, *et al.*), contrary to the usage of the New Testament. This word is not to be limited, as *e. g.* to God only (MEYER, *et al.*), to superiors (ESTIUS, *et al.*), or fellow Christians (CALVIN, WIESELER, *et al.*). [As γογγυσμός is the moral, so διαλογισμός is the intellectual rebellion against God (LIGHTFOOT).—H.]

Ver. 15. **That ye may become blameless and pure.** Ἵνα marks the end, γένησθε the way, which is *a becoming*, a process of development. Ἄμεμπτοι, *unblamable*, those (according to the Greek form) in whom there is nothing to blame (1 Thess. iii. 13), represents the moral integrity as manifesting itself outwardly; ἀκέραιοι (from κεράννυμι), *unmixed* (Rom. xvi. 19; Matt. x. 16), presents 'the same according to its inner character' (MEYER). The first is that from which we can judge of the second, for it is the condition of it; the inward answers to the outward.—**Children of God, without rebuke, in the midst of a crooked and perverse generation** [not *nation* as in the A. V.—H.] Τέκνα θεοῦ sums up both predicates, such *are* they as Christians: but in Christ (Eph. i. 5; Gal. iv. 5) they should *become* ἄμωμα (without μῶμος, Eph. i. 4; v. 27; Col. i. 22, *in quo non est, quod reprehendatur*), or ἀμώμητα (from μωμάομαι, 2 Pet. iii. 14, *qui reprehendi non potest*), and this in spite of and in their actual circumstances. Μέσον (here as a preposition, see WINER'S *Gram.*, p. 471) γενεᾶς σκολιᾶς καὶ διεστραμμένης. Comp. Acts ii. 40; 1 Pet. ii. 18; Matt. xvii. 17; Luke ix. 41. Γενεά is used *de ætatis alicujus hominibus*. The first adjective describes the outward, dishonest, perverted demeanor; the second the inward, distorted character. Manifestly there is an allusion here to a passage in the important chapter which serves as a basis of prophecy (Deut. xxxii. 5): ἡμάρτοσαν οὐκ αὐτῷ τέκνα μωμητά, γενεὰ σκολιὰ καὶ διεστραμμένη.—**Among whom ye shine as luminaries in the world.** [The active (φαίνειν) means *to shine* (see John i. 5; 2 Pet. i. 19; Rev. i. 16); but the middle means to *appear*, as in Matt. xviii. 27; 1 Pet. iv. 18 and James iv. 14. The A. V. does not always observe the distinction.—H.] Ἐν οἷς belongs *ad sensum* to γενεᾶς (WINER'S *Gram.*, p. 141). The verb, φαίνεσθε, not φαίνετε, describes their becoming visible, being recognized as God's children. Hence it is not *lucetis* (BENGEL), still less is it the imperative (PELAGIUS, ERASMUS, *et al.*). [Christians were not to be, but now actually *were*, as luminaries in a dark, heathen world (ELLICOTT).—H.] The apostle calls to their mind what they are, in order that they may show themselves to be such. But ὡς φωστῆρες introduces a new figure, to designate the immoral character of the world: Christians are the stars, illuminators, ἐν κόσμῳ, in the world, which in itself is as dark as night. Hence ἐν κόσμῳ is not to be joined with φαίνεσθε (DE WETTE), nor is φαίνονται to be supplied (RILLIET, *et al.*); neither is it equivalent to "in the heavens" (RHEINWALD), nor is it *dat. commodi*, "for the world" (STORR). [This form (φωστῆρες) occurs elsewhere in the N. T. only in Rev. xxi. 11, where it has the same sense.—H.]

Ver. 16. **Holding forth the word of life,** presents the mode of the φαίνεσθε. Λόγον ζωῆς receives illustration from the connection which exists between life and light (John i. 4: ἡ ζωὴ ἦν τὸ φῶς): life is light, Christ is the life (John vi. 48; xiv. 6) and the light (John viii. 62; ix. 5; xii. 46), and indeed the source of them; His followers are also light, but it is a derived light (Matt. v. 14); the essence of the gospel is light (Eph. v. 8; Col. i. 12), and the life is in the word, and as the thought breaks forth in the word, so also the light and the life. Accordingly ἐπέχοντες is used and not merely ἔχοντες. The Christian holds forth the word of life, living it, living out what is living within him. Hence τῷ λόγῳ προσέχοντες (THEODORET) is incorrect, for we have not the dative (Acts iii. 5); and so also is "holding fast" (LUTHER).—The aim and result is: **That I may rejoice in** [or, more literally, **for a rejoicing to me against**] **the**

day of Christ (εἰς καύχημα ἐμοὶ εἰς ἡμέραν Χριστοῦ). Comp. i. 10, 26. The cause of his rejoicing then will be: **That I have not run in vain, neither labored in vain** (ὅτι οὐκ εἰς κενὸν ἔδραμον οὐδὲ εἰς κενὸν ἐκοπίασα). The first expression, which recalls the contests of the *stadium* or race, denotes his zeal and the wide reach of his activity (not confined to one place); the second (derived from κοπός, *toil*) indicates the labor and effort which his ministry involves. The modifying οὐκ εἰς κενόν follows: *in vain, i. e. without fruit or result* (2 Cor. vi. 1; Gal. ii. 2; 1 Thess. iii. 5), which thus occasions the repetition, and does not merely arise from his feeling of joy in the consciousness that such is the result (MEYER).

Ver. 17. **But if also I be offered.** Ἀλλά introduces an antithesis which εἰ shows to be conditional. What this antithesis is, καί before σπένδομαι shows. ["My labors have been severe, unintermitted. *But* not content with this I am willing (if that is reserved for me) to suffer a martyr's death."—H.] The meaning of σπένδομαι is: *I am poured out as a drink-offering*, presented as a libation, as in 2 Tim. iv. 6. Comp. Numb. xxviii. 7; xv. 4 sq. [The present tense represents the act as in progress. "If I am being poured out," *etc.*—H.] The libation-wine, set apart from its common use, serving as an expression of joy (Ps. civ. 15; Eccles. x. 19), as an image of quickening grace (Prov. ix. 2; Isaiah lv. 1), as a sweet savor (2 Cor. ii. 15; Rom. xv. 16), serves to represent the Apostle (separated from them by his δεσμοί), as giving up his personal and official *ego*, his life and his desires, pouring out in a martyr's death his blood as a sweet savor. The Apostle's death by the sword is here alluded to, the present marking it as impending (i. 20). Καὶ connects this death by martyrdom with ἔδραμον and ἐκοπίασα, his sufferings with his labors; the latter have not been fruitless, and the former also shall not be so.—Hence the following is added: **Upon (in) the sacrifice and service of your faith.** Ἐπί points to the circumstances of the σπένδεσθαι; this takes place in τῇ θυσίᾳ καὶ λειτουργίᾳ. Both are united under one article, and are hence conceived of as a unity. The second is the priestly service (Luke i. 23; Heb. viii. 6), hence the first is the act of offering, not *victima* (WIESINGER). The offering itself is designated by the genitive: τῆς πιστέως ὑμῶν, with respect to which the Apostle exercises his priestly functions, presenting it to God, while he himself is the accompanying drink-offering, since his blood is poured forth. As the former results in his glory, so now this results in his joy. [The Hebrews, in offering their sacrifices, poured out often a libation or drink-offering at the same time. See Ex. xxix. 40; Numb. xxviii. 7. The costume of the thought in this passage is evidently derived from that practice. 'The faith of the Philippians, according to the Apostle's allusion, is viewed as a sacrifice which they have brought to the altar for the purpose of presenting it to God. The Apostle himself with reference to his agency in their salvation, officiates as the priest who offers this sacrifice for them. The act of presenting it is styled here a λ ε ι τ ο υ ρ γ ί α, *i. e.*, as the word imports, *a sacerdotal service*, or *ministry* (see Luke i. 23; Heb. viii. 6). Paul declares now, in the ardor of his affection for the Philippians, that if it be necessary in order that he may discharge his priestly office more perfectly, or that the sacrifice of their faith may be more acceptable unto God, that his blood should be shed as a libation for them, he is willing to *die* in their behalf. He has in view the possibility of his martyrdom, and the effect which he hopes may result from that event, in strengthening their faith and preparing them for heaven.—H.] RILLIET's rendering of σπένδομαι, I am sprinkled, is incorrect, for it is the present tense; ἐπί has not the sense of "to" (WIESINGER), or *super* (VAN HENGEL), since θυσία is not *victima*. There is no antithesis here to i. 25 (DE WETTE); of which no reader would readily think, for what intervenes (i. 26–ii. 1 sq.) makes that connection at too remote places, or to i 25, as if he had hoped to live to see the perfection of his readers, but now supposes the opposite (MEYER, WIESINGER, *et al.*), or as if he had thought at first that he should live to see the coming of the Lord (VAN HENGEL) which is not here in question. It should not be joined with the following χαίρω (BENGEL).—**I rejoice, and rejoice with you all,** χαίρω καὶ συγχαίρω πᾶσιν ὑμῖν. THEOPHYLACT: οὐχ ὡς ὁ ἀποθανούμενος λυποῦμαι, ἀλλὰ καὶ χαίρω ὅτι σπονδὴ γίνομαι. Paul rejoices in the prospect of a martyr's death; but not for himself merely; he rejoices with the Church also, which will thus experience and acknowledge the blessing of martyrdom. MEYER, contrary to the *usus loquendi* of the New Testament (Luke i. 58; xv. 6, 9; 1 Cor. xii. 26; xiii. 6, where it means in each case to rejoice *with others*) takes συγχαίρω as *congratulor* together with the Vulg., BENGEL, *et al.* [This is also LIGHTFOOT's interpretation.—H.]

Ver. 18. **For the same cause** (τὸ δ' αὐτό, governed by the verb) presents the cause of the joy to which in conclusion he earnestly exhorts them from his example. [Instead of being grieved that they should be such gainers at his expense, he would have them share his joy in being permitted to yield up his life with such gain to himself and such benefit to them.—H.]—**Do ye also rejoice, and rejoice with me,** καὶ ὑμεῖς χαίρετε καὶ συγχαίρετέ μοι. These are imperatives, not indicatives (ERASMUS). The following explanations are wrong: *gratulamini mihi, libato* (BENGEL); *subauditur* κατά with τὸ δ'αὐτό (BEZA); τὸ δ'αὐτό=ὡσαύτως (RHEINWALD, RILLIET, WIESINGER, who cites Matt. xxvii. 44). BENGEL: *martyrii præstantia.*

DOCTRINAL AND ETHICAL

1. A great blessing rests upon fellowship with Christians, whether they be mature or not (ver. 12), for it tends to the development of Christian character and life; but not merely upon fellowship with those who are present to the senses: the spiritual man ought to make his influence reach to the absent also. The more he does this the better.

2. In connection with faith which comes from the preaching of the divine word (Rom. x. 17: ἡ πίστις ἐξ ἀκοῆς, ἡ δὲ ἀκοὴ διὰ ῥήματος θεοῦ), obedience is demanded (ὑπακοή, ver. 12: ὑπηκούσατε).

This gives keenness to the tender conscience, which dreads to disregard or to seem to cast contempt upon God and His gifts (μετὰ φόβου καὶ τρόμου). *Quamvis enim gratis in uno Christo per fidem apprehenso servemur, tamen per viam justitiæ ad salutem contendere nos oportet, cum filii dei ejus spiritu ducantur* (BEZA), hence they must follow, because in His strength they are able to do it. We belong to God through Christ, and we should, by obedience to Him and to His word, prove this relationship.

3. Our salvation is as much God's work as our own. The beginning of a new life in the soul is entirely an act of God, which the Holy Spirit effects in our spirit, but not in our consciousness; yet in such a manner that we become conscious of it as an act of God. We do not create ourselves men; God creates us (HARLESS, *Ethics*, p. 229). He works in us constantly the willing and the doing. But we can resist Him, withdraw ourselves from Him. He does not work irresistibly, determinatively. But because He works thus in us, we may not remain idle, we must be fearful lest we lose this work of grace, fearful on account of our weakness, and the dangers in and around us, and must cherish and follow this willing and working effected by God.

4. [NEANDER:—Paul always represents the salvation of man as something which can be accomplished only through the grace of God as the work of God in man. But he adds (ver. 13) a more exact designation of the temper of heart with which Christians should work out their salvation, *viz.*, "with fear and trembling." This would not be appropriate if he were speaking of what lay merely in the hand of man, in which case all would depend upon his own strength. It is because Paul is conscious of the weakness and insufficiency of all human strength, because he presupposes that man can do nothing without God, and must constantly watch over himself, lest through his own fault he lose the aid of divine grace, without which all human efforts are in vain; it is for this reason that he designates this temper of mind as one of fear and trembling, as the feeling of personal accountability and helplessness, of insecurity and instability in ourselves, by which we may be ever admonished to continual watchfulness, and to ever-renewed waiting upon God as the fountain of all our strength. Hence, as the ground of such an admonition, he appeals to this consciousness that we can of ourselves do nothing, that it is God who alone bestows upon us the power to will and to perform what is needful to our salvation; that all, indeed, depends upon his sovereign will. This feeling of dependence, the ground-tone of the Christian life, is ever to be maintained. It is this which must combat the presumption of a vain human self-reliance, which, finding itself deceived in the result, so easily gives place to dejection and despair. (See vers. 12, 13.—H.].

5. The goal is reached by a gradual process (ver 15: γένησθε). *Renovatio non est talis mutatio, quæ uno momento statim omnibus suis partibus perficiatur ac absolvatur, sed habet sua initia, suos progressus, quibus in magna infirmitate perficitur.* (GERHARD, *loc.* xii. 9, § 126). *Fiunt in conversione inchoationes similes conceptioni, non tamen solum concipi, sed et nasci opus est; nihil tamen horum fit sine gratuita dei misericordia* (AUGUSTINE).

6. Φόβος καὶ τρόμος may not be omitted, for in the *renovatio* just as full a view is given of the *magna potentia Dei* as of the *magna infirmitas hominis.* But γογγυσμὸς καὶ διαλογισμός must be absent, for the first springs from self-confidence, contentment with one's self, the second from mistrust towards God and His gifts as the source of power; the first excites a sullen will towards God, the second turns the confused spirit away from God, and ends in despair.

7. Every Christian has a mission in the world, to let his light shine round about him, and to be anxious that the darkness of the world, though it is around him, shall on this very account not be and remain in him.

8. The word of God must, as a *word of life*, manifest itself actively in the personal traits of the Christian, that there may be an eloquent sermon without word of mouth, in the still, noiseless walk and character.

9. As death is no loss to the Christian, still less is the martyr's death, which is rather a ground and cause of thankful joy for the Church and for the martyr himself.

HOMILETICAL AND PRACTICAL.

The work of thy salvation is (1) God's work wrought upon thee and in thee; (2) the work of the Church, within which it takes place; (3) thine own work, since thou consentest to it.—God does not give thee the flower and the fruit of salvation, but the seed, the sunshine and the rain. He does not give houses, nor yet beams and squared stones, but trees, and rocks, and limestone, and says: Now build thyself a house. Regard not God's work within thee as an anchor to hold thy bark firmly to the shore, but as a sail which shall carry it to its port.—Fear thy depression and faint-heartedness, but take courage at thy humility before God. Consider God's gifts, thy employment of them, the final reckoning before Him. Ever become more and more what thou really art, a light in the world.—Even in sorrow and the deepest pain, overlook not the reasons for joy.

STARKE:—Behold the character of righteous children, scholars, and hearers, who in their parents and teachers really see God, and therefore are obedient, as well in their absence as in their presence, since they have the everywhere-present God before their eyes and in their hearts. Our Christianity does not lead one to hide himself in deserts and convents, and thus to remain blameless, but in the midst of the perverted, degenerate world to guard himself from sin. Such knighthood will God have from us.—When the joy of the children of this world ceases, then the joy of the faithful first really begins; and the ability to rejoice in extreme sufferings, even in death itself, is a proof of the truth and excellence of the Christian religion.

RIEGER:—We ought never to forget the danger of being lost, to which we are exposed so long as we live in a body of sin and death, and amid the temptations of the world; and therefore we ought not to regard ourselves as beyond fear and trembling.—God does not compel and overpower us by His working, like a block. Man can do nothing without God, and God will do nothing without man and his awakened will.—As surely as God does nothing against His honor, so surely will He do nothing against our salvation.—Doubting is opposed to faith, murmuring, to love. Even now, at the departure of favored children of God, the grace which has been made known in them sweetens perceptibly all sorrow over their loss, and prevents any wish to bring them back again.

Gerlach:—The believing Christian is awakened and moved by God's power. It is mighty in him. But he ought also to give himself up to it without reservation, neither opposing God's will by murmuring, a disposition directly contrary to it, nor concealing his disobedience behind doubts, subtleties, and questions.

Schleiermacher:—We ought to fear and tremble for ourselves as soon as we perceive the thought of future blessedness becoming dim in our souls, or the longing for it becoming languid in our hearts.—Every one who has such fear of that which may bring upon us adversity, every one who through this fear denies the Redeemer before men, should consider that it was the will of our dying Redeemer that His followers should take His cross upon them as their own. But we can take it upon us only in the faithful and unwearied service of truth and goodness, and of all that we recognize as the will of God.

Menken:—The willing is of God and the ability to do is of God; but the using, the action, the life in conformity with such divinely awakened willing and divinely bestowed ability, is ours, is dependent upon us, upon our faithfulness.—He who could think that God indeed works in him the willing but not the performing, or that to-day he gives the willing, but the performing not until after days and years, or even not until the future life, would in that error utter a falsehood concerning God, and would deny Him.—No disposition of heart in which love and faith are wanting accords with the spirit of truth and holiness.—So also no work is good and pleasing to God by which love and faith are injured.—There is something lovely and benevolent about a man who performs every good deed as freely, as joyfully, as kindly, as if it had not been a duty at all, as if no law had enjoined it, no fear compelled it, as if, instead of proving difficult, it had cost no self-denial and no effort, as if it had sprung forth with delight and joy from his very nature, from the rich treasure of his goodness and his love. How ungracious and unlovely on the other hand is every word, and work, and endurance, in which we detect compulsion, secret reluctance, and vexation, an inward, restrained murmuring, that says to us plainly enough: all this would not be done, were it not compelled.—The worth and the good conduct of the child of God should not be the pitiable product of favorable circumstances, not that miserable, godless virtue which is ever dependent on outward circumstances, and changes as often as they change.—The Holy Scriptures contain not an empty, unpractical theory, not a rule for those who dwell in heaven, but instruction for us who live in the midst of the world, who are on the field of battle, and whose life, on account of our own inward character and relation to the world, can be nothing else but a struggle, and who can attain to freedom and peace only through manifold victories.—It was in general characteristic of the Apostle to be moved, awakened, strengthened and exalted by nothing so quickly, so deeply, so powerfully, in the depths of his heart, as by a glance forward to the day of Christ (ver. 16).

Heubner:—With real Christians there should be no need of any Mentor, of any higher power whose presence alone could compel them to obedience; they should do the right, no matter whether any one sees or not. With many, doing right is but an eye-service, and with such the law itself is at bottom only one more bugbear.—Christianity does not enjoin anxious scrupulousness and gloomy self-mortification, but it forbids bold assurance and defiant self-confidence. This thought—it is possible for thee to lose thy salvation—can never be fearful enough to us. We should tremble at the idea—it is possible for thee to be cast off from God.—Man must strive as though he could do all, as though all depended on himself. Joy and love in obedience characterize the Christian as a child of God, as a son in distinction from a slave.—Christians should stand in contrast with their age, should constitute the *élite*, and serve as models for others around them.—The fickle sparkle at times; the truly pious burn evenly on.—The service of sin consumes also—but it destroys the best part of the man.

Passavant:—Fear and trembling, before the face of the thrice Holy One; before an unholy world, which ensnares us on every side with the allurements of sin, so that we become partakers of its sins; before ourselves, before this heart which, consciously or unconsciously, joins so readily with Satan and the world in lust and malice, which conceals within itself so many a lust, so many a lie, and so many a power of evil—a manifold tinder of destruction.

Meyer:—Only blessed! is the inscription over every pious Christian's door, as it is over the pastor's study, over font, altar, pulpit, grave. Strive that thou mayest be blessed.—(1) Your salvation *your* care; (2) your salvation *God's* work. The *defiant* heart has heard the admonition to penitence, "work out!"—the *timid* heart, the assurance, "it is God!"

IV. SECTION THIRD.

The conduct of the companions and assistants of the Apostle.

(CHAPTER II. 19–30.)

Timothy and his approaching mission to them.

(CHAP. II. 19–24.)

19 But I trust [hope][1] in the Lord Jesus to send Timothy shortly unto you, that I
20 also may be of good comfort, when I know your state. For I have no man like-
21 minded, who will naturally [sincerely] care for your state. For all seek their own,
22 not the things which are Jesus Christ's. But ye know the proof of him, that as a
23 son [child] with the [a] father, he hath served with me in [for] the gospel. Him
therefore I hope to send presently [immediately][2] so soon as I shall see[3] how it
24 will go with me. But I trust in the Lord that I also myself shall come shortly.

[1] Ver. 19. [Our English Version often confuses the renderings of ἐλπίζω and πέποιθα with each other. See the notes on Philem. ver. 23, p. 23 (LANGE's Series).—H.].

[2] Ver. 23. [" Presently," by an old English usage="immediately," as in 1 Sam. ii. 16; Matth. xxvi. 53. See EASTWOOD and WRIGHT'S *Bible Word Book*, p. 38. This change in the meaning of the English word conceals from the reader the relation in which "shortly" (ταχέως) in ver. 19, and "immediately" here (ἐξαυτῆς) stand to each other.—H.].

[3] *Ibid.* [On the form ἀφίδω, see the EXEGETICAL NOTES below.—H.].

EXEGETICAL AND CRITICAL.

Ver. 19. **But I hope** (*ἐλπίζω δέ*) in spite of the martyrdom, (*σπενδέσθαι*, ver. 17) which he apprehends. He regards a favorable result as possible, but only because he hopes **in the Lord Jesus** (*ἐν κυρίῳ Ἰησοῦ*) who is the ground of his hope (1 Cor. xv. 19), so that he is confident of being able to dispense with Timothy, and to send him shortly to them (*Τιμόθεον ταχέως πέμψαι ὑμῖν*). This also took place, since the second epistle was written to him after this. *Ταχέως* is limited by ver. 23. The simple dative *ὑμῖν* is stronger than *πρὸς ὑμᾶς*, not merely equivalent (VAN HENGEL), for the latter is only local, while the former marks his longing for the Philippians—their attachment to each other.—**That I also may be of good comfort**, gives the purpose (*ἵνα*) of the mission; *κἀγώ*, found only here, refers to the effect of the letter in allaying the anxiety of the church concerning Paul, who also needed the same alleviation with respect to them (*εὐψυχῶ*, also found only here), for the church is exposed to many dangers (i. 27-30; iii. 1-21; iv. 2).—**When I know your state.** *Γνούς* indicates definite knowledge, the object of which is *τὰ περὶ ὑμῶν*. He needs and expects to receive through Timothy good news as well as certain information. He ascribes special importance to Timothy's communications, for not only had Epaphroditus been a long time away from Philippi (vers. 25-30), but he wished also to learn the effect of this present letter, and Timothy understood him perfectly, and was aware of all that concerned and interested the Apostle.

Ver. 20. **For I have no man like-minded,** *οὐδένα γὰρ ἔχω ἰσόψυχον.* [The comparison here is between Timothy and other persons, not between him and Paul; since the object of the remark clearly is to state why the Apostle sends Timothy rather than any one else.—H.]. This last reason alone he makes prominent, and hence unfolds it still further.—**Who will sincerely care for your state.** *Ὅστις* describes the character of Timothy: *such a one as that, etc.*, and *ἰσόψυχος* (found only in this place in the New Testament), referring through *ἔχω* to the Apostle, is more closely defined in its mode of action, entirely like *φίλος ἴσος τῇ ψυχῇ μου* (Deut. xiii. 6). *Γνησίως* marks the uprightness and purity, the freedom from false, self-seeking arts, by which he will show his solicitude for them (*τὰ περὶ ὑμῶν μεριμνήσει*) when he comes. The sympathy with which he will enter into their relations and circumstances (*τὰ περὶ ὑμῶν*, not *τὰ ὑμῶν*, 2 Cor. xii. 14), your estate, your possessions. [The verb is future with reference to the concern for them which Timothy would manifest on his arrival among them.—H.]

Ver. 21. **For all** (*οἱ πάντες γάρ*) answers to *οὐδένα*. The article merely denotes a limitation. Those only are referred to who, from their situation being in the Apostle's immediate circle at the time, would be compared with the like-minded (*ἰσόψυχος*) Timothy.—**Seek their own, not the things which are Jesus Christ's** (*τὰ ἑαυτῶν ζητοῦσιν, οὐ τὰ Χριστοῦ Ἰησοῦ*), hence do not act sincerely (*γνησίως*). Comp. ver. 4. We are not to think of the hardships of the journey to which they preferred their own comfort (the Greeks), or that *οἱ πάντες* is equivalent to "many," "the most" (GROTIUS, *et al.*), or that they are *Philippensibus cogniti* (VAN HENGEL), or that the word 'more' is to be understood with ζητεῖν, (ERASMUS), although self-seeking has its gradations. No reference is made to those designated in i. 15, 17. It would not have occurred to Paul to send any of them. Those spoken of in i. 14, might be of the number. Of those mentioned in Col. iv. 10–14; Philem. ver. 24, Demas probably is the only one who was with him. This view seems to be confirmed by the fact that the Apostle cannot send Timothy away immediately (vers. 19, 23).

Ver. 22. **But ye know the proof of him** (τὴν δὲ δοκιμὴν αὐτοῦ γινώσκετε). Timothy was indeed known to the Philippians, and had been with them (Acts xvi. 1, 13; xvii. 14); hence the verb is indicative, not imperative (Vulg., *cognoscite*). On δοκιμήν, *indoles spectata*, see Rom. v. 4; 2 Cor. ii. 9; ix. 13.—The proof consists in this: **That as a child with a father, he hath served with me,** ὅτι ὡς πατρὶ τέκνον σὺν ἐμοὶ ἐδούλευσεν. Instead of saying simply ἐμοί, he proceeds with σὺν ἐμοί in a *variatio structuræ* (WINER'S *Gram.*, pp. 422, 577), in order to indicate that he is speaking of a service shared with himself, which is more nearly defined by the additional clause: **for the gospel** (εἰς εὐαγγέλιον), its advancement, (comp. i. 5).

Ver. 23. [By μέν here Paul opposes his sending of Timothy to his own coming as he hopes (δέ, next verse).—Οὖν, *therefore*, since the Apostle would be thus relieved (εὐψυχῶ, ver. 19), and Timothy (τοῦτον) had such qualifications for the service. Both grounds of the inference should be recognized.—H]. What follows here defines more closely the ταχέως in ver. 19. [The "shortly," "speedily" there, is relative with reference to the result of the crisis of which he now speaks as near at hand.—H].—**Him therefore I hope to send immediately,** (τοῦτον μὲν οὖν ἐλπίζω πέμψαι). Τοῦτον sums up the characteristics mentioned in vers. 20, 22.—**So soon as I shall see how it will go with me,** (ὡς ἂν ἀφίδω τὰ περὶ ἐμέ). For the form ἀφίδω instead of ἀπίδω, see WINER'S *Gram.* p. 45. It is like ἀφελπίζοντες in Luke vi. 35. The verb, according to its signification, points to the distance (*prospicere*), to see forward to the issue; it indicates his tender anxiety to send Timothy as soon as possible. Ὡς, *as*, in point of time, and with ἄν, *as soon as ever* his relations change, or there is a definite prospect of the issue, one or the other of them will come.—Ἐξαυτῆς sc. ὥρας (Acts x. 33; xi. 11; xxi. 32; xxiii. 30), emphatic limitation of πέμψαι. [He would send Timothy at once on being able to make him the bearer of good tidings. As LIGHTFOOT remarks ὡς ἂν . . . . ἐξαυτῆς is=*at once when*.—H.]

Ver. 24. **But I trust in the Lord** (πέποιθα δὲ ἐν κυρίῳ). Δέ answers to μέν in ver. 23. Although he hopes he will be able to send Timothy, yet he has confidence in the Lord (ii. 19): **That I also myself shall come shortly** (ὅτι καὶ αὐτὸς ταχέως ἐλεύσομαι); thus not merely Timothy, but he himself will come to them. Comp. i. 25, 26; Philem. ver. 22. [The Apostle expects not only to be set at liberty as Timothy will be sent to inform them, but to be able to use his own liberty for the purpose of coming to them.—H.] Here also there is an alternative, a presentiment of death and a hope of freedom, a wavering between martyrdom and a restored, free activity.

DOCTRINAL AND ETHICAL.

1. Friends should maintain fellowship with each other even when they are far apart in body. This is essential to the true welfare of each.

2. Letters and messengers are the means of communication, but in each case truth is our ultimate reliance as in personal intercourse, and this is found in its full extent only where there is a deep interest in the cause of Christ, and where selfishness does not reign.

3. Greater than the sorrow for weak and false brethren should be the joy over one *true* friend.

4. Even the apostolic church and the apostles had to suffer from the selfishness which hindered their complete prosperity: perfection is not reached at the beginning but only at the end.

5. Hope and confidence are to be based only upon the Lord, and are justifiable even in time of trouble, even when our hopes are not realized in the form that we expected, when indeed the future is shaped for us in exact opposition to our ideas.

HOMILETICAL AND PRACTICAL.

Where love for the brethren is founded on faith in the Lord—the basis of true fellowship—there will a lively hope in Him as the Ruler of the world manifest itself, giving confidence that the course of events shall result in the welfare of the church and of the individual. We see this illustrated in the case of Paul imprisoned at Rome, who, though of a melancholy, choleric temperament, was always hopeful. Candor in judging persons and things is as great as it is rare. It is based on perfect purity. Even the subtlest selfishness pales before it. A teacher in the church, a minister of the word of Christ, has especially to guard himself from selfishness, both in its most refined and its noblest forms.—Hope in the Lord, and hope all that thy heart desires, if it find pleasure in the Lord, but reckon not upon thy heart or thy hope.

STARKE:—Not our own, not our humors, not our desires, but what is Christ's will, the advancement of His kingdom, must we seek as paramount in ourselves and in others, if we would be saved.—Since there is so many 'a slip between the cup and the lip,' we ought to speak cautiously of future events, saying: I hope so, if God will, *etc.* See James iv. 13 ff.

SCHLEIERMACHER:—All special love of one person for another, so far as it is truly brotherly, must be purely Christian.

MENKEN:—Such a man as Paul, in his holy, heavenly disposition, in the quiet, true greatness of his character, in the earnestness, purity and majesty of his life, his willing and his working, could not have many equals.

HEUBNER:—True friendship is rare; for a friendship such as makes two hearts one, requires not merely a similarity of certain general principles in duty and religion, but a similarity of inclinations, sentiments, and of essential principles. No one has more false friends than Jesus. Thus how rare, even among Christ's servants, is an entirely pure, unselfish mind! The coarsely selfish serve their belly, Mammon; the more refined their honor, their system, their school.

2. The return of Epaphroditus to them.

(CHAP. II. 25–30.)

25 Yet I supposed it necessary to send to you Epaphroditus, my brother, and companion in labor, and fellow-soldier, but your messenger, and he that ministered to
26 my wants. For he longed [was longing] after you all, and was full of heaviness
27 because (that) ye had heard that he had been sick. For indeed he was sick nigh unto death: but God had mercy on him; and not on him only, but on me also, lest
28 I should have sorrow upon sorrow.[1] I sent him therefore the more carefully [speedily], that, when ye see him again, ye may rejoice, and that I may be the less
29 sorrowful. Receive him therefore in the Lord with all gladness; and hold such
30 in reputation [honor]: because for the [sake of his][2] work (of Christ) he was nigh unto death, not regarding[3] [hazarding] his life, to supply your lack of service toward me.

[1] Ver. 27. Ἐπὶ λύπην in A B C D E F, *et al.;* ἐπὶ λύπῃ in K has but slight support.

[2] Ver. 30. The manuscripts give ἔργον alone, or in connection with κυρίου (ℵ A), Χριστοῦ (B), or θεοῦ, also with the article. Probably all the additions are glosses. [For the absolute use of τὸ ἔργον see Acts xv. 38. "The authorities being very evenly divided, neutralize each other. All alike are insertions to explain τὸ ἔργον" (LIGHTFOOT). ELLICOTT is inclined to retain τοῦ Χριστοῦ.—H.]

[3] Ver. 30. Παραβολευσάμενος in ℵ A B D E F G, *et al.;* παραβουλευσάμενος in C K L, and some other manuscripts. The first *lectio* is the more difficult. See the exegesis. [MEYER, ELLICOTT, ALFORD, WORDSWORTH, LIGHTFOOT adopt παραβολευσάμενος.—H.]

EXEGETICAL AND CRITICAL.

Ver. 25. **Yet I supposed it necessary**—ἀναγκαῖον δὲ ἡγησάμην. Δέ points to the sending of Timothy and the visit of Paul, which may indeed be near at hand, but still are uncertain, more especially Paul's visit. Ver. 26 states the reason for his supposing it necessary to send him.—**Epaphroditus** (Ἐπαφρόδιτον) is not mentioned elsewhere, and is not identical with Epaphras, (Col. i. 7; iv. 12; Philem. ver. 23). [Epaphras had his circuit of labor in Phrygia or Asia Minor (Col. iv. 12), while Epaphroditus, as we see here, had his circuit in northern Greece or Macedonia. The names, however, are not decisive, as they may be different forms of the same name.—H.] The name signifies "lovely," "charming," and was not uncommon (*Tac. Ann.* XV. 55; *Seut. Domit.* § 14). He was no unimportant person to Paul and the Philippians. The Apostle, it will be noticed, commends him very highly.—**My brother, and companion in labor, and fellow-soldier** (τὸν ἀδελφὸν καὶ συνεργὸν καὶ συστρατιώτην μου).—The pronoun belongs to all three nouns. The first designates him as the partner of Paul's faith, the second as his partner in office or labor, the third as sharer of his conflicts and dangers; a climax proceeding from a more general to a more definite relationship. On συστρατιώτης, see Philem. ver. 2; 2 Tim. ii. 3–5. On συνεργός see iv. 3; Col. iv. 11; 1 Cor. iii. 9. On ἀδελφός without ἐν κυρίῳ (i. 14) see i. 12; iii. 1, 13; iv. 1, 8, 23; Col. i. 1; Eph. vi. 23.—**But your messenger, and he that ministered to my wants.**—Ὑμῶν as emphatic precedes (opposed by δέ to μου), and belongs to both substantives (ἀπόστολον καὶ λειτουργὸν τῆς χρείας μου). The first designates him as the deputy or messenger of the Philippians, as in 2 Cor. viii. 23. It cannot mean here an Apostle (Vulg., ERASMUS, *et al.*). The second designates him as the servant of the Philippians, and his errand is more fully defined by τῆς χρείας μου, so that we have it stated by whom and for what purpose he was appointed. The word is general in its meaning, as in Rom. xiii. 6, where rulers are called λειτουργοί, while in ver. 4 διάκονος is used. So also λειτουργία in 2 Cor. ix. 12, λειτουργεῖν, Rom. xv. 27, have a general signification.—**To send to you** (πέμψαι πρὸς ὑμᾶς, not ὑμῖν, as in ver. 19).—The verb does not signify *remittere* (GROTIUS: *simplex pro composito*). The idea of sending back yields entirely to the idea of sending away.

Ver. 26. **For he was longing after you all.**—Ἐπειδή introduces the reason of his mission (comp. 1 Cor. i. 21, 22; xiv. 16; xv. 21).—Ἐπιποθῶν ἦν πάντας ὑμᾶς marks his constant longing for the whole church and its individual members. An intimate acquaintance with the church and close relation to it are presupposed. Though the Apostle would gladly retain him, yet he is induced to send him to Philippi, lest this longing which had seized him after his sickness, should bring on a relapse in his weakened state. The imperfect is used with reference to the time of their receiving the letter, and of the arrival of Epaphroditus; for at the time of writing he is still in the state of mind described. [Whether he suffered this sickness at Rome, or on his journey from Philippi to Rome, is uncertain. Perhaps the latter view agrees best with the probable interpretation of ver. 30.—H.]—**And was full of heaviness, because ye had heard that he had been sick.**—Καί adds still another reason. Ἀδημονῶν (from ἀ *privativum* and δῆμος, 'foreign,' 'wretched,' like the German "*elend*," without country, homeless, in distress, as in Matth. xxvi. 37; Mark xiv. 33, the reason of which is: *διότι ἠκούσατε ὅτι ἠσθένησεν*. How the Philippians had heard this, and whence Epaphroditus had received his information, is not known, and is in no way indicated.

Ver. 27. **For indeed he was sick**—*καὶ γὰρ ἠσθένησεν*.—[The *καί*, says LIGHTFOOT, implies that the previous *ἠσθένησεν* understates the case. —H.] This addition confirms the report of his sickness which they had received, and at the same time supplements it: **nigh unto death** (*παραπλήσιον θανάτῳ*). This is an adverbial limitation, but neither elliptical, so that *ἀφίκετο* is to be supplied (DE WETTE), nor a solecism (VAN HENGEL).—**But God had mercy on him** (*ἀλλ' ὁ θεὸς ἠλέησεν αὐτόν*).—His recovery is, in the estimation of the Apostle, first of all an act of grace towards Epaphroditus.—By way of supplement he then adds: **And not on him only, but on me also**—*οὐκ αὐτὸν δὲ μόνον, ἀλλὰ καὶ ἐμέ*. *Δέ* introduces something explanatory, as in ver. 8, and often. See WINER'S *Gram.* p. 443.—**Lest I should have sorrow upon sorrow.**—*Ἵνα* introduces the purpose of the *ἠλέησεν*: *μὴ λύπην ἐπὶ λύπην σχῶ*. The *λύπη* which still remains is his bonds, his imprisonment, and consequent suffering (i. 12-26); the other, which has been removed, is the distress occasioned by his companion's sickness and apprehended death. *Si ad vincula accessisset jactura amici* (GROTIUS).—The view that one sorrow (*λύπη*) springs from his sickness, the other from his death, is incorrect (CHRYSOSTOM, ERASMUS, *et al.*).

Ver. 28. **I sent him therefore the more speedily**, *or* **earnestly**, *i. e.*, with the greater despatch (*σπουδαιοτέρως οὖν ἔπεμψα αὐτόν*).—The *οὖν* refers to the recovery of Epaphroditus, and to his intense longing after Philippi, which are the reasons for his speedy departure. With the comparative must be supplied: "than I should have done, had you not been disturbed by hearing of his sickness" (WINER'S *Gram.* p. 243). Comp. i. 12.—The Apostle's purpose is: **That, when ye see him again, ye may rejoice** (*ἵνα ἰδόντες αὐτὸν πάλιν χαρῆτε*).—Paul wishes the Philippians to rejoice anew, since their anxiety on account of the illness of Epaphroditus was removed. *Πάλιν* belongs to *χαρῆτε*, since as a rule it stands either before or immediately after the word to which it belongs. See GERSDORF, *Beiträge*, p. 491 sq. It should not be joined with *ἰδόντες*, especially as he was not sent that the Philippians might see him again.—The joy of the Philippians will react upon the Apostle: **And that I may be the less sorrowful** (*κἀγὼ ἀλυπότερος ὦ*).—"There is a delicate blending here of his own interest and sympathy with that of the beloved Philippians" (MEYER); *quum sciam, vos gaudere* (BENGEL). While he is in bonds he cannot be *ἄλυπος*, but yet he is less sorrowful (*ἀλυπότερος*), since the sorrow (*λύπη*) with regard to the anxiety and condition of the Philippians is removed.

Ver. 29. **Receive him therefore in the Lord with all gladness.**—The *προσδέχεσθε*, emphatic by position, requires a reception of Epaphroditus (*αὐτόν*), which shall most fully correspond (*οὖν*) with Paul's purpose in sending him (ver. 28, *ἵνα—χαρῆτε*), and one which shall be worthy of a Christian church (*ἐν κυρίῳ*, and comp. *ἐν κυρίῳ ἀξίως τῶν ἁγίων*, Rom. xvi. 2); for it should be *with all joy* (*μετὰ πάσης χαρᾶς*), without any admixture of chagrin or discontent on account of the sickness of Epaphroditus, or of his coming too soon or too late.—**And hold such in honor** (*καὶ τοιούτους ἐντίμους ἔχετε*). THEOPHYLACT remarks very justly: *ἵνα μὴ δόξῃ αὐτῷ μόνῳ χαρίζεσθαι, κοινῶς παραίνει πάντας τοὺς τὴν αὐτὴν ἀρετὴν ἐπιδεικνυμένους τιμᾶν*. Yet he has Epaphroditus in view as the individual of the class referred to (MEYER). Hence the suspicion that the Philippians were inclined to undervalue others (WIESINGER, with reference to ii. 3) has no support here.

Ver. 30. **Because for the sake of his work he was nigh unto death**—goes back at once to the person intended. The reception and honor required for Epaphroditus, are based upon (*ὅτι* his work (*διὰ τὸ ἔργον*); for this and nothing else brought upon him the severe illness (*μέχρι θανάτου ἤγγισεν*; and ver. 27, *ἠσθένησεν παραπλησίον θανάτῳ*). Under *τὸ ἔργον* we are to understand, according to the context (ver. 25: *ὑμῶν ἀπόστολον καὶ λειτουργὸν τῆς χρείας μου*; and ver. 30: *τῆς πρός με λειτουργίας*), the commission assigned to him by the church as the bearer of their gifts to the Apostle, and his zeal in the performance of that service. Hence it is not his activity in teaching, *opus a Christo ei demandatum* (VAN HENGEL); or labor for the gospel (SCHENKEL); or the enmity of Nero (the Greek interpreters), both of which are opposed to the context, since ver. 25 designates Epaphroditus as Paul's *συνεργός* and *συστρατιώτης* on account of his office and conduct in general, not especially in Rome, while the latter view contradicts also the history (Acts xxviii. 30, 31). Whether we are to limit his work to his sojourn at Rome (MEYER) may be doubted. Why may it not include his journey also, which certainly was an arduous one?—**Hazarding**, *or* **staking his life** (*παραβολευσάμενος τῇ ψυχῇ*) states the way in which he came so near losing his life. This verb occurs as seldom elsewhere as the other reading (*παραβουλευσάμενος*); yet that (*παραβολεύσεσθαι*) has a less familiar sound than *παραβουλεύεσθαι*, and has also better witnesses, and a sense that offers itself less readily. *Παραβολεύεσθαι* is *παράβολον εἶναι*, "to be a fool-hardy" or "reckless person," as *περπερεύεσθαι* is *πέρπερον εἶναι*, "to be a boaster, braggadocio" (1 Cor. xiii. 4). See WINER'S *Gram.* p. 93. *Τῇ ψυχῇ* is dative of the respect in which (WINER'S *Gram.* p. 215). It is his life, not money, property, time, which he put at hazard, or (to keep nearer to the word) squandered. We see in this prodigality the measure of his zeal. Whether the season of the year, his haste, means of travel by land and water, were concerned in the case, is not indicated, is simply unknown. *Παραβουλευσάμενος* would mean *male consulens vitæ* (LUTHER), since he regarded his life so lightly). TISCHENDORF. (ed. VII. maj. II. p. 473) compares CÆSAR (*Bell. Gal.*): *adeo esse perterritos nonnullos, ut suæ vitæ durius consulere cogantur*, and the verbs *παραφρονεῖν*, *παραλογίζεσθαι*, and finds this rendering the more suitable, because there is then only *temeritas*, not guilt, in a holy work. Yet we are the less to assume the reproach of a censurable *temeritas* in παραβολεύεσθαι, from the fact that the watchers by the sick* in the ancient church were named *parabolani* (from παραβάλλεσθαι, whence παράβολος and then παραβολεύεσθαι, are derived); yet certainly the name implied no reproach, but was meant solely to recognize their fearless courage. The conclusion states the object of the participial clause.—**To supply your lack of service toward me.** Ἵνα introduces the motive for such exposure (παραβολευσάμενος τῇ ψυχῇ) which is that he *might fill up*, (ἀναπληρώσῃ), *etc.* Parallel to this is 1 Cor. xvi. 17: ὅτι τὸ ὑμέτερον ὑστέρημα αὐτοὶ ἀνεπλήρωσαν. Comp. 2 Cor. xi. 9; Philem. 13; also Col. i. 24: ἀνταναπληρῶ τὰ ὑστερήματα τῶν θλίψεων τοῦ Χριστοῦ. The verb denotes not merely filling, but filling *usque ad oram*, and being emphatic by position, gives prominence to the act. The object is τὸ ὑμῶν ὑστέρημα, which differs from τὸ ὑμέτερον ὑστέρημα, by bringing to view the lack of personal ministration as defined by the genitive (τῆς πρὸς μὲ λειτουργίας). The service (λειτουργία) according to the expression itself, and the context, is the pecuniary relief or supplies which the Philippians could not bring and present in person, but were obliged to remit through Epaphroditus. Luther: "in order that he may serve me in your stead." The apostle finely and delicately views the absence of the Philippians as a deficiency in that service, and bespeaks their grateful sympathy in the affliction of their delegate who had performed his mission with equal courage and skill (MEYER). [In designating the absence of the Philippians in the presentation of their gift as something which was wanting to make it complete, he expresses no censure, but shows merely his affection for those of whose personal intercourse he found it so painful to be deprived, (SCHENKEL). — H.] Hence it is incorrect to join ὑμῶν with λειτουργίας, to understand this last word in general of every service (RILLIET: *les services, dont j'avais besoin*) in disregard of the limitation furnished by the context, or even as *res necessariæ*, and τὸ ὑμῶν ὑστέρημα as *defectus qui subvenitis* (HÖLEMANN.)

DOCTRINAL AND ETHICAL.

1. The best men and Christians often show a union of opposite virtues; for example, Epaphroditus. The finest delicacy of soul, which if alone might seem excessive and effeminate, allies itself to a manly courage, which sets at naught life itself. The deepest love of the church does not exclude a most faithful attachment to its great Apostle, nor anxiety for the present moment forbid sympathy for a distant community. One may reverence and acknowledge superior men, and yet give all the glory to God alone; may be anxious for his own soul, and yet give himself to the welfare of the church, and the common service of its membership.

2. God looks not upon the individual merely in his sorrow. Every instance of God's help is an act of His compassion for the sake of others, as well as of the sufferer; because we are members together, and have joy whenever God causes any one member to rejoice.

3. [REV. J. TRAPP:—Epaphroditus was sick nigh unto death, and Paul distressed on that account. This should not have been if St. Paul could have cured him, as he did others. This shows that the Apostles cured the sick, and did miracles, not by their own power, or at their own pleasure, *etc.*—H.]

HOMILETICAL AND PRACTICAL.

All that thou doest with respect to others regard as a duty which the Lord Himself demands of thee. By the faithful performance of duty, rightly apprehended, thou dost promote the welfare of those with whom God has placed thee.—Above all be a brother to thy neighbor, and thou wilt be his helper not in joys and labors alone, but also in suffering and victorious endurance. Observe how clear a vision true Christian love has in all our relations, even the most difficult, and how strong it is even in the most trying times. The thread which we are to grasp, to hold firm, never escapes its sight; nor does strength to do what is right, and what is salutary, and beautiful, and lovely at the same time, fail its arm. Whether God's hand smites thee or preserves thee, still feel the pity of the Father's heart which stretches out the arm and lifts the hand.

STARKE:—Neither nature nor grace produces stoics, unsusceptible men; but the susceptibility of friendship, which already exists between kinsmen and friends, is sanctified and perfected by grace.—Unbelief looks to nature and medicine as the only remedies in sickness; faith looks to the providence of God also, by virtue of which He comes to the aid of man's nature, as well as of medicine and care, with a special influence and blessing.—When believers look upon one another, they see also the inner, renewed nature, through the covering of the outer man; and because a tender love exists between them, the sight of each other refreshes, quickens them.

RIEGER:—We must not expect grace to lift us above all alternations of feeling into a state of entire tranquility.—It is a mistake to suppose that one must be equally well equipped at all times. Even in the holy soul of our blessed Saviour there were changes of feeling.

SCHLEIERMACHER:—At the bottom of all love between individuals there must be love for the entire body to which they belong as living members; on the other hand, this love for the whole body is the consequence of affection for the individuals.

MENKEN:—One might think that this tenderness of feeling on the part of Epaphroditus went almost too far; on the contrary, we are to notice also here that one possessed of such extreme sensibility may yet be a strong man, and that a very tender heart may nevertheless be a very firm heart. It was not a trifling act for a Chris-

* [The most natural supposition is that Epaphroditus brought upon himself this sickness, which was so nearly fatal, in consequence of some special exposure on the journey, or of the fatigue incident to travelling with such despatch, in his impatience to reach the Apostle. It does not comport so well with our ideas of Paul's character to ascribe it to his "anxious attendance on the Apostle at Rome" (ELLICOTT). Paul did not exact, hardly was willing even to accept, such self-denying services from others. For exemplifications of Paul's delicate regard for the safety, health and comfort of others, the reader may see Dr. HOWSON'S *Lectures on the Character of St. Paul*, pp. 78-83 (London, 1864).—H.]

tian, one of a sect everywhere spoken against, everywhere hated and oppressed, which found no protection under Jewish or Gentile rule, to travel from Philippi to Rome in order to carry aid to a Christian teacher, an Apostle, yea, the hated and now imprisoned Paul, over whose approaching death his enemies were already rejoicing, and take his stand publicly before the world, by the side of this man, and say, "I am his friend."—They knew that by faith and prayer one can move heaven and earth, but they did not regard faith and prayer as amulets, or talismans, that are able to expel all darkness and distress from a Christian's life, and to raise him above all humble waiting on God's help, above all subjection of his own will to God's will.

HEUBNER:—Life, especially the life of a faithful servant of Christ, possesses great value. For such a life we ought to pray; and it is an act of God's grace when it is preserved to the church.

PASSAVANT:—If one were separated ever so completely from all other men, still he is a warrior and combatant, since in his own heart are the worst enemies of his heavenly peace.

V. SECTION FOURTH.

Warning against Judaistic teachers and wicked deceivers.

CHAPTER III. 1—IV. 1.

1. *The disposition of these teachers in contrast with that of the Apostle.*

(CHAP. III. 1–16).

(1) The Apostle warns his readers against the disposition of these false teachers, especially their pride (2-7); points out plainly the opposition between righteousness which is of the law and that which is of faith (8-11); declares with humility that he is yet striving after perfection (12-14), and concludes by exhorting them to unity (15, 16).

1 Finally, my brethren, rejoice in the Lord. To write the same things to you, to
2 me indeed is not grievous, [irksome] but for you *it is* safe. Beware of [the] dogs, be-
3 ware of [the] evil workers, beware of the concision. For we are the circumci-
sion, who worship (God) in the Spirit [of God[1]] and rejoice [glory] in Christ
4 Jesus, and have no confidence in the flesh. Though I might [can] have
confidence (also) in the flesh. If any other man thinketh that he hath whereof he
5 might trust in the flesh, I more: circumcised[2] the eighth day, of the stock of Israel,
of the tribe of Benjamin, an Hebrew of the Hebrews; as touching the law, a Pha-
6 risee: concerning zeal,[3] persecuting the church; touching the righteousness which
7 is in the law, blameless. But what things were gain to me, those I [have] counted
8 loss for Christ. Yea, doubtless, and I count all things (but) loss for the ex-
cellency of the knowledge of Christ Jesus my Lord: for whom I have suffered the
loss of all things, and do count them (but) dung [refuse] that I may win
9 Christ, and be found in him, not having mine own righteousness, which is of the
law, but that which is through the faith of Christ, the righteousness which is of
10 God by [upon] faith; that I may know him, and the power of his resurrection,
11 and the fellowship of his sufferings, being made conformable[4] [being conformed]
unto his death: if by any means I might attain unto the resurrection of the dead.[5]
12 Not as though I had already attained, either were already perfect: but I follow
after, that I may apprehend [lay hold upon] that for which also I am apprehended
13 [was laid hold upon] of [by] Christ Jesus. Brethren, I count not myself to have
apprehended[6] [to have laid hold upon] but (this) one thing: (*I do*,) forgetting
14 those things which are behind, and reaching forth unto those things which are be
15 fore, I press toward the mark for the prize of the high calling of God in Christ Je-
sus. Let us therefore, as many as be perfect, be thus minded: and if in anything
16 ye be otherwise minded, God shall reveal even this unto you. Nevertheless,
whereto we have already attained, let us walk by the same rule,[7] let us mind the
same thing [in the same let us walk].

[1] Ver. 3. Θεοῦ is found in ℵ A B C, and most of the authorities, whereas θεῷ has but slight support, and is evidently a correction. [The evidence, says TISCHENDORF, is clearly on the side of the former.—H].

[2] Ver. 5. [The approved text is περιτομῇ and not the nominative περιτομή. See the notes below.—H].

[3] Ver. 6. ζῆλος has the support of ℵ A B D* F G, *et al.* A few manuscripts have ζῆλον. Is it a copyist's error (comp. 2 Cor. ix. 2. MEYER)? The passage here would seem rather to require τὸ ζῆλος in 2 Cor. ix. 2, [instead of ὁ ζῆλος, masculine. See WINER'S *Gram.* p 65].

[4] Ver. 10. Συμμορφιζόμενος is found in ℵ A B, *et al.* On the other hand, συμμορφούμενος (E K L, *et al.*) and συνφορτειζόμενος (F G, *et al.*), *cooneratus*, have but slight support.

[5] Ver. 11. Τὴν ἐκ νεκρῶν, is well attested by ℵ A B D E *et al.*, better than τῶν νεκρῶν, and need not appear strange after ἐξανάστασις, though Paul has elsewhere ἀνάστασις τῶν νεκρῶν. [See the exegetical notes *infra.*—H].

[6] [Apprehend meant formerly "to take in the hand," or "by the hand" (a Latin sense of the word). Thus Jeremy Taylor (*Holy Living*, ii. 6) says: "There is nothing but hath a double handle, or at least we have two hands to apprehend it."—H].

[7] Ver. 16. Στοιχεῖν, for which συνστοιχεῖν also occurs, has after it κανόνι, τὸ αὐτὸ φρονεῖν, in ℵ C, but in some other copies has the words before it, while in others again the words appear only in part. No doubt ii. 2, and Gal. vi. 16, have led the copyists to change the text for the sake of uniformity.

EXEGETICAL AND CRITICAL.

Ver. 1. **Finally** (τὸ λοιπόν) as *formula progrediendi* begins (BENGEL) as in iv. 8; Eph. vi. 10; 2 Cor. xiii. 11; 1 Thess. iv. 1; 2 Thess. iii. 1), a section usually near the end. Hence in the glow of feeling the Apostle always adds "my brethren" (ἀδελφοί μου or ἀδελφοί). It does not conclude what immediately precedes (SCHENKEL), nor does it so necessarily indicate the end, that ver. 2 follows as a digression (MEYER).—**Rejoice in the Lord** (χαίρετε ἐν κυρίῳ). This is of the first importance, and corresponds with the ground-tone of the letter (see Introd. §§ 1, 2, p. 4; and comp. iv. 4; ii. 17, 18, 28; i. 18, 25). Their joy should have its origin and element in Christ (Rom. xiv. 17; 1 Thess. i. 6). That the emphasis falls upon this expression is shown by the final exhortation (iv. 1) στήκετε ἐν κυρίῳ (iv. 2), which lies at the foundation of that given here, and appropriately follows the warning against the false teachers who would separate them from the Lord.—**To write the same things to you, to me indeed is not irksome but for you it is safe** (τὰ αὐτὰ γράφειν ὑμῖν, ἐμοὶ μὲν οὐκ ὀκνηρόν, ὑμῖν δὲ ἀσφαλές). We infer from ὀκνηρόν (from ὄκνος 'sluggishness,' 'delay,' like πονηρός, *qui aliis* πόνους *facit*), which in Matt. xxv. 26; Rom. xii. 11, signifies 'slothful,' that an unpleasant task is meant, and that may consist in a formal repetition of his words. 'Ασφαλές (from σφάλλω, *labo, vacillare facio*), properly "firm, secure," (Heb. vi. 19; Acts xxi. 34; xxii. 30; xxv. 26), or 'adapted to secure,' 'make safe,' presupposes warnings against imminent dangers. It is clear that Paul, 'who writes the same things' (τὰ αὐτὰ γράφει), only for the sake of the Philippians, would prefer not to be compelled to do so; it is, therefore, no feeling or confession of poverty of thought (BAUR). It is also evident that τὰ αὐτὰ γράφειν does not refer to consolation, exhortation, which would not be to him burdensome (ὀκνηρόν). Hence it is not the preceding exhortation to rejoice that is meant (BENGEL, WIESINGER, and others). Both adjectives lead us to think of the warning as directed against false teachers in Philippi. But in this letter Paul as yet has written nothing about these teachers, since those mentioned in i. 15, 17 sq. are in Rome and may be endured, whereas those here are of the most dangerous character. It is most natural to think of another letter of Paul's to Philippi, especially as POLYCARP says of Paul (Phil. iii.): ἀπὼν ὑμῖν ἔγραψεν ἐπιστολάς, εἰς ἃς ἐὰν ἐγκύπτητε δυνήσεσθε οἰκοδομεῖσθαι. He also says in another passage (Phil. ii.), preserved only in a Latin translation: *Ego autem nil tale sensi in vobis vel audivi, in quibus laboravit beatus Paulus, qui estis in principio epistolæ ejus, de vobis enim gloriatur in omnibus ecclesiis.* The meaning of this is not: "Ye are in the beginning of his letter," but according to 2 Cor. iii. 1-3: "Ye are from the beginning, in the beginning, his letters, letters of recommendation." Why may not an epistle to the Philippians have been lost, as well as that to the Laodiceans (Col. iv. 16), and one to the Corinthians (BLEEK, *Studien und Kritiken*, 1830, p. 625; WINER'S *Realw.*; p. 673)? The view that *quæ præsens dixeram* should be supplied (PELAGIUS, ERASMUS, and others) is untenable; for he does not say καὶ γράφειν, nor can we suppose, with HEINRICHS and PAULUS, that from τὰ αὐτὰ γράφειν to iv. 20, we have an *esoteric* letter to his more intimate friends, while the remainder is an *exoteric* letter to the church. This is an arbitrary notion, and does not help us at all to explain the language; "it is a manifest historical and psychological misconception," says MEYER, "if we only think of Paul's relations to the Philippians." [Paul had been at Philippi twice after his founding of the church there (Acts xx. 1, 2) where this city must have been among "those parts" mentioned in that passage, and again on his return to Macedonia after the three months in Greece, (vers. 3, 6); and on these occasions he must have given to the Philippian Christians much and varied oral instruction. The γράφειν as present will bear the emphasis—"to be writing as I now do"—and this could be opposed to the warnings which they had heard from his lips, when among them. The act of dictating and writing to them would thus be tacitly opposed to the easier task of merely speaking to them. He would submit cheerfully (οὐκ ὀκνηρόν) to the trouble of repeating his instructions in every form, with the pen or the voice, if he could only by such or any other means secure them against the dangers to which they were exposed. So, among others, CALVIN and WIESINGER. Prof. LIGHTFOOT understands the expression as referring to the Apostle's reiterated warnings against dissension in this letter, and Bishop ELLICOTT of his exhortations, expressed or implied, to rejoice in the Lord.—H.] In χαίρετε ἐν κυρίῳ we see Paul's aim, in οὐκ ὀκνηρόν his readiness, in ἀσφαλές the church's danger and want, and in τὰ αὐτά (not τὸ αὐτό) the variety or compass of his teachings.

Ver. 2. **Beware of [the] dogs, beware of [the] evil-workers, beware of [the] concision.** Βλέπετε, followed as here by a direct accusative, strictly means 'behold,' 'fix your eye upon;' and so in 1 Cor. x. 18; i. 26. See WI-

NER's *Gram.*, p. 223. The proper Greek for 'beware of' would require ἀπό with the genit. after βλέπετε (Mark viii. 15; xii. 38). The one sense here involves the other; *videte et cavebitis* (BENGEL). The threefold repetition marks the Apostle's earnestness and the importance of the warning (WINER's *Gram.*, p. 609), while it corresponds *gradatione retrograda* (BENGEL) to the three clauses (ver. 3) which describe only a single class of teachers, and hence not three different kinds of false teachers (VAN HENGEL). The first substantive (τοὺς κύνας) was a term of reproach with heathen and Jews, and implies 'impudence, shamelessness.' (in Matt. xv. 26, τοῖς κυναρίοις, less severe); among the Jews it (κύνας) implied also uncleanness (Matt. vii. 6; Rev. xxii. 15), and among the heathen that of ferocity and malevolence. It is most natural to retain here the biblical idea, *viz.*, profane, impure, shameless, thereby indicating the moral character of the teachers in question. Hence it is not to be understood of mere shamelessness (CHRYSOSTOM), or this together with covetousness (GROTIUS), or ferocity or violence (RILLIET), and least of all a special class: *homines a Christi professione ad Judæorum superstitionem reversi, imitatores canum ad vomitum suum redeuntium* (VAN HENGEL). Τοὺς κακοὺς ἐργάτας designates their activity, not as πονηρόν, evil to others, but as evil in itself, unprofitable, injurious (comp. δόλιοι ἐργάται, 2 Cor. xi. 13). See the contrast in 2 Tim. ii. 15. VAN HENGEL is incorrect: *qui se a Christo quidem non avertunt, sed superstitione illa divinam corrumpunt doctrinam.* Τὴν κατατομήν, *paranomasia nam gloriosam appellationem* περιτομῆς *vindicat Christianis* ver. 3, *κατατέμνα de concisione vetita,* Lev. xxi. 5; 1 Reg. xviii. 28; *non sine indignatione loquitur* (BENGEL). See WINER's *Gram.*, p. 638. The language here states the result of their activity; with their circumcision they effect only an outward mutilation. This ironical and sarcastic *paranomasia* (found often in Paul as well as in LUTHER) marks only the quality, not the quantity (BAUR), of the circumcision, and is to be taken passively in its concrete sense, *i. e.* the mutilated, not the mutilators. The reference is not to idolatry (BEZA, *et al.*), or to a separation of faith from the heart (LUTHER), a sundering of the church (CALVIN, *et al.*), and still less to a class of teachers: *Judæi, fiduciam suam in carnis circumcisione potentes atque ita ad Christum venire nolentes, sed illum contemnentes et spernentes* (VAN HENGEL). It is certain that they were Judaists, as in Galatia, and were active at Philippi, and though they had no success and no adherents at Philippi, yet were dangerous opponents of Paul's view of Christianity. The severity of the Apostle's language contrasts strongly with his joy and friendliness with reference to the Philippians, but was justified by the fact that a spiritual field so fair and hopeful was threatened and endangered by such disturbers. The condition itself of the church furnished a reason for his sharpness against them. The contrast in ver. 3 sheds further light on this point.

Ver. 3. **For we are the circumcision** (ἡμεῖς γάρ ἐσμεν ἡ περιτομή). *Causa, cur,* ver 2, *alios tam longe secludat* (BENGEL). [Paul justifies here (γάρ) his refusing to recognize the Judaists as the advocates of true circumcision. They are destitute of the marks of those who answer to that character. They substitute an outward form for the spirit of true worship, and rely upon their own works for acceptance, instead of the righteousness offered to them in the gospel; whereas the circumcision that God accepts is that of the heart and not of the letter (Rom. ii. 29), and is the seal or evidence of the justification which man obtains by faith and not by deeds of the law (Rom. iv. 11 sq.). Christians fulfilled both of these requisitions for obtaining the favor of God, and hence they also were entitled to be called the circumcision.—H.] Ἡμεῖς precedes with emphasis. The Apostle means himself and his beloved church, which was composed for the most part of Gentiles. Hence ἡ περιτομή is to be understood in the purely spiritual sense, that is, Christians who have received circumcision of the heart (Col. ii. 11; Rom. ii. 25–29). Comp. 1 Cor. vii. 19; Gal. iii. 28; v. 6; vi. 15.—These are further characterized: **who worship in the Spirit of God** (οἱ πνεύματι θεοῦ λατρεύοντες). The verb is used absolutely, as Heb. ix. 9; x. 2; Acts xxvi. 1; Luke ii. 31, of the worship of God which the instrumental dative defines more fully as spiritual, and the genit. θεοῦ refers to the Holy Spirit in opposition to the human spirit. It is contrasted with the σάρξ in its moral sense. Comp. John iv. 23, 24; Heb. ix. 14; Gal. iii. 3; Rom. xii. 1 (τὴν λογικὴν λατρείαν). Hence the dative does not designate the rule (VAN HENGEL). WINER's *Gram.*, p. 216. Comp. 1 Cor. ix. 7.—**And rejoice [glory] in Christ Jesus** (καὶ καυχώμενοι ἐν Χριστῷ Ἰησοῦ). For the form of expression see Rom. ii. 17: v. 11; 1 Cor. i. 31; iii. 21; 2 Cor. x. 17. They are here contrasted with the κακοὶ ἐργάται.—**And have no confidence in the flesh** (καὶ οὐκ ἐν σαρκὶ πεποιθότες) denotes their moral position as opposed to the κύνας, the impure, insolent, while that which precedes marks their religious sphere. Οὐκ implies a direct negative: *qui non confisi sunt,* whereas μή would have made it hypothetical (*si non confisi sunt*). See WINER's *Gram.*, p. 485.

Ver. 4. **Although I might have** (more strictly **am having** = **have**) **confidence also in the flesh.** Καίπερ is restrictive here only in Paul, more frequently in the Epistle to the Hebrews (v. 8; vii. 8; xii. 17). Ἐγώ singled out from ἡμεῖς, ver. 3 (the truly circumcised whether outwardly or not), places the Apostle, who is a Jew as the false teachers were (ver. 2), not one of the heathen as was the greater part of the Philippian Church, in contrast with these teachers, as having confidence in the flesh (ἔχων πεποίθησιν ἐν σαρκί) *de jure,* not *de facto.* His actual confidence is based not upon the flesh, upon outward advantages, but upon Christ (hence καί before ἐν σαρκί, *i. e.*, also in *it* as well as Him), though not without his reasons for that other confidence and a right to it. Hence the participle does not denote the past (VAN HENGEL), nor is it to be resolved into 'could have' (SCHENKEL), nor is πεποίθησις merely *argumentum fiduciæ* (BEZA, CALVIN, *et al.*). In σαρκί special reference is made to circumcision. [This rite is named because it was the watchword, as it were, of those who, in their system of salvation, exalted good works above the merits of Christ (see

Gal.)—H.]—**If any other man thinketh that he hath whereof he might trust in the flesh, I more,** introduces a comparison between Paul's condition and that of the others. Ἐι τις ἄλλος is entirely general, leaving his readers to apply it to the Judaists. Δοκεῖ denotes the subjective, arbitrary judgment, as in Gal. vi. 3; 1 Cor. iii. 18; viii. 2. No appeal can be made to Gal. ii. 6, 9 (SCHENKEL), for there the meaning is 'to be found such by others, to have that repute.' Πεποιθέναι ἐν σαρκί denotes the actual πεποίθησιν ἔχειν, contained in the perf. With ἐγὼ μᾶλλον we are to supply δωκῶ πεποιθέναι ἐν σαρκί; comp. 2 Cor. xi. 23.

Ver. 5. Now follow the specifications which justify this claim. His first advantage is: **Circumcised the eighth day** (περιτομῇ ὀκταήμερος). The dative (not nominative, as if the abstract were used for *circumcisus* (BENGEL), which is true only in the collective sense) denotes the respect in which (Eph. ii. 3: τέκνα φύσει ὀργῆς). WINER'S *Gram.*, p. 215. The adjective designates Paul in contrast with proselytes, as a Jew by birth, who had been circumcised on the eighth day, according to the law (Gen. xvii. 12; Lev. xii. 3).—*In censum nunc venit splendor natalium* (VAN HENGEL), the second advantage: **Of the stock of Israel, of the tribe of Benjamin, an Hebrew of the Hebrews** (ἐκ γένους Ἰσραήλ, φυλῆς Βενιαμίν, Ἑβραῖος ἐκ Ἑβραίων). These all belong together according to the sense and the construction, for the preposition is not repeated before φυλῆς. As SCHENKEL well remarks: The theocratic full-blood (Rom. xi. 1; 2 Cor. xi. 22) is contrasted with the Idumean half-blood. Comp. Eph. ii. 12. The tribe of Benjamin enjoyed and conferred a distinction, because unlike the Ephraimites it had remained faithful to the theocracy. Besides this his Jewish extraction (εὐγένεια) was also perfect: his mother also was a Jew, and not a foreigner. It is incorrect to understand this of Hebrew-speaking parents (the Greek interpreters), which the context does not support, or of a *tota majorum series ex Ebræis* (GROTIUS), which would be unnecessary if he sprung from the people of Israel, from the tribe of Benjamin.—The third advantage: **As touching the law a Pharisee.** Κατά denotes the reference, as τὰ κατ' ἐμέ (Eph. vi. 21). WINER'S *Gram.*, p. 401. Comp. Acts xxii. 3; xxvi. 5. His religious position, his relation to the law, is marked as strict, rigorous; for the Pharisees observed it conscientiously and scrupulously. Νόμος is not = αἵρεσις, *disciplina*, θεσμοί (GROTIUS and others).

Ver. 6. The fourth advantage: **Concerning zeal, persecuting the Church** (κατὰ ζῆλος διώκων τὴν ἐκκλησίαν) describes his moral conduct in the relations above mentioned. The participle is to be taken substantively as οἱ ζητοῦντες in Matt. ii. 20. It is not equivalent to διώξας (GROTIUS). That which is the greatest sin of the Apostle's life, in his own estimation (1 Cor. xv. 8, 9; 1 Tim. i. 13-16), he reckons by a sort of irony in this controversy with the Judaizers, as a glory to himself.—The fifth advantage: **Touching the righteousness which is in the law, blameless** (κατὰ δικαιοσύνην τὴν ἐν νόμῳ γενόμενος ἄμεμπτος) presents the moral result. The righteousness referred to here (as the result of his conduct) is that which rests in the law, is based upon and determined by it; hence essentially that which is ἐκ νόμου (ver. 9), and not 'righteousness under or in the condition of law' (DE WETTE). In this respect he is 'blameless' (ἄμεμπτος) according to men's judgment (*communi hominum existimatione*, CALVIN). It does not fully embrace Paul's meaning to say: *se nihil fecisse, quod morte aut verberibus castigandum esset* (GROTIUS). Γενόμενος, put for emphasis before the adjective, signifies '*becoming*, striving himself to be,' upon which, as the context teaches, he places value in the presence of God, but only when he opposes the carnal pride of these false teachers. To find here an obvious, though weak and lifeless imitation of 2 Cor. xi. 18-27, and to call this passage tame and without interest (BAUR), indicates a perverted taste (MEYER).

Ver. 7. **But what things were gain to me,** presents forcibly Paul's own position in contrast with (ἀλλά) that of these teachers. In ἅτινα, *quæcunque*, which is emphatic as the following ταῦτα shows, are included the preceding privileges and others of the same class.—These formerly ἦν μοι κέρδη, **were actually gains,** as the verb, emphatic by position, indicates. By μοί Paul means himself, as when he was Saul of Tarsus, and there is no need of weakening the sense by taking the pronoun (μοί) as the dative of judgment (ERASMUS, *et al.*) The plural κερδῆ is used *ob rerum varietatem*, but there is no reason for supplying *non vera lucra, sed opinata* (VAN HENGEL) which is no more implied in the plural than in μοί, since ἦν precedes.—**These [have] I counted loss for Christ** (ταῦτα ἥγημαι διὰ τὸν Χριστὸν ζημίαν). The perfect, after the emphatic ταῦτα, denotes an *actio præterita, quæ per effectus suos durat*, and implies the inward decision which has resulted in action. It does not refer to the act in itself, but to the act as a result of conscious freedom. Hence it is not *abjeci, repudiari* (VAN HENGEL), which ii. 3 does not confirm. Both the collocation and the signification of the words are to be observed. As to the order, we notice that διὰ τὸν Χριστόν stands between ἥγημαι and ζημίαν: Christ must first be known, then the ταῦτα are esteemed ζημία. With respect to the words we remark the following: (1) that with the accusative διά marks the reason (WINER'S *Gram.*, p. 398); (2) that τὸν Χριστόν denotes the well known, historical Christ, and (3) that ζημίαν calls to mind Acts xxvii. 10 (πολλῆς ζημίας οὐ μόνον τοῦ φορτίου καὶ τοῦ πλοίου, ἀλλὰ καὶ τῶν ψυχῶν ἡμῶν), and ver. 21, where reference is made to what had been thrown into the sea. Hence it is *jactura*, after the figure of a merchant who throws his κέρδη overboard, as ζημίαν, in order to save his life. The various kinds of gain (κέρδη) are esteemed as one loss of life, so far as these (ταῦτα) separate and keep one away from Christ.

Ver. 8. **Yea, doubtless, and I count all things loss.** Ἀλλά contrasts the present (ἡγοῦμαι) with the perfect (ἥγημαι). Μέν *rem præsentem confirmat*, οὖν *conclusionem ex rebus ita comparatis conficit*, (so also MEYER) and καί connects the present with the preceding perfect. WINER'S *Gram.*, p. 442. [The stricter translation according to this view, is: 'But therefore also I count,' *etc.* The present (ἡγοῦμαι) reaffirms his former judgment: He has still the same view of the worthlessness of all reliance on outward forms and privileges.—H]. The contrast does not lie in πάντα (RILLIET), for this only embraces the ἅτινα in its widest scope.—The reason why he thus holds all things to be 'loss' (ζημίαν εἶναι) the subsequent clause unfolds: **For the excellency of the knowledge of Christ Jesus my Lord** (διὰ τὸ ὑπερέχον τῆς γνώσεως Χριστοῦ Ἰησοῦ τοῦ κυρίου μου). The explanation which belongs to διὰ τὸν Χριστὸν does not lie in the relation defined by the preposition (that being simply repeated), but in that with whom it effects the relation. The substantive participle (τὸ ὑπερέχον) designates in comparison with those gains (κέρδη) one of far surpassing value, which results from a knowledge (τῆς γνώσεως) of the Redeemer both in His Person (Χριστοῦ Ἰησοῦ) and in His relation to each individual (τοῦ κυρίου μοῦ). CALVIN wrongly takes it *ad exprimendam affectus vehementiam*.—**For whom I have suffered the loss of all things.** [It is the aorist in Greek, 'suffered,' which refers to the definite epoch in Paul's life when he experienced the change in his views and relations which he here describes.—H]. In δι' ὃν he returns again to the person of Christ, on which, after all, everything depends, not on the subjective knowledge. Τὰ πάντα, where the article recalls πάντα just mentioned, is the limiting accusative after the passive ἐζημιώθην, which states a result consequent on this altered view of his character and wants. Luther incorrectly renders it: 'I have counted loss;' and VAN HENGEL: *cujus causa factum est, ut me illis privarem omnibus*.—But the Apostle has not merely endured this passively, for he adds: **And do count them refuse that I may win Christ.** Καὶ ἡγοῦμαι indicates his activity, conviction, knowledge, the ground of which is still *for whom* (δι' ὅν). Σκύβαλα (from κυσὶ βαλεῖν) εἶναι marks the absolute worthlessness more strongly than ζημίαν εἶναι which concedes a relative value: *ζημία, jactura fit æquo animo, σκύβαλα properi abjiciuntur, posthac neque tactu, neque adspectu dignanda.* (BENGEL). [Another derivation is that from σκῶρ, σκατός, 'dung,' 'filth,' which some good etymologists adopt, though the other is generally preferred.—H]. The aim and purpose of such a judgment is ἵνα Χριστὸν κερδήσω, *that I may gain Christ*, who replaces all losses.—The future does not exclude present possession, but yet implies a fuller appropriation, which the present does not satisfy. Χριστόν is stronger than simply *Christi favorem* (GROTIUS)

Ver. 9 attaches itself closely to that which precedes.—**And may be found in him,** καὶ εὑρεθῶ ἐν αὐτῷ. BENGEL well observes: *qui omnia, ne se ipso quidem excepto, amittit, Christum lucrifacit et in Christo lucrifit; Christus est illius et ille est Christi. Plus ultra loquitur, Paulus quasi adhuc non lucrifecerit.* It is incorrect to take the objective gaining of Christ (ἵνα κερδήσω) placed emphatically after the subjective, *i. e.*, the being found (εὑρηθῶ) opposed to ἡγοῦμαι, as equivalent to *sim*, (GROTIUS) or to restrict it to *judicum dei* (BEZA). How he will be found is stated in what follows.—**Not having mine own righteousness, which is of the law.** Μή is used with ἔχων in the first place, because it belongs to a final clause, but also because it expresses a judgment concerning Paul: 'as one who does not have.' See WINER's *Gram.*, p. 482 sq. VAN HENGEL incorrectly joins it closely with εὑρέθω: *ut deprehendar in ejus communione non meam qualemcunque habere probitatem*, while RHEINWALD and others explain it as 'holding fast.' It is *habens* as a specific modal-limitation of εὑρέθω ἐν αὐτῷ.—Ἐμὴν δικαιοσύνην τὴν ἐκ νόμου describes the righteousness (δικαιοσύνην) under two aspects: first, ἐμήν, emphatic by position, corresponding to τὴν ἰδίαν δικαιοσύνην (Rom. x. 3) 'his own,' 'self-acquired,' to which is opposed ἡ ἐκ θεοῦ or ἡ τοῦ θεοῦ (Rom. x. 3); secondly, τὴν ἐκ νόμου with reference to the medium, as in like manner δίκαιος ἐκ πίστεως (Rom. iii. 26) and answering to τὴν διὰ πίστεως (comp. Rom. iii. 21, 22, 26; iv. 5; ix. 32; x. 3, 5, 6).—Hence he at once adds to the latter the opposite characteristic. **But that which is through the faith of Christ,** ἀλλὰ τὴν διὰ πίστεως Χριστοῦ. Here righteousness (*i. e.*, of faith) is described as the *causa apprehendens* or means of securing the benefits of Christ's work.—But for the sake of completeness he now adds still under the antithetic ἀλλά: **The righteousness which is of God upon faith** (τὴν ἐκ θεοῦ δικαιοσύνην ἐπὶ τῇ πίστει). It is not a righteousness proceeding from the subject, but from God (*causa efficiens*), which rests on faith as its basis. The article τῇ renders the *gen. objecti* (Χριστοῦ or εἰς Χριστόν), and the article τήν before ἐπὶ τῇ πίστει unnecessary, because this limitation is immanent in the conception as the faith-righteousness. WINER's *Gram.* p. 135. MEYER incorrectly connects this clause (τὴν ἐκ θεοῦ, *etc.*) with ἔχων, and SCHENKEL, with εὑρέθω ἐν αὐτῷ. So remote a connection is itself against both views. We reject also the following: *In fide* (Vulg.), *per fidem* (GROTIUS), *propter fidem*, (DE WETTE), *conditione hujus ipsius fidei posita* (VAN HENGEL).

Ver. 10. **That I may know him** (τοῦ γνῶναι αὐτόν). This knowing of Christ is what the righteousness of faith proposes, without which such knowing is impossible, in the possession of which therefore he would be found, that he may be able to know Christ. In like manner in Rom. vi. 6, one clause with ἵνα is joined to another with τοῦ and the infinitive. Thus the process of the knowledge of Christ (ver. 8) is given. CALVIN, BENGEL, and others, join this clause incorrectly with ἐπὶ τῇ πίστει. The excellence of this knowledge lies first of all in its object, the person of the Lord, a practical, experimental acquaintance with Him. What follows αὐτόν is epexegetical.—**And the power of His resurrection; and the fellowship of His sufferings** (καὶ τὴν δύναμιν τῆς ἀναστάσεως αὐτοῦ καὶ τὴν κοινωνίαν τῶν παθημάτων αὐτοῦ). The first denotes the *vis et efficacia* which the resurrection of Christ has upon those who know Him, which they experience when they embrace by faith the resurrection of the Lord; whereby God declared Him to be the author of justification and righteousness to all and every one who believes, (Rom. iv. 25; viii. 11; 1 Cor. xv. 17; 2 Cor. ii. 14; iv. 10, 11; Col. iii. 1, 2). Hence the new life, the striving for that which is above, the conversation in heaven (ver. 20), spring up in and with the righteousness of faith. Hence ἀνάστασις is not to be regarded as *exortus* (BENGEL);

or δύναμις to be understood as the power which effects the resurrection (GROTIUS); nor is reference had to the certainty of our resurrection and exaltation (HÖLEMANN, *et al.*) The other expression, τὴν κοινωνίαν τῶν παθημάτων αὐτοῦ, indicates a participation in the sufferings of Christ, a συμπάσχειν (Rom. vii. 17. See Gal. ii. 20: Χριστῷ συνεσταύρωμαι; 2 Tim. ii. 11) a suffering for Christ's sake and in fellowship with Him. Thus suffering alone does not lead to glory as dying does not save or make us blessed. With Him! But as there is no resurrection without death, so also is there none without suffering (WIESINGER). Hence this thought, which logically should come first, takes the second place, emphatically intimating that the second is something not to be overlooked if one desires the first. The reference is not merely to a similar disposition in suffering (VAN HENGEL), or to an appropriation by faith of the merit of Christ, (CALOV), nor is it to be explained as if it were written τὴν δύναμιν τῆς κοινωνίας (HÖLEMANN). These two things, the power of the resurrection of Christ and the fellowship of His sufferings, are objects of the knowledge which only the righteous by faith possess. Hence such knowledge transcends all other advantages (ver. 8).—**Being conformed unto his death,** συμμορφιζόμενος τῷ θανά τῳ αὐτοῦ. The nominative with τοῦ γνῶναι, without its relation to the subject being more closely defined is unusual. It would properly be the accusative of the subject, but is a *constructio ad sensum*, as if it had been ἵνα γνῶ. Comp. John viii. 54; and for the opposite construction Acts xxvii. 10. WINER'S *Gram.*, p. 572; see on Eph. iv. 2. The present participle points to an incipient present accomplishment, which the verb shows to be outwardly similar to the death of Christ. Paul had been exposed in the cause of the gospel more immediately to a violent death, at the hands of the heathen in league with the Jews; he might at length die a martyr's death. It is not therefore to be carried forward beyond the nearer clause, to which it actually belongs, to one more remote, which has its own limitations; nor does it denote a condition yet to be attained, or an inward ethical relation of likeness to the death of the sinless Redeemer (SCHENKEL).

Ver. 11. **If by any means** *or* **perchance,** εἴ πως, *si forte*, denotes a hope which naturally connects itself with what has been said of the power of the resurrection of Christ, of fellowship with His sufferings, and of the Apostle's, own impending death by martyrdom. The problematical form of the expression shows his humility in view of the glory which is the object of this hope. We are not to suppose any hesitation, or doubt, but only the exclusion of moral certainty.—**I might attain unto the resurrection of the dead.** Καταντήσω as in Acts xxvi. 7. Εἰς τὴν ἐξανάστασιν τὴν ἐκ νεκρῶν is simply the resurrection of the righteous to blessedness. The first preposition in the substantive ἐξανάστασις, found only here, (the verb ἐξαναστήσαν in Mark xii. 19; Luke xx. 28; Acts xv. 5), points to the place whence the dead come forth (ἐκ τῆς γῆς). BENGEL hypercritically refers ἐξανάστασις to the resurrection of Christians, and ἀνάστασις to Christ's resurrection. Our passage gives no support to the distinction between a first and second resurrection. Comp. 1 Cor. xv. 23; 1 Thes. iv. 16. ["The general resurrection of the dead," says Prof. LIGHTFOOT, "whether good or bad, is ἡ ἀνάστασις τῶν νεκρῶν (*e. g.*, 1 Cor. xv. 42); on the other hand, the resurrection of Christ and of those who rise with Christ, is generally [ἡ] ἀνάστασις [ἡ] ἐκ νεκρῶν (Luke xx. 35; Acts iv. 2; 1 Pet. i. 3); the former includes both the ἀνάστασις ζωῆς and the ἀνάστασις κρίσεως (John v. 29); the latter is confined to the ἀνάστασις ζωῆς." To infer that the righteous only are to be raised at the last day would contradict the express declaration of Christ in John v. 26–29; and of Paul in Acts xxiv. 14, 16.—H]. VAN HENGEL'S view is singular: *si forte perveniam ad tempus hujus eventi, hence: live to the time when the dead shall rise.*

Ver. 15. **Not that I have already attained [laid hold of] or am already [or have become] perfect.** Οὐχ ὅτι guards against the error of supposing that Paul would say of himself ἤδη ἔλαβον ἢ ἤδη τετελείωμαι. The object of ἔλαβον is not named, hence is to be drawn from the context: τὸ γνῶναι αὐτὸν (ver. 10), τὸ ὑπερέχον τῆς γνώσεως Χριστοῦ Ἰησοῦ (ver. 8). Ἔλαβον naturally denotes complete, secure possession; as if he were entirely penetrated by such knowledge, and it had entirely penetrated him, as if it had accomplished in him its perfect moral effect. The explanatory τετελείωμαι defines the meaning. With this modest literal account of his experience we are not to connect the figurative βραβεῖον in ver. 14, which does not come forward till after the intervention of several other clauses (the Greek interpreters, BENGEL, MEYER, and others); and also not τὴν ἀνάστασιν (RHEINWALD) *jus ad resurrectionem beatam* (GROTIUS), καταντᾶν (MATTHIES), all of which belong to the future, or Χριστόν (THEODORET), moral perfection (HÖLEMANN). BENGEL well remarks: *in summo fervore sobrietatem spiritualem non dimittit apostolus.*—**But I follow after if I may also apprehend [lay hold of] that** (διώκω δέ, εἰ καὶ καταλάβω). Διώκω means (as in Rom. ix. 30; 1 Cor. xiv. 1; 1 Tim. vi. 21; 2 Tim. ii. 22) *studiosi appeto*, in contrast with (δέ) ἔλαβον, and having the same object. The εἰ shows the striving to be with humility. Καί points back to ἔλαβον; καταλάβω is stronger: *cum quis plene potitur* (BENGEL); laying hold firmly (MEYER). Comp. Rom. ix. 30; 1 Cor. ix. 27.—**Because also I was apprehended [laid hold of].** The ground on which he hopes to lay hold of (ἐφ ᾧ), as in Rom. v. 12; 2 Cor. v. 4 (WINER'S *Gram.*, p. 394), hence equivalent to διότι. It is inappropriate to supply τοῦτο as the object of καταλάβω, **for which,** καὶ κατελήμφθην ὑπὸ Χριστοῦ (RILLIET, WIESINGER, and others); for the Apostle's thought relates not so much to the reciprocal acts of 'laying hold,' and 'being laid hold of,' as to the effectual initiative which Christ has taken; and equally out of place is the idea of 'being laid hold of for Christian perfection.' The tone of the passage, which is not dialectic, reflective, speaks against such interpretations as: 'under the condition,' (MATTHIES), *quo ut pervenire possim* (GROTIUS). LU-

THER's rendering is unphilological. 'After that,' and CALVIN's *quem ad modum*. We are to recognize a suggestive and fine allusion in κατελήμφθην to the manner of Paul's conversion (Acts ix. 3 ff.). [This reference appears to me doubtful.—H.]

Ver. 13. **Brethren,** ἀδελφοί. *Familiariter fatetur* (BENGEL). **I count not myself to have laid hold of,** ἐγὼ ἐμαυτὸν οὐ λογίζομαι κατειληφέναι. A repetition of ver. 12, which emphatically excludes himself (Acts xxvi. 9; John v. 30, 32; vii. 17; viii. 54). The perfect as distinguished from καταλαβεῖν, denotes the having laid hold and kept hold. He resolutely discards all certainty and self-conceit, not so much on account of his readers and of their conduct (ii. 2-4), as WIESINGER thinks, but for their sakes in view of false teachers among them, or who might appear among them.

Ver. 14 answers to ver. 12 *b*. **But one thing,** ἓν δέ, introduces the antithesis of οὐ λογίζομαι; hence we are to supply λέγω (LUTHER), or λογίζομαι κατειληφέναι brought forward; for what follows he maintains to be true of himself in opposition to what he has denied to be so. There is no ground for inserting ποιῶ (BENGEL, WINER's *Gram.*, p. 620, *et al.*); nor διώκω (VAN HENGEL). Ἓν refers to the whole following sentence, not merely to one member of it, *viz.*, the two participial clauses (MEYER).—**Forgetting those things which are behind, and reaching forth unto those things which are before, I press toward the mark,** (τὰ μὲν ὀπίσω ἐπιλανθανόμενος, τοῖς δὲ ἔμπροσθεν ἐπεκτεινόμενος κατὰ σκοπὸν διώκω). The finite verb, as in ver. 12, is first of all defined more closely by two participles, which stand emphatically before it. The first clause is negative: 'forgetting that which lies behind;' the second is positive: 'reaching out to what lies before;' the first designates a purely spiritual act; the second describes a spiritual act by the posture of the body. Ἐπεκτεινόμενος indicates the bent-forward posture of one stretching himself out towards an object. BENGEL: *Oculus manum, manus pedem prævertit et trahit.* The concrete expressions (ἔλαβον, διώκω, καταλάβω, τὰ ὀπίσω, τὰ ἔμπροσθεν, ἐπεκτεινόμενος, σκοπόν) gradually pass over more and more into the figure of a runner who in view of the goal before him and in thinking of the prize, forgets the space that lies behind. At first these expressions are such as readily attach themselves to the figure—perhaps it already lay at the bottom of them—in the end they are borrowed directly from the figure, so that τὸ βραβεῖον naturally follows as a part of the description. Hence in τὰ ὀπίσω the reference is not to the advantages mentioned, vers. 5, 6 (PELAGIUS, *et al.*), for these as attributes of the flesh (σάρξ) must be given up before the race begins, nor is it to the labors of the apostleship (THEODORET), but to the past attainments of the Christian life (MEYER). Τὰ ἔμπροσθεν, according to the figure the space yet to be traversed, is the life: future experience, not the goal itself, which is pointed out by κατὰ σκοπόν. The dative (τοῖς ἔμπροσθεν) shows upon what the gaze is fixed, while the preposition (κατά) indicates the direction, so that the goal is always thought of beyond the intermediate steps: it is thus = goalward (MEYER), *versus metam* (WINER's *Gram.*, p. 400).—**For the prize of the high calling of God in Christ Jesus.** Εἰς τὸ βραβεῖον presents now the object towards which his thoughts and efforts are directed. See 1 Cor. ix. 27; comp. Col. iii. 15. How the genitive τῆς ἄνω κλήσεως τοῦ θεοῦ ἐν Χριστῷ Ἰησοῦ is to be understood, a due attention to the subject and the figure shows. By ἡ ἄνω κλῆσις is meant the heavenly calling (Heb. iii. 1: κλῆσις ἐπουράνιος) in opposition to τὰ ἐπὶ τῆς γῆς (Col. iii. 2), and as usual κλῆσις denotes an action (Eph. i. 18; iv. 1, 4; Rom. xi. 29; 2 Tim. i. 9; 2 Thes. i. 11; 1 Cor. i. 26; vii. 20). If its nature and character are thus determined, so now is its author (τοῦ θεοῦ). Comp. 1 Thes. ii. 12. The medium is presented by ἐν Χριστῷ Ἰησοῦ (WINER's *Gram.*, p. 135 sq. Comp. Col. i. 4.) To connect this clause with διώκω (CHRYSOSTOM, MEYER) is against both the sense and the construction. Accordingly τῆς κλήσεως is genitive of the subject, which holds forth τὸ βραβεῖον, but not the genitive of apposition (SCHENKEL). [On the games of the Greeks and Romans, from which the Apostle has drawn his illustration, see GAMES in Dr. Smith's *Dictionary of the Bible.* —H].

Ver. 15. **Let us therefore, as many as be perfect, be thus minded.** Ὅσοι οὖν τέλειοι begins the practical application as an inference (οὖν) from the preceding. Τέλειος is to be distinguished from τετελειωμένος: *ille, cursui habilis, hic, brabeo proximus, jam jam accepturus* (BENGEL). The first word designates a character or condition objectively determined without measuring its subjective development or degree; whereas the second determines the measure of that growth or progression. It designates like ἅγιος (Eph. i. 1) the Christian state of which the context treats, ver. 12 (τελείωσις), Heb. vii. 11. See 1 Cor. xiv. 20; Matth. v. 48; Col. iv. 12; Jam. i. 4; iii. 2; Heb. v. 14. "As the ἅγιον εἶναι is the strongest obligation to ἁγιασμός, so the τέλειον εἶναι presents the strongest incentive to strive after the τελειοῦσθαι" (WIESINGER). The nature or extent of the perfection (τέλειοι) appears in vers. 9, 10. The question is one not of absolute, but only of relative perfection. Οὖν points back to the entire passage (1. 14), not merely to 12–14 (MEYER). By ὅσοι each individual is left to judge for himself whether he belongs to the τέλειοι or not. There is no reason for understanding the expression as ironical, and since he includes himself, as self-irony (SCHENKEL). Nor can the Apostle refer to intelligence only (GROTIUS, *et al.*), for the point under remark is the righteousness of faith. Hence, too, a comparison with immature believers or beginners in the Christian life, νήπιοι (1 Cor. ii. 6; iii. 1; xiv. 20; Heb. v. 13, 14) as MEYER supposes, is irrelevant. Τοῦτο φρονῶμεν has reference to the moral disposition. BENGEL: *hoc unum* (ver. 14). Unlike the false teachers the church should be of the same mind as the Apostle. The reference is not to τὸ βραβεῖον (VAN HENGEL); the point in question is the true way of striving after the βραβεῖον.—**And if in anything ye be otherwise minded,** (καὶ εἴ τι ἑτέρως φρονεῖτε) supposes a case in which the members of the church differ among themselves in their views or spirit in regard to points which are incidental or formal, and not essential, (it is ἑτέρως, not ἕτερον, as if to distinguish between form and substance), but still not rightly, as surely might be the case according to i. 9–11. The context does not indicate in any way how this has taken place.—Those of whom Paul speaks are not νήπιοι (*aliter ac perfecti*, BENGEL) nor those who have been led astray (GROTIUS); nor yet are the errors entirely indifferent (SCHENKEL), for ἀποκαλύψει authorizes a hope of correction or recovery; nor is it: *si quid boni per aliam viam expetitis* (VAN HENGEL).—**God shall reveal also this unto you** (καὶ τοῦτο ὁ θεὸς ὑμῖν ἀποκαλύψει is a confident hope, not a wish (LUTHER). Καί also points to other things that He has already revealed. The verb indicates an immediate disclosing to the human spirit by the Spirit of God, which next to the teaching (διδάσκειν) of the church men need in order to understand ethical truth. See Eph. i. 17.

Ver. 16. **Nevertheless, whereto we have already attained, let us walk in the same.** [For the rendering of this verse, see remarks on the text.—H]. Πλήν (as in i. 14; and iv. 14) limits the hope by a *conditio sine qua non*, which is εἰς ὃ ἐφθάσαμεν τῷ αὐτῷ στοιχεῖν. The infinitive as in German: '*nur—wandeln!*' is to be construed as an imperative (WINER's *Gram.* p. 316), but not connected with ἀποκαλύψει (ŒCUMENIUS), or with what follows (RILLIET). The verb, according to its derivation from στοῖχος, *row, order*, (from στέχω, to ascend), signifies 'to walk with and after one another,' and is construed with the dative (Gal. v. 25, πνεύματι; vi. 16, τῷ κανόνι τούτῳ; Rom. iv. 12, τοῖς ἴχνεσιν). Hence the meaning of τῷ αὐτῷ στοιχεῖν is: 'to walk together with each other according to or in the same.' Τῷ αὐτῷ is more closely defined by εἰς ὃ ἐφθάσαμεν. This verb means to arrive at, to reach, hence has to do with an act completed at a definite time, which the tense marks as belonging to the past, while the act denoted by στοιχεῖν is continuous, reaching from the present into the future. The common rule by which they are to act is that which they have experienced or gained in the Christian life—the gospel, truth, Christ, God's Spirit and life—and indeed in its entire range as the indefiniteness of the expression indicates. Thus there is no reference to the βραβεῖον, or any single thing, and the sense is: Should energy become even violence; mildness, softness; earnestness, stubbornness; reserve, exclusiveness; fidelity, narrowness; freedom, laxity; in any one point (all which is τὶ ἑτέρως φρονεῖν), only hold fast to the gospel, the Lord and His word, to the essential truth of the same, to that of which we have become partakers.

DOCTRINAL AND ETHICAL.

1. Christianity plants and nourishes essentially and chiefly joy, true joy, joy in the Lord, in His word and work, His life and gifts, His excellence and glory.

2. Irony and humor in sacred things (ver. 2: κατατομή—περιτομή) hold almost the same place that the imprecatory Psalms hold among the prophetic; the former invoke on the enemies of God and His kingdom what the latter predict. Irony and humor are an expression of the difference which exists between reality and truth, a difference sharply recognized and as sharply uttered, without mercy for the delinquent, but with a tender regard for those who are to be instructed. They occur especially in the style and thoughts of genial men distinguished for faith, at the same time full of deep earnestness as well as tender love, like Paul and Luther (whose *Drecket Drecketal*, instead of *Dekret Dekretal*, MEYER compares here with Paul's sarcastic paranomasia). They are to be distinguished from *ridicule* which only seeks to provoke laughter against one, and thus to achieve a petty triumph, and from derision and scorn which have their origin in contempt. It is not an allowed ridicule or scorn—allowed to an Apostle, even a duty, but in general to be condemned (SCHENKEL)—that is here employed. The greatness of the danger and of the interests at stake, the hot struggle at an endangered post, a true and lively sense of justice, the deepest sympathy with those for and around whom the contest is raging, and great spiritual keenness, sagacity, and depth of feeling, occasion the hard, telling, crushing expression (see ver. 3).

3. Two things are as important as they are difficult: to determine the *extent* of one's advantages and gifts, and the *worth* and relation of the same. Birth and lineage, family, tribe and nationality on the one hand, and the moral character determined by them on the other, Paul reckons together as excellencies and gifts of the same kind, and holds them all in slight esteem compared with what he has in Christ. The morality of men belongs to the province of the natural life; it depends on birth, family, position, culture, time and circumstances, and gives reason, as does every favor for humble thankfulness, but not for proud boasting (vers. 3-5).

4. The righteousness of faith has its advantage over righteousness of the law in the author to whom it owes its origin, that is God Himself; in the *medium* through which it is wrought, faith which embraces and clings to the Mediator; and in the *experiences* which it works, and which reach into the eternal glory, that is, Christ's life and sufferings, with whom the believer has sympathy (ver. 10).—The worthlessness of the righteousness of the law does not consist in this, that law and advantages, such as birth, family, nation, morality, are in themselves valueless, but in the fact that man of himself, the natural man, without Christ, in his perverseness, does not rightly estimate them (ver. 7-9, and Rom. vii. 7-24).

5. Progress consists in advancing from the possession of faith to that of knowledge, which is not merely an intellectual thing, but an experience of the whole man, a transforming of impressions into views or judgments, and then onward through suffering with Christ to glorification with Him who perfects His servants even as He completed His own course. The first points out the material or means of progress, the second its form or sphere, while the end is the permeating of the entire man by the dead and again risen Lord (vers. 11–14).

6. The progress of the Christian to eternal glory has its *origin* in the fact, that he has been called from above by God in Christ, and has been laid hold of by Him; its *continuance* in the fact,

that he holds firmly to Christ without contentedly looking back upon what has been already won, but with his face earnestly set towards the goal with the feeling that he has not yet reached it; and its *end* in the fact, that the exalted Lord receives him into His glory. It is thus an onward movement in one direction, without elation or depression, or a deviation to the right or left (vers. 13, 14). To him belongs the χαίρετε ἐν κυρίῳ who obeys the στήκετε ἐν κυρίῳ (iv. 1).

7. He who has the truth-loving heart will never want the helping guidance and revelation of the Spirit of truth; and as certainly will he have his waverings and his need of this help (vers. 15, 16).

8. [It seems appointed that much of the highest instruction should come to us (even in the Bible) through the sufferings and struggles of individual men. *Perseverance in the Christian life* is, after all, the basis of St. Paul's character. "I therefore so run, not as uncertainly; so fight I, not as one that beateth the air; but I keep under my body, and bring it into subjection; lest that by any means, when I have preached to others, I myself should be a castaway." "Not as though I had already attained, but I follow after. This one thing I do, forgetting those things which are behind, and reaching forth unto those things which are before, I press toward the mark for the prize of the high calling of God in Christ Jesus." (DR. HOWSON'S *Lectures on the Character of St. Paul*, p. 212 f.)—H].

HOMILETICAL AND PRACTICAL.

Warn thy hearers constantly by holding up before them first of all what the Lord commands, and by leading them to observe what they have lost, and by whom they have been deprived of it.—Never glory in the gifts of the Lord, but only in the Lord of the gifts.—Do not leap over the valley of sorrows through which the way to the heights of glory passes.—Thou art never complete, never think thyself complete; what thou hast and art is ever less than what thou shouldest have and be.—Far-seeing, circumspect, self-inspecting, watch all waverings in thyself, that thou mayest not depart from the one way of salvation.

LUTHER:—Thoughtless, full, surfeited souls, if they have once heard a word of God's, act as if it were an old thing, and yawn for something new, as if they were able to do all that they have heard. This is a dangerous plague and wicked artifice of the devil, who thereby renders men confident, secure, over-curious, and ready for every error and schism; and they are guilty of the vice of slothfulness (ἀκηδία) in the service of God (ver. 1).—Flesh and blood say: Something new, else it becomes tiresome. Nay, says Christ, but *think of me.* The word of God rightly received into the heart, produces neither fulness nor satiety, but greater desire the longer it is known (ver. 1).

JEROME SCHURF:—*Sic mutatam et corruptam esse ecclesiæ doctrinam, quia concionatores existimarint gloriosum esse, non repetere eadem, sed alia et nova afferre redeuntibus iisdem festis.*

STARKE:—God has no respect of persons; before Him the slave has as much worth as the master, the peasant as the noble, the subject as the prince. We see this, indeed, in death, which is God's provost, who uses even justice, and punishes the master with the slave.—It is a humility which becomes those to whom God has lent many talents, and who have also increased them by usury, to act as if they knew it not, and so to give God all the glory.—To boast of one's race, lineage, rank, and external advantages, is a vain ostentation; but we may well praise those on account of their family and descent, who also possess the faith and virtues of their ancestors.—False prophets may perhaps be blameless in their outward walk; but without circumcision of the heart, it is only a coat of whitewash over an old, unsightly wall.—Righteousness of the law is good, but it does not merit blessedness, which is bestowed as a gift only through faith in Christ.—Whoever fancies that he has advanced so far in Christianity that he needs nothing more, may perhaps in God's school hardly sit upon the lowest form. Christians have ever to be learning, and cannot finish their education during their entire life (ver. 15).—In religious matters we ought not to depart a hair's breadth from the prophetic and apostolic doctrine; and thus many errors may be prevented.

RIEGER:—As with the two scales of a balance, when one rises the other falls; and what I add to one, diminishes the relative weight of the other; so as one adds to himself he takes away from the pre-eminence which the knowledge of Christ should have. What he concedes to Christ makes him willing to abase himself, to resign all confidence in his own works. Therefore the sharp expressions, 'to count as loss, as dung,' become in experience not too severe; for to reject the grace of Christ, to regard the great plan of God in sending His Son, as fruitless, were indeed far more terrible (ver. 8).

GERLACH:—The inner and outer life of the Christian upon earth, is a life of suffering in the sorrow which he feels for the sins of others, for his own, and for the distress of others, and for the oppression, conflicts, and even apparent defeats of the children of God. These sufferings are the sufferings of Christ Himself, not merely similar to His; He bears them with His members. His conflicts and their conflicts are the same; it is one cause for which, and one strength in which, they strive; it is one victory and one crown which He has won, and which He gives to them (ver. 10).—'What is behind' signifies in this figure not merely the world and sin, which we have forsaken, but also our own virtue, the actual progress which we have made, on which we are prone to dwell with self-complacency, and so to become unmindful of our great deficiencies and sins (ver. 14).—True Christian perfection, therefore, in this world, the token of a mature Christian, is that, certain of his election in Christ he yet does not regard himself perfect, but painfully perceives the wide space which still intervenes between the righteousness imputed to faith and the sanctification of his entire heart and life, and unceasingly strives to reach the goal.

SCHLEIERMACHER:—Are now the expression of the Apostle John, "Little children, love one another," as he explains it, and the expression of the apostle Paul, "Rejoice in the Lord," one and the same? And are both such that one can say of them with confidence, that they never weary the speaker, and that they always strengthen the hearer?

MENKEN:—The ever recurring exhortation of the apostle to rejoice in the Lord, was adapted to assure them that Christianity is something bright, cheerful, and joyful, to make them certain, confident in their knowledge and walk in opposition to those who imagine that one must mix a bitterness, narrowness, and legal servitude with the mildness, breadth and freedom of the new covenant and its gospel.—There is no one among us, however limited his powers may be, whose weakness and incapacity may not be changed into wisdom and knowledge; his timidity into firmness and fearlessness; his hardness and unloveliness into gentleness and amiability, through our Lord Jesus Christ, who of God is made unto us wisdom, and righteousness, and sanctification, and redemption. Hence the Christian religion is vastly different from human morality.—The choice of the best part is never repented of.—As in the life of the body the question is not, whether the man will breathe or not, whether he will make use of the light that is in the world to see or not; but as it is understood, that according to the laws of nature he must breathe, if he will live, and must open his eye to the light, if he will see; and as there is no way of supporting life outside of the atmosphere, and no medium for perceiving the world of matter, except the light; so is there no other way of becoming partakers of the divine light and life except Christ, and no room for the question whether man can do without Christ or not.—All men are under sin and death, and no one comes to the divine light and life, to his own source and end—to God, except through Christ.—The forgiveness of sins is not indeed deliverance from sin, but it is the sure pledge and earnest of future complete deliverance, and is necessary, and must form the beginning.

HEUBNER:—The preacher should not be ever thinking of something new, but of what is useful, edifying. The Sophists made it a charge against Socrates that he repeated the same things.—Lavater's principle of saying at least something in every sermon, which he was certain he had never said before, *i. e.*, something that he had never before spoken either so plainly, or so urgently, or with such a particular application (though the kernel of the sermon must always be the same) is not at variance with that of the Reformers; for they also do not exclude variety in the contents, or diversity in the form of the sermon.—Spiritual sloth may creep over even the converted, so that the Bible becomes dull to them. Bunyan himself complained of this.—What a vast difference between blamelessness before God, and legal blamelessness before men! How can one deceive himself therein!—How many an ecclesiastic buries himself in his studies, while he might be sowing seed for eternity by oral instruction, visits, and the teaching of children. The more earnest in conversion and sanctification, the humbler is our state of mind, and clearer our knowledge of our imperfections, because we then first see and understand how lofty and distant is this goal of perfection, and how great is the work of sanctification. The Christian does not please himself with the conceit that he has already laid hold of, or attained it; this folly is far from him.—The influence of grace is mighty, but not irresistible.—The most advanced Christian thinks least of himself.—The Christian is not yet in quiet possession; he should not rest on his laurels.—The Christian knows that he is ever in arrears, and so long as there are debts still remaining, so long must he also work.—I look not back like Lot's wife towards the Sodom I have left, nor long like the Israelites after the flesh pots of Egypt. Both kinds of looking back are idle and ruinous, for they make us slothful, they lead to unfaithfulness.—Perfect Christians, in the proper sense of that language, are those who know the goal and the way thither, *i. e.*, Christ, and have begun with earnestness to press towards it.—The hope of spiritual growth is conditioned on fidelity, conscientiousness, and adherence to known truth.

PASSAVANT:—Every one who will not deceive God or himself knows in his own heart out of what darkness the light broke forth with him, and out of what darkness old and new, it has long continued to break forth.—Paul forgets what is behind, *viz.*, three things: 1) those objects of pride which he formerly regarded as gain and glory; 2) the sins of his past life in general, and especially the many and great sins which he had committed as a persecutor and blasphemer of the Church; and 3) his progress hitherto in the new divine way of life.

AHLFELD:—The genuine warrior of Christ may not stand still: 1) he knows that he has not yet obtained the prize; 2) in the pursuit of it he never becomes weary; 3) he journeys towards the city of God, having the same mind as his brother.

HARLESS:—Three great foes of Christian and social virtue; 1) the conceit of being perfect; 2) the weakness of looking back; 3) obstinacy and destructiveness of self-will.

LEHMANN:—True progress in the Christian life. 1) From what *origin* must it proceed? Laid hold of by Christ! 2) By what *rule* must it shape itself? I have not yet obtained! 3) What *end* must it seek? The prize of the heavenly calling (vers. 12–14).

[ROBERT HALL:—As every person either has, or expects to have some spring of joy or source of consolation, there is nothing which so much determines our character as *that* from which we expect this to rise. So if we wish to know ourselves we must examine where this spring or source lies.—We see from the Apostle's account of his experience, that it is very possible for a person to have great zeal for modes, and forms, and ceremonies, and yet be totally ignorant of the spirit of true religion. Real religion is one thing; an attachment to forms and ceremonies another. We may be very zealous for one particular creed, opinion, sect or denomination, and with the credit and conceit of our wisdom yet be very defective in the Christian spirit. This temper leads to malignity of feeling. There may be sufficient in such religion for us to hate one another, but not enough to cause us to love each other. Let us "worship God in spirit, rejoice in Christ Jesus," and be taught to value the great truths and promises of the Gospel as all in all (vers. 1, 2, 6).—H].

(2). *The destiny of false Christians in contrast with that of true believers.*

(CHAPTER III. 17—IV. 1).

17 Brethren, be followers together of me [become imitators of me] and mark them
18 who walk so as ye have us for an ensample. For many walk, of whom I (have)
19 told you often, and [but] now tell you even weeping, that they are the enemies of
the cross of Christ; whose end is destruction, whose God is their belly, and whose
20 glory is in their shame, who mind earthly things. [1]For our conversation [citizen-
21 ship] is in heaven; from whence also we look for the [a] Saviour the Lord Jesus
Christ; who shall [will] change [transform] our vile body [the body of our humiliation], that it may be fashioned like[2] unto his glorious body [the body of his
glory], according to the working whereby he is able even [also] to subdue all
IV. 1 things unto himself.[3] Therefore, my brethren dearly beloved and longed for,
my joy and crown, so stand fast in the Lord, my dearly beloved.

1 Ver. 20. [The *γάρ* here has the support of all the oldest manuscripts, though the passage is cited by many early writers, as if *δέ* was the connective.—H].

2 Ver. 21. Before *σύμμορφον* some *codices* insert *εἰς τὸ γενέσθαι αὐτό*, manifestly an interpretation.

3 *Ibid.* ℵ A B *et al.* have *αὐτῷ*. A few copies read *ἑαυτῷ* [adopted in the received text.—H].

EXEGETICAL AND CRITICAL.

Ver. 17. **Brethren, become imitators of me**, *συμμιμηταί μου γίνεσθε, ἀδελφοί.* 1 Cor. iv. 16: *μιμηταί μου γίνεσθε.* They are to look to the Apostle, to follow him, with him to act on the principle of following the light which they have (*τῷ αὐτῷ στοιχεῖν*, ver. 16). This result is not achieved at once, but by degrees (hence *γίνεσθε*, '*become*'). The *συν* refers to the Apostle's associates, as is evident from what immediately follows (THEOPHYLACT: *συγκολλᾷ αὐτοὺς τοῖς καλῶς περιπατοῦσιν*). [The "associates" are those whom the Apostle would have the Philippians to imitate, together with himself (*τύπον ἡμᾶς*); and the import of *συν* more naturally is='be ye all a company of imitators' (ELLICOTT).—H]. Hence it is not: *una cum Paulo* (BENGEL), *omnes uno consensu et una mente* (CALVIN), or superfluous (HEINRICHS). *Brethren, ἀδελφοί*, indicates the fervor of the appeal.—**And mark them who walk so**, (*καὶ σκοπεῖτε τοὺς οὕτως περιπατοῦντες*) associates others with Paul, who are models for the church, since they walk as he does.—**As ye have us for an ensample** (*καθὼς ἔχετε τύπον ἡμᾶς*) embraces Paul and those who walk like him. *Ἡμᾶς* is thus neither Paul alone, especially as it stands after *μου*, while besides, we should have in that case *ἔχουσιν*, instead of *ἔχετε*, nor Paul and Timothy (SCHENKEL), nor Paul and all approved Christians (MATTHIES), nor *ut ego meique socii* (VAN HENGEL). The singular (*τύπον*) is found not only where one is spoken of (1 Tim. iv. 12; Tit. ii. 7), but also in regard to a plurality (1 Thes. i. 7; 2 Thes. iii. 9). In 1 Pet. v. 3 *τύποι* occurs where several are meant. The singular here indicates that they all present the same image, belong to the same category. In *καθώς* lies unquestionably an argumentative force='in the measure' (MEYER).

Ver. 18. The Apostle confirms his exhortation by two contrasts (vers. 18-21).—**For many walk** (*πολλοὶ γὰρ περιπατοῦσιν*), since there are many wicked persons who strive to lead others astray, consider us, not them. [They should heed his expostulations the more because there were so many (*πολλοί*) whom they could not safely imitate. "The persons here meant are not the Judaizing teachers, but the anti-Roman reactionists. This view is borne out by the parallel expression, Rom. xvi. 18: *τῷ κυρίῳ ἡμῶν Χριστῷ οὐ δουλεύουσιν ἀλλὰ τῇ ἑαυτῶν κοιλίᾳ*, where the same persons seem to be intended; for they are described as creating divisions and offences (ver. 17), as holding plausible language (ver. 18), as professing to be wise beyond others (ver. 19), and yet not innocent in their wisdom: this last reproach being implied in the words *θέλω δὲ ὑμᾶς σοφοὺς εἶναι εἰς τὸ ἀγαθόν, ἀκεραίους δὲ εἰς τὸ κακόν.* They appear therefore to belong to the same party to which the passages vi. 1–23; xiv. 1—xv. 6, of that epistle are chiefly addressed. For the profession of "wisdom" in these faithless disciples of St. Paul, see 1 Cor. i. 17 sqq.; iv. 18 sqq.; viii. 1 sqq.; x. 15" (LIGHTFOOT). See the remarks on ver. 18.—H]. *Περιπατεῖν* is not neutral here as in 1 Pet. v. 8, *circulantur* (HEINRICHS), 'go about' (MEYER). It could not stand absolutely after *οὕτως περιπατοῦντες*. Paul wishes to describe more closely the moral walk of those in question, but he is led away from the adverbial construction by the first relative clause, and proceeds in relative clauses to speak of the end, motive, and character of this walk. Hence neither *κακῶς* (ŒCUMEN.) nor *longe aliter* (GROTIUS), is to be supplied, nor is the concluding limitation (*οἱ τὰ ἐπίγεια φρονοῦντες*) to be joined with the verb to relieve the difficulty (CALVIN); nor are we to assume that since *περιπατοῦσιν* in itself needs no qualifying term, the sentence proceeds with entire correctness with the subjoined limitations of the subject (MEYER). Those, whose example the Philippians should shun (πολλοί) are according to the entire description members of the church, not false teachers, as in iii. 2; at the most they are those who, led astray by such teachers, have become in turn corrupters of others.—**Of whom I told you often, but now tell you even weeping,** (οὓς πολλάκις ἔλεγον ὑμῖν, νῦν δὲ καὶ κλαίων λέγω.) [The imperf. shows the habit=" was accustomed to speak of." This is an instance of Paul's repeating in his letter what he had said in person when he was among the Philippians. See the remarks on ver. 1. The Apostle in this passage, refers evidently to his former warnings, when he was at Philippi.—H]. To understand the remark of passages in the letter itself (iii. 2; i. 15), is untenable; for these here are different persons from those referred to in the passages mentioned. To πολλοί corresponds πολλάκις. Why he now weeping repeats that which he had formerly said without tears, is well explained by CHRYSOSTOM, ὅτι ἐπέτεινε τὸ κακόν. [The evil in the meantime had become more serious.—H]. He writes with deeper emotion, with streaming eyes.—**That they are the enemies of the cross of Christ** (τοὺς ἐχθροὺς τοῦ σταυροῦ τοῦ Χριστοῦ) we are to join with οὓς ἔλεγον. [On this construction see WINER'S *Gram.*, p. 530.—H]. Paul thus designates those to whom the cross is an offence or foolishness; formerly they may have been Jews or heathen, but now they are Christians, who wish to know nothing of the "fellowship of Christ's sufferings," (κοινωνία τῶν παθημάτων Χριστοῦ, ver. 10), to whom the 'sufferings of Christ' (παθήματα τοῦ Χριστοῦ, 2 Cor. i. 5) are offensive, who are not willing to suffer with Him, (συμπάσχειν, Rom. viii. 17), nor allow the world to be crucified to them and themselves to the world (Gal. vi. 14), nor crucify their flesh together with its lusts and desires (Gal. v. 24). The Apostle is speaking of immorality of life, ethical errors, while ver. 19 (ὧν ὁ θεὸς ἡ κοιλία) indicates an Epicurean, careless life (ἐν ἀνέσει ζῶντες καὶ τρυφῇ, CHRYSOSTOM). No reference is made to their doctrine of the cross (THEODORET); or even to theoretical errors, or intellectual misconceptions. The reference is not to those who are not Christians (RILLIET) or *hostes evangelii* (CALVIN).

Ver. 19. **Whose end is destruction** (ὧν τὸ τέλος ἀπωλεία) is first mentioned. *Hoc ponitur ante alia, quo majore cum horrore hæc legantur; in fine videbitur. Finis, ad quem cujusvis rationes tendunt, ostendit sane, quæ sit ejus conditio* (BENGEL). Ἀπωλεία, the opposite of σωτηρία (i. 26) is passive. BENGEL incorrectly regards *salvator* as the equivalent term, and HEINRICHS takes the meaning to be: their end is to destroy Christianity. The end is described by τὸ τέλος (2 Cor. xi. 12-15) as their own peculiar, appointed end.—**Whose God is their belly,** (ὧν ὁ θεὸς ἡ κοιλία). The belly is termed their God, as being their highest concern, the master whom they serve (Rom. xvi. 18). Κοιλία from κοῖλος, *cavus*, is *venter* (Matt. xv. 17; Mark vii. 19; Luke xv. 16) *uterus* (Luke i. 41, 44; ii. 21; John iii. 4; Matt. xix. 12), and also *intima hominis* (John vii. 38). It embraces here the organs of sensual desire and of gluttony, not excluding licentiousness, nor referring exclusively to it: so that this passage comprehends more than 1 Cor. xv. 32.—**And whose glory is in their shame** (καὶ ἡ δόξα ἐν τῇ αἰσχύνῃ αὐτῶν). Καί takes the place of ὧν. Ἡ δόξα signifies the honor and glory which belong peculiarly to them; that which they conceive to be glory, but which is actually and truly their shame, and will in the end prove to be such. BENGEL well remarks: *Deus et gloria ponuntur ut parallela. Sic venter et pudor sunt affinia. Id colunt isti, cujus ipsos maxime pudere debebat et suo tempore pudebit misere.* But there is no reference to circumcision, the genitals (BENGEL, *et al.*) It is not intimated that they have perverted Christian truth to palliate their moral laxity (WIESINGER). —**Who mind earthly things.** The individualizing article οἱ introduces the comprehensive characteristic: τὰ ἐπίγεια φρονοῦντες. The nominative is the logical subject (MEYER), and it is not vocative (WINER'S *Gram.*, p. 183).

Ver. 20. **For our citizenship is in heaven** (ἡμῶν γὰρ τὸ πολίτευμα ἐν οὐρανοῖς ὑπάρχει). The confirmatory sentence (γάρ) points back like vers. 18, 19, to ver. 17, and states why the Philippians should look to Paul and to those who walk as he does (ἡμῶν as in ver. 17 ἡμᾶς). [Their souls are mundane and groveling. They have no fellowship with us; for *we* are citizens of a heavenly commonwealth. The emphatic position of ἡμῶν contrasts the false adherents of St. Paul with the true (LIGHTFOOT). On the state of the text see the notes.—H.] Πολίτευμα, found only here, in the N. T., denotes according to its termination and its derivation (from πολιτεύεσθαι i. 27) citizenship, commonwealth, the rank and rights of a citizen. Comp. πολιτείαν ταύτην ἐκτησάμην, Acts xxii. 28. True Christians have nothing to do with an earthly possession and existence simply, but are citizens of the heavenly (ἐν οὐρανοῖς) Jerusalem (Gal. iv. 26; Rom. v. 2; viii. 24; 2 Thes. ii. 8; Heb. xii. 22, 23) even here. We are not to join ὑπάρχει with ἐν οὐρανοῖς, as if the citizenship did not exist here at all, but to regard ἐν οὐρανοῖς as descriptive of the character of the πολίτευμα rather than the place. Hence this sentence does not confirm the conclusion of ver. 19 (WINER'S *Gram.* p. 453, MEYER, *et al.*); for it is not pertinent to say 'for this very reason I warn you against them,' since he does not warn but exhorts them. It does not confirm καθὼς ἔχετε τύπον ἡμᾶς (WIESINGER), but συμμιμηταί μου γίνεσθε καὶ σκοπεῖτε τοὺς οὕτως περιπατοῦντες (ver. 17). Nor does it present the higher glory of the true Christian as the cause of his deep sorrow over the misconduct of the enemies of the cross (SCHENKEL), since καὶ κλαίων is too subordinate a remark. Again, πολίτευμα is not ἀναστροφή, *walk*, (LUTHER) nor does it refer to the Messiah's kingdom which has not yet appeared (MEYER), for it exists already even upon earth, and only waits for its completion.—**From whence also we look for a Saviour, the Lord Jesus Christ.** Ἐξ οὗ, an adverbial expression, equivalent to *unde* (Vulg., WINER'S *Gram.*, p. 141 sq.) refers to ἐν οὐρανοῖς, not to πολίτευμα (BENGEL); but is not equivalent to *ex quo* (ERASMUS), nor even to ἐκ ὧν (MATTHIES). Καί before σωτῆρα indicates that He is looked for (ἀπεκδεχόμεθα, an awaiting, *ad finem usque, perseveranter exspectare*, Rom. viii. 19, 23,

25; 1 Cor. i. 7; Gal. v. 5) not merely as κύριος in their πολίτευμα, in contrast with the θεός of the enemies of the cross, but also as a Saviour, in contrast with their 'destruction' (ἀπώλεια). Comp. Luke xviii. 7, 8; xxi. 28. Καί points neither to a relation corresponding to what has been said of their citizenship (MEYER), nor to 'conduct' (WIESINGER), which does not agree with ἀπεκδεχόμεθα.

Ver. 21. **Who will transform the body of our humiliation** (ὃς μετασχηματίσει τὸ σῶμα τῆς ταπεινώσεως ἡμῶν) explains how the Lord will manifest Himself as σωτήρ. The reference is to a future transformation which relates to the σχῆμα or fashion of the body (ii. 8; 2 Cor. xi. 13, 14; 1 Cor. iv. 6); and not to its identity. Hence Paul does not speak of the body alone as the object of the change (τὸ σῶμα) but adds the genitive of characterization (WINER'S *Gram.*, p. 187 sq.), namely, τῆς ταπεινώσεως, as in Col. i. 22: σῶμα τῆς σαρκός; Rom. vi. 8; τῆς ἁμαρτίας; vii. 24; τοῦ θανάτου τούτου. CHRYSOSTOM well observes: πολλὰ πάσχει νῦν τὸ σῶμα, δεσμεῖται, μαστίζεται, μυρία πάσχει δεινά. But we must also include here the carnal, the sinful in man's nature; for it is that especially which makes up the ταπείνωσις ἡμῶν. Not merely the body, but we ourselves (note the ἡμῶν) suffer these things, which constitute this humiliation, that cleaves to the body. The object or result of the transformation is now stated. —**That it may be fashioned like unto the body of his glory,** σύμμορφον τῷ σώματι τῆς δόξης αὐτοῦ. The breviloquence (or adj., instead of a sentence) is like 1 Thess. iii. 13; Matt. xii. 13. See WINER'S *Gram.*, p. 624 sq. Out of this arose the variation noted in the critical remarks. The body is now no longer σῶμα τῆς ταπεινώσεως, but has become σῶμα τῆς δόξης, and as that was ours (ἡμῶν) so this is his (αὐτοῦ). The body comes forth from our present humiliation, and becomes a participant in the glory of Him who has transformed it. This is to be effected by the change which makes it like, conformed to, the body of His glory; hence through a transformation into His image (Rom. viii. 29), which begins even here (2 Cor. iii. 18: μεταμορφούμεθα). [The body is that which exhibits His glory not merely because He has it in His glorified state, but because His glory in that state so pre-eminently appears in the spiritual body with which He is there clothed, and which stands forth as the type of the spiritual body into which every one of His true followers will be transformed.—H.] HÖLEMANN joins ἡμῶν with σῶμα, αὐτοῦ with σώματι. HAMMOND explains σῶμα as the church; LUTHER supposes only the weakness and frailty of the body to be meant, MEYER, the change which first begins at the time of Christ's second advent. All of these views are more or less faulty. He has the power necessary to produce such a transformation.—**According to the working whereby he is able also to subdue all things unto himself.** On κατὰ τὴν ἐνέργειαν, see Eph. i. 19, where τοῦ κράτους τῆς ἰσχυος αὐτοῦ is added, while here we have τοῦ δύνασθαι αὐτὸν καὶ ὑποτάξαι αὐτῷ τὰ πάντα. Since all things are and must be subject to Him. He can *also* (καί) transform the (body μετασχηματίζειν); for the καί connects that verb with ὑποτάξαι. It is an *argumentum a majori* (ὑποτάξαι αὐτῷ τὰ πάντα) *ad minus* (μετασχηματίζειν). Comp. 1 Cor. xv. 25–28; 50–57. It is incorrect for HÖLEMANN to connect δύνασθαι and ὑποτάξαι by καί, as if Paul would say that He is able to do all things and subject all things to Himself. [Τὰ πάντα is stronger with the article: not only this, but *all the things* together which require infinite power (comp. ver. 8).—H.]

CHAP. IV. Ver. 1. **Therefore** (ὥστε) introduces the conclusion, as in ii. 12. The section extends from iii. 1 to iv. 1, not merely from iii. 17 to iii. 21 (MEYER); for στήκετε ἐν κυρίῳ points back to χαίρετε ἐν κυρίῳ. [So extended a reference of ὥστε is uncommon and not necessary here. In view of the glorious destiny which awaits those whose citizenship is above, they should persevere and not frustrate such a hope (vers. 20, 21). Comp. 1 Cor. xv. 58.—H.]—**My brethren dearly beloved and longed for, my joy and crown,** is an expression of his love and recognition of them. Ἀδελφοί μου indicates the relation of fellow-believers with respect to the personal fellowship, which not only renders the Philippians an object of special love (ἀγαπητοί), but also of earnest longing (καὶ ἐπιπόθητοι; comp. i. 8). [The Apostle's separation from them was so painful because his affection for them was so strong—H.] Χαρά marks the personal, στέφανός μου the official relation: they are the joy of his *heart* and the honor of his *office* (SCHENKEL). The first expression refers to the present, the second reaches onward into the future. [The στέφανος among the Greeks was the emblem of victory, and not of regal power or dignity, which was denoted by διάδημα. On this distinction see SMITH'S *Dictionary of the Bible*, vol. i. p. 597 (Amer. ed.) Hence "his converts will be his wreath of victory;" for it will appear that he "did not run in vain," (ii. 26), and he will receive the successful athlete's reward. Comp. 1 Cor. ix. 25 (LIGHTFOOT).—H.]—**So stand fast in the Lord** (οὕτως στήκετε ἐν κυρίῳ); *i. e.*, as I and those who walk with me stand (iii. 17) and as I have exhorted you (iii. 1 sq.) Comp. i. 27. BENGEL, incorrectly, *ita, ut statis, state* [which disagrees with ii. 17.—H.].—**Beloved** (ἀγαπητοί) thus repeated shows his ardent affection for them.

DOCTRINAL AND ETHICAL.

1. The instinct of imitation gives force to the power of example; and the Apostle here does not present merely his own apostolic character, but joins with himself those who walk with him.—Sympathy and community of feeling render specially effective an example which embodies ethical views and principles. Hence precisely in the section where the citizenship of Christians in heaven is brought forward, this appeal is specially appropriate. Manifold as may be the forms of life in individuals, they are yet features of one image; they harmonize with each other, are not discordant; the many reflect one type (τυπός). The power and frequency of evil example (1 Cor. xv. 33) make it the more necessary to regard the Apostle's exhortation.

2. Enmity to the cross of Christ, which takes offence at Christ's form as a sufferer, and His

path of suffering wherein His followers ought to walk, has its ground not exclusively indeed, but to a great extent, in a sensual character, subject to the lust of the world, by which many are governed even in the church. From an occasional, easy, and subtle service of the senses it may come to be uninterrupted and overbearing. Gentleness towards the natural man is cruelty towards the spiritual. Forbearance towards sensual desire ends in the loss of eternal glory, and that which passes current under the forms of conventional propriety, is in truth often a shame and disgrace.

3. The stand-point in the Christian life which fixes the eye on the future, the familiarity with God which maintains a close connection with the church, militant on earth but triumphant in heaven, and does not suffer the child of God to forget his eternal inheritance, affords the surest protection against evil example, and gives to good example its strongest attractive power.

4. [NEANDER:—The earthly mind Paul would say (vers. 19–21) must be far from us, who are Christians; 'for our conversation,' (more correctly 'citizenship') is in heaven.' His meaning is, that Christians, as to their life, their walk, belong even now to heaven; in the whole direction of their life existing there already.—This he deduces from their relation to Christ, their fellowship with Him to whom they are inseparably united, so that where He is there are they also. While here, they are sustained by the consciousness that Christ now lives in heaven, manifested to believers, though hidden from the world. Thither is their gaze directed, as their longings rise towards a Saviour, who will come again from thence to make them wholly like Himself, to fashion them wholly after His own glorious pattern, to transform them wholly into the heavenly. Hence Paul says: "From whence also we look for the Saviour, the Lord Jesus Christ; who shall change the body of our humiliation, that it may be fashioned like unto his glorious body, according to the working whereby he is able even to subdue all things unto himself." There is not presented here a resurrection, as a restoration merely of the same earthly body in the same earthly form; but, on the contrary, a glorious transformation, proceeding from the divine, the all-subduing power of Christ; so that believers, free from all the defects of the earthly existence, released from all its barriers, may reflect the full image of the heavenly Christ in their whole glorified personality. in the soul pervaded by the divine life and its now perfectly assimilated glorified organ. —H.]

5. [CHR. WORDSWORTH:—Christ, at His own transfiguration, gave a pledge and glimpse of the future glorious transformation of the risen body, and thus prepared the apostles to *suffer* with Him on earth, in order that they may be *glorified* forever with Him, in body and soul, in heaven (*N. T. Commentary*, vol. ii. p. 357).—H.]

HOMILETICAL AND PRACTICAL.

In lack of faith is found the cause of lack of joy.—There is no true renewal without humbly going to the cross of Christ. The bodies of many who profess to be renewed, are temples of the god of the belly and of his servants to whom Christ's cross is so entirely an offence, that they are even its enemies.—He who does not see the Easter sun rising behind the cross on Golgotha is no true Christian, does not cling fast to the good example of the apostles, and the faithful in the church, and becomes himself an evil example which may frighten away and even destroy others.

STARKE:—Not all who point out the way to heaven will themselves be received into it. Many helped to build the ark of Noah who did not enter it.—Thou rejoicest when thou canst lay off an old garment and put on a new one: why art thou troubled because thy body shall experience corruption? By this means it lays aside not only what is worthless but attains to a glorious transformation (ver. 21).

RIEGER:—Our house, home, city, and fatherland where we belong, the seeking and hoping for which govern all our thoughts, are not mere fancies to be grasped only by the imagination, but exist in heaven; God has prepared them there; and faith in His word affords us a complete representation of them.

GERLACH:—Every one who is not redeemed by Christ's cross from sin and from the present evil world, serves his flesh and minds earthly things, though his imagination take ever so exalted flights, though he be a philosopher, or a slave to grovelling lusts.—No Christian can find perfect rest until even the last trace of sin is overcome and destroyed: hence his life upon earth is a life of waiting and longing.

SCHLEIERMACHER:—If a man still values and seeks sensual good he is then an enemy of the *cross* of Christ. If he has earthly honor in view, and desires to distinguish himself before the world, he is then an enemy of the *shame* of Christ which accompanied His sufferings.—Eternal life is not to be thought of apart from a man's reconciliation with himself and with Christ, who has left peace as His most beautiful legacy to His followers.

HEUBNER:—They who will not recognize the crucified Redeemer as their only righteousness, who are proud of their legal virtue, are as much enemies of the cross of Christ as those who from a fleshly mind will not follow the crucified Redeemer, nor crucify their flesh together with its lusts and desires.—Pride and the lust of the world can make a man an enemy of the cross of Christ.—The holiest thing may become an offence to a corrupt heart, and excite violent opposition.—Even evil examples must be salutary to the Christian, because they deter him from evil: they present it to him in all its fearfulness and render him anxious for himself.—The man who opposes the cross of Christ, labors for his own ruin.—That which is honorable with God, the worldly man does not understand at all.—The present body disturbs the heavenly life; and hence this body is to be glorified. The future body will promote, facilitate the spiritual life. We are to attain to a complete likeness to Christ, even the body is to become like His; but as the condition of this the soul here must first resemble His soul. The power of Christ extends to the new creation of our bodies and of the world.—Though difficult, the Christian may guard himself against the destructive influence of evil examples. 1) He has no lack of good examples around him; 2) He sees the fearfulness of evil examples; 3) He has a heavenly calling.—There is a Christian use of bad examples as well as good.

PASSAVANT:—This is the three-fold divine working of the one Redeemer; He has redeemed His people from the *curse* of sin through His blood; He redeems them more and more by His Holy Spirit from the *power* of sin, and He will finally redeem them from all *misery* and all oppression in this evil, godless world, and bring them to His heavenly kingdom.

[NEANDER:—Each one is required to apply to his own life the measure of spiritual discernment bestowed upon him (ver. 16).—All progressive revelation of the Spirit, all new light of which man is made partaker, presupposes a faithful application of what has previously been given (ver. 15).—If each one were careful to put in practice with strict fidelity his own measure of Christian knowledge, without contending with others about matters wherein they differ from himself, how many schisms might have been avoided in the church, how many differences might for its interest have been overcome and adjusted!—H.]

VI. SECTION FIFTH.

Concluding exhortations designed to secure co-operation between the Philippians and the Apostle.

CHAPTER IV. 2–20.

(1). *Exhortation to unity addressed to individuals.*

CHAP. IV. 2, 3.

2 I beseech Euodias [Euodia][1], and [I] beseech Syntyche, that they be of the same
3 mind in the Lord. (And) [Yea][2] I entreat thee also, true yoke fellow, help those
[these] women,[3] who labored [strove] with me in the gospel, with Clement also, and
with other[4] [others] my fellow laborers, whose names are in the book of life.

1 Ver. 1. [On this change of the name see notes below. The Geneva version has the feminine form of the name instead of the masculine. STEPHENS' text has Εὐωδίαν, which means 'fragrance;' but the correct reading is Εὐοδίαν, 'good way,' according to all the uncial manuscripts.—H.]

2 Ver. 2. [The common text has καί, but ναί is undoubtedly the correct reading —H.]

3 *Ibid.* [Our English version misleads the reader here. In the Greek the first pronoun (αὐταῖς, 'them'), refers to Euodia and Syntiche, and the second (αἵτινες='since they') assign them to the class of co-laborers with Paul whose toil and conflicts (συνῆθλησαν) they had shared. The translation therefore might be: 'help them, since they labored,' *etc.*—H.]

4 *Ibid.* [For this use of 'other' (=others) see the note on ii. 3. Instead of the appositional form it may be rendered: 'the rest of my co-laborers.'—H.]

EXEGETICAL AND CRITICAL.

Ver. 2. **I beseech Euodia, and I beseech Syntyche**, Ἐυοδίαν παρακαλῶ καὶ Συντύχην παρακαλῶ. From the general exhortation (ver. 1) the Apostle passes to one addressed to individuals. The relation of the persons being known to the readers, it was unnecessary to describe it. The repeated παρακαλῶ, I *exhort* (not so correctly *beseech*) indicates that each of them needed the admonition; they were both in fault. The repetition is not merely *ad vehementiam affectus significandam* (ERASMUS). The names, common also elsewhere, belong to women, as αὐταῖς (ver. 3) demands; but the persons are otherwise unknown. GROTIUS incorrectly regards both as men. HAMMOND regards only the second as a man, and BAUER both as parties. SCHWEGLER regards the first as the Jewish party, the second as the Gentile Christian party; but they did not labor with Paul (συνήθλησάν μοι). The Apostle exhorts:—**That they be of the same mind in the Lord** (τὸ αὐτὸ φρονεῖν ἐν κυρίῳ). See ii. 2. On this agreement the Apostle lays special stress; it belongs to the στήκετε ἐν κυρίῳ. They must in some way have been alienated, but on what occasion, in what cause or manner, is not stated or hinted. Hence it cannot be said that, as the expression is borrowed from ii. 2, the motives for this estrangement must have corresponded to those mentioned in ii. 3 (WIESINGER, DE WETTE). With as little reason can it be said that they are deaconesses. [Those who hold that such an order existed in the primitive church generally think that these women belonged to it, and that their variance was the more unworthy on that account.—H.]

Ver. 3. **Yea I entreat thee also, true yoke fellow.** Ναί, very common as *particula affirmantis*, but as *particula obsecrantis*, only elsewhere in Rev. xxii. 20. It indicates the seriousness of the affair to the Apostle that he turns with his entreaties (ἐρωτῶ), to still another (καί σε) besides the women. It is not clear who it is that he invokes in γνήσιε σύζυγε. The substantive, in the N. T. found only here, is plain from its opposite, ἑτεροζυγεῖν (2 Cor. vi. 14), as also from the use of ζυγός (figuratively: Matt. xi. 29, 30; Acts xv. 10; Gal. v. 1; literally, 1 Tim. vi. 1; Rev. vi. 5); hence partner, associate, and the relation of this person to Paul is described as very close, as that of one who draws at the same yoke with himself. It is a stricter connection than that of συνεργός. The epithet γνήσιε describes the nature and character of this person (ii. 20) as genuine, pure, true. Hence it cannot appear strange that Paul did not address him by name: every one is supposed to know him. It is incorrect to regard σύζυγε as a name (CHRYSOSTOM, MEYER, distinctly; WIESINGER with hesitation), as a designation of Epaphroditus (GROTIUS), or of Timothy (ESTIUS), for these could not have been addressed as in Philippi; or arbitrarily of Silas (BENGEL), of the husband of one of two women (the Greek interpreters), or of Paul's wife (CLEMENS ALEX., ERASMUS, *et al.*) contrary to the history (1 Cor. vii. 8) and against the grammar (masculine form). [The noun may be masculine or feminine, but the adj. has properly three terminations, and must be masculine here. Other conjectures, on the supposition that an anonymous person is meant are, that it may have been Luke who appears to have been absent from Rome when the Epistle was written (see on i. 1) or Epaphroditus (LIGHTFOOT) at the side of Paul as he wrote, and whom he addressed (παρακαλῶ) at the moment.—H.] LAURENT's view (*Neutest. Studien*, pp. 134–137) is worthy of notice. In reply to the assertion that the name Syzygus does not occur, he remarks that names are not objects of literature, but products of social or civil life, as for example, Onesimus, Tryphena, and Tryphosa (Rom. xvi. 12). He explains the passage thus: "Thou, who, a genuine Syzygus, hast already by thy birth (γνήσιε) and thy name been called to be a yoke fellow and helper of all laborers in the vineyard of the Lord, lay hold now also of the work together with these two sisters, that they through thy aid may carry it forward with one spirit, not as heretofore, in discord! For Paul does not mean to blame them (as in ii. 20) but to praise them, and hence would not imply that he has only one γνήσιον σύζυγον in Philippi." Like Εὐοδία (way of faith), Syntyche and Syzygus appear to him to have been names received after baptism, as in the case of others, whose names are more familiar to us. [The best view after all seems to be that of MEYER, LAURENT, and others, that Syzygus or Synzygus (σύνζυγος) is a proper name, borne by one who had been associated with Paul in Christian labors, who was at Philippi when the Apostle wrote the letter, and was well known there as deserving the encomium which this appeal to him implies. Paul nowhere uses this word (σύζυγος) of any one of his official associates, being used in fact nowhere else in the N. T.; it is found here in the midst of other proper names (vers. 2, 3); and the attributive γνήσιε corresponds finely and significantly to the appellative sense of such a name. That such an alliteration is not foreign to Paul's manner, see Philem., vers. 10, 11. The name, it is true, does not appear anywhere else; but many other names also are found only in single instances, and certainly many names to us must have been in use among the ancients which have not been transmitted at all. Paul himself repeatedly mentions persons in his epistles who are named only once, and a catalogue of names might be made out from the Acts of the Apostles, of those whose whole history for us lies in a single passage. See MEYER's *Brief an die Philipper* on iv. 3.—H.]—**Help these women** (συλλαμβάνου αὐταῖς) presents the object of the request. The verb (Luke v. 1) signifies 'to take hold vigorously with,' 'to assist one,' *i. e.*, here to re-establish harmony. It is not *ut habeant, unde se suosque sustentent* (GROTIUS), against the context.—**Who strove with me in the gospel**, states the motive for helping these women in the work of reconciliation. Hence he adds αἵτινες=*ut quæ* (see Eph. i. 23). Ἐν εὐαγγελίῳ marks the sphere, as in 1 Thes. iii. 2, in which they had labored with him (συνήθλησάν μοι). The verb points back to the beginning of Christianity at Philippi, when the women embraced it (Acts xvi. 13), and had exerted themselves to advance it. They had contended at Paul's side for the gospel, and ought not now to strive against one another, against Christianity and against Paul; they are so useful and deserving in other respects, they should be right also in their relation to each other.—**With Clement also, and with my other fellow-laborers** (μετὰ καὶ Κλήμεντος καὶ τῶν λοιπῶν συνεργῶν μου), brings to view the fact that various persons at Philippi at that time were harmoniously engaged in behalf of the gospel, men, as Clement and others, as well as (καί-καί) women associated with them. Paul thus exalts the merits of Syntyche and Euodia who labored in such company. Clement was a Philippian; which is evident, but nothing further, not even that he was a teacher (MEYER). We have no right to suppose him to have been Clemens Romanus (Catholics), or Flavius Clemens, Domitian's *patruelis* (BAUR). He does not of course mention the λοιποὶ συνεργοί by name, because it is superfluous, as in the case of the γνήσιος σύζυγος. [The closer proximity and the nature of the thought connect μετὰ συνεργῶν μου with συνήθλησαν, rather than with συλλαμβάνου αὐταῖς. The position and influence of the women as co-partners in Christian service with Paul and his associates rendered the spectacle and effects of such strife the more deplorable, and thus enforced the appeal (συλλαμβάνου) to strive the more earnestly to promote harmony between them.—H.]. In his joy on their account he adds:—**Whose names are in the book of life**, ὧν ὀνόματα ἐν βίβλῳ ζωῆς. [We are to refer ὧν ζωῆς to τῶν λοιπῶν apart from CLEMENT, because the Apostle having named the latter would recognize the others though unnamed by him, as yet having their names written in heaven (MEYER, ELLICOTT and others). This expression does not of itself decide whether these other fellow-laborers were living or dead, but certainly it is altogether improbable that Clement was the only one of them who still remained. —H.] The figurative expression was suggested perhaps by iii. 20, for the registers of the citizens of Israel, out of which one's name was erased on his decease prepared the way for the expression ספר חיים (Exodus xxxii. 32; Isa. iv. 3; Ezek. xiii. 9; Ps. lxix. 29; Dan. xii. 1) which was adopted in the N. T. (Luke x. 20; Acts iii. 5; xiii. 8; xvii. 8; xx. 15) in order to mark the certainty of the eternal inheritance, the blessedness which is to be reached by faithful striving. [It is clear from the expression "blotting out of the book," (Rev. iii. 5) that the image suggested no idea of absolute predestination. For the use of the phrase in Rabbinical writers see Wetstein here (LIGHTFOOT).—H.] Ἐστί is to be supplied, not the optative (BENGEL). It is the joyful certainty, not a wish that Paul has in mind here.

DOCTRINAL AND ETHICAL.

1. The servant of the word of God ought not only to exhort the whole church from the pulpit, but also with a special care for souls to warn individuals.

2. The pastor in his oversight of souls should not stand alone, but be aided by others properly qualified. The lay-element should be cultivated for the service of the church.

3. Goodness at the beginning does not protect one from a fall afterward, nor courageous striving for the gospel from ill-natured arrogance towards others, nor the vanquishing of outward foes from weak indulgence towards one's self.

4. The unity of the church as a body must extend into the narrowest circle of neighborhood and home.

5. He who will exhort, incite others, must generously recognize what is praiseworthy, and attach himself to the good which already exists.

6. Women are to be highly esteemed in the church for their services; but they should act with men (μετά), and not work independently.

HOMILETICAL AND PRACTICAL.

STARKE:—There are peace-disturbers enough, but not so many peace-makers. To the work then! and help check those who love contention, and thus make peace!—Even women are to help in extending the kingdom of God with their prayers, gifts, good counsel, *etc.*, and to contend fearlessly for the gospel.

RIEGER:—A tried, approved mediator can often by the grace of God adjust many difficulties.

SCHLEIERMACHER:—Let us strive with all our powers to *extend* Christian fellowship, and yet not weaken it.

HEUBNER:—To have a genuine colleague is not a privilege granted to every one (ver. 3).

---

(2) *General exhortation to Christian joy.*

(CHAPTER IV. 4–7).

4, 5 Rejoice in the Lord always: (and)[1] again I [will] say, rejoice. Let your modera-
6 tion [gentleness] be known to all men: The Lord is at hand. Be careful for no-
thing; but in everything, by prayer and supplication, with thanksgiving, let your
7 request [requests] be known unto [before] God. And the peace of God, which pas-
seth [every] understanding, shall keep [guard] your hearts and [your] minds through
[in] Christ Jesus.

1 Ver. 4 [This 'and in the A. V. answers to καί in the common text, which is, however, unwarranted. For the asyndeton which thus occurs, see WINER'S *Gram.*, p. 537. See the notes below on ἐρῶ.—H.]

EXEGETICAL AND CRITICAL.

Ver. 4. **Rejoice in the Lord always** (χαίρετε ἐν κυρίῳ πάντοτε) takes up in connection with ver. 3 (ὧν ὀνόματα ἐν βίβλῳ ζωῆς) the theme of the epistle. See iii. 1. A tone of special emphasis rests on "always" (πάντοτε): there lies the difficulty and the glory of rejoicing in the Lord. —**Again I will say, rejoice** (πάλιν ἐρῶ, χαίρετε) repeats the command with emphasis.—BENGEL incorrectly joins πάντοτε with πάλιν.—[The verb (ἐρῶ) is future, not present, as in the A. V. This reiterated exhortation is the more remarkable when we recollect that Paul as he wrote or dictated the letter had his right arm chained to the arm of a Roman soldier, or at all events was a prisoner under the eye of a sentinel who never left him (see Acts xxviii. 20).—H.]

Ver. 5. **Let your forbearance be known to all men**, though without any external notation, connects itself logically with χαίρετε, since joy has of itself a tendency to make us mild and gentle: *gaudium in domino parit veram æquitatem erga proximum*, (BENGEL). Τὸ ἐπιεικὲς ὑμῶν is stronger than the substantive, ἐπιείκεια (2 Cor. x. 1; Acts xxiv. 4), and implies that this quality (τὸ ἐπιεικές) pervades the entire nature of the ὑμῶν. Comp. iii. 8; Rom. ii. 4; Heb. vi. 17. It signifies mildness, forbearance, (used with ἄμαχος, 1 Tim. iii. 3; Tit. iii. 2; between εἰρηνική and εὐπειθής, Jas. iii. 17; with ἀγαθός, 1 Pet. ii. 18), hence not 'becoming conduct' (MATTHIES). It is to be known to all (γνωσθήτω πᾶσιν ἀνθρώποις) without exception, to strangers, and so much the more to neighbors, because they have such occasion to see it manifested towards themselves and towards others. The context leads us to think more directly of the adjustment of difficulties, the removal of dissension (vers. 2, 3) for effecting which the gentleness which spares the delinquent is a great assistance. [The ἐπιεικὲς ὑμῶν stands in contrast to the ἀκριβοδίκαιος, as being satisfied with less than is one's due. ARIST. *Eth. Nic.*, v. 10 (LIGHTFOOT).—H.]—**The Lord is at hand** (ὁ κύριος ἐγγύς) in whom they are to rejoice, hence Christ, under whose eye they are to walk and act, who will also judge them: *judex vobis propitius, vindex in malos* (BENGEL). This is a strong motive to the exercise of forbearance. We are not to refer κύριος to God (CALVIN), since πρὸς τὸν θεόν follows in ver. 6, and the subject here is not that of the providence of God, but the παρουσία or advent of Christ. MEYER incorrectly joins it with what follows. [This nearness of Christ admits of other explanations. It may mean that He is ever near to His people as their efficient supporter and helper, so that with such an arm to defend them they have nothing to fear from the power or malice of their enemies (comp. Matt. xiii. 11; 1 Pet. iv. 7); or, more probably, that He is always near to them in point of time, will soon come to relieve them of their cares and trials, and receive them to their appointed rewards and rest in heaven (John xiv. 3; Rom. xiii. 11, sq.) See note on i. 7. There is no necessary, certainly no exclusive, reference here to a definite expectation of the near advent of Christ, and the end of the world.*—H.]

Ver. 6. **Be careful for nothing,** (μηδὲν μεριμνᾶτε) enjoins freedom from anxiety since *gaudium in domino legitimam securitatem in suis rebus parit* (BENGEL). Μηδέν, accusative of the object, excludes every subject of harassing care, whether fruitless labor or the events which precede the Lord's advent (ver. 5); hence not anxious solicitude merely is forbidden (GROTIUS).—**But in every thing** (ἀλλ' ἐν παντί) is the antithesis to μηδέν (comp. Eph. v. 24).—**By prayer and supplication, with thanksgiving, let your requests be known unto God,** (τῇ προσευχῇ καὶ τῇ δεήσει μετὰ εὐχαριστίας τὰ αἰτήματα ὑμῶν γνωριζέσθω πρὸς τὸν θεόν) is the antithesis of μεριμνᾶτε. He who rejoices in the Lord has not to do with 'earthly things' (τὰ ἐπίγεια, iii. 19). Τὰ αἰτήματα ὑμῶν, are the contents or objects of the prayers, *desideria vestra* (Luke xxiii. 24; 1 John v. 15). The verb γνωριζέσθω has a threefold limitation: 1) the way (τῇ προσευχῇ καὶ τῇ δεήσει) which the article points out as the appointed one, and its repetition as consisting of two parts or acts (on the difference see Eph. vi. 18); 2) the accompaniment: μετὰ εὐχαριστίας (comp. Eph. v. 4; Col. ii. 7; iv. 2), which should never be wanting in prayer and request; and 3) the direction (πρὸς τὸν θεόν) to whom the prayer should be directed. We are not to run to men with our complaints and lamentations. BENGEL well points out the connection of vers. 4–6: *tristitiam et curam comitatur morositas.*

Ver. 7. **And the peace of God, which passeth every understanding.** Καί adds now a promise. Joy in the Lord is accompanied by the *peace of God, etc.* The genitive marks the author (see Eph. i. 2; Col. iii. 15; and comp. WINER'S *Gram.*, p. 186), and the participial clause the value of the peace which as the context shows must be understood as an inward state or peace of soul, in contrast with violence (ver. 5), anxiety (ver. 6) and in connection with joy (ver. 4). Hence 'the peace' (εἰρήνη) is not harmony with one another (MEYER), which does not accord with the following predicates, nor reconciliation with God (ERASMUS), which peace of soul presupposes, and on which it is founded. This peace of God is a possession defined as ἡ ὑπερέχουσα πάντα νοῦν, *i. e.*, towering above (ii. 3; iii. 8; Eph. iii. 19) the reach of man's understanding, however strong it may be (πάντα νοῦν), (Eph. iv. 17). The comparison is between peace as the object of emotion and experience, and the understanding as the perceptive or rational faculty, and not between the incomprehensibility of this peace and the understanding (ERASMUS, *res felicior, quam ut humana mens queat percipere*, and so MEYER *et al.*) [According to MEYER'S view (1859) the comparison lies in the efficacy of God's peace, on the one hand, and of man's reason or understanding on the other, to lift the soul above disquietude and the power of the world. So essentially LIGHTFOOT: '*Surpassing every device* or *counsel*' of man, *i. e.*, which is far better, which produces a higher satisfaction, than all punctilious self-assertion, all anxious forethought. ELLICOTT translates: '*which overpasseth every understanding*,' *i. e.*, 'which transcends every effort and attempt on the part of the understanding to grasp and realize it.' The similarity between the language here and Eph. iii. 20 speaks almost decisively for the latter and more obvious interpretation: 'Who is able to do exceedingly abundantly above all that we ask or think,' αἰτούμεθα ἢ νοοῦμεν.—H.] We are not to think at all here of the doubting or perplexed understanding (DE WETTE).—**Shall keep your hearts and your minds in Christ Jesus,** characterizes the efficacy of the peace in question. The verb (φρουρήσει) signifies *to guard*, while the tense marks the continuance of this protection; it is a promise, assurance, not a wish (VULG., *custodiat, et al.*) The object τὰς καρδίας ὑμῶν καὶ τὰ νοήματα ὑμῶν, is the inner personality, made emphatic and exhaustive by the repeated article and pronoun. BENGEL: *cor sedes cogitationum*. Comp. 2 Cor. iii. 14, 15. Thus the whole and its parts, the principal and derivative, in the individual's life, are preserved *adversus omnes insultus et curas* (BENGEL); or ὥστε μένειν καὶ μὴ ἐκπεσεῖν αὐτοῦ, τῆς πίστεως (CHRYSOSTOM). Comp. 1 Pet. i. 5. [The νοήματα reside in and issue from the καρδία (comp. 2 Cor. iii. 14, 15): for in the Apostle's language καρδία is the seat of thought as well as of feeling (LIGHTFOOT).—H.] This result is ac-

* [NEANDER suggests still another, or at least a modified interpretation. The consciousness that "the Lord is nigh," furnishes a motive for the exercise of forbearance under provocation. His persecuted people walk in the sight of the Lord and dare not give way to passion in the near presence of Him, who endured every wrong with heavenly patience and long-suffering. This consciousness that the Lord is near will also restrain them from wishing to anticipate His justice, to take the work of retribution into their own hands.—H.]

complished ἐν Χριστῷ Ἰησοῦ, and hence apart from Him it does not spring from any inherent efficacy in the peace itself. Without His aid it is not possible to abide with Him, to obtain or to keep His gifts.

DOCTRINAL AND ETHICAL.

1. Joy in the Lord is the theme of this epistle, and the chief feature in the portrait of the Christian. On this frame of mind much depends: gentleness towards all men, in word and deed, since it causes many a provocation to pass unnoticed, or to be borne patiently; freedom from care and delight in prayer, for the Christian knows and frequents the way to God, and casts all his care upon Him who cares for him, being driven by care to prayer, and by prayer driving away care; inward peace, which God has wrought, and continues to strengthen in the soul.

2. Our consciousness of the nearness of the Lord, is strengthened by our very joy in the Lord, which is only perfected in the other world, so that we feel His coming to be a blessing, and desire it (ver. 5).

3. The prayer for what is lacking should never be separated from thanksgiving for what has been granted (ver. β).

4. All that moves, disquiets thee, may and should become a subject of prayer, but the sort of prayer, manifold as may be the reason for it, is definite, and not every prayer avails.

HOMILETICAL AND PRACTICAL.

STARKE:—Two things trouble us: sin and affliction; on the other hand we find here a double incitement to rejoice in the Lord; Rejoice!—A Christian must be no towering tulip, but rather a humble violet, dispensing everywhere a sweet perfume.—Thou lion and tyrant in thy house! When an honorable man, a stranger approaches thee, thou ceasest perhaps to scold, and curse, and rage: why hast thou not as much reverence for the Lord who is near thee?—To care is God's part, but to labor and in prayer to commit the issue to Him, is ours—To-day peace, to-morrow war! So it was formerly in the world, so it is now and so it will be to the end; but the peace of God is an eternal peace.

RIEGER:—Everything in the Lord's life, character, and experience is indeed a cause of joy to you. His condescension in His incarnation and birth, His walk in the world, His sufferings, cross, and death, His life and glory, His present concealment in God, His revelation from heaven ever near and nearer to us.—One may have the inward ground of joy in the Lord, though he has not the same susceptibility at one time as at another.—Yet joy in the Lord does not lead one to violent outbursts, or on the other hand to sit indolently, but to work, and it is this exercise which keeps it pure. A joyful follower of our Lord Jesus Christ, has to deal with different men, who in many ways have need of his forbearance.—Sometimes, indeed, even our reason performs good service against care, and promotes contentment of mind. But too often our reason is itself the fountain of many cares, or at least meets with cases where it is entirely helpless.—Out of the heart the life flows; if it is not protected it evaporates, and the senses bring in many a thing from the world, which has power to disturb our contentment.

GERLACH:—Let the Lord who in grace and judgment is ever near His people, care for all things. Address no prayer to Him, even out of the deepest distress, without thanksgiving; for even in the greatest misery you have more reason for thanksgiving and joy than for sorrow and complaint. Thus you can maintain joy in the Lord and gentleness towards men, at the same time.

[ROBERT HALL:—Seek repose by prayer. If your mind be overcharged or overwhelmed with trouble and anxiety, go into the presence of God. Spread your case before Him. Though He knows the desires of your hearts, yet He has declared He "will be sought after;" He will be "inquired of to do it for you." Go, therefore, into the presence of that God who will at once tranquillize your spirit, give you what you wish, or make you more happy without it, and who will be your everlasting consolation, if you trust in Him. He will breathe peace into your soul, and command tranquillity in the midst of the greatest storms. How much are they to be pitied who never pray. The world is to them all gloom and disappointment; for *there* they see none of the kindness and protection of our heavenly Father. We do not wonder that the sorrow of the world worketh death, with the distresses, afflictions, and disappointments to which human nature is exposed (ver. 6).—H.]

SCHLEIERMACHER:—What then are the chief things in the holy joy of Christmas? 1) Joy in the entire Lord and Redeemer. 2) A common feeling of love and joy (*a*) in the consciousness of the kindness and favor of God, our heavenly Father, which have been manifested in Christ Jesus; (*b*) in the purity and serenity of Christian joy. 3) Joy not over this or that aspect of heart and life, but over universal inward development.

PASSAVANT:—This gentleness manifests itself at one time as equanimity and patience under all circumstances, among all men, and in manifold experiences; at another as integrity in business relations; as justice, forbearance, and goodness, in exercising power; as impartiality and mercy in judging; as noble yielding, joyful giving, and patient enduring and forgiving.—As the epistle for the fourth Sunday in Advent.

HEUBNER:—The true joy of the Christian in Advent. 1. Its nature. It springs from the past, the present, and the future coming of the Lord. 2. Its effects: gentleness, freedom from care, disposition to pray, peace. It is the best preparation for Christmas.

LÖHE:—The approach of the festival as typical of the second coming of Christ greets us with a four-fold trumpet-blast: 1) Joy in Christ; 2) gentleness and goodness; 3) prayer and thanksgiving; 4) a prolonged sweet tone of peace, which is higher than all reason.

AHLFELD:—Supplication and thanksgiving are better than care. 1. Care gnaws the marrow and pith out of God's gifts. 2. Rise above it and leave it to your Lord. 3. Live in prayer and thanksgiving. He will gladly help you.

Law and Testimony. It is necessary to call solemnly to mind the much forgotten second coming of the Lord. 1) It brings holy joy in every way; 2) it is a rampart and wall against all hate and harm; 3) it inspires care-conquering prayer; 4) it enfolds us in God's peace.

PRÖHLE:—The Christian disposition of mind in the holy time of Advent. 1) Holy joy; 2) tender love of men; 3) firm trust in God; 4) divine peace.—Difference between the holy mind of Christians and the wanton mind of the world. 1) The sources: the former springs from believing, sanctified hearts; the latter from a fortunate gift of nature, or it is the fruit of the sinful flesh. 2) Expressions: the former in religious joys, in lawful earthly pleasures used with moderation, a gentle, loving spirit, with God before the eye and in the heart; the latter, in sensual joys and violent passions. 3) Duration: the former always, the latter now and then. 4) Effects: the former liberates from care and melancholy, and renders one inclined to and qualified for the good; the latter leads away from God into sin.—The Lord is near! The thought (1) sanctifies our joys; (2) dissipates our cares; (3) consecrates our prayers; (4) fills us with love and forbearance towards our neighbor.

[J. S. HOWSON:—The Apostle Paul illustrated his precepts by example. He was remarkable for his habit of combining thanksgiving with his prayers (see ver. 6).—I know of no more instructive study than to go over all the ground from Romans to Philemon, taking the structure of the Epistles as we find it, and noticing these streams of prayer and praise, sometimes as they appear separately, very frequently together. We have grand doxologies after the commencement of some great truth, or at the prospect of some glorious future, as in the letter to the Romans, (xi. 33); "O the depth of the riches; both of the wisdom and the knowledge of God!" or in the First to the Corinthians (ix. 57): "Thanks be to God which giveth us the victory, through our Lord Jesus Christ!" The habit strikes us more forcibly when the reference is to something *personal*. Thus, at the mention of the long-delayed, but at last accomplished meeting with Titus (2 Cor. ii. 14): "Now thanks be to God, which always causeth us to triumph in Christ!" Even in his statement of a fact, Paul uses a eucharistic form (Rom. vii. 25): "Who shall deliver me? I thank God through Jesus Christ our Lord." "Thanks be to God which put this into the heart of Titus." 2 Cor. viii. 16. "I thank God that I baptized none save Crispus and Gaius." 1 Cor. i. 14. "I thank my God, I speak with tongues more than you all." 1 Cor. xiv. 18. Even when he speaks of food, the name which he employs is: "That for which I give thanks." And what is said of thanksgiving may similarly be said of prayer. Thus, with the same kind of exuberant impulse, after a doctrinal statement: "For this cause I bow my knees unto the Father of our Lord Jesus Christ, that He would grant you to be strengthened with might by His Spirit in the inner man." Eph. iii. 14–16. So when he has been describing his projected journey: "Now the God of peace be with you." Rom. xv. 33. So when he has been giving advice to an individual: "Consider what I say; and the Lord give thee understanding in all things." 2 Tim. ii. 7. Evidently with St. Paul the law of Prayer is the law of Praise. Supplication and gratitude are almost always inter-linked together; or at least when one is present, the other is seldom far absent. "I will pray with the Spirit, and I will sing with the Spirit: I will pray with the understanding, and I will sing with the understanding." 1 Cor. xiv. 15. In the Christian life he clearly assumes that Thanksgiving will follow easily in the footsteps of Prayer, and that Prayer will be mindful to fill the place which has just been occupied by Thanksgiving. Two parallel sentences from the Ephesians may conclude this imperfect list of illustrations: "Giving thanks always for all things unto God and the Father in the name of our Lord Jesus Christ." Eph. v. 20. "Praying always with all prayer and supplication in the Spirit, and watching thereunto with all perseverance." Eph. vi. 18. Different as St. Paul's Epistles are in most respects from the Psalms of David, they resemble them in this combination. The lesson derived from both, and in both cases alike enforced by the writer's example, is this: "Offer unto God thanksgiving; and call upon Him in the time of trouble; so will He hear thee, and thou shalt praise Him," (Ps. l. 14, 15). See *Lectures on the Character of St. Paul*, p. 150 (London, 1864).—H.]

---

(3). *General exhortation to Christian progress.*

(CHAPTER IV. 8, 9)

8 Finally, brethren, whatsoever things are true, whatsoever things are honest [honorable] whatsoever things are just, whatsoever things are pure, whatsoever things
are lovely, whatsoever things are of good report; if there be any virtue, and if
9 there be any praise, think on these things. Those [The] things which ye have both
[also] learned, and received, and heard, and seen in me [these] do: and the God of
peace shall be with you.

EXEGETICAL AND CRITICAL.

Ver. 8. **Finally,** τὸ λοιπόν, introduces the conclusion, but does not strictly resume iii. 1 again (MATTHIES). [This expression indicates an approach to the end, and as MEYER remarks, its recurrence here shows Paul's reluctance to say the last word of farewell.—H.] It is here added how and wherein the peace of God (ver. 7) is to manifest itself; and as ver. 7 states what God does, so this declares what remains for men to do. (DE WETTE). The address, **brethren,** ἀδελφοί, is prompted by the fervor of his feelings; and to this fervor is due also the six times repeated ὅσα. [The words which follow here may be said to be arranged in a descending scale. The first four describe the character of the actions themselves, the two former, ἀληθῆ, σεμνά, being absolute, the two latter δίκαια, ἁγνά, relative; the fifth and sixth προσφιλῆ, εὔφημα, point to the moral approbation which they conciliate; while the seventh and eighth ἀρετή, ἔπαινος, in which the form of expression is changed (εἴτις for ὅσα), are thrown in as an after-thought that no motive may be omitted (LIGHTFOOT).—H.]—**Whatsoever things are true,** ὅσα ἐστὶν ἀληθῆ. The ὅσα indicates that all things, without exception, which the category embraces are meant; while ἐστίν implies their actual existence in contrast with the arbitrary supposition of men. 'Αληθῆ is the morally true, in harmony with the objective rule of morality in the gospels. See Eph. iv. 21. It should neither be limited by *in sermone* (BENGEL) nor be taken as merely subjective in the sense of sincerity (ERASMUS).—**Whatsoever things are honorable** (ὅσα σεμνά), designates things of a worthy character corresponding to the essence of the ἀλήθεια (1 Tim. ii. 2; Tit. ii. 2). [They are such as men esteem, regard with respect, veneration.—H.]—**Whatsoever things are just** (ὅσα δίκαια) signifies the things which accord with the law, as in Eph. iv. 24, and should not be limited by *erga alios* (BENGEL).—**Whatsoever things are pure** (ὅσα ἁγνά) describes the same qualities or acts intrinsically (2 Cor. vi. 6; vii. 11; Jas. iii. 17; 1 Tim. v. 22; 1 John iii. 3; ἁγνῶς i. 17). It is not simply 'chaste' (GROTIUS).—**Whatsoever things are lovely, whatsoever things are of good report** (ὅσα προσφιλῆ, ὅσα εὔφημα) comprises again a two-fold relation; both words have reference to the estimation of men, the first however designating what is valuable and dear to the heart of man, (προσφιλῆ), the second (εὔφημα) what is praised, esteemed among men, in word and deed. The first should not be supplemented by τοῖς πιστοῖς καὶ τῷ θεῷ (CHRYSOSTOM), or restricted by τῷ θεῷ (THEODORET), or interpreted as *benigna, quæ gratiosum faciunt hominem* (GROTIUS). The second does not refer to *quæ bonam famam conciliant* (ERASMUS), or to *sermones, qui aliis bene precantur* (STORR), which is opposed to the context.—**If there be any virtue, and if there be any praise,** sums up the preceding; εἴ τις ἀρετή refers to the first two pairs, καὶ εἴ τις ἔπαινος to the last pair. The former, ἀρετή, used of God, 1 Pet. ii. 9; 2 Pet. i. 3, here and in 2 Pet. i. 5, of men, signifies moral rectitude in disposition and action; the latter (ἔπαινος) the moral judgment of men, hence not *res laudabilis* (CALVIN, *et al.*); virtue (ἀρετή) calls forth praise (ἔπαινον): this presupposes that.—Thus what is in a Christian sense moral, is described in manifold relations, and the Apostle now says of it:—**Think on these things,** ταῦτα λογίζεσθε, not the same as φρονεῖτε. The Philippians should choose these things as the subject of their meditation, have them ever in their thoughts.

Ver. 9. The train of thought leads us here to the province of action.—**The things which ye have also learned, and received, and heard, and seen in me.** The first καί points to the ἐστίν with ὅσα. [Hence it does not signify *both* (A. V.), but *also, i. e.*, it adds the Apostle's example and teaching to the claims of the virtues themselves. LIGHTFOOT makes the first καί responsive to the third, and so connects the verbs in pairs.—H.] 'Εμάθετε καὶ παρελάβετε, refer to instruction, the former indicating the act in this process, as that of the Philippians, the latter, as that of Paul. The second intimates that the first could not have taken place without the second. 'Ηκούσατε καὶ εἴδετε refer to examples of which the Philippians had knowledge by report or from personal observation, and which καί joins with the instruction (ἐμάθετε). 'Εν ἐμοί belongs to both verbs, for Paul is an example in word as well as act. Therefore καί-καί-καί is not "as well as," nor ἐμάθετε *genus*, and the others *species* (HÖLEMANN), nor does ἠκούσατε refer to preaching (CALVIN, *et al.*).—**These do** (ταῦτα πράσσετε) is parallel to ταῦτα λογίζεσθε; both together, thinking and doing, are what Paul enjoins.—**And the God of peace shall be with you,** καὶ ὁ θεὸς τῆς εἰρήνης ἔσται μεθ' ὑμῶν. The particle connects the result (='and so,') with the injunction. The promise points to ver. 7. He has the peace of God as his protection, who has the God of peace with him and in him.

DOCTRINAL AND ETHICAL.

1. Salvation with all its inward wealth and manifold relations, is a unit. It harmonizes with the standard (ἀληθῆ) immanent in it, whereon depends its dignity, its worth (σεμνά), agrees with the rule made objective in the law (δίκαια), so that it is unspotted (ἁγνά), has its echo in the creature (προσφιλῆ), and in the circles formed by it (εὔφημα).

2. Salvation is obtained through a saving union of doctrine and example.

3. He who rightfully claims salvation in word, has resting upon him still more the duty of bearing witness to it in his life.

[ANDREW FULLER:—"The God of peace shall be with you" (ver. 9). We cannot experience the peace of God, and joy in the Holy Ghost, unless we have the testimony of our own consciences that in simplicity and godly sincerity we have had our conversation in the world.—What is this peace? The Christian, the minister who enjoys a well-grounded persuasion that he possesses the favor of Jesus Christ, whose confidence is in Him who sits at the helm of the universe, who walks with God and has the testimony of a good conscience, possesses the peace of God.—H.]

HOMILETICAL AND PRACTICAL.

STARKE:—Christians have no need of the teachings of pagan morality, for no virtue can be found, or anything else praiseworthy and glorious, which is not found in God's word.—Whoever will have the blessings of salvation, must submit to the divine plan of salvation.

SCHLEIERMACHER:—In regard to what is honorable, just, pure, lovely, and of good report, there is a true and a false standard, and for this reason the Apostle here places the true at the beginning, that when the following exhortations are presented this fact, which our experience so often discloses, may at once occur to the Christian, and he may be led to examine himself and see whether he also is everywhere seeking for the true.

HEUBNER:—The Christian should not be one, but many-sided; he should strive after all that is excellent.—The true type of Christian virtue rejects all falsehood.—KLOPSTOCK inserts ver. 8 in his ode to the Redeemer at the close of the Messiah.

[ROBERT HALL:—There are very different virtues. If we would be complete in our Christian profession, we must attend to *all* the virtues of it;—whatsoever things are true, honest, just, or lovely, as well as those sublimer things which more immediately respect God and Christ, and heaven and eternity. The beauty of the Christian character is not formed so much by the gigantic size of one virtue, as from the harmony and consistency of all. Never, then, let it appear which virtue has been most approved by you, but cultivate *every* virtue (ver. 8).—H.]

---

(4). The Apostle's thankfulness for the gifts of love which he has received from them.

(CHAPTER IV. 10–20).

His joy on account of such friendship (ver. 10); *correction of a possible misunderstanding on their part* (vers. 11–13); *grateful recognition of their kindness* (vers. 14–17); *and assurance of the divine blessing* (vers. 18–20).

10 But I rejoiced in the Lord greatly, that now at the last your care of me hath
flourished again; wherein ye were also careful, but ye lacked [were lacking]
11 opportunity. Not that I speak in respect of want, for I have learned, in whatsoever
12 state I am (therewith) to be content. I know both [also][1] how to be abased, and
I know how to abound; every where [in everything], and in all things I am in-
13 structed both to be full and to be hungry, both to abound and to suffer need. I
14 can do all things through Christ[2] [in him] who strengtheneth me. Notwithstanding
15 ye have well done that ye did communicate with [shared in] my affliction. Now,
ye Philippians, [also] know (also) that in the beginning of the gospel, when I de-
parted from Macedonia, no church communicated with me as concerning [for an ac-
16 count of] giving and receiving, but ye only. For even in Thessalonica ye sent once
17 and again unto[3] my necessity. Not because [that] I desire a [the] gift: but I de-
18 sire [the] fruit that (may) abounds to your account. But I have all, and abound:
I am full, having received of Epaphroditus the things which were sent from you,
19 an odour of a sweet smell, a sacrifice acceptable, well pleasing to God. But my
God shall supply all your need according to his riches[4] in glory by [in] Christ Je-
20 sus. Now unto God and our Father be glory forever and ever. Amen.

[1] Ver. 12. [We are to read καί after the first οἶδα, and not δέ as in the common text. The witnesses are decisive. So TISCHENDORF, MEYER, ELLICOTT, WORDSWORTH, and others decide.—H.]

[2] Ver. 13. Only a few manuscripts add Χριστῷ. ℵ (inserted afterwards) A B C *et al.*, omit it. It is an exegetical variation. [The change makes the expression like 1 Tim. i. 12, and that conformity may have been the motive for the change.—H.]

[3] Ver. 16. [Some good authorities omit εἰς after δίς, but it is undoubtedly genuine, having been overlooked in some copies in consequence of the successive similar endings.—H.]

[4] Ver. 19. [The older rendering is τὸ πλοῦτος instead of τὸν πλοῦτον. The manuscripts (LACHMANN, TISCHENDORF) fluctuate in some other places between the neuter and the masculine.—H.]

EXEGETICAL AND CRITICAL.

Ver. 10. **But I rejoiced in the Lord greatly**. Paul commences by adding (δέ) something else which concerns himself personally (ἐχάρην). He limits this statement in two ways; first, by designating the element (ἐν κυρίῳ) and secondly, the degree (μεγάλως) of his joy, the latter word being at the end for the sake of emphasis.—**That now at the last your care of me hath flourished again.** Ὅτι introduces the reason of his joy: ἤδη ποτὲ ἀνεθάλετε. This form of the verb is not found elsewhere. See WINER'S *Gram.*

p. 87. The verb (from ϑάλλω to bloom, be luxuriant, or to cause to bloom) signifies to become green again, or to make green again. [The figure was not suggested by the season of the year when the gift was sent (BENGEL), but the thought in its freshness budded into poetry (EADIE).—H.] The Philippians are regarded in the figure as a tree or field, wherein the concealed life has shown itself anew in the bestowal of the gifts of love, which are, as it were, the new buds or shoots of spring. The figure does not admit of the transitive signification (GROTIUS, with an appeal to Ezek. xvii. 24), and the context, which presents the reason for his great joy, forbids our referring it to a return of prosperity (MEYER, SCHENKEL: to thrive, prosper in their circumstances); and also forbids (for it contains no reproach) our regarding either the emphatic ἤδη ποτέ as *tandem aliquando* (MEYER), though it may be so taken in Rom. i. 10 where it stands with the future, or ἀνεϑάλετε as pre-supposing the readers to be deficient in sympathy, as it were withered, unproductive, ἀπομαρανθέντες ἐν τῇ ἐλεημοσύνῃ (ŒCUM. *et al.*) Under what circumstances the Apostle's welfare (τὸ ὑπὲρ ἐμοῦ) could not be a subject of the concern and care (φρονεῖν) of the church, is not stated, nor can it be conjectured. BENGEL, who however goes too far when he says *videtur legatio a Philippensibus tempore verno constituta, a quo metaphora sumitur*, observes very justly: τὸ ὑπὲρ ἐμοῦ *dicitur ut* τὰ παῤ ὑμῶν, ver. 18, and also *regitur a* φρονεῖν. Hence τὸ ὑπὲρ ἐμοῦ φρονεῖν is not to be taken as the accusative of relation (WINER'S *Gram.*, p. 317 sq.) In a word, a new life has sprung up in the church, which has led them to consider (φρονεῖν) how they can do something again for the Apostle (τὸ ὑπὲρ ἐμοῦ). If it could be suspected that any censure was intended here, what follows serves at once to remove that suspicion, for it excludes entirely all ground for such a thought. —**Wherein ye were also careful, but ye were lacking opportunity**. 'Εφ' ᾧ, which is always neuter with Paul, and indicates the basis of the φρονεῖτε (WINER'S *Gram.*, p. 392 sq.), has τὸ ὑπὲρ ἐμοῦ for its antecedent, while ἐφρονεῖτε, which the prefixed καί associates with their failure to contribute to his support, declares, that notwithstanding such omission, they had been thoughtful in the matter, so that they could not have been ἀπομαρανϑέντες ἐν ἐλεημοσύνῃ. It was not the disposition, but the outward circumstances that were at fault (ἠκαιρεῖσϑε δέ). The omission of μέν after ἐφρονεῖτε, to which δέ corresponds, states the palliating antithesis with greater point and vivacity. DE WETTE incorrectly explains φρονεῖν ἐπί as a thinking without doing, φρονεῖν ὑπέρ a thinking with doing. The action is not indicated by the preposition, but is expressed in ἀνεϑάλετε. We are not to refer ᾧ to ἐμοῦ for its antecedent, (CALVIN), nor to translate ἐφ' ᾧ *although* (LUTHER), or *sicut* (VULG.), or *post id* (GROTIUS). In what the unfavorableness of their condition consisted, is not stated or intimated. But Paul's joy on account of the change does not permit us to find it in the state of their resources, their temporal means, (MEYER, *et al.*), or in the want of an opportunity to transmit their gifts (ERASMUS). [The more precise translation of ἠκαιρεῖσϑε may be *ye were not having a favorable time:* which as already remarked leaves it uncertain in what respect it was unfavorable. Of the conjectures that of MEYER and others (see above) is as probable as any other. The want of something to send to the Apostle is less likely to have been the difficulty than the want of a suitable messenger. The commission as a fiduciary trust required honor and fidelity on the part of the agent, and was not to be entrusted to every one who might offer himself for the service. The journey too was a difficult one, involving perils by land and sea, and (as shown in all probability by the narrow escape of Epaphroditus himself) requiring courage and physical hardihood, which many would not possess though not deficient in other respects.—H.]

Ver. 11. **Not that I speak in respect of want**, (οὐχ ὅτι καϑ' ὑστέρησιν λέγω) denies that the relief of any personal want was the cause of his joy, which is not of a nature to depend on external circumstances. On οὐχ ὅτι see iii. 12. WINER'S *Gram.*, p. 597. On καϑ' ὑστέρησιν, see WINER'S *Gram.*, p. 402.—He now adds in confirmation:—**For I have learned in whatever state I am to be content** (ἐγὼ γὰρ ἔμαθον ἐν οἷς εἰμι αὐτάρκης εἶναι). Comp. 2 Cor. ix. 8; 1 Tim. vi. 6; Heb. xiii. 5. 'Εγώ is emphatic: with others it may be different. There is no reason for supplying *in tot adversis*, or *divinitus* with ἔμαϑον (BENGEL). 'Εν οἷς εἰμι means his condition at any time; and does not refer merely to his condition at that time, nor is ἐν οἷς to be taken as masculine (LUTHER, *with whom*). [Prof. EADIE reminds us that the great divine, Dr. Isaac Barrow, has four sermons on this text. See under HOMILETICAL and PRACTICAL.—H.]

Ver. 12. **I know also how to be abased** *or* **brought low**, (οἶδα καὶ ταπεινοῦσθαι) begins the account of his resignation, contentment (αὐτάρκεια). The order of the contrasts (ταπεινοῦϑαι, περισσεύειν) appears to adjust itself to the condition of the Apostle at the time when he wrote the Epistle. The knowing (οἶδα) is a consequence of the learning (ἔμαθον). On the facts see 2 Cor. iv. 8; vi. 9, 10. Καί adds to the general statement ἐν οἷς εἰμι, the more particular one.—**And I know how to abound**—*οἶδα καὶ περισσεύειν*. Here καί adds the opposite as having also been learned. Περισσεύειν harmonizes better with the context than would the more exact opposite of the preceding verb (ὑψοῦσϑαι). PELAGIUS: *ut nec abundantia extollar, nec frangor inopia.* GROTIUS: *in rebus exiguis patienter me gerere, rebus abundantibus cum modo uti.* The signification *excellere* (ERASMUS) is untenable.—**In every thing and in all things I have been instructed** *or* **initiated.** —'Εν παντὶ καὶ ἐν πᾶσι is to be explained by ἐν οἷς (ver. 11). Both then are neuter, embracing all states and every state. The first is not equivalent to *ubique* (Vulg.), nor is the second masculine (LUTHER: among all; BENGEL: *respectu omnium hominum*). The perfect of the verb (μεμύημαι) denotes the continuance of the state described. There is manifestly here a climax: ἔμαθον as pupil, οἶδα as companion, μεμύημαι as master. Only a gradation, however, is indicated in the extent and exactness of the knowledge, but there is no reference to a divine revelation (ESTIUS, BENGEL). The verb is followed by the accusative or dative; hence ἐν παντὶ καὶ ἐν πᾶσι only describes the condition, in which this knowledge manifests itself; what he has been taught is stated in the following infinitives, equivalent to accusatives after the verb.—**Both to be full and to be hungry, both to abound and to suffer need** (καὶ χορτάζεσθαι καὶ πεινᾷν, καὶ περισσεύειν καὶ ὑστερεῖσθαι).

Ver. 13. **I can do all things in him who strengtheneth me.**—Summing it all up, he says, πάντα ἰσχύω. [Πάντα is the 'quantitative' accusative after ἰσχύω (Gal. v. 6; James v. 16) defining the measure and extent of the action (ELLICOTT).—H.] Again, climacteric from knowledge to ability (Gal. v. 6; James v. 16), and πάντα is entirely general, extending even beyond the categories just mentioned. VAN HENGEL incorrectly restricts it to *omnia memorata.* It sounds like boasting, hence in humility he adds: ἐν τῷ ἐνδυναμοῦντί με. In himself there resides no such knowledge and ability; it has been bestowed upon him, he has it only in and from the Lord who alone creates it. Comp. Eph. vi. 10; 2 Cor. xii. 9; Acts ix. 22; Rom. iv. 20; 1 Tim. i. 12; 2 Tim. ii. 1; iv. 17.

Ver. 14. **Notwithstanding** (*better,* **nevertheless**) **ye have well done.**—Πλήν turns the attention from Paul to the Philippians and their gifts, which are now estimated positively. *Cavet, ne fortiter loquendo contempsisse ipsum beneficium videatur* (CALVIN). [Notwithstanding (πλήν) he did not need their bounty to relieve his wants, he is thankful for it, and commends their generosity.—H.]—Καλῶς ποιήσατε describes their contribution as a good deed, which the following more closely defines: **That ye shared in my affliction**—συγκοινωνήσαντές μου τῇ θλίψει. It was therefore a fellowship (a κοινωνεῖν) with the affliction (θλῖψις), which last denotes his hard condition, not merely want; hence it was compassion, interest, but as the emphatic position of μου indicates, for the sake of the person, in devoted love. *Composito verbo innuitur, etiam alios alio modo fuisse* κοινώνήσαντες (BENGEL). Comp. ver. 16; 2 Cor. ix. 11. [This sympathy on the part of the Philippians with the suffering representative of Christ and His cause is the very trait of character which the Judge selects for eulogy at the last day. See Matth. xxv. 35 sq. (EADIE).—H.]

Ver. 15. **Now, ye Philippians also know**—οἴδατε δὲ καὶ ὑμεῖς, Φιλιππήσιοι. The transition to the past is indicated by δέ; καί points to Paul, for they and he alike know what has been done by them. The insertion of the name of the church shows his deep emotion, and gives a marked emphasis, as 2 Cor. vi. 11. No contrast with other churches is implied (BENGEL).—**That in the beginning of the gospel, when I departed from Macedonia.**—Ὅτι introduces the object of their knowledge. Ἐν ἀρχῇ τοῦ εὐαγγελίου, a limitation of time which ὅτι ἐξῆλθον ἀπὸ Μακεδονίας, the first departure from Macedonia (Acts xvi. 11—xvii. 15), so defines, that it must be understood from the standpoint of the Philippians, since for them the existence of the gospel began when the Apostle preached in Macedonia. [The "beginning of the gospel" at Philippi implies that he visited the Philippians on some other and later occasion. This intimation tallies exactly with Acts xx. 2, 6, which states that Paul came to Philippi (since μέρη ἐκεῖνα in the former passage would include that city), both on his second journey from Macedonia to Greece, and on his return from Corinth to Asia Minor and Jerusalem.—H.] It is incorrect to regard ἐξῆλθον as used for the pluperfect (VAN HENGEL, WIESINGER, *et al.*), which is forbidden by ἐν ἀρχῇ τοῦ εὐαγγελίου, and besides ver. 16 does not refer merely to the gifts sent to Corinth.—**No church communicated with me for an account of giving and receiving, but ye only,** οὐδεμία μοι ἐκκλησία ἐκοινώνησεν εἰς λόγον δόσεως καὶ λήψεως, εἰ μὴ ὑμεῖς μόνον. Only the words λόγον δόσεως καὶ λήψεως are difficult. The context, especially ver. 17, explains εἰς λόγον as meaning *for account of;* for the genitives, like the words *debit* and *credit,* receipts and expenses, point to the keeping of accounts as the source of the phraseology (CICERO, *Læl.* 16: *ratio datorum et acceptorum*). Hence BENGEL incorrectly takes the meaning to be *quod attinet* (*limitat*), as if in other ways than with gifts of love, other churches had indeed communicated with him. Further, it is the present giving and receiving of Paul and the Philippians that are spoken of: he gives the gospel and receives their gifts, they bestow their gifts and take gifts from him, God's word. Hence it is not a giving of the Philippians and receiving of Paul in the matter of the gifts of love (GROTIUS, *et al.*), or a giving of Paul and receiving of the Philippians, in *rebus spiritualibus* (the Greeks, *et al.*), nor are we to think of gifts of money from Paul to the Philippians (RHEINWALD), or, least of all, that with Paul the page headed δόσις, with the Philippians that headed λῆψις remained blanks (MEYER), for the two run into each other, and we are not to think merely of the temporal.

Ver. 16. **For even in Thessalonica ye sent once and again unto my necessity.**—Ὅτι is *quia* (Vulg.), or *nam* (LUTHER), and confirms εἰ μὴ ὑμεῖς μόνοι. It does not depend on οἴδατε, it is not 'that' (VAN HENGEL, *et al*). Ἐν Θεσσαλονίκῃ states that it was in Thessalonica that the gifts came to him, so that the designation of place can indeed be joined with ἐπέμψατε, but rather belongs with μοι (WINER's *Gram.* p. 414), and the prefixed καί, with an allusion to ἀρχῇ τοῦ εὐαγγελίου, denotes the early period of this contribution, while καὶ ἅπαξ καὶ δίς (1 Thess. ii. 18) renders the repetition of their giving prominent with a hint at the rapid succession of the gifts. [The *both once* and *twice* is emphatic, *i. e.,* not *once* only, but *twice* (DE WETTE, ELLICOTT). The καί, *also,* connects other and later instances of their liberality with the gifts which he received so early and promptly at Thessalonica immediately after his departure from Macedonia. We read in 2 Cor. xi. 9 that while Paul was at Corinth, after having preached in Macedonia, where Philippi was situated, he received supplies from that province. The particular place from which he received them is not named in that passage, but as the Apostle declares here that no other church aided him in that way, we must conclude that the bounty which he acknowledges in the Epistle to the Corinthians is that which he tacitly accredits here to the Philippians.—H.]—Εἰς τὴν χρείαν designates the need of the Apostle, the article indicating that it was a present need, and also known to the Philippians.

Ver. 17. **Not that I desire the gift** (οὐχ ὅτι ἐπιζητῶ τὸ δόμα) denotes that he was not concerned about the definite material present. The verb is simply *quæro*, the preposition denoting the direction, as in ἐπιποθῶ (i. 8). The present tense denotes 'the constant, characteristic tendency: that is not his case' (MEYER). Hence it is not *studiose quæro* (HÖLEMANN).—**But I desire the fruit,** ἀλλὰ ἐπιζητῶ τὸν καρπόν.—Emphatic repetition of the verb in the antithetical clause. ['I do *not* want the gift, I *do* want the fruit,' *etc.* (LIGHTFOOT).—H.] 'The fruit' suggests the idea of the gift, the present, as seed sown which will be followed by a harvest (Gal. vi. 18), and points to a manifold reward (MEYER). But there is no reference to the Christian life as first bringing forth the gift (RILLIET).—**That abounds to your account,** τὸ πλεονάζοντα εἰς λόγον ὑμῶν, describes the fruit as one that grows for the advantage of the Philippians: that what they have entered as δόσις is registered to them as λῆψις; they may therefore receive from Paul, from other churches, from the Lord Jesus Christ and God Himself, what will prove a blessing to them for time and for eternity. On πλεονάζειν see Rom. v. 20; vi. 1; 2 Cor. iv. 15; 2 Thess. i. 3. To this εἰς λόγον ὑμῶν belongs, which is not equivalent to εἰς ὑμᾶς, *ratione vestri* (BENGEL), and not to ἐπιζητῶ (VAN HENGEL), nor is καρπός here equivalent to τόκος, interest (MICHAELIS), for the context gives no occasion to adopt this meaning, though λόγος is to be held as implying 'account.'

Ver. 18. **But I have all, and abound. I am full.**—'Απέχω δὲ πάντα is an expression of his complete content: he has all that (Matth. vi. 2; v. 16; Phil. 15) he needs or desires, so that he has nothing left to wish for. It is not "receipt" (ERASMUS), also not *habeo autem omnia* (Vulg.). With a climactic force καὶ περισσεύω is added: I have yet more than I need and wish, am even filled (πεπλήρωμαι), have abundance around and within. Not outward abundance is meant, but complete inward satisfaction.—**Having received of Epaphroditus the things which were sent from you** (δεξάμενος παρὰ 'Επαφροδίτου τὰ παρ' ὑμῶν) points to the mode in which he had come into this state.—He describes their gift as: **An odor of a sweet smell, a sacrifice acceptable, well pleasing to God.**—'Οσμὴν εὐωδίας (comp. Eph. v. 2), θυσίαν δεκτὴν, εὐάρεστον τῷ θεῷ, represents the gift under the image of an offering. The dative belongs equally to both expressions. Comp. ii. 17; Rom. xii. 1; Heb. xiii. 16; 1 Pet. ii. 5. Every gift and act of love should be regarded as an offering made to God in thankfulness, and hence it is that they are acceptable, well pleasing to Him.

Ver. 19. **But my God shall supply all your need** (ὁ δὲ θεός μου πληρώσει πᾶσαν χρείαν ὑμῶν) attaches itself to τῷ θεῷ. God allows no offering to be made to Him in vain, especially when it is a gift to one whose God He is. Comp. i. 3. Paul's God will repay the Philippians for having so contributed to his aid that he could say πεπλήρωμαι. Hence πληρώσει measures, as it were, the recompense to them by his πεπλήρωμαι, and πᾶσαν χρείαν ὑμῶν responds to εἰς τὴν χρείαν μοι (ver. 16). The reference is not merely to bodily want (CHRYSOSTOM), or even to spiritual (PELAGIUS), but to bodily and spiritual combined, and the recompense also should not be restricted to the other world (MEYER).—The πληρώσει is now qualified.—**According to his riches in glory in Christ Jesus.**—The limitation is three-fold: (1) κατὰ τὸ πλοῦτος αὐτοῦ shows the relation of the recompense to the gift of the church; (2) ἐν δόξῃ states the kind of recompense: in a glorious way; (3) ἐν Χριστῷ 'Ιησοῦ presents the medium by which it is effected. It is incorrect to join ἐν δόξῃ with πλοῦτος (GROTIUS, *et al.*), since αὐτοῦ stands between, and with πλοῦτος we should have had the genitive δόξης (Eph. i. 14; iii. 16; Col. i. 27; Rom. ix. 23). [The adverbial sense of ἐν δόξῃ has hardly any parallel elsewhere. The *constructio prægnans* affords a better meaning (LIGHTFOOT): in the state of glory where they would ultimately be, and partake of Christ's glory at the right hand of the Father; and it is in Him (ἐν Χριστῷ 'Ιησοῦ) as the sphere of their existence that they attain this exaltation and blessedness.—H.]

Ver. 20. **Now unto God and our Father be glory for ever and ever. Amen.**—The doxology here forms a natural conclusion: τῷ δὲ θεῷ καὶ πατρὶ ὑμῶν recalls ὁ θεός μου (ver. 19), who is also the God of the Philippians, and not merely God, but also our Father. See on i. 2. With ἡ δόξα supply εἴη. See Eph. iii. 20, 21; Rom. xi. 36. The glory which He has shall also be acknowledged even εἰς τοὺς αἰῶνας τῶν αἰώνων, an expression equivalent in sense to εἰς πάντας αἰῶνας, Gal. i. 5; 1 Tim. i. 17; 2 Tim. iv. 18; Heb. xiii. 21; 1 Pet. iv. 11; v. 11.

DOCTRINAL AND ETHICAL.

1. The Christian life, both of individuals and of churches, can no more be without its waverings, its ebb and flow in the stream of its activity, than nature can fail of its winter, spring, summer and autumn (ver. 10). This should be no cause of stumbling.

2. The manifestations of Christian activity are a cause of joy less on account of the material benefits they confer, than on account of the power of love and of life which they evince: and this is the reason why they are not to be lightly esteemed.

3. Both traits of character are important: dignity in circumstances of misfortune and trial, without weakness and without ill-humor; and nobility of soul in the midst of abundance, without pride or arrogance. The last of these, perhaps, is more difficult to acquire than the first.

4. Man can of himself do nothing in matters of morality, but in Christ, who strengthens him, he can do all things (John xv. 5).

5. There is a certain *solidarity* of earthly and heavenly interests, bodily and spiritual, like that which exists between the body and the soul. Romanism, in its proneness to a false ascetism, underrates the former. Socialism and Communism, which attach themselves only to this life, deny the latter. The lower or temporal interests should be subordinated to the higher or

spiritual; they should be servants, not masters, under the control ever of a mind which maintains its ascendency over the earthly and present. These higher interests cannot be replaced by the lower; they should not be displaced by them.

6. The gift of love is in form and product the true gift, and should be regarded as a sacrifice brought to God and well-pleasing to Him (ver. 18).

7. [AUGUSTINE:—I have learned from Thee, O Lord, to distinguish between *the gift* and *the fruit*. The *gift* is the thing itself, which is given by one who supplies what is needed, as money or raiment. But the *fruit* is the good and well-ordered will of the giver. It is a *gift*, to receive a prophet, and to give a cup of cold water; but it is *fruit*, to do those acts in the *name* of a prophet, and in the *name* of a disciple. The raven brought a *gift* to Elias when it brought him bread and flesh; but the *widow fruit*, because she fed him as a man of God (ver. 17).—H.]

HOMILETICAL AND PRACTICAL.

STARKE:—What virtuous pagans have learned from nature, as in a shadow, that they should not allow themselves to be lifted up by fortune and abundance, nor let their courage sink in misfortune and want, is a knowledge which true Christians have by reason of their faith, in all truth, fulness, and purity.—Thou desirest to know nothing of Christ's power in overcoming sin, and ever excusest thy deeds as effects of human weakness: but if thou art a true Christian, and thus in Christ, thou art strong enough to conquer all things. If thou hast not this strength, then is Christ also not in thee.—God is a rich Proprietor, to whom thou lendest what thou dost give to the poor, and who will recompense thee a hundred-fold, if not in this world, yet certainly in eternal glory (ver. 19).

RIEGER:—From that which one endures, something also should be learned. Nature is content with little, grace with even less. Most desires are first aroused by comparison with others.—So soon as I turn away from Christ, any thing can overthrow me. So soon as I am in Christ, I can withstand all things.

SCHLEIERMACHER:—The Apostle's boast: 1) what he boasts of himself; 2) how he gives Christ the glory.

HEUBNER:—In many a one the spiritual impulse seems at times dead, as the life in flowers and trees, but in favorable weather it breaks out again in buds, blossoms and fruits. Even the manifestation of that which is good is controlled by circumstances (ver. 10).

[ISAAC BARROW:—He who has the consciousness of fulfilling the condition, will secure the effect of that promise: "Seek ye first the kingdom of God and His righteousness, and all these things shall be added unto you."—This is what supported the Apostles and kept them cheerful under all the heavy load of distresses which lay on them: "Our rejoicing is this: the testimony of our conscience, that in simplicity and godly sincerity—we have had our conversation in this world."—It is an evil conscience that giveth an edge to all other evils, and enableth them sorely to afflict us, which otherwise would but slightly touch us.—The contemplation of our future state is a medicine to work contentedness and to cure discontent. Considering heaven and its happiness, how low and mean, how unworthy of our care and affection, will these inferior things appear.—What is any loss, any disgrace, any cross in this world to me, who am a citizen of heaven, who bear a capacity and hope of the immense riches, the incorruptible glory, the perfect and endless joys of eternity? "For this cause," says Paul, "we faint not—while we look not on the things which are seen, but on the things which are not seen; for the things which are seen are temporal, but the things which are not seen are eternal." And he says again: "I reckon that the sufferings of the present life are not worthy to be compared with the glory which shall be revealed in us."—H.]

VII. CONCLUSION:

Salutation and Benediction (iv. 21–23).

CHAP. IV. 21–23.

21 Salute every saint in Christ Jesus. The brethren who are with me greet [salute]
22 you. All the saints salute you, chiefly [but especially] they that are of Cæsar's
23 household. The grace of our [the[1]] Lord Jesus Christ be with you all [your spirit[2]].
Amen.[3]

[1] Ver. 23.—[The A. V. reads ἡμῶν after κυρίου, but on no sufficient authority—H.]

[2] *Ibid.*—Instead of μετὰ τοῦ πνεύματος ὑμῶν some manuscripts read μετὰ πνευμάτων υμῶν. [LACHMANN and TISCHENDORF adopt the former in their text. MEYER regards μετὰ τοῦ πνευμάτος ὑμῶν as borrowed from Gal. vi. 18. The English Version translates the common μετὰ παντῶν ἡμῶν, which is not well supported.—H.]

[3] *Ibid.*—'Αμήν is found in ℵ A D E K L. The subscription in ℵ is πρὸς φιλιππησίους, and in B the same with ἐγράφη ἀπὸ Ρώμης added, while K subjoins δι' 'Επαφροδίτου.

EXEGETICAL AND CRITICAL.

Ver. 21. **Salute every saint in Christ Jesus,** *ἀσπάσασθε πάντα ἅγιον ἐν Χριστῷ Ἰησοῦ.* He desires to single out every member of the church as embraced in this greeting; and hence he uses the singular (*πάντα*), and does not write *πάντας τοὺς ἁγίους.* The nearer limitation, *ἐν Χριστῷ Ἰησοῦ,* belongs to the verb (Rom. xvi. 16; 1 Cor. xvi. 20; 2 Cor. xiii. 12: *ἐν ἁγίῳ φιλήματι*). It is to be a Christian salutation; *ἅγιος* does not need any limitation (Van Hengel, *et al.*), as Eph. i. 1 shows. — **The brethren who are with me salute you,** adds salutations (*ἀσπάζονται ὑμᾶς*) entrusted to him by others, *οἱ σὺν ἐμοὶ ἀδελφοί, qui mihi vincto ministrant, qui me visitant, qui mecum hic in evangelio laborant* (Estius); hence the smaller circle (i. 14), which, however, we are not to divide into travelling companions (as Luke, Titus and others) and those who lived in the place (as Clemens, Euodia, *et al.*) (Van Hengel).

Ver. 22. **All the saints salute you** (*ἀσπάζονται ὑμᾶς πάντες οἱ ἅγιοι*), all Christians in Rome who did not happen to stand in personal or official relations with himself.—**But especially,** *μάλιστα δέ,* marks a greeting delivered to him with great earnestness.—**They that are of Cæsar's household,** *οἱ ἐκ τῆς Καίσαρος οἰκίας.* Since *οἰκία* most naturally means house, then palace, the imperial servants are probably meant. Neither the context nor the history gives us reason to understand the word in the sense of family, as in 1 Cor. xvi. 15, and to suppose the members of the imperial family, the relatives of the Emperor, to be referred to (Baur, Van Hengel). Still less appropriate is it to suppose the Prætorians to be meant (Matthies), as in i. 13. The expressions 'palace' and 'prætorium' do not admit of being interchanged. It is not correct to think of Cæsarea and the *βασίλειον τοῦ Ἡρῴδου* on account of *Καίσαρος* (Böttger, *et al.*). Who they were and why they sent an especial salutation is not stated. [Neander conjectures that possibly they may have been natives of Philippi, or have known some of the Philippian Christians who had been at Rome. Perhaps we are not to seek so far for an explanation. The Apostle's 'especially' (*μάλιστα*), which so emphasizes the greeting of 'those of Cæsar's household,' may represent the tone of hearty earnestness with which they spoke up, as he was writing or dictating the letter, and asked them to send their kiss of love (*ἀσπασμός*) to these Philippians of whom they had heard so much from the Apostle. For this the parties need not have had any personal knowledge of each other. As servants in the palace (especially if Paul was quartered in that neighborhood) they may have been brought into relations of special intimacy with Paul.*—H.]

Ver. 23. **The grace of the Lord Jesus Christ be with your spirit. Amen.**—*Ἡ χάρις τοῦ κυρίου Ἰησοῦ Χριστοῦ μετὰ τοῦ πνεύματος ὑμῶν. Ἀμήν.*—Entirely like Gal. vi. 18; Rom. xvi. 24; 1 Thess. v. 28; 2 Thess. iii. 18; 2 Cor. xiii. 13. [This remark must be understood of a similarity in the import and not the form of the salutations.—H.]

DOCTRINAL AND ETHICAL.

1. Salutations are tokens of personal interest and living fellowship which should not be lightly esteemed.

2. It is important that the grace of the Lord be in us, not merely that we be surrounded by it.

HOMILETICAL AND PRACTICAL.

Starke:—The Apostolic salutations teach that the Christian religion does not make men unfriendly and stubborn, but courteous and friendly.—A Christian salutation is a benediction, and not merely a custom: the fashionable world uses instead its empty compliments.—O Rome! Rome! how greatly hast thou changed! Formerly thou hadst true saints even in the household of a pagan and tyrannical emperor; but now hast thou false saints, especially in and around the so-called chair of Peter and at the court of his supposed successor.

Gerlach:—Thus among the slaves of the emperor Nero there existed a believing and loving community of Christians who felt a special interest in foreign churches. Perhaps it is on account of this noteworthy circumstance that Paul brings them forward so prominently.†

Heubner:—Christianity had forced its way into the very presence of the emperor, had found entrance among the servants of the court. Whether Seneca was among them or not is unknown. Christianity finds its way every where, and the worst places are not closed to grace.

Nitzsch:—The salutations of the saints which the Apostle delivered in such numbers and so earnestly rest—1) on faith and a confession of the one true church of the Lord; 2) they are an expression of the feeling of our communion, of our higher, heavenly relationship in the family of God; 3) they furnish significant proofs of Christian love.

* [Some have supposed that Seneca may have been one of the members of the Emperor's household, to whom Paul here refers. On this question of the possibility of an acquaintance between the Apostle and the philosopher during Paul's captivity at Rome, Professor Lightfoot has an extended *Dissertation* in his *Commentary on Philippians*, pp. 268-331. The discussion involves an elaborate examination of the spirit and teachings of Stoicism as compared with those of the Gospel. The essay is indeed one of great value.—H.]

† [It was their own request, and not Paul's act, which made them prominent (see on ver. 22).—H.]

THE

EPISTLE OF PAUL

TO THE

COLOSSIANS.

BY

KARL BRAUNE, D. D.

GENERAL SUPERINTENDENT AT ALTENBURG, SAXONY.

TRANSLATED FROM THE GERMAN, WITH ADDITIONS,

BY

M. B. RIDDLE, D.D.

THE

EPISTLE OF PAUL TO THE COLOSSIANS.

INTRODUCTION.

§ 1. CONTENTS OF THE EPISTLE.

1. SYNOPSIS.*

I. ADDRESS AND SALUTATION (I. 1, 2).

II. **PART FIRST**: MENTION OF THE GROUND OF CHRISTIAN FELLOWSHIP AND WARNING AGAINST APOSTASY (I. 3.—II. 23).

1. *Thanks to God for the faith and love of his readers from the beginning* (i. 3—8). Paul prayerfully gives thanks for the faith of the Colossians in Christ and their love to the brethren, which rests upon Christian hope (vers. 3—5a), and in joy at the preaching of the gospel, which they had forthwith embraced (vers. 5b—6), as brought to them by Epaphras, who had told the Apostle of it (vers. 7, 8).

2. *Earnest supplication for the progress of the church in true knowledge, especially of the Being and Work of Christ* (i. 9—23). The immediate object of the supplication is fuller knowledge of the Divine Will (ver. 9), in order to upright Christian walk in gratitude (vers. 10-12) for the Redemption in Christ (vers. 13, 14), whose Person is then set forth as to His inmost Being (ver. 15), His efficiency in creation (ver. 16) and Providence (ver. 17) and as Head of the Church (ver. 18), in order to mark how heaven and earth were embraced in the Redemptive Work of Him (vers. 19-20), in whom they also have now a part (vers. 21-23).

3. *Joy of the Apostle in his sufferings and labors* (i. 14-29). Paul rejoices that the sufferings of Christ are becoming ever more complete through his own (ver. 24), and sketches his ministerial relation in furtherance of Christ's cause (vers. 15-20).

4. *Anxiety of the Apostle lest they be led away through false wisdom* (ii. 1-15). After a free expression of his concern about the spiritual health of the church (vers. 1-3), he briefly sketches the situation (vers. 4, 5), then exhorts to faithfulness in walk (vers. 6, 7), warns against apostasy (ver. 8) and praises the glory of Christ and His Work (vers. 9-15).

5. *Two special warnings* (ii. 16-23): against carnal legal service (vers. 16-17), against superstitious angel-worship (vers. 18, 19), with a comprehensive conclusion (vers. 20-23).

*** [The following is a popular summary:**
I. The doctrinal part: I.—II. 3 (corresponding with Eph. I.—III).
II. The warning: II. 4.—23 (with no parallel in Eph.).
III. The practical part: III, IV. (corresponding with Eph. IV.—VI).—R.]

III. PART SECOND: EXHORTATION TO TRUE VITAL SANCTIFICATION (III. 1.—IV. 6).

1. *The foundation and prospect of a genuine Christian sentiment and walk* (iii. 1–4). Fellowship with the exalted Redeemer points to "things above" (vers. 1–3) and has an elevating prospect (ver. 4).

2. *General Exhortations* (iii. 5–17): a) *negatively*, to put off the carnal nature (iii. 5–11), first and fundamentally, as respects the lusts and possessions of earth (vers. 5–7), then in social relations with one another (vers. 8–11); b) *positively*, to practice Christian affection toward each other, and to glorify Christ in word and work (iii. 12–17). The social virtues of the new man are set forth (vers. 12–14), their tone given (ver. 15) and helps described (vers. 16, 17).

3. *Special Exhortations* (iii. 18–iv. 1);
a) to wives (ver. 18) and husbands (ver. 19);
b) to children (ver. 20) and fathers (ver. 21);
c) to servants (vers. 22–25) and masters (iv. 1).

4. *Concluding Exhortations* (iv. 2–6) in relation to prayer (vers. 2–4), conduct (ver. 5), speech (ver. 6).

IV. CONCLUSION. (IV. 7–18.)

1. *Personal intelligence* (vers. 7–9).
2. *Salutations* and *Messages* (vers. 16, 17).
3. CLOSING WORDS (ver. 18). [AUTOGRAPH SALUTATION, EXHORTATION AND BENEDICTION.—R.]

2. The FUNDAMENTAL THOUGHT, as BÄHR justly remarks, is: "Christ the Head of all things." Upon this Paul places himself in open antagonism to error (ii. 6–23), as well as to deduce clearly and definitely thence the lines, both of his doctrine—quietly arranged without expressed antithesis (i. 9–23)—and of his directions respecting Christian walk (iii. 1.—iv. 1). The Epistle to the Ephesians on the other hand sets Him forth as "the Head of the Body." In both Christ is the centre, with this modification only, that in this Epistle the *Christliness* [*Christlichkeit*] is more prominent than the *churchliness* [*Kirchlichkeit*], the *life* of the church more than its *nature*.

§ 2. CHARACTER AND SIGNIFICANCE OF THE EPISTLE.

1. What is said of the Epistle to the Ephesians (Introd. § 2, 1) is applicable here with this difference: there the overflowing fulness of the thought struggles with the expression, here in parallel passages we find a briefer, acuter, indeed a more *clear* and *mature* encasing of the thought.* The independence of the author is quite unmistakable. We find evidence of it in the pithy brevity which controls both thought and language, while it is not less apparent in the ἅπαξ λεγομένοις,† which are either altogether without analogy (ii. 8: συλαγωγεῖν; ii. 18: καταβραβεύειν), or remind us of parallel passages only that we may recognize his gift of language as ii. 4: πιθανολογία (2 Cor. ii. 4); i. 23: μετακινεῖν (2 Cor. xv. 58); iii. 1: σπλάγχνα οἰκτιρμοῦ (Phil. ii. 1); compare also the order in iii. 11: Ἕλλην καὶ Ἰουδαῖος, which is altogether exceptional.

2. References more or less definite to the situation of the Apostle (i. 24–29; ii. 1; iv. 3, 10, 18), and to his relation to the Colossian Church (i. 4, 9; ii. 1), to its origin (i. 7, 8), its full membership (iii. 18; iv. 1) and simple organization (iv. 17), its external relation to neighboring Churches (iv. 13), to friendly and sympathizing persons (iv. 9–14), as well as to its internal condition as respected Christian life (i. 4–6, 8, 9; ii. 6, 7) and threatened danger from false teachers (ii. 8–23), afford a firm basis for a clear sketch of the situation. (See § 4.)

3. In contrast with the *Universalism* of the Epistle to the Ephesians, there prevails in our

*
Col.	Eph.	Col.	Eph.	Col.	Eph.
i. 4.	i. 15.	i. 15.	i. 7.	iii. 12, 13.	iv. 2, 3, 32.
i. 5.	i. 13.	i. 16.	i. 21.	iii. 16.	v. 19, 20.
i. 9.	i. 8, 17.	ii. 19.	iv. 15, 16.	iii. 18—iv. 1.	v. 22—vi. 9.
i. 10.	iv. 1.	iii. 5, 6.	v. 5, 6.	iv. 2–6.	vi. 18–20.
i. 11.	iv. 9, 10; i. 19.	iii. 8.	iv. 31.		v. 15; iv. 29.
i. 13.	ii. 2; vi. 12; i. 6.	iii. 9, 10.	iv. 22, 25.		

† [ALFORD, New Testament, Vol. III. *Proleg.*, p. 40, gives a list of ἅπαξ λεγόμενα, thirty-five in number, and then remarks the fact that *nineteen* or *twenty* occur in the second chapter—introduced there by the nature of the subject. At the same time he attributes many to Paul's style, to the σεμνότης of controversial tone.—R.]

Epistle a *Monism*: the Person of Christ, and again and again the Person of Christ, and this exclusively. Hence instead of "the Word of God" (i. 25; Rom. ix. 6; 1 Cor. xiv. 36; 2 Cor. ii. 17; iv. 2), or "of the Lord" (1 Thess. i. 18), "of truth" (i. 5), "of wisdom," "of knowledge" (1 Cor. xii. 8), "of the Cross" (1 Cor. i 18), "of reconciliation" (2 Cor. v. 19), we find here alone (iii. 16) "the Word of Christ." The Epistle is thoroughly Christological; Christ's Person is the Lord of Eternity, ruling heaven and earth, the visible and invisible (i. 14–16, 19; ii. 9), who by entering into our race and the history of humanity (i. 18), has reconciled all things and all classes to God (i. 20, 21), has so spanned all centuries of development, that out of Him and before Him even the highest mental culture and noblest morality are but rudiments, elements of the world which pass away (ii. 8); in Him are given Peace (i. 20), Life (i. 18; ii. 13; iii. 1–3), Salvation and Bliss (i. 22; iii. 4), likewise all virtue (iii. 5–14) in all the moral relations of life (iii. 18; iv. 1), and this is done by the ethical method of faith (i. 23; ii. 13), in obedience to His word (iii. 16), in vital fellowship with Him (ii. 11–15; iii. 1–4), and in prayer (iv. 2), so that Christ *for* us becomes Christ *in* us (ii. 13–15; iii. 3, 4).

4. The *judgments* respecting this Epistle confirm the preceding statements, as well as mark its significance. This is in part the same as that of the Epistle to the Ephesians (Introd., § 3), so far as they coincide, but consists peculiarly in this, that Christianity is here set forth as the full bloom of true wisdom and the norm on which all false wisdom is put to shame, and at the foundation is placed the connection of the most profound truth with the simplest Christian walk.—CALVIN calls it on account of the first chapter: an incomparable storehouse; COCCEIUS: *brevis epistola, sed nucleum evangelii continens et opposita omnibus postea subingressis completis.*—BÄHR: "vivacity and strength, depth and fulness of thought, often struggling with the words, great natural talents, which however are pervaded, illuminated and exalted by the Spirit of God. But a pithy, compact brevity appears as especially characteristic in this Epistle. It breathes the spirit of tenderest love and joy in all sorrows and afflictions. Although bowed down by external circumstances, which made it impossible for him to go into all the world, bearing the name of Jesus unto all the Gentiles, the inward joyousness and elevation of the great Apostle to the Gentiles increased but the more."—BÖHMER (*Isagog.*, p. 160) passes this judgment on our Epistle: *viva, pressa, solida, nervis plena, mascula.*—STEIGER finds this Epistle *fresher*, the connection with the news just received not effaced, and sees in the Epistle to the Ephesians only echoes from this.—Even DE WETTE uses the "rich brevity" of the Colossian Epistle to condemn that to the Ephesians as a "verbose expansion" of it.—SCHENKEL remarks that the structure of words and sentences throughout is original.—The opposing, dissenting judgments are partly in regard to details, partly based upon pre-conceived views (see § 3) rather than upon the Epistle itself, and hence cannot be deemed of any weight.—[ALFORD, comparing it with that to the Ephesians, calls it: "his caution, his argument, his protest; so to speak, his working-day toil, his direct pastoral labor." Hence we have here "system defined, language elaborated, antithesis and logical power." WORDSWORTH, in making the same comparison, says: "The Apostle is both a builder and a soldier. He builds up the truth in one Epistle, and he wars against error in the other. He has his sword girded at his side in the Epistle to the Church of Colosse.—Almighty God, in His Wisdom and love, controlled and overruled these evils for endless good to the Colossian Church, and to the Church Universal of every age and country, by the ministry of St. Paul in the present Epistle." DAVIES even suggests, that these errors, as reported to him, gave a stimulus to his thoughts, and made him "aware of depths in the gospel of Christ and of aspects of the Person of Christ which he had not so clearly apprehended before." Certainly these twin Epistles are the most profound of all the Pauline Epistles. This not less so than the other, for here Christ's Person is more prominent, there Christ's Body.—R.]

§ 3. THE AUTHOR OF THE EPISTLE.

1. The Epistle itself specifies the Apostle Paul as its author, both in the address (i. 1) and in the text (i. 24), as in Eph. iii. 1 (comp. Introd., § 4), and in the conclusion (iv. 18). It refers to the sufferings he had to endure as an Apostle (i. 29), and especially from the Jews as the Apostle to the Gentiles (iv. 11), to his imprisonment (iv. 3, 10, 18), refers particularly to the same circle of companions, as Philem. 24, men who are known otherwise as his friends, such as *Timothy*

(i. 1), *Epaphras* (i. 7, 8; iv. 12, 13), *Tychicus* (iv. 7–9), *Onesimus* (iv. 9), *Luke* (iv. 14), as well as to two others, *Mark* (iv. 10) and *Demas* (iv. 14), one of whom had been the cause of serious blame and decided contention, indeed of separation from his companion *Barnabas* (Acts xiii. 13; xv. 37–40), while the other afterwards forsook him (2 Tim. iv. 10). Finally the Epistle sets forth the fundamental features of the same errors, which are combatted by the Apostle in the Epistle to the Ephesians and the Pastoral Epistles, and yet in such a way that the points of agreement and diversity are readily perceived (§ 4, 5).—Accordingly the Epistle, both in form and contents, bears the stamp of Pauline origin.

2. *The testimony of the early Church*, as in the case of the Epistle to the Ephesians (Introd., § 4, 2) is in favor of the Pauline authorship. The occurrence of πρωτότοκος πάσης κτίσεως (i. 15) in the writings of JUSTIN, who suffered martyrdom A. D. 163, and of THEOPHILUS, Bishop of Antioch, who died A. D. 181, may be of more importance for the history of doctrine, than for historical criticism upon this Epistle, yet the fact must be noted in connection with the testimony of the Canon of MURATORI (Eph. Introd., § 4, 2), which was drawn up about A. D. 160, a catalogue of what was generally received. This cites our Epistle as Pauline. IRENÆUS († 202), who quotes iv. 14, CLEMENS ALEXANDRINUS († 220), TERTULLIAN († 220), ORIGEN († 254) cite it as Pauline; EUSEBIUS reckons it among the ὁμολογούμενα. It is even found in the Canon of MARCION, and the Gnostics did not question its genuineness. BÄHR is right in saying: "It could not occur to any considerate person to doubt its genuineness or make a critical plaything of it." [ALFORD: "That this Epistle is a genuine work of St. Paul, was never doubted in ancient times: nor did any modern critic question the fact, until SCHRADER (*der Apostel Paulus*, V. 175 sq.) in his commentary pronounced some passages suspicious, and led the way in which BAUR and MEYERHOFF followed."—R.]

3. MEYERHOFF (*der Brief an die Kolosser mit vornehmlicher Berücksichtigung der drei Pastoralbriefe kritisch geprüft.* 1838) accepts the Epistle to the Ephesians as genuine, to contest the genuineness of that to the Colossians, while BAUR (*Paulus*, 1845, pp. 417–457) rejects both as an unpauline pair. The charge that the language is unpauline fails in view of the "original many-sidedness" (SCHENKEL) of the Apostle; the charge of poverty in thought and quotation from the Epistle to the Ephesians, as well as that of controversy against Cerinthus, are met by correct and discriminating exegesis of the passages in question. If BAUR finds in the false teachers at Colosse, according to this Epistle, later post-apostolic Ebionites, and in its doctrinal drift, as in that of the Gospel of John, a Gnostic tendency, so that it is to be regarded only as a pseudo-apostolic movement of Gnosticism against Ebionitism, it may be replied, that the doctrine respecting Christ as the centre of the entire spiritual world, and the idea of the πλήρωμα are not sufficient to prove the presence of unpauline Gnosticism, since we find here, only that more fully developed and advanced Christology, the foundation of which was already laid in Rom. i. 3, 4; viii. 34; 2 Cor. iv. 4; nor is the opposition to the necessity of circumcision to salvation, and to exaggerated asceticism, evidence of post-pauline origin, since the former had already been opposed in Gal. ii. 3, 4, and the latter in Rom. xiv. 1, 2. The thought that in the death of Christ all diversities and antitheses are abrogated, must not be taken in the sense of a mere external Universalism, separated from the Pauline anthropology and restricted to a coalition of Gentiles and Jews. It is not foreign to the Apostle, but occurs also in Gal. iii. 27, 28; vi. 14, 15, where there is also a reference to baptism as symbolizing death. It would be difficult to receive or justify the opinion, that in the mention of Mark and Luke (iv. 10, 14), there was a purpose of recommending their Gospels and giving prominence to their harmony with each other and with Paul. The open antagonism of the Epistle to the Judaizing tendency directly contradicts the assertion that its main design was to mediate between Jewish and Gentile Christians. Whatever may be peculiar and special in this as compared with other Pauline Epistles, affords no just ground for denying that it is a product of the same author, especially of this vivacious and spirited Apostle.—EWALD (*Sendschreiben des Apostel Paulus*, p. 466 sq.) finds the plan, thoughts and argument Pauline, but takes exception to such words as ἐθελοθρησκεία, ἀνταναπληρόω, to the infrequent use of inferences and causal particles, also to the reference of the reconciling work and death of Christ to angels (i. 20), and hence is of the opinion, that after a preliminary conference about the contents, the composition of the Epistle was left to Timothy as co-author, Paul, how-

ever, dictating the words towards the conclusion and adding his autographic salutation. But according to i. 23, 25; ii. 1, 5, this view is inadmissible, and, notwithstanding 2 Cor. i. 1; Phil. i. 1; Philem. 1; 1 Thess. i. 1; 2 Thess. i. 1, inapplicable to those Epistles also. It will appear from the exegetical remarks that peculiarities of language are not unpauline, because not occurring in antecedent Pauline Epistles.—MEYER, with a reference to ERASMUS (*non est cujusvis hominis Paulinum pectus effingere; tonat, fulgurat, meras flammas loquitur Paulus*), aptly remarks: "The *forging* of such an Epistle as ours would be more wonderful than its genuineness." [For a detailed answer to Meyerhoff's objections, see EADIE, *Liter.* III., though, as he concludes, "the attacks on this Epistle are of no formidable nature." ELLICOTT forcibly remarks: "To class such an Epistle, so marked not only by distinctive peculiarities of style, but by the nerve, force, and originality of its argument, with the vague productions of later Gnosticism, is to bewray such a complete want of critical perception that we can scarcely wonder that such views have been both very generally and very summarily rejected." See DAVIDSON, *Introd.*, Vol. II., p. 427 sq. —R.]

§ 4. THE CHURCH AND ITS CIRCUMSTANCES.

1. *Topographical Remarks.* COLOSSE, in the vicinity of Laodicea and Hierapolis, was the locality of the Church addressed in this Epistle. This is evident from ii. 1; iv. 13, 16. The opinion of Erasmus and others, that Rhodes is meant, the inhabitants of which are termed Κολοσσαεῖς, on account of the Colossus, is singular enough [and were there any evidence to support it, the variation in the title of the Epistle (see below) would overthrow it.—R.]

COLOSSE is situated in the southwestern part of Asia Minor, in Greater Phrygia (*Phrygia pacatiana*), on the river Lycus, near the spot where it disappears in a chasm, out of which it soon emerges again to empty itself into the Meander. At the distance of half a day's journey were several populous cities. The most prominent among these, especially in the time of the Romans and in Church History, was Laodicea; STRABO (1st century, A. D.) counts it among the μέγισται πόλεις. HERODOTUS calls Colosse: πόλις μεγάλη εὐδαίμων καὶ μεγάλη, but STRABO includes it among the smaller towns (πολίσματα), which lay near Laodicea (THEODORET: μητρόπολις αὐτῆς (Colosse) καὶ γείτων ἡ Λαοδίκεία); though PLINY counts it among the *celeberrimis oppidis*, yet he names it only among the *oppidis*. OROSIUS, who describes the earthquake of the time of Nero in the year 66, mentions Laodicea and Hierapolis first and Colosse last, among the cities affected by it; whether because the smallest, or the least injured by it, is doubtful (*tres urbes—terræ motu conciderunt*). TACITUS misstates the date of the earthquake (60), but expressly mentions Laodicea only, as soon recovering itself without the help of the State or foreign aid, and flourishing anew. THEOPHYLACT († after the middle of the 11th century) calls it Χῶναι; it is now named *Chonas.* [ALFORD: "For a minute and interesting description of the remains and neighborhood, see SMITH'S *Dictionary of Anc. Geography, sub voce.* From what is there said it would appear that Chonæ is in reality about three miles south from the ruins of the city." See also PAULY, *Realencycl.*, Vol. II., p. 518; STEIGER, *Einleitung*, p. 1–33; EADIE, *Col.* p. x., and CONYBEARE and HOWSON, *St. Paul,* Vol. II., p. 383, note, and p. 390, note. The authors last named refer to a legend respecting the opening of the chasm, mentioned above, by the archangel Michael during an inundation from the Lycus, and the church built in his honor, as a curious illustration of the tendency to "angel-worship" rebuked by the Apostle, ii. 18.—R.]

Whether the name should be written: Κολοσσαί or Κολασσαί is doubtful. Codex Sinaiticus [א.] gives the former in the title* and i. 2 (Κολοσσαεῖς); but in the headings of the pages and the subscription Κολασσαεῖς. The former is found upon coins and in classical authors, and seems to be the correct form, the latter appears to be the vulgar form, afterwards the more common one. [All modern editors apparently adopt this explanation of the variation. LACHMANN, TISCHENDORF, ELLICOTT give *a* throughout; ALFORD and WORDSWORTH follow the varied spelling of א. and B.—R.]

2. *Missionary History.* Paul came to Phrygia in his second missionary journey (Acts xvi. 6: "throughout Phrygia and the region of Galatia"), also in his third missionary journey (Acts

*[ALFORD, III. *Proleg.* p. 34 and p. 196, 4th ed., gives Κολασσαεῖς as the reading of א. in the title. A consultation of the Imp. Ed. in the Library of the Union Theo. Sem., N. Y., proves the correctness of BRAUNE'S statement in every respect.—R.]

xviii. 23: "over all the country of Galatia and Phrygia in order, strengthening all the disciples"), visiting the churches which he had founded in his second journey. Hence there is a possibility, or even probability, that Paul had been in the valley of the Meander and Lycus at Laodicea and Colosse, but nothing more, especially as Phrygia had many divisions: Pisidian Phrygia, mountainous Phrygia, the districts of Amorium, Eumenia, Synnada, and the region about and beyond Laodicea to Apamea and yet further. On the contrary our Epistle, in i. 23, where mention must have been made of the fact, if Paul had ever been in Colosse, says nothing of it, but rather expresses (ii. 1), and in several other places (i. 3–7; ii. 5), pre-supposes that Paul had not been there and that the Church had not been founded by him. This takes away all weight from that possibility or probability, which SCHULZ, WIGGERS and others, following THEODORET, have accepted as fact. For the acquaintance with Philemon, Epaphras and other individuals can readily be accounted for; this acquaintance might easily have been formed at Ephesus and other points, in consequence of the extended movement produced by the gospel, or during business journeys made to these points, with which Colosse was connected by commercial ties. [Dr. LARDNER is the principal English supporter of the view that Paul was the founder of the Church; his argument is given in full and answered by EADIE and ALFORD. WORDSWORTH also adopts this view. See his Introduction to the Colossians. BARNES deems it "in the highest degree probable." But it seemed attended with more difficulties than the other view, which is now held by most biblical students. See DAVIDSON, *Introd.*, Vol. II., p. 396 sq.; ALFORD, III. *Proleg.* p. 35 sq.; also EXEG. NOTES on ii. 1.—R.]

3. *Local affairs.* a) *Epaphras*, a Colossian (iv. 12: "one of you"), who had probably been won to the gospel by Paul during his two years' residence in Ephesus, which was connected in various ways with the important city of Laodicea, had proclaimed the gospel and founded churches in Colosse, Laodicea and Hierapolis (i. 7; iv. 12, 13). He is certainly no unimportant personage; Paul describes him as his helper (i. 7), refers to his correct teaching (i. 4, 7; ii. 6), to his indefatigable, energetic zeal (iv. 12), which had impelled him not merely to prayer to God (iv. 12) on behalf of the Church, but also to go to the Apostle at Rome and share his imprisonment (i. 8; Philem. 23), and which made him shun no labor for the neighboring churches in Laodicea and Hierapolis also (iv. 13).

b) The *Church* was composed mainly of Gentile Christians (ii. 13), for which reason Paul the Apostle to the Gentiles regarded it also as his Church and labored for it (i. 27; ii. 1, 2. Comp. Rom. xv. 20; 2 Cor. x. 15, 16). He had already made or caused to be made to them certain written or oral communications now unknown to us, "touching" Mark (iv. 10). Although allusions to the Mosaic law are not entirely wanting (ii. 10, 13, 14, 16, 21), there is neither quotation, nor proof, nor even a reminiscence from the Old Testament.—Paul praises the Church, which (ii. 16) stands better than the Galatians (Gal. iv. 10), for their Christian deportment (i. 2, 4, 6; ii. 5); his relations with them were altogether undisturbed (i. 8, 25; iv. 7–9, 10); but they needed admonition (i. 9–12; ii. 2, 20; iii. 1–4; iv. 12). False teachers, whom the Church yet in its first love opposed, threatened to ruin it. We cannot, however, infer from iii. 16 that worship had degenerated into lip-service (THEOPHYLACT), nor from iii. 13, that there was variance in heart (SCHENKEL).—The Apostle wrote only "to the saints at Colosse" (i. 2), not "to the Church" (1 Cor. i. 2; 2 Cor. i. 1; Gal. i. 2; 1 Thess. i. 1; 2 Thess. i. 1), nor does he add, as in Phil. i. 1, "with the bishops and deacons," but through the Church exhorts a certain Archippus. Ecclesiastical relations seem to be as yet in an incipient state. According to i. 5, 9; ii. 6, the Church had been formed not long before, probably toward the close of Paul's stay in Ephesus, some time before A. D. 60, about four or five years before the Epistle was written; had it been formed earlier, Paul would certainly have visited it from Ephesus.

4. *Ethnography* and *Religious history* give us data respecting the kind of false teachers at Colosse and the consequent danger. The Phrygians, an ancient people, were highly gifted, and surrounded by a corresponding grandeur of nature. They were skilful not only in agriculture and trade, in the manufacture and dyeing of woolen stuffs, but also in arts and sciences, especially in music and the art of healing. Besides the mother-tongue, the language of the Greeks and other neighboring nations were in use among them. They had their grammarians and rhetoricians. Resembling their neighbors, the Ionians, in susceptible, impressible, mobile disposi-

-tion, they readily adopted the various elements of culture. The worship of nature, of the *great mother*, Gaia, of the tower-crowned Cybele, and of Bacchus, was domesticated among them. Here Hellenic Philosophy, which proceeded from the earliest school, the Ionic, and sought the fundamental principle of all things in nature, first in the path of Materialism, then of Idealism, oscillating between Dualism and Pantheism, hostile not to religion, but to Polytheism, came in contact with the Oriental Philosophy. Here the syncretism of that period of transition from the old to the new, Christian age, found ample nourishment. Besides under Antiochus the Great two thousand Jewish families had been transplanted into Phrygia and Lydia. There was in addition a tendency to serious and sombre fanaticism, and to reliance on physical, especially telluric and sidereal influences. [As a further indication of their tendencies, EADIE notes the fact that "the reveries of Montanus originated there about the middle of the second century, and spread rapidly and extensively. The leading features of Montanism were a claim to ecstatic inspiration, the gift of prophecy, the adoption of a transcendental code of morality, and the exercise of an austere discipline. Its votaries were often named Kataphrygians, from the region of their popularity."—R.]

5. With these data we may now learn from the Epistle itself, what was the heresy of the false teachers at Colosse. The polemics of our Epistle point: *First*, to perverted and perverting doctrine *within* the Church (ii. 19: "not holding the Head"), as the admonition also is not respecting apostasy from the Church, but disturbance of the growth in Christ, of the progress in Christian knowledge and Christian life (i. 23; ii. 6). *Secondly*, these false teachers have a Judaistic tendency, they would cling to Jewish laws of food and feasts and seasons (ii. 16), they recommend circumcision (ii. 11) and teach Jewish separatism. *Thirdly*, an asceticism is required, severe and astringent indeed, but *Fourthly*, resting upon a Dualistic view, since it identifies matter with evil, regarding it as eternal, and seeks not sanctification of the life and character by ethical means, but subjugation, mortification of the flesh by physical or chemical or dietetic methods (ii. 23; iii. 6). *Fifthly*, with this is connected the idea that *angels* as *immaterial* beings are objects of adoration (ii. 18), and an Ebionite view of Christ appears, which mistakes and denies His relation to God the Father, to the spiritual world and to creation at large (i. 15, 16, 19; ii. 9), and mistakes and degrades the significance of the objective fact of the crucifixion, that makes peace and reconciliation (i. 20, 22; ii. 14). *Sixthly*, the heresy appeared in the form of a speculation, adapted to the spirit of the age, with the pretensions of a system, which would profoundly, acutely and triumphantly present the entire truth (ii. 8, 18).

Accordingly we are not to regard them as Jews, either with Pharisaical tendencies (EICHHORN) or with a syncretic leaning to Christianity after the manner of the Chaldean Magi or Alexandrian Neo-Platonists (HUG, SCHNECKENBURGER), or as Essenes (CHEMNITZ, FLATT, THIERSCH and others). Nor can we regard them as heathen philosophers in general (TERTULLIAN), or in particular as Epicureans (CLEMENS ALEX.), Pythagoreans (GROTIUS), Platonists or Stoics (HEUMANN); nor yet as Gnostics who represented a definite system. Nor was *Cerinthus* intended (MEYERHOFF), nor Ebionite Gnosticism (BAUR), and Cabbalism (HERDER, OSIANDER) as little. The errors were rather incipient, occasioned by the thoughts, with which the atmosphere of both the age and the people was charged. This much is true: that in Simon Magus we have a personage, in whom the attempt had been made at a systematic combination of Christianity with the Oriental theosophy (PRESSENSE: *Die ersten drei Jahrhunderte*, 2, pp. 128–136); he is the first heretic and Cerinthus the next. But in our Epistle, as in those to the Ephesians, to Timothy and Titus, all is still in flow; here and in the Epistle to the Ephesians as yet within the Church, in the pastoral Epistles without it, and afterwards more widely, sharply and solidly developed. [EADIE: The winged seeds were floating in the atmosphere, and falling into a soil adapted to them, and waiting as if to receive them; in course of years they produced an ample harvest.—R.] Comp. MANGOLD: *Die Irrlehrer der Pastoralbriefe*, 1856. [See DAVIDSON, *Introd.*, Vol. II., pp. 407–424, and EADIE, *Introd. to Col.* Comp. DAVIES' *Essay on the traces of foreign elements in the doctrine of* this and cotemporaneous Pauline Epistles. The same author says: "a meeting of the Persic or Zoroastrian religion with Judaism was sufficient to account for all the dangerous teaching referred to in the Epistle to the Colossians—traces of such a meeting are to be found in the Jewish literature antecedent to the time of Christ." As he indicates that this is the germ of subsequent Gnosticism, he uses it to oppose those who claim a post-apostolic date for this Epistle, on the ground of its opposition to Gnosticism, Whatever may have been the origin of these theosophic tendencies, Phrygia was the region where Judaism and Orientalism would most readily combine in errors such as are opposed by the Apostle.—R.]

§ 5. TIME AND PLACE OF COMPOSITION.

Compare § 2, 1 and INTROD. to *Eph.* § 6.

[Braune there claims priority for the Epistle to the Ephesians Undoubtedly both were written about the same time. Which was first is almost entirely a matter of conjecture. Yet the probabilities, as set forth in the Introd. to the Ephesians, outweigh those drawn from "the nature of the contents of this Epistle" by ALFORD, ELLICOTT and DAVIDSON. "The more directly systematic and doctrinal" Epistle might precede quite as readily, as "the more directly individualizing and polemical" one.—R.]

§ 6. LITERATURE OF THE EPISTLE.

Besides the more general works mentioned Introd. Eph., § 7, the following must be named: MELANCHTHON: *Enarratio epistolæ Pauli ad Col. Corpus Reform* XV. pp. 1221–1282.—JUNKER: *Histor. krit. und philol. Commentar über den Brief Pauli an die Kolosser*, 1828.—BÖHMER: *Isagoge in ep. a Paulo ad Col. data theologica, historica, critica*, 1829, and *Theologische Auslegung* of the same Epistle, 1835.—Especially we mention: BÄHR: *Commentar über den Brief Pauli an die Kolosser*, 1835.—STEIGER: *Kleine Paulinische Briefe*, Thl. I.: *Der Brief an die Kolosser*, 1835.—HUTHER: *Commentar über den Brief Pauli an die Kolosser*, 1841.—Compare also: RHEINWALD: *De pseudo doctoribus Colossensibus*, 1834.—SCHNECKENBURGER: *Besträge zur Einleitung in's N. T.*—Besides the practical expositions which include this Epistle (Introd. Eph. § 7): STEINHOFER: *Tägliche Nahrung des Glaubens aus der Erkenntniss Jesu nach den lehrhaften Zeugnissen des Briefs an die Kolosser.*—SCHLEIERMACHER: Sermons on the Colossians (*Works*, Vol. II. 6, pp. 191–401).—KÄHLER: 36 *Betrachtungen über den Brief Pauli an die Kolosser.*—PASSAVANT: *Praktische Auslegung des Briefes Pauli an die Kolosser* (a posthumous work), 1865.

[For a list of commentaries on the whole Bible and the New Testament, see LANGE'S *Com. on Matthew*, General Introd. p. 19. Of especial value for this Epistle: CALVIN, DE WETTE, MEYER, BENGEL, HENRY, BARNES, ALFORD, WORDSWORTH. On the Epistles of St. Paul: MACKNIGHT, CONYBEARE and HOWSON (London and New York). Of special English works, the oldest are BYFIELD: *Expos. Col.*, London, 1615.—ELTON: *Exposition*, London, 1620.—BISHOP DAVENANT (member of the Synod of Dort): Learned and exhaustive prelections in Latin, 1727 (translated into English, 1831).—DAILLE, *Sermons*, translated by John Owen, 1672, also Edinb., 1865, and Philadelphia, Presb. B. Pub.—WATSON: *Practical Discourses*, 1834.—Bishop DAN. WILSON, *Expository Lectures*, London, 1845, with special reference to prevailing errors.—CARTWRIGHT: *Notes of Sermons*, Edinb., 1864. These are all mainly practical.—Later exegetical works of great value: EADIE: *Commentary on the Greek Text of the Colossians*, London and Glasgow, 1856. (Very full and reliable.)—ELLICOTT: *Critical and Grammatical Commentary on Philippians, Colossians and Philemon, with a revised translation*, London and Andover, from 2d Eng. ed., 1865. (Clear, discriminating and judicious, fully sustaining the author's reputation as a critic, grammarian and exegete, largely used in the additions to the present work.) —J. LLEWELYN DAVIES: *The Epistle of St. Paul to the Ephesians, the Colossians and Philemon; with introductions and notes, and an essay on the traces of foreign elements in the theology of these Epistles*, London, 1866. (An attempt to use the Oriental studies so common in England in elucidating these Epistles which seem to have encountered ancient Oriental tendencies.)—There are no special American works on this Epistle.—R.]

THE

EPISTLE OF PAUL TO THE COLOSSIANS.*

I. ADDRESS AND SALUTATION.

Chapter I. 1, 2.

1 Paul, an apostle of Jesus Christ [Christ Jesus][1] by the will of God, and Timo-
2 theus *our* [ὁ, the] brother, To the saints and faithful [or believing] brethren in
Christ which [who] are at Colosse:[2] [.] Grace *be* unto you, and peace, from God
our Father and the Lord Jesus Christ.[3]

* Title: Πρὸς Κολοσσαεῖς, ℵ. and others; πρὸς Κολασσαεῖς, A. B. K. and others. [The latter is adopted here by Lachmann, Tischendorf, Meyer, Alford, Wordsworth. Alford incorrectly cites ℵ. in support of the latter reading, both in his *apparatus criticus* and *Proleg.* p. 34, Vol. III.—R.] Comp. Introd. § 4. 1.

1 Ver. 1.—Χριστοῦ Ἰησοῦ in ℵ. A. B. F. G. [Lachmann, Tischendorf, Alford, Ellicott.—R.]; better supported therefore than Ἰησοῦ Χριστοῦ.

2 Ver. 2.—[Κολοσσαεῖς is to be retained on the authority of ℵ. B. D. F. L. (Alford, Wordsworth); Κολασσ. Lachmann, Tischendorf, Ellicott. The order of the E. V. is not that of the original: "To the saints in Colosse and believing brethren in Christ."—R.]

3 Ver. 2.—Καὶ κυρίου Ἰησοῦ Χριστοῦ, wanting in no other Pauline salutation, occurring in precisely the same form (except in the pastoral Epistles), is sustained by ℵ. A. C. E. G. and others, but omitted by other important authorities and critics (Tischendorf). The original absence of the phrase is less explicable than the subsequent omission in some MSS. [Rejected by Meyer, Alford, Wordsworth, Ellicott.—R.]

EXEGETICAL AND CRITICAL.

Vers. 1. 2a. Address. **Paul, an Apostle of Christ Jesus by the will of God.**—See Eph. i. 1. To this church, not founded by himself and to its false teachers, he thus defines his official position as the Apostle called immediately by the ascended Son of God: hence "Christ Jesus."

And Timotheus the brother.—On this see Van Oesterzee (Lange's *Commentary*) 1 Timothy. The same phrase is added, Philem. 1. and 2 Cor. i. 1; in 1 Cor. i. 1: "and Sosthenes the brother"; Phil. i. 1: "Paul and Timotheus, servants of Jesus Christ"; 1 Thess. i. 1 and 2 Thess. i, 1: "Paul and Silvanus and Timotheus"; Gal. i. 1, 2: "Paul an Apostle—and all the brethren that are with me." Since "my" is not added as in Rom. xvi. 21, "Timotheus my workfellow," this last passage compels us to understand the word ἀδελφός in the simple sense of "Christian brother," with no more special relation to Paul, than that of one Christian to another (as ver. 2, ἀδελφοῖς). The Apostle writes, not merely in virtue of his peculiar authority as an Apostle, but together with tried associates; he includes with himself his helpers and friends. To him the Christian brother is a friend and assistant, with whom he has consulted and now acts respecting the case of this church, without resigning or impairing his independence (i. 24; ii. 1; iv. 7). Timothy is not on this account the writer of the Epistle, which Paul dictates to him (Steiger), else according to Rom. xvi. 22, Tertius should have been named in the address, Rom. i. 1; and must each of the Epistles to the Thessalonians have been dictated to two persons? or the Epistle to the Galatians to the whole circle of Paul's companions? for Gal. vi. 11 is the usual autograph salutation. See Schmoller *in loco* (Lange's *Commentary*, Gal.) and Laurent: *Neutestamentliche Studien*, p. 4 sq. Nor can Timothy be regarded as the dispatcher of the Epistle (Schenkel), and certainly ὁ ἀδελφός does not mean "fellow Apostle" (Chrysostom: οὐκοῦν καὶ αὐτὸς ἀπόστολος). [So Theophylact. Wordsworth, supporting the view that Paul was the founder of the Colossian church, says: "In the case of all the *other* Epistles, where Timothy is thus introduced, it is certain that he had been with St. Paul at the places, and was well known to the churches to which those Epistles were sent." "If Timothy had not been at Colosse, it is hardly probable that, being still a young man, he would have been associated with the Apostle in this address to the Colossian church." "This opinion is also confirmed by the words ὁ ἀδελφός, *the brother*, signifying that he was well known to them as such, and was *their* own brother as well as St. Paul's.

Timothy is introduced as 'Timothy *the brother*' in the Epistle to *Philemon*, who lived at Colosse." EADIE:—"So well known was he as 'the brother,' doing the Apostle's work, carrying his messages, bringing correspondence to him, endeared to him in so many ways, and representing him in his absence, that the church of Colosse could not wonder at his name being associated with that of Paul."—R.]

Ver. 2. **To the saints in Colosse.**—See Eph. i. 1. [See BEVERIDGE, Vol. VI. Serm. II., p. 401, where he answers the question, "What is it to be a saint?"—R.]—**And faithful brethren in Christ.**—After defining their relation toward God, the relation of the members of the church to each other is noted in the word "brethren." This is one, mediated and maintained by Christ, while the adjective πιστοῖς describes its internal, true and vital character. At all events "in Christ" must be joined with "brethren" or better with "saints," ἁγίοις, here used as a substantive, and hence having the local attribute joined to it; it must not be joined to πιστοῖς, which is not = faithful (STEIGER). [The E. V. might be amended—to read "believing" instead of "faithful," but the ordinary reader would then be more likely to regard "in Christ" as connected with it rather than with "brethren" or "saints." Alford joins ἐν Χριστῷ to ἀδελφοῖς and suggests, to account for the omission of the article before ἐν X. that the idea ἀδελφὸς-ἐν-Χριστῷ was familiar.—R.] A comparison with Eph. i. 1, 2, shows, amid all the similarity, the unmistakable original independence.

Ver. 2b. *The Greeting.* **Grace be unto you, and peace, from God our Father and the Lord Jesus Christ.**—Comp. Eph. i. 2. [The final phrase, hitherto rejected by most modern editors, has found a new and important support from Cod. Sinaiticus. While the reason given in the critical note for retaining it should have due weight, the testimony of CHRYSOSTOM and THEOPHYLACT must not be disregarded: "Yet in this place he does not insert the name of Christ."—THEOPHYLACT adds: "Although it is his usual way to insert it." The reason he subjoins: "Lest the Apostle should revolt them at the outset, and turn their minds from his forthcoming argument," EADIE properly terms "silly;"—especially since, as WORDSWORTH, referring to Chrysostom, remarks: "It is observable that in the beginning of this Epistle—addressed to a church where the name of Jesus Christ was disparaged by many, and written in order to vindicate His Dignity—the Apostle repeats the word Christ four times"—not including this instance, where both adopt the briefer reading.—R.]

DOCTRINAL AND ETHICAL.

All Christians are brethren. In addition to the remarks on Eph. i. 1, 2, one thing must here be noted; the fact that Paul, the Apostle of Christ Jesus, describes with the same name of *brother*, Timothy, whom he places beside himself, and the Colossian Christians to whom he writes with apostolic authority. From this we infer:

1. The Church founded by Jesus Christ is presented to our view as a "family of God," in which all the members are children of God and brethren to each other.

2. Compared with the difference from God, all differences between the members so far disappear that all are simply brethren.

3. Even in the organism of the church those members, distinguished immediately and by special authority, do not pass out of this fraternal relation; that most important office of the church, the apostolate, is but an accident of the brotherhood; the Christian position is the basis of position in the Church and surpasses it.

4. On fraternal fellowship and love depend all relations of life, all the gradations of that fundamental form which God has established in the earthly human community; each should feel that he is incorporated in the family.

5. True fraternity is not the result of natural family feeling, nor of any form of human community, but the product of God's Spirit in Christ.

6. But the brotherly love, which embraces all united in the faith, does not in the New Testament mode of life make the special personal relation of friendship stand out more sharply; the disciple of Christ has none other as friend than the disciple of Christ, but has all, who are such, without distinction as friends. Yet as soon as the church is enlarged numerically, there must naturally appear, within the great circle, personal affinities, and chosen companionship. Notwithstanding what is remarked above, biblical justification of these is not wanting, since the Lord Himself chose three of the Twelve to be nearest to Himself, and of these but one leaned on the bosom of Jesus. So Paul, among many whom he loved, had no one so "like-minded" as Timothy (Phil. ii. 20), and in the beginning of the apostolic history we see Peter and John more closely united together than to the others (PALMER: *Moral*, p. 400 sq.).

HOMILETICAL AND PRACTICAL.

If we can pray "Our Father," we are and we have brethren. "Father" bids us know and feel and conduct ourselves as children, "our" as brethren.

STARKE:—First, we must be certain of the will of God, then we must follow it cheerfully, whether the world look sweet or sour.—We must not think that we alone can do all, so that nothing goes right but what we alone do. Each must be of such a mind, as to bear a helper beside him.—Whoever fears the Lord from childhood and diligently uses God's Word, like Timothy may soon become a man in Christ, though in years still a youth.

SCHLEIERMACHER:—The Scriptures know nothing of those who were especially saints, preeminent above others, but all who through Christ are brought back into living fellowship with God, are saints.

[PASSAVANT:—It is not: *believers on Christ*, but *in Christ;* the Apostle views Christians as through faith firmly founded *in Christ*, vitally and deeply rooted in His heavenly Being, members of His body, flesh of His flesh, and spirit of His Spirit, life from His life.—*On the greeting.* Notice everywhere in the writings of the New Testament and especially in the Epistles of Paul, this thorough, unsearchable and indissoluble union of the Father and the Son; from eternity one Being, one Life, one Work of one Eternal Power and Love—and in this Eternal Blessed unity of the Father and the Son was from the beginning decreed and provided and bestowed all that should become to us the *peace* of eternity: the grace coming unto us.—RIEGER:—Fellowship with God through faith makes saints, fellowship with one another makes brethren in Christ.—HENRY:—He thought himself engaged to do his utmost, as an Apostle, because he was made so by the will of God.—As all good ministers, so all good Christians are *brethren* one to another—toward God they must be *saints*, and in both *faithful*.—SCHENKEL:—Why Christians are called saints: 1) how humbling, 2) how exalting this designation.—R.]

[Christians are brethren, whatever difference of age or opinion (Paul and Timothy), in spite of distance and degrees of knowledge and piety (Paul and the Colossians); because all are "brethren in Christ."—R.]

II. FIRST PART.

Mention of the ground of Christian fellowship and warning against apostasy.

CHAPTER I. 3—II. 23.

1. Thanks to God for the faith and love of his readers from the beginning.

(CHAPTER I. 3–8).

3 We give thanks to God and [omit and][1] the Father of our Lord Jesus Christ, praying
4 always [always, when praying] for you,[2] Since we heard of your faith in Christ
5 Jesus, and of the love which ye have[3] to all the saints, For [on account of] the hope
which is laid up for you in heaven, whereof ye heard before in the word of the truth
6 of the gospel; Which is come unto you [lit.: is present unto you], as *it* is in all the
world; and[4] bringeth forth fruit [is bringing forth fruit and increasing],[5] as *it doth*
[*it is*] also in [among] you, since the day ye heard *of it* [it], and knew the grace of
7 God in truth: As ye also [Even as ye][6] learned of Epaphras our dear fellow servant,
8 who is for you[7] a faithful minister of Christ; Who also declared unto us your love
in the Spirit.

1 Ver. 3.—Θεῷ πατρί, B. C. and other MSS. and the oldest versions. ℵ. [with A. K. L.] and others insert καί, as in Eph. i. 3; Rom. xv. 6; 2 Cor. i. 3; xi. 31 in a similar connexion; here it is an interpolation. [Τῷ πατρί is another reading, not well supported. Lachmann, Tischendorf, Alford, Ellicott (though not with perfect confidence) reject καί; Wordsworth retains it.—R.]

2 Ver. 3.—Περί, ℵ. A. C. [K. L., Tischendorf, Alford, Ellicott, Wordsworth—R.], the less supported ὑπέρ [Lachmann—R.] probably from ver. 9, and because more significant. [See EXEG. NOTES on the above emendation.—R.]

3 Ver. 4.—Ἣν ἔχετε, ℵ. A. C. and others, supported by the context, [so all recent editors—R.]; τήν is poorly supported, probably from Eph. i. 15. [The italics of the E. V. are therefore unnecessary.—R.]

4 Ver. 6.—Καὶ ἔστιν on the authority of F. G. K. L. and the oldest versions, supported by the context. [Tischendorf, Meyer, De Wette, Ellicott.—R.] Καί is omitted in ℵ. A. B. C. and others [by Lachmann, Alford, Wordsworth—R.], and is the less difficult reading.

5 Ver 6.—[Καὶ αὐξανόμενον, supplied on the authority of ℵ. A. B. C. D.[1] F. L., many versions and all modern editors.—R.]

7 Ver. 7.—After καθώς, ℵ. A. B. C. D. omit καί. It is a "mechanical repetition" from ver. 6. [So modern editors. E. V. retains it in "also," which should be omitted. Καθώς="even as," here (Ellicott).—R.]

7 Ver. 7.—Ὑπὲρ ὑμῶν, C. E. F. K. L. and ℵ. corrected and in nearly all versions. The otherwise well supported ἡμῶν, ℵ. A. B., is an error of the transcriber, accounted for by the prevalence of the first person. [Tischendorf, Ellicott, Wordsworth. Alford, quoting Ambrosiaster (4th century, *vice apostoli*), reads ἡμῶν, following Lachmann.—R.]

EXEGETICAL AND CRITICAL.

The immediate object of thanksgiving (vers. 3-5). Ver. 3. **We give thanks.**—As a rule the Apostle begins with thanksgiving; this is precisely as in 1 Thess. i. 2; but in 1 Cor. i. 4, though the address reads: "Paul—and Sosthenes," we find εὐχαριστῶ (so also Phil i. 1-3). The plural is not then conditioned by the mention of Timothy in the address (MEYER, SCHENKEL), yet it is not=εὐχαριστῶ (BAEHR). Plural and singular forms are not used arbitrarily by the Apostle; the choice depended upon the predominance of the Apostle's individual feeling, or of the common sentiment of those participating: and this certainly includes not merely him or those named in the address, but the church in the house or place where the Apostle was. [ELLICOTT says: "we, *i. e.*, I and Timothy," but intimates that the context always fully accounts for the selection of singular or plural. So EADIE, ALFORD. CONYBEARE contends for the singular meaning of the plural throughout all the Epistles—which is inadmissible.—R.]

To God the Father of our Lord Jesus Christ.—See Eph. i. 3.—**Praying always for**

you defines more particularly "we give thanks;" the participle marks the thanksgiving as part of the prayer, and the adverb renders it prominent, that the former was never wanting in the latter. "Always" is not to be joined with the participle "praying" (GREEK FATHERS, BENGEL, LUTHER, etc.) [ALFORD, ELLICOTT, E. V. The majority of modern commentators join it with the verb,—EADIE renders: "We bless God, the Father of our Lord Jesus Christ always, when praying for you."—R.] Still less is "for you" to be joined with "we give thanks" (BAEHR). The latter cannot be decided by Rom. i. 8; 1 Cor. i. 4; 1 Thess. i. 2, while the former opinion is confirmed by Eph. i. 16. On the difference between περί and ὑπέρ, see Eph. v. 2; vi. 18.

Ver. 4. *The occasion of thanksgiving.*—**Since we heard**, ἀκούσαντες.—This second participle (aorist) sets forth what had preceded the thanksgiving, while the first one (present) appends what had accompanied it. See WINER'S *Gram.* p. 323.* The plural here marks the fact as publicly known, not merely made known to the Apostle and his friends.

Of your faith in Christ Jesus, and the love which ye have to all the saints.—"Your faith in Christ Jesus" is the first ground of this thanksgiving; your faith, resting on Christ, moving itself in Him; the phrase "in Christ Jesus" limits "faith" as Eph. i. 15, not ὑμῶν (DE WETTE). The preposition does not affect the meaning of "faith," so that it becomes "believing constancy" (LUTHER), but it only denotes that the object is to be regarded, not as the end of effort (εἰς), but as the element and ground. [ELLICOTT: "In Him as the sphere or sub-stratum of the πίστις, that in which the faith centres itself. The omission of the article gives a more complete unity to the conception, 'Christ-centred faith.'" ALFORD: "the immediate element of their faith, not its distinctive character, is the point brought out."—R.] On the remainder of the clause, "and of the love which ye have to all the saints," see Eph. i. 15.—[The reading: ἣν ἔχετε carries "more affectionate commendation" (ALFORD) than the simple article of the Rec. It draws attention to the love and points to its persistence (ELLICOTT).—R.]

Ver. 5: describes this love more closely.—**On account of the hope which is laid up for you in heaven.**—[Joined to "love."—R.] Since διὰ τὴν ἐλπίδα is joined grammatically to ἣν ἔχετε, Paul has not written ἀγάπην τήν as in the parallel passage, Eph. i. 15, but subjoined the relative clause. "The hope" is characterized by the clause "which is laid up for you in heaven," as objective, like the ἐλπὶς βλεπομένη (Rom. viii. 24), "that which is hoped for," which is preserved, set aside (ἀπό), *in deposito reconditum* (LÖSNER), as a securely placed treasure (CHRYSOSTOM: τὸ ἀσφαλὲς ἔδειξεν; BENGEL: *sine periculo*), or rather as a reward and prize according to 2 Tim. iv. 8; 1 Pet. i. 4; Matt. xix. 21; comp. Heb. ix. 27; vi. 18. On "in heaven," see Eph. i. 10. Accordingly this hope gives a motive for the love in its activity as well as its extent; it does not depend upon the present, on temporal life and possessions, nor on the men, the brethren whom it reaches. It is certain of the eternal, heavenly, divine possessions and salvation, and has in these enough. "Hope" is not therefore the third with "faith" and "love" (STEIGER and others), nor does it furnish a motive for faith (BAEHR and others); least of all for the thanksgiving (BENGEL: "from the hope is manifest how great the ground of thanksgiving for the gift of faith and love"). [So EADIE, BARNES. The E. V.—"for the hope" seems obscure. Both "on account of" (EADIE, ALFORD), and "because of" (ELLICOTT), leave the reader uncertain as to the connection, which is the main difficulty here.—R.]

Whereof ye heard before, ἣν προηκούσατε.—In the ἅπαξ λεγόμενον: προακούειν, according to the context the πρό refers to the object, "the hope laid up" which is future and concealed. MEYER is therefore incorrect: before you had this hope; HEINRICHS: *alio doctore (Epaphra) ante me;* BÖHMER, HUTHER: before the Epistle was written; SCHENKEL: before he had received tidings of their faith. The interpretation (GROTIUS): *prima rudimenta accepistis,* as if προακούειν described the first instruction of catechumens, is unwarranted. [Braune seems to follow DE WETTE and OLSHAUSEN in their view of the force of "before," "before the fulfilment of the hope," but as EADIE well remarks "such an exegesis is a species of truism." ELLICOTT: "not before any definite epoch, but merely at some undefined period in the past," "formerly."—EADIE gives the sense of "*already,*" as intimating that this hope had been made prominent in preaching, and they of course heard of this in hearing the gospel; a view to be preferred as giving more point to the passage and fully accordant with the context.—R.] To "laid up in heaven" corresponds what is joined to "heard before," viz:

In the word of the truth of the gospel—through which the "hearing before" has its guarantee. This expression is another briefer and independent setting forth of Eph. i. 13, "after that ye heard the word of truth, the gospel of your salvation." The hearing before of the hope is mediated by the preaching (ἐν τῷ λόγῳ) of the truth (τῆς ἀληθείας), which is the substance of the λόγος, but is taken out of nothing other than the gospel (τοῦ εὐαγγελίου), to which the truth belongs. It is not proper to follow the parallel passage, which is grammatically different, and take "of the gospel" as a genitive of apposition to "in the word of truth" (STEIGER), or to "the truth" (BAEHR), [ELLICOTT: "a defining genitive, allied to the genitive *possessivus* (genitive *continentis*), which specifies, and so to say, localizes the general notion of the governing substantive: 'the truth which was preached in and was announced in the gospel'".—R.] Nor is "the word of the truth"=*sermo verax* (ERASMUS), or "the preaching of truth" (HUTHER, BLEEK), nor "of the truth of the gospel"=genuine gospel (STORR), nor is λόγος defined as to its substance by ἀληθείας as absolute truth, as to its form by εὐαγγελίου as "proclamation of salvation" (SCHENKEL).

The deeper cause of thanksgiving (vers. 6–8). Ver. 6. **Which has come unto you**—*lit.*, is present unto you. This is spoken of the gospel.

* [The original references are to the 6th German edition; altered throughout to the 7th German ed., 1867.—R.]

Παρών notes its being present (1 Cor. v. 3; 2 Cor. xiii. 10); with πρὸς ὑμᾶς, 2 Cor. xi. 8; Gal. iv. 18, 20, here εἰς ὑμᾶς. In the passages quoted the Apostle stands before them, turned towards them; here he speaks of the gospel, that penetrates into them; he describes the steady, constant and finally entire penetration of the gospel, which is not forced through with one blow. [The preposition conveys the idea of its having *reached* them, the participle implies its abiding there (ELLICOTT).—R.] The added clause: **as it is in all the world,** renders prominent the simple fact of the presence of the gospel in the world. The preposition ἐν marks the distinction between its presence in the world, and in Colosse, where it has already wrought what it should and would. "In all the world" indicates the whole world as the field, in which the gospel is found and which it will permeate. It is not confined to one part, had already begun its efficacy in the most diverse places, among Jews and Gentiles. Hence it is no synecdoche, "meaning the most noted parts of the world, as Rom. i. 8; x. 18" (GROTIUS), nor only the Roman Empire, nor popular hyperbole (MEYER). [ALFORD: "No hyperbole, but the pragmatic repetition of the Lord's parting command.—R.]

And is bringing forth fruit and increasing.—[ALFORD, omitting καί, calls the paragraph broken and unbalanced.—R.] It is not merely *in* all the world, but efficient there also. We have here the usual transition from the participial construction to that of the finite verb (WINER'S *Gram.*, p. 505 sq.); the participle with εἶναι indicates continuance and duration (WINER'S *Gram.*, p. 326 sq.). [So in English, hence the literal rendering: "is bringing forth fruit and increasing" is preferable.—R.] THEODORET: καρποφορίαν τοῦ εὐαγγελίου κέκληκε τὴν ἐπαινουμένην πολιτείαν, αὔξησιν δὲ τῶν πιστευόντων τὸ πλῆθος. The figure is borrowed from a tree which both bears fruit and grows (Matt. vii. 17; xiii. 32; Luke xiii. 19). The former word refers to the faith, the love, the Christian virtues, which the gospel produces in the internal and external life, the latter to the extension and the multiplication of its adherents (Acts vi. 7; xii. 24; xix. 20). [The former the *intensive*, the latter the *extensive* progress of the gospel. ELLICOTT.—R.]—**As it is also among you,** introduces Colosse as a part of the field, in which the gospel is and is working ("in all the world"), and furnishes a proof that the gospel is, and how it is, "in all the world." Hence ἐν ὑμῖν is "among you," not "in you" (LUTHER). "Bringing forth fruit and increasing" must be supplied. ["*It doth,*" supplied in E. V., is to be changed to "*it is,*" to correspond with the participial form of the verb in the former clause.—R.]

Since the day ye heard it, and knew the grace of God in truth.—[Braune, following DE WETTE, supplies no object after "heard," making "the grace of God" the object of both verbs. MEYER, STEIGER, EADIE, ALFORD, ELLICOTT, supply: "the gospel," which is to be preferred. E. V. "of it," is unsatisfactory; they must have heard the gospel, as well as heard of it, before it would bring forth fruit among them.—R.] On the construction ἀφ' ἧς ἡμέρας, see WINER'S *Gram.*, p. 130. The first proclamation of the gospel was followed by the acceptance of it, and from that time forth the Christian life and character of the Church developed internally and externally in constant progress. The object is "the grace of God," the substance of the *evangelical* preaching (ver. 5), the marrow of the gospel over against the law. "In truth" is an adverbial qualification of the verbs "heard" and "knew." The gospel is proclaimed *vere et sincere absque fuco*, οὐκ ἐν ἀπάτῃ καὶ λόγοις εἰκαίοις * (GREEK FATHERS), and is accepted *non simulate, sed vere.* It implies a contrast to the false teachers and is not = ἀληθῶς, "truly," nor to be joined with "grace" (STORR and others), nor = in the gospel (GROTIUS) [BARNES.—R.]. Nor is it to be joined only to "knew" (MEYER and others), nor to "heard" alone (BAEHR and others). [ALFORD: "in its truth, and with true knowledge." So EADIE: "the words ἐν ἀληθείᾳ describe the teaching of Epaphras, or represent that genuine form, in which, by his preaching, the grace of God had been exhibited at Colosse." This makes it qualify the verb "knew," and at the same time define "the grace of God" by presenting the element, in which the gospel was proclaimed.—R.]

Ver. 7. **Even as ye learned of Epaphras.**—Καθώς refers to "in truth" [ALFORD: "in which truth"—R.], and describes the manner in which they had learned from Epaphras. The verb, the object of which must be "the grace of God," marks the intermediate step between "hearing" and "knowing" and describes the earnest, constant effort of the Colossians, to which the activity of Epaphras corresponds.—Epaphras a Colossian or Phrygian (iv. 12: "one of you"), with Paul in his imprisonment (Philem. 23: "my fellow prisoner"), is not identical with Epaphroditus, the Macedonian, a preacher of Philippi † (Phil. ii. 25; iv. 18), as GROTIUS arbitrarily assumes; here indicated as the founder of the Church in Colosse, but otherwise entirely unknown to us. Even should we accept the reading καί before ἐμάθετε, we could not, with WIGGERS,‡ treat it as though it were καὶ ἀπὸ Ἐπαφρᾶ (as in Rom. v. 7; Eph. iv. 4), in order thus to maintain that there had been a proclamation of the gospel in Colosse before that of Epaphras. Still less does the καθώς resume the preceding καθὼς ἐν παντὶ τῷ κόσμῳ, as though Epaphras had only told that the gospel was every where proclaimed (THEODORET). The preposition ἀπό indicates that the Colossians had gladly met Epaphras and heard him speak. The words which follow are a confirmation of the preaching of Epaphras: **our dear fellow servant, who is for you a faithful minister of Christ.**—"Our dear fellow servant" describes him in his position toward Christ (δοῦλος) [no thought of his imprisonment with Paul (CONYBEARE)—R.], and toward Paul with his helpers (σύν—ἡμῶν), and in his relation to them (ἀγαπητοῦ), as an excellent minister, who, entirely dependent on the Lord, and independent of men, labored as a colleague with the Apostle and his

* ["Truly and sincerely, without dissimulation, not in deceit and rash words."—R.]

† [CONYBEARE. II. 385: "Epaphras is the same name with Epaphroditus" (?)—"but this can scarcely be the same person." *etc.*—R.]

‡ [*Studien und Kritiken.* 1838. p. 185.—R.]

fellow laborers, especially for the Church at Colosse (ὑπὲρ ὑμῶν), from the beginning, with proper fidelity (ὅς ἐστιν πιστός) in the service of Christ (διάκονος Χριστοῦ). [The reading of the Rec., ὑπὲρ ὑμῶν, "for you," "on your behalf," is not only better supported, but avoids the repetition of the other reading, while it is as strong a commendation of Epaphras to the Colossians, to say that he had been a faithful minister of Christ for them, as to say that he had been faithful *vice apostoli*.—R.]

Ver. 8. **Who also declared unto us your love in the Spirit.**—The declaration is made prominent. Epaphras has not only seen in Colosse, but spoken in Rome to Paul in a detailed, perspicuous way, as a witness respecting "your love in the Spirit." The love was "not carnal, but spiritual" (ŒCUMENIUS), "fruit of the Spirit" (Gal. v. 22: Rom. xv. 30); Spirit is of course the Holy Spirit (as Rom. xiv. 17). Hence it is not the spirit of man, the inner man, nor a "love which depends on an internal sentiment and disposition, a love sincere and earnest" (A LAPIDE, BÖHMER and others), and since the context must decide what is the object of the love, it is to be regarded as "love of the brethren" (ver. 4), including love to the Apostle, but not this latter exclusively (BAEHR, BLEEK and others); the following "we also" at least cannot decide this to be the meaning, since the Apostle does not pray merely in reciprocity. It is improper to join ἐν πνεύματι with δηλώσας (WAHL), as though Epaphras had narrated it through inspiration, or to explain it, *per spiritum sanctum* (GROTIUS). [EADIE properly expounds "love" as denoting the Christian grace of love, hence "in the Spirit." ALFORD: "the chief gift of the Spirit," "thus in the elemental region of the Spirit;" ELLICOTT: "genuine and operative only in the sphere of His blessed influence." —R.]

It is unmistakably the object of Paul in this honoring description, to establish as firmly as possible in every direction the authority of Epaphras; his doctrine is right, his relations to the Apostle hearty and intimate, his interest for the Colossians active and pure, undisturbed from the first. He seems to have been suspected by the false teachers. Paul gives prominence to these facts, in order to shame the errorists, to warn and guard the Church against them; for their sake and that of the cause, he enters particularly upon the efficiency and conduct of Epaphras. ESTIUS: "Lest they might suffer themselves to be led away from the doctrine which they had learned from him by new teachers."

DOCTRINAL AND ETHICAL.

1. *Faith* and *Love* are the chief points, in judging of the condition of the Christian Church. Faith must not only be directed *to* (εἰς) Christ, but be a life *in* (ἐν) Christ; it is the foundation and source of love, by which it worketh [Gal. v. 6.—R.]. This love must be "in the Spirit" (ver. 8), that it may be pure, and extend "to all the saints" (ver. 4), that it may be large-hearted, not limited by sensuous, arbitrary and selfish sympathies. Living, active faith in Christ alone leads to such purity and extent of love, because the believer has first of all love to God, the Father of Jesus Christ (and through Him his Father), and from a faith on the love of God in Christ, which enjoys the love of the Father and Son, he gains a love to all, in whom the same faith is active, who have become and still are the objects of the same mercy, altogether irrespective of the stage of results accomplished, however manifold the degrees of its strength may be. It overleaps party lines and difference of creeds, and prays in truth: Our Father, which art in heaven. In "*Father*" lies the doctrine of *faith*, in "our" the ethics of *love*, in "which art in heaven," the impulse and motive of *hope*.

2. *The activity of this love*, growing out of faith, which embraces all Christians as brethren, as children of the Father, has its mainspring in the hope of salvation, secure for us in heaven. This is *Christian eudæmonism*, which indeed has in view the salvation of our own souls, the perfection and blessedness of our own personality, yet not selfishly, but seeks and knows in fellowship with all believers; nor yet externally, sensualistically, like a Turk or heathen German, but internally, in the spirit of the mind; nor yet here, but in heaven, not in time, but in eternity, hence not as a materialist or atheist burning for good fortune and earthly pleasure; and finally not in our own strength, as it has been attempted "in godless virtue," but as a gift of the gracious God through Christ.

3. *Faith grows from the preached word of gospel truth.* Since faith as to its essence is God's word become living in the heart of man, since it grows out of this word as from a seed, its establishment and growth depends altogether upon the preaching of this word of God (λόγος, ver. 5), which alone contains the truth indispensably necessary for the soul, presenting the grace of God, which is the marrow of the gospel (ver. 5: τῆς ἀληθείας τοῦ εὐαγγελίου, ver. 6: τὴν χάριν τοῦ θεοῦ). This and not the preaching (SCHENKEL) is the vital principle of Christianity, which penetrates ever more deeply into the believers, producing in them and in the life of the church the fruits of virtues, both active and passive, ever extending more widely, ever permeating more thoroughly every one and all things (ver. 6). ["To keep the figure of the Apostle, it was like a tree, whose fruit, falling to the earth, germinated, so that there sprang up a youthful and healthy forest on all sides of it" (EADIE).—R.] Preaching is only the principal means, to which we must hold fast in simplicity and freedom from all perversion, deterioration or obscuration.

4. *The teachers or preachers of the gospel* must labor as belonging to Christ, as entirely dependent on Him (ver. 7: δοῦλος) yet attached to Him (διάκονος); they are not servants *of* the church (SCHENKEL), but only of Christ; *servants*, but *for* the church (ὑπὲρ ὑμῶν), in doctrine (vers. 6, 7), in supplication to God (ver. 3), and in the varied intercourse with men, among whom they would advance their cause. They should never forget that they do not stand alone and for themselves, but in fellowship (ver. 7: σύνδουλος), that as colleagues they should esteem and love each other, that one should rejoice without envy in the other, as Paul in Epaphras, who meekly flies to

him, and should fraternally suffer with each other, as Epaphras with Paul. [HENRY:—"Thus he puts an honor on an inferior minister, and teaches us not to be selfish, or think all that honor lost which goes beside ourselves. We learn in his example not to think it a disparagement to us, to *water* what others have *planted*, or build on the foundation others have *laid*."—"Observe Christ is our proper master and we His ministers. He does not say your minister, but the *minister of Christ for you*. It is by Christ's authority, but for the people's service."—R.]

HOMILETICAL AND PRACTICAL.

Even where we must fear and blame and warn, an opportunity for thanksgiving is not wanting. —In the general prayer for Sunday service belongs the petition for love toward *all* men; however easy towards *some*, it is just as difficult towards *all*.—Do not suffer a preacher, colleague or friend to be misunderstood and falsely judged, for speaking well of him belongs to obedience to the Ninth Commandment; neither break out blindly against him, that misunderstands the neighbor whose cause you would advance.—Rejoice when you see the word of God efficacious, and learn to wait patiently, as a husbandman for the fruits.

STARKE:—He who does not believe on Jesus Christ, does not believe on God at all; so though the Jews and Turks think they believe on God, yet they in no wise do; for they do not believe on Jesus, on whom we must believe before we can assure ourselves of grace and salvation from God. — [Always to pray, and always to give thanks are the Christian's needful duties.—If teaching and learning are of the right sort, then God's word hath good speed.—Not all loving is praiseworthy; love in the Spirit is commended. —R.]

RIEGER:—In the eyes of the world the character of a philanthropist, embracing all in his love, will indeed bring us more honor and glory than love to the saints; for this implies a distinction which the world does not willingly admit. The world has a love to which a Jew or Turk is more acceptable than a saint.—If we consider only the yet feeble beginnings of faith, the still prevailing temptations, we may doubt whether we have cause to rejoice and thank God. But by looking out to the mark of hope, which is set before us, the grace to us becomes very great.—It is certainly unspeakable how much the world, now so unbelieving and unthankful, does yet enjoy of the fruits of the gospel; how many arts and sciences, milder customs and laws would not exist, had not the gospel made the first advance in that direction.

SCHLEIERMACHER:—Faith, since it is active, becomes not only love to Christ, but also love to all, who belong to Christ.—We see how readily we allow ourselves to be led into all manner of divisions and limitations of love, which have less ground than then existed in the difference between Jewish and Gentile Christians. It is better to study such a love to *all* saints, and not one that extends to the few who exactly and specially agree with us, however great enjoyment there may be in it.—[The gospel is a germ, made fruitful by God, which cannot be received, without its making an impression on the spirit.—R.]

PASSAVANT:—There is generally an unspeakably beneficent, tender feeling in giving thanks from the heart for a benefit.—Thanksgiving will be the bliss of eternity. The beginning, the first steps thereto must be made on the porch, else we shall have no voice nor place, no life above in the holy choirs.—It may often be long: days, years, decades may pass as we hear and know the gospel, before we obtain a living knowledge of the grace of God, that permeates our heart and mind and life.—"There are men," says Pascal, "who admire external greatness alone, as if there were no mental greatness; others can only admire mental greatness, as though there were not one infinitely higher, to be found in wisdom."

[LISCO:—The Apostolic thanksgiving and the praise therein contained has no other purpose than encouragement, 1) to continued steadfastness; 2) to further advance in all good.—HENRY: —Ver. 3. In our thanksgiving we must have an eye to God as God (He is the object of thanksgiving as well as prayer), and as the Father of our Lord Jesus Christ, in whom and through whom all good comes to us.—Vers. 4, 5. Faith, hope, and love, are the three principal graces in the Christian life, and proper matter of our prayer and thanksgiving.—We must love *all the saints*, bear an extensive kindness and good-will to good men, notwithstanding lesser points of difference and many real weaknesses.—Ver. 6. All who hear the word of the gospel, ought to bring forth the fruit of the gospel.—Wherever the gospel comes, it will bring forth fruit to the honor and glory of God. We mistake, if we think to monopolize the comforts and benefits of the gospel to ourselves.—Ver. 8. Faithful ministers are glad to be able to speak well of their people.—R.]

[EADIE:—Ver. 5. "For the hope." Every blessing which the gospel makes known has futurity in its eye,—and the Christian life, in the meantime, is one as much of expectation as of positive enjoyment.—Ver. 6. The gospel bore choice and noble clusters of fruit. It is not a ceremonial to be gazed at, or a congeries of opinions to be discussed. It is essentially a practical system, for its ethics are involved in its creed and worship.—The gospel was ecumenical, but the error which menaced them was only provincial in its sphere.—Ver. 8. Love is to be regarded as the crown and consequence of all the other graces. The Spirit of Him who is Love takes possession of the believing bosom, and exerts upon it His own assimilating power. A Christian community may be congratulated upon its love.—R.]

[SCHENKEL:—The true Christian idiosyncrasy of a church: 1) Its ground—faith in Christ; 2) its fruit—love to the saints; 3) its power—hope of the heavenly treasure of eternal life.—The gospel of Jesus Christ, the tree of life for humanity: 1) The fruit, which it brings; 2) the extension, which it gains.—The power of the gospel: 1) It consists in the word of the grace of God. 2) It is conditioned by a faithful proclamation and simple apprehension of it.—R.]

2. Earnest supplication for the progress of the Church in true knowledge, especially of the Being and Work of Christ.

(Chapter I. 9–23.)

9 For this cause we also, since the day we neard *it*, do not cease to pray for you,
and to desire[1] that ye might be filled with the knowledge of his will in all wisdom
10 and spiritual understanding [in all spiritual wisdom and understanding]: That ye[2]
might walk worthy of the Lord unto all pleasing, being fruitful in every good work,
11 and increasing in [by][3] the knowledge of God; Strengthened with all might
[strength][4] according to his glorious power [the power of his glory],[5] unto all pa-
12 tience and longsuffering with joyfulness [joy];[6] Giving thanks unto the Father,
which [who] hath made us meet, to be partakers [for the portion, εἰς τὴν μερίδα][8] of the
13 inheritance of the saints in light: Who hath delivered us from [out of] the power
of darkness, and hath translated *us* into the kingdom of his dear Son [the Son of
14 his love];[9] In whom we have redemption through his blood [omit through his
15 blood],[10] *even* the forgiveness of sins: Who is the image of the invisible God, the
16 firstborn of [before] every creature: For [Because] by [in] him were all things cre-
ated, that are in heaven, and that are in [on] earth, visible and invisible, whether
they be thrones, or dominions, or principalities, or powers: all things were created
17 by him, and for him: And he is[11] before all things, and by [ἐν, in] him all things
18 consist [subsist]. And he is the head of the body, the church: who is the begin-
ning, the firstborn[12] from the dead; that in all things he might have the pre-emi-
19 nence. For it pleased *the Father* that in him should all fulness dwell [Because in
20 him *God* was pleased that the whole fulness should dwell]:[13] And, having made
peace through the blood of his cross, by him to reconcile all things unto himself:
21 by him, *I say*, whether *they be* things in [on] earth, or things in heaven. And
you, that were sometimes alienated and enemies in *your* mind by wicked works
22 [lit.: as to *your* understanding in wicked works], yet now hath he reconciled,[14] In
the body of his flesh through [his] death,[15] to present you holy and unblamable and un-
23 reprovable in his sight: If [If at least, εἴγε] ye continue in the faith grounded and
settled, and *be* not moved away from the hope of the gospel, which ye have heard,
and which was preached to every creature[16] which is under heaven; whereof I Paul
am made a minister.[17]

1 Ver. 9.—Καὶ αἰτούμενοι is wanting in B. [On the order of the latter part of the verse see Exeg. Notes.—R.]

2 Ver. 10.—[Ὑμᾶς, inserted after περιπατῆσαι, Rec. Tischendorf, Wordsworth. Rejected by Lachmann, Meyer, Scholz, Alford, Ellicott, on the authority of ℵ. A. B. C. D. F. The subject "ye" necessarily supplied in the finite construction of our language.—R.]

3 Ver. 10.—Instead of the more difficult reading: εἰς τὴν ἐπίγνωσιν, of D.[3] E.[2] K. L., we find in ℵ. B. [C. D. F. G.] τῇ ἐπιγνώσει, which with Meyer is to be regarded as an explanation. [Braune's German text: *in der Erkenntniss*, is certainly a typographical error for *in die Erkenntniss*. The reading ἐν with the dative has little support. Εἰς with the accusative, which Braune adopts, is that of Tischendorf (eds. 2 and 7, not 1). But Lachmann, Griesbach, Scholz, De Wette, Alford, Ellicott follow the preponderant uncial authority and read τῇ ἐπιγνώσει, all of them previous to the discovery of ℵ., which confirms this reading. I have therefore altered the English text to express the force of this reading (instrumental dative).—R.]

4 Ver. 11.—["Strengthened with strength;" δυνάμει δυναμούμενοι.—R.]

5 Ver. 11.—[The hendiadys of the E. V. is generally considered unfortunate. Coverdale, Rhemish: "the might of His glory."—R.]

6 Ver. 11.—["Joy;" Wickliffe, Rhemish, Eadie, Alford, Ellicott.—R.]

7 Ver. 12.—B. inserts καλέσαντι καί before ἱκανώσαντι [retained by Lachmann only.—R.]. D.[1] F. G. read καλέσαντι only, omitting ἱκαν. The first appears to have been interpolated, then the subsequent omission.

8 Ver 12.—["For the portion," more literal than E. V., following the versions of Wickliffe, Coverdale and the Rhemish—"for the share," "for the part," *etc.*—R.]

9 Ver. 13.—["Son of his love," preferred by all modern commentators, avoiding the hendiadys of the E. V.—R.]

10 Ver. 14.—[Ellicott: "διὰ τοῦ αἵματος αὐτοῦ rests only on cursive manuscripts, and is rightly omitted by nearly all modern editors." From Eph. i. 7.—R.]

11 Ver. 17.—[Wordsworth reads ἔστι. "exists," instead of ἐστί, "is." "Subsist," Alford, Ellicott.—R.]

12 Ver. 18.—Ἐκ is to be retained before τῶν νεκρῶν with B. and the corrector of ℵ.—B. alone has the article ἡ before ἀρχή.

13 Ver. 19.—[The rendering of Alford, given above, coincides with that of Braune. See Exeg. Notes.—R.]

14 Ver. 21.—B. and others have ἀποκατηλλάγητε. The reading ἀποκατήλλαξεν, ℵ. A. C. and others, seems to

be an emendation on account of the construction. [The preponderance of authority is on the other side. Lachmann adopts the reading of B., but Rec., E. V., Tischendorf, Alford, Ellicott, Wordsworth follow the mass of MSS. See EXEG. NOTES.—R.]

15 Ver. 22.—Αὐτοῦ after θανάτου, ℵ. A., is properly omitted in B. [Τοῦ θανάτου is="his death" here.—R.]

16 Ver. 23.—Τῇ is omitted after πάσῃ in ℵ. A. B. C. and others. The corrector of ℵ. adds it.

17 Ver. 23.—Instead of διάκονος, the reading of ℵ. B. [? A.] is κήρυξ καὶ ἀπόστολος, yet διάκονος is added in the margin of ℵ.

EXEGETICAL AND CRITICAL.

The immediate object of supplication: full knowledge of the Divine will. (ver. 9.)—Ver. 9. **For this cause** refers to the entire paragraph, vers. 3–8. What the Apostle had heard of the Colossians moved him to the petition. This is required by the contents of the petition and by the accords: "since the day we heard" (ver. 9), to which the object must be supplied from above ("your faith in Christ Jesus and love to all the saints"); ver. 6. "since the day ye heard" and ver. 4. "since we heard:" and also "do not cease to pray for you" (ver. 9), and ver. 3, "praying also for you." After his thanks to God, Paul now gives the purport of his prayer. Certainly ver. 9 is not connected with ver. 8 alone, where the love of the Colossians to himself is spoken of: because he had heard this, he now prays for them (BLEEK); as though Paul, like the Pharisees, prayed only for those who loved him.

We also, as in "we give thanks" (ver. 3), is Paul and those with him, hence not Timothy merely (MEYER, SCHENKEL), nor is he excluded (BAEHR). Καί, "also," refers chiefly to Epaphras, who represents and labors for the Colossians (vers. 7–8), and then to the Colossians also, who were won to the gospel (ver. 6) and have love to the brethren (vers. 4. 8). It does not therefore indicate merely the reciprocity of intercourse between the Colossians and Paul (SCHENKEL, MEYER). [It has here its slightly *contrastive* force (ELLICOTT), and marks the change of subject; "we on our part" (ALFORD).—R.] It is not to be separated from ἡμεῖς and joined to διὰ τοῦτο (DE WETTE), nor by any means to προςευχόμενοι (BAUMGARTEN-CRUSIUS).

[**Since the day we heard.**—ELLICOTT: "incidental definition of the time with reference to ἀκούσαντες, ver. 4. EADIE: "The receipt of the intelligence produced immediate results and led to prayer. The effect was instant—and it was not spent with a single impulse." The prayer was continuous also.—R.]

Do not cease to pray for you, and to desire.—On οὐ παυόμεθα with the participles, see Eph. i. 16. [ELLICOTT: "an exactly similar affectionate hyperbole."—R.] The first verb denotes the wish (2 Cor. xiii. 9; 3 Jno. 2; Acts xxvii. 29), addressed to any one, then in general a prayer expressing a wish; the second, the supplication, entreaty, the medium with its reflection; *sibi expetere*, the pressing hearty petition from a sense of fellowship. [It seems a better distinction to regard the first as general, the second as special, "the one prayer in its ordinary aspect, the other direct request." Καί "brings into prominence a special after a general" (ALFORD). The comma of the E. V. answers the same purpose here.—R.]

That ye might be filled.—(BENGEL: "He made mention of his supplications generally ver. 3; he now expresses what he supplicates." Ἵνα indicates the aim of the petition, the purpose of the petitioner, hence not simply its purport (against HARLESS, Eph. 17). [On ἵνα after verbs of praying, see ALFORD, 1 Cor. xiv. 13. "The *purport* and *purpose* become *compounded in the expression.*" ELLICOTT: "Ἵνα has here its secondary telic force, the subject of the prayer is blended with the purpose of making it."—R.] Πληρωθῆτε pre-supposes the imperfect state of those prayed for, and from its position at the beginning renders prominent the importance of progress to fulness. It occurs in this Epistle alone five times, here; ver. 25; ii. 10; iv. 12, 17; in Ephesians (i. 23; iii. 19; iv. 10; v. 18), and in Philippians (i. 11; ii. 2; iv. 18, 19), each four times.

With the knowledge of his will.—Τὴν ἐπίγνωσιν is an accusative of reference, like Phil. i. 11; so σκηνοποιὸς τὴν τέχνην (Acts xviii. 3). [ELLICOTT: "accusative of the remoter, the quantitative object in which the action of the verb has its realization." "The genitive marks the absolute *material* out of which the fulness was realized, the accusative as it were, the domain of which the fulness was evinced."—R.]. See WINER'S *Gram.* p. 216. Further it is not = τῇ ἐπιγνώσει, since they were not to be filled with the knowledge, but their knowledge should be full, perfect. The word itself describes the knowledge which grasps and penetrates the object (MEYER), as ver. 10; ii. 3; iii. 10. [WORDSWORTH: "ἐπίγνωσις, full knowledge is more than γνῶσις, it is a gift and grace of the Holy Spirit. This word occurs oftener in this Epistle than in any other of St. Paul. He may perhaps have used it as a contrast to the false γνῶσις or *gnosticism* of the false teachers, who were beguiling the Colossians with the speciousness of their vain philosophy. They in their theories promise γνῶσις, but the Apostle gave ἐπίγνωσις by his ministry." DE WETTE suggests, the former is a mere impractical and theoretical, the latter full and living knowledge.—R.] "Of his will," since it concerns the purpose of the prayer, is God's will, and, according to the context (ver. 10), the will of God respecting the walk and conversation of the Christian in the world. Hence not the redemptive decree, as Eph. i. 9 (STEIGER and others), not the will of God which operates on us and is efficient in us, but the will of God to be obeyed by us, hence not the will of the majority (SCHENKEL). [The immediate context "in all wisdom," is against this limitation of "His will." The result of full knowledge was to be worthy walk, but the knowledge was not therefore to be limited to His will respecting walk. As a fact Christian walk is based on a far wider knowledge.—R.]

Paul now sets forth the mode in which this "being filled" was to be consummated: **In all spiritual wisdom and understanding.**—Hence this is not to be joined with "walk" (ver. 10), which is otherwise defined (THEODORET and others). See Eph. i. 8: "in all wisdom and prudence." Σύνεσις is not identical with φρόνησις (Sirach. i. 4; σύνεσις φρονήσεως); the latter refers more to the God-given organ, the former more to the activity of man in using it; the latter more to the original gift, the former obtained rather by exercise. [The former is perhaps seen more in practically embracing a truth, the latter more in bringing the mind to bear upon it (ELLICOTT). — R.] The adjective "spiritual" belongs to both substantives. It indicates that the "being filled" cannot be effected by any purely natural development of human mental life from its own power. The wisdom is not "fleshly" (2 Cor i. 12; 1 Cor. i. 26), nor is the understanding of this character; yet neither are of themselves spiritual," they become so only through the Holy Ghost. [EADIE and ALFORD join πνευματικῇ to συνέσει alone, but it seems better with ELLICOTT to join both adjectives to both substantives. On σοφία and σύνεσις, the general and particular, ELLICOTT remarks: "both appear to have a practical reference; the former is, however, a general term; the latter its more special result and application."—R.]

The aim of the petition: Christian walk. Vers. 10–12. They were not to rest with "knowledge of His will," but advance.

Ver. 10. **That ye might walk.**—The infinitive, περιπατῆσαι, depending on πληρωθῆτε is epexegetical (WINER'S *Gram.* pp. 298, 301); it is not necessary to supply εἰς or ὥστε. The closer definition follows.—**Worthy of the Lord** refers to Christ [as always *apparently* in St. Paul's Epistles (ELLICOTT).— R.], the model of the Christian. Neither 1 Thess. ii. 12, "worthy of God," nor Eph. iv. 1, "followers of God," will justify us in understanding it otherwise.—**Unto all pleasing** describes the manner of the worthy walk, giving prominence to the purpose (εἰς). Ἀρέσκεια, only here, in a good sense, describes in classical authors the conduct of the ἄρεσκος, the obsequious, *i. e.*, obsequiousness. The context requires that it be understood as "pleasing Christ" not God, in spite of Matt. v. 48 (SCHENKEL). Since Christ can be pleased in everything, "all" is added.

This is confirmed by the following characteristic of the Christian walk: **Being fruitful in every work.**—[Braune reads, "being fruitful and increasing in every good work," a collocation in conformity with his view of the text and his exegesis. The order of the E. V. seems to preserve the symmetry and present the meaning better.—R.] On the nominatives καρποφοροῦντες καὶ αὐξ., instead of the more exact accusatives, to agree with ὑμᾶς implied after περιπατῆσαι, see Eph. iv. 1, 3. Here it is readily explained, yet not by joining the participles to πληρωθῆτε (BENGEL); the two participles are united as in ver. 6; first bearing fruit, then growing more, as in a tree, in order to greater fruitfulness. The sphere of both is denoted by "in." The prepositional phrase, standing first for emphasis, is not to be joined with "pleasing" (OECUMEN, STEIGER and others), but with the verbs [or according to the view of ALFORD, ELLICOTT and others, with the verb "being fruitful"—undoubtedly to be preferred if the instrumental dative is retained. See below.—R.] By "good works" we are to understand, works required by the will of God, growing out of faith, demanded, not merely by law, but by relations, circumstances, by the inward impulse of the conscience and the Holy Ghost.

[**And increasing by the knowledge of God.**] The advance is made into, up to the knowledge of God. This indeed depends upon their being "filled with the knowledge of His will" (ver. 9). Their being fruitful and increasing in every good work aids thereto. Hence LUTHER is incorrect; and be fruitful in every good work and increase in the knowledge of God. [The order of the E. V. is the same.—R.] Advance is made from knowledge to knowledge in the Christian walk, wherein the spirit of God guides into all truth (Jno. xvi. 13; xiv. 26). Εἰς is neither = κατά (BÖHMER nor = ἐν (BEZA), nor = the dative which HUTHER and others read. [The close union of the two participles above and the preceding exegetical note are based on the less supported reading: εἰς τὴν ἐπίγνωσιν. The better reading is τῇ ἐπιγνώσει (instrumental dative). This is to be joined with αὐξανόμενοι, "increasing by the knowledge of God." As the main reason for retaining the reading of the fewer MSS. is that it is more difficult, ALFORD remarks, supporting τῇ ἐπιγνώσει: "this is by far the most difficult of the three readings, the meaning of ἐν and εἰς being very obvious, the former pointing out the element, the latter the proposed measure of the increase. And hence, probably, the variations. It is the knowledge of God which is the real instrument of *enlargement*, in soul and life, of the believer—not a γνῶσις which φυσιοι, but an ἐπίγνωσις which αὐξάνει." So OLSHAUSEN, DE WETTE, HUTHER, EADIE, ELLICOTT.—R.]

Ver. 11 gives a second definition of the walk, almost exactly like the first in its construction. —**Strengthened with all strength,** ἐν πάσῃ δυνάμει δυναμούμενοι. The verb, which occurs only here, marks those walking worthy of the Lord as energized in activity, not in one direction, but in all: in will, affection and perception, in understanding, in home and calling, in all external relations. [Braune seems to regard ἐν as indicating the element, and δύναμις as subjective (so ALFORD). It seems more natural and accordant with the phrase immediately following, to take ἐν as instrumental and δύναμις as objective, *i. e.*, strength from God. So MEYER, EADIE, ELLICOTT (THEODORET is quoted by the latter), and E. V.; in either case "all" implies that the energy extends to every department.—R.] The paranomasia, as well as the construction like that of the previous clause, forbid the separation of the prepositional phrase from the verb, to join it with what precedes.

According to the power of His glory, κατὰ τὸ κράτος τῆς δόξης.—Power is requisite, the Christian does not have it in himself; the measure of it is not inconsiderable, it increases. God alone gives it in proportion to the Power which He has, in comparison with whose glory, majesty, grace and mercy, we are and have nothing. His glory ever reveals itself more and more to him who walks worthy of the Lord. The motive and measure of our strength is in the might of the majesty of God, whom we know ever better. Hence δόξα and ἰσχύς (Eph. i. 19; vi. 10, "according to the power of his might") are not to be considered as parallels and the former limited here to the Ruler's dignity (STEIGER), nor is the phrase="glorious power" (LUTHER, BAEHR, [E. V.], and others), as though it were ἔνδοξον κράτος.

Unto all patience and long-suffering with joy.—Through growing strength progress is made in directions the most various (πᾶσαν, all) "unto patience" (ὑπομονήν) which is not merely suffering (ὑπέχει, Jude. 7. only) *i. e., sustinere.* Ὑπομένειν means the mind in suffering; ὑπομονή denotes this constancy and patience of the mind. Hence we find, not the patience of God, but "the God of patience" spoken of (Rom. xv. 5), it is not God, who demands, but who dispenses "patience" (TITTMANN, *Syn.*, I. p. 194). "Patience" is opposed to displeasure without power to help or change; "long-suffering," to displeasure with power to punish, to avenge, to alter and avert. CHRYSOSTOM: "one is long-suffering towards those whom it is possible to requite, but patient towards those whom he is unable to requite." In the former case the objects are usually men, in the latter, circumstances. It is incorrect to make "patience" refer to the extent, and "long suffering" to the continuance of the feeling (SCHENKEL), or to contrast timidity with the former and irritability with the latter (HUTHER), or to ignore the distinction (MEYER, BLEEK). [ELLICOTT renders εἰς, "to insure, to lead you into," marking the final destination; EADIE: "in order to." See his notes *in loco*, on the distinction between "patience" and "long suffering."—R.] That which is characteristically Christian in both is: "with joy," which is impossible in such a case without the power of God. In "patience and long-suffering" the Christian is glad, and certain of the victory of his cause, of his reward with God both in his own heart and in heaven. It must not then be joined with "giving thanks" (ver. 12), as is done by the Greek fathers, ESTIUS, HUTHER, MEYER, SCHENKEL, BLEEK. [And also by TISCHENDORF, LACHMANN, ELLICOTT, on the ground of the parallelism in the structure of the clauses.—R.] "With joy" would be entirely superfluous in that connection; the parallelism is not compulsory, and besides it is not "*in* joy," indicating the element, but "with (μετά), which shows that it is only an accompaniment with "patience." [As DE WETTE says: by such a connection "we lose the essential idea of joyful endurance—and the beautiful train of thought, that joyfulness in suffering expresses itself in thankfulness to God" (ALFORD). —R.]

The *third definition* follows (vers. 12–14).—Ver. 12.—**Giving thanks to the Father who hath made us meet.**—Even in sorrow, let there be thanksgiving; let not Him be forgotten who giveth gifts and is the Father. It is incorrect, to take the participle, not as coördinate with "being fruitful," "increasing," "strengthened," but as connected with "do not cease," ver. 9 (Greek fathers, CALVIN, BENGEL); or to supply "of our Lord Jesus Christ" (ver. 3) after "Father" (MEYER) [ALFORD, ELLICOTT.—R.], instead of regarding Him, in accordance with the context, as our Father, who however is and proves Himself such in Christ: *qui idoneos fecit, fueramus enim inidonei*, 2 Cor. iii. 6 (BENGEL). "Us" includes the Apostle and his companions and his readers, who are Christians.—For what has He made us meet?—**For the portion of the inheritance of the saints in light.**—"For" (εἰς as above) marks the aim the "making meet," which (as aorist) shows that it is already, even though incipiently, attained. Τὴν μερίδα describes the "portion," share, which falls to one personally (Luke x. 42; xii. 43), and "the inheritance" (τοῦ κλήρου) describes the whole of which the Christian is partaker, as given *sorte non pretio* (BENGEL), as undeserved. The expression is borrowed from the Old Testament (Ps. xvi. 5, "the portion of my inheritance, μερὶς τῆς κληρονομίας); as the chosen people obtained Canaan (ἡ γῆ τῆς κληρονομίας) through the grace of God, and each Israelite his part in the distribution of the land, so the Christian obtains his portion in and of the kingdom of heaven. "The saints" then describes the possessors of the heritage. The position of ἐν φωτί forbids our connecting it with ἱκανώσαντι, "making meet" (Greek fathers, STEIGER, MEYER), which besides is accomplished in another way than "in light;" or with "inheritance" (BEZA, HUTHER, BLEEK), or with "portion" (BENGEL). It is a closer description of the sphere in which "the saints," the Christians, (ver. 2) are found in their walk (ver. 10), in order to mark the extent of the benefit conferred upon them through the "making meet," which is the occasion of the thanksgiving. Comp. Eph. v. 8, 9, 11; iv. 18. According to the context the result is the principal point here, not the means, which are introduced afterwards, but without any exposition of "in light" or any reference to it. Hence it is incorrect, to contrast with Christians as the "saints in light" other saints in darkness, under the law in the Old Testament, which is contrary to the *usus loquendi* and to Pauline views (GROTIUS: thus is shown the distinction of the law and the gospel), or to refer it to future glory (SCHENKEL:= ἐν τῇ δόξῃ). [This last view is the popular one; "light is taken to mean "heaven," and the passage interpreted as a thanksgiving for what God has done to prepare us for an inheritance in heaven, or inheritance with the saints in heaven. Obviously this is forbidden by the context. EADIE, who joins it with "inheritance" as descriptive of it, ALFORD, who connects it with the whole phrase "portion - - saints," and ELLICOTT, who indicates a preference for joining it with "inheritance of the saints," all avoid this mistake. The saints are now "in light," and the inheritance *is* "in light." "In light" as the sphere of their walk, the saints enjoy their "inheritance" which is "begun here and the meetness conferred in gradual sanctification, but completed hereafter."—R.]

God's act and gift, as the foundation and beginning of the Christian walk, more accurately defined (vers. 13, 14).

Ver. 13. **Who hath delivered us out of the power of darkness.**—"Who" refers back to "Father." His act is first, "hath delivered us," *i. e.*, has drawn, snatched us out of danger (see PASSOW, *Lex.*). CHRYSOSTOM: "He does not say delivered, but snatched (ἐῤῥύσατο), showing our and their great misery and captivity." ZANCHIUS: "This is more than: he has liberated. For those are liberated, who are willing and desirous and deserving of being made free; those who are seized are often unwilling, as Lot from Sodom; he magnifies both the grace and the power of God." "Out of the power of darkness" denotes the power under the dominion of which Christians were before Redemption. The first substantive describes the organized power, the second its character, as Eph. ii. 2: "the power of the air;" vi. 12: "powers of this darkness." [ALFORD: "power *i. e.*, in the territorial sense; darkness—not to be understood of a person but of the character of the region." ELLICOTT: "evil and sin viewed objectively." DAVIES refers here to the dualism of the Zend-avesta.—R.] Necessarily opposed to this is "the power of His glory" (ver. 11), and as a consequence "the saints" are "in light." Here we find a justification of the exposition given above.

And translated us into the kingdom of the Son of his love.—But He did not stop with this "deliverance" (καί); He has "translated" (μετέστησεν) us. The word denotes a local change, hence a change of relation, determining the conduct and walk. "Into the kingdom" is in contrast with "out of the power," and "the Son of His love" with "darkness." "The Son of His love," which recalls both in phrase and connection Eph. i. 6, occurs only here, and sets forth the Son with the greatest emphasis as the Object of His love, upon whom His entire love flows, and through Him therefore upon us. The Son is not conceived of here as "out of" the love, born out of its substance (AUGUSTINE), [*i. e.*, "Love considered more as an essence than an attribute."—R.]; nor is it=His beloved Son (Matt. iii. 17; xvii. 25; xii. 18). [Nor "His dear Son" (E. V).—R.] Not only is the "power" His, but the "kingdom" also, the Messianic kingdom of heaven, which is already actually present here, but not completed in the Christian Church, and therefore not identical with it. This is not then to be understood of the church (BAEHR, HUTHER and others). ["The term has a reference neither purely metaphorical (the church), nor ethical and inward, nor yet ideal and proleptic (MEYER), but —semi-local and descriptive —nor is this wholly future" (ELLICOTT).—R.]

Ver. 14 gives the *modus translationis* (THOMAS AQUINAS): **In whom we have redemption, even the forgiveness of sins.**—Like Eph. i. 7, except that "through his blood" is omitted here [retained in Rec. and E. V.—R.], the means of redemption not being made prominent; and that ἁμαρτιῶν is deeper and more internal than παραπτωμάτων. Paul's freedom and independence are unmistakable. [The exact force is: "In whom we are having the redemption" (ELLICOTT).—R.] Such a possession is the result of the act of God which changes our relation to Him [through the Redeemer whom the Apostle then describes.—R.]

The exalted relation of the Mediator to God and the world. Vers. 15–17. BENGEL: "He describes the glory and eminence of Christ above the highest angels; and scatters those germs from which he afterwards confutes the worshippers of angels. This so full knowledge of Christ is comprehended only by those who are experienced in the mystery of redemption."

Ver. 15. **Who is.**—"Is," not "was" or "became;" hence we have here defined, not what He became at His appearing in the flesh, but what He *is*, and is personally (τοῦ υἱοῦ—ὅς). [Undoubtedly the subject of the whole passage is "the Son of God's love" (ver. 13); and this subject must be taken in its widest and most complex relations, whether as Creator or Redeemer, the immediate context defining the precise nature of the reference (ELLICOTT). MEYER very justly remarks: "It must be noted that Paul is viewing Christ according to His present Being, *i. e.*, according to His present and permanent status of exaltation, and hence he expresses not what Christ was, but what He is." Yet it cannot be denied that while this is true, there must be a distinction made in referring the various predicates to the subject, for even MEYER in objecting to this says: "The only correct reference is to His whole Person, which in the theanthropic status of his present heavenly Being *is* continuously what His Divine nature (considered in itself) *was* before the Incarnation, so that by virtue of the identity of His Divine Nature, we can attribute the same predicates to the Exalted One as to the Logos." He thus himself implies a distinction, which he will not permit in Paul's language. In claiming as we do with the Fathers generally, BENGEL, ELLICOTT, BLEEK, WORDSWORTH and many others, that the immediate reference throughout this verse is to the λόγος ἄσαρκος (against MELANCHTHON, BARNES, EADIE, and ALFORD, who refer it to the λόγος ἔνσαρκος), we by no means deny that all which is here predicated is, now and forever, true of the Son of God's love, but guard against a false interpretation of the predicates themselves. Admitting that such a distinction can be made, we find a reason for the above reference in the fact that ver. 16, which gives a reason for the statements of this verse, must be referred to the Logos, or to the whole Person of Christ, "by virtue of the identity of His Divine Nature." The grammatical connection with ver. 14, which refers to the λόγος ἔνσαρκος is not so close. The subject then in this verse is the Son of God's love, as He was before the incarnation, and as He still "is."—R.]

The image of the invisible God, εἰκὼν τοῦ θεοῦ ἀοράτου (2 Cor. iv. 4). The first thing is His relation to God, immanent and permanent. Εἰκών is not in itself something visible (PHILO: θεοῦ λόγον εἰκόνα λέγει θεοῦ). Comp. Gen. i. 26, 27. God's image in man is not that which is perceptible by the sense, only thus cognizable. Compare the expression with μορφὴ θεοῦ, ἴσα θεῷ (Phil. ii. 6), and ἀπαύγασμα τῆς δόξης καὶ χαρακτὴρ τῆς ὑποστάσεως αὐτοῦ (Heb. i. 3). It denotes likeness to and equality with the invisible God (Jno. i. 18; 1 Tim. vi. 18), who cannot be perceived absolutely without a Mediator and a revelation, hence is invisible to angels and the redeemed (Heb. xii. 14). The context here differs entirely from Jno. i. 14. Here we must think of the Exalted One, transported from our sight, who yet already existed before the creation. Thus the "Son of His love" is further described (THEOPHYLACT: *μόνος—καὶ ἀπαράλλακτος εἰκών*). The revelation, the making known, the rendering visible of the Father is put in the second place. It is not to be viewed as the chief point here, nor as the sole ground of this expression (Jno. xiv. 9), as CALVIN, SCHENKEL and others prefer; nor is it to be entirely denied (BAEHR, HUTHER). [It is worthy of note that here, as in all the terms used in the Scriptures to express His relation to the Father, there seems to be an implication of revelation (*λόγος, ἀπαύγασμα χαρακτήρ, μορφή*, and even in *πρωτότοκος π. κτ.*) On this relation, immanent and permanent, the actual revelation in the Person of Jesus Christ, indeed the context implies, in all other ways, seems to rest. Still we must be careful not to limit the meaning to this actual revelation as EADIE, BARNES and others do, for as Braune remarks:—R.] it is a sad dilution to interpret: God has as it were made Himself visible in Him (DE WETTE), in Christ it is manifest that God is wise, powerful, good and the like (GROTIUS).

The first-born before every creature, *π ρ ω τ ό τ ο κ ο ς π ά σ η ς κ τ ί σ ε ω ς*.—[So Ellicott. Braune's exegesis is better set forth by: the first begotten before every creature. — R.] This second predicate defines His relation to the created world. *Π ρ ω τ ό τ ο κ ο ς* distinguishes Him as the Son *from* the creation (*κτίσις*); it is = *πρωτόγονος*, "first begotten" (PHILO), but not = *πρωτόκτιστος, πρωτόπλαστος* (among the Alexandrians, ORIGEN). It is joined with the first predicate, closely uniting *with* God and distinguishing *from* the creation. (THEODORET: "not as having creation for a sister, but as begotten before all creation." CHRYSOSTOM: "not significant of glory and honor, but only of time.") It is synonymous with *ἀρχή* (ver. 18; Rev. iii. 4). The genitive *κτίσεως* depends on *πρῶτος* as *πρῶτός μου*, Jno. i, 15, 30 (WINER's *Gram.* p. 229). [So MEYER. It must be here remarked that WINER does not expressly sanction this view of this passage. It would not perhaps be strictly correct to say that the genitive is governed by *πρῶτος* in composition, although the Greek syntax favors such government in composition. BENGEL even governs this genitive by the *πρό* found in *πρῶτος*. ELLICOTT's view is a safe one: "genitive of the *point of view*, rendered more intelligible by the latent comparative force involved in *πρῶτος*," though even this is but a circumlocutory statement of its dependence on *πρῶτος*, As the word is Alexandrian, the syntax has been supported by Hebrew usage, though the broad use of the Greek genitive scarcely requires this.—R.]

Since *π ά σ η ς* denotes every kind of creature, angels and men, Christ existed before all. He does not begin the series of a category, as "first begotten of the dead" (Rev. i. 15), "among many brethren" (Rom. viii. 29), but He is antecedent, conditioning the creation. [It is doubtful, whether it is better to take *πάσης κτίσεως*, collectively: "the whole creation," or individually: "every creature," the context favors the former, so ALFORD; the polemic aim of the Apostle, the latter, so ELLICOTT.—Braune makes this predicate refer exclusively to priority in time. On this ELLICOTT speaks of "His deigning by the mouth of His Apostle to institute a *temporal* comparison between His own generation from eternity and their creation in time," but he admits "the possibility of "a secondary and *inferential* reference to priority in dignity." ALFORD seems to include both views; "not only first-born of His mother in the world, but first-begotten of His Father before the worlds — He holds the rank, as compared with every created thing, of first-born in dignity." To the view which makes the latter thought the chief one, as held by WHITBY, BARNES, EADIE ("the acting President of the Universe and therefore the first-born of every creature"), it may be objected; 1. that it confuses the aspects in which this verse refers to the Son of God's love, see above; 2. it gives to *πρωτότοκος* a secondary and figurative meaning, where a more literal one seems more appropriate; 3. it ignores, or at least throws too far into the back-ground, the relation to the Father which is not only expressed in *πρωτότοκος*, but given further prominence by the close connection with the preceding clause; hence those who adopt it consistently refer that predicate also mainly to the revelation of the Father in Christ, rather than to the relation of the Son to the Father. Yet it must be admitted that there is an inferential reference to priority in dignity, a consequence of the priority in time of the Begotten to every creature; not only so, but as Braune well remarks: He **is** antecedent, conditioning the creation—for the context, giving a reason (*ὅ τ ι*) for this verse, goes on to set forth in detail His relation to the creation. So that while His priority in time shows His independence of creation, creation is not independent of Him, as He is here described. In this His relation to the Invisible God is to be found the ground or condition of the whole creation. The 16th verse asserts that He is the *causa conditionalis*, this one seems to intimate that in virtue of His relation immanent and permanent to the Father, as the Image and Only Begotten, He holds the relation to the creation subsequently defined. So WORDSWORTH quotes Theophilus, Bishop of Antioch: "when God desired to create the world, He begat the world as *προφορικὸν, πρωτότοκος πάσης κτίσεως*." While He is thus placed out of the category of the created, He is the more intimately linked with "every creature."—R.]

Therefore the view of the Arians that He is the first creature is incorrect, as also that of the Socinians, GROTIUS and others, who refer *κτίσεως* to the new moral creation, in which case *καινή* would not be wanting (2 Cor. v. 17). To make of the two predicates but one and join *πρωτότοκος* as an adjective to *εἰκών* (SCHLEIERMACHER, *Stud. und Krit.* 1832, p. 497) is not only harsh, but grammatically inadmissible. To read *πρωτοτόκος*, "first bringer forth" (ISIDORE of Pelusium, ERASMUS and others), is not allowable, since this is applied only to the female sex, and *πρῶτος* in that case would be irrelevant.

Ver. 16. **Because in him were all things created.**—This verse justifies the explanation given above. *Ὅ τ ι* adds the reason that *ante omnem creaturam genitum esse filium, non creatum*, before every creature the Son was begotten, not created: "in Him were all things created." The emphasis is placed upon "in Him." The verb requires us to understand the fact of creation as here spoken of; the historical act, as the aorist denotes. Acts x. 6 has ἔκτισε τὸν οὐρανόν κ. τ. λ., while xiv. 7, reads: τῷ ποιήσαντι τὸν ουρανόν. The same interchange occurs Gen. vi. 7; Deut. iv. 22, Sirach xv. 14; xxiv. 9 [LXX]. SCHLEIERMACHER should not therefore affirm that κτίζειν is not used in Hellenistic Greek of the original creation, but means to give order, arrangement. This creation is ἐν αὐτῷ, not ὑπ' αὐτοῦ, which would indicate the first cause. This is not the Son, but the Father, as the thought in the word is efficient in the Son, out from whom the creation is accomplished; but there is no thought of emanation, hence ἐξ αὐτοῦ is not used. It is here indicated that the accomplishment of the creation rests in Him, its immediate instrumental cause is to be sought in Him, but not the last, *principalis*. 'Εν αὐτῷ is not to be referred to the κόσμος νοητός, the *idea omnium rerum*, which was in Him (SCHLEIERMACHER and others), nor is it = δι' αὐτοῦ (USTERI); nor does ἐκτίσθη refer to the new moral creation, which reference is not supported by Eph. iv. 23, where the context is entirely different. ['Εν αὐτῷ here denotes, not the *causa instrumentalis* nor *causa exemplaris*, but *causa conditionalis*, as the conditional element pre-existent and all-including. ALFORD, ELLICOTT.—R.] Τὰ πάντα is the existing all, the totality of things [the universe, ALFORD.—R.], πάντα would be all that actually is (WINER'S *Gram.* p. 105). A specification as regards *place* follows: **in heaven and that are on earth,** τα ἐν τοῖς οὐρανοῖς καὶ τὰ ἐπὶ τῆς γῆς.—Thus Paul writes instead of οἱ οὐρανοί or ὁ οὐρανὸς καὶ ἡ γῆ, not excluding these however, because to him all depends upon this, that nothing was created without Him; He stands in such a relation to the whole creation that He was before it and it exists first through Him. There is no reason for understanding by this, *habitatores qui reconciliantur* (WETTSTEIN), or only living creatures (BAEHR) or rational creatures. On τοῖς οὐρανοῖς see Eph. i. 10. We cannot conclude from the precedence of οἱ οὐρανοί that emphasis is placed upon the creation of angels (THEOPHYLACT), nor from the omission of "under the earth," that God has not created for the lower world (*Unterwelt*); the context gives no warrant for this.—**Visible and invisible.**—This is added to describe the *nature* of what was created. There is no reason for referring both exclusively either to earthly (SCHLEIERMACHER), or to heavenly things (THEODORET); nor are the former alone visible, and the latter invisible, since among the visible we must reckon sun, moon and stars, and among the invisible human souls. The Apostle places the highest, "things in heaven," first, but here the more important follows, because he intends to give a specification of the angels. It must be borne in mind that τὰ πάντα is described. Hence "invisible" does not refer merely to the heavenly world of spirits (MEYER), though this is the main reference (BLEEK).—**Whether they be thrones, or dominions, or principalities, or powers,** εἴτε θρόνοι, εἴτε κυριότητες, εἴτε ἀρχαὶ, εἴτε ἐξουσίαι. Εἴτε, thus repeated, specifies the world of angels, to which we arrive through "invisible;" at the same time it indicates an uncertainty respecting the classes of angels, or that nothing essential depends upon this classification. In Eph. i. 21, we find ἀρχή, ἐξουσία, δύναμις, κυριότης; δύναμις is not found here, nor θρόνος there. This latter word occurs here only in the New Testament, but is applied by the Rabbins, by Dionysius the Areopagite and *testamentum* Levi, to the angels in the seventh or highest heaven. These classes may be regarded as different orders, joined in pairs; θρόνοι, the highest, κυριότητες, the lowest, ἀρχαί and ἐξουσίαι, the intermediate. [ELLICOTT, comparing Eph. i. 21, "where the order *seems* descensive," says, "we may *possibly* infer that the θρόνοι are the highest order, *etc.*, if indeed all such distinctions are not to be deemed precarious and presumptuous. It may have been suggested by some known theosophistic speculations of the Colossians, but more probably was an incidental revelation, which the term ἀόρατα evoked." PEARSON thus gives the intent of the passage and the force of εἴτε: "Lest in that invisible world, among the many degrees of the celestial hierarchy, any order might seem excepted from an essential dependence upon Him, he nameth those which are of greatest eminence, and in them comprehendeth the rest."—R.] SCHLEIERMACHER most incorrectly applies ἀόρατα to earthly empires, civil orders and legal conditions (MELANCHTHON similarly), and understands here magisterial offices and other functions of persons in power.

All things were created by him and for him, τὰ πάντα δι' αὐτοῦ καὶ εἰς αὐτὸν ἔκτισται. [Literally, all things have been created through Him and to Him.—R.] Solemn recapitulation (MEYER). The perfect, setting the past in relation to the present, is chosen instead of the aorist, noting the *factum*, because we have here a dogmatic consideration of the completed and now existing creation (WINER'S *Gram.* p. 255). Hence also we have not merely δι' αὐτοῦ (instrumental), but εἰς αὐτόν, indicating Him as the τέλος of creation. BENGEL: *ἐν denotat prius quiddam quam mox διά et εἰς. Notatur initium, progressus, finis.* Comp. Rom. xi. 36; 1 Cor. viii. 6, where εἰς αὐτόν refers to God, as here to Christ, to whom the κυριότης τῶν πάντων is committed (Matt. xxviii. 18; Phil. ii. 9; 1 Cor. xv. 27), who is the delegated Regent of the world (MEYER). Εἰς denotes not simply *for* Him, but also *to* Him, in Him (WINER'S *Gram.* p. 390). That He is Lord over all is but one side therefore; the other is, that to Him the whole is directed, and thus is developed, exalted, glorified. To His exalted dignity is joined the glorifying of what is created, the participation of the creatures in His glory and blessedness. [ELLICOTT: ἐν αυτῷ, *causa conditionalis;* δι' αὐτοῦ, *causa medians;* εἰς αὐτόν, *causa finalis* or *finis ultimus.* ALFORD: "He is the end of creation, containing the reason in Himself, why creation is at all and why it is as it is."—R.]

Ver. 17 accordingly adds: **And he is before all things.**—Αὐτός and ἐστι are emphatic from their position. ["He Himself is" or "exists."—R.] Both the permanence of the existence of Christ and His pre-existence are affirmed. The *usus loquendi* requires only, that it be understood of *time*, the context, of the *whole;* compare Jno. viii. 58. The Vulgate is incorrect: *ante omnes*, and Luther, *vor Allen*, [*i. e.*, before all beings.—

R.] So also the Socinians, SCHLEIERMACHER and others, who limit the meaning to superior rank, which is indeed sufficiently implied in such an assertion of priority.—**And in him all things subsist.**—[The E. V. here as in ver. 15, unfortunately renders ἐν, "by."—R.] The verb is used of things held together, as milk, which runs. So 2 Pet. iii. 5; γῆ ἐξ ὕδατος καὶ δι' ὕδατος συνεστῶσα τῷ τοῦ θεοῦ λόγῳ. Without Christ all things would fall asunder. The perfect, following ἔστι, has the force of the present—put together and now subsisting. The reference is to organic permanence, the continuance of the composition of the things of the world "in Him," because He holds together what He has created. [ELLICOTT: "the causal sphere of their continuing existence, —not *exactly* identical with ἐν αὐτῷ above. Christ was the conditional element of their *creation*, the causal element of their persistence."—R.] It does not refer to a consolidation of earthly relations (SCHLEIERMACHER), nor to the acknowledgment and rule of the Lord in the new world (BAUMGARTEN-CRUSIUS).

The relation of the Mediator to the Church. Vers. 18–20.

Ver. 18. **And he is the head of the body, the church.**—"And He," αὐτός, [is emphatic, possibly involving an antithesis to some errors of the Colossian Church (ALFORD, ELLICOTT). The subject is "the Son of God's love," the passage requiring a reference to the λόγος ἔνσαρκος, the now glorified Christ.—R.] "Is": in form this is a resumption of ver. 17, connected closely with that verse, but in matter it refers back to the starting-point, ver. 14, so that, just as in vers. 15, 16, the corresponding relative clause (ὅς ἐστιν) follows, together with its proof (ὅτι). The parallel of thought—Christ, the Son of God, is before and over the world, as He is Head of the Church —is echoed in the chain of parallel clauses. On "the Head of the Body, the Church," see Eph. i. 22, 23. The second genitive is unquestionably *appositional* (WINER'S *Gram.*, p. 494, and Eph. iv. 9). In the parallel passage: "Head over all things," *etc.*—the relation of Christ to the world is defined by "over all things." On the Church as an organism, a Body, see Eph. iv. 12; v. 23, 30; that the world might not be considered this Body, "the Church" is added. It does not refer to the family of God in heaven and on earth (RÖSSELT); this is too spiritualistic, is contrary to biblical realism and *usus loquendi*.

Who is the beginning, the first-born from the dead, ὅς ἐστι ἀρχή, πρωτότοκος ἐκ τῶν νεκρῶν.—"First-born," πρωτότοκος, here is somewhat different from ver. 15,—in the more exact sense of one beginning a series. Hence ἐκ can be omitted, as in Rev. i. 5. The preposition marks the fact, conceived of as in Eph. v. 14: "arise from (ἐκ) the dead;" as ἀπὸ τῶν νεκρῶν also occurs, to denote the separation of the living from the dead. The reference is not to those merely who have died within the church (SCHENKEL); for when the dead revived in the Old Testament times, they were not "first-born from the dead," since they died again; it is otherwise in the case of Christ. [ELLICOTT distinguishes this passage from Rev. i. 5, where the preposition is omitted: "first-born not only of, but out of the dead"—He left their realm and came again as with a new begetting and new birth into life."—R.] It is pre-supposed, but not stated either in the text or context: "because He restores life to others" (CALVIN. THEODORET: "the phrase hints also at the resurrection of us all"). [EADIE retaining his view of πρωτότοκος, as referring to priority in dignity, remarks: "as He rose from the midst of the dead, He became their chief,— came out from among them as their representative. His people rise in virtue of His power. He is not only the pledge, He is also the pattern." This is undoubtedly true, but only implied here. —R.] By "first-born," which was not chosen without a reference to ver. 15, ἀρχή, a word of wide signification, is here more closely defined as "the Beginning," while the personality is at the same time thus emphasized as the principal thing. Comp. Jno. xi. 25. So Gen. xlix. 3: "Reuben my first-born" (ἀρχὴ τέκνων μου=πρωτότοκός μου, Deut. xxi. 17). It is therefore="the first-fruits of them that slept" (ἀρχὴ τῶν κεκοιμημένων, 1 Cor. xv. 20), "first that should rise from the dead" (πρῶτος ἐξ ἀναστάσεως νεκρῶν, Acts xxvi. 23); hence to be taken as referring to time, with a secondary reference, however, to a power efficient in a succeeding series (Rev. iii. 14; xxii. 13); in which it differs from ἀπαρχή. Hence it is neither *principium* (BAEHR, STEIGER, HUTHER), nor Regent of the world (FLATT), nor author of the Church (BAUMGARTEN-CRUSIUS), nor "beginning of the second and new creation" (CALVIN). Nor is "of the resurrection" to be supplied (DE WETTE), since the Apostle had far more in view than "the dead," nor "of the church" (SCHENKEL), since there is nothing to indicate this; nor is "first-born" an adjective joined to "beginning" (SCHLEIERMACHER). [While ἀρχή has here a primary temporal reference, and is further defined as a Personality by πρωτότοκος, there is an argumentative force in the relative "who" involving a secondary reference to "the church" which immediately precedes. So ELLICOTT, EADIE, who insists upon this too exclusively, however. ALFORD: "He is the 'beginning,' in that in Him is begun and conditioned the church." WORDSWORTH suggests the two-fold sense of ἀρχή; 1. *principium*, beginning. 2. *principalitas*, dominion, rule. In the first sense, Christ is the source of life to the church: in the second, the Principality of all things, therefore even in His manhood superior to the angelic principalities and powers (against the false teachers).—R.]

That in all things he might have the pre-eminence.—["In order that (ἵνα) in all things he (αὐτός, emphatic,) might become (γένηται) pre-eminent."—R.] Ἵνα denotes the purpose of God working herein; it is not=ὥστε (ESTIUS, BAEHR). What He is, is the basis for something else, which is accomplished in the purpose—which becomes (γένηται); hence such permanent relations are here concerned, as took shape historically, and are adapted for definite ends, to be realized in time (STEIGER). In that He is the Risen One, it is the design of God, that He becomes ἐν πᾶσιν αὐτὸς πρωτεύων, *He*, emphatically, and none other, *sine locum tenentibus, sine vicario* (BENGEL), and "in all," on all sides, in wisdom, holiness, might, death-overcoming power, dominion and glory, as respects the world as well as the church. The *First*, for ever and for every one. The verb πρωτεύω occurs only here in the New Testament and denotes strongly, "to have the first rank." [ALFORD: "The word is a transitional one, from priority in time to priority in dignity, and shows incontestibly that the two ideas have been before the Apostle's mind throughout," though, as ELLICOTT suggests, this being a result, the same meaning does not necessarily belong to πρωτότοκος.—R.] 'Εν πᾶσιν must be neuter, as Tit. ii. 9, 10; 1 Tim. iii. 11; iv. 15; 2 Tim. ii. 7; iv. 5; Hebrews xiii. 4, 18,=παντί (1 Cor. i. 5; 2 Cor. iv. 8, etc). Did it refer to νεκρῶν, it must have the article. Hence *inter omnes* (BEZA and others) is incorrect.

Ver. 19. **Because in him God was pleased that the whole fulness should dwell.**—As in ver. 16, ὅτι introduces the ground of the last clause, and thus mediately of the whole preceding verse. It is not therefore a proof of the relative clause exclusively (STEIGER), nor is this to be excluded (MEYER). 'Εν αὐτῷ εὐδόκησεν πᾶν τὸ πλήρωμα κατοικῆσαι may be simply rendered; the finite verb εὐδόκησεν leads to a will, a personal author as final cause, over against a becoming of necessity: on this account Θεός is the self-evident subject, hence not specially indicated; ἐν αὐτῷ is to be joined with κατοικῆσαι, it is placed first emphatically, and denotes the same as in the foregoing; πᾶν τὸ πλήρωμα is the accusative subject of the infinitive, and according to the context, without the necessity of supplying anything, the whole fulness of Him, who had formed the decree (Eph. iii. 19: "all the fulness of God;" Col. ii. 9: "of the God-head"). [With this rendering, the E. V. agrees, but supplies *Father* instead of God, marking, it is true, an obvious antithesis between Christ (the subject hitherto), and the new one. But the impersonal form of the verb is not strictly correct. ELLICOTT renders: "the whole fulness of God was pleased to dwell," making πᾶν τὸ πλήρωμα the subject of the finite verb. The question is only a grammatical one, as the dogmatical result is the same in either case. See ELLICOTT *in loco*.—R.] On πλήρωμα, compare Eph. i. 10; on κατοικῆσαι, Eph. iii. 17; on εὐδόκησεν, Eph. i. 5. To regard πληρωμα as the fulness of the Gentiles and totality of Israel (SCHLEIERMACHER), is as unfounded, as to understand it, from the terminology of Valentin, of the complex of Æons (BAUR). HOFMANN also is in error, in understanding it as the fulness of that which is, making Christ the subject of εὐδόκησεν; too artificial. [WORDSWORTH, after giving two interpretations: 1. that God the Son was pleased; 2. that God was pleased, with a preference for (1), adds "on the whole, we may perhaps affirm, that the Apostle designedly placed εὐδόκησεν here without any limitation of a nominative expressed, in order to bring out the truth more fully that the εὐδοκία is to be ascribed to the Father in the Son, and to the Son in the Father, and that there is perfect unity in will and operation in both."—R.]

Ver. 20. **And by him to reconcile all things unto himself.**—*Locus hic torquet interpretes et vicissim ab illis torquetur* (DAVENANT). The force of καί is clear: "this indwelling (ver. 19) is the foundation of the reconciliation" (BENGEL). Δι' αὐτοῦ, *i. e.*, Christ, is placed emphatically first, denoting the known mediation. The main difficulty is found in ἀποκαταλλάξαι εἰς αὐτόν. The verb occurs only here, ver. 21 and Eph. ii. 16; here with εἰς αὐτόν, in the last passage with τῷ θεῷ. Καταλάσσειν, Rom. v. 10; 2 Cor. v. 18, 19: τῷ θεῷ, ἑαυτῷ; 1 Cor. vii. 11: τῷ ἀνδρί. The meaning is: to reconcile, strengthened by ἀπό. So that the one reconciled is freed, removed from something; open, conscious, outspoken enmity is not meant, rather concealed unconscious estrangement and separation of one or two parts (HOFMANN): but it is found only in him who is reconciled, not in him who reconciles. See on Eph. ii. 16. With MEYER we hold as follows: sin began among the angels, and came, was brought from the angelic world to the race of men (Jno. viii. 44; 2 Cor. xi. 3; Eph. i. 10); thereby the whole creation was disturbed in its harmony, "was made subject to vanity," in "the bondage of corruption," and suffered according to the saying: *delirant reges, plectuntur Achivi* (comp. Rom. viii. 19–22). In Christ the act of reconciliation is accomplished, and this reconciliation is to unfold itself in all directions unto the *palingenesia* (Matt. xix. 28; 2 Pet. iii. 15), to the coming (*Parusie*) of Christ (1 Cor. xv. 24, 28). The aorist infinitive denotes the historical fact; εἰς αὐτόν instead of the usual dative ἑαυτῷ marks the direction, and consequently the gradually accomplished development. We meet here the comprehensive and classical idea of reconciliation, which is considerably modified with respect to the universe, as well as to the human race and the angelic world, as is afterwards indicated. It is therefore incorrect to identify ἀποκαταλλάξαι with ἀνακεφαλαιώσασθαι, Eph. i. 10 (MELANCHTHON, GROTIUS, BAEHR and others), or in accordance with this view, to apply εἰς αὐτόν to Christ (LUTHER and others) and not to God, as the context requires. [E. V., "to Himself," correctly applies it.—R.] Nor is τὰ πάντα to be limited to intelligent beings, or to men only (A-LAPIDE and others) or to *universam ecclesiam* (BEZA); nor does the verb mean; "the removal of reciprocal enmity" (STOLZ, SCHLEIERMACHER and others). [ELLICOTT, while objecting to any dilution of "reconcile," or limitation of τὰ πάντα, cautions against the irreverence of far-reaching speculations on the reconciliation of the finite and infinite. "It *does* say that the eternal and incarnate Son is the '*causa medians*' by which the absolute totality of created things shall be restored into its primal harmony with its Creator—more than this it *does not* say, and where God is silent it is not for man to speak." EADIE: "The one Reconciler is the head of these vast dominions, and in Him meet and merge the discordant elements which sin had introduced The humanity of Jesus bringing all creatures around it, unites them to God in a bond which never before existed—a bond which has its origin in the mystery of redemption. Thus all things in heaven and earth feel the effect of man's renovation." The view of Braune, that this will find its full development at the coming of Christ, is not in opposition to the above view. See EADIE and ALFORD, also DE WETTE.—R.]

Having made peace through the blood of his cross.—Εἰρηνοποιήσας naturally and grammatically agrees with the latent subject of εὐδόκησεν, God. The verb, only here, like the substantive εἰρηνοποιός (Matt. v. 9) is clear in its meaning. The aorist participle indicates the modality of "reconcile," as Eph. i. 19. Both acts are contemporaneous, conceived of as one, this does not ante-date the other [as E. V. implies—R.]. "Through the blood" marks the act as one of royal judgment and priestly sacrifice (Rom. iii. 25: Heb. iv. 14, 18, 20; 1 Pet. i. 19); while "of His cross" marks the shedding of blood as a consequence of the punishment to which He devoted Himself, in humblest obedience (Phil. ii. 18), in innocence for our sake, in holiness to make us holy. Both denote the definite, historical act, over against all spiritualistic conceptions, as well as Christ's suffering and death over against our moral or ascetic works. In order to preclude any materialistic or magical views of the blood of Christ, Paul reaffirms; **by him**, thus making prominent the Person of Him, who had shed His blood, and thereby made peace with God. ["I say" added in E. V. conveys the meaning.—R.]—Besides this repetition, designed to guard against false views, there is added, in explanation of the object, which has been and shall be reconciled, made partaker of the peace: **Whether there be things on earth, or things in heaven** (comp. ver. 16).—Here "earth" stands first, because he has been just speaking of the act on earth, by which the reconciliation begins. It is not easy to determine how the reconciliation of angels may be conceived of, since it cannot be applied to wicked ones, who remain unreconciled and are condemned, and the good need no reconciliation, only sustaining power. This difficulty leads us to refrain from any explanation, which would be at best a mere surmise. [See above on τὰ πάντα, which is specified here. ELLICOTT remarks: "How the reconciliation of Christ affects the spiritual world—whether by the annihilation of '*posse peccare*,' or by the infusion of a more perfect knowledge, or (less probably) some restorative application to the fallen spiritual world—we know not, and we dare not speculate." WORDSWORTH specifies a fourfold reconciliation, 1. Between God and man. 2. Between angels and man. 3. Between Jew and Gentile. 4. Between man and the inferior creatures. Under the last particular he refers to the attempt of false teachers to mar this work of universal reconciliation, by forbidding the *free use of the creatures*, chap. ii. 20, 21. This is open to the objection stated below.—R.] The disjunctive force of εἴτε forbids the idea of reconciliation of the two parts with each other (ERASMUS), nor do "things on earth," "things in heaven," favor the view, that Jews and Gentiles had become hostile to each other on account of heavenly and earthly things, matters of Divine worship and principles related thereto, but should now be reconciled (SCHLEIERMACHER). Nor does this refer to the reconciliation of the Jews and Gentiles to each other and with the world of spirits, nor to the final conversion and blessedness of the demons (ORIGEN), nor to a tendency at least thereto (OLSHAUSEN).

Application. Vers. 21–23.

Ver. 21. **And you.**—Καὶ ὑμᾶς, as Eph. ii. 1, to begin a new sentence. There is an anacoluthon in the construction, since the reading is ἀποκατηλλάγητε, not ἀποκαταλλάξαι. See critical note[14]. [The additional note gives the authorities for the reading Braune rejects. So great is the preponderance in its favor, that the translator feels bound to differ from the author here. The anacoluthon is not so strong with this reading; ὑμᾶς is the object of the verb, though νυνὶ δέ intervenes.—R.] There is no reason for joining "and you," with its immediate attributive, to the preceding sentence (LACHMANN and others). [The better punctuation is that of E. V. and most modern editors, beginning a new sentence or paragraph here.—R.] Καί is not merely a copulative particle (and); but is = "even," "precisely," as the following characteristic requires: **that were sometime alienated and enemies**, ποτὲ ὄντας ἀπηλλοτριωμένους καὶ ἐχθρούς.—With ποτέ he refers to their past condition, and with emphasis, as its position indicates, in praise and thanksgiving; the participle is imperfect. On "alienated," see Eph. ii. 12. Neither "from the commonwealth of Israel," from that passage, nor "from the life of God," from Eph. iv. 18, is to be supplied (BAEHR); the context clearly suggests "from God." But more than alienation is mentioned, they had passed into enmity of which the former is the germ; ἐχθρούς is therefore active, enemy against God (Rom. viii. 7). It is incorrect to consider it as passive, *invisos deo* (Rom. v. 10, STEIGER), since it is enmity, not on the part of God, but of men, which is extirpated, out of which they are delivered in the reconciliation.—**As to your understanding in wicked works,** τῇ διανοίᾳ ἐν τοῖς ἔργοις τοῖς πονηροῖς.—Their enmity is thus described. The article refers to a known previous disposition and mode of conduct. The simple dative is one of *reference;* "in" marks the sphere in which the alienation and enmity manifested itself. Both belong to "alienated" as well as "enemies." On διάνοια, see Eph. ii. 3; iv. 18; 1 Jno. v. 20. [ELLICOTT: "the higher intellectual nature especially as shown in its practical relations." "Understanding," "mind" (as distinguished from heart in E. V.) is the correct rendering, though Braune, referring it to the state rather than to the faculty itself, has *Gesinnung*, disposition.—R.] This manifests itself actively; in it the "wicked works" have their ground and soil. [The form τ. ἔργ. τοῖς πον. emphasizes the character of the works.—R.] The phrase includes all works which are done contrary to God's command, or if formally in accordance with the law, yet from carnal appetites and propensities. It is incorrect to govern τῇ διανοίᾳ by ἐχθρούς (ERASMUS: "enemies to reason") or to consider it as the ground: through their disposition (MEYER), through their reason (LUTHER), since the cause of the enmity cannot be found in this organ or in this disposition, which is a product as respects the enmity. Nor does ἐν ἔργοις depend on διανοίᾳ (BEZA, BAEHR).—**Yet now hath he reconciled,** νυνὶ δὲ ἀποκατάλλαξεν.—[Braune, reading ἀποκαταλλάγητε renders: "now you are reconciled."—R.] Νυνί marks the present which begins with the reconciliation, when the readers have become partakers of it; δέ marks the resumption of the thought uninterrupted by the parenthesis [describing their previous condition—R.], like the Latin *inquam*. "Reconciled" is an act through Christ, (ver. 20) not of Christ (Greek fathers, CALVIN, CALOV., others). Compare 2 Cor. v. 19. [The subject throughout is God.—R.]

Ver. 22. **"In the body of his flesh through death.**—This sets forth in twofold manner the way or the means of reconciliation. *First:* "In the body of his flesh." This describes the earthly, sensible, historical appearance of Christ. Sirach xvi. 23: ἀνθρωπος πόρνος ἐν σώματι τῆς σαρκὸς αὐτοῦ, where σαρκός refers to the sensual lusting. Here the reference is to the Redeemer and Reconciler, who had taken upon Him our flesh and blood and appeared in the life and history of our race; ἐν is to be taken locally. [ALFORD: "The situation or element of the reconciliation." ELLICOTT: "the *substratum* of the action is pointed to by ἐν."—R.] It is entirely foreign to the context to suppose "of his flesh" is in contrast with the body "of the church," as ver. 20 (BENGEL). The antithesis is less docetic false teachers according to ii. 23 (STEIGER), or the glorified body of the Risen One, 1 Cor. xv. 44 (SCHENKEL), or exaggerated doctrine of angels (MEYER), than this, that the work of Redemption was far too easily separated from the person of Christ and His historical, human nature in the form of a servant. The expression is evidently anti-spiritualistic. *Secondly:* "through death," [the means, instrumental cause.—R.] renders prominent the exit from this natural life, in short, the suffering and death referred to in ver. 20; the entrance into this life through birth must have corresponded with such an exit. Hence it is not strange that Paul speaks often of the latter, but never of the former *ex professo*.

To present you holy and unblameable and unreproveable in his sight.—The end to be attained. "To present you" depends on the verb "reconciled." What has occurred to the Christian in this reconciliation is something to be preserved, unfolded, perfected. The God who effects reconciliation, effects more, as Eph. v. 27. The subject is not the subject of the passive ἀποκαταλλάγητε, but of the active [*i. e.*, of the verb ἀποκατάλλαξεν, as most read—R.]; the accusative ὑμᾶς is the object not the subject of the infinitive (MEYER, SCHENKEL). Certainly the immediate result of the reconciliation, the righteousness imputed for the sake of Christ, is not meant (HUTHER and others). The three adjectives ἁγίους καὶ ἀμώμους καὶ ἀνεγκλήτους mark the continued effect of the reconciliation, *viz.*, moral purity in three directions. As "holy," ἅγιοι, they are consecrated to God, live to God, die to the world, have conducted and shown themselves as such; as "unblameable," ἄμωμοι, they are free from the faults and stains of sin; as unreprovable, ἀνέγκλητοι, they are not accused by their neighbors. BENGEL is not incorrect in his: *erga deum, respectu vestri, respectu proximi.* [ALFORD and ELLICOTT follow MEYER in referring the first to the *positive*, the latter two to the negative side of holiness. DAVENANT deems it the aggregation of three similar ideas. On the whole Braune's view, which is that of EADIE, is much preferable. —R.] "In his sight," κατενώπιον αὐτοῦ, refers undoubtedly to the Judgment, hence according to the context we may apply it to Christ. Comp. 2 Cor. v. 10. [ALFORD seems most correct; referring it to the day of Christ's appearing; but before His *i. e.*, God's presence. ELLICOTT doubts the former reference, but renders: "before Him, God not Christ." The passage undoubtedly refers to *justitia inhærens*, as the necessary result of the reconciliation which gave to the believer *justitia imputata*. So CALVIN, but, as HOOKER judiciously remarks, "whensoever we have any of these (actual, inherent or imputed holiness) we have all—they go together."—R.]

Ver. 23. **If at least ye continue in the faith.**—God's act for and upon them is not carried out to a blessed consummation without subjective advance and personal activity. Εἴγε marks a condition, about which there is no doubt. [ALFORD: "assuming that."—R.] It is the mildest, most delicate method of calling attention to the necessity of faith (BLEEK), and seems to belong to "present," rather than to depend on the finite verb, ver. 21 (BENGEL). See on Eph. iii. 2; iv. 21. Ἐπιμένετε τῇ πίστει is construed, as Rom. vi. 1; xi. 22, 23; 1 Tim. iv. 16. [Stronger than μένετε, implying with the dative, *rest* at a place, perseverance to and rest in the end, "persist" (ALFORD, ELLICOTT).—R.]. The article marks the faith as definite; an indefinite one, after their own pleasure, does not suffice.—**Grounded and settled and be not moved away from the hope of the gospel.** —["Grounded and settled and not being moved away" is the literal construction. The E. V. seems to make "moved away" co-ordinate with "continue."—R.] The modality of the persistence is thus denoted: 1. Τεθεμελιωμένοι (see on Eph. iii. 18), whose antithesis is χωρὶς θεμελίόυ (Luke vi. 49: "without a foundation"), refers to an objectively given foundation, placed upon which they still stand. This is a reference to Christ, to God's grace in Him, not to the hope (MEYER). 2. Ἑδραῖοι *dicit internum robur, quod fideles ipsi habent; quemadmodum ædificum primo quidem fundamento recte solideque inniti, deinde vero sua etiam mole probe cohærere et firmiter consistere debet* (BENGEL), 1 Cor. xv. 58. [These two denote the positive side of the modality of their persistence; then the negative follows.—R.] 3. Μὴ μετακινούμενοι ἀπὸ τῆς ἐλπίδος εὐαγγελίου marks, through the present participle passive, what is very possible, likely to enter every moment from without and within; circumstances, purposes and suggestions, as well as lusts and selfish thought and desire can easily move, so that they are moved away from the hope of the gospel, held up before them as an aim (not a point of support—SCHENKEL), and both sure and glorious as belonging to the gospel (see on Eph. i. 18). [ALFORD makes the hope subjective, but grounded on the objective, and the genitive possessive. ELLICOTT says: "the hope arising from, evoked by the Gospel,"—subjective, therefore: "τοῦ εὐαγγ. is the genitive of the origin or the originating agent"—which is preferable. EADIE thus discriminates between the three expressions: "the first epithet alludes to the cause, the second to its effect, the third depicts a general result,—as the use of μή seems to indicate." Μή is usual and proper, however, in such a sentence as this—see WINER's *Gram.* p. 443.—R.] Μετά refers to the inward change in being moved, ἀπό to removal from the given object, thereby effected. — **Which ye have heard**, denotes a fact which takes away all excuse, they know it, it has been told them. [ELLICOTT objects to "have" in the E. V. without reason, as the inexcusableness rests upon the fact that it has already been heard, thus best expressed.—R.]—It has been made efficient for them, and not for them alone: **And which was preached to every creature which is under heaven**, =in the whole world. The command of Christ, Mark xvi. 15: "preach the gospel to every creature" has begun to be carried out. "Preached to every creature" is not hyperbolical (MEYER), nor is κτίσις to be limited to the Gentiles. [ALFORD incorrectly renders: "in the whole creation." EADIE and ELLICOTT call this hyperbole, though agreeing with Braune's next remark. —R.] The Apostle prophetically sees as accomplished what has as yet only begun, and marks the universality of Christianity. *Sane undiquaque vulgatum evangelium Christi, ne quid cogitarent Colossenses de mutanda fide, quæ jam ab omnibus esset recepta* (ERASMUS). [On the phrase, "which is under heaven," ELLICOTT remarks, that it characterizes the κτίσις as ἐπίγειος, including, however, thereby, all mankind.—R.]

Whereof I Paul am made a minister.—See on Eph. iii. 1. [MEYER makes here "three considerations" enforcing their "not being moved away"—It would be, 1) inexcusable for themselves, because they had heard the gospel; 2) inconsistent with the universality of the gospel "preached to every creature;" 3) contrary to the personal relation of the Apostle to the gospel, "whereof I Paul," etc.—R.]

DOCTRINAL AND ETHICAL.

1. *Christian knowledge.* The progress of Paul's thanksgiving for the faith and love of the Church to supplication for their advance in true knowledge derives its motive from the end in view, *viz.*, Christian walk. Herein is implied: *First:* the basis of Christian knowledge is the Christian morality of the perceiving subject, in its fundamental traits and principles, in faith and love. Here it begins, and hence advance is made to and in the former. The subject of knowledge must also be correctly situated on account of the object of knowledge, and the organ of knowledge in the knowing subject must, at the same time, be first acted upon, that it may enjoy healthy activity and the reward of sound knowledge. Yet is faith itself an immediate knowing, and love, a desire which directly grasps the objects of faith, so that what makes an impression in faith, can be intelligently conceived. *Second:* the *object* of Christian knowledge is the will of God, in the unity of that will in creation, law and redemption, hence in the visible and invisible, in the temporal and eternal, in the moral and intelligent world, both what was designed in creation and redemption, and what was commanded in word as precept. *Third:* the *effect* of Christian knowledge is essentially a re-action upon the Christian walk, and thus they reciprocally further each other. *Fourth:* the way to Christian knowledge is essentially a life of practical morality. *Fifth:* its *course* is like that of the Christian life, a gradual advance, moving and developing itself in various experiences, temptations and circumstances.

2. *The Christian walk* has its *ground* in the fact of redemption, which has been decreed and ordained by God the Father, mediated and accomplished through the Son; its *beginning*, in the appropriation of this fact of objective redemption and subjective acceptance; its *standard*, in the example of our Lord Jesus Christ; its *motive*, in pleasing this Lord; its *activity*, in good works, according to the various relations of life in which we are placed; its *modality* in this, that what is done, is done from inward constraint and not from calculation; its *development*, in this, that it perceives more clearly each moment the will of God, grasps it more securely, retains it more firmly, proves it more widely; its *genuineness*, in the joy with which it bears and forbears, and controls itself with ever increasing strength; its *tone*, in gratitude for what God had done to and in and for One, and its *aim* in the eternal heritage in heaven, of which an earnest is given within us.

3. *The Apostle's conception of God.* *God*, who is the beginning and end for the Christian, is conceived of, not as absolute *substance*, but as an *absolute Person*, in substance a Spirit, in character *Love*; here especially in the latter aspect. He has His will, and His εὐδοκεῖν (ver. 19) wills itself as the good, wills it with energy and almightiness, and accomplishes His will in general and particular alike. In this recession (*Zurücktreten*) of the absolute substance behind the freedom of the absolute Subject, the right of Pantheism and Emanatism is taken away, in the precession (*Vortreten*) of His almighty and saving Love, that of Deism and Naturalism. The personality of the Living One, and the Life of the Absolute Person are the cardinal points of the Christian's belief in God. Against Indifference "the whole fulness" of God (ver. 19) speaks. By this is meant the fulness of Love and Holiness, of Wisdom and Power, of Grace and Majesty and Blessedness, which bursts forth in the works of Creation, Redemption, Sanctification and Glorification, but which neither is nor can be exhausted in the world; although immanent in the world, He far transcends it. Only in the Son of His Love is "the whole fulness" to be seen and found. Hence there is a reference to a Triune relation, since such fulness of God, the Living One, did not first come in flow with the creation, but moved already in Him, who is before and above all creatures.—The self-existence of God the Father, who is αἴτιος πάντων τῶν ὄντων, is indicated; on Him the Son Himself depends and His activity in the works of Creation and Redemption.

4. *The Person of Christ* is more accurately described in a threefold relation:

a) *His relation to God* is set forth in the phrases: ὁ υἱὸς τῆς ἀγάπης αὐτοῦ, "the Son of His Love," (ver. 13); εἰκὼν τοῦ θεοῦ ἀοράτου, "the image of the invisible God," (ver. 15). The first expression marks Him as the object of the Father's love, which has in Him, nothing that can grieve it, holy as it is, or that it must first subdue; thus His Holiness, Sinlessness are implied, on account of which it is He, in whom the forgiveness of sin is obtained. The other phrase leads into the substance of the glory of God, manifesting itself first and most of all in Him, and denotes also His Divine Personality; He is indeed the Image of a Personality, so that he must both have existence and be a Person, especially as "all the fulness" of God is said to dwell in the Son of Man. It may be conceded to HOFMANN (*Schriftbeweis*, I. 153-158), BEISCHLAG (*Christologie des N. T.*, 228-233), SCHENKEL and others, that the historical Christ must be made the subject for the most part (ver. 13). [See EXEG. NOTES on ver. 15.—R.] But what gives to this One His position in history and His Dignity, lies above this history in his super-terrestrial position and intrinsically Divine Dignity. Indeed the historical events pre-suppose the relation of the Son to the Father, His Divinity, and do not first constitute Him the Son, or God the Father, or Him a Person, who did not exist before, or was not yet a Person nor the Son of God.

b) *His relation to the world* is described by πρωτότοκος πάσης κτίσεως, "first-born of every creature" (ver. 15), and further explained by the confirmatory clause (ver. 16), "in him were all things created"—"by him and to him" (ἔκτισται), and sharply defined in ver. 17: "He is before all things and in him all things subsist." In the given connexion there is *first*, a temporal definition (πρὸ πάντων), so that here His pre-existence is decidedly and expressly asserted, in agreement with Jno. xvii. 5: "πρὸ τοῦ τὸν κόσμον εἶναι, "before the world was;" i. 1: ἐν ἀρχῇ, "in the beginning;" Eph. i. 4: "before the foundation of the world." *Second:* Prominence is given to the Personality, denoted both by πρωτότοκος and the creation of God "*in*," "by" and "to Him," as in Jno. i. 1: πρὸς τὸν θεόν; viii. 58: ἐγὼ εἰμί. So that the Apostle here treats of a pre-existent Person, not merely of a pre-existent principle, or of a historical Person, as though the pre-existent principle first became personal in Jesus at the Incarnation, or the personality had previously been only ideal. Compare THOMASIUS. *Christi Person und Werk*, pp. 60-66. *Thirdly*: His Creatorship excludes any creatureship in Him, and the identity of the Creator and Redeemer is so affirmed, that He who became man is placed more under the idea "God" than the idea "man." On this account Theodoret aptly says, "not as having creation for a sister, but as begotten before all creation." *Fourthly:* Our text defines Him, not as Him, ὑφ' οὗ all things were created, and yet as active in the creation: δι' αὐτοῦ; He is not simply an archetype of the creation for the Creator. *Fifthly:* He is emphatically indicated as the foundation and centre of the world and its history, its stability, and development. [CHRYSOSTOM interprets this passage and Eph. ii. 22: "as teaching that Christ is the Living Centre, to which all things in creation converge, the Divine Keystone in the arch of the Universe, on which the whole fabric leans; but he warns his readers against supposing that Christ Himself is *consubstantial* with the creatures whom He made and upholds" (WORDSWORTH).—R.]

c) *His relation to the Church* is described by "Head of the body, the Church;" "beginning;" "first-born from the dead." On the first expression, see on Eph. i. 22. It is the organizing power, dwelling in Him, through which the Church has come into being. The other expression refers to the victory over death, as the fact upon which the secure status of the Church rests; as indeed Paul appears especially as a witness of the resurrection, wherever as Apostle he founds churches. All views which will not recognize and appreciate the Person of Christ as the centre of His work and His Church, as Divine in origin and nature, as eternal, pre-terrestrial and super-terrestrial, efficient both in Creation and Redemption, degenerate into a false speculation against which this Epistle to the Colossians contends. The question is not raised here, not even a hint given, how we are to conceive of Divinity and humanity united in One; nothing is said upon this point; hence Nestorian error does not lie so near, as SCHENKEL thinks, but rather Arian or Sabellian or Gnostic or another spiritual error, which volatilizes the eternal reality of the Person of Christ, or a dualistic one, which overshadows and crowds out the act of the Redeeming Subject by asceticism or legality, the so-called virtue of the subject to be redeemed.

5. *The Work of Christ*, with respect to God, from whom the world has apostatized through sin, is described as an ἀποκαταλλάξαι τὰ πάντα, "reconciling all things;" with respect to the state into which the world has fallen through sin, as ἡ ἀπολύτρωσις, "the redemption," and as to its *beginning* and *principle*, as ἡ ἄφεσις τῶν ἁμαρτιῶν, "the forgiveness of sins." First of all, the ultimate *cause* of Reconciliation and Redemption is God the Father (ver. 13: ὃς ἐῤῥύσατο, ver. 19: εὐδόκησεν—ἀποκαταλλάξαι), as in creation. The *Mediation* of these belongs, as in the creation, to the Son of God, as Theanthropos in His historical Personality (ver. 20: by Him—and that "through the blood of His Cross," ver. 22: "in the body of His flesh through death"); His Person has central importance, His suffering and death is *the climax.* He entered into the fellowship of humanity, which is the object of Divine wrath, endured in this fellowship the wrath of God resting upon it, gave Himself as a Sacrifice, holy and innocent, proved in His self-denying obedience, in His office as Saviour, that just as His Son in whom He was well pleased became man, so it was the man in whom He was well pleased,—so that the Father for the sake of this One could turn His complacency upon the whole race which through Him dies to sin, and turns to God in grateful love.

The work of Redemption, as to its *Object*, relates to the totality of the creatures, although it begins in the human race; as to its *Purpose*, it tends to a restitution of the creation, or to a bringing back of the creation to the path which it has forsaken, toward its proper consummation. The former marks the extent of the corruption of sin. Man is a prey to the "power of darkness," which forms the antithesis to the kingdom of Love, so that darkness, which is opposed to Love, is to be conceived of, rather, as moral, than intellectual. Will, as well as knowledge, religiousness and morality, social and political relations, are effected and corrupted, and this can not only be affirmed of heathen (ver. 21 : ὑμᾶς), but is applicable to Jews (ver. 13 : ἡμᾶς). In the presence of this Redemption in Christ the advantages of Israel over the Gentiles disappear. The purpose of Redemption is directed, chiefly, to the internal sanctification of men, to the forgiveness of sin, extirpation of it and its consequences, to justification before God in the judgment within the conscience, and in the future at the last day (ver. 21). But it extends in ever wider circles, in order to permeate the whole creation, and bring all creatures and all relations to happiness and blessedness with Him into eternity. [To avoid any misconception, see EXEG. NOTES on ver. 20.—R.] Hence no dualistic view finds any justification here, in fact, dualism is anti-christian. The overcoming of the antagonisms, which are easily recognized, is thus set forth as a possibility and an indispensable task, and this is accomplished by ethical means, from the reconciliation of the world to the transformation of the world. [HENRY: Christ is the Mediator of reconciliation, who promises peace, as well as pardon, and brings into a state of friendship and favor at present, and will bring all holy creatures, angels as well as men, into one glorious and blessed society at last.—R.]

6. *The Church* in which the Redemption, objective in Christ, and accomplished by Him, is, and will be subjectively appropriated, is presented in our text in a two-fold aspect;

a) as respects its *region*—the militant and triumphant church, referred to in the expression, (ver. 18); ἀρχή, πρωτότοκος ἐκ τῶν νεκρῶν;

b) as respects its *inner life: cœtus vocatorum et fidelium*, referred to in the expression (ver. 12): ἅγιοι ἐν φωτί, "saints in light." The *organism* of the church is indicated by the expression (ver. 18): "Head of the body, the church." Its *extent* is denoted by the former reference, its *vitality* by the latter, and its mission is to further, subjectively, the purpose of the work of Christ. It is by no means indifferent *how* one stands in the church and holds to her; but it is just as little without important influence, *whether* or *that* one belongs to her, as it is indifferent in what nation or family one is incorporated.

7. The *morality* of the individual within the church of Christ is defined as objectively caused (ἅγιος, "holy"), subjectively internal (ἄμωμος, "unblamable"), and constantly referred to God (ἀνέγκλητος κατενώπιον αὐτοῦ, "unreprovable in his sight"); and on that account conditioned by *faith*, which must prove itself in a two-fold manner, in its life and its substance, as right and correct, as genuine and true, as *fides qua* and as *fides quæ creditur;* it is indeed the *word of God become alive* in the Christian. This, at the same time, explains, why and that faith must be stable and independent of time and human opinions; it depends upon permanence.

8. *The Word of God*, which should be heard and proclaimed, requires living persons who have been filled and moved by it, whom it has first served, to serve it in turn. Here we find a direction for the establishment of public worship, in which the exposition and proclamation of the Word should not be wanting, as well as for the labors of Bible Societies, that should circulate God's Word, not merely in black and white, as copies from the press, like booksellers, and bookbinders, but in accordance with the organism and mission of the Church, in connexion with the efforts of Home and Foreign Missions.

HOMILETICAL AND PRACTICAL.

There is an order in prayer. Luther sets it forth in his explanation of the second Commandment [Luther's small catechism, the 2nd answer —on our Third Commandment.—R.]: "In all necessities call, pray, praise and give thanks." The call for help, the cry of distress, the entreaty, which necessity presses out, is the easiest, briefest, first, the prayer of an elementary pupil; the petition in perplexity for a *need* is an affair of the apprentice, who has learned first to pray for himself, and when further advanced, to offer supplications of unselfish love for others. The journeyman knows how to *give thanks* for gifts received, but the master *praises* the *giver*, not forgetting Him in His bounty. Whoever can and does do this, will not slight the easier part. Paul always goes from praise to thanksgiving, and from thanksgiving to supplication. He begins with the former, nor does he neglect the latter. Do you also? [The Apostle's order is that of mature Christian experience. But the other is that of the learner. It is also that of the Psalms. They usually begin with petition and end with praise. They were written in the times of preparation for Christ. How often Christians revert to David's method. The Old Testament still leads us to the New,—we pray first like the Psalmist, then like the Apostle.—R.]

Theory succeeds practice, as Philosophy follows Poetry. To live the truth is more than to know the truth. To perceive the truth is rather a matter of the sanctified will, than of the well-stored memory or the isolated intellect.—Being filled with the knowledge of the truth, is to know both what is nearest and what is most remote. Reason is both a telescope, to look into distant eternal things, and a microscope to inspect and understand the things at hand, in house and heart, in life and business, but to adjust the glasses aright is not hers, it belongs to the will, it is not an intellectual, but a moral act. Christian living is not the product, but the producer of Christian thinking.—The more you do, the more you become.—Only when bearing fruit, does the Christian grow.—Self-redemption is a falsity, and forgiveness of sins, without Christ, a lie. The folly of the sixteenth century, when people bought absolution with money, is laughed at, but why should we not also ridicule the blindness of the nineteenth century, when people forgive their own guilt and sin, and fancy they get absolution at a still cheaper rate. Those who credit Christ, no longer have a creditor in God; in this privilege unbelief has no share.—The Christian cannot divide or divorce God and Christ, God and the world, Creation and Redemption, Christ's Person and Work, this world and the next, faith and love, faith and God's word, faith and forgiveness, faith and bliss, religion and morality, church and Christianity, sin and corruption, grace and salvation, salvation and sanctification, though it is he who accurately distinguishes them.—The truth in Christ is the greatest paradox of life; the cross is a throne, death is life, weakness is strength, defeat is victory, gain is loss.—Christ, who satisfies all the needs of the human heart, begins with pardon, with grace that ends in blessedness with God. He blesses man in himself and goes on until He completes the whole creation—to the choirs of angels.—The Bible is the jewel of all the literature of the world; in the ring of the Bible the gospel is the diamond.—The news and knowledge of the Holy Scriptures come to us in personalities, and in him who understands them they become again personal.

STARKE:—You flatter yourself that you are a good Christian because you do nothing wicked! Is a tree good then, that does not bear thorns and thistles? If you are not diligent in good works, your Christianity is nothing, your imagination is vain, your hope is lost. We must grow in knowledge, grow in the power of God, grow in spiritual walk and in holiness. If a new-born child does not grow perceptibly, it is a bad sign. So it is with a Christian also.—To be patient in so many sufferings of this present time, and long-suffering amid so many adversities are excellent gifts of God. But those are far advanced, who endure evil not only with patience, but with joy also.—Eternal life is an inheritance, hence it can be trifled away with sin, but not earned with good works. For a little child, though it have done nothing as yet, comes to its inheritance as well as the larger ones, who have done much.—Sad condition of men through the fall of Adam! once monarchs over all creatures, they must now be subject to the devil and his empire.—[Believers also are first born, and enjoy the liberty of the First Born.—The dignity of believers surpasses that of angels, for they are united with the Son of God, who is higher than all angels.—R.]

RIEGER:—Darkness, ignorance, doubt, inability man traces to himself; vexation and impatience break out of this darkness. But the gospel first makes known that behind this there is concealed a rule and power of darkness, out of which a deliverance is required, deliverance accomplished by means of right and justice moreover.—It was not done by the Father's sending the Son into the world, as a great witness of His love, to tell much of His name, and thus lead us away from our hostile disposition toward God, or direct us to confidence in Him: but God laid our sins and those of the whole world on this our Mediator, accepted His obedience, His sufferings, His sacrifice and the shedding of His blood as a ransom-price for us.—There is no doubt the corruption in heathenism was greater than now, although we, who spring from Christian, perhaps specially sainted parents, are still wicked and born sinners; yet much is ameliorated in our hereditary disease, and the favorable opportunity for us to find God as Love, is much facilitated. But this must be regarded rather as an advantage of our age, and not one of our persons. Through neglect of this grace of our age, we may become again as bad and worse than a heathen.—[The praise of the blood of Christ reaches to our being presented holy and unreprovable before God.—R.]

HEUBNER:—The heart of a Christian is a large heart. Paul had already entered into intimate fellowship with this Church, although he had never seen it. What attracts the heart of one Christian to another? How easily true Christians at once understand each other!—The more fruitful our walk, the more does our knowledge of God grow. True knowledge can come only out of and with action. It is not only the knowledge that increases, but the power is enlarged, the capacity of enduring, holding out in conflict, as well as of cherishing kindly sentiments toward enemies—and of doing both with joy. We must live ourselves into Christianity.—Those who do not desire to become holy or to be "made meet," may be external adherents, but are not citizens of the kingdom of heaven.—Christ is *before* all with respect to time; He does not belong to the series of beings created in time. This "*before*" *of priority* naturally includes the "before" of *preëminence.*—Justification precedes, sanctification follows: the heart must first be stilled, then it can collect itself and prepare for sanctification. The latter is the end of the reconciliation. Why then will we ever invert this order? Because we would ascribe pardon to our merit, and not to the merit of Christ.

SCHLEIERMACHER:—A mind, that would fully apprehend the truth of the gospel, will soon mark a voice in itself, when something important and essential is omitted, while on the other hand, good sense will soon warn us, if we allow ourselves to be misled, so as to insert in the Scripture, through artifice, something which is not there.—Only when *He* has become to us the knowledge of the Divine will, is there a walk worthy of Him.—Expanded knowledge is itself a consequence of fruitfulness in good works.—The more plain the will of God becomes to us, the more we see what God has laid upon us to do; so much the more do we encounter opposition, the more difficult it becomes to instil the same view into others, and the more does this spiritual conduct of life enter into spheres which appear foreign to it.—Oh that we so investigated the Scriptures, that it tended to edification!—Paul makes sanctification dependent upon "being grounded" in faith, and upon not being "moved away" from the hope of the gospel, which is no other than that of the consummation of the kingdom of God in Christ.

PASSAVANT:—At the time of the council of Constance, three cardinals in their ride met a poor shepherd weeping on the beach. They asked him why he wept so. "Out of gratitude," he answered, pointing to a worm, "that God has made me a man and not a poor worm like that." What would have been the gratitude of the poor shepherd, had the cardinals revealed to him, that God could, besides, make him meet for the inheritance of the saints in light.—Darkness is a kingdom, and this kingdom has its principalities and powers, and their artifice and malice is great; their might is great and the abyss is deep.—Many a one may appear pure and refined in conduct and culture, whose conscience sleeps, whose heart deceives itself; it is a dream of rest and peace, a false dream of life: sin can scatter over the whole life of a sinner her poppy leaves.—There exists among highly cultivated minds, among educated people, an alienation from God, and in consequence an enmity, which seems to arise not so much from the ordinary sinful flesh, as from the temerity and pride of the thinking or subtilizing faculty in us, which indeed is also flesh. ["One can—and the inconsistency is not rare—worship Jesus Christ as God, and yet not have acknowledged Him as God formally and with the understanding; the heart makes Him God, the understanding makes Him man, still with most men the heart cannot cure the mind of its error, but is rather led astray itself." Quotation in Passavant.—R.] "To extend the law of Christ," says Theodorus, "they did not use carnal weapons. The power of convincing speech alone attested the power of these divine precepts. Every where exposed to the greatest dangers, they endured in all cities, through which they passed, the most shameful and cruel mal-treatment: scourge and rack, prisons, executions and martyrdoms of all kinds were daily their lot: yet though the executioner could kill the bearers of the divine message, they could not kill the message itself. It proved still mightier after their death: the gospel survived with equal vital power the efforts and the rage of Barbarians and Romans: out of the funeral pile where they would bury the memory of those fishermen and tent makers, it went forth yet more brilliantly and gloriously."

[HENRY:—The Apostle heard that they were good, and he prayed that they might be better.—1. That they might be knowing, intelligent Christians. 2. That their conversation might be good. 3. That they might be strengthened. Vers. 12 sq. Here is the summary of the doctrine of the gospel concerning the great work of our redemption by Christ. It comes in here not as the matter of a sermon, but as the matter of a thanksgiving.—He does not discourse of the work of redemption in the natural order of it; for then he would speak of the purchase of it first, and afterwards of the application of it. But here he inverts the order; because in our sense and feeling of it, the application goes before the purchase. We first find the benefits of redemption in our own hearts, and then are led by those streams to the original and Fountainhead.—They who are not saints on earth, will never be saints in heaven. All who are designed for heaven hereafter, are prepared for heaven now. They who have the inheritance of sons, have the education of sons, and the disposition of sons.—This meetness for heaven is the earnest of the Spirit in our hearts; which is part of payment, and assures the full payment.—The greatest enemies to God, who have stood at the greatest distance and bidden Him defiance, may be reconciled, if it is not their own fault.—There was such a value in the blood of Christ, that on account of Christ's shedding it, God was willing to deal with men upon new terms, and bring them under a covenant of grace; and *for His sake* and in consideration of His death upon the cross, to pardon and accept to favor all who comply with them.—This gospel may be preached to every creature; for it excludes none who do not exclude themselves.—Paul was a great Apostle; but he looks upon it as the highest of his titles of honor, to be a minister of the gospel of Jesus Christ.—R.]

[BURKITT:—Ver. 10. Our fruitfulness should be an universal fruitfulness, an humble and self-denying fruitfulness, a proportionable fruitfulness, an abounding and abiding fruitfulness; this is to be fruitful in every good work.—Ver. 12. This meetness is a spiritual blessing, a transcendent favor, a discriminating favor, an everlasting favor; eternity will be too short to spend in the admiration of it; let such as are interested in it, now begin the work upon earth, of giving thanks to the Father for it.—R.]

[EADIE:—Ver. 10. Superabundance of one kind of fruit is no compensation for the absence of another. "Every good work" is inculcated. Such fruitfulness is not exhaustive. The tree grows healthfully while its fertility is so great.—Ver. 11. That peculiar position which necessitates the exercise of "patience and long suffering" should not induce despondency, as if it were inevitable fate, to be sullenly submitted to, but rather should there be joy that this Divine power is communicated, and that the mind is upborne in triumph, and enabled to hope and wait in quiet expectation.—Ver. 12. None but the saints, as being "light in the Lord" can dwell in that light. They who enjoy it are made meet for social intercourse. Selfishness vanishes before universal love, the intense yearnings of a spiritual brotherhood are developed and perfected.—Ver. 13. The one kingdom of God has an earthly and a celestial phasis. It resembles a city divided by a river, but still under the same municipal administration and having one common franchise.—Ver. 14. Forgiveness is more closely connected with redemption than any other blessing; it comes at once from the cross to the believing soul.—Vers. 15–19. The sentences in which Paul describes the rank and prerogative of Christ are like a bursting torrent. How he exults in the precious theme, and how his soul swells into impassioned panegyric!—Had the Divine Being remained alone, His glory would have been unseen and His praises unsung. Christ fitted up these "all things" "for Himself," in order that He might exhibit His glory, while He diffused happiness through creatures of innumerable worlds, and enabled them to behold His mirrored brightness and to reflect it.—At every point of His existence, it may be said of Him, "He is." What faith in power and extent should not be reposed in such a Saviour-God!—In all things He has the pre-eminence. None like Christ is the decision of faith, none but Christ is the motto of love.—Every grace as it is needed, and when it is needed, in every variety of phasis and operation, is wrapt up in that fulness which dwells in Christ.—Ver. 20. Blood shed on earth creates feuds to be extinguished only by other blood; but the blood of Christ's violent and vicarious death brings peace, restores alliance between heaven and earth.—Ver. 21. Man does not win his way back to the Divine favor by either costly offering or profound penitence. God re-unites him to Himself; has not only provided for such an alliance, but actually forms and cements it. The incarnation rightly understood, enhances the Redeemer's greatness.—Ver. 23. Thus a life of faith is one of hope. The loss of faith is the knell of hope.—Man is not acted on mechanically by the grace of God, but his whole spiritual nature is excited to earnest prayer and anxious effort. The confidence of success inspirits them.—R.]

[BARNES: Vers. 9-11. It is a good time to pray for Christians when they are already prosperous, and are distinguished for zeal and love. We have then encouragement to do it.—Vers. 12-13. No words can express appropriately the goodness of God in thus making us heirs of light.—Vers. 15-18. In the affections of our hearts let the Saviour in all things have the preeminence. None should be loved by us as Christ is loved.—Ver. 19. In all our wants let us go to Christ, in whom all fulness dwells.—Ver. 20. What a glorious work is that of the gospel! It reconciles and harmonizes distant worlds.—R.]

[ROBERT HALL:—Ver. 19. In Jesus Christ "*all* fulness" dwells, for the supply of spiritual destitution. Fulness of *knowledge:* knowledge is the great distinction of the mind, and here is all spiritual knowledge. Christ is Himself the wisdom of God; to know HIM is to attain at once the highest knowledge. Fulness of *holiness;* holiness is the proper riches and beauty of the soul; and the subjects of Christ are created anew in holiness after His image. Fulness of consolation; the greatest comforts that ever visited the troubled heart of man are those which flow from Christ as their fountain. Fulness once more, as it respects the *inheritance* in reserve; of which the saints have at certain seasons a *present* sense and foretaste, though the light of eternity is required to display its real extent, to display the *accessible* fulness of the *present* Saviour.—R.]

AHLFELD: He who places the full Christian grace before his soul, will strive the more earnestly to possess it. 1) Wherein does it consist? 2) How may I gain what I still lack?—CARSTEN: Peace through His blood on the cross. 1) Between God and man, 2) Heaven and earth, 3) in each human breast—or 1) The world reconciled with God, 2) Heaven opened, 3) Conscience stilled.—LÖHE: A ladder that reaches from heaven to earth. 1) God the Father has set it through the Son of His Love; 2) the highest round, at first concealed, shines in the light of sanctification; 3) the second in that of justification; 4) the third in the bloody scene of Golgotha; and our Redemption.—KÖHLER: Thanksgiving for the benefit of Redemption; 1) end; 2) mode; 3) means; 4) Person of Redemption.

ZIMMERMAN: Strife of two kingdoms for the souls of sinners; 1) God the Father devised the struggle concerning us; 2) God the Son has won the victory and kingdom for us; 3) whoever abides in Him, has escaped the enemy.*

On the epistle for the 24th Sunday after Trinity [vers. 9-14. The Prot. Episcopal Book of Common Prayer, following that of the Church of England, uses vers. 3-12.—R.]—HEUBNER: The great change wrought in man by Christianity. 1) *Its nature:* a) new light, full of knowledge and wisdom; b) a new virtuous walk, worthy of God; c) the translation into a new kingdom; d) the eternal Redemption. 2) *The consequences:* a) what is the reason, if we have not yet experienced this change? b) what have we to do?—RAUTENBURG: The question respecting our growth in Christianity. 1) *Can we*—2) *will* we grow? 3) *Have* we grown?—Paul prays for the believers in Colosse: 1) that, 2) what, 3) where and when he prayed for them.—KAPFF: What is eternal blessedness? 1) Redemption for all evil; 2) blessed fellowship with God and all saints; 3) unspeakable joy and honor in the glory of the heavenly kingdom.—LORENZ: Darkness and light. 1) Man according to nature; 2) man according to grace.—FLOREY: Light, the believer's inheritance. 1) They *have* the light of *truth;* 2) they *walk* in the light of *virtue;* 3) they come into the light of blessedness.—BECK: How a share in the glorious power of God 1) makes us meet; 2) admonishes us to thanksgiving.

[BEVERIDGE: Ver. 12. The happiness of the saints in heaven. 1) What kind of persons they are, who are or shall be happy in the other world; they are saints. 2) The happiness they enjoy there; the inheritance in light. 3) They who desire to enjoy that happiness must be duly qualified for it; "made meet." 4) All who are so qualified must ascribe it wholly to God, and give Him thanks for it; "giving thanks," etc.—STEINHOFER: The economy of the Triune God in the work of our blessedness. 1) What God has determined according to the counsel of His own good pleasure; 2) what in His Son from all eternity for our salvation; 3) what actually takes place in us to the praise and glory of His name.—The three glorious names of Jesus (Begotten before every creature, first-born from the dead, Head of the Body) should awaken us 1) to an humble joy, 2) a complete faith, 3) a tender love to Him.—LISCO: The actual union of God with the human nature in Christ the ground of the most intimate re-union of humanity with God through Christ.—SCHENKEL: A fruitful teacher's duty to pray unceasingly for his people.—The Christian should not rest until he has fully known the will of God, 1) in its highest designs and ends; 2) according to its manifold methods and means.—How Christian life and Christian thought reciprocally condition each other. 1) Without Christian thought the Christian life is not plain. 2) Without Christian life Christian thought is not correct.—The blessing of Redemption: 1) Wherein it consists (forgiveness of sins); 2) whereby it is obtained (through the blood of Christ.)—Jesus Christ, the Risen One, the Head of the church: 1) Its Founder, 2) its Upholder, 3) its Ruler.—Jesus Christ, according to God's good pleasure, the Bearer of all fulness of humanity and of man. Consider then 1) His glory, 2) our poverty.—The threefold witness for the truth of the gospel: resting 1) on the antiquity, 2) the extent, 3) the power of the proclamation of the same.—R.]

* [These divisions are made to rhyme in German—a fashion in sermonizing that happily has not yet come into vogue in America: 1) *Gott der Vater hat den Kampf um uns ersonnen,* 2) *Gott der Sohn hat Sieg und Reich fur uns gewonnen;* 3) *wer in Ihm bleibt, der ist dem Feind entronnen.*—*R.*]

3. Joy of the Apostle in his suffering and labor.

(CHAPTER I. 24–29.)

24 Who [I][1] now rejoice in my [the][2] sufferings for you, and fill up that which is
behind [ὑστερήματα, deficiencies] of the afflictions of Christ in my flesh for his body's
25 sake, which is the church; Whereof I[3] am made [became][4] a minister according to
the dispensation of God which is [was] given to me for you, to fulfil the word of
26 God; *Even* [*To wit*] the mystery which hath been hid from ages and from genera-
tions [the ages and from the generations],[5] but now[6] is made manifest to his saints:
27 To whom God would [willed to] make known what *is* the riches of the glory of this
mystery among the Gentiles; which[7] is Christ in [or among][8] you, the hope of
28 glory: Whom we preach, warning every man, and teaching every man in all wis-
dom; that we may present every man perfect in Christ Jesus [in Christ]:[9]
29 Whereunto I also labor, striving according to his working, which worketh in me
mightily.

[1] Ver. 24.—Before νῦν some MSS. read ὅς, which is wanting in ℵ. A. B. C.; more likely to have been added for closer connexion with the preceding context, than to have been omitted. [Alford suggests that it is from the preceding termination. Rejected by all modern editors, though retained in E. V. Instead of "Who" read "I," or better "Now I rejoice."—R.]

[2] Ver. 24.—[The E. V. follows Rec., which inserts μου after παθήμασιν. This reading is supported by no uncial authority except ℵ[3].; rejected by all modern editors, hence not noted by Braune. The E. V. undoubtedly gives the true sense.—R.]

[3] Ver. 25.—ℵ. reads Παῦλος after ἐγώ, but not B. and others; probably from ver. 23, *causa nexus*.

[4] Ver. 25.—["Became," Alford, Ellicott, Coverdale (Test.).—R.]

[5] Ver 26.—[The article of the Greek should be retained in English, to give definiteness: ages and generations "before us," Alford.—All older English versions omit it, however.—R.]

[6] Ver. 26.—[Rec. with A. D. K. L., Lachmann, Tischendorf, Ellicott, Wordsworth, read νυνί; ℵ. B. C. F., Alford, νῦν.—R.]

[7] Ver. 27.—[Ὅς is the reading of ℵ. C. D. K. L. Rec.; adopted by Tischendorf, Meyer, Ellicott, Wordsworth; ὅ is supported by A. B. F. G., Lachmann, Alford. Braune renders *welcher*, thus adopting the former reading.—R.]

[8] Ver. 27.—[Ἐν ὑμῖν, literally "in you," but here "among you" also. Braune: "*bei Euch*." See EXEG. NOTES.—R.]

[9] Ver. 28.—[Ἰησοῦ is wanting in ℵ.[1] A. B. C. D.[1] F. G.; rejected by Tischendorf and modern editors generally. E. V. follows Rec., which inserts it. Uncial authority slight.—R.]

EXEGETICAL AND CRITICAL.

The joy in suffering. Ver. 24.—**Now I rejoice in my sufferings for you.**—"Now" marks the present, which is described by "in my sufferings for you;" precisely therein, surrounded, encompassed by sufferings "I rejoice." [EADIE: "'at the present time,' with the chain upon my wrist:—not, however, as if he had been sorrowful at a previous period."—R.] At other times he had his joy without bonds, in full freedom of activity for the gospel. The object of joy is not denoted by ἐν, but by ἐπί with the dative, Matth. xviii. 13; Luke i. 14; Acts xv. 21; 1 Cor. xiii. 6; xvi. 17, or by διά, Jno. xi. 15; 1 Thess. iii. 9. Only in Luke x. 20; Phil. i. 18 is the object introduced by ἐν τούτῳ. The object of his joy is that his sufferings had good fruit among the Gentiles. Comp. Phil. i. 12–20. It was in Rome that he had learned this; hence "now." The bitterness of sorrow cannot disturb his joy at the sweetness of the fruit. See Eph. iii. 1. Hence it is incorrect to consider νῦν a particle of transition (BAEHR), or of consecution, or τὰ παθήματα as the object of the joy (GROTIUS, HUTHER and others). Nor is ὑπέρ="instead of" (STEIGER), or "on account of" (*wegen*, STOLZ), or to be joined with χαίρω. The reference is neither to the occasion of the sufferings of the Apostle to the Gentiles, nor to his example, but to the fact, that his sufferings are for the good of the Church, as indicated by what follows. [EADIE agrees with STOLZ: "on account of." He was imprisoned because of his preaching to the Gentiles. This is true, but ALFORD's view agrees better with the text, context and Braune. "The preposition cannot here imply substitution—but strictly *in commodum vestri*, that you may be confirmed in the faith by—not my example merely—the glorification of Christ in my sufferings." So WINER: *zum Vortheil*, *Gram.* p. 358.—R.]

And fill up that which is behind of the afflictions of Christ.—["And am filling up fully the lacking measures of the sufferings of Christ," ELLICOTT.—R.] Καί leads us forward from the subjective feeling to the objective state of the case (MEYER), but not from the particular (ὑμῶν) to the whole (LUECKE); nor is it=καὶ γάρ (BAEHR), nor yet=*sed* (BENGEL). By τὰ ὑστερήματα (Phil. ii. 30; 1 Thess. iii. 10; 1 Cor. xvi. 17; 2 Cor. viii. 13, 14; ix. 12; xi. 9); we are to understand arrears, which must be cancelled ["deficiencies," ALFORD—R.]; where such are found is indicated by τῶν θλίψεων τοῦ Χριστοῦ. As in 2 Cor. i. 5 ("the sufferings of Christ") the meaning here is, sufferings which Christ endured.* The Apostle, whom Christ had asked, when he persecuted the Church (Acts ix. 14), "why persecutest thou me?" and who in the Epistle to the Ephesians (i. 22; v. 33; iv. 12) calls Him the Head of the Church, and this His body, could speak thus without fear of being misunderstood. What befalls His own, the Master accepts as done to Himself (Matt. x. 40-42; xxv. 31-46). Hate and persecution He had announced to them beforehand (Jno. xv. 18-21; xvi. 1-4). What the servants suffer is aimed at the Master. He takes it to Himself. All enemies of the Church are His enemies also, who shall be put under His feet (1 Cor. xv. 25). See WINER'S *Gram.* p. 178. MELANCHTHON: *non quod ad meritum, quod plenissimum est solius Christi, sed quod ad militiæ societatem attinet.* Here the Apostle treats of historical matters, phenomena and facts, behind which we must ever hold fast to a real, though invisible connexion of the Head with His Church—(here just as in Phil. iii. 10; Rom. viii. 17; 2 Cor. iv. 10 sq.; 2 Tim. ii. 11; 1 Pet. iv. 13)—with respect to the historical development, the course of the Kingdom through the world. There is nothing whatever to indicate atonement with God [*i. e.*, by means of these sufferings of Christ, the "deficiencies" of which Paul was filling up; this interpretation made this "a proof text for the doctrine of indulgences" among the medieval Romanists—it is doubtless thus understood still among them.—R.] As little as *τὰ ὑστερήματα* describes any lack or insufficiency of afflictions in themselves, so little stress can be laid upon the choice of the specially significant expression (*θλίψεις*) instead of the more general *παθήματα* (2 Cor. i. 5). It is incorrect to understand *τοῦ Χριστοῦ* as meaning: similar to the sufferings of Christ (HUTHER and others), or for the sake of Christ (BÖHMER and others), or borne *auctore et auspice Christo* (LUECKE), or the Church directly. On *ἀνταναπληρῶ*, placed first on the main idea, BENGEL makes the excellent remark: *fixa est mensura passionum, quas tota exantlare debet ecclesia; quo plus igitur Paulus exhausit, eo minus et ipsi et posthac et ceteris relinquitur; hoc facit communio sanctorum.* While *ἀναπληροῦν* occurs more frequently in the New Testament, *ἀνταναπληροῦν* is found here only, and is rare anywhere. The preposition *ἀντί*, according to the context, refers to a filling up in view of arrears, and marks the extent and weight of the Apostle's sufferings. It cannot be regarded as referring to Christ (instead of Christ, or: as He for me, so I now suffer for Him [*vicissim*]), or to the Church; not even to the fact that he had formerly persecuted Christ and afflicted the Church; although he now as a sufferer completed the sufferings which come on the Church, while as a persecutor he had formerly brought such upon it. TITTMANN (*Syn.* I. p. 230) and WINER (*de verb. comp.* III. p. 22) explain: *alterius quod deficit loco et vice supplere;* not indicated here. [EADIE gives the clearest statement of the various interpretations, and mentions those who uphold them. His own view, which agrees in the main with that of BRAUNE, ALFORD, ELLICOTT,—and of many of the best commentators from CHRYSOSTOM to our day, will appear from the following extracts: "The personal sufferings of Christ are over, but His sufferings in His people still continue. The Apostle in suffering for the sake of the Church, felt that he was filling up the measure of those afflictions. The double compound verb denotes to fill up in relation to; to fill up with something which meets the exigence, or is equivalent to the want. The Apostle filled up the sufferings of Christ not with some foreign agony that had no relation to the defect; but the process of supplement consisted of sufferings which met the deficiency, in quality and amount.—Filled up what was yet wanting in the Saviour's sympathetic sorrows." So Augustine on Psalm lxi.—See Doctrinal notes below.—R.] A further and fuller definition of *ἀνταναπληρῶ* is given in the next clause: **In my flesh for his body's sake.**—[In support of the above view, WORDSWORTH aptly remarks: "Hence the Apostle says, that I may fill up what is lacking of Christ's sufferings in His *Body;* not in the *Head.*"—R.] The two phrases belong together; "flesh"—"body" denote the reciprocal relation; the former describes the person of the Apostle on the side which is affected by the sorrow (Gal. iv. 4; 2 Cor. iv. 11), the latter the organism to which benefit accrues from the sorrow endured, from the bearing of the sorrow; the individual sacrifice for the whole (MEYER) is the intent of these adverbial phrases. Comp. Eph. iii. 13. STEIGER incorrectly joins these phrases with "the afflictions of Christ as one idea: the verb requires closer definition rather than this. [So ELLICOTT: *ἐν τῇ σαρκί μου* defines the seat, and inferentially the mode of the "filling up,"—in exquisite contrast (MEYER) with the *σῶμα*, which defines the *object* of the action.—R.]—**Which is the church,** is simply an explanation (see Eph. i. 22), as *ὑπὲρ τοῦ σώματος ὑμῶν* is an explanation of *ὑπὲρ ὑμῶν.*

The ministerial position of Paul. Vers. 25-27.

Ver. 25. **Whereof I became a minister,** *ἧς ἐγενόμην ἐγὼ διάκονος.*—See ver. 23. This vocation of suffering for the Church he must endure as its minister; as servant, not as master, as servant of the gospel and of the Church, *qui evangelio servit, idem ecclesiæ servit* (GROTIUS). [EADIE: "of which Church;" ELLICOTT: "*ἧς* has a faintly explanatory force,—'I fill up, *etc.*—the Church, being an appointed

* [MEYER: "Τοῦ Χριστοῦ is a subjective genitive. Paul describes his own sufferings, according to the idea of 'the fellowship of the sufferings of Christ' (1 Pet. iv. 13; comp. Matt. xx. 22; Heb. xiii. 13), as 'the afflictions of Christ,' in case the Apostolic suffering was essentially of the same kind, which Christ had endured (the same cup, of which Christ had drunk, the same baptism, with which Christ had been baptized). The sum of these afflictions is conceived of as a definite measure, as is frequent in classical usage in similar figurative representation.—'I rejoice in my sufferings, which I endure for you, and how great and glorious is that which I am engaged in accomplishing through these sufferings! the full completion of that which is lacking on my part in the fellowship of the sufferings of Christ.' Very naturally his triumphant consciousness, this feeling of the greatness of the matter, led not only to the choice of the highly significant word ἀνταναπληρῶ, but to this description of the Apostle's own afflictions in the most honorable and sublime manner, as the 'afflictions of Christ,' since in their kind and character they are none other than those endured by Christ Himself."—R.]

minister thereof'—in ver. 23 the διακονία referred to the εὐαγγέλιον, here to the Church by which the εὐαγγέλιον is preached."—R.] As servant, which he became: **according to the dispensation of God which was given to me for you.**—Κατὰ τὴν οἰκονομίαν τοῦ θεοῦ [*gemäss der Haushalterschaft* (stewardship, ALFORD) *Gottes*.—R.] defines his ministry as that of an οἰκόνομος, God as οἰκοδεσπότης, His (τοῦ θεοῦ) is the οἰκονομία entrusted to him, he and his office belong to God. It is therefore the office, not the management, *dispensatio* (Eph. i. 10; iii. 2). [ELLICOTT: "not the *disposition* of God, but the spiritual function, the office of an οἰκόνομος."—The word is difficult to render accurately in English. "Dispensation" can remain, not from its fitness, but in lack of a better.—R.] Hence "which was given to me." A comparison of Rom. xv. 15 ("the grace that is given to me of God") with 1 Cor. iii. 10 ("the grace of God which is given unto me") enables us to perceive that the emphasis is laid upon this, that the office, which was given to him, was of God, not that God had given it to him. The expression regards the Church [*Kirche*] as the house of God in connexion with the view that the congregation [*Gemeinde*] is the body of Christ, as in Eph. i. 22 sq. and ii. 21 sq.).—The added phrase, εἰς ὑμᾶς ["for you," "towards you" (ALFORD)—R.], gives the reference, the direction of the office, which God had determined, and takes the readers as denoting, concretely and immediately, the heathen world to which they belonged.

To fulfil the word of God.—This is his allotted duty. The infinitive depends on δοθεῖσαν. [Infinitive of design.—R.] In the object the gospel is included, and thus the idea of a message, which should be carried in all directions. Hence "fulfil" implies the figure of a measure to be filled. BENGEL: *ad omnes perducere. Paulus ubique ad summa tendit.* Comp. Rom. xv. 19. There indeed the locality is given; here it is indicated also by εἰς ὑμᾶς, which precedes. Hence it is not=to fulfilling the promises (BEZA), that was not the affair of the Apostle, nor=to proclaim fully in extent and contents (OLSHAUSEN), nor=to preach fully (LUTHER), nor=to complete, as if finish the teaching of Epaphras (FRITZSCHE), nor=to teach as גָּמַר (FLATT, BAEHR and others), nor yet=to realize (STEIGER),=to work out (DE WETTE),=to bring to full faith (CHRYSOSTOM, who connects εἰς ὑμᾶς here). [ALFORD seems to incline to the view of Chrysostom, but rejects the assumed connection: "to fulfil the duty of the stewardship, in doing all that this preaching of the word requires." ELLICOTT: "to give its fullest amplitude to, to fill up the measure of its fore-ordained universality, not perhaps without some allusion to the οἰκονομία, which could thus be fully discharged." So MEYER and EADIE. See HOMIL. NOTES.—R.]

VER. 26 defines more closely the word of God as to its purport.—**The mystery which hath been hid from the ages and the generations.**—See Eph. iii. 9, 4: i. 9. The synonymous phrase (καὶ—γενεῶν), alone is new, and unique in the New Testament (yet see Eph. iii. 5, 21; Acts xv. 21). Beside the ages of the world, the generations of men living in them are brought into special prominence, and thus the concealment from the beginning of human history is marked. BENGEL incorrectly refers αἰῶνες to angels, γενεαί to men. [ELLICOTT: "the mystery was the divine purpose of salvation in Christ, and more especially as the context seems to show '*de salvandis gentibus per gratiam evangelicum*' (DAVENANT).—The Apostle does not say, πρὸ τῶν αἰώνων, from eternity. The expression is historical. The counsel was *formed* πρὸ τ. αἰ., but *concealed* ἀπὸ τ. αἰ." EADIE seems to be incorrect in limiting "mystery" here to the salvation of the Gentiles, though it has a special reference to this.—R.]

But now is made manifest to his saints.—The Greek liked the transition from a participle to a finite verb, of course with due regard to the structure of the thought, WINER'S *Gram.* p. 505. [Here the transition gives prominence to the second member of the sentence, and sharpens the contrast.—R.] Eph. iii. 5 is parallel. Special emphasis rests upon νυνὶ δέ on account of the antithesis. In contrast with ἐγνωρίσθη, which refers to knowledge, and ἀπεκαλύφθη, which refers to special spiritual revelation, ἐφανερώθη is the most general and comprehensive expression, certainly not without a reference to the historical actualization, to the fact of evangelical preaching (2 Tim. i. 10). [MEYER observes that this manifestation took place in different ways, partly by revelation, partly by preaching and exposition, and partly by all combined. EADIE and ALFORD seem disposed to limit it to direct manifestation by Divine power, "at the glorification of Christ and the bestowal of the Spirit." But the whole context refers to Paul's ministry, hence the more extensive view, which includes preaching, is to be preferred.—R.] Thus "His saints" means all Christians, and must not be limited to the Apostles on account of the parallel passage (BAEHR, STEIGER, and others). Nor should "saints" be taken indefinitely (HUTHER), because the mystery of the reception of the Gentiles into the kingdom of God was not known by many Jewish Christians. The word is not ἐγνωρίσθη, "known;" these were only a minority at best, and their misconception was rather respecting the mode, the immediacy of the entrance of the Gentiles. [DAVENANT applies it to the *elect*, which though true enough, is not pertinent here, see below.—R.]

Ver. 27. **To whom God willed to make known,** οἷς ἠθέλησεν ὁ θεὸς γνωρίσαι.—This relative clause marks the design of God. Ἠθέλησεν* is not to be limited to free grace, as the Greeks and Reformed claim. [CHRYSOSTOM, CALVIN, BEZA, DE WETTE—modern commentators, even EADIE, object to pressing such a meaning. ALFORD: a legitimate *inference*, but not an *exposition*.—R.] Simply=it was His will. His

*[Buttman thus distinguishes θέλω and βούλομαι: the former expresses "will combined with choice or purpose," the latter "mere inclinations." Prof. Hitchcock, however, claims (see his valuable note on τοῦ θελήματος, Eph. i. 9) that in the wide range of volition expressed by θέλω, the element of spontaneity is always included, while βούλομαι always implies deliberation. The former can be used of a brute, the latter of a rational being only (Ammonius). This view, if adopted, would lead to a slight modification of Braune's exegesis, though it would also exclude the limitation to free grace. Perhaps care should be taken in applying the distinction to what is predicated of God.—R.]

design in the "making manifest" was "to make known." Thus the view respecting the former verb is corroborated. The relative clause does not limit the force of ἅγιοι, to those who should know: οἷς is: as to whom, [*quippe quibus* (MEYER): as being persons "to whom," etc. "Seing that to them it was God's will," etc. (ELLICOTT).—R.]. The object of γνωρίσαι is: **what is the riches of the glory of this mystery among the Gentiles.**—"What is the riches" is *quæ suit divitiæ* not *quales*. On ὁ and τὸ πλοῦτος, see WINER'S *Gram.* p. 64. The Apostle is speaking of the wealth "of the glory of this mystery." Δόξα is the main idea, which must not be weakened: on it depends a "wealth," while it depends "on this mystery," and comes with the revelation of it. Hence it is incorrect to render: "glorious riches" (LUTHER) and *gloriosi hujus mysterii* (BEZA). Δόξα is glory, not to be limited to "bliss" (MICHAELIS), "glorious results" (CHRYSOSTOM), nor yet to be extended to God's Being, His wisdom and grace (DE WETTE), the Divine self-revelation (SCHENKEL). CALVIN is excellent: "He teaches that these riches had appeared, particularly among the Gentiles; for what could be more deserving of admiration, than that the Gentiles, who for so many ages had been sunk in death, and whose condition might seem altogether desperate, should suddenly be received into the family of God, and receive the inheritance of salvation?" [On the meaning of δόξα, see ALFORD and ELLICOTT.—The former, following MEYER, makes it identical with δόξα below—the latter distinguishes it, more correctly. Both would not restrict it to either a subjective or objective meaning; it partakes of both.—R.] On this account "among the Gentiles," is to be joined with "is," which must be supplied, not to "this mystery." Among the Gentiles the riches of the glory of this mystery revealed in the gospel appeared in the sharpest contrast with the deepest shadows (OLSHAUSEN).

Two phrases in apposition make the sense clearer. *First:* **which [or who] is Christ in you,** [*bei Euch*, "among you—R.]—"Christ among the Gentiles, the greatest paradox in that age" (BENGEL). First "without Christ," "without God." "Children of wrath by nature" (Eph. ii. 12, 13) now He is among, in them (Eph. iii. 17). Ἐν ὑμῖν corresponds to ἐν ἔθνεσιν, "Christ" to "the riches of the glory of this mystery," and ὅς marks this reference, though it conforms to the following name, not to τὸ πλοῦτος (WINER'S *Gram.* p. 157). [Hence the various readings do not affect the sense.—R.] The reference to "this mystery" (HUTHER) [ALFORD, ELLICOTT.—R.] is too restricted, and not well-founded in grammar or fact. By "Christ" we must understand not the knowledge of Christ (THEOPHYLACT), nor the doctrine of Christ (GROTIUS) nor yet "from Christ" (FLATT), but Himself, His Person. "You" means the Gentiles, not simply the Colossian readers, as in ver. 25.—*Secondly:* **the hope of glory,** in exegetical apposition with "Christ," in whom the Gentiles have the surety for the future fruition of the glory of salvation: in Him we have here as seed, what we shall have in Him there as harvest. Entirely like 1 Tim. i. 1, "Jesus Christ, our hope." ["Glory" here is future blessedness, above it has a more general reference, see EADIE, ELLICOTT.—R.] "Christ—your life," iii. 4, is similar. Jno. xi. 25. Comp. Eph. i. 18; ii. 12; Rom. viii. 24. BENGEL: *Christus in nobis, per se lætissimum; sed multo lætius, respectu eorum, quæ revelabuntur.*

Paul's labor. Vers. 28, 29. **Whom we preach,** ὃν ἡμεῖς καταγγέλλομεν.—The emphasis must be laid on ἡμεῖς, which might be wanting, did not the Apostle speak in opposition to false teachers. At the same time, he notes that he does not stand alone. It does not refer directly to Timothy (MEYER), nor to Epaphras; it is doubtful whether Paul thought of particular persons. Certainly BLEEK is mistaken in his view that he thought particularly of no other one than himself. [So CONYBEARE, who insists ever upon the singular force of ἡμεῖς.—R.] The singular which follows (ver. 29: κοπιῶ) forbids such an opinion. ERASMUS incorrectly places the emphasis upon ὅν; "this one, not Moses or angels."

Warning every man and teaching every man.—This gives the modality of the καταγγελεῖν. Both participles [νουθετοῦντες and διδάσκοντες] are used, iii. 16, in another order. The first aims to affect the will, using what is already known, the other to foster knowledge, beginning indeed with what is known; it denotes the imparting of information, linked with what is known, or the extension and deepening of knowledge, and here indeed, in the second place after νουθετοῦντες, on the basis of experiences and occurrences in the present and past, with a view to the future and eternity. Eph. vi. 4; Acts xxvi. 18; Rom. iii. 23–26. Both embrace repentance and faith—not the first participle the former, and the second, the latter (MEYER). [So ELLICOTT, and ALFORD, "but not too closely or exclusively."—R.] Nor is the first alone moral, and the second only didactic (SCHENKEL). BENGEL too is incorrect, νουθετοῦνται, *qui jam docti sunt*, διδάσκονται, *rudes*. [For the other views, see EADIE, who, while regarding the first term as the more general, and the second as the more special,—agrees in the main with BRAUNE'S view as given above.—R.] Both are more closely defined: **in all wisdom,** ἐν πάσῃ σοφίᾳ.—See Eph. i. 8. There is no reason for joining it to διδάσκοντες alone, (DE WETTE, MEYER) [ALFORD, ELLICOTT and apparently EADIE.—R.], and the view is a perversion, which finds in it the object of the instruction (ESTIUS and others). "Wisdom of words" (1 Cor. i. 11; ii. 1–4) is excluded, but insight into the individuality of one to be taught and admonished, into his condition, and into the method by which it can be successfully done. [ALFORD: "the method of teaching." ELLICOTT: "in every form of wisdom—the characteristic element in which the teaching was always to be, and to which it was to be circumscribed." CHRYSOSTOM: μετὰ πάσης σοφίας. These views are correct, but should be extended to "warning" as well.—R.]

That we may present every man perfect in Christ.—Ἵνα gives the end of the "preaching," mediated by the "warning" and "teaching." As in ver. 22, παραστήσωμεν, which is placed first for emphasis, is used with reference to the Judgment; so earnest a matter is it; it has not to do with men's judgment. The offering of a sacrifice is not found in the context. "Every man" is repeated for the third time: every individual the Apostle bore on his heart. BENGEL: *hoc toties positum maximan habet δεινότητα ac vim, et causam continet. cur etiam ad ignotos scribat.* As "perfect" each should there appear, and indeed, as the context and ver. 22 require, in his whole being, not simply in knowledge (CHRYSOSTOM [CALVIN] and others), or in justifying faith (OLSHAUSEN). Perfection is possible only "in Christ," who alone conditions and effects this, in life and nature. By this he excludes all those false methods of voluntary asceticism, to which the false teachers guided. [Such a reference is considered doubtful by ALFORD and ELLICOTT, "in Christ" being so frequently used by the Apostle.—R.]

Ver. 29. **Whereunto I also labour.**—["To which end."—R.] The proclamation of Christ is the Apostle's life-work (ε ἰ ς ὃ) and not simply a service, and also (κ α ί) a painful labor (κ ο π ι ῶ). [Καί, also; besides preaching, etc.—I labor also. The relapse to the singular—"has an individualizing force, and carries on the reader from the general and common labors of preaching the gospel, to the struggles of the individual preacher" (ELLICOTT).—R.] This is strengthened by **striving**, ἀγωνιζόμενος.—By this he means both the *internal* conflicts of soul (iv. 12; ii. 1 sq.) in care, prayer, sympathy and earnestness for sanctification, and the *external* "fightings" (1 Tim. iv. 10; 1 Thess. ii. 2; Phil. i. 30). CHRYSOSTOM adds μετὰ πολλῆς σπουδῆς τουτέστιν μετὰ πολλῆς τῆς ἀγρυπνίας. MEYER [EADIE, ALFORD.—R.] incorrectly limit it to internal, GROTIUS, BAEHR and others to external conflict.

According to his working, which worketh in me mightily.—"According to his working" (ἐ ν έ ρ γ ε ι α ν α ὐ τ ο ῦ according to the context: Christ's) denotes, that Paul is not led and limited to his own strength, but strives according to the measure of the energy of Christ, which too worketh mightily in him, Eph. iii. 20, Phil. iv. 13. *Paulus per se non valeret, pro eo ac Christus in eo operatur, pellet* (BENGEL). It is both humility and certainty of victory. As little as αὐτοῦ should be considered as referring to God (CHRYSOSTOM and others), so little is the participle to be taken as passive (ESTIUS) and ἐ ν δ υ ν ά μ ε ι (comp. Rom. i. 4) to be referred to miracles (VATABLE). [ELLICOTT, quoting CALVIN, thinks there is no reason for excluding miracles summarily, though he admits such a reference would be only secondary. EADIE makes the phrase specify "the mode of operation." "The occurrence of the noun and a correlate verb intensifies the meaning"—Such a "working" would be "in power." "Its ample energies clothed him with a species of moral omnipotence."—R.]

DOCTRINAL AND ETHICAL.

1. *The sufferings of the Church are the sufferings of Christ.* The connexion of Christ, as Lord and Head, with the Church, His Body is so close, that the sufferings of the Church are the sufferings of Christ. "We know that the unity of the head and the members is such, that the name *Christ* sometimes comprehends the whole body" (CALVIN). "The head feels pain before the other members: thus experience teaches. For if you tread on a man's little toe, or hurt any other one of the most insignificant members, you notice it at once in his countenance. So Christ, our Head, takes the pains of us, His members, as if they were His own, and it burdens Him, as though it befell Himself, when any sorrow meets us" (LUTHER). [WORDSWORTH quotes Augustine on Ps. lxi., as follows: "Jesus Christ is one Man with His Body and His Head; the Saviour of the Body and the members of the Body are twain in one flesh; they are one in *suffering*, and when the iniquity of the world is past, they will be one in *rest*. Therefore the sufferings of Christ are not limited to Christ; nay, rather the sufferings of Christ are not except in Christ. For if you understand Christ to be both Head and Body, the sufferings of Christ are all in Christ. Hence the Apostle says '*Ut suppleam quod desunt pressurarum Christi in carne meâ.*' Whosoever therefore thou art, if thou art a member of Christ, whatsoever thou sufferest, was lacking to the sufferings of Christ. Therefore that suffering of thine is added because it was lacking; thou art filling the measure, not making it flow over. Thou sufferest so much in thyself as was to be poured in the universal passion of Christ, who suffered in our Head, and who suffers in His members, that is, in us. The whole measure of suffering will not be filled up till the world comes to an end."—R.] Two opinions present themselves here in opposition at either extreme: That of MEYER, that persecutions are indeed *directed* against Christ, but He, the victorious Ruler in Glory, cannot be *passively affected* by them; and SCHENKEL's, that He, as Head of His Body, must even now *share its feelings.* The former view sunders them, and makes of Christ's sympathy a mere phrase; the latter so confounds them in one, that the sympathy of Christ is marred and soiled by the susceptibility of the militant Church, instead of this being alleviated, purified and exalted by that.

2. *The atoning and the enduring sufferings of Christ.* A distinction must be made between the sufferings of Christ, which *atone for sin* and *extirpate* its *corruption*, and those which *endure sin* and its *evils.* The former, which He vicariously and representatively bore for us, are not here spoken of. The Romanists (CAJETAN, BELLARMINE, and others) are in error, in referring this passage to these only, and then regarding Paul's sufferings as supplementary to those of Christ, and hence, as also atoning and substitutionary, founding upon this their dogma of a storehouse of *superfluous good works* and *indulgences.* According to Jno. xix. 30, "It is finished," Christ's propitiatory sufferings need no supplement and completion; neither do His sufferings remove merely the guilt of original sin, nor is atonement for sins after baptism to be sought through the saints; one needing redemption himself, cannot make atonement. [For authorities on both sides of this controversy, consult the notes of EADIE, ALFORD and WORDSWORTH.—R.] This passage does not speak of those redeeming sufferings, of the sufferings of Christ in the theological, doctrinal sense, but in the *historical* sense, of the

sufferings of Christ in the world, of the sufferings of His Church from the world. These have a sum and extent not yet concluded, which are diminished in the onward progress to final victory, so that what the world, exhausting itself in its enmity, does to the members of Christ, turns out to the advantage of the Church, in so far as these members bear and forbear in the fellowship of their exalted Lord, the victor who sympathizes with triumphant sympathy. It is by just such *suffering heroes* in the Church, that she is helped out of manifold sorrow.

3. The *Word of God* is, as to its *nature*, *revelation* of a mystery, which would otherwise have been hidden from men, as to its tenor, *testimony* respecting Christ for all men. And this tenor is *universal*, directed to all men, is *mediated* by the proclamation of historical facts, *begins* within the man, and reaches beyond the germs and conflicts of time into perfection in eternity.

4. The *ministry of the Word* is an ordinance of God in and for the Church He has formed. It pre-supposes the revelation of Christ in the world, in the history of humanity, has to do with the proving of the same for each and every one by means of a proclamation, which takes hold of and advances the whole man, morally and intellectually, in will and knowledge. It should preserve, as its end, the internal sanctification and perfection unto the final Judgment, and is conditioned by the personal labors of the minister, as Christ's energy in him.

5. *Special care for Souls* is very important ["every man"—R]. It begins with Christ's special care.

HOMILETICAL AND PRACTICAL.

The Christian has to be thankful for so many and so great things, which he cannot lose, that in the sorrows of time, with the prospect of eternity and bliss, he is not joyless, but should be constantly rejoicing.—The Christian may rejoice, where men rejoice, and *can* rejoice, where it is impossible for men. He can rejoice, when he has his child in his arms,—and over its bier also. It is a great mistake to suppose that a certain melancholy and restraint of lively emotion is joined with Christian faith and piety.—Christian joy is the echo of a higher joy, which drowns the tumult of earthly sorrow.—The springs of joy in Mount Zion and Calvary cause it to flow on without interruption, and inexhaustibly.—The Christian's sorrow can and will bring good to the whole body and cause of Christ; in this the world's enmity but wearies and exhausts itself, to make the Christian come forth ever brighter. —The minister of the Word labors with the Eternal on the Eternal, for eternity, more than the artist; but only when He who has contrived eternal Redemption, works upon him, and he does not resist Him.

STARKE:—Preachers are not lords of the faith, but servants of the church, who have to direct all their service to the edification of the church.—The gospel is indeed made known to all the world, but is *known* in its truth and power only by those, who let themselves be brought thereby to faith. —Christ is in His believers, and this is the greatest mystery.—If many a teacher did not interlard his discourses with uncertain stories, fables, figures and other things of human wisdom, they would sink deeper into the hearts of men.

RIEGER:—The joy of the Apostles amid their sufferings was a fruit of the sorrow of Jesus under His. In our sufferings there must often be revealed to us, amid fear and sorrow, the weakness of our flesh, but often also, amid great peace and conscious joy, the manifold power of God and His Spirit of glory. Both are wholesome. Let one force or affect nothing, but accept what and as God finds it necessary.—One must so serve the church, that the gospel be derogated in no respect; yet one must not, under the pretext of the gospel, lord it over the people, but be a helper of their joy.

GERLACH:—In a few significant words the Apostle here brings to our view the activity of a genuine preacher of the gospel; 1) he preaches the mystery of the grace of God in Christ; 2) he admonishes all sinners to repentance; 3) he instructs even the plainest, poorest, most ignorant men; 4) he seeks to guide all to perfection, will withhold the higher light and life from none, keep none in a lower grade, is never satisfied with himself, nor permits himself to be satisfied with the state of others; 5) is ever conscious that a life of labor, especially of conflict too, is allotted to him; and 6) in this life confides only in the power of God working in him mightily, which is promised him, and hence gives God the glory for all.

SCHLEIERMACHER:—He could compare his sufferings with the sufferings of Christ, because they too had their cause in the antagonism of men to the preaching, which Christ had begun, and because to him they also were a work of obedience. Now too there are more views of Redemption, more representations of the manner of the liberty of the Sons of God, and yet there is ever more to be revealed of this mystery.

HEUBNER:—Suffering for atonement, Christ alone and fully bore; but suffering for our preservation and for the extension of the kingdom of Christ, every Christian must bear; since Christ has left a share to each.—The gospel sermon is a universal enlistment of souls for Christ. No man is too bad. Empty and hungry souls are led to Him, with Him to be satisfied and sanctified.

PASSAVANT:—"I do not fear the crowd of men, nor the angry outbreak of the world," wrote Matamoras, the Spanish martyr (November, 1862), from his prison in Granada; "as a Christian I have strength enough to lift myself above the raging torrent of earthly anger;—not through my own might, through my own powers, no, but through the strength our loving Father bestows upon me in Jesus; through Jesus, who is my Shield, an impenetrable shield, against which the whole world is weak."—Among the poor heathen of those times as of ours, could be seen only ignorance, hollow deceits, brilliant errors and lies; crying, devilish sins and proud vices raged among the refined Greeks and the proud men in all classes of the spoiled people. The light, or the uncertain, distorted ray of a former light, was limited to the narrow circle of nobler minds; the yet beautiful, rare fragments of the shattered truth remained a private possession of their pupils: the more lovely souls in every nation had only the uncertain legends of the poets as a solace: the priestly utterances, the arbitrary wisdom of the sage, as light on the path of life to death; many, perhaps very many sought salvation and peace at the dumb altar of "the unknown god."—The mystery since then has been made known to myriads of myriads; yet only the smaller part have comprehended it; to the saints alone has it been revealed in their hearts.—Without this "Christ in us" all hope beyond earth is but empty fancy, vanity and delusion; Christ among us and the clearness of His heavenly kingdom about us, only an unknown foreign land into which we have no desire to enter. Then our Christianity is but a borrowed, beautiful garment, which neither fits us nor hides our nakedness.

[SCHENKEL:—Ver. 24. The joy of the Christian in sorrow: 1) Its ground; 2) Its kind.—The blessing of persecution for the church of the Lord: 1) wherein it consists; 2) whereon it rests.—Ver 27. Christ lives among us: 1) A mystery to the unbeliever; 2) the comfort and joy of all believers.—Ver. 28. The task of the evangelical sermon; 1) as to its contents; to warn and to teach; 2) as to its form; "every man in all wisdom;" 3) as to its end; to "present every man perfect in Christ."—Ver. 29. The duty of the evangelical preacher: 1) wherein it consists—in labors and striving; 2) whereby its fulfilment becomes possible—through the help and power of Christ.—R.]

[BURKITT:—Such as are eminent in the church, and, as ministers of the gospel, do lay out themselves more abundantly in the church's service, must expect to meet with a measure, and a full measure of suffering beyond others.—Observe the subject, the manner, the end of St. Paul's preaching. Also his pains and diligence; the gracious help and blessed success he had, humbly and thankfully acknowledged, and ascribed to God.—R.]

[HENRY:—The preaching of redemption 1. to whom it was preached (ver. 23), 2. by whom it was preached. 1) Whence Paul had his ministry (ver. 26); 2) for whose sake he has his ministry (ver. 25); 3) what kind of a preacher Paul was; a suffering preacher (ver. 24), a close preacher (ver. 28), a laborious preacher (ver. 29). 3. The gospel which was preached (ver. 26, 27). 1) A mystery long hidden, 2) now made manifest to the saints.—The meanest saint under the gospel understands more than the greatest prophets under the law.—The ground of our hope is Christ in the word, or the gospel revelation, declaring the nature and methods of obtaining it. The evidence of our hope is Christ in the heart, or the sanctification of the soul and its preparation for the heavenly glory.—R.]

[EADIE:—In the Divine arrangement of the spiritual house, the Apostle held a function which had special reference to the members of the gentile churches. He would not be confined within the narrow circuit of Judaism; the field on which his soul set itself was the world.—The Apostle says of himself that he did not preach, but that he fulfilled the gospel. He carried out its design—he did not narrow its purpose—he opened for it a sweep and circuit adapted to its magnificence of aim, and its universality of fitness and sufficiency. As an instrument of human regeneration, he brought it to perfection —The glory of Christians is yet to come, but it is certain. Such glory is too bright for earth, and is therefore to be enjoyed in a scene which shall be in harmony with it. Christ is the hope of this glory.—The process of sanctification begets at once the idea and the hope of perfection.—The apostolic preaching was precise and definite. The one theme was Christ, "Him first, Him last, Him midst." Not simply His doctrine, but Himself.—What in other spheres is enthusiasm, in the Christian ministry is sobriety.—The sublime motive to present every man perfect in Christ, through the preaching of Christ, could only be realized by the conferment of Divine qualification and assistance.—BARNES:—In such a work it is a privilege to exhaust our strength; in the performance of the duties of such an office, it is an honor to be permitted to wear out life itself. Doing this, a man when he comes to die will feel that he has not lived in vain.—R.]

4. Anxiety of the Apostle about their being led away by false wisdom.

(Chap. II. 1–15.)

1 For I would that ye knew what great conflict I have for[1] you and *for* them at
2 Laodicea, and *for* as many as have not seen[2] my face in the flesh; that their
hearts might be comforted, being knit together[3] in love, and unto all riches[4] of the
full assurance [lit., of the fulness of assurance] of understanding, to the acknowledg-
ment [full knowledge] of the mystery of God, and of the Father, and of Christ
3 [or omit all after God],[5] in whom [or which] are hid all the treasures of wisdom and
4 knowledge. And this I say, lest any man [that no one, μηδείς][6] should beguile you
5 with enticing words. For though I be absent in the flesh, yet I am with you in
the spirit, joying and beholding your order, and the steadfastness [firm foundation]
6 of your faith in Christ. As ye have therefore [or As then ye have] received Christ
7 Jesus the Lord, *so* walk [walk] ye in him: rooted and built up in him, and estab-
lished in the faith [or by faith],[7] as ye have been taught, abounding therein[8] with
8 thanksgiving. Beware lest any man spoil you [lit., lest there shall be any one that
maketh you his booty][9] through philosophy and vain deceit, after the tradition of
9 men, after the rudiments of the world, and not after Christ. For [Because] in him
10 dwelleth all the fulness of the Godhead bodily. And ye are complete [made full,
11 πεπληρωμένοι] in him, which [who][10] is the head of all principality and power: in
whom also ye are [ye also were] circumcised with the [a, article wanting] circumci-
sion made without hands, in putting off the body of the sins [omit of the sins][11] of
12 the flesh, by [in, ἐν] the circumcision of Christ; buried with him in baptism,
wherein [or in whom][12] also ye are risen with *him* [were raised] with *him* [or to-
gether] through the faith of [in] the operation of God, who hath raised him from
13 the dead. And you, being dead in your sins and the uncircumcision of your flesh,
[insert you][13] hath he quickened together with him, having forgiven you [us][14] all
14 trespasses; blotting [having blotted] out the handwriting of ordinances that was
against us, which was contrary to us, and took [he has taken, ἦρκεν][15] it out of the
15 way, nailing [by nailing][16] it to his cross: *and* having spoiled principalities and
powers, he made a shew of them openly [with boldness],[17] triumphing over them
in it.

[1] Ver. 1.—Περὶ ὑμῶν is to be preferred as the more difficult reading to ὑπὲρ ὑμῶν which ℵ. A. B. C. read, probably taken from i. 24. [The authorities are as follows: περί, D.[1] D.[3] E. F. G. K. L., most cursives, Tischendorf, Meyer, Ellicott, Eadie, Wordsworth; ὑπέρ, ℵ. A. B. C. D.[2] Lachmann, Alford. Retaining the former, "for"="about".—R.]

[2] Ver. 1.—['Εώρακαν (an Alexandrian form of the perfect) is adopted by Lachmann, Tischendorf, Meyer and later English editors on the authority of ℵ. A. B. C. and others.—R.]

[3] Ver. 2.—[Instead of συμβιβασθέντων. (Rec., grammatical emendation, uncial authority slight) συμβιβασθέντες is well sustained, adopted by all modern editors.—R.]

[4] Ver. 2.—[Instead of πάντα πλοῦτον, (Rec.) modern editors adopt one of two readings; πᾶν τὸ πλοῦτος, Lachmann, Tischendorf, Meyer, Ellicott, Wordsworth: πᾶν πλοῦτος. Alford on the authority of ℵ.[1] B. The former is preferable as it accounts of the reading πάντα, το being changed to τα. The neuter form has a distinct meaning.—R.]

[5] Ver. 2.—Τοῦ θεοῦ is found in several cursive manuscripts which usually agree with B. To this B. adds: χριστοῦ [adopted by Lachmann, Tischendorf, ed. 1, Meyer, Huther, Wordsworth, Tregelles, Ellicott, "with considerable confidence."—R.] ℵ. adds πατρὸς χριστοῦ; a later hand: καὶ πατρὸς τοῦ χριστοῦ; A. C. insert πατρὸς τοῦ χριστοῦ; some cursive manuscripts and versions: πατρὸς καὶ τοῦ χριστοῦ; Rec. with E. K. L. καὶ πατρὸς καὶ τοῦ χριστοῦ. We find besides ἐν χριστῷ and ὅ ἐστιν χριστός. See Exeg. Notes. [Amid so great variety, we may yet conclude, 1. that the longer reading of Rec., followed by E. V., is not the true reading. 2. That the simplest explanation of the great variety is, the original text was the shorter τοῦ θεοῦ, the rest being glosses. So Braune, Tischendorf, ed. 2. 7. De Wette, Alford and many others. But 3, this reading having no uncial support, there remains a strong doubt in favor of another one of the many. Of these the most probable as well as best supported is that of B., τοῦ θεοῦ χριστοῦ. For a defence of the former, see Alford, who confesses his inability to fix the reading on any external authority; of the latter, Meyer, Ellicott, and the editors they respectively quote. The rendering, in case the latter be adopted, is still doubtful; either "of God, Christ" or "of God, even Christ" *i. e.*, Christ in apposition with "mystery." See Exeg. Notes.—R.]

[6] Ver. 4.—ℵ. A. B. C. D. and others have μηδείς, [Tischendorf and modern editors generally.—R.]; better supported than μήτις, [Rec.—The above reading indicates stronger probability of their being deceived.—R.]

[7] Ver. 7.—Τῇ πίστει. B. D. [Lachmann, Tischendorf, Meyer, Alford. Ellicott.—R.] ℵ. and many others insert ἐν [Rec. Wordsworth—R.], which seems to have been taken from the foregoing context. [The simple dative may be either instrumental, Braune, Meyer—"by faith," or of reference, Alford, Ellicott. See Exeg. Notes.—R.]

[8] Ver. 7.—'Εν αὐτῇ is to be retained with B. [D.[3] E. K. L. Tischendorf, ed. 7, Lachmann, Meyer, Ellicott, Wordsworth.—R.] It is wanting in ℵ. but ἐν αὐτῷ is added by a later hand.

[9] Ver. 8.—[The E. V. is too condensed. "You" is emphatic, the more so, as the correct reading seems to be τις ὑμᾶς ἔσται, B. K. L. Rec., Tischendorf, ed. 7, Meyer, Alford, Ellicott, Wordsworth. Not ἔσται ὑμᾶς, Lachmann, Braune apparently.—R.]

[10] Ver. 10.—[Ὅς is the reading of ℵ. A. C. K. L., Rec. Tischendorf, Meyer and others. ὅ, B. D. E. F. G. Lachmann "Which," E. V., stands here for "who."—R.]

[11] Ver. 11.—[Τῶν ἁμαρτιῶν of the Rec. is generally rejected as an explanatory gloss. Uncial authority very slight.—R.]

[12] Ver. 12.—[Ἐν ᾧ may mean "wherein" or "in whom." If the latter be adopted, read "risen together" instead of "with Him." See EXEG. NOTES;—βαπτίσματα is to be retained with most authorities and editors, instead of βαπτισμῷ, Alford.—R.]

[13] Ver. 13.—Ὑμᾶς is to be retained with ℵ. [A. C. K. L., Lachmann, Tischendorf, Meyer, Alford, Ellicott, Wordsworth.—R.] B. has ἡμᾶς. Some [Rec. D. F.] omit both as unnecessary.

[14] Ver. 13.—[Ὑμῖν of the Rec. is not well supported, Wordsworth retains it; ἡμῖν. ℵ. A. B. C. D. F. K., Tischendorf and most modern writers. Ellicott says: "Both external and internal arguments suggest the more inclusive ἡμῖν."—R].

[15] Ver. 14.—[The perfect should be retained by rendering "hath taken," so Tyndale, Coverdale and other versions.—R.]

[16] Ver. 14.—["By nailing" preserves the modal force as well as the relation of time implied in προσηλώσας.—R.]

[17] Ver. 15.—[This alteration is the only one required to make the English text harmonize with Braune's exegesis. The various renderings that are substituted for "spoiled," as well as the marginal reading of the E. V., "in him" for "in it," are discussed in the EXEG. NOTES.—R.]

EXEGETICAL AND CRITICAL.

Winning exordium full of tender concern for the spiritual health of the Church. Vers. 1–3.*

Ver. 1. **For I would that ye knew** (1 Cor. xi. 3; Phil. i. 12; Rom. xi. 25).—"For" links this to the foregoing, and according to the context, to "striving" (i. 29); with good reason did he speak of conflicts in this Epistle, since he was anxious about the Colossians also.

What great conflict I have for you.—Ἡλίκον (only in Jas. iii. 5, where it is used twice of little fire and great wood), derived from ἦλιξ (one of the same age, a companion), describes the manner, the vehemence and importance rather than the extent (MEYER and others), as πηλίκοις (Gal. vi. 11 †)=*qualibus*. HESYCHIUS: ποδαπόν, ὁποῖον. [ELLICOTT: qualitative adjective.—R.] Ἀγῶνα ἔχω denotes the continuance of his anxiety. [EADIE: "intense and painful anxiety." Any reference to outward sufferings (ELLICOTT) is very doubtful.—R.] Περὶ ὑμῶν indicates the readers as the object: what is more prominent in ὑπέρ, viz., for their benefit, is put in the back ground. **And them at Laodicea** adds a neighboring church in the same situation (see Introd. § 4.).

And as many as have not seen my face in the flesh.—On ἑώρακαν (see WINER'S *Gram.* p. 73). Ver. 2: αὐτῶν, requires us to understand this of persons belonging together and grouped together. It is improper to imply it either to those unknown to Paul in other places, in contrast with those in Colosse and Laodicea (THEODORET, SCHULTZ in *Stud. und Krit.*, 1829, p. 135 sq.), Paul having been in both places, or to those Colossians and Laodiceans who remained unknown to him (ROHR, WIGGERS). Paul merely adds a category for his readers; they had not seen him. [ALFORD: καί is not copulative, but generalizing. See his remarks on the grammatical inference that Paul had not been at Colosse—so most modern editors.—WORDSWORTH is decided in favor of the other view, following THEODORET. The passage so naturally suggests the thought that Paul had not been there, as to require far stronger evidence than has yet been adduced to sustain any other view.—R.] He adds to πρόσωπόν μου (1 Thess. ii. 17; iii. 10) ἐν σαρκί, since the contrast between spiritual presence and lack of personal acquaintanceship (ver. 5) readily suggested this concrete strengthening (bodily face). The reason for it is not to be found in the spiritual physiognomy (OLSHAUSEN), nor is it to be joined with ἑώρακαν (CHRYSOSTOM and others). It marks rather, that the readers need not be surprised at the Apostle's concern, when they did not know each other, that he included all Christians, known and unknown, in his sympathy as brethren, than that the motive of his concern was the fact of his not having himself founded and instructed this Church (SCHENKEL), or his having only an uncertain idea of it (BLEEK). BENGEL: *Paulus se omnium gentium debitorum statuit.*

Ver. 2. **That their hearts might be comforted.**—This is the purpose of the conflict (ἵνα). The verb means accurately, "to call upon," then "to admonish" (Phil. iv. 2), "to entreat" (Philem. 10), [rendered "beseech" in both cases in E. V.—R.], "to comfort" (2 Cor. i. 4), so that trust, confidence, strength is there, not doubt, uncertainty, wavering (iv. 8 · Eph. vi. 22); hence also "to strengthen, confirm" (Jas. iv. 3; Isa. xxxv. 3). [ALFORD insists that the idea of confirming predominates here. But MEYER, EADIE, ELLICOTT agree in upholding the usual meaning —R.] The Apostle regards the danger from false teachers as misfortune, affliction (CHRYSOSTOM: οὔτε κατηγορῶν οὔτε ἀπαλλάττων αὐτοὺς κατηγορίας). This comfort and tranquillity should first affect the heart, the centre.—**Being knit together in love.**—Συμβιβασθέντες according to the sense, as though it were αὐτοί, iii. 16; Eph. iv. 2, 3, WINER'S *Gram.* p. 532. On the meaning, comp. ii. 19; Eph. iv. 16. The participle denotes the way, the mode of the comfort; union in love according to the context: *in amore fidelium mutuo*, brotherly love, as the ethical element (MEYER) in which the "knitting together" was consummated. The Vulgate (*instructi*) is incorrect, and LUTHER also: comprehended (coördinate to "comforted").

And unto all riches of the full assurance of understanding, to the full knowledge of the mystery of God [**even Christ.**

* [" From the construction of this Exordium I venture to assert that there is no rule laid down by Aristotle, Cicero, and other masters of eloquence, concerning the framing of introductions, which is not adhered to in this brief opening. For three things are required of them in a legitimate Exordium: That it be adopted to render the hearer *attentive*, and *docile*, and to *conciliate his affection*." DAVENANT.—R.]

† [The meaning of πηλίκοις (Gal. vi. 11) has been much discussed. See *in loco*. It is very doubtful whether *qualibus* is strictly correct.—R.]

ELLICOTT. **God Christ**, WORDSWORTH.—R.]—Καί joins coördinately the end (εἰς) of the union, and in a two-fold direction; formally and quantitatively, "all riches of the fulness of assurance of understanding," materially and qualitatively, "to the full knowledge of the mystery of God." It is not sufficient to maintain, to know individual matters, the understanding must extend to the whole, in its fulness, and must attain to knowledge of the mystery. Comp. i. 9; Eph. iii. 18; in fellowship we advance to full knowledge.—On πληροφορία, see 1 Thess. i. 5; Heb. vi. 11; x. 22; it denotes full conviction, excludes incompleteness, includes joyous self-certainty. [EADIE: "the fixed persuasion that you comprehend the truth, and that it is the truth which you comprehend." What is commonly termed "assurance of knowledge," rather than "assurance of faith."—R.]—On "the mystery of God" see Eph. i. 9. If Χριστοῦ is inserted, this could not be regarded as dependent on θεοῦ (against HUTHER, MEYER, SCHENKEL), since the article is wanting, and every clear ground for it in the text, but only as in apposition to θεοῦ, so that Christ is called God, a singularity which is not Pauline, notwithstanding Rom. ix. 5; Eph. v. 5; Tit. ii. 13 (against STEIGER)—nor is it in apposition to μυστηρίου, as a gloss indicates. [Rejecting the reading of the Rec. as untenable, but one other than the shortest, has a claim upon our attention, the one referred to above: τοῦ θεοῦ Χριστοῦ. Braune refers to the three interpretations suggested. The first: the "mystery of the God of Christ," is harsh, as well as open to the grammatical objection he urges. The second is defended by WORDSWORTH, following HILARY: "the mystery of the God Christ," *i. e.* the mystery of the Divine nature of the Man Christ Jesus. His notes are worthy of attention. The third, making Χριστοῦ in apposition with μυστηρίου seems far preferable: "the mystery of God, even Christ."—It is well supported by ELLICOTT, and the gloss above referred to (ὅ ἐστιν Χριστός), is not without weight in determining the reading and the interpretation. Even MEYER, in adopting the interpretation "the mystery of the God of Christ," says: *In Christ* God has comprehended and consummated the decree of Redemption (the μυστήριον). To him who has acknowledged God as the *God of Christ*, the divine mystery is thereby revealed." Of course the meaning of μυστήριον is widely extended by taking Ellicott's view. It includes not simply the mystery of the Incarnation, but also of Redemption as involved in the Incarnation. The next verse can certainly be interpreted more readily, if this view be accepted.—R.]

Ver. 3. **In which**—Ἐν ᾧ refers to μυστηρίου. [E. V., "in whom"—(with the marginal reading "wherein,") refers it to Christ. If Χριστοῦ is retained above, and then taken in apposition to μυστηρίου, the meaning is the same. Unless the reference be to Christ in some direct way, it seems scarcely likely that Paul would say that in it were, "hid *all* the treasures of wisdom and knowledge." So wide a predicate is best applied to Christ.—R.]—**Are.**—Εἰσίν stands first for emphasis, to lay stress upon the fact that in God all mysteries are actually present.—**All the treasures of wisdom and knowledge**, πάντες οἱ θησαυροὶ τῆς σοφίας καὶ τῆς γνώσεως.—Σοφία is the practical wisdom, to which every Christian attains, γνῶσις is the dialectic science, which is found only in a mentally gifted and cultivated Christian. [Σοφία, the more general, γνῶσις, the more special, MEYER, EADIE, ALFORD, ELLICOTT.—R.] CALVIN is incorrect: *duplicatio ad augendum valet.* BENGEL: θησαυροί, *hinc* πλοῦτος, σοφία *hinc* σύνεσις, γνῶσις *hinc* ἐπίγνωσις. Hence the mystery must needs be revealed for the treasures are **hid**, ἀπόκρυφοι, in it. The adjective is a closer definition of the existence of the treasures in the mystery, and not a description of the treasures in themselves, therefore not an attributive joined to θησαυροί (BENGEL, MEYER, SCHENKEL). [ALFORD defends most fully the interpretation: "the secret treasures." EADIE upholds the view not noticed by Braune, that the treasures are "laid up." ELLICOTT, whose notes here are valuable, makes it a "secondary predicate of manner," *i. e.*, the treasures, *etc.*, *are* in the mystery or in Christ, they are so *suddenly;* until revealed and made the object of "full knowledge" as above (ver. 2). This recognizes the emphatic position of the verb, takes the adjective in its natural meaning, and accords better with the context. It seems to be Braune's view. DAVIES refers to the *gnostical* stamp of the terms in this verse. There is probably an allusion to the false doctrine at Colosse.—R.] The church did not need another system of doctrine, only more profound exposition.*

Brief sketch of the Situation. Vers. 4, 5.

Ver. 4. **And this I say**, refers to vers. 1–3, not to ver. 3 alone (ŒKUMEN, CALVIN, BAEHR and others). In ver. 5 he proves his λέγω by his sympathy. The danger which environs his readers, on account of which he cannot be silent, corresponds with his inward conflict about and for them: **that no one should beguile you.**—The verb (παραλογίζηται, only here and Jas. i. 22,) denotes, through παρα, as in παραβαίνω, παράδοξος, a deviation, violation, of the λόγος, the λογίζεσθαι, to miscalculate, to be deceived through sophisms (PASSOW, *sub voce*).

With enticing words, ἐν πιθανολογίᾳ denotes especially the danger. Πιθανός means "adapted to convince, persuading," like πειθός, and λογια denotes the mode in which this skill appears, viz.: in speech; it is stronger than ἐν πειθοῖς σοφίας λόγοις (1 Cor. ii. 4); it is found here only and *in malam partem.* LUTHER is incorrect—"with rational speech." The formal side of the false doctrine, the sophistical, rhetorical, insinuating method is noted, there is nothing from which the purport of the false doctrine can be inferred. [ELLICOTT: "the preposition ἐν has that species of instrumental force, in which the object is conceived as existing in the means," rather than indicating merely "the element in which the deceit works" (ALFORD).—R.]

Ver. 6. **For though I be absent in the flesh, yet am I with you in the spirit.**—Comp. 1 Cor. iii. 5. External, bodily absence, and spiritual presence, strongly marked by σὺν ὑμῖν, are here contrasted. There is no hint

* [In view of the errors which assailed them, the verse implies that they needed to know, "not more *than* Christ, but more *of* Christ."—R.]

here of a previous presence at Colosse (WIGGERS, *Stud. und Krit.* 1838, p. 181). [Nor does ἐν πνεύματι refer to the Holy Spirit, even secondarily (DAVENANT).—R.] There is no proof here of the danger of enticement to which the Colossians were exposed, nor of the greatness of the Apostle's anxiety, though these are involved. This proof lies in what follows; a description of the possessions endangered through the dangerous false teachers: **joying and beholding your order and the steadfastness of your faith in Christ.**—"Joying and beholding" describe the mode of Paul's presence. The joy is emphasized by the position, in order to point to the noble possessions which it concerns: his joy on this account enchains him, so that he stands there as a spectator. The representations made by Epaphras were sufficient to bring him into this attitude, although he was then unknown and absent. The object of the "joying and beholding" is, *first*, "your order;" its opposite is ἀταξία. It is the external appearance of the Church in good order—fixed, orderly deportment (1 Cor. xiv. 40); ὑμῶν, placed first, indicates the contrast with the false teachers, who disturb such order. *Secondly*, "and the steadfastness of your faith in Christ," describes sharply and definitely the internal state of the Church. Στερέωμα, *firmamentum*, like τάξις, is a military word, a fortification into and upon which they could and should fall back; perhaps suggested by ἀγῶνα (ver. 1). 1 Pet. v. 9: στερεοὶ τῇ πίστει is similar. It is incorrect to regard the participles as a hendiadys: *cum gaudeo videns* (BENGEL), or *gaudeo videns* (GROTIUS), nor is καί causal: *quia video* (CALVIN), nor explicative: to wit (WINER'S *Gram.* p. 438), nor can the order of words be called illogical. Neither should another object than that of βλέπων be given to χαίρων: his spiritual presence with the readers (MEYER, SCHENKEL), or about you (WINER), [apparently ELLICOTT, see ALFORD also.—R.] Στερέωμα is not=στερεότης (HUTHER and others). [ALFORD: not any abstract quality, but as all nouns in -μα, the concrete product of the abstract quality.—R.] Finally we cannot limit this to a part of the Church (FLATT) which was unseduced, or apply it to the whole, hypothetically, were this the case (BAUMGARTEN-CRUSIUS). [ELLICOTT: "after these words we have no reason for doubting that the church at Colosse—was substantially sound in the faith."—R.]

Admonition to fidelity in walk, vers. 6, 7.

Ver. 6. **As then ye have received Christ Jesus the Lord.**—The emphasis rests upon ὡς: on which account καθὼς is repeated (ver. 7). "Ye have been taught" there corresponds to "ye have received" here. Comp. ver 8: κατὰ τὴν παράδοσιν; Eph. iv. 20: ἐμάθετε; 1 Thess. ii. 13: παραλαβόντες—ἐδέξασθε. It is not then: have accepted [*angenommen habt*] (LUTHER and others): it refers to correct instruction. "Christ Jesus the Lord" [lit., the Christ, Jesus the Lord.—R.] sets forth the object, and "the summary of the whole confession" (MEYER), giving stronger prominence to the Person. "The Lord" marks, in apposition, what Jesus is for us, whom Paul had named "the Christ" over against God: τὸν κύριον is not to be interpreted, *ut dominum* (BENGEL and others). [ELLICOTT well remarks: "Though the reference seems mainly to reception by teaching, the object is so emphatically specified, as apparently to require a more inclusive meaning; they received not merely the *doctrinam Christi*, but Christ *Himself*, in Himself the sum and substance of all teaching."—R.]—From the favorable state of the Christian cause, the Apostle deduces (οὖν), according to the received instruction, the obligation: **walk in him!**—Ἐν αὐτῷ standing first, is emphasized; He is the Life-element. "Walk" includes in agreement, external and internal mode and conduct of life. "In Him" is still further explained by

Ver. 7. **Rooted and built up,** ἐρριζωμένοι καὶ ἐποικοδομούμενοι, [lit. "having been rooted and being built up."—R.]—The perfect denotes a concluded and still efficient fact,—the present, a continuing state, a process of becoming, a progressing development; hence it is not ἐποικοδομηθέντες (Eph. ii. 20) or τεθεμελιωμένοι (Eph. iii. 18). BENGEL: *præteritum pro initio, præsens etiam in progressu.* The figures are different, yet related. *Lucian de saltat.*, 34: ῥίζαι καὶ θεμέλιοι. Comp. Eph. iii. 18. Thus the readers are more closely characterized in their relation to Christ, and obligated to Christian walk. [The mixed figures mark "the stable growth and organic solidity of those who truly walk in Christ." "The accessory idea of the foundation is admirably conveyed by the ἐπί in the compound verb" (ELLICOTT).—R.] SCHENKEL is incorrect in beginning a new sentence here, because the participles do not correspond with "walk."—**In him,** is of course to be joined with both participles according to the figure. Christ is first regarded as the soil, and then as the corner stone, [foundation,—R.]; but not as the bond of the root-fibres and the parts of the building (SCHENKEL).

And stablished by faith.—To the objective ground of life, the subjective element is thus added. Βεβαιούμενοι, also in the present, denotes a progressing development, the means of which is indicated by τῇ πίστει: the Christian is fortified by means of appropriating faith; it is almost=διὰ τῆς πίστεως (THEOPHYLACT), and not the dative of reference: "as to the faith" (DE WETTE). [The former view is that of MEYER, and EADIE, if ἐν be omitted. ALFORD and ELLICOTT, rejecting ἐν, adopt the latter view. If ἐν αὐτῇ, below, be retained, "faith" must be considered subjective, a view which is preferable on other grounds.—R.]—**As ye have been taught.**—Καθώς connects with τῇ πίστει, and ἐδιδάχθητε reminds of Epaphras (i. 7).—**Abounding therein with thanksgiving,** is subordinate to "stablished," in order to denote the tone in which the "becoming established" acts upon the extension and enlargement of the measure of faith. [ELLICOTT: "mainly reiterating with a quantitative, what had previously been expressed with a qualitative reference.—R.] Hence περισσεύοντες ἐν αὐτῇ is *abundantes ea; i. e., fide* (Phil. i. 9; Rom. xv. 13; 2 Cor. viii. 7), which is felt to be a privilege, a great gift; ἐν εὐχαριστίᾳ=σὺν εὐχαριστίᾳ (ŒKUMEN). [ALFORD: "the field of operation in which that abundance is manifested." ELLICOTT more accurately distinguishes: "the *accompaniment* with which περισσ. ἐν πίστει was associated and as it were, environed."—R.] LUTHER incorrectly joins (*reichlich dankbar*) "abundantly thankful:" the position of the words and the context, which treats of faith, are against this.

Warning against apostasy. Ver. 8.

Ver. 8. **Take heed lest there shall be any one that maketh you his booty.**—The future indicative (ἔσται) denotes an impending danger, whose entrance is feared as certain. (Heb. iii. 12; comp. Luke xi. 35; Gal. iv. 11. WINER'S *Gram.* p. 469.) Ὑμᾶς ἔσται ὁ συλαγωγῶν is not=συλαγωγῇ: it marks the continuance of this state; it is not simply that one or another one deceives them, but there is one or another there, who in character and action is a deceiver, ever misleads others. WINER'S *Gram.* p. 326. Ὑμᾶς, emphatically placed, makes perceptible the advantages described in ver. 4, which they have above others [as well as indicating that they themselves were the booty to be carried away.—R.] The verb, occurring only here in New Testament, means *prædam abigere* (BENGEL: *qui non de vobis, sed vos ipsos spoliam faciat*): they themselves were made a spoil, lost to the Lord. LUTHER is incorrect; who may rob you; and the Vulgate (*decipiat*).

Through philosophy and vain deceit.—The means employed by the seducers. Since the preposition and article are not repeated, one means, a category is here presented. BENGEL: *quod adversarii jactabant esse philosophiam et sapientiam, id Paulus inanem fraudem esse dicit.* [Not "philosophy" in general, but what they called such, which was "vain deceit."—R.] In distinction from "enticing words," ver. 4, "philosophy" refers to the substance, the thought and doctrine (against THEODORET, CALVIN and others); in distinction from σύνεσις, ἐπίγνωσις, ἐπιστήμη (against TITTMANN), to a system; according to the state of the Church and the context, an Oriental, and according to vers. 11, 16, 18, somewhat Judaistic system, although the future (ἔσται) may point to one just arising. It is not to be regarded as Hellenic philosophy (TERTULLIAN), nor more particularly as Epicurean (CLEMENS ALEX.), or as Platonic and Stoic (HEUMANN), or Pythagorean (GROTIUS): nor yet as Gnosticism or Kabbalism (BRUCKER) whose germs were just discernible. Philo had already called the Jewish religion τὴν πάτριον φιλοσοφίαν, and Josephus speaks of the three doctrinal systems of the Essenes, Sadducees and Pharisees, as τρεῖς φιλοσοφίας; yet it is by no means equivalent on this account to *cultus divinus* (HEINRICH). Paul does not mean philosophy in itself (CALIXTUS: *si dicam, vide, ne decipiat vinum, nec vinum damno, nec usum ejus accuso, sed de vitando abusu moneo*), but a certain Judaistico-oriental one (MEYER)* which was in itself "vain deceit." Eph. v. 6. On this account the Apostle characterizes it more closely:

After the tradition of men, after the rudiments of the world.—Emphatically asyndetic, with the preposition repeated; co-ordinate clauses, which are to be joined, not with the verb, but with what immediately precedes. The first: κατὰ τὴν παράδοσιν τῶν ἀνθρώπων marks the origin as purely human in contrast with the revelation from God (BENGEL: *antitheton, deitatis*). The other: κατὰ τὰ στοιχεῖα τοῦ κόσμου marks the substance (BENGEL: *antitheton, corporaliter*, ver. 9). Τὰ στοιχεῖα, used in a physical sense 2 Pet. iii. 10, 12, is here, as in ver. 20; Gal. iv. 3, 9; Heb. v. 12, used in a spiritual, didactic sense; beginnings in education, the A B C of knowledge, upon which childish thoughts the Christian as a man looks down (1 Cor. xiii. 11). It is incorrect to interpret: principles of the moral life in the world (HUTHER); precepts of the world (LUTHER); *rudimenta legis ritualia* is too limited (SCHAUBACH: *Commentatio, qua exponitur quid στ. τ. κοσ. in N. T. sibi veluit*). Comp. on ver. 20. [WORDSWORTH'S interpretation, following that of the Fathers, is curious: "The physical elements, such as the Sun and Moon, regulating times and seasons; and according to superstitious observances of times, *Fasts, New Moons,* and *Seventh Day* Sabbaths ordered thereby, as if they were of the same importance as articles of faith, and equally necessary to salvation." ELLICOTT'S view is to be preferred: "all rudimental religious teaching of *non-Christian* character, whether heathen or Jewish or a commixture of both,—the first element *possibly* slightly predominating in thought here, the second in ver. 20." Whether the immediate reference be to Judaistic errors or not, the phrase must not be limited to Jewish worship (EADIE) or ritualistic observances (ALFORD), for the Apostle is not describing the things themselves, but giving the category (κατά) to which they belong. A careful investigation of his use of the phrase will not justify any such limitation. Comp. *Galatians*, pp. 96, 105.—R.]—**And not after Christ.**—Sharply conclusive, comprehensive negative. Comp. Eph. i. 21; 2 Cor. v. 17. Incorrect: after the doctrine of Christ (ERASMUS and others). [MEYER: "The activity of this συλαγωγεῖν does not have Christ as its objective norm." EADIE: "True Christian science has Him for its centre and Him for its object." On the whole verse the notes of WORDSWORTH are very full and interesting as grouping the patristic authorities respecting the angel-worship of the early heretics.—R.]

Praise of the glory of Christ and His work. Vers. 9–15.

Ver. 9. **Because in him dwelleth all the fulness of the Godhead bodily.**—Ὅτι confirms the warning against a doctrine which does not have its norm in Christ, supposing it can transcend Him and yet not attaining to Him. By "in Him dwelleth" (κατοικεῖ not κατῴκησε) Jesus, whose importance is to be portrayed, is described as a habitation, whose value rests upon what is at home there. ["In him" is emphatic, *in him* and in none other than him (ELLICOTT).—R.] This is then "all the fulness of the Godhead" (i. 19; comp. Rom. xv. 29; xi. 25). Θεότης

* [MEYER remarks: "This φιλοσοφία is not *philosophy in itself and in general*, however much it had, in its decay and according to its manifestation in that age, proven itself to the Apostle as folly in comparison with the wisdom of the gospel, but the *definite* speculation, *known* to his readers, which obtained in Colosse and that region, and which consisted of gnostic theosophy blended with Judaism (Essenism), designated by the name philosophy, on account of its ontological character, and in general, irrespective of its relation to the truth rightly so called; but perhaps put forward also by the false teachers themselves under this designation, which is the more probable, since Paul uses the word only in this passage." So EADIE, ALFORD and ELLICOTT substantially.—R.]

must be distinguished from θειότης (Rom. i. 20); the former, *vocabulum abstractum significantissimum* (BENGEL), means *Deitas*, Godhead [*das Gottsein*], the Divine Essence; the latter, *Divinitas*, Divinity [*Göttlichkeit*], the Divine Quality; what is here viewed metaphysically is regarded in i. 19, charismatically (MEYER). Θεότης is not to be understood as meaning God's will (the SOCINIANS), Divine grace and gift (SCHLEIERMACHER), nor does "all the fulness of the Godhead" refer to the Christian Church (HEINRICH, SCHENKEL and others). Σωματικῶς, placed last for emphasis, limits "dwelleth," which refers, in the present, to the permanent state of the present and exalted Christ, founded (i. 15) upon His nature, and is to be regarded, in contrast with "rudiments of the world" (ver. 8), and "shadows" (ver. 17), as indicating the full nature of the matter, and from the relation of οἶκος and σῶμα (2 Cor. v. 1 sq.) with a reference to the Incarnation (HOFFMANN, *Schriftbew.* II. pp. 27 sq, 533; SCHMID, *Bibl. Theologie*, 2, p. 301). Hence it is neither= οὐσιωδῶς (CYRIL, STEIGER, HUTHER), since there is no contrast between οὐσία in Christ and ἐνέργεια in the prophets, nor=ἐν τῷ σώματι, whether this be referred to the Church (SCHENKEL) or to the body, which He assumed of the Virgin, that is now glorified (MEYER): before the Incarnation He was ἐν μορφῇ θεοῦ (Phil. ii. 6). Beyond Christ there is no eternal truth; beyond Him is away from Him. [WORDSWORTH interprets: 1, *substantially and truly* (Hilary); 2, *bodily*, in distinction from "soul" (Council of Antioch),—quoting Augustine, who combines both views. But the literal interpretation is far preferable: "in bodily fashion" (ELLICOTT). "Before His Incarnation the fulness dwelt in Him, as the λόγος ἄσαρκος, but not σωματικῶς, as now that He is the λόγος ἔνσαρκος" (ALFORD). If this be the correct view, then with MEYER we must regard the present, κατοικεῖ, as referring the whole expression to the glorified Christ. He also finds an apologetic design in the emphasis given to the adverb, "bodily," since the false teachers, "by their doctrine of angels (comp. ver. 10), appear to have spiritualistically split up the πλήρωμα τῆς θεότητος."—R.]

Ver. 10. **And ye are made full in him.**—[Perhaps to bring out the double predication involved in the position of the words, it were better to render: "And ye (*being*) in Him are made full."—R.] Καί is a simple copulative, making the clause depend upon ὅτι. Ἐστέ (not γίνεσθε) standing first is pregnant: "ye are," need not first become so; the "being" is more strongly marked than the subject, in contrast to Christ; hence ὑμεῖς is not expressed. It is not the imperative (GROTIUS and others): *Beneficium Christi, non nostrum officium* (CALOV.). But only in Him are they πεπληρωμένοι. ERASMUS: *Christo cum sitis semel insiti*; BENGEL: *ipse plenus, nos replete.* LUTHER is incorrect: *vollkommen.* [E. V. also—"complete." EADIE's translation is given above; ALFORD: "filled up;" ELLICOTT, as above, also "filled full,"—Rhemish, "in Him replenished." —R.] The perfect excludes the further effect of the fact. Neither τῆς θεότητος (THEOPHYLACT and others) nor *sapientia et virtute* (BENGEL) is to be supplied; the first is not indicated by the text, which does not read καὶ ὑμεῖς, nor the second by the context. Divine Truth, Power, Life are treated of. Comp. Eph. iii. 19; Jno. i. 16.—[MEYER: "Out of the 'fulness of the Godhead' which dwells in Christ, flows the being made full of the Christian, which therefore has its ground in none other than Christ and in nothing else than fellowship with Him. Filled *with what?* The answer is self-evident to the consciousness of the reader. It is the *charismatic* πλήρωσις, which Christians in virtue of their vital union with the Lord have received and continually possess, out of the *metaphysical* πλήρωμα dwelling in Christ, out of the 'fulness of the Godhead.'"—R.]

Who is the head of all principality and power.—This affirms the absolute dignity of Christ over against the angelic world (ver. 18). Comp. i. 18. In Him they may, must have enough.

Ver. 11. **In whom ye also were circumcised.**—[Καί, "also," emphasizes the fact stated by the verb, which is a historical aorist: hence "were" not "are" (E. V.).—R.] The reference is to their entrance into Christianity, to conversion, regeneration in Christ. The Christian is circumcised, not indeed as the Judaistic teachers required, with the Jewish circumcision, but: **with a circumcision made without hands,** περιτομῇ ἀχειροποιήτῳ ["not hand-wrought," ELLICOTT.—R.]—The Jewish external rite was χειροποίητος (Eph. ii. 11). Comp. Rom. ii. 28, 29; Deut. x. 16; xxx. 6; Jer. ix. 26; Ezek. xliv. 7; Acts vii. 51. He then sets forth, wherein this spiritual circumcision of the heart, which is better than the Jewish, consists: **in the putting off the body of the flesh, in the circumcision of Christ.** —[The E. V. not only retains "of the sins," but is faulty in punctuation; the second ἐν also it renders "by," when it is parallel to the first.—R.] The first clause is in contrast with the externality, the second with the "hand" that performs it; according to the former this circumcision is a moral advance, according to the latter an act of Christ. "In the putting off the body of the flesh" describes the body on which it takes place, as belonging to the flesh (σάρξ), entirely corresponding with the context, and parallel to "the body of sin" (Rom. vi. 6), which lives in the flesh, so that it is not indifferent (see Eph. ii. 3). The material, earthly body is not spoken of here, as in i. 22, but the sinfully sensuous organism, "the old man" (Rom. vii. 14). The substantive ἀπέκδυσις (only here) is emphatic and in contrast with the circumcision, which severs only a small part. It is joined with τοῦ σώματος, which naturally neither means, *massa*, totality (CALVIN and others), nor refers to Christ's body and His death (SCHNECKENBURGER), since αὐτοῦ is wanting. LUTHER, retaining τῶν ἁμαρτιῶν, renders incorrectly: "the sinful body in the flesh."—"In the circumcision of Christ" presents nothing new or important, except in the genitive, which denotes the author (THEODORET: αἴτιος) of the circumcision. [ELLICOTT: "*the originating cause;* Christ by union with Himself brings about the circumcision and imparts it to believers."—R.] It is incorrect to apply it to the circumcision to which Christ was subjected (SCHÖTTGEN), or to view Christ only as the Mediator of it (MEYER). Nor should we on account of ἀχειροποιήτου apply it to baptism (STORR [ALFORD apparently], and others).

Ver. 12. **Buried with him in baptism.**—The participle συνταφέντες, following περιετμήθητε (ver. 11), denotes the progress of the entrance of conversion. "Putting off the body" reminded of death; "being buried" was readily suggested. Αὐτῷ, governed by σύν in composition, denotes the fellowship with Christ, which is consummated "in baptism," that is a water bath and a water grave for the "old man." Comp. Rom. vi. 3, 4. We live Christ's life, with and through Him, symbolically, ethically, spiritually, but actually and really. ["Burial implies a previous death." "The reality of death is evinced by burial." "This point of burial they had reached—when they were baptized—for then they personally professed a faith which implied the death of sin within them" (EADIE). The reference to burial in connexion with baptism, suggests, that death to sin had already taken place, hence this ordinance has not in itself any efficacy "in the putting off the body of the flesh." There is no doubt that the participle describes an action nearly contemporaneous with that of the preceding verb. This rite would speedily follow the "putting off;" though ALFORD is scarcely correct: "the new life being begun at baptism."—Braune admits, as must be done, an allusion to *immersion* in baptism, but enters into no discussion as to the *mode;* the question is not deemed so important in Germany as it has been made here. EADIE says: "Whatever may be otherwise said in favor of immersion, it is plain that here the burial is wholly ideal.—Believers are buried in baptism, but even in immersion they do not go through a process having any resemblance to the burial and resurrection of Christ." ALFORD correctly admits an allusion to the κατάδυσις and ἀνάδυσις in baptism, but adds, "To maintain from such a circumstance that *immersion* is *necessary* in baptism, is surely the merest trifling, and a resuscitation of the very ceremonial spirit which the Apostle here is arguing against." A fair exegesis must allow that the passage proves immersion to be baptism; whether baptism is immersion turns on something else than exegesis; see controversial works on both sides of the question. A list will be found, LANGE'S *Com.* Matthew, p. 560.—R.]

In whom ye were also raised together through the faith.—[So Braune renders. The aorist συνηγέρθητε, must be rendered "were raised." Whether raised "together" or "with Him," depends upon the reference in ἐν ᾧ: in baptism or in Christ.—R.] Ἐν ᾧ is parallel to ἐν ᾧ (ver. 11), and refers like ὅς (ver. 10) to Christ and not to baptism; καὶ συνηγέρθητε does not confirm the latter reference, but requires the former, since καί renders prominent an advance from the "burial" in immersion at baptism—the new life would not enter with the immersion but with the emersion, and we should find ἐξ οὗ or δι' οὗ [*i. e.*, were the reference to baptism.—R.]. The fellowship with the life of Christ ("raised together") rests upon union with His Person (ἐν ᾧ). [So DAVENANT, MEYER, EADIE. For the other view, see ALFORD and ELLICOTT *in loco.*—R.] Hence there is no pleonasm here (DE WETTE), nor any reference to the resurrection of the body, which is an ideal possession before the *parousia*, but becomes a reality with it (MEYER, the Greek Fathers: καὶ γὰρ ἐγηγέρμεθα τῇ δυνάμει, εἰ καὶ μὴ τῇ ἐνεργείᾳ). Συνηγέρθητε denotes an accomplished fact, corresponding with that accomplished in baptism, and like this, actual, but according to the context, spiritual, ethical. After the negative side of dying to sin, the positive side of a new life is set forth, prominence being given to the subjective appropriation, διὰ τῆς πίστεως, hinted at already in ἐν ᾧ. BENGEL is excellent: *ut mors est ante resurrectionem, sic baptismus natura præcedit fidem adultam.* The genitive depending on πίστεως: **of the operation of God**, can only set forth the object, since only this (Eph. iii. 12; Phil. i. 27; iii. 9; Rom. iii. 22; Gal. ii. 16, 20; iii. 22), or the believing subject (ver. 5; i. 4; 1 Thess. i. 3, iii. 2) is denoted by the genitive. [ELLICOTT, while taking this as the genitive *objecti*, considers the statement of MEYER, referred to above, and endorsed by EADIE and ALFORD, as not *perfectly* certain.—R.] LUTHER is incorrect: "which God works."

God is then characterized: **who hath raised him from the dead**, because the syllogism runs: Has God raised Christ, then can He also bring me to new life (comp. Eph. i. 19, 20). It is precisely through faith in such an "operation of God," that this is experienced.

Ver. 13. **And you being dead in your sins.**—["When you were dead," ELLICOTT.—R.] See on Eph. ii. 1-5. Here the "being *dead*" is more strongly marked, than the "*being;*" there the simple dative marks the cause of this condition, here the results manifesting the condition are added; there inward motions (ἁμαρτία) are added to outward transgressions (παραπτώματα), here is added: **and the uncircumcision of your flesh** (the preposition "in" is supplied in thought).—This means the uneradicated, sensuous, sinful nature which marked the heathen. "Uncircumcision" according to the context is ethical, spiritual (Deut. x. 16; Jere. iv. 4), and is more closely characterized by the genitive. This is epexegetical, σάρξ being used, as in ver. 11, in the ethical sense, so that the carnal nature is regarded as their uncircumcision (BLEEK). BENGEL: *exquisita appellatio peccati originalis.* MEYER is incorrect in taking νέκρους and ἀκροβυστία literally, and σάρξ as indifferent. [MEYER seems to place the moral significance in τῆς σαρκός, hence ἀκροβυστία, which is their state still, is now indifferent (ALFORD). This gives to ἀκροβ. its literal meaning. EADIE takes the whole phrase literally: "Uncircumcision of the flesh was the physical mark of a heathen state." ELLICOTT gives a slight ethical force to σαρκός, which he considers a possessive genitive—they were heathens, unconverted heathens as their very bodies could attest. Braune's view seems more in accordance with the context.—R.]

You hath he quickened together with him, συνεζωποίησεν ὑμᾶς σὺν αὐτῷ. See on Eph. iii. 5. Ὑμᾶς [omitted in Rec.; "you" to be inserted in E. V.—R.] and σύν ["together with"—R.] are repeated as an emphatic reminder to the readers. MEYER incorrectly takes the verb in its literal sense [doubtless to correspond with his interpretation of the preceding context—R.], and HEINRICH makes Christ the subject, when the context requires "God," quite as much as it refers to the new spiritual life beginning with regeneration, which is eternal life to be perfected at the resurrection. [ELLICOTT also makes "Christ" the subject, rendering "with Himself." His interpretation of the whole passage is modified by this view, which he ably defends; see his notes *in loco*, which are highly suggestive. Still the predicates throughout are better applied to God; those in this verse, "quickened" and "forgiven," being so generally ascribed to God, that the burden of proof rests with those who take the other view. As they have not succeeded in showing a preponderance of reasons in its favor, it is safer to consider "God" the subject (comp. MEYER).—R.]

The mode of the life is described; **having forgiven us all trespasses,** χαρισάμενος ἡμῖν πάντα τὰ παραπτώματα (CHRYSOSTOM: ἃ τὴν νεκρότητα ἐποίει).—The objective act of reconciliation and justification is referred to, and its universal efficacy denoted by "us" [not "you," the Colossians merely, but all believers.—R.] At the same time the connection between the new life beginning with pardon and justification, and the propitiation of the wrath of God and reconciliation of man with Him is hinted at. BENGEL: *cum hac liberatione a peccato conjuncta est liberatio ab opprobrio peccati* (ver. 14) *et liberatio a potestate tenebrarum* (ver. 15).

Ver. 14. **Having blotted out the handwriting of ordinances that was against us.**—"Having blotted out" (ἐξαλείψας), joined like the preceding participle to "quickened together," is contemporaneous,* and describes significantly the act of Divine grace. The verb (here and Acts iii. 19; Rev. iii. 5; vii. 17; xxi. 4) means to wash out, then to obliterate. "The handwriting against us" is the law obligating us and proving our debt, witnessing against us, a bond [*Schulddokument*], (Job v. 3; ix. 5). It means God's law among Gentiles and Jews (Rom. ii. 14, 15), not the Mosaic law merely (MEYER); hence we cannot here distinguish between the moral and ceremonial law, and refer this exclusively to the former (LUTHER), or to the latter only (CALVIN), which is also a moral affair, and affects the conscience. "All trespasses" are here treated of [hence "the whole law" DAVENANT, ELLICOTT—R.], and Christ's death for the Gentiles also, indeed here with special reference to them. The dative τοῖς δόγμασιν (see Eph. ii. 15; ἐν δόγμασιν) denotes the contents of the handwriting, written with well-known commandments (MEYER), as Gal. vi. 11. This is explained by the adjectival and verbal character of the word χειρόγραφον. [The verbal element governing the dative. MEYER would make the dative instrumental; ELLICOTT makes it the dative with reference to, that in which the hostile aspect was specially evinced," objecting decidedly to the government by the verbal element. EADIE and ALFORD agree with Braune: "The simple dative of form, that distinctive and well known form which the handwriting assumed.—R.] The dative is not=consisting in commandments, (CALVIN), nor instead of the genitive (CASTELLIO), nor to be joined to καθ' ἡμῶν (CALOV.), nor connected with both the preceding expressions (WINER'S *Gram.*, p. 206); as little does it belong to "having blotted out" in the sense: with reference to ordinances (STEIGER, HARLESS on Eph. i. 1), or through the gospel doctrine of faith (the Greek fathers). SCHENKEL joins it with what follows appealing to Acts i. 22: διὰ πνεύματος ἁγίου οὓς ἐξελέξατο, and BLEEK also without sufficient grounds.

Which was contrary to us.—This relative clause is only an emphatic repetition of καθ' ἡμῶν (MEYER), and not to be distinguished from it as is done by BENGEL: *contra esse et inimicum esse differunt, sicut status belli et ipsa pugna.* [ELLICOTT: "an expansion of the preceding: it was hostile not merely in its direction and aspects, but practically and definitely." There is no idea of secret hostility, *sub contrarius.*—R.]

And he has taken it out of the way.—The perfect denotes the completed, still efficient fact; the handwriting is not only blotted out, it is removed entirely, and this continues to be so. Thus the transition from the participial to the finite construction is explained (as i. 26; WINER'S *Gram.* p. 533). The mode of taking it away is described: **By nailing it to his cross** ["to the cross."—R.] It was the law rather than Christ, which was slain and done away with on the cross, because He bore the curse of the law, took away its condemnation. Men slew Christ, but the Lord slew the law on the cross. Gal. ii. 13; 2 Pet. ii. 24. [There seems to be no ground for the opinion, that there is here an allusion to the cancelling of a bond, by driving a nail through it, although WORDSWORTH expresses the thought thus strikingly: "He nailed the bond of our debt to the Tree, and as by the Tree in Paradise we became debtors to God in the first Adam, so by the Tree in Calvary we received remission of our debt in the Second Adam."—R.]

Ver. 15. **And having spoiled principalities and powers.**—Ἀπεκδυσάμενος, found only here and iii. 9. It denotes the result of the contest against the wicked angels (comp. i. 16; ii. 10; Eph. ii. 2; vi. 11, 12), and has an emphatic position at the beginning of the sentence before the finite verb. BENGEL: *qui angelos bonas colebant, malos timebant; neutrum jure.* The verb is well rendered by the Vulgate: *exspolians.* The middle signification, which is unmistakable in iii. 9, falls into the back ground here. [Two points are open to discussion here: 1. What is the meaning of ἀπεκδυσάμενος? 2. What is the reference in τὰς ἀρχὰς καὶ τὰς ἐξουσίας? 1. The more common interpretation is as above, "having spoiled," but WORDSWORTH, ELLICOTT, ALFORD, render "having divested himself of," "putting off," giving the middle sense. 2. Of what did He divest Himself? Here the commentators above mentioned differ. WORDSWORTH and ELLICOTT, taking Christ as the subject, refer "principalities and powers" to opposing hostile powers of evil, and follow Hilary, Augustine, in explaining thus: the powers of evil had power against Christ, as mortal in His flesh: He divested Himself of His flesh, by thus doing He di-

[* MEYER with reason insists that it is not contemporaneous, but means: "after he had blotted out," etc. "The divine work of redemption in Christ must occur before the forgiveness, through appropriation of it by the believers, could take place."—R.]

vested Himself of them. See WORDSWORTH's full notes upholding this view. Still it seems to be a forced interpretation. ALFORD does not admit that these principalities and powers are infernal potentates. He considers that the angelic agency (Gal. iii. 19) in the giving of the law is referred to, and these "put off" by the abrogation and taking away of the law, God manifesting Himself henceforward without a vail in the exalted Person of Jesus. This too seems forced. The view so strongly supported by MEYER, which takes God as the subject, "spoiling" as the meaning of the participle, and the infernal powers as referred to in "principalities and powers," is preferable to either of the others, on the ground of simplicity and accordance with the subsequent context.—R.] Thus deprived of their power, stripped of their armor as it were, in their helplessness: **He made a shew of them with boldness.**—Ἐδειγμάτισεν (only here and Matt. i. 19) has God as its subject, who now as in a triumph makes a show to their shame and His honor: the subject being the same as that of ἀπεκδυσάμενος, it is not repeated. Ἐν παῤῥησίᾳ is "frankly and freely" (*frank und frei*), and denotes the confidence and certainty of the complete, permanent victory (comp. 1 Jno. ii. 28) [LANGE's *Commentary*, p. 82.—R.] "Openly" (LUTHER) [and E. V.] is already found in the verb. [The idea of putting to shame (παραδειγματίσαι) does not necessarily belong to the simple verb. ALFORD, to carry out his view of the object of the verb, renders ἐν παῤῥησίᾳ "in openness" of speech, declaring and revealing by the cross, that there is none but Christ the Head of all principalities and powers. For this there seems to be no good support.—R.]

Triumphing over them in it.—Here θριαμβεύσας αὐτούς means "triumphing over them," while 2 Cor. ii. 14: θριαμβεύσας ἡμᾶς has the force of the Hiphil: "making us to triumph." "Them" means the persons conceived of as "principalities and powers." Ἐν αὐτῷ denotes the place of contest, the cross (ver. 14). It is not*=*in Christo* (BENGEL), [ALFORD, margin of English Bible—R.]. It was precisely "the cross, this symbol of shame and sorrow, which was the place of victory over the enemies of God" (SCHENKEL).

[On the whole verse, see EADIE. Both he and Braune agree entirely with MEYER, whose exegesis of this passage is highly satisfactory. WORDSWORTH is unusually full and valuable on this section, though his comments belong more properly to the homiletical department. ELLICOTT's exegesis is modified by his taking Christ as the subject throughout.—R.]

DOCTRINAL AND ETHICAL.

1. *Paul's care of the Churches.* Great is the sympathy of Paul, who not only has in eye and mind, as the Epistles to the Corinthians show, all the members of a Christian congregation, but fraternally remembers in prayer and paternally cares for with his counsel, all congregations of the Church of his Lord, even those personally unknown to him, whenever, as in this case, through the coming of Epaphras to him, a way of God's pointing out is opened to him. He does not step aside from his calling, from his immediate sphere of duty, but takes root in the soil appointed to him and bears fruit, but fruit for many without, as far as in him lies, for all. No one can appeal to the Apostle and his part in the great work, who does not take root and bear fruit in his own immediate calling, as though it were too narrow for him.

2. *Error a calamity.* The Apostle regards error and entanglement therein as calamity and sorrow, which begins with wavering and uncertainty, and has its root in moral deficiency. Hence his sympathizing solicitude, hence his παρακαλεῖν directed to their καρδίας (ver. 2). [EADIE: "The conflict of error with truth could not but lead to distraction and mental turmoil; and in proportion to their misconception of the gospel, or their confusion of idea with regard to its spirit, contents and aim, would be their loss of that peace and solace, which the new religion had imparted to them."—R.]

3. *Christian unity.* That saying of RUPERTUS MELDENIUS in the seventeenth century: *in necessariis unitas, in non necessariis libertas, in utrisque caritas*, could have been taken from ver. 2, where "in love" sets forth the subjective, and "unto full knowledge of the mystery of God" the objective *moment* of true unity. The "mystery" is the "necessary" matter, in which there must be unity; for *a*) as to its *nature* it is entirely *God's affair*; *b*) as to its *purport* it is the fulness of *all wisdom and knowledge*, the treasury of all truth in the world and the plan of salvation in the kingdom of God; *c*) as to its *position* it is a *fact revealed and revealing in Christ*; *d*) as to its *end*, it *reaches* into *eternity*; *e*) as to its *mission*, it *guides* protectingly through *time* with its errors and dangers; *f*) as to its *requirements*, it concerns *believing acceptance* and *living* therein. [Be-living, which is implied etymologically and practically in believing.—R.] Accordingly the one *centre* of both the mystery and the unity is Christ in His Being and work. [Still more if we adopt the reading which makes Christ Himself the mystery. The one "necessary" matter, about which there must be unity, is the answer to the question, "what think ye of Christ?"—R.]

4. *The Being of Christ* is all the fulness of the Godhead in bodily reality (ver. 9). This Pauline statement is related to the Johannine; "the Word became flesh;" the latter gives prominence to the historical incarnation, the former to the permanent state of the Exalted One.

5. *The Work of Christ* is pre-supposed as that of a mediator, who suffered death upon the Cross as an atonement for us, whom God the Father has raised again, in order that this fact of salvation should be made of benefit to us; it is essentially of an ethical nature.

6. *Salvation* is essentially *a new life*, the cause of which is God (the subject in vers. 13–15), the mediation of which is in Christ, resting *objectively* upon *Christ's death on the Cross*, whereby forgiveness of sin has been provided, the accusations and curse of the law done away, the power of the kingdom of darkness broken, and beginning *subjectively* with faith, the principle of the new life,

*[The original omits "not," but it is an obvious typographical error, which I have corrected without hesitation.—R.]

types of which are found both in the Old Testament and the life of Christ. The circumcision of the Old Testament corresponds with baptism in the New; both point, *formally*, to a putting away, the former partially, to a separation, the latter *totally*, to a dying, since the immersion points to the burial of Christ (vers. 11, 12; Rom. vi. 34); *materially*, both apply to the flesh, on which the sinful nature depends; the dying, being buried and rising again of Christ are events in His life which the believer, in contrast with the world, in and about him, must experience in his inner, moral life. In Christ, therefore, that is fulfilled, which before Him was only hinted at, prefigured; and only from Him and in Him, by means of faith, can the participation in this fulfilment be gained. [EADIE: "The Apostle looks on circumcision and baptism as being closely connected—the spiritual blessing symbolized by both being of a similar nature; though, probably, it would be straining this connection to allege it as a proof that baptism has been in all points ordained for the Church in room of circumcision."—To this may be added that just so far as we can refer to this passage in support of any mode of baptism, to the same extent we can find in it a proof of the connexion between baptism and circumcision. If we press it in the first direction, we must also in the second, as Braune does. Whatever may be gained from it in support of immersion, is equally gained for pædo-baptism.—R.]

7. *Sin* has so widely developed its power, that not only does every man stand under that power, but each man entirely: he is dead in his sinful doing and sinful being (ver. 13), so that he must be born again. It is the first power, which Christ endured to the uttermost and, sinlessly, victoriously, overcame on the cross in His propitiatory death. With the pardon of sin the new life begins.

8. *The law*, given on account of sin and against it as an external one, is contrary to man in his sin as his accuser. In Christ it is fulfilled, in Him it is satisfied. Against Him it can present no accusation and no guilt: He is the Fulfilled. Bodily law, which He has at once upheld and torn; upheld on the side of righteousness, torn and done away with on the side of the accuser and the curse. Only when the law is satisfied, is it done and done away; this has taken place in Christ and takes place only in Him.

9. *The kingdom of darkness*, the spiritual powers of evil have in sin their power over man, but lost it on the sinless Redeemer; in the atoning death of Christ, they gained a victory which was their defeat. Only he who lives to the flesh, remains under the dominion of the Evil one: whoever dies to sin and the flesh with Christ is snatched from this and has a share in the victory of Christ.

10. *All mental culture*, even the bloom of an organic science, of a *philosophy*, a love of wisdom, which is merely the intellectual product of the human mind, which does not proceed out of a moral life founded on Christ's life and rooted in Him, is idle, empty deceit and illusion. That which is most elegant, most noble and great without Christ is only elementary, imperfect in comparison with what He offers: the simplest, plainest of what is offered in Him, exceeds that in value. An humble Christian has and can do and knows, more and better than an unchristian philosopher. What is Christian alone is worthy of humanity, humane. As truly Christian life surpasses any other nobly moral life, so truly Christian opinion is more important and more truthful than any otherwise important speculative knowledge.

HOMILETICAL AND PRACTICAL.

Do not meddle in spheres and activities, which do not concern you, but, with the gifts entrusted to you, labor in the calling to which you are appointed; do not seek only for intimate friends of the same mind and station as yourself, perhaps in wider circles, to make amends for those indolent or opposed about you.—Take no offence at the ocean depth of the mystery of Redemption in Christ; the pearls of truth and wisdom, thou canst only find there. Before the truths become a harvest which we gather in, they are dull clouds in the distance, or ore in the depths.—What thou receivest as seed, return as blossom, what thou receivest as blossom, return as fruit.—Only the fellowship which has its cement in love, has its eternal end in true knowledge.—Entering into worldly mental culture without, thou not only losest something, but art thyself lost; lost to God and bound to human principles; you forego a blessed eternity, as you gaily go down the stream of time. No stand-points are more inferior than those without Christ, however well esteemed they may be of men.—Three powers are to be feared: 1) the power of Satan who stands behind the flesh and its motions; 2) the power of the flesh, that breaks out in sin; 3) the power of the law, that appears against our sin as accuser.

CALVIN:—Ver. 15. No tribunal so magnificent, no regal throne so glorious, no triumphal pomp so splendid, no chariot so sublime, as was that gibbet upon which Christ overcame death and the devil, the prince of death, whom He utterly bruised under His feet.

STARKE:—There are three excellent peculiarities, which must be found in a preacher, and also in *any* Christian, if he would make others know a matter; 1) that he himself be certain of its truth; 2) that he be able rightly to convince others of the same; 3) that he have a good end in view.—As a mother, who has children suffering in various degrees of sickness, attends most to the one who lies lowest, but never on that account permits herself to neglect or slight the others, so an instructor cares most for those hearers, who are in the most dangerous circumstances; yet not so as to forget or neglect the others.—See what belongs to genuine Christianity; a wealth and certainty of faith, a knitting together of hearts in love, a walk in Christ.—When we rightly know and have Christ, we know and have enough, though we know and have nothing else.—God's word is an inexhaustible mine full of treasures and riches; seek! dig! test! you will find one after another unto your spiritual and eternal delight.—Rational speeches are not always the truth, nor are learning and skill always a certain evidence of truth.—If we are rooted in Christ, we must prove by bearing fruit as trees of righteousness. Are we built on Christ, we must stand steadfast and unmovable, so that no winds and rains of affliction can overthrow us. A good inflow makes a good outflow; he who takes in much, can and must also give out much. Since then believers receive so much from and in Christ, so their active gratitude must flow copiously forth in unremitting obedience. — The Church is not a school of sages, where each can display the fanciful dreams of his reason.—In matters of faith the reason is an unfaithful and deceitful guide, that delivers us to error and delusion. The gospel is the true Christian philosophy, transcending all science, all human institutions, from which it can accept no law.—God is the creditor, we His debtors. 1) He is Omniscient, we cannot conceal a debt from Him; 2) He is almighty, He can exact the debt by force; 3) He is just, He will and must be paid; 4) He is omnipresent, none can escape Him. Who must not fear on this account?

GERLACH:—To every man, unenlightened, following his own wisdom, the mystery, plainly as it is revealed in the gospel, is closed, as to the blind eye the sun at mid day does not shine. But whoever knows how to study this great book, Jesus Christ, God manifest in the flesh, finds all knowledge therein. Humility opens the book, faith reads it, and love understands it.—[Jesus Christ; 1) The *way* on which the Christians walk; 2) the *root* from which they draw all their life-sap, 3) the *foundation* on which their whole inner life should rest.—R.]

RIEGER:—In natural things man prefers seeing all with his own eyes, and resting on his own observation rather than on what others can tell him. In the kingdom of grace however, one must be of such a tender heart, that he from the "being knit together in love," accepts much that others have experienced.—Among the Corinthians there was more of intelligence and knowledge, but less of submissive love reaching to others. On this account he pruned their knowledge and guided them to growing strength in love. Among the Colossians there was more of tractable love, but without sufficient light. Hence he had a conflict, that their obedient love should not be abused, but that they might acquire minds expert in examination.—The Apostle's word of incitement: walk in Him, means more than following in His footsteps, it signifies, that for such a walk as He walked, all strength is derived from Christ, that the walk is a fruit borne from Christ the vine.—In the time when God permitted the heathen to walk their own ways, He yet granted some footprints, from which something of Him and His truth could be made an object of search. On the part of God these were given as serviceable rudiments, but on the part of men they did not remain purely so. And if now-a-days any one will extol these as the choice relics of antiquity, it is as though some one should devote himself to a heap of sweepings, to find there a lost pearl.

SCHLEIERMACHER.—Ripeness of understanding in regard to the kingdom of God and intelligence respecting the things of this world are not together (Matt. xi. 25; Luke xvi. 8).—Love furthers the growth and maturity of the understanding.—[Why we continue in Christ? He has 1) not only the words of eternal life, but 2) the power of eternal life.—R.]

HEUBNER:—Unity, firm knitting together, incorporation in love, increases the "*plerophy*" [πληροφίας fulness, made an adjective in E. V. ver. 2.—R.]: the correct, firm conviction, the confidence in our insight, when we are certain of the matter.—External discipline and order must ever accompany faith in the life of the Church. Paul mentions their "order" first, because it first meets the eye.—In Christian faith there must be constancy. Growth therein is necessary, but change is destructive.—Man may learn to know himself from the wisdom of the world, but it cannot help him.—He who has the fulness, can give abundantly. In Christ we have abundance, all others let us hunger. Christ's word satisfies, contents the soul.—All, whom Christ has not awakened, are to be regarded as still dead.—[He who remains under Christ's standard, conquers.—R.]

PASSAVANT:—What now-a-days is so gladly shunned by many pious people, sometimes as dangerous, again as unprofitable, the Apostle here holds to be necessary, aye, he labors and struggles to bring souls thither. He would know of no poverty of spirit, which, made up of sheer laziness and cowardice, is willingly satisfied with superficial knowledge of saving truth: he insisted rather upon that riches of knowledge and of spirit, which contributes to the genuine poverty of an humble spirit. He would know of no blind or dim faith, but of open seeing eyes. He sought to produce in the Colossians a clear understanding, a plenitude of knowledge,—that their knowledge might suffer from no defects, be diseased from no obscurations or fluctuations, that might profoundly penetrate and gaze into the mystery of God and the Father.—Gratitude then helps us to stand, and joyously stand fast before every foreign spirit, before every foreign power, in every temptation and conflict; it is a rock, from which the darts of unbelief rebound. When the Roman proconsul on the judgment-seat urged that holy man Polycarp to curse Jesus Christ to save his life, the martyr answered, "For eighty-six years I have served Him: He has never yet done me harm. How can I blaspheme my King, who has saved me?"—"Vain deceit," Paul calls all human worldly wisdom and doctrine, which knows nothing of one true God; "tradition of men, rudiments of the world," all that oriental philosophy, which with its old and new twilight, its destructive atmosphere, marred the divine doctrine, it would enlarge and complete,—"vain deceit," that Jewish leaven, which through its ancient consequence, through use and abuse of the Mosaic ordinances and principles, threatened to rob the disciples of their new freedom, or stint them therein, to put again upon them "a yoke which neither their fathers nor they themselves were able to bear."—

For the Reformation festival [October 31st, anniversary of the nailing of Luther's theses on the church-door at Wittenberg, 1517.—R.] (ver. 6–9). How do we prove ourselves abundantly grateful for the regeneration of our Church? If we 1) hold fast to the ground of salvation, which it proclaims to us; 2) use the means of salvation, which it offers to us; 3) walk in the way of salvation, which it prescribes to us.

[BISPING:—Ver. 6. Notice that Paul here says, "ye have received *Christ*," not the doctrine of Christ. True faith is a spiritual communion; for in faith we receive not only the doctrine of Christ, but Himself, into us: in faith He Himself dwells in us: we cannot separate Christ, as Eternal Truth and His doctrine.—R.]

[BISHOP ANDREWES:—Ver. 14. If one be in debt and danger of the law, to have a brother of the same blood, made of the same woman, will little avail him, except he will come also "under the law," *i. e.*, become his surety, and undertake for him. And such was our estate. "The handwriting," our bond, we had forfeited. This debt of ours was no money debt, we were not *sub lege pecuniariâ*, but *capitalii;* and the debt of a capital law is death. He paid that to the full, and having paid it "blotted out the hand-writing," cancelled the sentence of the law.—R.]

[HENRY:—Ver. 1. We can think, and pray and be concerned for one another at the greatest distance; the communion of the saints is a spiritual thing.—Ver. 2. The prosperity of the soul is the best prosperity. Great knowledge and strong faith make a soul rich. The more intimate communion we have with our fellow Christians, the more the soul prospers.—Vers. 6, 7, a sovereign antidote against seducers.—They who pin their faith on other men's sleeves, and walk in the way of the world, are turned away from following after Christ.—It is not enough to put away some one particular sin, but we must put off the whole body of them.—We have communion with Christ in His whole undertaking. We are both buried and rise with Him, and both are signified by our baptism; not that there is anything in the sign or ceremony of baptism, which represent this burying and rising, any more than the crucifixion of Christ is represented by any visible resemblance in the Lord's Supper.—Christ's death was the death of our sins; Christ's resurrection is the quickening of our souls. The Redeemer conquered by dying. See His crown of thorns turned into a crown of laurels. Never had the Devil's kingdom such a mortal blow given to it, as was given by the Lord Jesus.—R.]

[BURKITT:—Ver. 1. The men of the world little understand, and less consider, what burthen of care lies upon the ministers of Christ, for, and on behalf of the whole Church of Christ in general, which is continually in danger of being corrupted by false teachers, who everywhere lie in wait to deceive.—Ver. 15. Christ's bloody cross was a chariot of triumph unto Him. Lord! whilst thou wert bleeding and racking upon the gibbet for us, thou wert then rejoicing and triumphing for the benefits redounding to us.—R.]

[EADIE:—Ver. 1. Like the caged bird beating its bared and bleeding breast against the wires of its prison, as it hears the repeated cry of its unseen young ones, the Apostle turned ever and anon toward those churches—nor did he idly chafe in his confinement, but he wrote this letter.—Ver. 4. The traveller who has already made some progress, but who begins gradually to doubt and debate, to lose faith in himself, and wonder whether he is in the right way at all, is prepared to listen to the suggestions of any one who, under semblance of disinterested friendship, may advise to a path of danger and ruin.—No philosophy ever dreamed of such an awful expedient as God robed in humanity, and in that nature dying to redeem His guilty creatures—whose name, nature and legal liabilities He had assumed: and such a scheme never found a place in any system of jurisprudence—what men have sought in deep and perplexing speculations on the order and origin of all things, they will find in this mystery.—The hallowed sphere of walk is "in Him," but beyond this barrier are sin and danger, false philosophies and mazy entanglements.—Any philosophy not "after Christ" must be earthly and delusive. It has missed the central truth—is amused with the stars, but forgetful of the sun.—Though the scar of circumcision might attest a nationality, it was no certificate of personal character—but wherever "the flesh" was parted with, there was the guarantee of individual purity and progress.—The nails which killed Christ pierced the sentence of doom,—gave egress to the blood which canceled it, and inflicted at the same time a mortal wound on the hosts of darkness.—R.]

[BARNES:—We should be on our guard against the seductive arts of false teachers. It is, in general, a safe rule for a Christian to abide by the views which he had on the great subjects of religion when he became converted (ver. 6). Then the heart was tender—there are some things in which the heart judges better than the head.—If at any time we can ascertain what are the prevalent views of Christ, we can easily see what is the prevailing character of the theology of that age.—Vers. 11–15. Christ has laid us under the highest obligations to serve Him. He has enabled us to put off our sins; He has raised us from spiritual death to spiritual life; He has removed the old ordinances that were against us, and has made religion easy and pleasant; He has subdued our enemies and triumphed over them.—R.]

5. Two special warnings.

(Chapter II. 16–23.)

16 Let no man therefore judge you in meat, or in drink [in eating or in drinking],[1]
or in respect of a holyday, or of the new moon, or of the sabbath *days* [of sabbaths]:[2]
17 Which[3] are a shadow of things to come; but the body *is* of Christ [Christ's].
18 Let no man beguile you of your reward in a voluntary humility [arbitrarily in humility][4] and worshipping of angels, intruding into those things which he hath not[5]
19 seen, vainly puffed up by his fleshly mind [lit., the mind of his flesh], And not holding the Head, from which [whom][6] all the body by joints and bands having nourishment ministered [being supplied], and knit together, increaseth with the increase
20 of God. Wherefore [omit Wherefore][7] if ye be dead with Christ from the rudiments of the world, why, as though living in the world, are ye subject to ordinances,
21, 22 (Touch not; taste not; handle not; Which all are to perish with the using;) [for destruction in the consumption:][8] after the commandments and doctrines of men?
23 Which things have indeed a shew [repute] of wisdom in will-worship, and humility, and neglecting [unsparingness][9] of the body; not in any honour to the satisfying of the flesh [only to the satisfying of the flesh].[10]

[1] Ver. 16.—[Βρώσει ἢ ἐν πόσει, the act of eating or of drinking. See Exeg. Notes. The reading is doubtful; ℵ. A. C. D. F. K. L. Rec. most versions; Lachmann, Tischendorf (ed. 7), Ellicott, Wordsworth read ἤ. B. Tischendorf (ed. 2), Alford, Braune: καί. The critical defence of the former reading is: "the common association of βρῶσις and πόσις would very naturally suggest the displacement of ἤ for the more usual καί"—of the latter: καί would readily be altered to ἤ to suit the rest of the sentence. Both are so plausible, that the reading ἤ can safely be adopted on uncial authority. As to the meaning as affected by the readings, see Exeg. Notes.—R.]

[2] Ver. 16.—[Σαββάτων, literally "sabbaths," here=the singular.—R.]

[3] Ver. 17.—ℵ. A. D. E. F. read ἅ; B. has ὅ, which is to be preferred as the more difficult reading. [So Lachmann, Meyer. Alford is undecided, but gives ὅ in his text. Ellicott considers the reading ὅ not improbable, but insufficiently attested. Here also it is best to follow the mass of uncial MSS., with Rec. Tischendorf, and others. E. V. "which are" is correct in that case.—The reading Χριστοῦ (τοῦ omitted), Tischendorf, Ellicott, is preferable. Hence "Christ's," poss. gen. Eadie, Ellicott, Rhemish, Lachmann and Alford insert τοῦ (ℵ. A. B. C.).—R.]

[4] Ver. 18.—[Θέλων. Braune renders "*willkürlich.*" There is such diversity in interpretation that nothing more definite could be given in the text, and this will serve to show the one point of agreement among our modern commentators, *viz.*, that the E. V. is incorrect.—R.]

[5] Ver. 18.—Μή is added in ℵ., where it was originally wanting, as in A. B. and others; but it is not to be omitted, [Οὐκ is also found, but μή is the proper form of the negative here. See Exeg. Notes. The reading of Rec. has preponderant external authority, 6 MSS., nearly all cursives: supported by most versions, Tischendorf, Ellicott. Lachmann, Meyer, Alford reject the negative,—and this view affects the exegesis of the latter two.—R.]

[6] Ver. 19.—[Ἐξ οὗ, masculine, Christ the Personal Head, hence "whom;" "which" in E. V. doubtless stands for "whom."—R.]

[7] Ver. 20.—[Οὖν of Rec. and the article before Χρ. "have the authority of *all* the MSS. against them and are properly rejected by all modern editors" (Ellicott).—R.]

[8] Ver. 22.—[The E. V. is indistinct,—the rendering given above presents the interpretation of Braune, Eadie, Alford, Ellicott, Wordsworth. The parenthesis should perhaps include this last clause only.—R.]

[9] Ver. 23.—[Ἀφειδίᾳ, "unsparingness." So Eadie, Ellicott ("unsparing treatment"), Alford, Davies, and older English versions similarly.—R.]

[10] Ver. 23.—[This is the interpretation of Braune, Meyer, Ellicott and others. See Exeg. Notes. More modifications might well be made, but this slight change sufficiently indicates the view upheld below.—R.]

[The text of this short passage, containing not less than 9 ἅπαξ λεγόμενα, is remarkably well established and free from variations.—R.]

EXEGETICAL AND CRITICAL.

The first warning, against a fleshly legality. Vers. 16, 17.

Vers. 16. **Let no man therefore judge you.**—Since the personality of the readers is strongly emphasized by the position of the words: τις ὑμᾶς in sharp contrast, "therefore" refers to what was said above (vers. 1–15), especially to their endowments and position in Christ: not merely however to the doing away of the Mosaic law (Meyer and others). Bengel: *ex. v.* 8–15 *deducitur igitur.* Κρίνειν means "to judge;" the connexion defines it more closely: allow no one the right to judge and to condemn you, if you do not respond to such demands. The warning is found in this,—permitting their action to be determined by this (Bleek). *Neminem, qui vos judicare conatur, audiatis* (Bengel). He treats of Christian, gospel freedom. Luther: Let no one make conscience for you (see also Rom. xiv. 22). It is not therefore=κατακρινέτω (Baehr).

In eating or in drinking.—Ἐν denotes the sphere, the point where the judgment was exercised, as Rom. ii. 1. Βρώσει and πόσει set forth the act of eating and drinking—food is βρῶμα; drink, πόμα (Rom. xiv. 17; 2 Cor. ix. 10; 1 Cor. viii. 4; x. 4; Heb. ix. 10). As the Mosaic law had (Lev. vii. 10–27) prohibitions respecting food alone, and forbade wine only to the Nazarites (Numbers vi. 3), and during the time of priestly service (Levit. x. 9), the false teachers had certainly gone beyond this and heightened asceticism for Christians (Matt. xxiii. 24; Rom. xiv. 21). It is a false view, that there is here only a consonance without further significance (DE WETTE). Whether all indulgence in meat (OLSHAUSEN) or in wine (SCHENKEL) was forbidden, does not appear from the context.

Or in respect of a holyday, or of the new moon, or of sabbaths.—After "eating and drinking," joined with the copulative καί, the disjunctive union with ἤ follows, because the Apostle passes over to another matter. [It is true that eating and drinking may form one category, but in view of the doubtful reading, there is no sufficient critical or exegetical ground for preferring to make the above distinction.—R.] Ἐν μέρει, in respect of, in the point of (2 Cor. iii. 10; ix. 3; comp. WINER'S *Gram.* p. 571), denotes the category, which includes the species: ἑορτῆς, *festum annum*, νομηνίας, *in mense*, σαββάτων, *in hebdomade* (BENGEL); the diversity is indicated by ἤ instead of καί. The threefold order of 1 Chron. xxiii. 31; 2 Chron. ii. 4; xxxi. 3, is transposed. Comp. Gal. iv. 10. It is incorrect to apply it to *partial* observances of festivals (CHRYSOSTOM and others), or to make it=*vicibus festorum* (MELANCHTHON), or=*ne ulla quidem eorum ex parte* (SUICER); BEZA and others inexactly interpret by *respectu*. [The E. V. "in respect of" is exact enough, as it certainly suggests the idea of a category,=in the matter of.—R.] Christians should not permit themselves to be bound to Jewish festivals in their worship of God; neither to the three great annual feasts, nor the new moons, nor the Sabbath; σάββατα=σάββατον, Matt. xii. 1; Luke iv. 16; Acts xiii. 14; xvi. 13; it does not refer to the triple Sabbath (jubilee year, Sabbatic year, weekly Sabbath, HEUMANN [BARNES]). BENGEL: *hic significanter positus; nam sabbata dicuntur dies singuli hebdomados.* Thus IGNATIUS contends against the σαββατίζειν as well as against Judaism in the Epistle to the Magnesians, 9. [The passage reads in English: "no longer observing Sabbaths, but keeping the Lord's day."—EADIE:—"nor were they to hallow the 'Sabbaths,' for these had served their purpose, and the Lord's Day was now to be a season of loftier joy, as it commemorates a more august event than either the creation of the universe, or the exodus from Egypt. The new religion is too free and exuberant to be trained down to 'times and seasons' like its tame and rudimental predecessor. Its feast is daily, for every day is holy; its moon never wanes, and its serene tranquility is an unbroken Sabbath." The Jewish Sabbath was kept by the early Christians as well as the Lord's Day. The practice was condemned finally at a council in the neighboring city of Laodicea. —WORDSWORTH: "σαββάτων, the *Seventh Day* Sabbath, the Jewish Sabbath, which as far as it was the *seventh day Rest*, had been filled by Christ resting in the grave. The *position* of the day is changed, but the *proportion* remains unchanged, and has received new strength and sanction by its consecration to Christ under the gospel in the *Lord's* Day."—R.]

Ver. 17. **Which are a shadow of things to come.**—This verse is a proof of the warning. Ὅ [see critical notes; the meaning is the same if the reading ἅ be adopted.—R.] comprises all as a unit, and means: this (eating, drinking, feasts according to the precepts of the laws of Moses) is "a shadow of things to come." Σκιά, *umbra vitæ expers* (BENGEL), is not=σκιαγραφία, sketched in outline with charcoal, "*silhouette*" (CALVIN and others), since its antithesis here is not εἰκών, but σῶμα. It denotes the typical in the Mosaic law, not exactly the unsubstantialness (MEYER) or the transitoriness (SPENER), and not at all the darkness (MUSCULUS); for it gives certain intimation of the substance of the reality, and truth of the "things to come" (Heb. viii. 5; x. 1). Ἐστίν denotes the permanent nature of the former things; it is not=ἦν, but the commands and institutions have and retain a typical meaning. Τὰ μέλλοντα are future things, the things of αἰὼν μέλλων, not like this (SCHENKEL), nor is ἀγαθῶν to be supplied, from Heb. x. 1. These things cast a shadow into the αἰὼν οὗτος, so that the light, as well as the μέλλοντα, standing in the light, are before us. So long as one walks in the shadow, holds to it, he is not in the αἰὼν μέλλων, which began with the appearing of Christ, not to begin first with His *parousia* (MEYER); for there is added:

But the body is Christ's (WINER'S *Gram.* p. 495).—This refers to the presence of the αἰὼν μέλλων, which had already entered. However, he, who still holds to the ordinances of the law, and allows himself to be governed by erring and erroneous men, not by Christ, does not hold to Him, is not yet in the Messianic kingdom and age, as he may and should be. The passage treats of a point of view rather than a point of time. See 1 Jno. ii. 8 [LANGE, *Comm.* p. 53.] "But the body" is in contrast with "shadow," fulfilment, full substance and life of "the things to come." Ἐστίν is to be joined to Χριστοῦ; to Him as Head and Lord (vers. 6, 19) it belongs; He has the direction of the "things to come," is the antithesis of τις (ver. 16). It is neither: *ad Christum pertinet, ab eo solo petenda est* (GROTIUS), *ex Christo pendet* (STORR), appeared in Christ (HUTHER), nor is σῶμα to be repeated with Χριστοῦ (BENGEL), certainly it is not=the Christian Church (SCHENKEL); as little is σκιά the Jewish Church. [WORDSWORTH: σῶμα is *substantial reality*. ALFORD incorrectly asserts that the Apostle could not thus have spoken, if the ordinance of the Sabbath had been, *in any form*, of lasting obligation in the Christian Church. Against this view, see ELLICOTT *in loco* and his references, also WORDSWORTH, Sermon 44, Christian Sunday.—R.] The joining of this clause to the following verse (Greek Fathers) is objectionable, because it obviously belongs to the antecedent context, and does not belong to ὑμᾶς.

Against superstitious worship of angels (vers. 18, 19).

Ver. 18. **Let no man beguile you of your reward.**—Μηδείς corresponds with μή τις, ver. 16, and introduces a warning. [EADIE remarks the uniform use of the singular in these warnings, as contrasted with the plural used in Galatians. "Either he marks out one noted leader, or he merely individualizes for the sake of emphasis." Probably the latter.—R.] Here too the stress is laid upon the object ὑμᾶς, placed in an emphatic position. Καταβραβευέτω corresponds with κρινέτω (ver. 16). The word is rare, but Attic (*Demosthenes adv. Midiam, c.* 25), hence not a Cilician provincialism (JEROME); βραβεύειν is to be a βραβευς [*i. e.*, the awarder of prizes in the games.—R.], to perform such an office, παραβραβεύειν is to do this partially, unjustly, in favor of or against a competitor, καταβραβεύειν denotes definitely the hostile intent against one entitled to the prize. The prize (βραβεῖον, Phil. iii. 14: "of the high calling of God in Christ Jesus;" 1 Cor. ix. 24) is the imperishable crown (1 Cor. ix. 25); "of righteousness" (2 Tim. iv. 8; ii. 5), "of life" (Jas. i. 12), "of glory" (1 Pet. v. 4). Hence it is not to be interpreted as Christian freedom (GROTIUS) or the honor and prize of true Christian worship (DE WETTE), nor is the verb=κατακρίνειν (BAEHR and others). The following thought is not remote from, but not in, the passage; *Ne quis brabeutæ potestatem usurpans atque adeo potestate abutens, vos currentes moderetur. perperamque præscribat, quid sequi; quid fugere debeatis, brabeum accepturi* (BENGEL—similarly BEZA). LUTHER is incorrect: let no one frustrate you in your aim; Vulgate also: *nemo vos seducat.*

Arbitrarily in humility and worshipping of angels.—Θέλων characterizes the design of the false teachers as to its ground. The participle denotes, what is joined to θρησκεία in the compound ἐθελοθρησκεία (ver. 23): the wilful desiring, having pleasure in "humility and worshipping of angels." Θέλειν ἐν is =חָפֵץ בְּ 1 Sam. xviii. 22; 2 Sam. xv. 26; Rom. x. 9; 2 Cor. ix. 8; Ps. cxlvii. 10. It is not to be complemented with τοῦτο or τοῦτο ποίειν (=καταβραβεύειν, MEYER). Nor is it to be explained *cupide* (ERASMUS). The former is both a pleonasm and brachylogy at once: the latter is contrary to usage. To join it with ἐμβατεύων (LUTHER) is inadmissible. [ELLICOTT follows MEYER and renders: "desiring to do it," but objects to any imputation of malice.—He characterizes the view supported by Braune (AUGUSTINE, OLSHAUSEN and many others) as distinctly untenable and contrary to all analogy of usage of θέλειν in the New Testament; yet his own interpretation is open to the objections made above. ALFORD renders: "of purpose," joining it with καταβραβευέτω, following THEOPHYLACT. The interpretation of MEYER, ELLICOTT, *et al.*, he deems "flat and spiritless;" that of Braune, he terms "a harsh Hebraism—irrelevant." If the view of θέλειν, given on p. 35, note, be correct, then Alford's interpretation is inadmissible. Braune's exegesis accords best with the distinction there made. They arbitrarily, spontaneously, from the evil impulses of their own nature, indulged in these things. This is relevant, for this made them dangerous.—R.] The context indicates that the first substantive, elsewhere used in a good sense (iii. 12; Eph. iv. 2; Phil. ii. 3; Acts xx. 19; 1 Pet. v. 5), has here a bad sense: false, affected humility, behind which much spiritual pride may hide. The other substantive (θρησκείᾳ) means worship, adoration, Jas. vi. 26, 27; Acts xxvi. 5 [E. V. "religion."—R.], the object of which is set forth by the genitive. Comp. Wisdom, xiv. 27; xi. 16; Maccab. v. 6. WINER's *Gram.* pp. 176, 233. In the Old Testament the angels repeatedly appeared as mediators between God and man, and as representatives of men with God (Job v. 1; xxx. 23; Zach. i. 12; Tobit xii. 15). In the Testimony of the VII. Patriarchs (PHILO) they appear as interceding, helping beings; among the later Jews the opinion is current, that the law was delivered to Moses through angels (BLEEK on Heb. ii. 2). The Fathers refer to the fact that the Jews supplicated angels and councils declare themselves on this point* (BÖHMER in *Herzog's Realencyclop.* 4. p. 31). [See EADIE *in loco.* It was at Colosse that special worship was given in after days to the archangel Michael, for an alleged miracle wrought by him, *viz.*, opening a chasm to receive the river Lycus. And at a council held in the neighboring city of Laodicea, the practice referred to in the text was condemned.—(CONYB. and HOWS. Am. ed. II. p. 390, note 2).—R.]—"Humility" is to be regarded as so connected with angel worship, that the latter is proof of the former, since the mediation of angels was claimed in approaching God (THEODORET), or because the Majesty of the Only Begotten demanded it (CHRYSOSTOM). It is a mistake to take "humility" in a good sense, but as irony (STEIGER and others), or τῶν ἀγγέλων as *genitive subjecti* (LUTHER: spirituality of the angels, SCHLEIERMACHER, religion of the angels), or to weaken it to *studium singularis sanctitatis*, or to understand by it demons, demigods (ESTIUS). ["The Catholic interpreters, Estius and A-Lapide, make a strong effort to exclude this passage from such as might be brought against the worship of the saints" (EADIE), but the connection of the two substantives gives it a direct application to this error. —R.]

Intruding into those things which he hath not seen, ἃ μὴ ἑώρακεν [ἑόρακεν] ἐμβατεύων, is a further definition of καταβραβευέτω. The verb [participle] occurs only here; to step upon a place, hence spiritual regions through speculation; it is used of the entrance of the gods and their seating themselves (PASSOW *sub voce*); in distinction from ἐμβαίνειν, it denotes a confident, immediate stepping up, which the description of the regions entered (ἃ μὴ ἑόρακεν)—the transcendental—emphatic from position—shows to be unjustifiable. [The E. V. "intruding" is sufficiently accurate, though Braune's "*sich versteigend*" is more so.—R.] The negative μή instead of which οὐ occurs also, is correct in the relative clause after μηδείς (WINER's *Gram.* p. 448). Without the negative it may be referred to ὁράματα (Acts xx. 10, 12; x. 3); or ὁράσεις (Acts ii. 17) with MEYER: but if ὀφθείς (Acts ix. 17) must also be so understood according to the context, still ἃ ἑόρακεν (comp. 1 Jno. iv. 20) cannot be rightly referred to enthusiastic fancies. [These passages above cited speak of "visions;" to interpret thus would imply either that these visions were in themselves "illusions," or in their influence became "delusions." ALFORD

*[BARNES erroneously asserts: there is no evidence that any class of false teachers would deliberately teach that *angels* were to be worshipped.—R.]

renders: "standing on the things which he hath seen" *i. e.*, "an inhabitant of the realm of light, not of faith;" which as ELLICOTT observes "is ingenious, but not very plausible or satisfactory." The difficulty in such interpretations arises from following another than the true reading. The canon respecting *lectiones difficiliores* may be pushed too far.—R.]

Vainly puffed up by the mind of his flesh, is the third trait, more closely characterizing "humility." Εἰκῇ, *temere* (Rom. xiii. 4) or *frustra* (1 Cor. xv. 2; Gal. iii. 4; iv. 11), is here joined with φυσιούμενος in the former sense. [ELLICOTT: "bootlessly, without ground or reason." So Braune: "*ohne Ursache.*" "Vainly" may imply vanity in the cause or the result; here the former.—R.] On account of its position it cannot be joined with ἐμβατεύων (STEIGER and others). His obscurity is groundless, since it rests upon his own mind, is caused by his own spirit (ὑπὸ τοῦ νοός), and the more so, since "the mind" (νοῦς) is determined by, entirely in the service of and belonging to, "the flesh" (τῆς σαρκὸς αὐτοῦ), which while unredeemed serves evil (Rom. vii. 14, 25), and commands the "mind," possesses and rules it, instead of being possessed and ruled by it. CHRYSOSTOM: ὑπὸ σαρκικῆς διανοίας [followed by the E. V., "fleshly mind."—MEYER: "It must be noticed that the matter is so represented that the σάρξ of the false teacher seems *personified* (comp. Rom. viii. 6), as though it had its own νοῦς, under the influence of which he is made proud. The *pride* of these people consisted in this, that with all their supposed humility, they allowed themselves to fancy, as is generally the case with fanatical tendencies, that they could not be satisfied with the simple knowledge and obeying of the gospel, but could attain to a peculiar, higher wisdom and sanctity."—R.]

Ver. 19. **And not holding the Head.**—This is the fourth trait to be connected with the "worshipping of angels," denying Christ and the church [*die Christlichkeit und Kirchlichkeit.*]—The object is Christ, to whom the false teachers did not hold fast as Head, hence as before and above all, angels as well. The negative οὐ, not μή as before, denotes a matter of fact (WINER's *Gram.* p. 452). BENGEL: *Qui non unice Christum tenet, plane non tenet:* but he may yet belong to the church.—**From whom all the body** [or **the whole body.**—R.]—According to the parallel passage, Eph. iv. 15, ἐξ οὗ refers to Christ, hence is masculine, not neuter (MEYER) [So EADIE following MEYER: "not personally as Jesus, but really or objectively." But "the following verse seems to imply distinctly the contrary" (ELLICOTT).—R.] The preposition which is to be joined with αὔξει denotes the cause from which proceeds what it predicated, *viz.*, the growth, and not a remote one, only conditioning it from without, but indicating the most intimate vital connection between them. "All the body" includes the whole church (*Gemeinde*) without exception; there is no member that does not derive its growth from the Head. [It is a question whether the reference here is to the body in its entirety, or to the body as including every member. ELLICOTT and EADIE favor the former view, ALFORD and BRAUNE the latter, which is preferable, as the whole passage is against false teachers, who did not deny the unity of the church, but slighted the fact that each member "must hold fast the Head for himself" (ALFORD). There is then the greater reason for taking "from whom" personally. MEYER, followed by EADIE, refers ἐξ οὗ both to the verb and the participles, which reference does not correspond so well with the above views.—R.]

By joints and bands being supplied and knit together, διὰ τῶν ἁφῶν καὶ συνδέσμων ἐπιχορηγούμενον καὶ συνβιβαζόμενον, characterizes the body, the church, as Eph. iv. 16. The first participle belongs to ἁφῶν, the second to συνδέσμων. Both substantives, joined without a repetition of the article, form a category. Ἁφαί are the nerves, σύνδεσμοι the muscles: the former afford help, the latter compactness, firmness. Wherein the assistance consists is not expressly stated, the context only intimating vital activity in general (MEYER), not "nourishment" [E. V.] however, (GROTIUS). Ἁφαί do not refer to faith (BENGEL), σύνδεσμοι to prophets (THEODORET) or believers (BÖHMER), for faith is the life and the persons are the members.—[The fact that the two substantives are joined without a repetition of the article, is against the assignment of a participle to each. As ELLICOTT remarks: "The distinctions adopted by Meyer, *et al.*, according to which the ἁφαί are especially associated with ἐπιχορ., and referred to Faith, the συνδέσ. with συμβ., and referred to Love—are plausible, but perhaps scarcely to be relied upon. As in Eph. the passage does not seem so much to involve special metaphors, as to state forcibly and accumulatively a general truth."—In the parallel passage, Eph. iv. 16, Braune seems to interpret ἁφαί, "joints." To limit it specifically to "nerves," seems to be incorrect. EADIE: "We may understand it not merely of joints in the strict anatomical sense, but generally of all those means, by which none of the parts or organs of the body are found in isolation." He is not correct in giving a middle sense to ἐπιχορηγούμενον: "furnished with reciprocal aid." Both participles are passive; as present they denote "that the process is now going on" (ALFORD).—R.]

Increaseth with the increase of God, αὔξει τὴν αὔξησιν τοῦ θεοῦ—[lit., "increaseth the increase of God." Accusative of cognate substantive and genitive *auctoris.*—R.] By this God is described as He who effects the growth from Christ (1 Cor. iii. 6, 12; vi. 18; WINER's *Gram.* p. 232). The most appropriate preposition for Christ in this figure is ἐξ, for God ὑπό. Hence it does not refer to growth well-pleasing to God (CALVIN), [nor "godly growth," CONYBEARE and HOWSON.—R.] But the folly and danger of the false teachers is sharply marked.

Comprehensive conclusion. Vers. 20–23.

Ver. 20. **If ye be dead with Christ from the rudiments of the world.**—Sketch of their Christian state, in accordance with the context and the preceding passage (vers. 1–15). BENGEL: *continuatur illatio v. 16 coepta.* Εἰ is a rhetorical "if, as is actually the case" (WINER's *Gram.* p. 418). There are here two definitions of "being dead:" how? "with Christ;" to what? "from the rudiments of the world." The motive for "being dead" is given in vers. 11, 12, and for "with Christ" in ver. 19 (the Head) and vers. 10–15. For the sake of distinctness, and at the same time to mark the "dying" as an emancipation (BENGEL: *concise: mortui et sic liberati ab elementis*), the preposition ἀπό is repeated from the verb, where otherwise the dative would be found (Gal. ii. 19; Rom. vi. 2). "The rudiments of the world" are here those rudiments in which they lived before they became "in Christ," when they were still heathen; they should not fall away into such again, seduced by Judaistic false teachers. See on ver. 8.—MEYER incorrectly supposes that Christ also was "dead from the rudiments;" he overlooks that Gentile Christians are referred to; Christ is indeed "the end of the law," but has not to die to it.

Why, as though living in the world, are ye subject to ordinances?—"Why" introduces, emphatically in the form of a question, the conclusion that it was wrong. Comp. Gal. iv. 8–10. "As living in the world," like "when we were in the flesh" (Rom. vii. 5), describes their standpoint before conversion, to which they are returning; ὡς denotes the justifiable conclusion and comparison=*quippe qui*, "as though." Δογματίζεσθε is the middle (LUTHER: why do ye allow yourselves to be caught with ordinances?); the verb is=δόγμα τιθέναι, like νομοθετεῖν. It can be neither: one decrees to you (MEYER);* nor: you lay ordinances upon yourselves (BLEEK); they did not do this, nor does it correspond with the situation, while the former does not correspond with the intention of the intensive question, as if it concerned only a sketch of the fact, and not a rousing of the readers against it.

These ordinances are now noted concretely as to their purport: Ver. 21. **Touch not, taste not, handle not,** μὴ ἅψῃ, μηδὲ γεύσῃ, μηδὲ θίγῃς.—The triple reference forming a climax, marks the urgency of the demand for abstinence (MEYER). The reference to ver. 16 allows the omission of the objects, meat and drink, which are required by the second verb γεύσῃ. It is incorrect to apply "touch not" to sexual pleasure (FLATT); this cannot be justified by 1 Cor. vii. 1; 1 Tim. iv. 3, against the context, *viz.*, the former part of ver. 22. The suppression of the object is not to be accounted for by the fear and dissimulation of the false teachers, who did not name it themselves (STEIGER), nor thus: that Paul had not thought on any definite object. The objects he sets forth in paraphrase:

Ver. 22. **Which all are for destruction in the consumption,** ἅ ἐστιν πάντα εἰς φθορὰν τῇ ἀποχρήσει.—This relative clause sketches the forbidden objects, all of them (ἅ—πάντα); ἐστιν, placed first for emphasis, denotes that their nature is,—"appointed to destruction, perishable" (εἰς φθοράν), by being used up (τῇ ἀποχρήσει). This verdict reminds us of Matth. xv. 17; Mark vii. 18, 19; 1 Cor. vi. 13. Hence these words must be considered the Apostle's judgment to show, and that not without irony, the perversity of the notion, that through eating and drinking moral detriment originated (CHRYSOSTOM: εἰς κόπρον γὰρ ἅπαντα μεταβάλλεται). They cannot be regarded as the words of the false teachers (VATABLE, SCHENKEL), who will not suffer them to be touched, nor as parenthesis* (MEYER). Nor is ἅ to be referred to δόγματα, implied in δογματίζεσθε above (AUGUSTINE [BARNES] and others), nor is εἰς φθοράν to be explained as moral corruption (DE WETTE), since it merely describes destruction, decomposition, here of sensuous things. Although ἀποχρήσει must not be taken as the simple noun, it must however be distinguished from παράχρησις and κατάχρησις, "abuse." [The view Braune upholds is so generally adopted by modern commentators and so far preferable that it seems unnecessary to notice the others particularly. The practical bearing of the passage is obvious to any, who discover its true meaning. That this true meaning has not always been discovered by American Christians is evident from the fact that some still cite: "Touch not, taste not, handle not," in support of "total abstinence" from beverages which can intoxicate. Whatever may be the expediency of such a principle, it is one against which, as a binding rule of universal application, this passage, rightly interpreted, *might* be used. To use it in its favor is contrary to all fair dealing with the word of God,—a wresting of the Scripture, excusable only on the ground of ignorance, if in these days such ignorance be not rather an aggravation.—R.]

After the commandments and doctrines of men, κατὰ τὰ ἐντάλματα καὶ διδασκαλίας τῶν ἀνθρώπων, sets forth a modality of δογματίζεσθε, marking it as in contrast with God's law and word in Christ, indeed with the law of Moses, beyond which they have gone. "Doctrines" is added in justification of "commandments;" the latter are more restricted, the former more extended; the latter are results, the former set forth the premises and consequences. Matt. xv. 7; Mark vii. 7. [ELLICOTT: they were submitting to a δογματισμός not only in its preceptive, but even in its doctrinal aspects.—R.]

Ver. 23. **Which things have indeed a repute of wisdom.**—"Which things" refers to "commandments and doctrines of men," and denotes, not single commandments, *etc.*, but the whole category of human ordinances. Ἐστὶν λόγον μὲν ἔχοντα σοφίας is a concession (μέν), to which the antithesis (δέ) is wanting; still to the very significant λόγος we have the correlate τιμῇ, to λόγον ἔχοντα corresponds ἐν τιμῇ τινι, and on this account to μέν the following οὐκ corresponds. Hence λόγος here must mean "report," as Luke v. 15; Jno. xxi. 23; Acts xi. 22. So Herodot. 5, 66 (GRIMM, *Clavis, sub voce* p. 260). CHRYSOSTOM: λόγον φησὶν, οὐ δύναμιν, ἄρα οὐκ ἀλήθειαν. The Vulgate therefore: *rationem*

* [MEYER (followed by ALFORD) regards the verb as passive, finding here, not a reproach but a warning of the readers, who have not yet been led away. In that case, "as living in the world" indicates the wrong view which the false teachers take of the Christian position. There is much force in his objection to the common view, as implying that they were living as if in the world, a reproach which does not correspond with the tone of the rest of the Epistle. However the implication may only be, that if they allowed this to continue, they would be returning to the world. —R.]

* [The parenthesis of the E. V. seems unnecessary. It was probably designed to connect "ordinances" and "after the commandments of men" more closely. If any clause be parenthetical, it is this one, and MEYER, ALFORD and ELLICOTT so regard it, agreeing entirely, however, with the exegesis of Braune.—R.]

habentia, and LUTHER: "appearance" [E. V.: "show"] are incorrect. [ALFORD: "possessed of a reputation,"—ELLICOTT: "do have the repute"—are enjoying the repute of wisdom.—R.] The omission of a clause introduced by δέ is an anacoluthon, but not strange, since the clause is unmistakable (WINER'S *Gram.* p. 535). 'Εστὶν ἔχοντα is used instead of ἔχουσιν, to mark the weakness of men in permitting themselves to be so readily deceived and blinded, and contains a charge against such in general rather than against those in Colosse. Bengel improperly joins ἐστίν with πρὸς πλησμονήν, and resolves ἔχοντα into: *cum habeant, ut sit incisum*; so SCHENKEL also.

In will-worship, and humility, and unsparingness of the body, ἐν ἐθελοθρησκείᾳ καὶ ταπεινοφροσύνῃ καὶ ἀφειδίᾳ τοῦ σώματος.—"In," standing only at the beginning, denotes that all three belong together. Compounds with ἐθέλο are frequent (see Passow's Lexicon) and describe, according to the word, something done freely, voluntarily, on one's own responsibility, arbitrarily, factitiously, affectedly; ἐθελοθρησκεία is self-imposed, arbitrary worship (ver. 18). The object is not added, because self-evident: God. The false teachers in question would worship Him through the mediation of the adoration of angels. Compare ἐθελοπερισσοθρησκεία, by which EPIPHANIUS (*haer.* 1, 16) describes the piety of the Pharisees. Ταπεινοφροσύνη, as in ver. 18, denotes the humility which appeared with ostentation, hence only apparent, external. 'Αφειδία σώματος denotes the unsparing austerity towards the body through ascetic abstinence. Such mortification is based upon contempt of the creatures, false views of matter as the seat of sin. The first substantive denotes the religious aspect of their conduct, the second, the moral in relation to men, the third, the same as respects earthly things. In such ways they gained a repute of wisdom.

In opposition to this repute, the Apostle adds his judgment: **not in any honour**, οὐκ ἐν τιμῇ τινι. Here belongs ἐστίν, which follows ἅτινα, in order to contrast with "the repute of wisdom among the people," the Apostle's judgment, *viz.*: the repute is without honorable grounds, without true honor. This is strongly affirmed; there is nothing at all in it which is really honorable; hence "in any honor" is a sharp negation (οὐκ) of will-worship, humility and unsparingness of the body.—To this negative Paul adds a positive statement: **[only] to the satisfying of the flesh**, πρὸς πλησμονὴν τῆς σαρκός.—The former clause denies "the repute of wisdom" as a just repute; this gives a motive for the negation, in connexion with "unsparingness of the body." The false doctrine tends (πρός) to a satisfying (in contrast with "unsparingness") of the fleshly nature (τῆς σαρκός opposed to σώματος). It is incorrect to render: "not giving to the flesh the honor due to its necessities" (LUTHER and others). Πλησμονή implies blame (BENGEL: *fere excessum denotat*) and cannot= πρόνοια (Rom. xiii. 14). The distinction between τοῦ σώματος and τῆς σαρκός, and the omission of τοῦ σώματος after ἐν τιμῇ τινι must not be overlooked. GROTIUS singularly deduces praise from this: *habent ista rationem non stultam, si adsint cautiones, si sponte ista suscipiantur non abominando ea, quæ deus creavit,—cum ea modestia animi, quæ alios aliter viventes non damnet,—si hoc sibi propositum habeant, dure tractare corpus neque carni obsequi ad saturitatem.*—[Braune's view is that of MEYER, and is to be preferred, 1) as least ungrammatical; 2) as giving the best correlate to μέν; 3) preserving the distinction between σῶμα and σάρξ; 4) bringing out the bad sense of πλησμονήν and thus conveying the sharp condemnation, that asceticism, while it appears to subdue the body, serves only to gratify the flesh and its evil nature. For other interpretations see EADIE, ALFORD, ELLICOTT. The latter agrees most nearly with Braune.—R.]

DOCTRINAL AND ETHICAL.

1. *Fasts* and *Feasts* are placed together by the Apostle (ver. 16), while as a rule fasting and prayer occur together; Acts xiii. 3: "when they had fasted and prayed;" xiv. 23: "prayed with fasting;" 1 Cor. vii. 5: "fasting and prayer" (A. B. however omit the former). He forbids the one or the other, as little as Christ (Matt. vi. 5, 16); he does not annul the decree of the apostolic council (Acts xv. 20, 28), in which also the ethical and ritual are united. But he opposes *first*, asceticism which extends to "unsparingness of the body," *secondly*, an arbitrary abstinence from the means of nourishment ordained for eating and drinking, demanded equally from all, *thirdly*, those fasts connected with certain arbitrarily chosen days in the year, month and week. He thus opposes that *dualistic* view of the world, which does not regard and treat matter as the creature of God, which undervalues the body and its life, and in spite of its "unsparingness of the body" serves only "to the satisfying of the flesh;" he demands the maintenance of individual freedom and would commit all abstinence to the free moral resolution (as Rom. xiv. 2 sq., 1 Cor. viii. 1 sq., 1 Tim. iv. 3), and—as far as such abstinence is justified, and may be occasioned or required by internal or external circumstances, by the discipline necessary for the individual, or occurrences that affect him,—he would not have it mechanically and arbitrarily bound to special days, least of all that it should be regarded as of moral merit or as a work of supererogation, transcending or retrieving the purely moral law and moral conduct of life. The Christian should not bind his conscience to men, but only to God's word and God's law. Holy days and seasons should be determined by the great facts of salvation and the great acts of God, and not arbitrarily chosen. Thus we must judge both the Romish worship overrun with fasts and saints' days, and the Methodist and Baptist sects adhering to the Reformed Church. [The author, being a Lutheran, refers to the entire neglect of even such anniversaries as Christmas, Easter and Pentecost.—The special reference to the Methodists and Baptists must be confined to Germany,—and indeed in this country there is no applicability in his allusion to their adherence to the Reformed Church. It is true that until lately the prevailing practice of many churches in America would fall under the condemnation he hints at, and even now these historic days are observed

socially rather than religiously, as holidays rather than holy days. The Lord's Day has always been kept in a truer position. I may add that "fasting" is practically ignored as a Christian duty from extreme antagonism to arbitrary fast days, but while the American Church has allowed "no man to judge" "in eating," it has permitted strict judgment "in drinking" to lay a burden on the conscience. Paul places both in the same category (ver. 16). However expedient abstinence may be, this passage (vers. 16, 20–23) forbids the infringement on Christian freedom which is quite common.—R.]

2. *The distinction and the connexion of the Old and New Testament* economy are here described. The former is "the shadow of things to come" (ver. 17) and "the rudiments of the world" (ver. 20), which are given in heathenism as well as Judaism; contrasted with the former, the New Testament economy is "the body," with the latter it is "perfection" (τελείωσις). Christianity is called "the power of God and wisdom of God" (1 Cor. i. 24), at once to distinguish it from Judaism and to describe it as pre-announced, pre-intimated, prepared for in the same. The law is done away, not because it is in itself of no value, but because man is unable to fulfil it, obtains only in Christ, what he cannot attain without Him through the law. See Schmid, *Bibl. Theol.* II. 233–235; 322–325. Catholic and Reformed confessions fail in this respect; they regard the gospel as a *nova lex*, and permit the distinction between the Old Testament and New Testament to fall into the background: the former is pharisaical, the latter spiritualistic. [The position of the law in the Reformed confession does not seem to me to warrant this remark. See the Heidelberg Catechism, Ques. 2, 91, 92. Belgic conf., xxiv. xxv. Perhaps others are more open to this charge. See also Form of Concord, VI.—R.]

[3. *The observance of the Lord's Day* cannot be affected by the warning of Paul (ver. 16). It is certain that the persons who were judging them, were pressing the duty of observing the Jewish Sabbath, not the Christian Lord's Day. It is equally certain that the observance of a weekly day of rest is written in God's physical and social laws for man, as plainly as in the Decalogue. Nor can we escape the conclusion that the fourth Commandment is but a reminder of a previous institution, so that even those who might contend that the whole Mosaic law is abrogated, as a guide to Christian life, do not escape this enactment. But since the Christian would live gratefully, he still finds the rule in God's "holy, just and good" moral law, and sees in his very frame as well as in the frame-work of society, an additional reason for appropriating to "rest in God's service," one day in seven, rejoicing therein, since it now marks the great fact of his Lord's resurrection, and since his Master has Himself explained how it should be observed.—R.]

4. *The importance of the doctrine respecting angels* (Philippi: *Kirchl. Glaubenslehre* I. p. 279 sq.), without which the doctrine respecting Satan remains incomprehensible, is as great as the danger from the rationalistic denial of angels, springing from a Sadduceean view of the world, and the Romish adoration of angels, growing out of Essenic and dualistic heresy. The latter soon appeared in the Church. In Laodicea (at the council held between 343 and 381), it was forbidden in the 35th Canon. Ambrose first encouraged it (*observandi sunt angeli*). Augustine warns against it: *imitandos eos potius, quam invocandos*, and refers to the distinction between *cultus religiosus* and *non religiosus*. This, the second council of Nicæa (787) turned in favor of the adoration of angels, and the distinction established between λατρεία, invocation, and τιμητικὴ προσκύνησις, δουλεία, pious veneration, must now serve as a support for the heathenish adoration of angels and worship of the saints (*Conc. trid. sess.* 25. *Cat. Rom.* 3. 2; 8. 10). Our symbols maintain: *angelos a nobis non esse invocandos, adorandos* (*Articles of Schmalkald* II. 2). [See Reformed Confessions and catechisms generally.—R.]

5. *Christ the Head of the Church*, is for her the foundation of all religious and moral life: she needs no other mediator with God.—

6. *The Church is a living organism*, not an establishment or institution. It is a unity of many members; it rests upon an act and work of God in Christ, is from God and to God, has as its end education for perfection and glory hereafter; and possesses, in the word and sacraments and the proper administration of the same, suitable means for the attainment of this end. As to its inmost being, it is a vital relation of the congregation [*Gemeinde*] to the ever present, spiritual-physically present Lord (Harless. *Ethik.* 6. *Aufl.* p. 564). [By "*Geistleiblich*"—which is untranslatable, Braune means the presence of Christ in the eucharist according to the Lutheran view. Vital union with Christ the Head is not less insisted upon by those who hold the really Calvinistic view.—R.] It is an organization (but not the source), for the facilitating and furthering of *Christliness* [*Christlichkeit*], and the sense of this fellowship founded and maintained by Christ with the corresponding conduct is *Churchliness* [*Kirchlichkeit*], which is indissolubly connected with Christliness. As Church and Churchdom [*Kirche und Kirchenthum*] are so distinguished, that the former, as a Divine act, legally and rightly, takes form in the latter, so there is a two-fold Churchliness; one holding fast to the revelation of grace and ordinance of salvation in Christ, the other adhering to the legal forms of a special Churchdom, which has been and is being humanly and historically developed. The former has its source in the invisible Church, the fellowship of the Spirit, the latter in the visible church, which is the fellowship of law, and hence only human, secondary, accessory; it is not the realization of the idea of the Church, but merely a help and external support (Stahl: *Rechts-und Staats lehre*, p. 164). All ecclesiastical canons *non imprimunt credenda, sed exprimunt credita.* But in thus distinguishing, rightly, the ordinances of salvation and of the Church, Christliness and Churchliness, and the latter again in this two-fold manner, care must be taken not to undervalue the latter, as well as not to overvalue it.

7. *The principle of Christian liberty* especially and of Christian life in general is, that one neither makes nor permits to be made an arbitrary law, and so exercises his Christianity upon all that is created, ordinances as well as gifts, that

the creature is used in humble obedience to God's will, without the fleshly nature exalting itself. Asceticism degenerates into mere mechanical morality, casuistic hair-splitting about the divine law, an externalizing of self-discipline and self-exertion, a stirring up of spiritual pride. Under austerity respecting externals is concealed effeminacy with regard to heart-emotions, and in the unsparing plaguing of the body the flesh is fondled.

[8. *The connection of the two warnings.* There is instruction in the connection of precepts in Paul's writings. Here are two warnings, one against fleshly legality, the other against worship of angels, both condemned as having a "show of wisdom"—but tending only to the satisfying of the flesh. The connection is not obvious, yet side by side the two errors have existed with the same result. In germ at Colosse, in full flower in the medieval church, and in modern times, in America especially, fanatical binding of the conscience respecting articles of diet and drink, and "intruding into things not seen," craving for other "spiritual manifestations" than those coming from the Head, have taken root and flourished in the same localities, together with "a show of wisdom" and an intense "satisfying of the flesh." Error has its affinities and its unchanging law of development no less than truth.—R.]

HOMILETICAL AND PRACTICAL.

Christ wants no legal man, who through zeal in good works will earn the love of God, but a spiritual man, whose faith through grateful love to God is diligent in every good word and work.—In winter fruit trees look more alike than in spring, summer and autumn; where life and liberty are wanting, there is monotony in faith and walk; while lifeless liberty makes every diversity prominent.

STARKE:—That is the devil's way, to judge and make conscience where none should be made, and to make none where it should be. Let us hold to Christ alone, and put no man or creature as mediator with Him; but hold to Him truly too, so that we have His witness, whether we have received of His Spirit to abide in us.—Will worship is worthless.

RIEGER:—Sincerity, which seeks God and clings to His Word, seizing salvation in Christ, as if it were I only in the world, whom it concerned; unity, joining itself to all who are called and pressing to the same goal with the same serviceableness; freedom, which binds and is bound by none in things that can neither hinder nor further me in the ordained course. —Each one has a corner in his heart where rash prejudices can hide, to break out swiftly in natural and spiritual things, so that we can quickly stumble at one thing, or thoughtlessly depreciate another.—[Self-will makes even humility, a vain puffing up.—R.]

GERLACH:—While one lives in the world, he serves its rudiments. Of these God made use in His law to typify in that time of childhood higher, eternal truths. But when the full light of truth has risen, to serve these is to be in bondage to the world. All this is renewed in Christendom, whenever Christ, as the only Mediator is supplanted or thrown into the background by other sub-mediators.

SCHLEIERMACHER:—The right way can only be the one way, in the likeness of the Divine Love to maintain the bond of love among each other, and in common with those who are our brethren to seek and to lead a spiritual life.—[The difficult wisdom of the gospel, which so few attain: rightly distinguishing the internal from the external, substance from shadow, spirit from letter.—R.]

PASSAVANT:—Habit and custom, the regular return of religious exercises and festivals, regular Sabbaths, periodical communion seasons, even set hours of meditations, even family worship otherwise so necessary in addition to public worship,—how easily do all degenerate into empty form and external posture without spirit and life.—He who does not hold to the Head, but holds rather to the thoughts of his own wisdom and the dreams of his own fancy, relying upon systems of human philosophy, upon highly gifted minds, or on the poesy of the human imagination, desiring to seek and find there all that is noble and exalted, salvation, joy, heaven itself, thereby denies and disowns the one great Reconciler and Redeemer, His Truth, His Love, His Right and His Glory: he loses in his folly and ingratitude the whole wealth of the Word of God; he takes the shadow instead of the body, the sheen for the true light, a self-made life for the true Life, God's Life in us.

HEUBNER:—The Christian should maintain freedom of conscience. He should not depend on others, but follow his own conscience, not permitting himself to be bound to non-essential exercises. A superstitious over-estimate of things indifferent always leads away from Christ.—*Young Stilling*, although indulging in many fancies about spirits, remained faithful to the biblical principle, that all such attempts to open up the invisible world about him are culpable and opposed to the present probationary state of man. A Christian, clinging to Christ is secure against all such foolery, which would divert him from his aim.

WILHELM.—The holy simplicity of the Christian. It consists herein 1) that he keeps his goal uninterruptedly in view: 2) guards against all going according to his own choice: 3) studies true humility at heart.—LEHMAN:—Against what must we guard if we would not miss the mark of our heavenly calling? 1) Against our own choice in the matter of our blessedness; 2) against false humility; 3) against carnal mind. CLAUS:—Two great dangers on the path to the heavenly goal; 1) the error of human ordinances; 2) the pride of our own heart.

[BURKITT:—Abstinence is sinful when men abstain from some meats, upon pretence of holiness and conscience, as if some meats were unclean, or less holy in their own nature than others, or as if simple abstinence at any time were a thing acceptable to God in itself, without respect to the end for which it is sometimes required.—Men are most forward to that service of God, which is of man's finding out and setting up; man likes it better to worship a God of his own making, than to worship the God that made him; and likes any way of worshipping God which is of his own framing, more than that which is of God's appointing.—HENRY: Ver. 19. 1) Jesus Christ is not only a Head of Government over the church, but a Head of vital influence to it. 2) The body of Christ is a growing body.—R.]

[EADIE:—Ver. 16. Sensations of spiritual joy are not to be restricted to holy days, for they thrill the spirit every moment, and need not wait for expression till there be a solemn gathering, for every instant awakes to the claims and the raptures of religion.—Ver. 19. The church can enjoy neither life nor growth, if, misunderstanding Christ's person or undervaluing His work, it have no vital union with Him.—Ver. 20. Christ is the Head and to Him alone do we owe subjection.

What mean they? Canst thou dream there is a power
In lighter diet at a later hour
To charm to sleep the threatenings of the skies,
And hide past folly from all-seeing eyes? (COWPER).

Ver. 23. When Diogenes lifted his foot on Plato's velvet cushion and shouted "thus I trample on Plato's pride," the Athenian sage justly replied "but with still greater pride." The Apostle utters a similar sentiment. These corporeal macerations, as history has shown tend to nurse licentiousness in one age, and a ferocious fanaticism in another.—R.]

[BARNES:—Ver. 16. It is the solemn and sacred duty of all Christians to remit all attempts to make ceremonial observances binding on the conscience.—Ver. 18. "Pride may be pampered while the flesh grows lean."—WORDSWORTH: Ver. 18. Pride in its worst form; Pride dressed up in the disguise of lowliness. And this is the besetting sin of the human heart, which is more puffed up by false humility than by open pride.—R.]

[SCHENKEL:—The danger of constituting oneself a judge of the consciences of others; 1) why it is so near us; 2) why it must be so earnestly contended against.—Christ the only mediator between God and man: It is not humility, but pride, if we seek another.—The officious seeking after revelations outside the Revelation: 1) how dangerous; 2) how foolish it is.—The danger of spiritual pride; 1) Its source—the flesh; 2) its effects—inflation.—Who has died with Christ, can no longer live in the world: 1) The reason, 2) the power of this truth.—Will-worship: 1) a self-deception, 2) a deceiving of others.—Interference with allowable enjoyment by ordinances of men: 1) the *wrong* inherent in such interference; 2) the *impurity* to which it leads.—R.]

III. PART SECOND.

Exhortation to vital sanctification.

CHAPTERS III. 1—IV. 6.

1. The foundation and prospect of a genuine Christian mind and walk.

(CHAP. III. 1–4.)

1 If ye then be risen [were raised together][1] with Christ, seek those things which are
2 above, where Christ sitteth [is, sitting] on the right hand of God. Set your affection
3 [mind] on things above, not on things on the earth. For ye are dead[2] [died] and
4 your life is [or hath been] hid [κέκρυπται] with Christ in God. When Christ, *who*
is our life,[3] shall appear [or be manifested], then shall ye also appear [or be manifested] with him in glory.

[1] Ver. 1.—[So Ellicott, Alford. The former renders the whole verse: "If then ye were raised together with Christ, seek the things that are above, where Christ is, sitting on the right hand of God," which rendering is justified in the notes below. His note on the distinction between "which" and "that" is interesting.—R.]

[2] Ver. 3.—['Απεθάνετε; aorist, referring to definite past time, hence: "died"—as in ver. 1: "were raised."—R.]

[3] Ver. 4.—א. C. D.[1] E.[1] F. G. and others read ὑμῶν; while B. and many others have ἡμῶν. A. has a *lacuna* here. The authorities are equal, the internal grounds also; the former is more striking, fitting, the latter the stranger, more difficult reading; not like the other dependent on ver. 3. Certainly it cannot be referred merely to Paul and Timothy (Schenkel), but to Christians in general. [Braune, following Meyer, seems to prefer ὑμῶν; but with Rec., Lachmann, Tischendorf, and modern English editors, ἡμῶν ("our," E. V.) is to be preferred.—R.]

EXEGETICAL AND CRITICAL.

The injunction. *Vers.* 1, 2.

Ver. 1. **If ye then were raised together with Christ** takes up from the foregoing (ii. 12) a comprehensive thought, in a form reminding us of ii. 20, to make it the basis of the exhortation. "If," like ii. 20, is not a doubtful hypothesis, but fact (ii. 12), from which, as undeniable, a certain conclusion is deduced (οὖν). By "raised together with Christ" we must understand the ethical renewal (see notes on ii. 12). MEYER, who apparently refers this also to the corporeal resurrection, overlooks the "shall be manifested" (ver. 4), and errs in regarding "actual" and "objective" as identical notions in contrast with "ethical;" this latter is no less actual. [ALFORD, ELLICOTT, WORDSWORTH refer the aorist to "baptism." It refers to the definite point of time when this actual, "ethical" change took place. Is that necessarily at baptism? The two former object to the ethical sense on the ground that the injunction which follows would then be superfluous. Why should not a motive be drawn from this? What has been done for them is the ground for their doing, "seeking."—R.]

Seek those things which are above.—Τὰ ἄνω, placed first for emphasis, is like τὰ ἐπουράνια (Eph. ii. 6); to seek such things is a necessary consequence and requirement of being "raised together with Christ." BENGEL: *Christus a resurrectione statim contendit ad cœlum* (Jno. xx. 17). Comp. Phil. iii. 14, 20; Matt. vi. 20, 23; Rom. ii. 7.—**Where Christ is, sitting at the right hand of God.**—"Where" marks "the things above" as the region of the heavenly things of the Messianic salvation; "Christ is, sitting at the right hand of God" indicates both the exultation after deep humiliation and certain rest after severe conflict. Thus a motive is given for the exhortation. Comp. Ps. cx. 1. [The passage seems to abound in motives, though this is the principal one. The E. V. overlooks the fact that there are two enunciations: "Christ is there, and in all the glory of His regal and judiciary power" (ELLICOTT).—R.]

Ver. 2. **Set your mind on things above.**—The emphasis rests on the object; hence it is placed first here also. This is not mere repetition. After "seek" (ζητεῖν), which manifests itself in active and outward conduct, prominence is given to the cogitations of thought (φρονεῖν, Phil. iii. 15, 19). BENGEL: *qui vere suprema quærunt, non possunt non sapere suprema.*—**Not on things on the earth.**—This is=τὰ ἐπίγεια, "earthly things" (Phil. iii. 19), τὰ ἐν τῷ κόσμῳ, "the things that are in the world" (1 Jno. ii. 15). The earthly, that which is "to perish with the using" (ii. 22), should not be the object of inward care and thought; this is a sign of being "of the world," which is not=being "in the world" (Jno. xvii. 14, 16, 12). The use of earthly things is not forbidden, but we are bidden, in the right use of the earthly to mind and seek heavenly things. [THEOPHILUS: Four-footed beasts are like images of men who *mind earthly things;* but they who live righteous lives soar aloft, like birds, on the wings of the soul, and *mind those things that are above* (WORDSWORTH).—R.]

Ver. 3. *The Proof.* **For ye died**, *i. e.*, died to the world, to the earth (ii. 20: "from the rudiments of the world"). The aorist (ἀπεθάνετε) is used to denote an act that has occurred. Ye cannot then go backwards, live again or longer after the former fashion: your life is now another one.—**And your life is hid with Christ in God.**—"And" adds to the negative side, the having died, the positive side, "your life," which however is "hid." The perfect (κέκρυπται) denotes the continued relation, the verb itself marks the state of the existent life as still hidden, of course from the world, from men, from themselves also (1 Jno. iii. 2: "It doth not yet appear"): the coherence of the life of Christians is denoted by "with Christ," the inherence by "in God" (MEYER). Comp. 1 Pet. iii. 4: "the hidden man of the heart;" Acts xvii. 28: "in Him we live and move and have our being." [EADIE, against BARNES: "the idea of concealment, and not that of security, seems to be principally contained in the verb, for it is placed in contrast with open manifestation of Christ's appearance. But this concealment is no argument against present and partial enjoyment."—R.]—Evidently this is to be understood of eternal life, which has been awakened and is furthered in the present in consequence of the new birth. It remains concealed until its completion, which enters (ver. 4; Rom. viii. 19) with "the coming" (2 Thess. ii. 8; 1 Tim. vi. 14; 1 Cor. i. 7; 2 Thess. i. 7) of its Author and Finisher, Christ. The Greek fathers, CALVIN, GROTIUS, MEYER, incorrectly regard it as the life hereafter, [ALFORD: the resurrection life—R.], as if the Christian life were not already substantially, though incipiently, the life to be completed hereafter. GROTIUS is incorrect, *jus ad rem rei nomine appellat;* HEINRICH: *sicuti Christus;* ROSENMUELLER: *in mente dei.* [ALFORD: notice the solemnity of the repetition of the articles; and so all through these verses.—R.]

Ver. 4. *The exalted prospect.* **When Christ shall appear.**—Rapidly, without καί or δέ, this reminder and prospect is added, to animate their zeal. "When" marks the time, viz.: the appearing of Christ.—**Our life**—[the E. V. inserts "*who is*," thus bringing out the force of the passage.—R.] This is in apposition with "Christ," as "the hope of glory" (i. 27). It forms the basis of the conclusion ("then shall ye also appear"); hence it is added to signify not merely that Christ is a remote and sundered Cause, but Impulse, Power, Object and Substance of the Life itself (Phil. i. 21; Jno. xi. 25). BENGEL: *Ratio sub qua manifestabitur.* [EADIE is unfortunate in his interpretation: "shall appear in the character of our life." Christ is our life itself, the essence and the impersonation of it (ELLICOTT).—R.]

Then shall ye also appear with him in glory.—"Then" refers to "when" (BENGEL: *prius non debemus postulare*); "ye also" to "Christ." [ELLICOTT: The more verbally exact opposition would have been "your hidden life;" but this the Apostle perhaps designedly neglects, to prevent ζωή being applied as it has been applied, merely to the resurrection-life.—R.] "With Him," which might otherwise have been omitted, is emphatic. "Appear with Him in glory" is="glorified together" (Rom. viii. 17), there preceded by "suffer with Him," as this is by "died" (ver. 3; ii. 20: "with Christ"). Comp. 1 Cor. xv. 42–44, 53.

DOCTRINAL AND ETHICAL.

1. *Here and hereafter* no more fall into two incongruous parts, than the year with seed time and harvest, human life with childhood and riper age, man with body and soul, the church in in-

visibly visible manner, with its militant and triumphant congregations. It is more than indistinctness and superficiality, it is anti-christian error to say, as does Kaüffer (*De ζωῆς αἰωνίου notione*, p. 93): *vitam enim piam et honestam, quam homo Christianus in hac terra vivere possit ac debeat, Paulus dicere non poterat nunc cum Christo in deo* (*in cœlis puta, in quibus Christus nunc est*) *reconditam esse, atque olim in splendido Jesu reditu de cœlo revelatam iri: hæc nonnisi vitæ cœlesti conveniunt.* Such an affirmation grossly offends against the Lord's words (Jno. v. 24, "hath eternal life") and Paul's (Phil. iii. 20: "our conversation is in heaven). So "ethical" and "physical" are very different, but not incongruous ideas. The Ethos should become Physis, and the latter should be made ethical. The Hereafter is not locally separated, is not a limited place, but a spiritual life-sphere, whose rudiments and germs lie in the narrow corporeal life, as in a concentric inner circle. God's world cannot be *dualistically* split into a visible and invisible world; as little can it be separated by a *rationalistic* or *deistical* cross-cut into an upper and under world. He has created His world, the material world, to be glorified with a receptivity for eternal spiritual being, *finitum infiniti capax.*

2. *The Ethical Consequence* of the Christian view is: in the earthly life to begin the heavenly, in time to seek and to find eternity, faithful in the least, the perishing, to gain the greatest, the eternal. Aptly and elegantly says the Epistle to *Diognetus* (chap. v. 6 in Scholz: *Apostolic Fathers*, p. 170) of Christians; they inhabit—Being in heaven. Comp. the beautiful hymn of Richter: *es glänzet der Christen inwendiges Leben.*

3. *Only in and with Christ* can we be even here assured of and joyful in eternal life; the true life is Christ in us.

4. *The motive* to constancy and fidelity in such a life is the glimpse of future glory, not the slavish fear of perdition, but child-like confidence and joy in the glory of the heritage and the heritage of glory.

HOMILETICAL AND PRACTICAL.

Do not indefinitely seek what is above in heaven, but think of this, that there Christ is in glory with the Father, resting in the assurance of victory, taking part in the rule of the world. As the leaves that cool thee with their shade, shining in the sunlight and gaily rustling and dancing on the stem, were only born in the spring, begotten the summer before, in the sleeping eye, as in a cradle, so in the heat of life is hiddenly prepared thy life to be manifested above: so God creates thy life in the quiet depth of the heart through and with Christ.—Wouldst thou be one day in heaven, then must heaven be in thee here: first the kingdom of God is in thee, then thou in it.

STARKE:—*Ascendamus interim corde, ut olim sequamur et corpore* (Augustine).—Think not, that by earnest meditation on the kingdom of God, all duties of house and office must be laid aside. We can find a place for that, even when the body is outwardly busy. Indeed through spiritual care of the soul, external business is properly regulated, sanctified and blessed.

GERLACH:—As Christ has concealed Himself from the bodily eye, and now lives a higher, heavenly, divine life; so does the Christian united to Him through faith. But the life of Christ will not always be thus concealed.

SCHLEIERMACHER:—The old man and the new man: this is the great contrast in which Paul's entire proclamation of the gospel moved. The old man is both the man of sin and the man of the law; the new man is both the new creature in whom Christ lives, and he, who serves the righteousness, which comes through faith and avails before God.—The walk is manifest, the life is hid, we can conclude respecting the latter, only from what is manifested in the former.

PASSAVANT:—The world knows not, sees not, what a new being has arisen in the believer through the risen Christ. He feels the life of Jesus in his heart.—Highest stand the prophets, apostles, martyrs, who "overcame by the blood of the Lamb, and by the word of their testimony; and loved not their lives unto the death" (Rev. xii. 11). But all the rest, who have fought unto death, in patience and long-suffering, in holy fidelity, who are made kings and priests, will be called conquerors by their Head.

HEUBNER:—The higher, heavenly sense of the Christian proceeds from Christ, the Risen One, —this is its origin, its power—thither it goes also to His heavenly glory as its goal. He who has found the higher, forgets the lower.—PALMER:—The life in God: 1) a life of profound concealment, yet to be made manifest; 2) a life in blessed rest, yet with daily unrest and labor; 3) a life in heaven, yet with an appropriate blessing for earth.

GESETZ UND ZEUGNISS [a German theological periodical.—R.]: Live with Christ in God! 1) We have to make this way clear to ourselves; 2) to acquaint ourselves with the nature and quality of this life; 3) to inquire respecting the end, to which it develops itself.—The sign of spiritual resurrection; 1) heavenly mind; 2) divine life; 3) blessed hope.—The exhortation of the Apostle: Seek the things which are above! 1) How the Apostle explains it; 2) what grounds he adduces for it.—Our past and present and future [*Unser Sonst und Jetzt und Einst.*] 1) our *past;* a seeking and minding what is on the earth; a life without Christ and without God, manifest in sin and shame. 2) Our *present;* a seeking and minding what is above, where Christ is; a life hid with Christ in God. 3) Our *future;* a possessing and enjoying all that after which we here strive in faith; a life with God manifested with Christ in glory.

[ANDREWES: Vers. 1, 2. Christ is risen, and if Christ then we. If we so be, then we "seek;" and that we cannot unless we "set our minds." On what? On "things above," not on earth, but where "Christ is." And why there? Because where He is, there are the things we seek for, and here cannot find. There He "is sitting" and so at rest. And at "the right hand" so in glory. "God's right hand" and so forever. These we seek, rest in eternal glory. These Christ hath found and so shall we, if we begin to "set our minds" to search after them.—LUTHER: —Ver. 2. We live not in the flesh, but we dwell in the flesh. BP. DAN. WILSON:—Things on earth too naturally draw us down, attract us, fix us. Esau's red pottage prevails over the birthright. The guests in the parable turn away to their land, or oxen, or families. The Gadarene mind wishes Christ to depart from its coasts.—R.]

[EADIE:—The pilgrim is not to despise the comforts which he may meet with by the way, but he is not to tarry among them, or leave them with regret.—WORDSWORTH:—Be ye good trees. Now, in the world's eye, is your winter; to men ye appear like dry sticks. Your life is *hid* with Christ. Ye are dead in *appearance*, but not dead *in reality;* dead as to show of luxuriant leaves, but not dead in your spiritual root. Your root is Christ. His coming will be your summer. Then ye will put forth a glorious foliage. Ye will *appear* with Him in glory. And the leafy fig-tree of this world will be withered by His coming.—R.]

[BEVERIDGE: Sermon on ver. 2. 1) Why "not on things on the earth?" *a*) they are below you and unsuitable to you both as men and Christians; *b*) they can never satisfy your desires; *c*) are troublesome and disquieting; *d*) unimportant and unnecessary (can neither make you happy themselves, nor conduce thereto); *e*) fleeting and unconstant. 2) Why "on things above?" *a*) nothing was made or designed as a proper object for our affections but these; *b*) our relations "above;" *c*) our possessions. 3) What affections? *a*) our thoughts and meditations; *b*) our affection of love; *c*) our desires; *d*) our joy. Thus become holy and happy.—R.]

---

2. General exhortations.

CHAPTER III. 5–17.

a) Exhortation to put off the old fleshly nature.

(CHAP. III. 5–11.)

5 Mortify therefore your[1] members which are upon the earth: fornication, unclean-
ness, inordinate affection [lustfulness],[2] evil concupiscence [or shameful desire],[3] and
6 covetousness, which is idolatry: For which things'[4] sake the wrath of God cometh on the
7 children of disobedience:[5] In the which [Among whom][6] ye also walked sometime
8 [once], when ye lived [imperfect, were living] in them. But now ye also put off all
these; anger, wrath, malice, blasphemy [evil speaking],[7] filthy [abusive][8] communi-
9 cation out of your mouth. Lie not one to another, seeing that ye have put off the
10 old man with his deeds; And have put on the new *man*, which is renewed [is being
renewed][9] in [unto, εἰς] knowledge [,] after the image of him that created him:
11 Where there is neither Greek nor Jew, circumcision nor uncircumcision, Barbarian,
Scythian, bond *nor* [omit *nor*][10] free: but Christ *is* all, and in all.

[1] Ver. 5.—Ὑμῶν is wanting in ℵ. A. B. and others. [It is omitted by Tischendorf (ed. 2, not 7), Alford, and by Braune; retained however by Rec. Lachmann, Meyer, De Wette, Wordsworth, Ellicott; the latter remarks: "The great preponderance of MSS. and the accordant testimony of so many versions seem to render this otherwise not improbable omission here very doubtful."—R.]

[2] Ver. 5.—[Alford and Ellicott thus render πάθος: not merely "lust," but the disposition toward it.—R.]

[3] Ver. 5.—[" Evil concupiscence" is correct, but "shameful desire" would be more generally understood.—R.]

[4] Ver. 6.—Δι' ἃ on the authority of ℵ. B. C. and others, is better supported than δι' ὅ. [The former reading is adopted by Lachmann, Tischendorf, Ellicott: the latter by Meyer and Alford.—R.]

[5] Ver. 6.—The clause ἐπὶ τοὺς υἱοὺς τῆς ἀπειθείας, "on the children of disobedience," is wanting in B.; apparently taken from Eph. v. 6, where it is supported by all. [Rejected by Tischendorf and Alford. The uncial authority, ℵ. A. C. D. E. K. L., in support of it is so preponderant that it cannot safely be omitted. The two Epistles might well contain expressions exactly alike. Meyer retains it.—R.]

[6] Ver. 7.—['Ἐν οἷς refers to "the children of disobedience," if that clause be retained. If it be rejected, the E. V. is correct, but is incorrect as it now stands. (Braune, Ellicott.)—R.]

[7] Ver. 8.—["Evil-speaking" or "calumny" is evidently the meaning of βλασφημίαν here, as in Eph. iv. 31, where the E. V. reads: "evil-speaking."—R.]

[8] Ver. 8.—["Abusive," perhaps "foul-mouthed communication," is better than "filthy;" the idea of obscenity is not necessarily included in αἰσχρολογίαν.—R.]

[9] Ver. 10.—[The present participle here denotes a process going on. See EXEG. NOTES.—R.]

[10] Ver. 11.—Before ἐλεύθερος. A. and others read καί, a few also before Σκύθης, but both weakly supported. ["Nor" is unnecessarily supplied in the E. V.—R.]

EXEGETICAL AND CRITICAL.

The first exhortation concerning the relation to the pleasures and possessions of earth. Vers. 5–7.

Ver. 5. **Mortify therefore your members, which are upon the earth.**—"Mortify therefore" is joined to vers. 1–4, containing an inference from "were raised together" (ver. 1) and "died" (ver. 3). Their being dead has as its result a new life, in which a "making dead" (νεκροῦν) is possible and necessary. The verb (only here and Rom. iv. 19; Heb. xi. 12) is *reddere νεκρόν, i. e., cadaver omnibus viribus privatum* (πτῶμα), stronger than θανατοῦν (Rom. viii. 13). See TITTMANN, *Syn.* I. p. 168. [The aorist denotes a definite act, which ELLICOTT thus expresses: "kill at once;" ALFORD: "put to death."—R.] After the Christian died (ver. 3), he has as quickened (ver. 1), with the newly gained vital power, to kill the "members which are upon the earth." This expression corresponds with the context, and refers in its sense to "putting off the body of the flesh" (ii. 11). There the whole organism was brought into view, here the individual members; there "of the flesh" describes what here, in accordance with ver. 3, is described by "which are upon the earth" (BENGEL: where is found the sustenance of those members, of which collectively the body of sin consists). Because they are "fleshly," there is a motive for putting them to death. This must be understood in an *ethical*, not a *physical* sense (HUTHER, UNGER and others), not of the Church members as the vital activities of the body of the Church (SCHENKEL); for the Christian is not required to mutilate his body, nor are members or masses of members "who are on the earth," organs of the Church and its activity, since it is a creation of God; the words might be applied to Christians, who are worldly-minded, but, as regards these, νεκροῦν, putting to death, is a duty only in the view of fanatics.

[ELLICOTT thus aptly paraphrases: "As you died, and your true life is hidden with Christ, and hereafter to be developed in glory, act conformably to it—let nothing live inimical to such a state, kill at once the organs and media of a merely earthly life." Put to death the portions of your body, which are the instruments of sin, as respects the sphere (on the earth) of these sinful activities, and the actions and desires below specified: a duty very different from and more difficult than asceticism, or obedience to "the commandments of men" (ii. 21, 22).—R.]

The substantives, which follow in appositional relation to "members," show more specifically what is meant: **fornication, uncleanness, lustfulness, evil concupiscence, and covetousness, which is idolatry.**—BENGEL: "these (μέλη, members) are enumerated." There is no metonymy here (DE WETTE), nor are these the ethical ingredients inhering in the members (MEYER, WINER's *Gram.* p. 494). On the first two and the last substantives, see on Eph. v. 3. "Lustfulness" (πάθος) [not limited to unnatural lust, as Rom. i. 26.—R.] and "evil concupiscence" (ἐπιθυμία κακή) are to be referred, according to the context, to sexual sin; the former denoting rather the formal eagerness, the latter the intrinsic unworthiness, determined by the object; the former is always the latter also, but not *vice versa* (1 Thess. iv. 5: "in the lust of concupiscence," ἐν πάθει ἐπιθυμίας). [The latter being more general.—R.] The category introduced by "fornication," on account of its manifold and frequent manifestations (Gal. v. 19), is prominently set forth in detail; unnatural uncleanness is included in the last two substantives, but not specially described (ERASMUS and others).

By the side of "fornication" thus specified, the Apostle puts "covetousness" as a second category, indicated by the article. Bengel: *articulus facit ad epitasin et totum genus vitii a genere enumeratarum modo specierum diversum complectitur.* He gives prominence to this by means of the relative clause, which characterizes it and gives a motive for mortifying it. "Which" (*quippe quæ*, "which indeed;" WINER's *Gram.* pp. 111, 157). See on Eph. v. 5. It is incorrect to apply it to insatiable voluptuousness (ESTIUS and others) or to "gains from lust" (BAEHR and others). [Braune in the parallel passage extends the application of the relative clause to all the preceding forms of sin, which application is grammatically inadmissible here, though allowable there. Πλεονεξία, "covetousness," is marked by the article as the notorious form of sin, not merely introduced thus as forming a new category; for while it is another form of sin, there is an intimate connection in point of fact, "monsters of covetousness have been also monsters of lust." Covetousness has as its primary object—wealth—but there is no objection to expanding its meaning here, as TRENCH does. He intimates that the Greek Fathers use this word to designate both the sins of impurity and avarice, "even as the root out of which they alike grow; namely, the fierce and ever fiercer longing of the creature which has turned from God, to fill itself with the inferior objects of sense is one and the same." *Syn. N. T.* § 24. This is idolatry. It is worthy of notice too that idolatry and lust are connected historically, as well as in the O. T. *passim.*—R.]

Ver. 6. **For which things' sake the wrath of God cometh.**—Thus he adds a motive for the necessity of the exhortation, "mortify:" you must either kill or be killed. The relative refers to the sins mentioned above,* on account of which "the wrath of God cometh." See on Eph. v. 6. [Also for notes upon: **on the children of disobedience,** which Braune rejects here.—R.] The absence of "on the children of disobedience" denotes a reference to God's judgment on earth, under which the saints also suffer. The expression, which is to be distinguished from "the day of wrath" (Rom. ii. 5), and the context which is to be distinguished from 1 Thess. i. 10, "the wrath to come," does not refer to the future judgment (MEYER, BLEEK and others). [ELLICOTT, following Theophilus, refers it to punishment here and hereafter. There is this strong objection to Braune's view, that the New Testament does not represent the wrath of God as coming in any sense upon the saints. If the longer reading be adopted, his remark is also grammatically incorrect. Whatever interpretation be put upon ἐν οἷς, the following verse excludes the Colossian Christians from the threatened wrath.—R.]

Ver. 7. **Among whom ye also once walked.**—If "on the children of disobedience" be retained, the relative must be joined to that antecedent; otherwise it refers as δι' ἃ to the enumerated sins. "Once walked" denotes their conduct in different relations. See on Eph. ii. 2.—**When ye were living in them.**—[That is, in these sins, as the sphere of life. There is no tautology if the personal reference of the last clause be adopted.—R.] The verb, in emphatic

* [ALFORD, reading δι' ὅ, refers it to "idolatry" alone, and hence in his exegesis, makes it "the all-comprehending and crowning sin." MEYER, adopting the same reading, refers it to the whole immoral character just named.—R.]

position, marks the internal life with undisturbed gratification, while "walk" denotes the manifestations of it in thought, word and deed; the imperfect ("were living") refers to a continued state, the aorist ("walked") to the individual acts, corresponding thus with the meaning of the verbs. Their sinful walk was conditioned by their sinful nature, not merely by habit and circumstance. BENGEL: *Vivebatis tanquam in vestro principio, origine, elemento* (Gal. v. 25). Hence ἐν τούτοις and ἐν οἷς refer to the same antecedent. This is not tautological (MEYER) but emphatic: the first is not merely walking in heathenism, and the other a vicious life (SCHENKEL); the former is rather the "act" and the latter the "power" of sin (CALVIN) or the one "energy," ἐνεργεία, the other "habit of nature" (ESTIUS).—[It is obvious how much is gained in the exegesis of this verse, by retaining "on the children of disobedience." It then means: "Among which children of disobedience ye also walked, when ye were living in these sins." Surely with preponderant uncial authority, this exegetical advantage should decide in favor of retaining it, instead of being used to support the omission as *lectio difficilior*.—R.]

The second exhortation concerning their social relations to each other. Ver. 8–11.

Ver. 8. **But now ye also put off all these.**—"But now" (νυνὶ δέ), in contrast with "once," (ποτέ, ὅτε), is the present Christian state, which begins with conversion. Hence "put off" corresponds with "mortify" (ver. 5), or "put away from you" (Eph. iv. 31), and "ye also" puts the readers here beside other Christians, as in ver. 7 by other heathen. "All these" (τὰ πάντα) refers to what follows (WINER's *Gram.* p. 102); not to all those (ver. 5) and these also which follow (MEYER, SCHENKEL). [ELLICOTT, ALFORD follow MEYER, but Braune's view is more strictly grammatical. EADIE unfortunately makes the verb indicative instead of imperative.—R.]—**Anger, wrath, malice, evil-speaking, abusive communication out of your mouth.**—See on Eph. iv. 31. The last substantive is wanting there, but corresponds to αἰσχρότης καὶ μωρολογία (Eph. v. 4). It describes shameful speech in general, which, according to the context injures the neighbor, who hears it or of whom it is spoken, as "evil speaking" (βλασφημία). It is not to be applied to lewd speaking (HUTHER and others), at least not exclusively, though it may include it. The first three substantives form a climax, describing the internal condition, from perceptible excitement to passionateness which is its basis, then to deep-seated malicious nature; the other two refer to speech, hence to both is significantly added: "out of your mouth." It might be joined with "put off," but without any reference to the first three, since it would not be enough that among Christians these never found expression in words (SCHENKEL); they should not be found at all.

Ver. 9. **Lie not one to another.**—See Eph. iv. 25. Εἰς denotes the direction: belie not one another. [The practice is thus stamped as a social wrong (ELLICOTT). MICHAELIS observes that it is only in this Epistle and that to the Ephesians, that the Apostle warns his readers against *lying* (BARNES).—R.] The aorist participles which follow (vers. 9 b–11) give a motive for the injunction in vers. 8, 9 a.—**Seeing that ye have put off the old man.**—[The E. V. thus admirably expresses the force of the aorist participle ἀπεκδυσάμενοι.—R.] The aorist requires this as the Apostle's view: first, the experienced death and rising, then the active mortification of the members, first the experienced putting off the old man and putting on the new, then the active removal of what is contrary thereto, here a motive, drawn from what has preceded, is pre-supposed. Hence the Vulgate: *exspoliantes*, and BENGEL: "putting off," as if it were contemporaneous, are incorrect; LUTHER also: put off, as though it were an injunction. The verb is to be taken according to the parallel expression (Eph. iv. 22: ἀπόθεσθε) like the substantive ii. 11, and its object as in Eph. iv. 22. The old man, the sinful nature as it is before conversion and regeneration is to be laid off as a garment that has become useless, with all its peculiarities, hence: **with his deeds.**—Here is the stringent conclusion that what was detailed above must of course be put away. Comp. Rom. viii. 13; Gal. v. 24: "the flesh with the affections (παθήμασιν) and lusts."

Ver. 10. **And have put on the new man.**—The putting off and on, connected by καί, are to be regarded as contemporaneous, according to the principle: *natura et gratia non patiuntur vacuum* (nature and grace do not tolerate a vacuum); only in the domain of grace in distinction from the physical, the initiative is with the new man and in virtue of the divine power creating him. In contrast with παλαιός, old, we have in Eph. iv. 24, καινός, new, as not yet present, here νέος; παλαιός being therefore old, superannuated, senile; both are found in Eph. iv. 23, 24 (ἀνανεοῦσθαι—καινόν) and here in the adjective and added participle. The motive drawn from νέον, recent, young, as it were [newly entered and fresh state. ELLICOTT.—R.], lies in the danger prepared by the false teachers for Christians, who had been just now or not long converted.

The condition of the new man and his immediate task is more closely defined: **which is being renewed,** τὸν ἀνακαινούμενον.—The present participle denotes what is to go on in the present. The context requires the middle sense to denote the self-exertion, the active life. The new man is not anything complete at once, but in a state of vital growth, of further development, and that by the Holy Spirit (Tit. iii. 5). [This seems to contradict the last opinion that the participle is middle. ALFORD, ELLICOTT, WORDSWORTH all regard it as passive. The latter naturally suggests: "the new man was born in you at your *regeneration* in baptism, but needs the *daily renewal* of the Holy Ghost." Omit "in baptism," and the explanation will be generally received as correct. The passive or middle interpretation will be adopted as the stress is laid upon the divine or human side of the progressive work of sanctification, and yet as the Apostle is speaking of the new man, of our *becoming* holy, which lies back of active holiness, the passive is to be preferred. The new man is being renewed, rather than renewing himself.—R.] Comp. 2 Cor. iv. 16. The preposition ἀνά marks the further, upward, onward striving, which is then more closely defined:

Unto knowledge, after the image of him that created him.—"Unto knowledge" denotes the *end*, "after the image of Him that created him," the *norm*. According to ii. 2; i. 9, "knowledge" is not further characterized as a knowledge corresponding to the image of the Creator, for by thus regarding both clauses as one (HOFFMANN, MEYER), no natural sense is given. In this knowledge, which cannot be supplied by worldly wisdom, the new man must grow according to the image of his Creator, God; this image is Christ, since the Christian is a "new creature" (2 Cor. v. 17). There is an unmistakable allusion and reference to the first creation" (Gen. i. 26, 27). The second new creation is not to be separated from the first, the Christian is the genuine man, Christianity is true, God-willed humanity. [The latter clause is to be joined with "being renewed" (ALFORD, ELLICOTT). The final word "him" refers to the "new man." The passage means more than the restoration of the image of God lost by Adam. "It is certain that the image of God, in which Christ's Spirit re-creates us, will be as much more glorious than that, as the second man is more glorious than the first" (ALFORD). So EADIE *in loco*. Compare Eph. iv. 24.—R.]

Ver. 11. **Where there is neither Greek nor Jew, circumcision nor uncircumcision, Barbarian, Scythian, bond, free.**—"Where" refers to the region of the new creation in Christ, in contrast with the domain of creation without Christ; in the latter there is division, contrariety and discord; in the former union, fraternity. Just as in the parallel passage (Eph. iv. 25: "for we are members one of another"), this fellowship of the regenerate, the converted, requires truth and friendship among each other. It is incorrect to join "where," as =*qua in se*, to the yet remote "knowledge" alone, finding here its object now brought in (SCHENKEL). Ἔνι means, as in Homer: there is there, therein; *οὐκ ἔνι* denies division as respects nationality ("Greek and Jew"),* as respects religion ("circumcision and uncircumcision"), culture ("Barbarian, Scythian"), social status ("bond, free"). It is worthy of note, that, in nationality, the Greek who ruled in language is put before the Roman who held empire; in religion, Israel honored with revelation takes precedence; in culture, the step is from the uncultivated to the extreme savage (BENGEL: "Scythians, more barbarous than the Barbarians;" *βαρβαρώτατοι*), as in Rom. i. 14, the polished Greek not being again mentioned, while the summary is indicated by the omission of the conjunction; in the social category, the slave stands before the freeman to note the receptivity of the insignificant, and the exalting power of the gospel. Comp. Gal. iii. 28. [LANGE'S *Com.* pp. 88, 91.—R.]

But Christ is all and in all.—"But" presents the contrast to the condition in the region of the natural life; hence within the Church there is not difference, divisions; in spite of the distinctions, there is no schism there, but union, concord on the ground of unity; in all these four directions (*τὰ πάντα*), and in all the individual persons, the Christians ("in all," *καὶ ἐν πᾶσι*) is the same (*Χριστός*), "who alone occupies the whole, as the saying is, between stem and stern, and is both beginning and end" (CALVIN). Comp. 1 Cor. xv. 28; Gal. vi. 15. BENGEL: "Scythian is not Scythian, but Christ's; Barbarian is not Barbarian, but Christ's. Christ is all things, and that in all who believe. In Christ are new creatures." [MEYER: "The subject is placed at the end, for the greatest emphasis. *He*, the all determining principle of the new life and activity (*τὰ πάντα*) in all his believers (*ἐν πᾶσι*), forms the higher unity, in which all those old divisions and antitheses become without significance and as if no longer existing." ELLICOTT: "Christ is the aggregation of all things, distinctions, prerogatives, blessings, and moreover is in all, dwelling in all, and so uniting all in the common element of Himself."—R.]

* [The E. V. places the negation in the conjunctions. A more literal rendering would be: "There is not Greek and Jew, circumcision and uncircumcision," *etc.*—R.]

DOCTRINAL AND ETHICAL.

1. *Christian Exhortation.* All truly Christian exhortation to a moral life, internal and external alike, is directed mainly towards the right use of salvation as already possessed, towards its preservation in given circumstances, and the maintenance of conduct which meets the conditions of the rightly adjusted relations of the Christian. What is accepted and received as a germ through faith in the mercy of God in Christ, must be held fast, ever more vitally appropriated, nourished and developed practically in every direction. The regenerated believer, with the powers imparted to him by God, must now so work, that his action and conduct are as much his consenting, as God's continued action. Christ *for* us becomes Christ *in* us, and Christ *before* us becomes Christ *through* us.

2. *The world in and about the Christian.* With respect to its pleasure, sensual, especially sexual pleasure, he must strive after purity; with respect to its possessions, after contentment, in order not to fall away from God and under His wrath. [For the sin of sensuality is not only intimately connected with that of covetousness, but both are essentially idolatrous. Those "without God" (Eph. ii. 12) are "in the world," and the world's pleasures and possessions are put by them in the place of God.—R.]

3. *Towards his neighbor*, especially the brethren, there must be friendliness in disposition, word and truth.

4. *All sin must be repelled.* All that is opposed to what is required, both in its various shades from coarser to finer and finest, and in its different manifestations in act, word, thought, perception, from external to internal and inmost, must be contended against and repelled. *Only* what is sinful, yet *all* that is sinful, is contrary to Christianity and Christian character.

5. *Christ the point of unity.* Upon the absolute dignity of Christ and His central position toward the world (i. 17: "in Him all things subsist"), which points to His Divine Fulness (i. 19; ii. 9), to Him as the image of the Creator, rests the fact that He is the absolute point of unity, the central

and terminal point for men. What He is for the macrocosm He is also for the microcosm; He is the Second Adam, "a quickening spirit" (1 Cor. xv. 45). Hence the requirement to become a Christian and be a Christian must be deemed absolute for every man. Union with Christ is absolutely right, but it alone; contrasted with it all diversities as to nationality, confession, culture and station (ver. 11) are only relatively right; this they are, in so far as that absolute right remains unimpaired. Cosmopolitism in political and social life, union in denominational life are fruitless, or stunted products of the natural man working within the Church, when and where they do not recognize and maintain union with Christ, established above all unions. This is then the rule: one with Christ, united with one another. By this every Christian, that is every evangelical Christian, and every age, such as that of the Reformation, must be tested. [By it too must be tested many human organizations, which aim at uniting selfish men so as to contribute to the common good. Many social and political problems remain to be solved, but social science has not always remembered that "the putting on of the new man" alone brings man "where there is neither Greek nor Jew—bond nor free, but Christ all and in all."—R.] Compare the notes on Eph. iv. 22 sq.; v. 25; v. 5, 6.

HOMILETICAL AND PRACTICAL.

With every sin look at its concealed beginning in the heart, and its public issue in the judgment of God, who regards the heart.—Be not content with strength enough to prevent the sin of the heart from breaking out unto word and work. Be so ashamed of the past, that the present may not be as it was, and the future become far worse.—As a rule lying *to* others is closely connected with lying *about* others.

STARKE:—Improvement of the sinful life is as difficult for the flesh, as if the man should go to his death; for he is as much in love with fleshly lusts, as if this were his life. One of the chiefest members of the old man is "the lust of the flesh;" this secret poison hides in all. Though this fire be at once quenched in believers, yet, if they do not take care, the ever-glowing cinders may easily and quickly burst into a flame again. 2 Sam. xi. 2 sq.—Covetousness breaks not only the eighth and tenth commandments of the second table, but the first and second of the other also; hence the covetous are idolaters too.—Old rags we throw away; sin, which makes us so old and deformed and ugly before God, the Christian must so put away, that he not only restrains its outbreak, but also exhausts the spring itself, draining it more and more, even if he does not dry it up entirely.—[What a mark of our great corruption, that the tongue, which should be the means of doing our neighbor good, is so often the instrument to injure him.—R.]—The state of the regenerate is a putting off the old and a putting on the new man. Hence in a believer there are as it were, two men or a double nature, Spirit and flesh, which contend against each other. Gal. v. 17. The one from its corrupt propensity wills what is evil, the other from divine operation what is good.

RIEGER:—With *all* that belongs to the old nature, we are never done; yet we should not be grieved by the way: the quietest plan is with childlike mind to learn, and to regard the matter as ever in progress.—GERLACH:—The capacity for knowing and loving God is that alone wherein man excels the rest of creation, whereby he rules it. Is he a mirror of the Most High, then there is in him an image of God, which sin has not obliterated, but so polluted and marred that his own power can never more restore it.—When the image of God is restored in the soul, the partition-walls among men fall down.

SCHLEIERMACHER:—When Christians seem to us to be not yet permeated entirely by the new life in Christ, we may not thence infer an entire lack of the Spirit.—Paul admonishes them to put off their old members, not by virtue of the old man itself, but by virtue of the new and because the vital strength of the new man in them is presupposed.—This work of putting off the old man and putting on the new is a common one, and we should not believe in the fancy that somewhere it is wanting altogether.

PASSAVANT:—[Ver. 15. Covetousness which is idolatry can be found among Christians, in men who rejoice in a Christian education, and bow before the cross of Christ as the tree of life. The life of the covetous man is hid with his hoards in iron chests; the life of the Christian is "hid with Christ in God."—Ver. 7. It is better, if one has never walked in these things, if they have never been the elements of our life, for then our sanctification is easier. On this account we should learn the fear of God from our youth.]—Ver. 8. A single word, slipping from the mouth of the Christian can pollute the whole God-sanctified new man.—[Ver. 9. It is long before a tongue, hitherto unaccustomed to lie, becomes accustomed to the truth; this is the work of the Spirit of God, which is the Spirit of truth. —Ver. 11. God regards in us only His Son and His image, as He hates only the old man and his corruption.—R.]

[BURKITT:—Ver. 7. No argument will prevail more with a Christian to follow on the work of mortification closely for the time to come, than the remembrance of his long continuance in sin in time past.—Ver. 9. Lying makes a man like the devil, who was a liar as well as a murderer from the beginning.—Ver. 11. O blessed Jesus! Art thou thus all to me? I will labor to be all to thee; to give thee all that I am.—R.]

[HENRY:—Ver. 5. It is very observable, that among all the other instances of sin which good men are recorded in the Scripture to have fallen into; (and there is scarcely any but some or other in one or other part of their life, have fallen into;) there is no instance in all the Scripture of any good man charged with covetousness.—Ver. 9. Lying makes us like the devil (who is the father of lies), and is a prime part of the devil's image upon our souls.—Ver. 10. The new man is said to be renewed in knowledge; because an ignorant soul cannot be a good soul. Light is the first thing in the new creation, as it was in the first.—R.]

[EADIE:—Ver. 5. If the heart is dead let all the organs which it once vivified and moved die too—nay, put them to death. Let them be killed from want of nutriment and exercise.—This desire of having more, and yet more, is idolatry. What it craves it worships, what it worships it makes its portion.—Ver. 11. 1. Such distinctions do not prevent the on-putting of the new man. 2. In the church, prior and external distinctions do not modify the possession of spiritual privilege and blessing.—WORDSWORTH: —Ver. 5. You must be dead to earth, in order to life in heaven. While we mortify our members upon the earth, we quicken our members in heaven.—R.]

---

b) Exhortation to Christian love one toward another, and to glorifying the name of Christ in word and work.

CHAPTER III. 12–17.

12 Put on therefore, as the elect of God, holy [or saints][1] and beloved, bowels of
13 mercies [mercy], kindness, humbleness of mind, meekness, longsuffering: Forbear-
ing one another, and forgiving one another [each other],[2] if any man have a quarrel
[or complaint, μομφήν] against any: even as Christ[3] forgave you, so also *do* ye [*doing*
14 yourselves].[4] And above [But over][5] all these things *put on* charity [love],
15 which[6] is the bond of perfectness. And let the peace of God [Christ][7] rule in your
hearts, to the which also ye are [were] called in one body; and be ye thankful.
16 Let the word of Christ dwell in you richly [;] in all wisdom; [omit semi-colon]
teaching and admonishing one another in psalms and [omit and][8] hymns [*and*]
spiritual songs, singing with grace [in grace[9] singing] in your hearts to the Lord
17 [God].[10] And [everything] whatsoever ye do in word or deed, *do* all in the name
of the Lord Jesus,[11] giving thanks to God and the Father [God the Father][12] by
him.

[1] Ver. 12.—[Ἅγιοι, "saints," if used substantively as Braune holds. See EXEG. NOTES. There are several quite unimportant various readings in this verse; οἰκτιρμοῦ and πραΰτητα are preferable to οἰκτιρμῶν and πραότητα of the Rec.—R.]

[2] Ver. 13.—[Ἀλλήλων—ἑαυτοῖς; there is nothing in the E. V. to indicate that different words follow the two participles.—R.]

[3] Ver. 13.—Instead of ὁ Χριστός, C. [K. L., most versions, Tischendorf, Meyer, Ellicott, Wordsworth, Rec.], A. B. and others [Lachmann, Alford] read ὁ κυρίος. ℵ. ὁ θεός. Besides, θεὸς τοῦ Χριστοῦ, *deus in christo*, occur.

[4] Ver. 13.—[To supply an imperative, with E. V., breaks the construction unnecessarily. If anything be supplied in English it should be the auxiliary participle as above.—R.]

[5] Ver. 14.—[Ἐπὶ πᾶσιν δὲ τούτοις. "But over all these;"—"above all" is ambiguous.—R.]

[6] Ver. 14.—A. B. C. F. G. and others read ὅ; ὅς in ℵ. is a correction, as well as the later ἥτις; [Rec., grammatical emendation (Meyer, Alford).—R.]

[7] Ver. 15.—[Τοῦ Χριστοῦ on the authority of ℵ. A. B. C. and most versions, modern editors generally, instead of τοῦ θεοῦ, Rec., followed by E. V.—R.]

[8] Ver. 16.—Καί before ὕμνοις and ᾠδαῖς added from Eph. v. 19.

[9] Ver. 16.—[Braune omits the article before χάριτι and renders "in thanksgiving." But it is retained by most modern editors on the authority of B. and others. See EXEG. NOTES.—R.]

[10] Ver. 16.—[Τῷ θεῷ is the reading of the mass of MSS., adopted by most modern editors; κυριῷ, Rec. Lachmann, probably taken from Eph. v. 19.—R.]

[11] Ver. 17.—B reads κυρίου Ἰησοῦ, ℵ. inserts Χριστοῦ, others omit κυρίου. [Lachmann, Ellicott, Wordsworth follow the last reading; Tischendorf, Alford, Rec. that of B.—R].

[12] Ver. 17.—[Καί, probably from Eph. v. 20, is omitted in ℵ. A. B. C., by Lachmann, Tischendorf, Meyer, Alford, Ellicott, Wordsworth.—R.]

EXEGETICAL AND CRITICAL.

The virtues of the new man in intercourse with the brethren (vers. 12–14).

Ver. 12. **Put on therefore.**—To the "have put on the new man" (ver. 10) there is joined, as a consequence ("therefore"), the positive precept, which finds a motive, as a continuing and valid requirement, in the "being renewed;" although they have put on the new man, they have yet to take up anew the single parts. [ELLICOTT, following HOFFMANN, thinks οὖν has here more of its reflexive force, taking up what has been said and continuing it: "as you have put on the new man, put on all its characteristic qualities." But even this paraphrase implies a "moral consequence." "For although the putting on of the new man as a fact *has* historically occurred through the conversion to Christ, yet it has, according to the nature of the new man, its continued acts, which *should* occur, viz., through the appropriation of those virtues, which the new man as such must possess" (MEYER).—R.]

As the elect of God, [**holy** or] **saints and beloved,** conditions the justice of the precept and the indispensableness of complying with it. "As" gives prominence to the actual condition, relation, in which they stand.—"Elect of God" is used substantively as Matt. xxiv. 31; Mark xiii. 27; Luke xviii. 7; Rom. viii. 33; Tit. i. 1: "saints" (ἅγιοι) as Rom. i. 7; xv. 25, 26, 31; xvi. 2, 15; 1 Cor. i. 2, etc. Ἅγιος τοῦ θεοῦ (Mark i. 24; Luke iv. 34; Jno. vi. 69) is a description of the Christian; ἅγιοι αὐτοῦ ("His saints") also occurs (2 Thess. i. 10). The position of the genitive (τοῦ θεοῦ) however requires it to be joined with the first term ("elect"). "Beloved" is also used substantively as Eph. i. 6. The climax here is unmistakable: as to the ground, they are without desert "elect of God," as to their condition they are "saints," as to their relation to God, they are, as the perfect denotes, the continued objects of His love (1 Thess. i. 4; 2 Thess. ii. 13). BENGEL: "the order of words corresponds exquisitely with the order of things: eternal *election* precedes sanctification in time, the sanctified feel love, and then imitate it." The last, firmly founded on the preceding, has the stress laid on it. All three are correlatives of "putting on the new man," which pre-supposes the "election of God" (vers. 10, 11). Hence neither are the last two substantives and the first an adjective (BLEEK), nor the first subject and the two others predicates (MEYER, BENGEL). [So also EADIE, ALFORD and ELLICOTT. Either view is admissible on grammatical grounds. ELLICOTT urges that the force of the exhortation rests on their character as "elect," while ALFORD insists that as ἐκλεκτοί is a word, which must find its ground independently of us in the absolute will of God, it cannot be an adjunctive attribute of the other two. On the whole the view of MEYER, followed by the commentators just mentioned, and implied in the E. V., is preferable. For it seems better accordant with Paul's method of stating the truth of Divine grace, and with the position of the words to lay the emphasis upon the phrase "elect of God," and not to regard the three phrases as co-ordinate. "The consciousness of this extraordinary privilege, of being the elect of God, who as such are holy and beloved of God—how it must have affected the conscience of the readers and aroused them to the very virtues, corresponding with so high a position, which Paul here enjoins!" MEYER.—R.]

Bowels of mercy, kindness, humbleness of mind, meekness, long-suffering.—"Bowels of mercy" stands foremost; *viscera* with the quality of mercy, of which they are the seat. Phil. ii. 1, we find "bowels and mercies." The first word denotes what is inmost, most individual (Phil. i. 8; Philem. 12; 2 Cor. vi. 12: 1 Jno. iii. 17). Luke i. 78, "tender mercy of God" lit., "bowels of mercy of God" is similar. So Eph. iv. 32, "tender-hearted," "heart of mercy" (εὔσπλαγχνοι). The manifestations of mercy then follow, forming a climax; "kindness" which as the opposite of "severity" (Rom. xi. 22) helps outward need, "humbleness of mind" (ταπεινοφροσύνην) which recognizes our own unworthiness and the superiority or talent of a brother, "meekness," which as the opposite of "fierceness" (ἀγριότης), is mild toward faults which are blameworthy, and "long-suffering" which restrains itself so as to quietly bear reprehensible injuries in the hope of a better mind and consequent improvement on the part of the offender. See on Eph. iv. 2, 32. TITTMANN, *Synon.* I. 140–142. [Comp. TRENCH; *Syn.* New Testament, *sub vocibus.* He makes "meekness" to be at first in respect to God, then toward men as growing out of this. But in this case it is primarily toward man, though implying the other as its ground (ALFORD, ELLICOTT, while EADIE excludes the reference to God).—R.]

Ver. 13. **Forbearing one another and forgiving each other.**—These participles define the modality of the exhibition of the virtues just mentioned; they must be appropriated by practice which makes the master. The present tense indicates permanence. On "forbearing," see Eph. iv. 2, on "forgiving," Eph. iv. 32. "One another" (ἀλλήλων) marks the purely reciprocal, mutual enduring, forbearing; "each other" (ἑαυτοῖς) indicates at the same time also, that they have experienced such forgiveness from without, from Him who is their Example. That which is difficult to bear and forgive in others, is not simply what one does against us, but also what he does in general, what is displeasing, unpleasant, or offensive in his manner, whatever in his relations to us may give occasion for blame (μομφήν), so that the participles refer to all the preceding virtues, not to the last one only. BENGEL arbitrarily distinguishes: forbearing in present offences, forgiving past offences.

If any man have a complaint against any.—[Μομφή, only here in N. T., but classical: "ground of blame," "just cause of complaint." —R.] TITTMANN, *Syn.* I. 29, distinguishes ἄμεμπτος and ἄμωμος—each is free from blame, the former because it is perfect and absolute in its members, the latter because it is free from vice; in the former nothing more can be desired, in the latter there is nothing to be reprehended. On this account, as well as because πρός, not κατά, is here used, a more general relation than that of hostility is indicated; this must be regarded as referring in general to an experience occurring every where, yet mildly described hypothetically, that one can easily find something to blame in another, as is indicated above. [The Greek conditional protasis here used always implies that the hypothesis is correct.—R.]

Even as Christ forgave you, so also doing yourselves.—Χαριζόμενοι is to be supplied in thought (WINER's *Gram.* p. 526). Hence there is no parenthesis here, nor a disrupted sentence, as though an imperative were to be supplied. [The E. V. gives the imperative, which is objectionable; ELLICOTT preserves the construction by rendering as above—R.] This expression is explained, ii. 13; Eph. iv. 32. Here we have "Christ," in Eph. i. 1: "God in Christ;" this variation will explain ii. 13. BENGEL is excellent: *Christus, cui maxima fuerat nobiscum querendi causa.* Accordingly "the grace (χάρις) of the Lord Jesus Christ" is often spoken of. "As" denotes the mode of forgiveness, as Luke vii. 37–47; xxiii. 34, not the accomplishment of reconciliation with God by His death.

Ver. 14. **But over all these things put on love.**—"Love," as in i. 4, 8; Eph. iv. 2, is to be taken as "brotherly love," which must come over all those virtues, upon them (ἐνδύσασθε, ver. 12). [So E. V. supplies "put on," though "above" may or may not have the local or semi-local (Ellicott) force, which ἐπί here conveys. Eadie renders "in addition to," weakening the force of the passage. Wordsworth quotes Clement, who apparently refers "love" to "love to God."—R.] In reference to this "love," the Apostle adds: **which is the bond of perfectness.**—By the neuter [ὅ, not ἥτις—R.] the putting on of love as an act, is denoted. [The article is wanting—hence Braune renders "a bond." Ellicott says the omission may be due to the verb substantive.—R.] Σύνδεσμος, the encircling band, reminds us of a girdle, put over the clothes to hold them together. The genitive therefore adds those virtues included under the category of "perfectness," as Acts viii. 23: "the bond of iniquity;" Eph. iv. 3: "bond of peace." It is parallel with "in love" (Eph. iv. 2). Comp. Rom. xiii. 10: "love is the fulfilling of the law." The Pythagoreans called friendship "the bond of all the virtues." Hence ὅ is not to be rejected and ἥτις substituted (Bleek), nor ἀγάπη to be regarded as neuter (Meyer); ii. 19 is not a parallel case, since there the masculine is used, and the construction is according to the sense, as Christ is conceived of under κεφαλή. Nor is love to be regarded as the upper garment (Meyer), nor "bond" as "sum total" (*Insbegriff*, Olshausen), nor as the efficient cause of "perfectness" (Schenkel); nor yet is the genitive to be taken attributively as that of quality (Grotius). [To refer "which" to the putting on of love is a doubtful interpretation. It does not agree so well with the figurative representation of the Apostle, who has already been speaking (ver. 12) of what they were to put on, and seems to be mentioning here the last garment required to complete the attire. To make the act of putting on the "bond of perfectness" would be an unnecessary obscuring of the metaphor; especially as we may readily take ἀγάπη absolutely. There is the same objection perhaps to Meyer's view, that love is here represented as an upper garment, but a close-fitting upper garment might well be, at the same time, the bond which enclosed and held together all the others. Adopting this view, we may not only say, that love itself is "that bond which unites all the graces into completeness and symmetry" (Eadie), but "without love there is no perfectness; this has its *conditio sine qua non* in the including of all its other parts in love" (Meyer). Love is the principal of all the other virtues, but is here named last, as if supplementary, because of the figure. Braune's view of the genitive, which is that of Meyer, is to be preferred to that of Ellicott, who regards it as a genitive of the subject: "love is the bond which belongs to, is the distinctive feature of perfection." Alford well remarks: "Those who find here justification by works, must be very hard put to discover support for that doctrine."—R.]

The frame of mind in which Christian love is to be exercised. Ver. 15. **And let the peace of Christ rule in your hearts.**—This is not a command, but only a wish, the fulfilment of which is of importance. The subject, which in Phil. iv. 7 is "the peace of God," is that peace wrought by God through Christ in the Holy Ghost, which, according to Jno. xiv. 27 ("my peace I give unto you"), can be accurately termed "of Christ." (See Winer's *Gram.* p. 175.) It is the calm of the soul resting on the consciousness of having a reconciled God and Father, in Christ the Saviour.—[Ellicott says, the idea in Phil. iv. 7 "is substantially the same, except that perhaps peace is there contemplated as in its antithesis to anxious worldliness, while here it is rather to the hard, unloving and unquiet spirit that mars the union of the one body." It must not be limited to, though it certainly includes, mutual concord.—R.]—The verb βραβεύω, "to be an umpire," and as such to award the prize as well as regulate the contest, marks the administrative activity in distinction from the legislative found in βασιλεύειν. [The idea of presiding, ordering, ruling, is to be retained; the reference to bestowing (Wordsworth), or even winning a prize, which some commentators find here, is forbidden by the phrase which follows.—R.]—The phrase "in your hearts," ἐν ταῖς καρδίαις ὑμῶν, is not="in you," ἐν ὑμῖν (ver. 16); it refers to the inner, most individual relations, where the peace of Christ is to rule; it is not therefore to be referred to the unity of believers among themselves (Greek Fathers, Calvin, Grotius, Meyer).

To the which also ye were called in one body.—["To the which," almost=for, into it (Ellicott).—R.] This peace is the immediate end of the calling; this calling is marked by "also" (καί), which joins it to "rule," as that to which the rule of peace has to correspond. The result of the consummation of the calling on the part of God, and of its acceptance on the part of men, is described by "in one body" This refers to the Church as the body of Christ (Eph. iv. 4; ii. 16); which is the sphere and place, in which this calling is consummated and the called are to move. Therefore it is not=εἰς ἓν σῶμα (Grotius), nor is the Church as an organism the object of the Divine calling (Schenkel), which is addressed to individual persons. The calling in itself and the implanting in the Church constitute a benefit, important on account of the peace joined with it, and obligating to friendliness toward the brother, who has become partaker of the same; hence Paul adds: **and be ye thankful** [*sc.* to God.—R.]—Comp. ii. 7; iv. 2; Eph. v. 4. Knowledge of the benefit of the calling and the peace, together with gratitude therefor, must increase. The adjective (εὐχάριστοι) does not occur elsewhere in N. T. Incorrectly rendered "amiable," "friendly," by Jerome, Erasmus, Baehr, [Calvin].

Helps to the exercise of Christian love. Vers. 16, 17.

Ver. 16. **Let the word of Christ dwell in you richly.**—"The word of Christ" is the word which He has spoken and caused to be proclaimed (1 Thess. i. 8; iv. 15; 2 Thess. iii. 1), and which communicates the inward peace, directing and leading to right conduct toward the brethren: "the word through which ye were called" (Bengel); elsewhere called "the word of God," (i. 25; 1 Cor. xiv. 36; 2 Cor. ii. 17; iv. 2) from its highest cause, "of truth" (Eph. i. 5, 13) from its purport, "of life" (Phil. ii. 16) from its effect. But it must have a permanent locality, "as in a temple" (BENGEL): let it dwell "among you," as the context demands. It is not="in your hearts" (ver. 15) "in you" (THEODORET, BEZA and others). [EADIE: "within you;" MEYER, ALFORD: in you as a church, which seems to be Braune's view. Preferable on the whole, and suggestive of the truth, that want of general diffusion of the word of Christ among the people "richly," much prevents their obeying the following precept.—R.] "Richly" relates to substance, hence, not used in a stunted, abbreviated eclectic fashion. ["Not with a scanty foothold, but with a large and liberal occupancy" (EADIE).—R.] It does not refer to frequency of use, or to the members of the Church=among many (SCHENKEL).

In all wisdom teaching and admonishing one another in psalms, hymns and spiritual songs.—["In all wisdom" is joined with what follows. The construction is thus rendered more harmonious; the preceding clause has its emphatic adverb last, and the two qualifying participial clauses each begin with an adverbial phrase of manner. EADIE, following the pointing of TISCHENDORF, joins "psalms," *etc.*, with the second clause, but this destroys the correspondence, while the objection he urges, in regard to psalms and hymns as the material of instruction, is not in keeping with his own quotation from Basil's encomium on the Psalms.—R.] The participles, which are to be joined with "you" in the nominative, just as in Eph. iv. 1-3 (WINER'S *Gram.* p. 532), refer to the application and use of the word present among them, describe the manner in which the word dwells among them. This explains "speaking to yourselves" (Eph. v. 19). The first verb indicates the intellectual, the other the moral reference. To both belong the definition of manner "in all wisdom" (comp. i. 28), which is placed first emphatically, and the asyndetic datives which define the means to be used [or "the vehicle in which" the teaching and admonishing was communicated (MEYER).—R.]. These means act the more instructively and effectively, the more familiar one is with them, for the hymn grows out of the word of God and of Christ, and these grow into such songs, as the Bible, the Psalter and Church history attest. TERTULLIAN: *Post aquam mannalem et lumina, ut quisque de scripturis sacris vel proprio ingenio potest, provocatur in medium canere.* Comp. Eph. v. 19. The reference is to public worship, to the use of the word of Christ and singing at the *agapæ* and in the family circle; it should not be limited to the latter (MEYER).

In grace singing in your hearts to God.—[Braune adopts the reading ἐν χάριτι, and therefore renders "in gratitude" (*Dankbarkeit*), but with LACHMANN, TISCHENDORF, MEYER, ALFORD, ELLICOTT, WORDSWORTH, it is better to retain the well supported article: τῇ χάριτι then refers to Divine grace, the element to which the singing was to be circumscribed,—that which should accompany it.—R.] The clause corresponds in its structure with the foregoing; "in all wisdom,"—"in grace," the participles, then the closer definition; they are coördinate therefore. It is altogether improper to join both with "be ye thankful," making "let the word . . . richly" parenthetical, or to connect "in psalms," *etc.*, with this clause (SCHENKEL), on the ground that singing instruction is inconceivable, or to join ἐν χάριτι with πνευματικαῖς (LUTHER: spiritual, lovely songs). Since "singing" on account of "in your hearts" (see ver. 15) must be referred to something internal, and "to God" indicates its direction, "in grace" must be a closer definition of the singing; "in gratitude," as 1 Cor. x. 30. The meaning of χάρις is like *gratia.* It cannot mean "in gracefulness" (iv. 6; Eph. iv. 29; ERASMUS, SCHENKEL), nor in grace, nor with the article: in the grace impelling thereto (CHRYSOSTOM, MEYER). [If the article be retained, this is undoubtedly the meaning; not only because *usus loquendi* favors such a view, but because the other meaning: "thankfully" would be a flat and unmeaning anticipation of "giving thanks" below (ALFORD).—R.] The opinion that the phrase "in your hearts" refers to the existing abuse of singing with the mouth (THEOPHYLACT) is not justified, since the reading is not τῇ καρδίᾳ, and the tone which accompanied instruction is here noted. [Yet the former clause seems to refer to singing with the mouth, and this to that "in the silence of the heart" (MEYER).—R.]

Ver. 17. **And everything whatsoever ye do in word or deed, do all in the name of the Lord Jesus.**—It is evident that "do" must be supplied with "all" (πάντα), and that "all in the name of the Lord Jesus" corresponds with "everything whatsoever" [πᾶν ὅ τι—the absolute nominative.—R.]; "everything whatsoever" referring to individual things, and "all" taking up the same collectively. On this account it is incorrect to explain it: "in every thing which ye do, do all in the name," *etc.* (MEYER), or that out of the doing in general the doing in particular proceeds (SCHENKEL). [EADIE makes the plural "individualing" also.—R.] The repetition as well as the position of πᾶν, together with the giving of a category ("in word or deed"), and the marking of the individual acts (ὅ τι) as well as the conditional form (ἐὰν ποιῆτε) require that it be understood of the entire action (BENGEL: *facitis lato sensu ponitur, ut etiam τὸ loqui incendat*) and this should be "in the name of the Lord Jesus." This is joined by "and" to "the word of Christ" (ver. 16). In addition to His Word, His Name, His Person should be availing to us; the former in us, and we in the latter, as in the life-sphere dearest to us, out of which we never go, the element which we cannot lack. See Eph. v. 20; Phil. ii. 10. The variation from "Christ" (ver. 16) and "Jesus" here makes us think of the model of the Incarnate One in the form of a servant. "In the name" is not "with invocation of" (CHRYSOSTOM and others). BENGEL extends it too far: *ut perinde sit, ac si Christus faciat, ver. 11, vel certi ut Christo omnia probetis.*

Giving thanks to God the Father by him.—The participle refers to the mood which should ever attend their "doing" (see ii. 7; Eph. v. 20), and which expresses itself in hymn and song. The repetition (vers. 15–17) marks the importance of "giving thanks." On "God the Father," see Eph. i. 3; v. 20; vi. 23; Col. i. 2. As "Father" is without any closer definition, it means of course, "of Jesus." [ALFORD, however, justly remarks: "the words must be taken as approximating in sense to that more technical meaning which they now bear, without exclusive reference to either our Lord or ourselves."—R.]—Δι' αὐτοῦ, "through him," is, according to Eph. v. 20,="in the name of the Lord," marking more strongly the mediation of the thanksgiving, the Christian sentiment (Rom. i. 8; vii. 25). There is nothing here to indicate opposition to angel-worship (THEODORET, BAEHR). [ALFORD: "'through Him,' as the one channel of all communication between God and ourselves, whether of grace coming to us, or of thanks coming from us. 'No man cometh unto the Father but by me' (δι' ἐμοῦ), Jno. xiv. 6." MEYER: "For Jesus, as the personal, historical Mediator of the Messianic Salvation through His atoning work, is therefore for the Christian consciousness the *Mediator* of thanksgiving; He it is, through *whose* favor the Christian can and does give thanks."—R.]

DOCTRINAL AND ETHICAL.

1. *Conduct determined by condition.** The Christian is "elect," "holy," "beloved." In the first there is a negative reference to the mass and world, out of which he is taken, in the second a positive reference to the same, asserting that he is consecrated to God, while the third declares, positively also, that he is an object of the love of God; the first denotes simply the occurred fact, the third gives prominence to the continued effect, while the second sets forth the *status*. The relation is constantly defined as passive; the Christian has experienced something, without previous merit or meritorious assistance. This conditions and promotes his conduct, with thankful zeal, in order to show in response what he has experienced, *viz.*, love. [The Apostle here as always (comp. Rom. viii.; Eph. i.) treats of "election" as a fact, which is made known to us, in order to awaken love in us. It is doubtless necessary that it be at times handled polemically and dogmatically, but he uses it most like Paul, who speaks of it as a fact, revealed by God, evidenced as true of persons by corresponding facts, *viz.*, Divine acts of grace which make men "holy and beloved," and in itself an act of Divine grace, which the Christian can so apprehend as to derive from it a constant motive to such Christian graces as the Apostle here enumerates. So far from being made thereby harsh, proud and unforgiving, they "*therefore*" put on bowels of mercy, kindness, humbleness of mind, *etc.*—R.]

2. *The new Christian condition or relation* is first of all a relation toward God, yet it at the same time influences essentially the relation between those concerned and transferred by it. It is precisely by this that it must prove itself, the religious by the social. First of all this relation of man to God brings a discord into the individual himself, because it divides him into the receding old man, and the advancing new man. The principle of the old man, selfishness, is made by this relation, to yield or become yielding to the principle of the new man, *viz.*, self-denying and world-denying love and the social virtues: mercy, kindness, humility, meekness, long-suffering, appear as necessary manifestations of the reality of the relations towards God. These virtues must show themselves toward the sins, faults and offences of a brother, just as God's love has shown and still shows itself toward us.

3. *Christian love is active.* In the social Christian virtues there is no weakness, effeminacy, indifference. It is not indifferent indolence but active *love*, energetically breaking out in these as its forms. The Apology for the Augsburg Confession, iii. § 110, rightly repels the assertion of the Romanists, that love justifies, since it does not establish the relation to God, only proves that it has been established, in and by the conduct toward the brethren.

4. *Christ*, in whom God's love has become and still becomes our portion, remains the only model, the exclusive norm.

5. *His peace in the heart, His word in the Church*, are the attendants of Christian love, the former as its tone, the latter as the means of promoting it; without the first, rest, confidence and joy were wanting, without the other, certainty, correctness and strength.

6. *The Christian Song*, deriving its contents and its growth from the word of God, promoted culture and progress in the Christian life; it is in itself a sermon from the Divine word, and has its value in the fact that it is such. The Christian entrusted with it, should use it in the wider and narrower circle of his associates. Produced by spiritual, natural endowments from the use of God's word and experience in life and heart, it is an excellent means of edification and growth for the new man. [The question of Psalmody and public praise, is to be settled by (ver. 16) and similar passages. *The word of Christ* is to be its substance; all that is not of the word of Christ is to be excluded, all that is, may be included. Hence the Psalter in the main source, but not the only one. "In all wisdom" is its mode, hence mere rhymes of a pious turn are not included. Its end is mutual edification, not entertainment, hence the hymn must be adapted to this end, and the singing of it "to edification." Those who cannot sing to edification may sing in their hearts, but the text implies that "this teaching and admonishing" is not the privilege of a few, but of Christians as a body.—R.]

7. *The walk in fellowship with Christ*, the practice of Christian virtues, advances us from the rudiments of a pupil to the perfection of a master. Not for merit, but for growth, Christian walk and Christian virtue are indispensable.

8. *Gratitude*, corresponding with the status into which we have been brought, with the glory of our relation to God, is most important and constant in Christian conduct. [Hence the excellence of those symbols, which treat of Christian morality under the head of the gratitude of God for redemption. See Heidelberg Catechism. This view guards alike against the extremes of antinomianism and legalism.—R.]

* [I have thus attempted to retain the neatness of Braune's sentence: "*Das Verhalten ist durch das Verhältniss bestimmt*," with indifferent success.—R.]

HOMILETICAL AND PRACTICAL.

The Christian's station, ornament, strength, tone and weapon.—All morality takes its rise in religion, which is essentially love, given of God, who gave Himself and accepted us, or peace, in which all the antagonisms within the personality of the man himself in his conscience and will, or between himself and the world or his neighbor, or the nearest of all, *i. e.*, God the Lord Himself, was and is taken away.—Love is not a garment, that can be thrown over other virtues, but the soul of all to hold them together, their germ and impulse, their strength and beauty.—Ought the word of God to do well in you, then live in it, and let it live into you.—It is rudeness of mind to have no taste for the sacred poetry of the Church, the flowering of the Divine word in a gifted human soul, and a misfortune to have no benefit of it in the joy and sorrow of life.—A stamp you must have, lo, nothing is current in his eyes but His own Image.

STARKE:—Nothing gives the devil so much room to come into the heart as hatred and anger; God's children drive out both by meekness and spit on the embers, so that they may not break out into a fire.—He who bids us put up the sword, allows us still a shield for our protection; He who has commanded us to be as doves, has desired that we be "wise as serpents."—A little child, that falls so often and so easily, is lifted up and carried; so gently and tenderly must weak Christians be dealt with. The world sets itself to righting and fighting, if attacked even by a cross word; but a Christian overcomes all by forgiving and yielding; he yields his own right [not the right, however,] and does not think of revenging himself.—That the wolf devours the lamb is nothing uncommon, but that one lamb eats another is deplorable and unnatural; we who are Christ's sheep will cherish love toward one another.—Behold the necessity of household devotion. All others have their assemblies, merchants, mechanics, *etc.*, yes even the Godless, that they may mock at God and His word, should not believers then establish their holy assemblies?—We must thank God not only for His benefits, but also for His fatherly chastisements. "Both in His gifts and in His chastisements, praise Him, who either wins thee by giving, that thou mayest not want, or punishes thee when wandering, that thou mayest not perish" (AUGUSTINE).

SCHLEIERMACHER:—Christian social life: 1) what the deeds peculiar to the new man are; 2) what is distributed to each by virtue of these peculiarities of the new man; 3) the common rule for every one.—Controversy does not divide love and is not against the Christian spirit, if it only proceeds from a desire after nothing save what is true and right.—Love "the bond of perfectness:" 1) by which all imperfections are balanced; 2) by which all that bears in itself only the appearance of the new man, not its true spirit, is overcome; 3) by which we become helpful to others.

PASSAVANT:—Forbearance may be difficult in certain cases; forgiveness is harder still.—However necessary this gift (God's word) from above is, it will be learned from daily experience, that the Christians here and there are a very sensitive folk, not permitting themselves to be easily admonished or exhorted, hence the so frequent halts and retreats.—The first Christians from among the Jews soon found in their Psalms from earlier ages, thoughts and words for the later inward experiences, for the thanksgiving, praise and adoration of their new life; and those who came out of heathenism, listened with wonder, when these words of the sacred singers were transferred into their own language, and learned thence the quiet joys and devotions of God's children in Israel. But soon too under their beautiful sky new Psalms and hymns in their own Greek tongue were born out of the deep inspiration and the holy and happy feelings of their redeemed souls. This glorious gift of spiritual song contributed greatly to the spread of the pure gospel in the age of the Reformation. The great Reformer of the Germans with his friends soon became their choristers, and it is a precious privilege to follow them and so many God-inspired men of after days in singing these beautiful Psalms and sweet hymns.

GENZKEN:—The choice communion garment of the children of God: 1) who gives it to them (ver. 15); 2) how it is woven (vers. 12-15); 3) how we should put it on.—HARLESS:—The proper self-education for the maintenance of divine love and divine peace: 1) constant practice in obedience to God's word; 2) sanctification of all our doings in the name of the Lord Jesus; 3) unceasing thanksgiving for God's unmerited grace in Christ.—SCHNUR:—Spiritual songs: 1) Eagles of Christianity; 2) missionaries of Protestantism; 3) heart-preachers of our nation; 4) mouth of our worship; 5) the Apostles in our houses; 6) the crown of our congregations.—WOLF:—The comfort and joy of the Christian in spiritual songs. They serve: 1) as witnesses of the truth from all stations for the strengthening of our faith; 2) as confessions from the inner life of experienced Christians for the soothing of our spirits; 3) as awakening voices of the Spirit to enliven our own meditation.—KÖHLER:—The new man, as St. Paul depicts him, outshines all the lustre of the world! 1) His richly-colored garment; 2) his golden girdle; 3) his heart's peace; 4) the weapons of his hand.—PRÖHLE:—Bible and hymn book, two precious household treasures; 1) their worth; 2) their use.—Love in all human unions, the most perfect bond: 1) the noblest; 2) the gentlest; 3) the firmest.—Exhortation to Christian families to engage in family worship; it is 1) a venerable custom inherited from our fathers, though unfortunately disappearing from many houses; 2) deeply grounded in the character of Christianity, as well as in the nature of the family circle; 3) of the most blessed influence upon the home life itself.

[BEVERIDGE:—Ver. 17. Doing all in the name of the Lord Jesus. 1) What is meant by "the name of the Lord Jesus." *a.* Lord of all, *b.* Jesus, Saviour. *c.* Lord Jesus by the Incarnation. *d.* Mighty works in His name. 2) And we ought to do all, *etc.*, *a.* only what God commands or allows. *b.* in a firm faith in His Holy name. *c.* for His glory. 3) Instances of things thus done in God's word. Religious assemblies, Sacraments, Thanksgiving, Censures of the church, Resisting the devil, even giving a cup of cold water. All that a Christian *may* do, can be done in His name.—R.]

[BURKITT:—Ver. 12. Humility is a certain evidence of our holiness, because it is a great part of our holiness.—Ver. 13. He must have no friends, that will have a friend with no faults, consequently Christians stand in need of forgiveness from each other.—Ver. 14. 1) The upper garment is larger and broader than the rest; so ought charity to extend itself to all persons and upon all occasions. 2) The upper garment is usually fairer than the rest; so doth charity shine brightest amongst all the graces. 3) The upper garment distinguishes the general orders and degrees of men; thus Christians are known by love, as by a livery; it is the bond that Christ's sincere disciples wear.—Ver. 16. If the heart and affections be not stirred in this duty of singing, the outward grace, though never so graceful availeth nothing.—R.]

[HENRY:—Ver. 12. They who owe so much to mercy, ought to be merciful to all who are proper objects of mercy.—There must not only be an humble carriage but an humble mind.—Ver. 13. We need the same good turn from others which we are obliged to show them.—Ver. 15. The work of thanksgiving to God is such a sweet and pleasant work, that it will help to make us sweet and pleasant towards all men.—Ver. 16. The gospel is the word of Christ, which is come to us; but that is not enough, it must *dwell* in us, or *keep house*, as a master, who has a right to prescribe and direct to all under his roof.—Ver. 17. They who do all things in Christ's name, will never want matter of thanksgiving to God the Father.—R.]

[EADIE:—Ver. 14. "Love the bond of perfectness." Bound up in this zone, every Christian excellence fills its own place, and keeps it, and the whole character is sound, does not distort itself by excess, nor enfeeble itself by defect.—Ver. 15. A peace, which is not the peace of Christ, is often rudely disturbed, for it is but a dream and a slumber in the midst of volcanic powers, which are employing the time in gathering up their energies for a more awful conflict.—Ver. 16. Such ought to be the habitual respect to Christ's authority, such the constant and practical influence of His word within us, that even without reference to Him, or express consultation of Him, all we say or do should be said and done in His Spirit.—Art, science, literature, politics and business, should be all baptized into the spirit of Christ.—R.]

[BARNES:—Ver. 16. He who is permitted to make the *hymns* of a church need care little who preaches, or who makes the creed.—Ver. 17. We are to engage in every duty, not only in the name of Christ, but with thankfulness for the privilege of acting so that we may honor Him.—SCHENKEL: —The victory of peace in the heart: 1) It comes *from Christ;* 2) it is accomplished *in the church;* 3) it is constantly attended by thanksgiving.—The proper Christian congregational singing: 1) The choice of hymns; 2) the kind of singing; 3) the source from which it should spring; 4) the end, which it should aim at.—The nature of Christian gratitude as shown: 1) In that, *for which* the Christian is thankful; 2) In *whom* he thanks; 3) In *whose name* he gives thanks.—R.]

---

3. Specific exhortations.

CHAPTER III. 18—IV. 1.

a) To wives and husbands.

(CHAP. III. 18, 19.)

18 Wives, submit yourselves unto your own [omit own][1] husbands, as it is fit [or as it
19 should be][2] in the Lord. Husbands, love *your*[3] wives, and be not bitter [or embittered] against them.

1 Ver. 18.—Some MSS. have inserted, probably from the parallel passage [Eph. v. 22], τοῖς ἰδίοις, omitted in א. A. B. C. and others.

2 Ver. 18.—['Ανῆκεν, imperfect, Ellicott renders as above.—R.]

3 Ver. 19.—א. A. B. and others omit ὑμῶν after γυναῖκας. [Retained by Lachmann, Meyer and others. In any case, "*your*" is required by our English idiom.—R.]

EXEGETICAL AND CRITICAL.

Ver. 18. **Wives, submit yourselves unto your husbands.**—See on Eph. v. 22. Αἱ γυναῖκες is found there also, while instead of ὑποτάσσεσθε, ὑποτασσόμενοι must there be supplied from the verse preceding. Τοῖς ἀνδράσιν does not refer to men as a category, but the given, proper men [*i. e.*, "husbands," as in E. V.—R.].

As it should be in the Lord.—The imperfect denotes this pre-supposition: that what was exhorted, was not as yet attended to (as Eph. v. 4. WINER's *Gram.* p. 254); hence it means: "as it should be," corresponding with the fellowship which has in Christ its life-sphere. This is applied somewhat differently in Eph. v. 22: "as unto the Lord." There the dignity of the man is made more prominent, by comparing the husband to Christ and the wife to the Church. It is incorrect to join "in the Lord" to "submit" (CHRYSOSTOM and others), or to take ἀνῆκεν as a perfect with a present signification (HUTHER, BLEEK also).

Husbands, love your wives.—See Eph. v. 25.—**And be not bitter against them.**—[ELLICOTT renders μὴ κικραίνεσθε, "be not embittered"—referring it to a state of mind, rather than to specific acts.—R.] This special warning concerns a foul blot in married life, when the husband, as head of the house, not as head of the wife, not in love to her, but ruled by the old man, either shows bitterness in word or deed, or in tone, to the wife, should she be wanting in humility and submission, or have violated or disregarded the household right of the husband; or treats her with indifference, neglect or harshness, without any fault of hers, from the cares and weariness of business, or the changing moods of the flesh, or mere habit. The preposition πρός, "against," denotes the direction only; it does not necessarily imply hostility towards the wife; she need only learn from his conduct, that in his false self-love he does not love her as himself, but as one unregenerate might do. BENGEL: *πικρία odium amori mixtum; multi, qui foris erga omnes humani sunt, tamen domi in uxorem ac liberos, quos videlicet non tement, occulta facile acerbitate utuntur, quæ ubi vincetur, specimen est magnæ mansuetudinis.*

[STEIGER would account for this special exhortation here and in Eph. by the supposition that the doctrine of the false teachers had developed a dangerous licentiousness. But had there been a polemic reference, the Apostle would have entered into the subject more fully, and not been content with these simple exhortations (MEYER). The social morality of these Asiatic cities was undoubtedly debased, but this was the case throughout the whole Roman empire. From this briefer form of the exhortation, ELLICOTT infers that our Epistle was written before that to the Ephesians.—R.]

DOCTRINAL AND ETHICAL.

Compare notes on Eph. v. 22, 23.

HOMILETICAL AND PRACTICAL.

STARKE:—That there are so few wedlocks which are properly regulated and rightly enjoyed on both sides, arises usually from the fact of the wife's avoiding submission, or of the husband's not knowing how to govern properly.—The male sex has usually more fire than the female, so that it can easily happen that a man in his power goes too far and deals too hardly with his wife.

RIEGER:—Most of the mistakes of married life are consequences of the sins of youth, especially of those seductive blandishments under which the marriages were formed.—Even that which is polluted, should any one in a time of ignorance be betrayed into a dubious union, may be washed away, cleansed and sanctified.—He who knows and considers his loveless heart, as God's word discloses to men their natural evil disposition, and by these two words especially: hard-heartedness and anger, will dig deeply and lay well the foundation in his love.—Negligence in affection is itself the first rupture of the marriage tie. But in love we have a fortress that can stand many an assault.

PASSAVANT:—It is exceedingly painful and saddening, to be forced by the reports of missionaries, to see at what a low grade of intelligence and in what a sorrowful condition in general, woman is kept among heathen nations—the Birmese perhaps and the Karens excepted—with what neglect and contempt and abuse she is treated.—Over the grave of many a great man, of many a sleeping saint, often too of one snatched as a brand from the burning, stands in lines, that angels read: he had a pious mother!—The man is the head; a high vocation, a higher power and strength, and a great responsibility! It pre-supposes quiet wisdom, earnest character, rational sway with benevolence—bearing, forbearing, patience, with mildness and friendliness;—and this cannot exist with a firm, faithful, ever equal love, without holy love toward the wife's soul, before the Lord.—This exhortation of the Apostle pre-supposes also, that there will be many an opportunity of becoming embittered, and that the wife's nature will be the occasion of it. Yet the husband should not allow himself to be overcome by the weaker vessel; but here there must be humility and bowing of heart before God every day.

HEUBNER:—Bitterness steals upon us at the very first in the closest unions, as we discover the weaknesses of another, or where there are many hastinesses. The husband can be easily led into this, if the wife does not gratify his wish.

[SCHENKEL:—Why Christian morality requires the submission of the wife in the household.—The dangers of bitterness in married life: 1) Its extent; 2) Its causes; 3) Its results.

SCHLEIERMACHER:—The regulation of household life. It should be so regulated, that 1) all that is done, is done in the name of Jesus; 2) that thanks are in every way given to God, through the conduct of our household life.—R.]

b) To children and parents.

(CHAP. III. 20, 21.)

20 Children, obey *your* parents in all things: for this is well pleasing unto [in][1] the
21 Lord. Fathers, provoke not your children *to anger* [omit *to anger*],[2] lest they be
discouraged [disheartened].[3]

1 Ver. 20.—[" The reading of Rec., τῷ Κυρίῳ, has not the support of any uncial MS., and is rejected by all modern editors" (Ellicott). Tischendorf (eds. 2 and 7) reads ἐστιν εὐάρεστον, but the order of ℵ. A. B. C. D. E. is εὐάρεστόν ἐστιν, followed by Lachmann, Meyer, Alford, Ellicott.—R.]

2 Ver. 21.—Instead of ἐρεθίζετε (B. and others,) ℵ A. and others have παροργίζετε, undoubtedly taken from Eph. vi. 4. [Lachmann and Scholz adopt the latter reading. The E. V. inserts "to anger"—now unnecessary, since "provoke" implies this in modern usage.—R.]

3 Ver. 21.—['Αθυμῶσιν, "disheartened," Eadie, Alford, Ellicott. Older versions render: "made feeble-hearted," "of a desperate mind."—R.]

EXEGETICAL AND CRITICAL.

Ver. 20. **Children, obey your parents in all things.**—See Eph. vi. 1. "In all things," κατὰ πάντα, here definitely expresses what is indicated in the parallel passage by the phrase, "in the Lord;" it is not to be limited (OECUMENIUS). It sets forth the principle, the rule, exceptions being left out of view (MEYER). [EADIE suggests, that as the reference is to Christian parents, who were to govern in a Christian spirit, the Apostle takes heed of an exception. On the exceptions see BISH. TAYLOR, *Duct. Dub.* III. 5. ELLICOTT remarks that ὑπακούειν includes not merely submission to authority, but obedience to a command. TITT. *Syn.* I. p. 193.—R.]

For this is well-pleasing in the Lord.—(Eph. vi. 1, "right".) Hence the reference here is to judgment and complacency, there to precept and authority. "In the Lord," before Him, as He looks at the matter. We need not supply τῷ θεῷ (Rom. xii. 2) in thought (DE WETTE), nor take ἐν κυρίῳ as the Christian qualification (MEYER) [ALFORD]; the former is not warranted by the context, the latter is contrary to usage and indistinct in itself. [ELLICOTT is more exact: the preposition defines the sphere in which the τὸ εὐάρεστον was especially felt and evinced to be so.—R.]

Ver. 21. **Fathers, provoke not your children.**—(See Eph. vi. 4: παροργίζετε.) The verb is used, 2 Cor. ix. 2, in a good sense, here in a bad sense; what is forbidden occurs through severe, unjust, capricious treatment. [We might render: "do not irritate your children."—R.] The motive for the warning is found in the result, which is marked as fixed and certain: **lest they be disheartened.**—BENGEL: "A broken spirit, the bane of youth." There is a lack of affection and confidence, pleasure and power for good and against evil.

DOCTRINAL AND ETHICAL.

Comp. on Eph. vi. 1–4.

HOMILETICAL AND PRACTICAL.

STARKE:—Disobedient children offend not only their parents, but God Himself; therefore they have no prosperity.—Children are not given for the service of parents, but parents are ordained for the benefit of children.—Actual chastisement should never be resorted to, until the child has been convinced of its guilt and well merited punishment, and God been earnestly implored to bless the infliction. The additional advantage thus gained is that meanwhile one's rising passion can be allayed and the punishment inflicted with proper moderation. The child, too, is thereby shown that the chastisement springs from love, and is more of an advantage than a punishment.—In the discipline of children, ignorance, weakness, hastiness, thoughtlessness and childish character must be distinguished from wanton wickedness.

RIEGER:—Our heavenly Father, the Father of our spirits, Himself carefully guards against our becoming disheartened under His chastisement, and nothing rejoices Him more than that we "cast not away our confidence;" and so also in the relations of parents and children, much depends upon our not being rendered morose by the faults, but taking courage in final triumph.

PASSAVANT:—In this obedience of children from the very cradle lies the foundation and beginning of all good discipline, of all welfare and blessing, external and internal, in the heart, in the family, in the state, in all phases and circles of social life.—Has many a yoke of early years been borne in the patience of faith, with what a peaceful gaze does one look back! Those who have grown old should again take it upon them, and as children kneel before their parents.

HEUBNER:—Christian nurture dare not intimidate, but should promote a noble frankness and openness.

[BURKITT:—God takes a mighty pleasure in the performance of relative duties; they are not only pleasing, but well-pleasing to Him; we are no more really than what we are relatively in the account of God; that which we call the power of godliness, consists in a conscientious performance of relative duties.—R.]

[HENRY:—Ver. 21. Let not your authority over them be exercised with rigor and severity, but with kindness and gentleness: lest you raise their passions and discourage them in their duty, and by holding the reins too strait, make them fly out with the greater fierceness. It is by the tenderness of parents, and dutifulness of children, that God ordinarily furnishes His Church with a *seed to serve Him*, and propagates religion from age to age.—R.]

[EADIE:—The child should feel that the punishment is not the result of fretful anger.—Children teased and irritated lose heart, renounce every endeavor to please, or render at best but a soulless obedience.—The twig is to be bent with caution, not broken in the efforts of a rude and hasty zeal. —SCHENKEL:—The evil effects of too severe a training of children. 1) In what they consist. 2) Whence they arise.—R.]

---

c) To servants and masters.

(CHAP. III. 22—IV. 1.)

22 Servants,[1] obey in all things *your* masters according to the flesh; not with eye-
service [eye services],[2] as menpleasers; but in singleness of heart, fearing God [the
23 Lord].[3] And whatsoever ye do, do *it* heartily [whatever ye do, do it from the
24 heart],[4] as to the Lord, and not unto men; Knowing that of the Lord ye shall re-
25 ceive the reward of the inheritance: [.] for ye serve [Serve ye][5] the Lord Christ.
But [For][6] he that doeth wrong shall receive[7] for the wrong which he hath done:
and there is no respect of persons.

IV. 1 Masters, give unto *your* servants that which is just and equal; knowing that
ye also have a Master in heaven.

[1] Ver. 22.—[Modern English commentators render δοῦλοι, "slaves" or "bondmen." As Braune makes it include (here and Eph. i. 1,) all servants, bond or free, the E. V. is sufficiently explicit.—R.]

[2] Ver. 22.—The reading, ὀφθαλμοδουλείαις, is well attested by ℵ. C. K. L. It is *lectio difficilior*, while the singular is probably taken from Eph vi. 6. [Tischendorf, Alford, Ellicott and others adopt the plural mainly on critical grounds; the singular is attested by A. B. D. F., adopted by Lachmann, Meyer, Eadie, Wordsworth.—On the different shade of meaning see EXEG. NOTES.—R.]

[3] Ver. 22.—ℵ. A. B. C. and others have κύριον; θεόν is weakly supported.

[4] Ver. 23.—ℵ. A. B. C. and others read ὃ ἐάν; the other reading καὶ πᾶν ὅ, τι ἐάν, is not sufficiently supported. ['Εκ ψυχῆς, "from the heart," Rhem.—R.]

[5] Ver. 24.—[Rec. inserts γάρ on insufficient authority. The verb δουλεύετε is imperative; Meyer, Eadie, Alford, Ellicott, Vulgate, *etc.*—R.]

[6] Ver. 25.—ℵ. A. B. C. and others read ὁ γάρ. Others read δέ [followed by E. V. This and the reading above rejected (ver. 24) stand or fall together, on exegetical as well as critical grounds.—R.]

[7] Ver. 25.—ℵ. A. C. and others [Alford; Wordsworth;] read κομιεῖται; B. and others [Tischendorf, Lachmann, Meyer, Ellicott], κομίσεται.

[8] IV. 1.—Οὐρανῷ is established by ℵ. A. B. C. and others, instead of οὐρανοῖς. [Lachmann, Tischendorf, Meyer, Alford, Ellicott, Wordsworth, adopt the singular; the plural apparently taken from Eph. vi. 9.—R.]

EXEGETICAL AND CRITICAL.

Ver. 22. **Servants.**—This point is treated in the most detailed manner, as though this were the state of the Church in the main: as Eph. vi. 5–8; also Tit. ii. 9, 10; 1 Pet. ii. 18–25 (comp. i. 18–21). Comp. also 1 Cor. i. 20, and 1 Pet. i. 1, according to which Peter wrote to the Church at Colosse also. The view of SCHENKEL: "it is possible, as MEYER supposes that this (*i. e.*, the minuteness) was occasioned by the flight and conversion of the slave Onesimus, a native of and fugitive from Colosse," is groundless. [Braune's opinion that δοῦλοι includes all servants, bond or free, seems correct (see Eph. vi. 5), but the free servants were the exception then. "Nothing is *said* for or against slavery in this passage," whatever may be implied.—R.]

Obey in all things your masters according to the flesh.—See Eph. vi. 5. "In all things" (κατὰ πάντα), as in ver. 20, is new. [WORDSWORTH remarks on this phrase in ver. 20 and here: "An example of a precept proceeding *on the charitable supposition* that the other party will do its duty; for if Parents and Masters order any thing contrary to God's law, then Children and Servants must 'obey God rather than men' (Acts v. 29)."—R.] Contrasted with "masters according to the flesh" is One "according to the spirit," "in heaven" (comp. ver. 24; iv. 1).

Not with eye services, as men-pleasers; but in singleness of heart, fearing the Lord.—"Not with eye services" marks by the use of the plural, the individual manifestations of eye service; found only here and in Eph. vi. 6 (singular). ["Here the concrete acts, there the abstract spirit" (ALFORD).—R.] It is contrasted with "but in singleness of heart," which is wanting in the dishonesty of "eyeservice;" "as men-pleasers" is contrasted with "fearing the Lord." ["The Lord," κύριον, κατ' ἐξοχήν, κατὰ πνεῦμα; the turn of the thought in the correct reading is lost both in the E. V. and the rendering above. MEYER: "The obedience of the Christian slave becomes man-pleasing towards his master, and eye-service in appearance, if it be not subordinated to the fear of Christ, the higher Master, and accordingly conditioned by this."—R.] The same words as in Eph. vi. 5, 6, but more sharply conceived. [EADIE, referring this to slaves exclusively, remarks: "The Apostle does not speak vaguely, but hits upon those vices which slavery is so apt to engender—indolence, eye-service and reluctance in labor."—R.]

Ver. 23. **Whatever ye do.**—Whatever ye do in servitude (BENGEL). The verse relates to individual and little things. See Eph. vi. 8.—**Do it from the heart, as to the Lord and not unto men.**—Ἐκ ψυχῆς, standing first for emphasis, and demanding glad, willing action, refers back to "in singleness of heart;" "as to the Lord," demanding constant mindfulness of the present heavenly Master, to "fearing the Lord;" while the absolute negative "not (οὐκ) unto men" refers to "men-pleasers." [MEYER: "*As to the Lord*, the point of view of the doing; this should be regarded as taking place for Christ, as service rendered to Him. And the relation to the human master (ἀνθρώποις, dative of the category) should not, in this method of regarding it, be taken into the account at all,—on the principle of not serving two masters,—hence οὐκ is not relatively, but absolutely negative." —R.]

Ver. 24. **Knowing.**—["Seeing ye know," *da Ihr wisset.*—R.]—The motive for such conduct (Eph. vi. 8).—**That of the Lord ye shall receive the reward [or recompense] of the inheritance.**—"That" sets forth the tenor of this Christian consciousness. "Of (ἀπό) the Lord" denotes that the Lord is the Possessor, Source and Origin, while παρά (Eph. vi. 8) indicates the immediate communication through the Lord (WINER'S *Gram.* p. 343). "Ye shall receive" points to the future, its signification referring to a reception of that which is lacking. "The recompense" (ἀνταπόδοσιν, only here; Rom. xi. 9: ἀνταπόδομα) with the article denotes a recompense in prospect, while the preposition (ἀντι) indicates that it is one compensating for the present privations by means of an inheritance, which is wanting to and yet wanted by the slave here; for "of the inheritance" (κληρονομίας) is an epexegetical genitive (WINER'S *Gram.* p. 494), as Jas. i. 12; Acts ii. 10. This inheritance is the full salvation, heritage of heaven, "although in this world you do not have an inheritance, yet you have part of the inheritance passing from the Master to the free" (BENGEL).

Serve ye the Lord [Master] Christ.—The Apostle's comprehensive conclusion. "Christ, who recompenses those serving Himself" (BENGEL). It is incorrect to join "of the inheritance" with "the Lord" (serve the Master of the inheritance), and also wrong to take the verb as indicative [as is done in the E. V., to which the incorrect reading γάρ has probably led. —R.]; neither find any reason or necessity in the context.

Ver. 25. In view of the importance of this matter, another reason is added: **For he that doeth wrong shall receive for the wrong which he hath done.**—The meaning of this general proposition (*locus communis*) clearly is that every one reaps what he sows (WINER'S *Gram.* p. 576); sowing wrong, he reaps wrong, as he reaps good when he sows good (Gal. vi. 8). This confirms the exhortation to serve Christ, for slaves and domestic servants alike; from it they should deduce the conclusion, to gladly obey. It is "contrary to the meaning," not to apply it to the slaves (MEYER, who renders ἀδικεῖν, to injure, limiting it to the masters. SCHENKEL). Paul admonishes the slaves here, while he encourages them Eph. vi. 8. [The reference is doubtful. ELLICOTT, ALFORD follow MEYER, and refer ἀδικεῖν to the master. The proposition is undoubtedly general, and has an application to both master and slave. The context seems to indicate the latter as the reference intended by the Apostle.—R.]—"Receive" refers to the judgment of the Lord, in which the "inheritance" is concerned, and "wrong which he hath done" (ὃ ἠδίκησε) marks the connection of the wrong on earth, and condemnation, destruction in eternity, where sin has transferred itself in its results and consequences.

And there is no respect of persons.—This means in this connection, that the low and insignificant as well as the high and distinguished are equal before God. The former often boast themselves of their poverty, as if on account of this they must be finally blessed and receive reward; "the insignificant often think, that they are to be spared on account of their insignificance" (BENGEL). This is not far-fetched (*aus der Luft gegriffen*, MEYER), but taken from the context. Eph. vi. 9 refers to masters. [The idea is indeed common among men, that God respects not the person of a rich man, but that of a poor man.—R.]

IV. 1. **Masters,** οἱ κύριοι.—See Eph. vi. 9.—**Give unto your servants that which is just and equal.**—Τὸ δίκαιον is what belongs to the slave of right—not historical, human right, but according to the regulations given within the domain of creation, and the rights thus set forth; hence what belongs to them as God's creatures, as human beings. "And" something truer and higher; "that which is equal," τὴν ἰσότητα, denotes the equality ordained within the domain of Redemption, according to which the redeemed are brethren (Philem. 16); this parity they should show in their treatment of the slaves. It is incorrect to regard it as merely "equity" (STEIGER, BLEEK) [ALFORD, "fairness"—R.], or "impartial treatment" (ERASMUS and others). [ELLICOTT says of the view of MEYER as given above: "This is ingenious and plausible, but not satisfactory," from its association with δίκαιον. There is this objection to it, that it limits the duty to Christian masters in their dealings with Christian slaves. See EADIE *in loco.* Notice the "dynamic" form of the middle παρέχεσθε: supply on your side, as far as you are concerned.—R.]

The motive is added: **knowing that ye also have a Master in heaven**, who is over you, and your Almighty, Omniscient, Just and Eternal Master. See on Eph. vi. 9.

DOCTRINAL AND ETHICAL.

Compare Eph. vi. 5–9.

[*These precepts in force where there are no slaves.* Through God's merciful Providence, the application of these precepts to a state of slavery has become unnecessary among us. But the relations of master and servant, employer and employee still exist, and there is as much need for the application of the Apostle's words to those who occupy these relative positions, as to servants and masters in the relation existing at Colosse. When we consider how much is said of the conflict between labor and capital, how large a part of the comfort and happiness of women in the household depends on the right conduct of these relations, we may be glad that Paul writes not merely for a state of slavery, but for all masters and servants, and at the same time regret that social science has so often attempted to settle troublesome questions of this kind, without the aid of Christianity. A large class are becoming not only unchristian but antichristian, because Christianity, which abolished slavery, has not yet been thoroughly applied to the relations of labor and capital.—Too many fancy that God is no respecter of the person of a capitalist, but takes the working man's part, whether justice be on his side or not.—R.]

HOMILETICAL AND PRACTICAL.

STARKE:—God in His wisdom has so classed men, that some are subjects and servants, while others command and should rule. This is not contrary to the equality of Christians, or to Christian brotherhood; they are still one in Christ. Therefore servants should not have so great a dislike to service, but serve with alacrity and with the heartier obedience, particularly as they are not slaves, but free.

RIEGER:—Him who fears God and honors God by keeping His commands, God honors in turn by giving him a suitable respect in the government of his own house. Men-pleasing and eye-service at first succeeds very well, but in the long run it becomes intolerable.

PASSAVANT:—A Christian may well tremble as he looks at his servant and asks himself: Why am I his master? Why is he my servant? The answer is: That I may take him just as he is, so bear and forbear with him as to sweeten his servile condition with all lenity and consideration, as to sanctify his calling to him, helping him out of his natural or habitual sins.

HEUBNER:—The character and doings of the Christian are soulful (ἐκ ψυχῆς). The doings of others are cold and dead.—Unrighteous servants will be punished too; God does not let Himself be led by weak sympathy into indulgence.

[SCHLEIERMACHER:—All improvements in the social relations of men must proceed, not from a disturbance of order and a violent throwing off of obedience, but from the greater power of love. —BURKITT:—Wink at some trivial miscarriages of servants. He must keep no servant that will have a servant with no faults.—R.]

[EADIE:—Ver. 22. Refractoriness on the part of the slave would at once have embittered his life, and brought discredit on the new religion which he possessed; but active and cheerful discharge of all duty would both benefit himself, promote his comfort and recommend Christianity. —Duplicity is the vice which the slave uses as his shield.—IV. 1. Let the great Master's treatment of you be your model of your treatment of them.—(Abridged) Three positions of the Apostle fatal to slavery: 1) He denies that slaves are an inferior caste (Homer, Aristotle); 2) certain duties to slaves spring from natural right; 3) in the Christian Church there is neither "bond nor free." Master and slave were alike the free servants of a common Lord in heaven.—R.]

---

4. Concluding exhortation.

Respecting prayer, walk and speech.

(CHAP. IV. 2–6.)

2 Continue [Persevere][1] in prayer, and watch in the same with thanksgiving;
3 Withal praying also for us, that God would open unto us a door of utterance [lit. of
4 the word], to speak the mystery of Christ, for which[2] I am also in bonds: That I
5 may make it manifest, as I ought to speak. Walk in wisdom toward them that are
6 without, redeeming the time [καιρόν, the opportunity].[3] Let your speech *be* always
with grace, seasoned with salt, that ye may know how ye ought to answer every
man.

[1] Ver. 2.—[Προσκαρτερεῖτε; the E. V. is scarcely strong enough.—R.]
[2] Ver. 3.—א. A. C. D. E. K. L. and others read δι' ὅ; B. and a few others δι' ὅν.
[3] Ver. 5.—[See EXEG. NOTES below and on Eph. v. 16.—R.]

EXEGETICAL AND CRITICAL.

The connection: These three exhortations do not apply to particular classes, but are of a general character. In fact they refer to that service in the gospel, which each member has to render; for they point to the ways in which the hindrances to that service may be removed. They are based upon the thought: if you do your duty as Christians in general and particular alike, you render service not merely as members of the congregation, but as servants of the Church, you are not merely to be regulated by the will and word of the Lord, but also do your part in helping others to do the same. This service is to be rendered by: Prayer, especially supplication for the Apostle, walk and speech. They are not therefore supplementary exhortations (MEYER), nor are they to be joined either to iii. 17, or to iv. 1—"ye have a Master in heaven" (SCHENKEL).

Prayer. Vers. 2–4. **Persevere in prayer.**—Like Acts i. 14; Rom. vii. 12. Καρτερέω, to be strong, πρός indicating the direction; it describes a strong persistence, an importuning of some one (Mark iii. 9; Acts viii. 13; x. 7). The meaning is the same as "pray without ceasing" (1 Thess v. 17).—**And watch in the same with thanksgiving.**—[*Lit*, "being watchful in it." —R.] The participle (γρηγοροῦντες) marks the modality of the perseverance in prayer; the verb enjoins lively circumspection according to the word of Christ: "watch and pray" (Matth. xxvi. 41; Mark xiv. 38). Comp. Eph. vi. 18; 1 Thess. v. 6; 1 Cor. xvi. 13; 1 Pet. v. 8. There should be watchfulness during the prayer ("in the same"), directed to God's benefits, thus "thanksgiving" would be united with it, if not as a constituent part (SCHENKEL), yet in the consciousness as a motive and tone (ii. 7; iii. 15, 17). [The first ἐν denotes the *sphere*, the second the *accompaniment.*—R.]. There is no warrant for joining "with thanksgiving" with "persevere" (BÖHMER).

Ver. 3. **Withal praying also for us.**—Eph. vi. 19, 20 is the parallel passage. "Withal" [ἅμα, at the same time—R.] denotes that this supplication should not be wanting as a constituted part of the prayer of the Colossians. "Us" (Eph. vi. 19, "me") includes not merely Timothy (MEYER and others), but other companions also, such as Epaphras. [The use of the singular in the immediate context forbids our limiting it to the Apostle himself. —R.]

That God would open unto us a door of the word.—["That" (ἵνα) blends the purport and the purpose of the prayer, the latter being more prominent. ALFORD, ELLICOTT.—R.] Eph. vi. 19 speaks of "utterance" (στόμα), but this passage does not. "Door" according to 1 Cor. xvi. 9; 2 Cor. ii. 12, means "free activity;" it is not =στόμα (CALVIN, BENGEL and others), and includes more than "boldly" (CHRYSOSTOM), which ver. 4 sets forth. Paul thought of his freedom and his coming to Colosse (Philem. 22). ["The Apostle longed for liberty, not for itself, but for the opportunity which it gave him of preaching the gospel. The opening of the door of his prison would be the opening of a door of discourse." EADIE.—R.]

To speak the mystery of Christ.—The infinitive is epexegetical of λόγον, as ver. 6 (WINER'S *Gram.* p. 298). See Eph. vi. 19; iii. 4. [EADIE: "An infinitive of result;" MEYER, ALFORD, ELLICOTT; "infinitive of purpose." This is preferable, and is a form of the epexegetical infinitive. "Τοῦ Χριστοῦ is a genitive *subjecti*, the divine mystery included in the appearing and the redemptive act of Christ, since the divine decree of Redemption, concealed before it was made known through the gospel, was accomplished in the mission and work of Christ." MEYER.—R.]

For which I am also in bonds, ["I have been and am bound."—R.]—"For which" (δι' ὅ) refers to "mystery," the preaching of which had brought him into bonds, and on account of which too he desired liberty. The perfect denotes that the imprisonment still continues; and "also," that this is added to other afflictions; while his activity is not destroyed (Eph. vi. 20, "I am an ambassador in bonds"), it is very much limited. ["Also" marks the extreme to which he had proceeded in his evangelical labors (ELLICOTT)—R.]

Ver. 4. **That I may make it manifest, as I ought to speak.**—"That" (ἵνα) marks "make it manifest" as the end, the purpose of the "speaking," as the common object requires. "It" is "the mystery of Christ," and the "speaking" will "make manifest" this. Hence the clause depends neither on "I am in bonds" (BENGEL), nor "praying" (BEZA). Paul wishes liberty (the opening "of a door of the word"), in order to be able to make it manifest. "As I ought to speak" refers to the apostolic activity in going from city to city, land to land (Rom. i. 13, 14; xv. 16), with "boldness" presupposed. "Ought" refers then to the Divine call to the Apostolate among the Gentiles, which includes zeal and intrepid candor.

The walk. Ver. 5. **Walk in wisdom toward them that are without.**—After what was to take place in the supplication for the Apostle and to be done by him, follows what they had to do actually and immediately, and this is first of all "walk without word." Hence this exhortation is not added without special connection (MEYER). The element in which the Christian is to move with his conduct is placed emphatically first; "in wisdom" (see Eph. v. 15; i. 8; Col. i. 9, 28; ii. 23. Comp. Matt. x. 16). The direction of the walk is denoted by "toward them that are without" (1 Cor. v. 12, 13; 1 Thess. iv. 12; 1 Tim. iii. 7); those who do not belong to the church, to the believers.—**Redeeming the opportunity.**—The participle gives a closer definition of the walk, inhering in the wise walk, as the present indicates. See Eph. v. 16. Here τὸν καιρόν stands first, because each favorable point of time is to be made use of, for furthering the kingdom of God, and winning others by such use of it. LUTHER is inexact: accommodate yourselves to the time. It is incorrect to regard it as referring to the shortness of time (CHRYSOSTOM), to the evil time (CALVIN and others), or to deny the reference to those without (MEYER), which is contrary to the context.

The speech. Ver. 6. **Let your speech be always with grace, seasoned with salt.**—The next means of intercourse, "your speech," is naturally in close connection; it is therefore to be regarded as directed toward "those without." It should "always" (πάντοτε, *i. e.*=ἑκάστοτε), according to the context ("every man"), toward well and evil-disposed people, at opportune and inopportune times (not as SCHENKEL thinks, in good or ill humor), have two peculiarities: "with grace," it should be invested with grace (Luke iv. 22; Eph. iv. 29) [ELLICOTT: χάρις was to be the *habitus orationis.* It does not mean Divine grace, but a result of it.—R.]; it should be "seasoned with salt." "Salt" has something sharp, energetic, but beneficial, which, as the perfect participle indicates, has been previously appropriated and continues to operate. According to the first peculiarity, the speech should not be repellant, but attractive; according to the second, not feeble and insipid, but apt, striking and interesting. The former has as its opposite, what is insolent and ugly, the latter, what is flat and powerless. The figurative expression is not therefore a strengthening or explanation of the literal one (MEYER). [The reference is not to the conservative power of salt, nor to wit, "Attic salt," but as salt makes food agreeable to the palate, so their speech should be commended to the hearers by a wholesome point and pertinency. ELLICOTT.—R.]

That ye may know, εἰδέναι, epexegetical to "speech," as λαλῆσαι (ver. 3). See WINER'S *Gram.* p. 298. [ELLICOTT: "expressive of consequence." —R.]—**How ye ought to answer every man.**—"How" indicates that this respects the form; the correct substance is pre-supposed. "Ye ought to answer every man" refers to intercourse in conversation with heathen, unbelievers, as the context (ver. 5) demands. It is applicable to the questions of unprejudiced, inquiring or evil-disposed unbelievers about points of doctrine, moral principles, Christian things or persons, and ecclesiastical ordinances. Comp. Acts xvii. 18 sq.; xxiv. 24 sq.; xxviii. 21 sq.; 1 Pet. iii. 15.

DOCTRINAL AND ETHICAL.

Comp. on Eph. vi. 18-20; on Eph. v. 15, 16; on Eph. iv. 29.

1. *Prayer* should have, as THOMAS AQUINAS says, three qualities, it should be assiduous, watchful and grateful. The perseverance, with which prayer uninterruptedly draws itself through all events, internal and external, like a thread, or encircles them like a chain, is its vital power; the watchfulness, the lively circumspection, the gratitude, are the quiet tone or firm basis of the same.

2. *Freedom* has no absolute value; the use and application made of it, gives it its value; and that just to the extent that in it the task set before its possessor is served or satisfied.

3. *Wisdom,* and that too in the silent walk, is demanded of the believer, toward the unbeliever, the opponent of the gospel; not from fear before him, but from solicitous love to those who should be won, should become what they are not as yet, brethren; from fear of God, who will save them also.

4. *In the speech of a Christian* in social intercourse with those, who are not yet or no longer brethren, but who may become so, two things are of importance with respect to Christian or ecclesiastical things: suavity and sharpness. The former depends on the character, the heart, the disposition, and the piety, the latter on the mind, the understanding, the culture and experience of the world; the former reckons upon benefiting, winning, the latter upon conviction, clearness, instruction; the one guards against unsatisfactory brevity, dogmatic harshness, injurious sharpness in wit or sarcasm; the other against gossipping length without meaning, garrulous pleasure without aim or end, tedious, flat and offensive talk without truth or shape.

HOMILETICAL AND PRACTICAL.

STARKE:—Prayer is the most excellent means of becoming skilled in all the duties of Christianity.—RIEGER:—Much depends not only upon what? but how? one speaks.—The Scriptures attach much importance to speech and the guarding of the tongue; and this has much influence upon the pollution or the unpolluted preservation of the rest of the walk.

GERLACH:—Salt is sharp, yet it gives to all food that pleasant taste, which renders it palatable. So the sharpness of Christian earnestness, of the fear of God's anger and punishment and of the desire for blessedness lends to all the words of the Christian their true grace and sweetness.—SCHLEIERMACHER:—Grace is that which attacks and befriends the soul: salt, the power of our words and life, that which penetrates the soul.

PASSAVANT:—The more trustful the prayer, the more open will the heart become for thanksgiving and praise; and the more thankful the heart, the more trustfully and filially will it pour itself out in prayer to the Lord.—Strong and firm, kind and pure, quiet and secure as those may be in heart and conscience, who stand without, they yet stand without, hindered by all sorts of spirits and by their own as well, exposed or given up to all change, all humors, all winds and storms, to a vain and perishing world separated from God, by which they are sooner or later deceived, misled and robbed, driven hither and thither now by waves and now by flames, where there is no help, no Helper and no God; they stand without that tabernacle of God among men, where alone truth and peace are to be found.—We may deal too imprudently, impatiently and roughly, without taking into account old habits and the stiff prejudices of years, unconcerned, whether we do good or harm, anger or appease by our demeanor, without showing any forbearance or affection toward those who have remained behind us, thus forgetting that once we were and lived no better, aye worse perhaps.—Or we may go too far the other way and not discern the spirits, may conduct ourselves without any prudence and foresight toward those of different views, acting toward those who are strangers to our faith, even opponents of it, with the greatest friendliness and intimacy, as if there were no dissimilarity between those without and those within: this is not the wisdom of the friends of the Lord.—A lazy weakness and leniency is not worthy of the truth, it brings scandal soon.

HEUBNER:—The more remiss in prayer, the more unfruitful is it.—The door of the heart is not to be broken through, the mind must open it.—Christianity recognizes some esoterics and exoterics.—What is Christian grace? Something different from the Grecian. It is the expression which arouses a sacred pleasure in the person and makes it sacred love felt.—NITZSCH:—Continue in prayer! 1) We should strive to follow in their fulness the occasions thereto afforded us by God; 2) Seek in definite needs and desires to strengthen and perfect our prayer before God, or, in respect to our pilgrimage in general as well as in special states, continue in prayer.

[BURKITT:—Ver. 2. Need will make us beggars, but grace only thanksgivers.—Ver. 6. Our speech must be seasoned; 1) With the salt of truth; 2) with the salt of wisdom and prudence. The people wondered of old at the gracious words which came out of Christ's mouth; and we may justly wonder at the graceless words which come out of the mouths of many that are called Christians. — HENRY: — Vers. 2, 3. The best and most eminent Christians need the prayers of meaner Christians, and are not above asking them.—Ver. 6. Though our speech be not always *of* grace, it must be always *with* grace.—R.]

[EADIE:—Ver. 2. Pray, wait, be not discouraged. Beware of spiritual sleepiness in devotion. There are many reasons of thanksgiving and not the least of them is the privilege of prayer itself.—Ver. 3. The Apostle was no Stoic, he felt the need of these prayers and set a high value on them. He knew the power of prayer. "For *us* he suffered. How dear then should his memory ever be to us."—Ver. 5. The world's Bible is the daily life of the Church, every page of which its quick eye minutely scans.—Zeal without knowledge is as the thunder shower that drenches and injures, not the rain that with noiseless and gentle descent softens and fertilizes.—Ver. 6. One kind of answer will not suffice for all, but each one is to be answered as he should be. Therefore the necessity of the "grace" and of the "salt."—BARNES:—Ver. 5. If you should have cheated a man out of never so small a sum, it is vain that *you* talk to him about the salvation of his soul. He wants no religion that will not make a man honest.—R.]

IV. THE CONCLUSION

CHAP. IV. 7–18.

1. Personal Intelligence.

(CHAP. IV. 7–9.)

7 All my state shall Tychicus declare unto you, *who is* a beloved brother, and a
8 faithful minister and fellow servant in the Lord; whom I have sent unto you for the
9 same [this very] purpose, that he might know[1] your estate, and comfort your hearts;
With Onesimus, a faithful and beloved brother, who is *one* of you. They shall
make known unto you all things which *are done* here.

[1] Ver. 8.—The reading γνῶτε–ἡμῶν, A. B. and others is better supported than γνῶ–ὑμῶν. In ℵ. τε is erased by another hand and η placed over ὑμῶν, though afterwards cancelled. [The reading which Braune rejects, (followed in E. V.) is best supported by versions and adopted by the following editors: Tischendorf, De Wette, Alford, Ellicott, Wordsworth. Griesbach, Scholz, Lachmann and Meyer adopt γνῶτε–ἡμῶν. Alford thus accounts for the corrections in ℵ. γνῶ–ὑμῶν was the original reading; ℵ.[1] inserted τε; ℵ.[3] erased it, altering ὑμῶν to ἡμῶν, but correcting it afterwards.—R.]

EXEGETICAL AND CRITICAL.

Vers. 7 and 8 are the same as Eph. vi. 21, 22, except that here **and fellow servant** is added after "faithful minister," having the same adjective and qualifying clause (**in the Lord**) as the latter. Thus Paul makes Tychicus prominent not, merely as brother, but also as colleague, not however, ascribing apostolic authority to him (SCHENKEL). [If the reading γνῶ–ὑμῶν be adopted, there is a further variation from Ephesians. Since the Colossian Church was in danger, it would seem more important that Paul should know their state, than that they should know his circumstances, and hence more probable that Tychicus was sent for the former purpose. This is a strong exegetical reason for preferring the reading followed in the E. V.; **that he might know your estate.** (See ALFORD and WORDSWORTH.)—R.]

Ver. 9. **With Onesimus, a faithful and beloved brother.**—On Onesimus, See LANGE'S *Comm.*, Philemon [p. 4, *et passim*]. Paul calls him "brother" on account of his faith, notes that he s faithful (can be relied upon), and is dear and valuable to him. To recommend him, he places him with Tychicus, who has only an official position in advance of him. Πιστός, as in ver. 7, must mean "faithful," not "believing," (BAEHR), which is implied in "brother."

Who is one of you.—He is thus described

and recommended as a Colossian, a townsman of the readers. [He who had been a fraudulent runaway slave is restored as "one of themselves," commended thus in an Epistle to be read publicly in Colosse and elsewhere (ver. 16). "How much native truth, courage, and beauty is there in Christianity, which enabled the Apostle to speak thus of a runaway slave, to the inhabitants of that city from which he had fled! What other religion in the world could have done this?" (WORDSWORTH).—R.]

They shall make known unto you all things which are done here.—[Τὰ ὧδε, "things here."—R.] In common and in agreement they will make known how it is here in general, as Tychicus will especially inform them of the personal circumstances, on account of which he was sent. This clause is thus readily reconcilable with the well attested reading. [According to the other reading, Tychicus was sent to learn officially concerning them, and to comfort them with his tidings, which Onesimus shared with him. ALFORD: "Is it likely with this re-statement (of ver. 7), that the same should be stated again in the middle of the sentence, which would be the case with the other reading (γνῶτε-ἡμῶν)?"—R.]

DOCTRINAL AND ETHICAL.

Comp. Eph. vi., 21, 22. What was common in faith on the Lord, is much more than what was diverse in station and culture. Even the position of an Apostle was not so exalted, that a Christian was not Paul's brother, and a servant of Christ his colleague.

HOMILETICAL AND PRACTICAL.

STARKE:—A Christian must not regard the former faults of his neighbor, occurring before his conversion, still less reproach him with them, rather praise and esteem the virtues, which God has granted him since.

[BURKITT:—Nothing endears persons so much to one another, as religion and the grace of God. These ties are stronger than those of nature. No such love as likeness occasions, especially likeness to God.—Happy it is, when the conversation of Christ's ministers is such, both in public and private, that they need not be ashamed to have it known, or that the Church may understand it.—R.]

[HENRY:—Ver. 7. It adds much to the beauty and strength of the gospel-ministry, when ministers are thus loving and condescending one to another, and by all just means support and advance one another's reputation.—Ver. 9. The meanest circumstance of life, and greatest wickedness of former life, make no difference in the spiritual relation among sincere Christians: they partake of the same privileges, and are entitled to the same regards.—R.]

---

2. Greetings and messages.

(CHAP. IV. 10–17.)

10 Aristarchus my fellow prisoner saluteth you, and Marcus, sister's son [cousin][1] to
Barnabas, touching whom ye received commandments: (if he come unto you, re-
11 ceive him;)[2] And Jesus, which [who] is called Justus, [.] who are of the circumcision.
These only [Of those who are of the circumcision, only these] *are my* fellow work-
12 ers unto the kingdom of God, which have been a comfort unto me. Epaphras,
who is *one* of you, a servant of Christ, [Christ Jesus][3] saluteth you, always labour-
ing fervently [ἀγωνιζόμενος, striving] for you in prayers, that ye may stand perfect
13 and complete [fully assured][4] in all the will of God. For I bear him record, that
he hath a great zeal [much labor][5] for you, and them *that are* in Laodicea, and
14 them in Hierapolis. Luke, the beloved physician, [or the physician, the beloved],
15 and Demas, greet you. Salute the brethren which [who] are in Laodicea, and
16 Nymphas, and the church which is in his[6] house. And when this epistle is read
among you, cause that it be read also in the church of the Laodiceans; and that
17 ye likewise read the *epistle* from Laodicea. And say to Archippus, Take heed to
the ministry which thou hast received in the Lord, that thou fulfil it.

[1] Ver. 10.—['Ἀνεψιός, cousin. Eadie and Ellicott suggest that the E. V. probably means this, i. e., *Geschwisterkind*. See EXEG. NOTES.—R.].

[2] [Ver. 10.—[The clause immediately following "Barnabas" is included in the parenthesis of the E. V., this is unnecessary.—R.]

[3] Ver. 12.—[א. A. B. C. L. insert Ἰησοῦ; Lachmann, Tischendorf, most modern editors.—R.]

[4] Ver. 12.—א. A. B. C. and others read πεπληροφορημένοι instead of πεπληρωμένοι. [So modern editors, Lachmann, Tischendorf and others. Braune renders it "*erfüllt*;" Eadie, Alford, Ellicott, Wordsworth: "fully assured" or "fully persuaded."—R.]

[5] Ver. 13.—א. A. B. C. and others read πόνον instead of ζῆλον. [Others κόπον, πόθον, ἀγῶνα. Modern editors have generally adopted πόνον, *multum laborem*. The word is rare in New Testament, hence the variety of readings.—R.]

[6] Ver. 15.—Αὐτοῦ is well attested by D. E. F. G. K. L. and others; ℵ. [A. C.] have αὐτῶν. B. reads Νύμφαν—αὐτῆς. The context requires the first, since Νυμφᾶν, the masculine name, is to be retained, and the explanation that the plural refers to Nymphas and family, is unnatural. [Lachmann follows B.; Meyer, Alford adopt the plural; Rec. Tischendorf, Eadie, Ellicott, Wordsworth: Νυμφᾶν—αὐτοῦ. The variation is of little importance, has probably arisen from a desire to identify the whole church of Laodicea with that in the house of Nymphas (Ellicott).—R.]

EXEGETICAL AND CRITICAL.

The *greetings*, vers. 10–14.

Ver. 10. **Aristarchus my fellow-prisoner saluteth you.**—According to Acts xix. 29; xx. 4; xxvii. 2, he was a Macedonian from Thessalonica, who had not shared the imprisonment in Cæsarea, but seems to have joined Paul on his departure for Italy, since when first mentioned again, according to Philem. 24, he was a "fellow-laborer" with the Apostle, hence not exactly in bonds (CHRYSOSTOM and others), but a voluntary companion of Paul in his imprisonment, as Epaphras is there called "fellow-prisoner," but not here.—Both seemed to have shared alternately the imprisonment of Paul. The word is further applied to captives in war, and corresponds with "fellow soldier" (Phil. ii. 25; Philem. 2). "Nothing better than this encomium" (CHRYSOSTOM). [This conjecture of MEYER respecting voluntary imprisonment is the most probable one. They may have undergone actual trial and thus exchanged places, but the reference to a bygone imprisonment (STEIGER) is unsatisfactory.—R.]

And Marcus, cousin to Barnabas.—This was the Evangelist; ἀνεψιός is *Geschwisterkind* [the relation between children of brothers and sisters], hence not cousin in the most extended sense, nor nephew (LUTHER). BENGEL: "Barnabas was better known than Mark; hence the latter is named from the former." [Perhaps better esteemed also.—R.] THEOPHYLACT: "he praises this one from his kindred; for Barnabas was great." On Mark, See LANGE'S *Comm.* Mark, [p. 4–7, Am. ed., where he is represented as the nephew of Barnabas, however.—R.]—**Touching whom ye received commandments.**—"Touching whom," Mark, not Barnabas (THEOPHYLACT): "ye received commandments" refers to a fact of earlier date, of which they are reminded. What, from whom, when and how? is and remains undetermined. BENGEL incorrectly takes ἐλάβετε as meaning *accipetis* after the manner of letter-writing, and supposes it took place with this letter through Tychicus and Onesimus; ἐντολάς forbids our referring it to letters of commendation (GROTIUS) [from Paul (DAVENANT) or the church of Rome (ESTIUS).—R.]; the plural and the omission of the article forbid our finding the command in what follows (CALVIN, BENGEL, and others). It is possible that there is a reference to the collections for the church at Jerusalem. We cannot infer from this, that there was an Epistle of Paul, since lost (REUSS). [In all probability these "commandments" had been written, and were of a commendatory nature, yet this is only conjecture.—R.]

If he come unto you, receive him.—A parenthesis, referring to a journey of Mark from Rome to Asia [ἐὰν ἤλθῃ implying that he would come.—R.], agreeable intelligence to the Colossians. We cannot accept the view of WIESELER, that Paul had anxiety lest Mark might not be well received on account of Acts xv. 38, 39, since all closer definition which would support this, is wanting. [Yet the thought is naturally suggested and is adopted by most English commentators. WORDSWORTH: "There would be something very graceful and affecting to their minds, on St. Paul's part, to St. Barnabas and to St. Mark. It would seem to say, Barnabas was tender-hearted to St. Mark his kinsman; he did for him a kinsman's part; and Mark, though he faltered for a time, has profited by his kinsman's kindness, and by my severity; and he has now returned to me, and to the service which he quitted for a time; never to leave it more. You may have heard of the separation which took place between Barnabas and me; you may have heard of Mark's dereliction of me. You will therefore rejoice to hear that now he is with me; I send you his greetings. I have given you commandments concerning him; and if he comes to you, I desire you to receive him."—R.]

Ver. 11. **And Jesus, who is called Justus:** unknown, not the one mentioned Acts xviii. 7 (THEOPHYLACT), who being described as "one that worshipped God" could not have belonged to the Jews.—**Of those who are of the circumcision.**—These three were Jews, who were attached to the Apostle to the Gentiles.—**Only these are my fellow workers unto the kingdom of God.**—He thus gives a motive for the last clause; Jewish Christian teachers were mostly anti-Pauline in their labors (Phil. i. 15, 17), hence he adds as a result for himself, and to distinguish them from such as were indeed fellow laborers for the kingdom of God, but not such as he could find comfort in: **which have been a comfort unto me.**—[ALFORD and ELLICOTT render: "which have proved a comfort unto me."—R.] Παραγορία, comfort, is found only here in the New Testament. He did not need a confirmation of the correctness of his doctrine; but comfort thus came to him. BENGEL: παραμυθία is in private grief, παραγορία is in public danger. [ELLICOTT objects, intimating that the latter admits of physical references, while the former is more ethical. There is some difference of opinion as to the punctuation of this verse, whether the stop should come after "circumcision" as in E. V. or after "Justus" (MEYER, LACHMANN, ALFORD). The meaning plainly is: that these three were Jews, and that these three alone of the Jewish Christians co-operated with him. Braune implies that others are here called "fellow-workers," but these three, distinguished by the last clause as having been a comfort, while EADIE, ALFORD and others think that he means to distinguish these alone as "fellow-workers unto the kingdom of God," *i. e.*, in its wide sense, as including the bringing in of the Gentiles. The former is preferable. WORDSWORTH remarks: "Therefore it does not seem probable that St. Peter was now at Rome."—R.]

Ver. 12. **Epaphras, who is one of you, a servant of Christ Jesus, saluteth you.**—

See i. 7; also above, ver. 9. Affection and sympathy were demanded by his place of nativity, recognition and regard by his office. Then follows the description of his devoted activity: **always striving for you in prayers.**—Comp. Rom. xv. 30. "For you" answers to "of you," the external union is not without internal sympathy. The verb denotes the ardor and zeal of Epaphras, as well as the danger of the Church.

That ye may stand perfect and fully assured in all the will of God—"That" marks the purpose of the prayer; "stand" renders prominent the constancy and firmness (Eph. vi. 11; Phil. i. 27). "Perfect," more fully defined by "and fully assured" [perfect participle] as a fact of experience and continued efficiency, and by "in all the will of God" *i. e.*, in all directions (WINER'S *Gram.* p. 105), as the vital sphere in which the "perfectness" and "fulness" were to move, limits the standing fast to the ethical department of the Christian's life. [On πεπληροφ., see ii. 2, πληροφορία; also 1 Thess. i. 5. —R.] "In all" *etc.*, is not to be joined with "stand" (BENGEL, MEYER, BLEEK); nor does ἐν mean "in virtue of," and "will" the decree of God (BAEHR).

Ver. 13. **For I bear him record.**—Attesting witness—**That he hath much labor for you.**—This refers to the trouble which he had in spirit, as "striving" (ver. 12), and also to the time and vital energy consumed for them. Hence not merely *labor* of the spirit (BLEEK), though proceeding from this. [ELLICOTT: "labor, not such as attends a combat (EADIE) but such as implies a putting forth all one's strength." WORDSWORTH: The sentence is like a reply to those at Colosse who might have *misinterpreted* the absence of Epaphras from his flock, into a sign of indifference to their welfare. This absence was not voluntary. Philem. 23.—R.]—**And them that are in Laodicea and them in Hierapolis**—On Laodicea, see Introd. § 4, 1. Hierapolis, also a Phrygian city on the Meander, near to and east of Colosse, famous for its warm baths. The place is now called *Pambuk Kulasi.* The activity of Epaphras was wide-reaching. [MEYER: "Certainly Epaphras had labored also in these neighboring cities as founder of the churches, or at least as an eminent teacher."—R.]

Ver. 14. **Luke, the physician, the beloved.**—This was the Evangelist; the first phrase defines his station, the second his relation to Paul and to the Church. He attended the Apostle from Cesarea to Rome (Acts xxvii. 1, WINER'S *Realwörterbuch,* II p. 34), but must not be confounded with Lucius (Acts xiii. 1). Lucas from Lucanus (WINER'S *Gram.* p. 97). [WORDSWORTH: "It would seem that St. Luke was known to the Colossians as a Physician. The neighboring city of Laodicea was a great medical school (Strabo. xii. p. 580). It may have had professional attractions for him." The suggestion that he may have been known through his Gospel implies that it had been already written, a point which cannot be discussed here. See LANGE'S *Commentary,* Luke p. 6, where SCHAFF favors the view that it was written during Paul's imprisonment at Cæsarea.—R.]

And Demas (Philem. 24; 2 Tim. iv. 10), who had not yet forsaken him. On account of the absence of any further description, BENGEL groundlessly supposes that the Epistle was dictated to him, and SCHENKEL, that the Apostle had already some disagreement with him, although in the cotemporaneous Epistle to Philemon (ver. 24) he is reckoned before Luke as a fellow laborer. [MEYER also deems this probable.—R.]

Messages. Vers. 15-17.

Ver. 15. **Salute the brethren who are in Laodicea.**—This shows the proximity and close union of the two Churches.—**And Nymphas, and the church which is in his house.**—"And" joins one person of Laodicea, giving him prominence, *viz.*, Nymphas, adding also, as the motive, this distinction: "and the church which is in his house." Comp. Philem. 2; Rom. xvi. 6; 1 Cor. xvi. 19. Such churches included not only the members of the family and intimate acquaintances (Greek fathers, ERASMUS and others), as if the reading were τῆς οἰκίας, but all those who assembled together there for worship. It is incorrect to understand by this the whole Church at Laodicea (BAEHR)="which are in Laodicea. GROTIUS improperly places Nymphas and his house in the neighborhood of Laodicea.

Ver. 16. **And when this epistle is read among you.**—Undoubtedly he means the Epistle to the Colossians lying before them (see WINER'S *Gram.* p. 102). The verb (ἀναγνωσθῇ) marks the reading as an understanding on the part of the readers answering to that of the author, referring to the meaning of what was written, while "*legere*" refers merely to the form, the letters taken together. "Reading it aloud to others" (*vorlesen*) is not implied in the word, but in the circumstances, as 1 Thess. v. 27, in the dative; 2 Cor. iii. 15; Acts xv. 21, in the times and the object.—**Cause that it be read also in the church of the Laodiceans**—"Cause that" gives prominence to the purpose as in Jno. xi. 27. This injunction grows out of the similar circumstances, explained and conditioned by the proximity and connection of the two Churches.

And that ye likewise read that from Laodicea.—"That from Laodicea" is placed first for emphasis to mark the antithesis. See WINER'S *Gram.* p. 511. "Ye likewise" places the Colossians beside the Laodiceans, after whom they also should read the Epistle. Evidently then a letter written *to* the Laodiceans is meant, which the Colossians should cause to be forwarded to them from Laodicea. See WINER'S *Gram.* p. 584. The context indicates that Paul had written it, since otherwise he would not have known that the Laodiceans had one, and what its contents were. He had probably written and sent it at the same time, counting upon the oral information of Tychicus (ver. 9), and was certainly induced to do so by Epaphras (ver. 13). But nothing further is known save the admission that it is lost, as indeed the Canon of Muratori cites an Epistle to the Laodiceans (comp. *Introd.* to *Ephesians,* § 5, 1). [As usual, where nothing is known, conjectures are abundant.—R.] The following opinions are inadmissible: that it was a letter written *from* Laodicea to Paul (ERASMUS, CALVIN) [so A. ALEXANDER, *Canon,* p. 296—R.]; or one written thence by Paul, as 1 Tim. (THEO-

PHYLACT); or the Epistles to Philemon (WIESELER, THIERSCH); that it was a purely private letter without appropriate doctrinal contents, a mere note, though of great value for the social relations and personal apprehension of those receiving it; that it was 1 John (LIGHTFOOT), or Hebrews (STEIN), or even Ephesians (BAEHR, MEYER, BLEEK) [CONYBEARE and HOWSON, I., 394–8, where this view is advocated at length—R.]. The Apocryphal Latin Epistle to the Laodiceans, first translated into Greek by ELIAS HUTHER (1699), and inserted in German Bibles before that of LUTHER, a poor bungling affair of twenty verses, cannot be the one referred to. [MACKNIGHT's conjecture, deemed probable by MIDDLETON, BLUNT and WORDSWORTH, is "that the Apostle sent the Ephesians word by Tychicus, who carried their letter, to send a copy of it to the Laodiceans, with an order to them to communicate it to the Colossians." WORDSWORTH remarks: that *all* St. Paul's Epistles were designed for *general* circulation. ELLICOTT *in loco*, after a clear statement, inclines to the view "that an actual Epistle to the Laodiceans is here alluded to, which possibly, from its similarity to its sister Epistle, it has not pleased God to preserve to us." EADIE: "Probably it was wholly of a temporary and local nature. An inspired writing is not necessarily a canonical one." The two leading hypotheses are: *a*) That it was the Epistle to the Ephesians, 1) regarded as an encyclical letter; 2) or, as addressed to the Laodiceans originally; 3) or circulating as MACKNIGHT suggests; all of which are open to great objections*). *b*) An Epistle now lost, for on exegetical grounds we must believe that it was a letter which the Laodiceans had or would have received, to come to Colosse from them. The latter is most probable, and does not involve the loss of a canonical book. (So BARNES.)—R.]

Ver. 17. **And say to Archippus.**—(Philem. 2, "our fellow soldier"). He was doubtless a Colossian.—**Take heed to the ministry which thou hast received in the Lord.**—An exhortation corresponding with the recognition in the other Epistle (Philem. 2), hence not a reproof, as though great attention were needful (SCHENKEL). Comp. 1 Cor. i. 26; x. 18; Phil. iii. 2. "Which thou hast received in the Lord" describes the kind of ministry meant; as to its origin, it was delivered to him (BENGEL: *vocatione mediata*), for the Church indeed, but not more closely described. It is arbitrary to regard it as the diaconate or administration of the episcopate during the absence of Epaphras (ESTIUS) [ELLICOTT and WORDSWORTH deem this not improbable—R.]; so also the opinion that he was a young man (EWALD), or now feeble from age (BENGEL). "In the Lord" is not="from the Lord" (BAEHR), nor "for the sake of the Lord" (FLATT), nor "according to the precepts of the Lord" (GROTIUS, who joins it with "fulfil"); it simply denotes the sphere in which the ministry moved, marking a responsible position. Comp. Acts xx. 24. [ALFORD: "The sphere of the *reception* of the ministry; in which the recipient lived and moved and promised at his ordination; not of the ministry itself." This is more accurate.—R.]

The purpose of taking heed to the ministry: **that thou fulfil it.**—It is not trajection: "that thou fulfil the ministry which thou hast received in the Lord" (GROTIUS and others). See 2 Jno. 8. Comp. Acts xii. 25; 2 Tim. iv. 5. Nor is there any reproof here, only exhortation, the circumstances of the Church being a motive for it; the service must be fully rendered to guard the Church from corruption. It must be noticed that the Church should thus speak to Archippus, in the words of the Apostle, however. [EADIE: "It was an admonition of Paul to Archippus through the Church." THEOPHYLACT finds in it also a command to the flock to recognize and obey the Pastor. This may be implied, but this interpretation belongs to a later age. See ALFORD, MEYER. Also WORDSWORTH, who quotes Theophylact with approval.—R.]

* [Comp. ALFORD III. Prolegg. pp. 17, 18, against 1) and 2), and ELLICOTT *in loco* against 3), which is by far the least improbable conjecture.—R.]

DOCTRINAL AND ETHICAL.

1. *Men may be against us, yet not against Christ.* In the various apprehensions of the all-important matter, affecting and effecting the salvation of the soul, *viz.*, Christianity and the Person of Christ, and amid all contrary and trying experiences, the clear view and impartial judgment should and will yet discover, that some are fellow-laborers, even if very few occupy precisely the same stand-point, and share the same views and methods. Only these three Jewish Christian teachers are comforting helpers and friends, yet he recognizes others still as his "fellow workers" unto the kingdom of God, and Paul does not regard *anti-pauline* Christians as anti-christian people. As little as anti-catholic is anti-christian, so little is all and every thing anti-Lutheran anti-christian also, or whatever and whoever is against you, against God and Christ.

2. *Hospitality* has now an entirely different form from that of earlier times, owing to the total change in circumstances. The character of this duty and custom remains unchanged in this respect, that to the poor and distressed as well as to friends and brethren, our house offers a place of friendly reception and hospitable help, according to the circumstances and needs of the case. Our house should not at times become a public house, but in the privacy of home we should still be good hosts for Christian sociality and Christian beneficence.

3. *Firmness* and *constancy* are, naturally, fundamental traits of the character of the Christian and the Christian Church, but their foundation and element must be the *will of God* in the various relations of life. The Christian should yield to no human opinion, to no thought of time, not to worldly wisdom or to the lust of his flesh and self-will. In God's "Will" we find our "Ought," and to this our "Can" must reach. [*In Gottes Wollen liegt unser Sollen, und darauf muss unser Können gehen.*]

4. *Fervent supplication* is a duty and important work, not without labor. In it not only is the heart elevated with its love, but it extends itself, it strengthens and nerves itself for skilful action. *Epaphras*, who approached God in supplication

for his Colossians, journeyed also to Rome to see Paul, and was interested in the neighboring churches.

5. *Every Church has its heads and leaders*, as well as its members, those known and esteemed and of wide reputation, and those unknown, unthought of, hidden ones. The former are not without the latter, are for them, and these too are with the former and for them also.

6. What was then said *to one Church* was of value to another, is of value to all, to the whole Church. The "form of a servant" in which single writings of the Bible appear, as occasional letters, as shared by the whole Scripture; in this we perceive the glory of the Lord, for such means suffice for His work.

7. *Independency.* Paul does not address his words to an Independent congregation of Christians. He places three congregations: Colosse, Laodicea and Hierapolis, together in union with himself and with each other.

8. Nor does Paul foster the *hierarchical spirit* of the clergy: the latter constitute a member of the body of the Church, to which the whole should furnish the impulse. The Apostle points from the Romish or Jewish Church of the clergy, to the evangelical Church of the people.

9. *The ministerial office* has a great responsibility on account of Him who imparts it, on account of Him in whom it is to be accomplished, and on account of those for whom it is to be fulfilled.

HOMILETICAL AND PRACTICAL.

It is of great value to know that good men think kindly of us. A greeting has in it something very beneficent. Do not forget to deliver it; do not consider such negligence a small matter. Be as careful about it as the Apostle.—Delight especially in those who gather others about them and serve the Church.—Do your part in helping every one to the conscientious performance of their ministry; show them especially their responsibility; remember, it is not enough that thou hast received, thou must fulfil, what thou hast received.

STARKE:—Every father should have and hold in his family a proper household church. That brings edification and blessing. Whoever tries it will find it so.—Reading the Word of God is not an especial privilege for this and that one alone, but for each and every Christian.—RIEGER:—We have children, households, entangling connections; and we ever say: to these too we must take heed. But "to the ministry," however, first and foremost.—SCHLEIERMACHER:—All associations of Christians in a society of personal friendship, which involve a dissimilarity to others, should end in such an understanding that each one, in his own place and in his own spirit, but joined in common love to the others, will forward the great work of blessing men through Christ.

PASSAVANT:—Ver. 10. Mark had struggled through and out of the old nature, and become a faithful servant in the gospel; we never go further in God's ways in vain.—Ver. 15. It was no slight evidence of the faith and love of this householder to Christ and His cause, that he received into his house the assembly of first Christians, these heathen converted out of darkness into light; such an one must assuredly anticipate many a pain and persecution.

[HENRY:—Ver. 10. We must forget as well as forgive.—Ver. 12. They who would succeed in prayer, must take pains in prayer.—Ver. 14. Luke was both a physician and an evangelist. Christ Himself both taught and healed, and was the great Physician as well as Prophet of the Church.—R.]

[EADIE:—Ver. 12. Love so pure and spiritual as that of Epaphras will produce an agony of earnestness.—Ver. 14. "Honor a physician with the honor due unto him for the uses which ye may have of him, for the Lord hath created him, for of the Most High cometh healing" (Ecclesiasticus xxxviii. 1, 2). It was indeed a common saying,—*ubi tres medici, duo athei.* Luke might have been an example to the profession.—R.]

[WORDSWORTH:—Ver. 14. This special mention ("the beloved") may have been designed by St. Paul to impart a Christian dignity to the medical profession, which was not held in high repute by the polite nations of antiquity; and to remind its practitioners, particularly those of Laodicea, to whom this Epistle was to be sent (ver. 16), of the honor and holiness of the medical calling, as ministering to the *human body*, which had been ennobled and consecrated by the *Incarnation* of Christ. Though special and *supernatural gifts of healing* were vouchsafed to the Church in those days, even then the *ordinary* means were not superseded, which were provided and bestowed by Almighty God for alleviating the sufferings of humanity through the art and skill of the Physician.—R.]

3. Closing words.

(Chap. IV. 18.)

18 The salutation by the hand of me Paul. Remember my bonds. Grace *be* with you. Amen.[1]

[1] Ver. 18.—Ἀμήν is wanting in ℵ. A. B. C. F. G. and others. It was afterwards added in ℵ.; and is found in D. E. K. L The subscription in ℵ. reads πρὸς Κολοσσαεῖς. others supplement it: ἀπὸ Ῥώμης (A.), ἐγράφη ἀπὸ Ῥώμης (B.[2]), ἐπληρώθη, ἄρχεται πρὸς Φιλιππησίους (D. E.), ἐτελέσθη πρὸς Κολοσσαεῖς, ἄρχεται πρὸς Θεσσαλονικαίους πρώτη (F. G.). [Rec.: πρὸς Κολοσσαεῖς ἐγράφη ἀπὸ Ῥώμης διὰ Τυχίκου καὶ Ὀνησίμου. The most accurate of all these spurious subscriptions.—R.]

EXEGETICAL AND CRITICAL.

Ver. 18. **The salutation by the hand of me Paul.**—Exactly like 1 Cor. xvi. 21; 2 Thess. iii. 17. Comp Gal. vi. 11. Bengel: "This verse Paul adds with his own hand, acknowledging what precedes as his own." The clause results rather from the Apostle's wish to add a word with his own hand, than, as Bleek supposes, from the wish of the Church to receive at least a few autograph words, to which he has acceded.

Remember my bonds—especially in praying. ["Every limitation is unwarranted" (Meyer).—R.] "My" is emphatic; he is more concerned about the preservation of his person in triumphant fellowship with the Lord, for His sake and that of His Church, than for release or the alleviation of his imprisoned condition. It is a final exhortation, touching in its simplicity, not a request for assistance (Heinrich). [The connexion between the autographic salutation and the exhortation must not be overlooked. It was the chain itself, linking his right hand to the soldier, rendering it difficult for him to write to those for whose sake he was in bonds. How natural to add, especially to these Gentile converts: "Remember my bonds." See Alford, Ellicott, Smith's *Dictionary Antiq.*, *Catena.*—R.]

Grace be with you.—"Grace," simply as Eph. vi. 24; 1 Tim. vi. 21; 2 Tim. iv. 22; Tit. iii. 15; Heb. xiii. 25. "With you" (μεθ' ὑμῶν), also as 2 Tim. iv. 22. The grace of God communicated in Christ is externally and internally with Christians.

DOCTRINAL AND ETHICAL.

1. More depends upon inner preservation of the person from fall and weakness than upon external deliverance from earthly distress.

2. From those who stake body, goods and life on the cause of the Kingdom of God, blessing in word and deed is to be experienced; they bless, having more than a benediction.

3. To such the Church not only owes gratitude and grateful thought, but can afford them joy and strength. So much depends on living communion with its reciprocal results.

HOMILETICAL AND PRACTICAL.

[Wordsworth:—St. Paul's bonds were providential. If he had been continually moving from place to place in missionary journeys, the Church might perhaps have never possessed this Epistle. She therefore has good cause to *remember his bonds* with thankfulness. The word of God here written is *not bound.* The fact that this Epistle was written by him in this state of durance and restraint, and yet designed to minister comfort to others, and that it has never ceased to cheer the Church of Christ, is certainly one which is worthy of everlasting *remembrance.*—R.]

THE END.